QUANTUM COMPUTING & TECHNIQUES

(Theory and Practice)

QUANTUM COMPUTING & TECHNIQUES

(Theory and Practice)

Dr. Rajiv Chopra

KHANNA BOOK PUBLISHING CO. (P) LTD.
PUBLISHEROFENGINEERINGANDCOMPUTERBOOKS
4C/4344, Ansari Road, Darya Ganj, New Delhi-110002
Phone : 011-23244447-48 Mobile: +91-99109 09320
E-mail : contact@khannabooks.com; Website : www.khannabooks.com

Dear Readers,

To prevent the piracy, this book is secured with HIGH SECURITY HOLOGRAM on the front title cover. In case you don't find the hologram on the front cover title, please write us to at contact@khannabooks.com or whatsapp us at +91-99109 09320 and avail special gift voucher for yourself.

Specimen of Hologram on front Cover title:

Moreover, there is a SPECIAL DISCOUNT COUPON for you with EVERY HOLOGRAM.

How to avail this SPECIAL DISCOUNT:

Step 1: Scratch the hologram
Step 2: Under the scratch area, your "coupon code" is available
Step 3: Logon to www.khannabooks.com
Step 4: Use your "coupon code" in the shopping cart and get your copy at a special discount
Step 5: Enjoy your reading!

Thanks,
Khanna Publishing House

Price: ₹ 598.00

ISBN: 978-93-55384-23-2

Quantum Computing & Techniques
(Theory and Practice)
by **Dr. Rajiv Chopra**

First Edition: 2025

To view complete list of books, please scan the QR Code:

Published by:
Khanna Book Publishing Co. (P) Ltd.
CIN: U22110DL1998PTC095547

Visit us at: www.khannabooks.com
Write us at: contact@khannabooks.com

Printed in Bharat.

FOREWORD

It is a matter of great pride that Dr. Rajiv Chopra, who is working as an Associate Professor in the Department of Computer Science and Engineering/AIDS/CS (DS) at Guru Tegh Bahadur Institute of Technology (GTBIT), affiliated to GGSIPU Delhi has written a textbook on "Quantum Computing and Techniques" for the emerging Engineers in the field of CSE/IT/CSE (DS)/AIDS/AIML as well as MSc.(C.Sc) of various Universities of India. He is the prolific author of 42 books out of which five are International Edition books. He has about 47 research publications in International Conferences as well as International Journals in Scopus, SCI-E / ESCI, UGC CARE, IEEE X'PORE, Thomson Reuters, Elsevier and so on. He has attended about 50 seminars, FDPs, workshops, symposium, conferences and webinars. The author is the Life Member of CSI, ISTE and CEGR. He has several certifications like Certification on 'Ethical Hacking' from Crezone Technologies Delhi, CSI, India, MS Azure-Cloud Certified, 'CEGR Certified Researcher', 'Certified Professional Data Engineer Assessment' certification by CareerNinja, 'Certified Java Assessment' certification by CareerNinja and 'Certified Python Assessment' certification by CareerNinja. Also, he is the co-guide of a Ph. D. (CSE) student (Degree awarded). He has been an invited speaker/ resource person at the webinar on "A Garden of Web-based System- Not a Silver Bullet" conducted by IEEE CS Madras, ACM Chennai and CSI Chennai, Member of Advisory Committee of ICTBIG-2023 organized by School of Computer Science and Information Technology, Symbiosis University of Applied Sciences, Indore, technically associated with IEEE MP Section, ACM Indore Section, CSI, UNESCO chair and Namibia University of Science and Technology. Several International Awards and Medals are to his credit like Award by IARDO Academic Excellence Award for Best College Teacher of the Year, Award by International Research Awards on New Science Inventions (NESIN 2020 Awards) for Certificate of Excellence as Best Researcher Award, Award by 'USA BOOK OF WORLD RECORD –Life Time Achievement Award', Award by 'LONDON BOOK OF WORLD RECORD- Prolific Author of CSE and AIDS depts.' Award by 'RABINDRA RATNA PURASKAR- LITERATURE' and also Award by 'CERTIFICATE OF WORLD BOOK RECORD-Prolific author of several books on CSE and Data Science'.

It gives me immense pleasure to give a foreword on the book entitled as 'QUANTUM COMPUTING and Techniques' by Dr. Rajiv Chopra under the publisher Khanna Book Publishing Company Pvt. Ltd. in order to help not only the students but also the faculties and researchers for them to clearly understand quantum computing and its applications in real life. Furthermore, the programs have been implemented and tested on IBM QISKIT TOOL that is an open-source tool for quantum programming. A Practical Lab. Manual has also been provided in the book in appendix so that quantum programming can be understood easily.

I hope that this book will serve the purpose.

Thanks

(Dr Om Pal)
Associate Professor,
Department of Computer Science,
University of Delhi

PREFACE

The field of technology is an ever-evolving landscape of technology. Quantum computing stands as a beacon of unprecedented potential. It is poised to reshape the future in profound ways. This brings quantum leap in our quantum research. The roots are embedded in the fascinating and often perplexing world of quantum mechanics. Quantum computing holds the promise of revolutionizing several facets of our existence. Hence, in this book we explore as to how our future will be transformed with the advent of quantum computing.

Several world giants like USA, UK, Russia etc. have already invested several billions of dollars in this field of quantum computers and hence quantum computing. Some of the benefits of quantum computing are as follows: -

- Better computational power.
- Better scientific research.
- Better AI and ML solutions.
- Supply chain optimization.
- Edge on Cryptography.

Quantum computers leverage the principles of quantum mechanics only to perform complex calculations at enormous speeds, better than classical and supercomputers too. This power of quantum computers will have a profound impact on the fields like cryptography, drug discovery, and optimization problems. Quantum computers can simulate the behaviour of molecules at quantum level with unparalleled accuracy. So, the researchers can now easily understand chemical reactions, solve complex physics and chemistry problems that were earlier computationally infeasible. Not only this, quantum computers can accelerate machine learning, deep learning and data science algorithms by processing large datasets more efficiently and effectively and also model training can be done at a faster rate now. So, better Natural Processing Language (NLP), better image recognition can be achieved now. Now days, another field namely, Quantum Machine Learning (QML) and Quantum Deep Learning (QDL) models may also uncover new patterns and insights in data that classical algorithms cannot do. Quantum computing ability to solve complex optimization problems rapidly has revolutionized logistics and supply chain management. It can efficiently optimize routes, distribution networks, inventory management, resulting in cost savings, reduced energy consumptions and mitigated environmental impact. This may have a vital positive effect on global trade too. Quantum computers take the level of cryptography high. It offers new opportunities for secure communications through quantum cryptography. Today, the need for quantum-resistant cryptographic protocols will grow, ushering in a new era of digital security.

The impact of quantum computing on data science can also not be ignored. Quantum computing and data science can revolutionize data analysis by processing, analysing and extracting insights from massive datasets more efficiently.

Mind-bending algorithms blended with neural networks enable instant recognition and verification of identities through neural signatures. It is an ultra-intelligent fusion of biometrics and encryption that assures the utmost security. Today, we are fuelled with quantum data exchange protocols.

An AI co-pilot, Polyglot programming and widgets are the new terms on the glossary of Google today.

Currently, we have stepped into the crossroads of quantum physics and cutting-edge machine learning to reshape data. Quantum Kernel-based machine learning with its trailblazing Quantum Support Vector Machines (QSVM) is ushering in a new era of data analysis and classification. We need to seamlessly integrate quantum principles into machine and deep learning today.

The field of quantum computers and quantum computing along with nanophotonics and nanosensors is one of the new technological frontiers which has generated enough excitation. It has also captured global imaginations. Recently, nanofridge has been suggested that can be placed inside a quantum computer so as to retain the charges of qubits. This has been done as qubits are found to be fragile. These nanostructured devices are attractive due to their ultra-small size (a few nm), extremely low power consumption, high response time, higher reliability, easy integration flexibility with other electronic devices and systems etc. In fact, nanophotonics merges nanoscience or nanotechnology methods with photonics. This enables superior light transmission, manipulation and detection on a nanometer scale.

In recent years, according to a survey, there has been enormous progress in cost-effective nanofabrication, nanogrowth and nanopatterning techniques that has supplemented the reality of different kinds of nanophotonic –based devices.

PASQAL's roadmap points to 10,000 qubits in 2026 with scalable logical qubits architecture. As recent research has demonstrated promising paths to Quantum Error Correction (QEC) for neutral atoms, the fault tolerant quantum computing era is moving closer for neutral atoms quantum computers.

Connecting the international quantum ecosystem is a vital part to become a global quantum technology leader. The company fosters international collaboration in quantum computing by connecting industry and academic hubs in Paris, France, Canada, and South Korea. PASQAL plays a key role in advanced neutral atoms quantum computing.

At the vanguard of technological advancement, quantum computing holds the potential to completely transform how we handle information and tackle challenging issues. Classical computing is approaching the limits of its capabilities. But quantum computing offers a tantalizing glimpse into a future where previously insurmountable challenges become tractable. In this book, I we explore into the promising landscape of quantum computing and delving into its potential applications and the road ahead.

Today, the impact of quantum computing extends across various sectors. For example, pharmaceutical companies can leverage quantum algorithms to simulate molecular interactions accurately that expedite drug development process. In financial field, quantum computing holds the potential to revolutionize portfolio optimization and risk management methods by efficiently processing vast datasets and complex algorithms.

IBM has plans to take the lead in quantum computing, with a new governmental partnership make this reality. Japanese news by Nikkei, reports on a leaked joint effort by IBM and Japan's National Institute of Advanced Industrial Science and Technology (AIST) that seeks to produce a quantum computer containing 10,000 qubits by 2029, vastly outclassing today's class-leading 133-qubit machines.

The 10,000 qubit machine explodes past IBM's quantum plan which doesn't even reach 2,000 qubits in commercial products until 2033 and beyond. IBM had previously planned on a 2025 release of a 1,000 qubit computer, Condor, but the prototype has been shelved now. The goal of the 10,000-qubit machine is to run quantum calculations without a traditional supercomputer as backup, as modern 133-qubit machines often make enough mistakes to need support computers checking their work.

To further educate those intrigued by quantum technology, I cover everything along with the applications of quantum computers. Thus, there is a desideratum to develop quantum computers. To ameliorate on this, I write this manuscript that is in your hand.

Dr. Rajiv Chopra

ACKNOWLEDGEMENT

In electrifying ecosystem of quantum computing the objective is to develop a book that inculcates resilience and independence in my students, empower them to face challenges and overcome them to face challenges and overcome negativity. The time has come now to consider suitable guardrails to ensure that quantum technology benefits the humanity and the planet. With quantum development still in flux, it is our responsibility in defining principles and practices.

My sincerest gratitude to all my readers like Professors and students for their steadfast support around the clock. Their cooperation and understanding has been pivotal in sustaining the vitality of my college community. I eagerly anticipate their continued partnership in the forthcoming years too.

I am profoundly grateful to my colleagues and students whose unwavering love and trust have been mine guiding light.

I would like thank the almighty GOD. Also the support given by my college, my colleagues, my students lie in the point of reference. Last but not the least; I would like to thank my parents, my wife and my two twin kids for their support and motivation while writing of this book. Believe me, while writing this book, I have considered myself to be a student of QUANTUM COMPUTING.

Warm Regards !!!

Dr. Rajiv Chopra

CONTENTS

Quantum Computing and its Components

1

1.1 MOTIVATION FOR STUDYING QUANTUM COMPUTING

With exponential data deluge, business problems are getting more and more complex. So, classical computers are not able to meet such requirements. Hence, researchers are banking on quantum computing and its ecosystem that harness the phenomena of quantum mechanics and that have speeds many millions of times that of the fastest supercomputers today. While a classical computer uses bits to process information, a quantum computer uses qubits to run multi-dimensional algorithms. **It means that a quantum computer does not have to wait for one process to end before it can begin another.** A lot of research on both hardware and software side remains to be done to realise the promise of quantum computing and to make them relevant for real-life applications. **Researchers claim that it has the potential to change the status-quo in any field involving complex and larger data sets.**

According to the reports of Tech Mahindra, "there will be a real shake up around 2025 for quantum and then it will be a decade of quantum." **The more the number of qubits, greater is its computational power (exponential).**

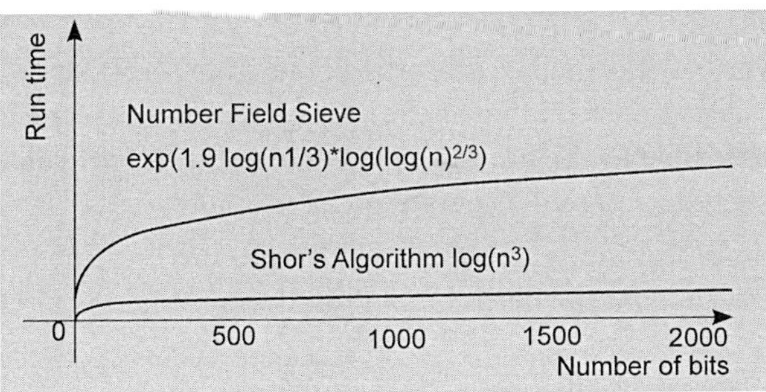

Fig.1.1: Classical Factorization algorithm v/s Shor's Quantum Algorithm comparisons

Due to traction in the world of Quantum computing, more and more traction is being gained now. Better speed-ups are possible with the Quantum Computing as compared to classical computers. In the graph of fig. 1.1 & 1.2, the time complexities of two large integer factorization algorithms—the Number Field Sieve (classical algorithm) v/s the quantum factorization algorithm developed by Peter Shor is shown. It is observed from the graph that Shor's algorithm provides a significant speed-up over the Number Field Sieve for a problem that is the foundation of current cryptography.

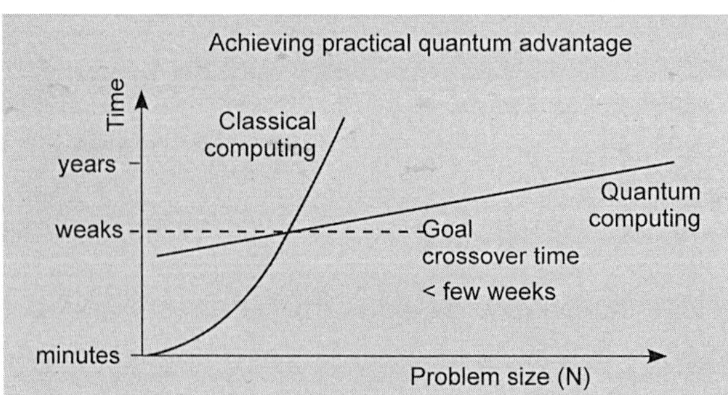

Fig.1.2: Classical Computing v/s Quantum Computing speed-up.

A great Physicist Richard Feynman once said **"If somebody tells you he understands quantum mechanics, it means he doesn't understand quantum mechanics".** So, we need to understand the hard and the mind-bending principles of quantum mechanics too. Actually, the story of quantum mechanics is a fable of wonder and bewilderment.

A British scientist Ernest Rutherford made a remarkable discovery about the nature of atom. He postulated that atoms look like tiny solar systems, made of a tiny nucleus with a positive charge and electrons negatively charged rotating like tiny planes around it. In 1920, Bohr came to Rutherford's lab. in Cambridge and Rutherford's model of atom became his passion. But there was a big glitch that he found. If classical Newtonian physics are applied to Rutherford's model where negatively charged electrons rotate around a positively charged nucleus, the electron will eventually fall inside and crash against the nucleus which will create a catastrophic paradox. **Please note that this means that nothing should exist because electron will crash in a matter of seconds.** Bohr observed this and decided to save Rutherford's model. Bohr postulates in a paper that electrons move in fixed orbits that cannot change. This is against the basis of Newtonian physics. However, this gave new ideas from the father of quantum mechanics, Max Planck. Now, Plank suggested that heat and light comes in units that cannot be divided, which he called **"energy quanta".** Plank's idea came from his efforts to solve the black-body radiation experiments where a body that completely that completely absorbs all radiation (heat) inside it has a cavity that allows some radiation to escape. **Also note here that as the heat increases inside the box, the frequency of the radiation reaches ranges visible to the human eye glowing at different colours.** It was a well-known fact at that time, all bodies produce fixed colours at given temperatures.

Plank used the **second law of thermodynamics also known as the Entropy to derive a formula for the experimental results derived from the black-body radiation problem.**

That is,

$$S = k \log W$$

Where S is **Boltzmann's entropy (S)**, k is known as the **Boltzmann's constant** and W is the **probability** that a particular arrangement of atoms will occur for an element be that a solid, liquid or gas.

Using Boltzmann's equation to compute Entropy, Plank gave a formula to match the results of the black-body experiment. **By dividing the total energy (E) in chunks proportional to the frequency (f), he derived with an equation: -**

$$\mathbf{E = h\nu = E_2 - E_1}$$

Where E is a chunk of energy, h is known as the Plank constant and ν (or f) is the frequency. Still he faced a problem i.e. Boltzmann's statistical method demanded that the chunks decrease to zero over time. This will nullify his equation and thus defeat its validity. After much struggle, Plank was bound to postulate that the energy quantity must be finite. And now Plank concluded that if this is correct, then **it implies that it is not possible for an oscillator to absorb or emit energy in a continuous range. It must absorb or emit energy in small indivisible chunks of E = hν which he called "energy quanta" and hence the term quantum mechanics.**

Bohr then applied Plank's idea of energy quanta to an atom (the smallest unit of matter). He stated that there is a relationship between an atom and light wherein an electron which rotates around the nucleus will emit of absorb light causing a quantum jump. A quantum jump, hence a transition between two states.

Soon there was a clash between these quantum giants and famous, Werner Heisenberg's Uncertainity Principle. Another blow came from Austrian Physicist, **Erwin Schrodinger** who came up with a new idea of **the atom not as a particle but as a wave.** This idea, however, gave rise to some arguments of **Louis de Broglie, a French scientist, who postulated that particles may exhibit wave properties and that duality may be mandatory to understand the nature of light.** De Broglie used both Einstein's popular equation for energy $E = mc^2$ and Plank's energy quanta **E = hν** to find a relation between the wavelength (λ) and the momentum (P) of a photon: -

$$E = mc^2 = (mc) * c$$

Given that (mc) is the momentum (P) of the photon and c (speed) = f (frequency) * λ (wavelength), the equation becomes: -

$$\mathbf{E = (P)\ (\nu\lambda)}$$

But hold on, Plank's relation states that the energy **E = hν; thus using basic algebra, de Broglie concluded that: -**

$$\mathbf{h * \nu = P * (\nu\lambda)}$$

$$\mathbf{h = P * \lambda}$$

$$\mathbf{\lambda = h / P}$$

Please understand that de Broglie showed that the wavelength of a photon decreases as the momentum increases. By analogy, he proposed that this relation was true not only for photons but for all particles.

Later, Schrodinger sought to find a function that could be applied to any physical system for which a mathematical form of energy is known. Thus, he created **a notorious wave function denoted by the Greek symbol, ψ (psi).**

The Schrodinger equation is:

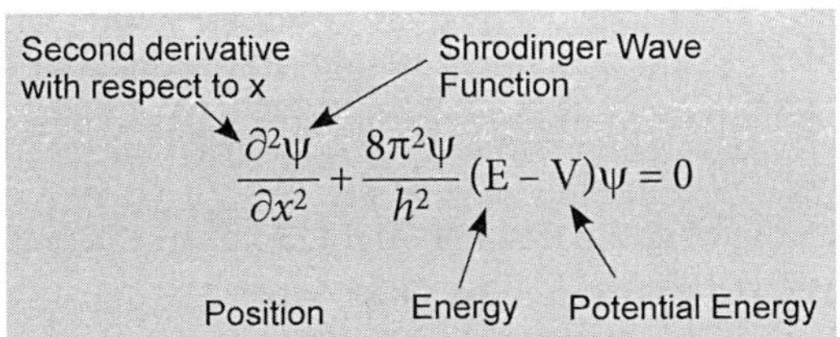

The solution to this equation is a wave that describes the quantum aspects of a system. Here, ψ is a wave function. The solution to the equation is based on the method of Eigen Values devised by Fourier. This is where any mathematical function is expressed as the sum of an infinite series of other periodic functions. The trick is to find the correct functions that have the right amplitudes so that when added together by superposition they give the desired solution.

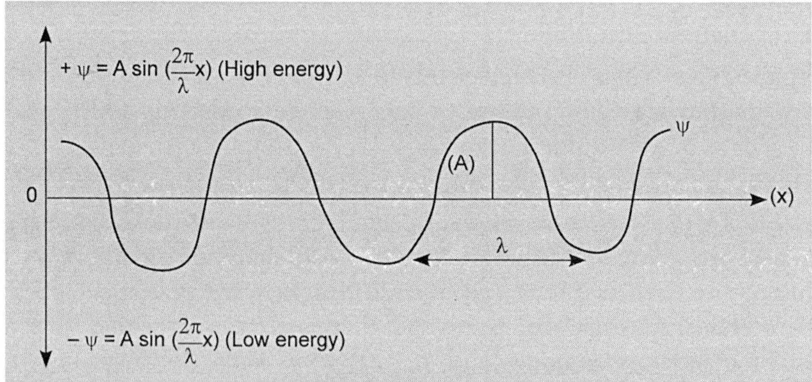

Fig.1.3: Schrodinger Equation waveform

Bohr and Heisenberg joined forces with Schrodinger with his notorious wave function. Schrodinger rejected Bohr and Heisenberg's theory of discontinuous quantum jumps in an atomic structure. **Schrodinger proposed that particles are in fact a superposition of waves.** This claim was later proved wrong by Lorentz. Bohr, Heisenberg and Schrodinger argued relentlessly until a point of exhaustion. Bohr wanted absolute clarity in arguments. He tried to force Schrodinger to admit that his interpretation was incomplete. But Schrodinger clinged to his classical view.

Heisenberg pondered about how the position of a particle cannot be known in Bohr's atom. After research, he found that to know where a particle is, you have to look at it, and to look at it, you have to shine a photon of light on it. But when you do this, it disturbs the particle position. Hence, the act of observing a particle changes its location. Heisenberg called this idea the **uncertainty principle. Heisenberg uncertainty principle states that " The uncertainty of a simultaneous measurement of the momentum and position is always greater than a fixed amount and close to Plank's constant, h."** Physicists commonly use to show the uncertainty principle in action with the help of a very famous **single slit experiment.** The uncertainty principle is very much significant as it unifies the rift between Schrodinger and Bohr laying down the foundation of modern quantum theory. **Please note that this means that an electron is a particle, as Bohr postulated but we don't know exactly where it is, as Heisenberg uncertainty principle states. Also note that the probability of finding it is given by the wave function (Schrodinger/ Born). Thus, there is a duality in the nature of the electron, both as a particle and wave.** And because of this rock-solid view of quantum mechanics emerges.

As we know that interference is another pillar of quantum mechanics. Richard Feynman once said about interference that **"The essentials of quantum mechanics could be grasped from an exploration of interference and the double slit experiment."** Everyone knows that at the beginning of the 19th century, there was a debate raging about the nature of light. Some like **Newton claimed that it was made of particles while other postulated that it behaves like waves.** To solve these types of problem Young came with his very popular Young's Double Slit experiment.

Entanglement is another pillar of quantum theory. Initially, it was believed that light behaves as a wave but Einstein proved that it also showed particle behaviour also known as **photons. The same was true about atoms too.** They behaved both as particles and waves depending on the instrument being used. **But please understand that both the conditions were necessary to obtain a complete picture which Bohr called complementarity.**

What if the particles were to be separated across very large distances, say, like from one side of the Universe to another? This naturally creates a paradox by violating a fundamental principle of science- **"The principle of cause and effect." The fact that all events in reality have a cause and effect and events can't be transmitted faster than the speed of light, the ultimate speed limit in the universe. Einstein called this principle as local causality or locality. This paradox will be known as the Einstein-Podolsky- Rosen (EPR) paradox.**

As Bohr came to know about it, he said that both the particles are to be considered as a single system. In other words, both particles become entangled, with space and time being meaningless in such a system. So, he said that the scenario of this atomic world is unknowable. **Also note that Einstein called the effects of entangled particles over large distances as "Spooky action at a distance".** However, the issues never got resolved and in 1965, John Bell gave new solutions to it.

Bell's Inequality—A Test for Entanglement

Bell proposed a set of inequalities to provide experimental proof of the existence of local hidden variables. Bell's inequality theorem states that **"No physical theory of local hidden variables can ever reproduce all of the predictions of quantum mechanics."**

Qubits along with superposition and entanglement capabilities enable intricate calculations and also transform the limits of data analysis. Actually, data science faces challenges in efficiently processing huge datasets due to limitations of traditional computing methods. In this age of exponential technological advancements, **the convergence of quantum computing and data science is a pivotal point of transformation. Please understand that the synergy between these two fields promises to revolutionize how we process, analyse and extract insights from massive datasets.**

Quantum computing and hence quantum computers rest on three pillars: -

(a) Superposition.

(b) Entanglement.

(c) Interference.

What is the current landscape of data science?

Data science is a cornerstone of decision-making, predictive analytics and pattern recognition across industries. Quantum algorithms have thrived but are limited by the classical hardware. Hence, the **symbiotic relationship** between quantum computing and data science cannot be ruled out. **Also note that the ability of quantum computers to perform complex computations exponentially faster than classical computers opens up new doors to accelerate data science applications like data analysis and decision-making processes.** The point to ponder is that the synergy between them encompasses quantum-enhanced ML algorithms, better optimization techniques and innovative data clustering and Dimensionality Reduction approaches.

Some applications of quantum computing and data science are as follows: -

1. Breaking current encryption standards and developing new, more secure encryption standards.
2. Simulating the behaviour of molecules—drug discovery.
3. Portfolio optimization, financial trading.
4. Better Weather forecasting.
5. Quantum computers can design new materials so as to capture and store carbon dioxide that comes out of a cloud platform.
6. Better, faster and efficient training of machine learning models.
7. Developing new machine learning algorithms.

Still the field of quantum computing is in its infancy. They are prone to errors. These challenges must be taken care of.

1.2 A BRIEF HISTORY OF COMPUTING INCLUDING 'TURING MACHINES'

A Turing Machine (TM) is an abstraction, a system with a finite number of internal states, a read-write head and a moving tape consisting of individual cells. Each cell contains a symbol. The Turing Machine starts in a certain state, looks at the symbol currently under the head and depending on the internal state and the current symbol; it may either erase that symbol and replace it with another symbol or leave it as it is. And then move the tape left or right and change its internal state. Mathematically,

Let Q_i and S_j denote the state and the symbol read at time t then Q_j, S_j and D, the new state, the symbol written and the direction of movement respectively, are given by-

$$Q_j = F\ (Q_i \text{ and } S_i)\ ,\ S_j = G\ (Q_i \text{ and } S_i),\ D = D\ (Q_i \text{ and } S_i).$$

The evolution of a computation carried out by a Turing Machine is given by the set of quintuples (Q_i, S_i, Q_j, S_j, D). It is completely specified by the original tape and the set (Q_i, S_i, Q_j, S_j, D).

Also there is a **Universal Turing Machine (UTM) that is capable of explaining any other Turing Machine.** This means that if we assume a set of quintuples describing the computation carried out by the original TM is available. We feed this UTM the description of the original TM (the set of quintuples) as well as the input tape of the original TM and an indication where to start and where to end.

Functions of TM

We think that the process of finding a solution to some problems can't be automated. Integrals of many functions can be found using Formulas but no general rules to obtain the analytic expression of the integral of an arbitrary function is known. There are some effective procedures to solve some problems while not for some other class of problems. FINDING AN EFFECTIVE PROCEDURE to carry out some computation means to find a TM able to carry out the same computation.

Let f(x) be a function of x. Now, the function f(x) is Turing computable if there is a Turing Machine T_f with a tape with a tape containing description of x and which will eventually halt with a description of f(x) on tape. The fundamental computational issue like **"Halting Problem"** can be reasoned now-**"For some input, x, a Turing Machine may not halt. It is not possible to construct a computable function which predicts whether or not the Turing Machine T_f with x as input will ever halt."**

A Probabilistic Turing Machine (PTM) is a Turing Machine in which some transitions are random choices among many alternatives. Note that a PTM is equivalent to a Turing Machine except that it has an instruction that allows it to choose an execution path randomly. For instance, a 'write' instruction where the value of the 'write' is random and equally distributed among the characters in TM_S alphabet. A classical computation carried out by a PTM can be represented as a tree where each node corresponds to a state of the PTM. **The root** of the tree reflects the starting configuration. Each **level** corresponds to a step of the computation. **An edge** represents a transition from one state to another i.e. a state can be reached from a parent state) at one level up in the tree) with a certain probability. The same state may appear multiple times at any level of the tree or at different tree levels. **Please note that the probability of reaching a state appearing multiple times at level i of the tree is the sum of probabilities of reaching individual instances of that state.** The probability of reaching an instance of a state of PTM is equal to the product of probabilities assigned to all edges leading from the root to the node corresponding to that state. **Also note that the sum of the probabilities of all states at any given level of the tree should be 1.** A computation is said to be well-defined if and only if the probabilities on the edges from a parent node and the children states do not depend on the position of the node in the tree. **Well-defined configurations can also be represented as Markov chains.**

Soon the Father of Quantum Computing—David Deutsch proposed the quantum model of computation named as Quantum Turing Machine (QTM). QTM is similar to the PTM model explained above but QTM is more powerful. **Also understand that the traditional / classical laws of probabilities that are being obeyed by the classical systems are now replaced by different laws specific to Quantum Systems.** A computation on a QTM is represented by a computational tree where each edge has associated amplitude i.e. a complex number with a magnitude at most 1. The amplitude associated with a node (state) **is the product of the amplitudes of all edges on the path from the root to that node. The amplitude corresponding to a state appearing multiple times at any level i of the tree is the sum of the amplitudes of all nodes corresponding to that state at that particular level of the tree. The probability of an instance of a state is the square of the amplitude of the corresponding node. Please keep in mind that the sum of the probabilities of all states at any given level of the tree should be one.** We require that a QTM always execute unitary steps. **Also note that the evolution of a QTM is unitary and reversible. It means that at each step, the amplitudes of possible states are determined by the amplitudes of the current state according to a fixed, local, unitary transformation similar to a stochastic matrix of Markov process.**

The Church-Turing principle states that **"all computing devices can be simulated by a Turing Machine".** This excellent thesis tells us that in order to study computability it is sufficient to restrict ourselves to a single abstract model, **the Turing Machine,** instead of investigating a potentially infinite set of physical computing devices. To conclude that if a function f(x) is computable or not, we have to find a TM that is able to carry out the computation as prescribed by the function f(x). **If such a machine exists we can be assured that the function is computable.**

1.3 MAJOR PLAYERS IN THE INDUSTRY (IBM, MICROSOFT, RIGETTI, D-WAVE ETC.)

Enterprises are preparing to Quantum leap today. The business scenario for quantum computing is a strong case. A practical quantum computer would open the doors of research in physics, chemistry, machine learning, deep learning, finance, healthcare and so on.

In 2020, D-Wave commissioned 451 Research to survey 253 enterprise decision makers based in US, UK, Germany and France on their quantum computing experiences and the potential for the quantum computing market. The survey shows that the industries are very much interested in the quantum ecosystem. To ensure for better and confidential survey, the respondents were not told that it's D-Wave doing this survey. In fact, the study was conducted through a multiple –choice web survey. In this survey,

- 59% of the respondents were IT executives or management.
- 20% were data scientists.
- 6% were R&D professionals.
- 7% were Information security specialists.
- Within this survey, 13 industry giants were represented.

As per the research of S&P Global Market Intelligence 2020, more than one in three enterprises (35%) surveyed are already experimenting with quantum computing. 4% are developing their own quantum computing applications.

- Nov-22 -IBM Unveils400 Qubit-Plus Quantum Processor
- Nov-22 -XANADU closes $100 Million fund raise, $1 billion valuation
- Nov-22 -Cold Quanta –Now Infleqtion–raises $110 Million Series B
- Oct-22 -Nobel Prize in Physics goes to pioneering Quantum Entanglement researchers
- Sept-22 -Four Quantum Pioneers share the Breakthrough Prize
- Aug-22 -QuantinuumStudy Shows Logical Qubits Can Outperform Physical Qubits
- Jul-22 -China's Origin Quantum secures $148 Million Series B Funding Round
- Jul-22 -Finnish Startup IQM raises €128 Million in Series A2 funding
- Jun-22 -XANADU'S Borealis demonstrates quantum advantage
- Mar-22 -Terra Quantum AG extends Series A funding to $75 Million
- Jan-22 -Atom Computing raises $60 Million Series B to build second-generation Quantum Computer

In another report, the top funded quantum Technology industries globally are as shown in the table below:-

Company	Segment	Description	Founded
IONQ SPAC[1]	Quantum Computers	Developer of a trapped ion quantum computer; spinout from University of Maryland.	2016
Ψ PsiQuantum	Quantum Computers	Company developing the first general purpose Quantum computer using silicon photonic qubits.	2016
SANDBOX AQ	Software	Enterprise SaaS company delivering solutions at the nexus of quantum tech and AI. Focus on sensing, security and optimization.	2022

Company	Segment	Description	Founded
QUANTINUUM	Quantum Computers	Combination of UK-based quantum software2 & OS company and Honeywell Quantum Solutions, specialized in Ion Trap quantum computers.	2021
SPAC[1]	Quantum Computers	California-based developer of hardware and software for quantum computers.	2013
D:Wave The Quantum Computing Company™ SPAC[1]	Quantum Computers	Full stack technology provider including cloud services, application development tools and other services.	1999
XANADU	Quantum Computers	Full-stack developer of quantum photonic processors and an open-source quantum software platform.	2016
IQM	Quantum Computers	Developer of scalable hardware for universal quantum computers, focusing on superconducting technology.	2018

Source: *The Quantum Insider Intelligence Platform. 2022*

Some more advancements observed in 2022 and 2023 includes-

- IBM announced new advances in quantum hardware and software and outlining its pioneering vision for quantum-centric supercomputing.
- IBM unveils 400 Qubit-Plus Quantum Processor.
- In news dated 2nd Aug. 2023, Russian scientists have asserted their interest in building close quantum technology collaborations with India and China. Putin proposed a "National Technology Project" for 2030 which includes establishing a roadmap for Russian Quantum technology development.
- Russian scientists eye Brics summit quantum lab with Indo-China role.
- 24th oct. 2023, Record-breaking Atom's quantum computer with more than 1000 qubits has been developed.
- Atom Computing has created the first quantum computer to surpass 1000 qubits, which could improve the accuracy of the machines.
- The world's **first quantum computer to exceed 1000 qubits** has more than double that of the previous record holder, IBM's Osprey machine, which has 433 qubits. Though having more qubits doesn't necessarily mean better performance, large numbers of them will be **needed for future error-free quantum computers that are useful,** unlike today's noise-filled research machines.
- The largest quantum computers, such as those from IBM and Google, use superconducting wires cooled to extremely low temperatures for their **quantum** bits, or qubits. On the other hand, the record-breaking machine from California-based start-up Atom Computing, which has 1180 qubits, uses **neutral atoms trapped by lasers in a 2-dimensional grid.**
- It is easy to **scale up the system and add many more qubits into the grid.**

- Any useful quantum computer in the future that is free of errors, a feature called **fault tolerance,** will need at least tens of thousands of **dedicated error-correcting qubits** working alongside the **programmable qubits.** Qubits in Atom Computing's machine keep their quantum state from collapsing, this feature is called fault tolerance, which is essential for error correction.
- According to the reports by Atom Computing, *"If we're only going to scale by dozens of qubits, like most of the trapped ion and superconducting systems have been scaling up until now, it's going to take a very long time to get to the fault tolerant era".*
- Atom Computing says that the team aims to **multiply the amount of qubits in the machine by around 10 every couple of years or so.**
- Neutral atom qubits provide **better quantum entanglement,** a strange quantum effect where qubits are linked so that measuring a property of one qubit reveals that of the other. They are also **more stable.**
- As of 2024, quantum computers will cost $15M to $40M (approx).

1.4 ORIGIN OF QUANTUM COMPUTING

I am reminded of a very good poem-

"Mirror, Mirror on the Wall,
Quantum Computing consumes Binary All"

Another set of lines appeal to my mind-

"Electrons, Photons little stars,
Quantum computing not so far"

Anyone trying to learn Quantum Computing (QC) is likely baffled by how to form its picture in a relatable way.

In one way, every computer is a quantum system but the quantum computer utilizes the true computational power that quantum mechanics depicts. The need is to separate the wheat from the Chaff. In 1982, Richard Feynman, quoted that-

"Nature isn't classical, dammit,
And if you want to make a
Simulation of nature,
You'd better make it
Quantum mechanical."

On Valentine's day, a Physicist wrote a few lines on quantum-

Roses are red.
Violets are blue.
My heart loves all,
The quantum in you.
Inside and out,

Atoms and space,
To think them all,
Makes my heart race.
Within each element,
There's is more going on.
Protons, neutrons,
And electrons.
Go deeper still,
And you will find quarks,
The building blocks,
Which give you your spark.
The quarks build atoms,
To make what you are,
The love of my life,
An ancestor of stars.
This quantum stuff,
Builds up to make you,
Red roses and
Violets of blue.
Quantum Quantum Quantum!!!

Even the world's largest supercomputers cannot solve problems of certain size and complexity. A new type of computing is the need that can harness quantum mechanics phenomena. And this is quantum computing.

In a classical computer, bits are either 0 or 1 but when it comes to a quantum computer, a bit is called as **Qubit** which has state |0> or |1> or both at a time. This situation is analogous to the tossing of a coin. When coin is tossed, it spins in air and the state of the coin is not yet known at that time of spinning. Until someone measures it states, a qubit is in superposition which means both 0 and 1 at a time. **Please note that if a classical computer does n-operations in 1 sec., a quantum computer can perform 2^n operations. Also, instead of dealing with a bunch of electrons, a quantum computer deals with a single electron or with small particles like photons.**

Consider an electron in a hydrogen atom. It can be in its ground state, represented as |0> or in its excited state, represented as |1>. In general, an electron in a quantum system may exist in a linear superposition of the ground and excited state. It is in the ground state (0) with a probability amplitude (α) and in the excited state (1) with a probability amplitude (β). **Such a two state quantum system is known as a qubit.** Its actual state, ψ, can also be any linear combination (or superposition) of these basis states.

The state space of a qubit can be imagined by using an imaginary sphere known as **Block Sphere.** It has a unit radius. The arrow on the sphere represents the state of the qubit. Its north and south poles are selected to represent the basis states |1> and |0> respectively. The other locations are superpositions of |0> and |1>. While the state of a classical bit can be either the north or the south pole of the equator, a qubit can be any point on the sphere. This is shown in figure 1.4.

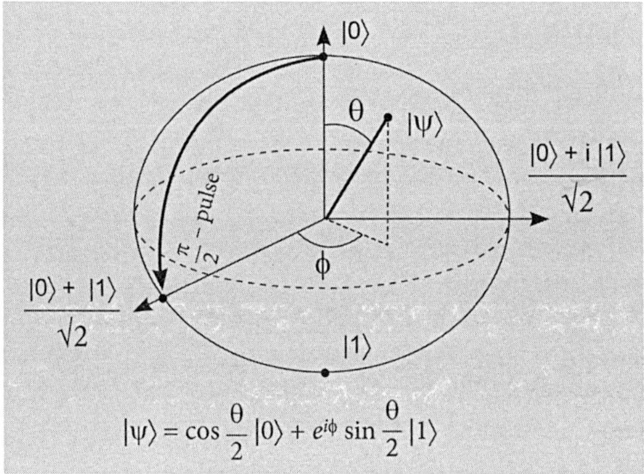

Fig.1.4: A Block Sphere

From figure-1.5, it is observed that the state of a qubit, $|\psi>$ is a vector, r, from the origin to a point on the 3D –sphere with a radius of one, called the Block Sphere. In block sphere, the position of a point is defined by θ i.e. the angle between the projection of the vector in the XY-plane and the x-axis. The block sphere representation of a qubit is-

$|\psi> \cos \theta/2\ |0> + e^{i}\theta \sin \theta/2\ |1>$ (a qubit)

where $0 \leq \theta \leq \pi$

and $0 \leq \phi \leq 2\pi$

The normalisation constraint is-

$|\cos \theta/2|^{2} + |\sin \theta/2|^{2} = 1$

Note that $|\psi> = |0>$ when $\theta = 0$

And $|\psi> = |1>$ when $\theta = \pi$

(regardless of ϕ)

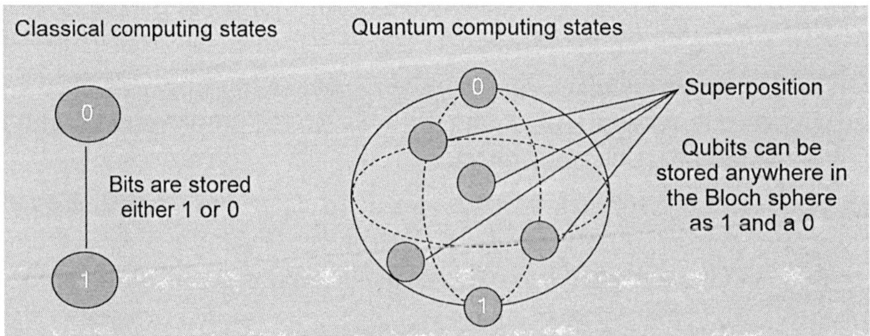

Fig.1.5: One Qubit

A bit can be in one of the two states, 0 or 1. The state $|\psi>$ of a qubit is represented as a vector from the origin to a point on Block Sphere. A qubit can be in a basis state, |0> or |1> or in a superposition state-

$$|\psi\rangle = \alpha_0 |0\rangle + \alpha_1 |1\rangle \text{ with}$$
$$|\alpha_0|^2 + |\alpha_1|^2 = 1$$

A 4-bit classical register can store one number from 0 to 15 at a time whereas a 4-qubit register can store all 16 numbers in a superposition. All values in a qubit register can be simultaneously accessed and operated on, thereby allowing a true parallel computing,

A quantum state in superposition can be given by a linear combination of $|0\rangle$ and $|1\rangle$ as follows: -

$$|\psi\rangle = \alpha_0 |0\rangle + \beta |1\rangle$$

where $|\psi\rangle$ is the state of the qubit.

and $|0\rangle$ and $|1\rangle$ are computational basis states.

The coefficients α and β are complex numbers. **They are called as probability amplitudes.** The actual probabilities are given by the absolute value squared of the associated amplitude. In other words, if 'α' is the probability amplitude of 0 state then the probability of the qubit being in 0 state is $\alpha\alpha^* = |\alpha|^2$, where α^* is the complex conjugate of α· Similarly, the probability of the qubit being in 1-state is $|\beta|^2$. Normalization requires that the sum of the probabilities must be 1 i.e.

$$|\alpha|^2 + |\beta|^2 = 1$$

The quantum state ψ, can also be be written as a unit column vector in a 2D complex plane. **Also note that the vectors |0> and |1> are orthogonal i.e. perpendicular to each other.** A qubit with state $|0\rangle$ is shown by the column vector $\begin{pmatrix} 1 \\ 0 \end{pmatrix}$

and a qubit with state $|1\rangle$ is represented by the column vector $\begin{pmatrix} 0 \\ 1 \end{pmatrix}$ i.e.

An arbitrary qubit state is represented by the vector $\begin{bmatrix} \alpha \\ \beta \end{bmatrix}$

Quantum computers are the computers based on quantum circuits that behave according to the laws of quantum mechanics. From these discussions we conclude that **the state of n qubits requires an energy that grows linearly with n while the energy required by a classical system which mimics the behaviour of the n-qubit system grows exponentially with n. Also understand that a thorough assessment of computational complexity must consider all computational resources, including energy, as opposed to the traditional complexity theory focussed only on time and space complexity.**

This concept of a computational system based on quantum properties comes from Nobel Prize winner Physicist Richard Feynman. In 1982, he proposed a quantum computer capable of using the effects of quantum mechanics. In 1995, Peter Shor in his research paper "Polynomial-Time Algorithms for Prime Factorization and Discrete Logarithms on a Quantum Computer" proposes a large prime factorization algorithm to run on a quantum computer.

As discussed above, bits in a classical computer are either 1 or 0 but when it comes to a quantum computer, a bit is called as **"qubit"** which has state $|0\rangle$ or $|1\rangle$ or both at a time. It is like a tossed coin that fell vertically and spinning. **Please understand that the state of the coin is not yet known because it is still spinning. In a similar fashion, until someone will measure its states, a qubit is in superposition which means both 1 and 0 at a time.**

Schrodinger's Experiment: Schrodinger's experiment explains the state of a quantum particle by taking a cat that is placed inside a box along with poisoned food. **Note that here there are many possibilities for the cat to be alive or dead.** Say, the cat being alive is |1> and cat being dead is |0> but we will know whether the cat is alive or dead only if someone opens the box which is tantamount to destroying the quantum state. **Hence, measuring a quantum bit turns it into a classical bit. There are many possibilities in this case. The cat may or may not eat the poisoned food. Instead, the cat can also die because of suffocation inside the box.** When it comes to differences then if a classical computer does n operations in 1 sec, a quantum computer can perform 2^n operations. **Also note that instead of dealing with a bunch of electrons, a quantum computer deals with a single electron or with particles so small, like photons.**

Let us now tabulate the differences between a classical/traditional/ conventional computer and a quantum computer in table 1.1.

Table 1.1: Comparisons between Conventional/ Classical Computers v/s Quantum Computers

Classical Computing	Quantum Computing
1. Classical computing is based on the classical electrical circuits being in a single state at a given time, either On or OFF.	1. Quantum computing is based on the phenomenon of quantum mechanics like superposition and entanglement, a phenomenon where it is possible to be in more than one state at a time.
2. Information storage is based on bits that are based on voltage or charge; low is 0 and high is 1.	2. Information storage and its manipulation is based on a quantum bit or qubit that is based on the spin of the electron or polarization of a single photon.
3. The circuit behaviour is governed by classical physics.	3. The circuit behaviour is governed by quantum physics or quantum mechanics.
4. Conventional computing uses binary bits 0 or 1 to represent information.	4. Quantum computing uses qubits i.e. 0, 1 and superposition state of both 0 and 1 to represent information.
5. CMOS transistors are the basic building blocks of conventional computers.	5. Superconducting Quantum Interference Device (SQUID) or quantum transistors are the basic building blocks of quantum computers.
6. These computers perform data processing in CPU =ALU + Registers + Control Unit.	6. In quantum computers, however, data processing is done in the Quantum Processing Unit (QPU) that consists of a number of interconnected qubits.

Note: If a quantum system comprises of three different states, then it is called as "qutrit". But if it contains "d" other state then it is called as "qudits". This is still an open area of research today.

1.5 OVERVIEW OF MAJOR CONCEPTS IN QUANTUM COMPUTING

There are three main major concepts of Quantum computing that are called as the **3-Pillars of Quantum Computing.** They are as follows: -

(a) Superposition.

(b) Interference.

(c) Entanglement.

Let us study these one by one now.

Superposition: Quantum superposition is the framework for understanding of all quanta phenomena. But if we go back to our classical physics, the concept of superposition is used on strings to describe that when two physical quantities are added together to make another third physical quantity that is entirely different from the original two. This concept of superposition was used in classical physics when we worked with **waves.** Also we performed an experiment in our secondary schools-- Two pulses on a string which pass through each other will interfere following the **principle of superposition.**

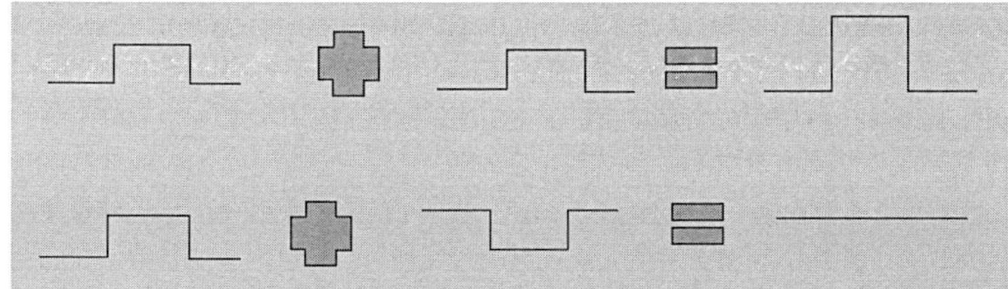

Fig.1.6: Classical superposition principle showing constructive and destructive interference

As an example, we were told by our Physics teacher that noise-cancelling headphones use superposition by creating sound waves with the same magnitude as the incoming sound wave but completely out of phase, thereby cancelling the sound wave. This is called as **destructive interference.**

Example 2: As an another application of classical superposition, consider the case of finding the total magnitude and direction of quantities like force, electric field, magnetic field etc. **For instance,** to compute the total electric force $\vec{F}_{total}$ on a charge q_2 produced by other charges q_1 and q_3 , one would sum the forces produced by each individual charge as follows:

$\vec{F}_{total} = \vec{F}_{12} + \vec{F}_{32}$. The challenge is that forces are vectors, so vector addition is needed and is shown in figure 1.7.

Fig.1.7: Classical superposition used to compute total electric force on a charge q_2 due to charges q_1 and q_3

Keeping these points in mind, we are now in a position to discuss about quantum superposition. **Quantum Superposition is a phenomenon associated with quantum systems that includes small objects like electrons, nuclei, photons** (elementary particles) **for which the wave-particle duality and other non-classical effects are seen. For example,** from physics, what we think is that an object can have an arbitrary amount of Kinetic Energy ranging from 0 to infinity Joules. This implies that a ball could be at rest or thrown at any speed. **But please note that according to quantum mechanics, the ball's energy is quantised i.e. it can have only certain values.**

To further explain the concept of quantum superposition, consider the case of tossing a coin. A coin has a 50/50 probability of landing as either heads or tails. **Note here that we can say that the coin is in a superposition of both heads and tails.** When it lands it has a **definite state—either heads or tails.** The word **state** in general means any particular way that a system can possibly be described. Like the coin can be either heads or tails or a combination of heads or tails while flipped in the air. **All of these cases are called as the states of the coin. And when the coin is being flipped in air, it is said to be in a state of superposition.** At any given time, a system can be described as being in a particular state. The state is related to its quantized values. For instance, a tossed coin is either in heads state or a tails state. As another example, an electron orbiting a hydrogen atom could be in a ground state or an excited state. **Please understand that a quantum system is special because it can be in a superposition of these definite states** i.e. both heads and tails simultaneously. The result of a measurement is to observe some definite state with a given probability.

Consider the famous Schrodinger's experiment wherein a Schrodinger's cat is placed in a closed box with a single atom that has some probability of emitting deadly radiation at any time. Because radioactive nuclear decay is a spontaneous process so it is impossible to predict for certain when the nucleus decays. Hence, you do not know whether the cat is alive or dead until you open and look inside the box. **It can be said that the cat is both alive AND dead with some non-zero probability. Note that this implies that the cat in a superposition state until you open the box and measure its state.** On measurement, the cat is obviously, either alive OR dead and we say that the superposition has collapsed to a definite and non-superposition state. **Please note that quantum systems can exist in a superposition state and measuring the system will collapse the superposition state into one definite classical state.** We cannot see quantum superposition with our eyes. In nutshell, we can say that: -

- A particle in a **quantum superposition** exists as a combination of different states at the same time.
- Each possible state has a given probability of being observed but **measurement destroys the superposition as only one definite state is observable.**
- **A 1-bit classical computer** can be (or store) in 1 of 2 states at a time: 0 or 1.

  A 1-qubit quantum computer can be in 2 states at a time. That is $2^1 = 2$.
- **A 2-bit classical computer** can store only 1 out of $2^2 = 4$ possible combinations.

  A 2-qubit quantum computer can store $2^2 = 4$ possible values simultaneously.
- **As a byte = 8 bits is the basic, standard unit used to store information in either system, then the number of values that can be stored simultaneously in a quantum computer would be 2^n where n is the number of qubits.**
- The following table 1.2 shows that qubits are powerful than classical bits-

Table 1.2: Qubits Simultaneously String Capacity

Bits/ qubits	Classic storage (bytes)	Quantum storage (bits)	Quantum storage (bytes)
4	1	16	2
8	1	256	32
32	4	4294967296	536870912
64	8	1.84467E+19	2.30584E+18

From table-1.2, it can be said that the amount of data that can be stored simultaneously in a quantum computer is record-breaking and this has given rise to a new tern **Quantum Supremacy.** It is at this point of junction that a quantum computer will be able to solve all problems that a classical/ conventional computer cannot.

In quantum mechanics, there is a fundamental principle of superposition. **It states that "Any two or more quantum states can be added together ("superposed") and the result will be another valid quantum state".** The point to ponder is now that as we already know that there are two quantum states, |0> and |1>. Can we add them, as |0> and |1> are vectors and adding two vectors is simple?

The answer is here. As we know that a vector is a geometric object that has a magnitude (or length) and a direction. Usually, they are represented by straight arrows, starting at one point on a coordinate axis and ending at different point. You can add two vectors by placing one vector with its tail at the others vector's ahead. The straight line between the yet unconnected tail and the yet unconnected tail is the sum of both vectors. That is,

Mathematically,

Let $$\vec{u} = \begin{bmatrix} u_1 \\ u_2 \end{bmatrix}$$

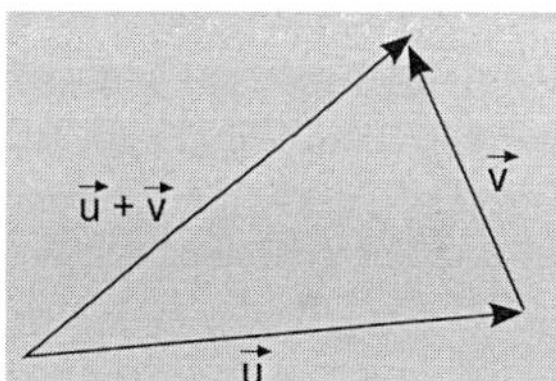

and $$\vec{v} = \begin{bmatrix} v_1 \\ v_2 \end{bmatrix}$$ be two vectors.

The sum of $\vec{u}$ and $\vec{v}$ is:

$$u_2 + v_2 = \begin{bmatrix} u_1 + v_1 \\ u_2 + v_2 \end{bmatrix}$$

Accordingly, our superposed state should be ψ:

$$|\psi\rangle = |0\rangle + |1\rangle = \underbrace{|0\rangle + |1\rangle}_{\text{superposition}} = \begin{bmatrix} 1+0 \\ 0+1 \end{bmatrix} = \begin{bmatrix} 1 \\ 1 \end{bmatrix}$$

*ψ ("psi") is a common symbol used for the state of a quantum system. We need to add weights to the quantum states |0> and |1>. Let us call them α and β. We weight |0> with α and |1> with β. That is,

$$|\varphi\rangle = \alpha|0\rangle + \beta\,|1\rangle = \begin{bmatrix} 1.\alpha + 0.\beta \\ 0.\alpha + 1.\beta \end{bmatrix} = \begin{bmatrix} \alpha \\ \beta \end{bmatrix}$$

Please note that amplitudes are proportional to probabilities. We need to normalize them such that-

$$\alpha^2 + \beta^2 = 1$$

If both states |0> and |1> should have the same weight, then

$$\alpha = \beta$$

Therefore, we can solve our equation to α:

$$\alpha^2 + \alpha^2 = 1$$
$$2.\,\alpha^2 = 1$$
$$\alpha^2 = ½$$
$$\alpha = 1/\sqrt{2}$$

And we insert the values for both α and β (both are equal). Let us try this quantum state now:

$$\varphi = 1/\sqrt{2}\,|0> + 1/\sqrt{2}\,|1> = \begin{bmatrix} 1/\sqrt{2} \\ 1/\sqrt{2} \end{bmatrix}$$

The corresponding array in Python will be therefore, [1/ sqrt(2) , 1/ sqrt (2)]. For this you must import sqrt. This means that the multiple measurements made on multiple qubits in identical states will not always give the same result. The equivalent representations of a quantum bit that when observed has the probability of α^2 to result in θ and β^2 to result in 1 are: -

$$|\varphi> = \alpha|0> + \beta\,|1> = \begin{pmatrix} \alpha \\ \beta \end{pmatrix} \text{ with } \alpha^2 + \beta^2 = 1.$$

In Python, the array [alpha, beta] denotes this state.

We are in a position to solve some problems now.

Example 1: Find out the state of qubit that has a 25% chance of resulting in 0 and 75% of resulting in 1?

Solution 1: This is the definition of a qubit in superposition. This qubit when observed has the probability of α^2 to result in θ and β^2 to result in 1.

$$|\varphi> = \alpha|0> + \beta\,|1> = \begin{pmatrix} \alpha \\ \beta \end{pmatrix} \quad \text{... (1)}$$

This is the required normalization. It requires the sum of the squared amplitudes (α and β) to equal 1.

$$\alpha^2 + \beta^2 = 1 \quad \text{... (2)}$$

Let us consider the probabilities 25% and 75% as fractions and equate them to α^2 and β^2 respectively.

$$\alpha^2 = 1/4$$

or

$$\alpha = 1/2 \quad \text{... (3)}$$

And

$$\beta^2 = 3/4$$

or

$$\beta = \sqrt{3}/2 \quad \text{... (4)}$$

Substituting euqtaions-3 and 4 in equation-1 we get:-

$$|\varphi> = 1/2\,|0> + \sqrt{3}/2\,|1> = \begin{bmatrix} 1/2 \\ \sqrt{3}/2 \end{bmatrix}$$

The corresponding array in Python will be therefore, [1/ 2 , sqrt (3)/2]. It represents the vector

$$= \begin{bmatrix} 1/2 \\ \sqrt{3}/2 \end{bmatrix}$$

For this you must import sqrt. And you can open Jupyter notebook and test these calculations.

Interference: Quantum Interference is a phenomenon which helps us bias the measurement of a qubit towards the desired state or set of states. We need to learn on how to manipulate quantum systems so that the paths leading to wrong answers interfere destructively and cancel out but the paths leading to the right answer reinforce each other. Quantum interference is what allows us to bias quantum systems toward the desired state. Quantum interference is a by-product of quantum superposition and it helps bias quantum measurement towards specific quantum states.

Entanglement: Consider an experiment set-up to measure the spins of two electrons, emitted in opposite directions following the decay of a two-electron singlet state with **zero total spin.** A singlet electron state corresponds to the anti-symmetric superposition state of a pair of electrons with **anti-parallel spins. The three possible superposition states of a pair of electrons with parallel spins i.e. with equal spin quantum numbers is called as a triplet. The total spin of a triplet state is equal to +1, 0 or -1.** The electrons have different quantum numbers s = +1/2 and s = -1/2 and **the total spin of the singlet state is zero.** For such a state, **the law of conservation of the angular momentum requires that the spin vectors of the two particles are oriented in opposite directions.** Hence, if we measure the spin of one of these two particles along a certain direction and find it in the state **"spin up", then along that direction, other particle must be in a state "spin down."** By measuring the spin of one particle and thus reducing its state vector to one of the Eigen vectors of the measurement basis, we automatically project the state vector of the other particle onto the same basis. **Please understand here that two particles emitted from the singlet are said to be entangled regardless of how far apart they travel before the spin measurements are made, the joint results will exhibit these joint probabilities. Also understand that these probabilities can be computed from the results of multiple measurements and such measurements have to be performed over several particle pairs, not just one pair.** In general, a large number of particle pairs can be prepared in a similar way and the measurements can be performed independently on the pairs. As per the laws of quantum mechanics, the results are expected to satisfy the same correlations. Hence, we can give another definition of a Quantum Computer. **"A quantum computer is a collection of prepared pairs of particles whose entanglement (correlations) satisfy all of the requirements for carrying out parallel computations described by a parallel algorithm."**

We can consider an algorithm designed to take the advantage of a specific entanglement. **Please note that the two entangled particles in a singlet state have total spin 0 because the spins of the individual particles about any axis are always opposite. Their spin will exist only as potentialities until an observer chooses a definite axis and performs the measurement.**

The term Entanglement was used by Schrodinger who was the first person to recognise this quantum effect. According to him, "**an entangled pair is a single quantum system in a superposition of equally possible states. The entangled state contains no information about the individual particles, only that they are opposite in states." Also note that an important property of an entangled pair is that the measurement of one particle influences the state of the other particle.** Einstein called this phenomenon as **"Spooky action at a distance."**

Quantum entanglement is a physical phenomenon that occurs when multiple qubits are correlated with each other. It can make quantum computers faster than classical computers. **The point to ponder is that the qubits can be entangled, providing hiden information that does not exist in the classical world.**

Consider an example of two fair coins. Classically speaking, if you flipped two fair coins many times, you would measure the outcomes HH, HT, TH or TT, each occurring with a 25% probability. However, by quantum entangling these two fair coins, it is possible to create a state $(1 / \sqrt{2})$ (|HH> + |TT>). Many other types of entangled states are possible but this is the one with famous example called as a **Bell state.** If you flipped this **"entangled"** pair of coins, they are entangled in such a way that only two measurement outcomes are possible: -

1. Both coins land on heads; or
2. Both coins land on tails; each outcome occurring with 50% probability. You would never see HT or TH !!!

Also note that if two entangled coins are separated by several miles of distance, one coin can be flipped and measured. In this scenario, if the measured coin produced the outcome heads then we automatically know that the other coin must also land on heads. If the measured coin produced the outcome tails then we automatically know that the other coin must also land on tails. Isn't this strange? If not, then it means that the two coins can transmit information instantaneously and even faster than the speed of light.

If the two coins are flipped at the exact same time, somehow the two coins know to land on the same side as the other even though there can be no classical communication between them. Now the question is that how does the other coin know what was measured on the other? Is information being somehow, transmitted faster than the speed of light? **Einstein called this behaviour a "spooky action at a distance". Also understand that it has since been shown that no information is being transmitted from one place to the other and hence no information is being transmitted faster than the speed of light. Instead the particles share non-classical information at the time of entanglement, which is then observed in measurement process.** The correlation between entangled qubits is the key that allows quantum computers to perform certain calculations much faster than the classical computers/ traditional/conventional computers.

Multi-Qubit states: Say, you are given multiple qubits. Then the total state of a system can be written together in a single ket. **For example,** if coin-1 is heads and coin-2 is tails, the two –coin state is expressed as |HT>. **So, in general we can say that a system of two qubits can be in a superposition of four classical states as follows: -**

$$|\psi> = \alpha_{00}\,|00> + \alpha_{01}\,|01> + \alpha_{10}\,|10> + \alpha_{11}\,|11>$$

These coefficients α_{ij} are called as the **amplitudes and are generally complex numbers. Measuring the two qubits will collapse the system into one of the four basis states with probability given by $\alpha^2{}_{ij}$**

We are in a position to solve a problem now based on superposition and entanglement.

Example 2: A system of two qubits is in a superposition state given by: -

$$|\psi> = \mathbf{1/\sqrt{2}\,|00> + ½\,|10> - ½\,|11>}$$

(a) **What is the probability of measuring both qubits as 1?**

(b) **If we only measure the first qubit and get a value of 1, what is the new state of the system?**

Solution 2:

(a) The probability of measuring both qubits as 1 is-

$$\text{Prob}\,(|11>) = (-1/2)^2 = ¼$$

(b) Since |00> is the only basis state of |ψ> that doesn't have a 1 in the first qubit, we eliminate the state |00> from the possibilities. This results in

$$|\psi`> = ½\,|0> - ½\,|11>.$$

(c) Finally, we re-normalize the state so that the probabilities add up to 1. Hence, the new state is-

$$|\psi`> = 1/\sqrt{2}\,|10> - 1/\sqrt{2}\,|11>$$

Also we have **non-entangled systems-** A system of particles that are not entangled with each other. In this case, changing one particle will not cause any change in the other particle. **For instance,** in basic classical system, flipping two coins and measuring one coin as heads does not tell you any information about whether or not the other coin will land on heads or tails. These events are said to be **independent.** If we want to compute the probability of |HT>, we would simply multiply the probability of getting H on coin-1 by the probability of getting T on coin-2. And this is given by: -

$$\text{Prob}\,(|HT>) = (1/2)\,(1/2) = 1/4$$

Please remember that non-entangled states are also called as the product states or separable states because they can be factored into a product of single-qubit states. Also the two single-qubit probabilities multiply to produce the two-qubit probabilities. Currently, it has been observed that there can exist quantum correlations in separable states that are not due to entanglement. **These are called quantum discord.**

Test for Entanglement: There are ways to test for entanglement without the need to factorise a multi-qubit state into single qubit states, namely, whether the trace of the density matrix for the subsystem squared is equal to 1.

Example 3: Is $|\psi> = 1/\sqrt{2}\,|00> + 1/\sqrt{2}\,|11>$ an entangled state? Explain.

Solution 3: Yes, it is an entangled state. To prove this let us examine qubit #2. The probabilities for measuring qubit #2 in the |0> or |1> states are originally 50/50 respectively. But if we measure qubit #1, then we know what the outcome of measuring qubit #2 will be with 100% certainty. The same argument holds if qubit #2 is measured first. **Please note that measuring one of the qubits affects the probability of measuring the other qubit in a certain state and so they are entangled.** Mathematically, an entangled state is a special multi-qubit superposition state that cannot be factored into a product of the individual qubits.

Example 4: Show that $|\psi> = 1/\sqrt{2}\,|00> + 1/\sqrt{2}\,|11>$ cannot be written as a product of two single qubits.

Solution 4: Assume that the state can be written as the product of two states. That is,

$$1/\sqrt{2}\,|00> + 1/\sqrt{2}\,|11> = (\alpha_0\,|0) + \alpha_1\,|1>)\,(\beta_0\,|0> + \beta_1\,|1>) \quad \text{..................(1)}$$

$$= \alpha_0\,\beta_0\,|00> + \alpha_0\,\beta_1\,|01> + \alpha_1\,\beta_0\,|10> + \alpha_1\,\beta_1\,|11> \quad \text{.......(2)}$$

Comparing the amplitudes on the left and on the right, the α_i 's and β_j 's must satisfy:-

$$\alpha_0\,\beta_0 = 1/\sqrt{2},\ \alpha_0\,\beta_1 = 0,\ \alpha_1\,\beta_0 = 0,\ \alpha_1\,\beta_1 = 1/\sqrt{2}.$$

But please note that this is not possible. For example, if we take **$\alpha_0\,\beta_1 = 0$, that is, either** α_0 **= 0 or $\beta_1 = 0$. If** α_0 **= 0 then** $\alpha_0\,\beta_0$ **= 0. But** $\alpha_0\,\beta_0$ **= $1/\sqrt{2}$,** in above given equation. A similar contradiction occurs with **$\beta_1 = 0$.** Hence, the initial assumption must be incorrect and this entangled state cannot be written as the product of two separate states.

Just as there are many ways of building a quantum computer, similarly there are many different ways of physically entangling particles. One method is called as **"Spontaneous parametric down-conversion" that shines a laser at a special non-linear crystal."** Figure 1.8 below shows how a non-linear crystal creates two photons with entangled polarizations.

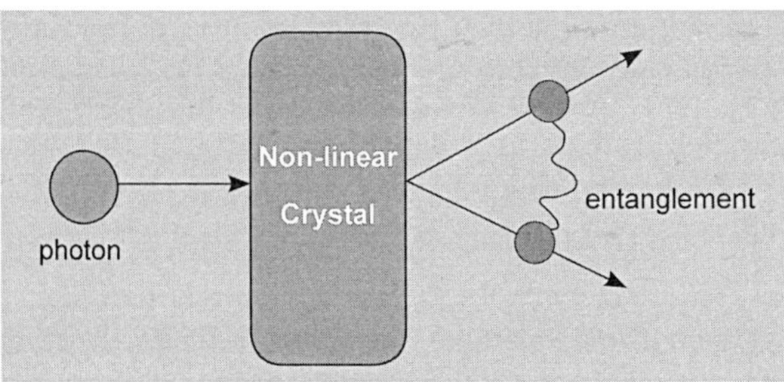

Fig.1.8: Two entangled photons created by a non-linear crystal

In this method, we shine a laser at a special non-linear crystal. The crystal then splits the incoming photon into two photons with correlated polarizations. **For example,** we can produce a pair of photons that always have perpendicular polarizations.

Schrodinger found that if a quantum system contains more than one particle then the superposition principle gives rise to the **phenomenon of entanglement, the interference of the system with itself. The result is an entangled system.**

Entanglement starts with two particles being generated in such a manner that the quantum state of each particle is linked to the other. **Please understand that if one particle in an entangled pair has a spin that is clockwise, the other particle will have a counter-clockwise spin. Also understand that the entangled particles are not treated as individual particles but rather as a whole. The state of this composite system is the sum or superposition of the product states of each local constituent.** Actually, there are many ways in which the particles become entangled. One such way is **subatomic particle decay.** It has been observed that if we separate two entangled particles then measure a property of one particle, like its spin and then measure the other particle's property then the two will be complementary. They are entangled. If no entanglement exists among particles then all qubits will work in isolation.

1.6 QUBITS AND MULTI-QUBIT STATE

As we know that classical bit is an abstraction of a physical system capable of being in one of the two states, 0 or 1. In classical computers, information is represented as the binary digits 0 or 1. These are called as **bits. For instance,** the number 2 is represented as 00000010. we place extra zeros in front to write every number with 8-bits, which is called one byte. Every classical computer translates these bits into human readable information. Computer hardware understands 1-bit as an electrical current flowing through a wire (in a transistor) whereas the 0-bit is the absence of an electrical current in a wire. These electrical signals can be thought of as "on" (bit 1) or "off" (0-bit). Computer then decodes these classical 1 or 0 bits into words or videos etc. On the other hand, Quantum bits or **qubits** are similar to bits only in that there are two measurable states called the 0 and 1 states. **But unlike classical bits, qubits can also be in a superposition state of these 0 and 1 states. The benefit of this is that certain calculations that would normally be performed on 0 or 1 separately on a classical computer could now be completed in a single operation using a qubit on a quantum computer. This will make computations much faster. Please note that although a single qubit is in a superposition of two classical bits, when a qubit is measured, the measurement actually only results in one classical bit of information –either 0 or 1. A qubit stores both 0 and 1 at the same time. A 64-bit classical computer means 2^{64} possible**

combinations. While 64-bit quantum computer means all 2^{64} states are being stored at the same time.

A **multi-qubit quantum system** can be formed by putting together a number of known quantum sub-systems. A sub-system based on a single qubit is generally described by its state that is defined to be a unit vector in some complex Hilbert space.

Mathematically, a multi-qubit system uses the concept of tensor product of vector spaces. The state space of the ith constituent of such a system is given by a separable Hilbert space, H_i. Each Hilbert space H_i has an orthogonal basis given by the following-

$$\{|i, k_i > k_i = k_i = 1, 2, \ldots\}, i = 1, 2, \ldots, n$$

The state space of the multi-qubit system is thus given as the tensor product space H defined by: -

$$H = H_1 \otimes H_2 \otimes \ldots \otimes H_n$$

where $\otimes$ represents the tensor product.

Also note that the basis states of a multi-qubit system are constructed from the basis-states of a single qubit using tensor product of vectors. The tensor product of two vectors u and v, assuming u and v are m-dimensional and n-dimensional respectively, has the dimension (m * n). Because in a single qubit system m = 2 = n, a two-qubit system has four basis states. These basis states are constructed from the single-qubit basis |0>, |1> using the following **rule: -**

$$|u> \otimes |v> = |u> |v> = |uv>$$

where u, v € {0, 1}.

For example, if the states of two qubits are given by: -

$$\Psi_1 = \alpha_0 |0> + \alpha_1 |1> \text{ and } \Psi_2 = \beta_0 |0> + \beta_1 |1>$$

Then the state of the composite system is given by: -

$$|\Psi> - |\psi_1> \otimes |\psi_2>$$
$$= \alpha_0 |0> + \alpha_1 |1> \otimes (\beta_0 |0> + \beta_1 |1>)$$

Now using the rule as given above-

$$|u> \otimes |v> = |u> |v> = |uv>$$

where u, v € {0, 1}.

Then, ψ can be written as-

$$|\Psi> = \alpha_0 \beta_0 |\mathbf{0}> |0> + \alpha_0 \beta_1 |\mathbf{0}> |\mathbf{1}> + \alpha_1 \beta_0 |\mathbf{1}> |0> + \alpha_1 \beta_1 |\mathbf{1}> |\mathbf{1}>$$

Hence, a two-qubit system has four basis states:

$$|0> \otimes |0>, |0> \otimes |1>, |1> \otimes |0>, |1> \otimes |1>,$$

For example, the **first state** in the **two-qubit system,** |0> $\otimes$ |0> **indicates that the first qubit is in state |0> and the second qubit is also in state |0>.** Similarly, for the state

|0> $\otimes$ |1> the first qubit is in the state |0> and the second qubit is in state |1>.

Using the **rule as stated above,** that is reproduced to easy understanding, as below: -

Rule: -

$$|u\rangle \otimes |v\rangle = |u\rangle |v\rangle = |uv\rangle$$

where u, v € {0, 1}.

The expression can be rewritten as-

$$|\Psi\rangle = \alpha_0 \beta_0 |0\rangle |0\rangle + \alpha_0 \beta_1 |0\rangle |1\rangle + \alpha_1 \beta_0 |1\rangle |0\rangle + \alpha_1 \beta_1 |1\rangle |1\rangle$$

And also as follows: -

$$|\Psi\rangle = \alpha_0 \beta_0 |00\rangle + \alpha_0 \beta_1 |01\rangle + \alpha_1 \beta_0 |10\rangle + \alpha_1 \beta_1 |11\rangle$$

Please note that every two-qubit state cannot be separated into two single-qubit states. In general, the state of a two-qubit system will take the form as follows: -

$$|\Psi\rangle = |00\rangle + c_1 |01\rangle + c_2 |10\rangle + c_3 |11\rangle$$

where

$$|c_0|^2 + |c_1|^2 + |c_2|^2 + |c_3|^2 = 1$$

Also remember that a collection of n qubits is called as a quantum register of size n. An n-qubit register has 2^n basis states, each of the form-

$$|c_0 \otimes |c_1 \otimes \ldots\ldots |c_{n-1}$$

with $c_i \in \{0, 1\}$.

A basis state can be represented by a number 0 to 2^{n-1}. For example, the state 1001 in a quantum register of size 4 is denoted by $|9\rangle_4$. A quantum register of n qubits can be in any superposition of 2^n states –

$$c_0 |0\rangle + c_1 |1\rangle + c_2 |2\rangle \ldots\ldots\ldots\ldots + c_2{}^{n-1} | 2^{n-1}\rangle$$

The point to ponder is that it is not possible to retrieve the states within a superposition because this process leads to the collapse of the superposition and produce just one of the original states $|j\rangle$ with probability $|c_j|^2$.

A quantum bit (or qubit) is a basic quantum object used to store information. A qubit, $|\psi\rangle$ is a vector in a 2D complex vector space i.e. with 2 components. We use Dirac's notation to represent a vector $|\psi\rangle$ as follows: -

$$|\psi\rangle = \alpha_0 |0\rangle + \alpha_1 |1\rangle$$

With α_0 and α_1 as complex numbers and with $|0\rangle$ and $|1\rangle$ being the vectors forming an orthonormal basis for this two dimensional vector space.

A classical bit can be in one of the two states, 0 or 1. Hence, we can represent the state of bit as $b = a_1 0 + a_2 1$, which has exactly 2 forms only-- $a_1 = 1$ and $a_2 = 0$. Also the value of bit is $b = 0$ or $a_1 = 0$ and $a_2 = 1$ and the value of bit is $b = 1$. On the other hand, the state of qubit can be represented by-

$$|\psi\rangle = \alpha_1 |0\rangle + \alpha_2 |1\rangle$$

where $|0\rangle$ and $|1\rangle$ is an orthogonal pair of the basis vectors called as **computational basis states.** The only constraints on the coefficients are that: -

(a) α_0 and α_1 are complex numbers, and

(b) $|\alpha_1|^2 + |\alpha_2|^2 = 1$.

And such a state is called as a **superposition of the basis vectors.** When we measure a classical bit we determine its state with a probability of 1 i.e. the bit is either in state 0 or state 1. The result is highly deterministic. In contrast, when we measure (or observe) a qubit we get the result as-

$$|0> \text{ with a probability } |\alpha_0|^2$$

$$|1> \text{ with a probability } |\alpha_1|^2$$

Now, for this to be true, we need **the vector length or the norm of the vector** to be equal to 1. Else the probabilities do not sum to unity. This means that-

$$|\alpha_0|^2 + |\alpha_1|^2 = \alpha_0^* \alpha_0 + \alpha_1^* \alpha_1 = 1$$

Then, we say that a qubit is in a **continuum of states between** |0> and |1> until we measure it.

For instance, a qubit can be in state-

$$½ |0> + \sqrt{3}/2 |1>$$

A measurement of qubit yields the result |0> with probability ¼ and |1> with probability ¾. **Please note that the superposition and the effect of measurement of a quantum state** (the state of the qubit) **means that there is hidden information that is preserved in a closed quantum system, until it is compelled to reveal itself to an external observer. Also note that we say that the system is closed until it interacts,** i.e. we perform an observation of the system. But the point to ponder is that how we use this hidden information? Till now we have chosen |0> and |1> vectors to represent a qubit. However, we can choose a different set of vectors also on orthogonal basis-

$$|+> = (|0> + |1>) / \sqrt{2}$$

and

$$|-> = (|0> - |1>) / \sqrt{2}$$

In this example, a qubit can be represented as follows: -

$$|\psi> = \alpha_0|0> + \alpha_1|1> = \alpha_0(|+>+|->)/\sqrt{2} + \alpha_1(|+>+|->)/\sqrt{2}$$

$$|\psi> = (\alpha_0 + \alpha_1)/\sqrt{2}|+> + (\alpha_0 - \alpha_1)/\sqrt{2}|->$$

Identity matrix Transformation of a Qubit

As we know the basics and shown basis vectors earlier. Now we show their duals also in matrix notation-

$$|0> = \begin{bmatrix}1\\0\end{bmatrix} \text{ and } |0> = (1\ 0)$$

$$|1> = \begin{bmatrix}0\\1\end{bmatrix} \text{ and } |1> = (0\ 1)$$

1.7 BRA-KET NOTATION

As studied earlier, a qubit is a quantum mechanical system based on the state of a particle. This can be the polarization of a photon, the spin of an electron or several other properties. Also we studied that, a typical way of representing the quantum state of a qubit is by a linear superposition of its two orthonormal basis states that are named as **basis vectors. Linear algebra says that "if two vectors are**

both orthogonal i.e. **perpendicular to each other,** and have a unit length (length =1), **the vectors are said to be orthonormal.**"

As explained earlier, that qubits can exist in a blended state. So, they are decorated with extra symbols to distinguish them from standard bits. In particular, we will label the idealized states as |0> and |1> respectively. The names **bra and ket** come from Paul Dirac. These are called as Dirac's notations. A vector is simply a list of numbers. The **dimension of the vector is the number of numbers in the list.** ***If the lists are written vertically, we call them column vectors or kets. If the lists are written horizontally then we call them row vectors or bras.*** **And the numbers that make up a vector are called as entries.**

There are many ways to represent the state of a qubit: -

1. Using Dirac's notation.
2. Using Block sphere.

Let us discuss the second method now.

1.8 BLOCK SPHERE REPRESENTATION

As we know that a classical bit can be in one of the two states, 0 or 1. That is, a qubit in a superposition state, $|\psi> = (|0> + |1>) / \sqrt{2}$. In figure 1.9, $\theta = 90^\circ$ and $\phi = 0^\circ$ whereas a qubit can be in a continuum of states represented as points on the Block Sphere (as shown in fig. 1.9(a) and 1.9(b)).

Imagine that if a coin is being tossed, then figure 1.9(a) on left shows the state of a coin, i.e. either 0 or 1. While fig. 1.9(b) shows 1-qubit where the north pole shows bit 0 i.e. tail while south pole shows bit 1 i.e. head. **Also note that the black dots on this block sphere shows the superposition states that can be in 0 and 1 state simultaneously. If we try to measure the state of these dots on the sphere then the system collapses to either 0 or 1 which contradicts the basic principle of superposition.**

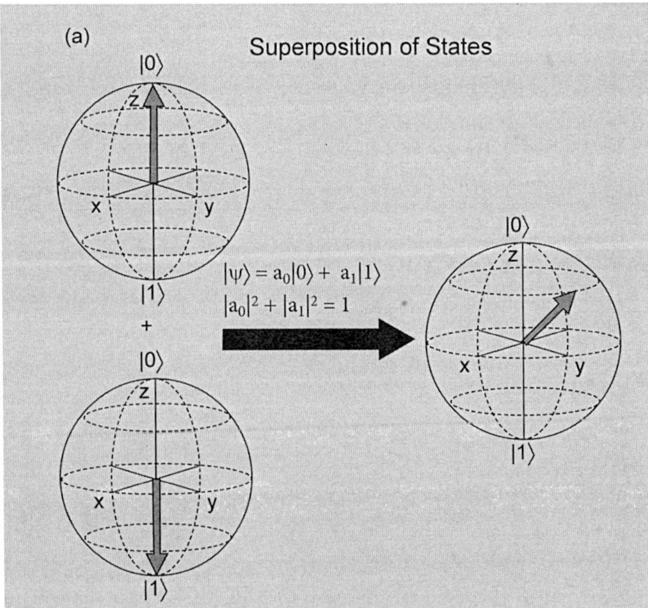

Fig.1.9: A qubit in a superposition state

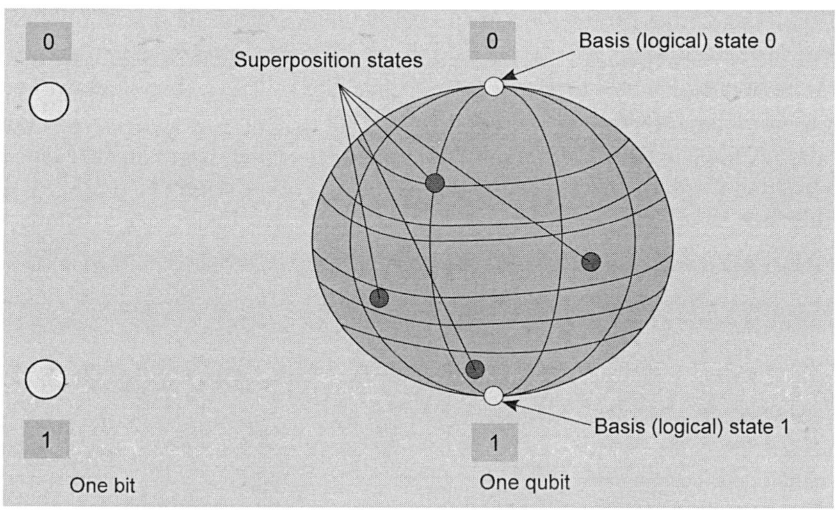

Fig.1.9 (a): One bit, **Fig.1.9** 9(b) One Qubit

The state space of a qubit contains the two '**basis' or "logical" states, |0> and |1>. Please note that the initial state of a qubit is always assumed to be one of the basis states. Also note that the classical information revealed by one qubit is the label of one of the two basis states while the contents of the quantum information encoded to a qubit is more richer.** Figure 1.9(a) and 1.9(b) shows both the cases. Fig. 1.9(a) shows that a bit can be in one of the two states, 0 or 1. **Fig.** 1.9(b) shows the state $|\psi>$ of a qubit being represented as a vector from the origin to a point on the Block Sphere. A qubit can be in a basis state, $|0>$ or $|1>$ or in a superposition state $|\psi> = \alpha_0 |0> + \alpha_1 |1>$ with $|\alpha_0|^2 + |\alpha_1|^2 = 1$.

Single qubit operations are defined as **rotations on the Block sphere.** It provides us another way to think about **a set of gates that satisfies universal computation is the one which enables us to reach any point on the Block sphere.**

1.9 MEASURING QUANTUM STATES

The effect of a measurement on the state of one qubit is very significant. A measurement forces a qubit in a superposition state to one of the two basis states. A qubit in the superposition state $|\psi> = \alpha_0 | 0> + \alpha_1 | 1>$ behaves like $|0>$ with the probability $p_0 = |\alpha_0|^2$ and like $|1>$ with probability $p_1 = |\alpha_1|^2$. This is shown in figure 1.10(a) and 1.10(b).

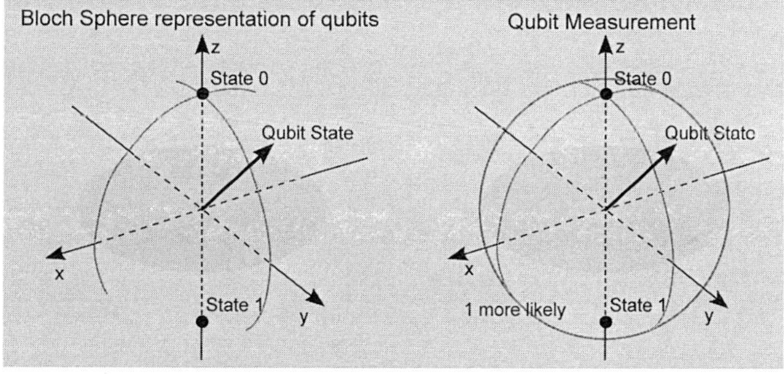

Fig.1.10 (a): Measuring Qubit states

Figure-1.10(a) shows that the vector shown on the block sphere may be at any position showing the qubit state in superposition. However, because the south pole shows state-1 while north pole shows state-0, so the state above the x-axis may represent 0 more likely while it shows 1 state more likely below x-axis. Hence, the problem of showing the qubit state at all instances of time (except north and south pole) can be done as shown in fig. 1.10(b). **Please remember that if we try to measure the qubit state on this block sphere then it will be in a superposition state. Scientists observed that if we try to measure the state of qubit then it collapses to either 0 or 1. This contradicts the principle of superposition too.**

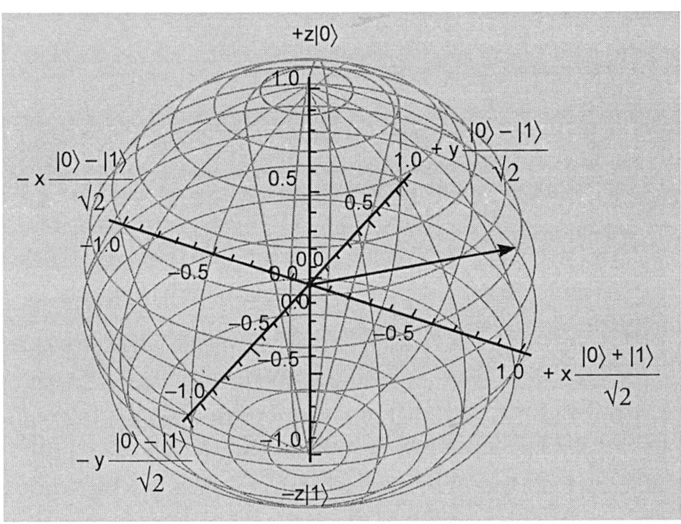

Fig. 1.10: (b) Writing of Qubit states

Quantum measurements of 1 qubit in state $|\psi\rangle = \alpha_0 \mid 0\rangle + \alpha_1 \mid 1\rangle$ are characterized by a set of linear operators with the associated matrices, $\{M_k\}$. And the probability that the outcome with index k occurs as a result of the measurement is: -

$$p(k) = \langle\psi \mid M^+{}_k M_k \mid \psi\rangle$$

Also note that sum of probabilities of all possible outcomes of the measurement must be equal to 1. That is,

$$\Sigma_k p(k) = \Sigma_k \langle\psi \mid M^+{}_k M_k \mid \psi\rangle = 1$$

Remember that the measurement causes the qubit to change its state. **And the point to ponder is that if the state of the qubit immediately prior to the measurement is** $|\psi\rangle$ **then after the measurement** M_k, it becomes $|\varphi_k\rangle$ i.e.

$$|\psi\rangle \rightarrow |\varphi_k\rangle = M_k |\psi\rangle / \sqrt{\langle\psi \mid M^+{}_k M_k \mid \psi\rangle}$$

Before measurement (↗ $|\psi\rangle$)   after measurement (↖ $|\varphi_k\rangle$)

There are only two possible outcomes of a measurement in the {|0>, |1>} basis. **Note that we can only observe the basis state |0> or |1>** (see figure-1.11)

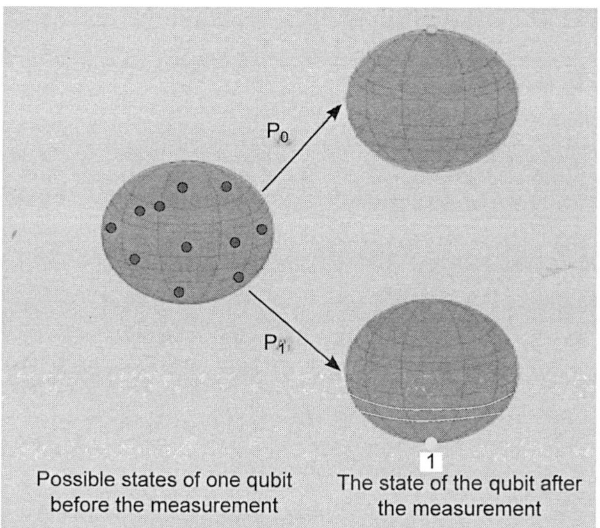

Fig.1.11: Measurement Effects

Therefore, the corresponding matrices of the measurement operators are as follows: -

$$M_0 = |0><0| = \begin{bmatrix} 1 \\ 0 \end{bmatrix} (1\,0) = \begin{bmatrix} 1 & 0 \\ 0 & 0 \end{bmatrix} \text{ and}$$

$$M_1 = |1><1| = \begin{bmatrix} 0 \\ 1 \end{bmatrix} (0\,1) = \begin{bmatrix} 0 & 0 \\ 0 & 1 \end{bmatrix}$$

Also note here that these two operators are Hermitian and also $(M_0^+.M_0) = M_0$ **and** $M_1^+.M_1 = M_1$**.** That is,

$$M_0^{'} = \begin{bmatrix} 1 & 0 \\ 0 & 0 \end{bmatrix} = M_0$$

$$(M_0^+.M_0) = M_0^2 = \begin{bmatrix} 1 & 0 \\ 0 & 0 \end{bmatrix} \begin{bmatrix} 1 & 0 \\ 0 & 0 \end{bmatrix} = \begin{bmatrix} 1 & 0 \\ 0 & 0 \end{bmatrix} = M_0$$

Also, we can now write that-

$$M_1^+ = \begin{bmatrix} 0 & 0 \\ 0 & 1 \end{bmatrix} = M_1$$

$$(M_1^+.M_1) = M_1^{\,2} = \begin{bmatrix} 0 & 0 \\ 0 & 1 \end{bmatrix} \begin{bmatrix} 0 & 0 \\ 0 & 1 \end{bmatrix} = \begin{bmatrix} 0 & 0 \\ 0 & 1 \end{bmatrix} = M_1$$

Referring to figure- 1.11 above, the probability of the outcome corresponding to |0> is as follows: -

$$p_0 = <\psi \mid M^+{}_0 M_0 \mid \psi> = <\psi \mid M_0 \mid \psi>$$

First of all, **we calculate the effect of applying the operator M_0 to the qubit state** $|\psi>$ **: -**

$$M_0 |\psi> = \begin{bmatrix} 1 & 0 \\ 0 & 0 \end{bmatrix} \begin{bmatrix} \alpha_0 \\ \alpha_1 \end{bmatrix} = \begin{bmatrix} \alpha_0 \\ 0 \end{bmatrix}$$

Also note that the bra vector $<\psi| = (\alpha^*_0 \;\; \alpha^*_1)$ **is the dual of the original vector,** $<\psi|$

So, we get: -

$$M_0 |\psi> = \begin{bmatrix} \alpha_0 \\ 0 \end{bmatrix} = \alpha_0 \begin{bmatrix} 1 \\ 0 \end{bmatrix} = \alpha_0 |0>$$

Hence, we can say that **the state of the qubit after applying the measurement operator,** M_0 is as follows: -

$$|\varphi_0> = M_0 |\psi> / \sqrt{<\psi| M^+{}_0 M_0 |\psi>}$$
$$= \alpha_0 |0> / |\alpha_0>$$
$$= (\alpha_0 / |\alpha_0|) . |0>$$

Similarly, **the probability of the outcome corresponding to** $|1>$ **is-**

$$p_1 = <\psi| M^+{}_1 M_1 |\psi> = <\psi| M_1 |\psi>$$

Similarly, **we calculate the effect of applying the operator M_1 to the qubit state** $|\psi>$ **: -**

$$M_1 |\psi> = \begin{bmatrix} 0 & 0 \\ 0 & 1 \end{bmatrix} \begin{bmatrix} \alpha_0 \\ \alpha_1 \end{bmatrix} = \begin{bmatrix} 0 \\ \alpha_1 \end{bmatrix}$$

Or

$$M_1 |\psi> = \alpha_1 |1>$$

Then we can write as follows: -

$$p_1 = <\psi| (M_1 |\psi> = (\alpha^*_0 \;\; \alpha^*_1) \begin{bmatrix} 0 \\ \alpha_1 \end{bmatrix} = |\alpha_1|^2$$

So, the state of the qubit after applying the measurement operator M_1 is-

$$|\varphi_1> = M_1 |\psi> / \sqrt{<\psi| M^+{}_1 M_1 |\psi>}$$
$$= \alpha_1 |1> / |\alpha_1>$$
$$= (\alpha_1 / |\alpha_1|). |1>$$

The completeness condition is hence satisfied, because-

$$p(0) + p(1) = |\alpha_0|^2 + |\alpha_1|^2 = 1.$$ Hence, proved.

1.10 A PAIR OF QUBITS AND BELL STATES

John Bell (1964), proposed a method to test for the existence of the proposed hidden variables. Let us understand this theorem of quantum mechanics namely **Bell's inequality or Bell's theorem** with the help of an example. Consider two photons that are entangled. Bell claimed that the only way to account for the perfect correlation in quantumly entangled particles, without invoking non-locality, was that there must be pre-existing values.

Consider now a system of 2-qubits in a 4D complex vector space. In this Hilbert space of dimension four (H_4), we choose as a basis, the 4 vectors |00>, |01>, |10> and |11>. A vector (on block sphere) describing the state | ψ> **of 2-qubit system is a linear combination of the basis vectors with complex coefficients** $\alpha_{00}, \alpha_{01}, \alpha_{10}$, and α_{11}, i.e.

$$|\psi\rangle = \alpha_{00}|00\rangle + \alpha_{01}|01\rangle + \alpha_{01}|00\rangle + \alpha_{10}|10\rangle + \alpha_{11}|11\rangle$$

Please note that when we measure a pair of qubits we project the state |ψ> of the system to one of the four basis states |00>, |01>, |10> and |11> with corresponding probabilities $|\alpha_{00}|^2$, $|\alpha_{01}|^2$, $|\alpha_{10}|^2$, or $|\alpha_{11}|^2$ respectively. That is,

Ψ or states	Probability
|00>	$|\alpha_{00}|^2$
|01>	$|\alpha_{01}|^2$
|10>	$|\alpha_{10}|^2$
|11>	$|\alpha_{11}|^2$

Also note that the normalization condition reflects that the norm of the vector |ψ> is one. Hence, the sum of probabilities must also be one: -

$$|\alpha_{00}|^2 + |\alpha_{01}|^2 + |\alpha_{10}|^2 + |\alpha_{11}|^2 = 1$$

The point to ponder is that before the measurement, the state of the two qubits is uncertain whereas after the measurement the state is certain. It is **|00>, |01>, |10> and |11> which is analogous to our classical 2-bit system which takes one of the four values, 00, 01, 10, or 11.**

So, we observed that it is not possible to measure the qubit when it is in superposition. There is no hard and fast rule that we must observe both qubits. But what happens if we observe only first qubit and then only second qubit? Two cases arise here: -

Case-1: Measure/ observe first qubit only.

Case-2: Measure/ observe second qubit only.

Case-1: If we measure only the 1st bit, then we expect the system to be left in an uncertain state because we did not measure the second qubit which can still be in a continuum of states. The first qubit can be 0 with probability-

$$p'_0 = |\alpha_{00}|^2 + |\alpha_{01}|^2$$

or 1 with probability-

$$p'_1 = |\alpha_{10}|^2 + |\alpha_{11}|^2$$

The normalization condition is satisfied, the sum of the two probabilities is unity-

$$p'_0 + p'_1 = 1$$

Say, $|\psi'_0\rangle$ **is the post-measurement state when the first qubit is measured to be 0 and** $|\psi'_1\rangle$ **when the first qubit is measured to be 1.** The two **post-measurement states** are as follows: -

$$|\psi'_0\rangle = (\alpha_{00}|00\rangle + \alpha_{01}|01\rangle) / \sqrt{|\alpha_{00}|^2 + |\alpha_{01}|^2}$$

$$|\psi'_1\rangle = (\alpha_{10}|10\rangle + \alpha_{11}|11\rangle) / \sqrt{|\alpha_{10}|^2 + |\alpha_{11}|^2}$$

Let us now measure the 2nd qubit only.

Case-2: The second qubit can be 0 with probability: -

$$p''_0 = |\alpha_{00}|^2 + |\alpha_{10}|^2$$

or 1 with probability-

$$p''_1 = |\alpha_{01}|^2 + |\alpha_{11}|^2$$

Again the normalization condition requires that-

$$p''_0 + p''_1 = 1$$

Now, the two post-measurement states are: -

$$|\psi''_0\rangle = (\alpha_{00}|00\rangle + \alpha_{10}|10\rangle) / \sqrt{|\alpha_{00}|^2 + |\alpha_{10}|^2}$$

$$|\psi''_1\rangle = (\alpha_{01}|01\rangle + \alpha_{11}|11\rangle) / \sqrt{|\alpha_{01}|^2 + |\alpha_{11}|^2}$$

Special state of a two-qubit system-

When $\alpha_{00} = \alpha_{11} = 1/\sqrt{2}$

And

$$\alpha_{01} = \alpha_{10} = 0$$

This state is called as a Bell state and the pair of qubits is called as an EPR pair, (Einstein, Podolsky and Rosen) were the first ones to consider the strange behavior of states like Bell states. If the 2-qubit system is in this state, when we measure the first qubit the two possible outcomes are 0 with probability ½ and 1 with probability 1/2 . The corresponding post-measurement states are as below: -

$$|\psi''_0\rangle = |00\rangle$$

And

$$|\psi''_1\rangle = |11\rangle$$

Conclusions: The two measurements are correlated. Once we measure the first qubit we get exactly the same result as and when we measure the second one. **The two qubits need not be physically constrained to be at the same location and yet because of the strong coupling between them, measurements performed on the second allow us to determine the state of the first. There are four special states called as the Bell states.** They form an orthonormal basis: -

1. $|\beta_{00}\rangle = (|00\rangle + |11\rangle) / \sqrt{2}$
2. $|\beta_{01}\rangle = (|01\rangle + |10\rangle) / \sqrt{2}$
3. $|\beta_{10}\rangle = (|00\rangle - |11\rangle) / \sqrt{2}$
4. $|\beta_{11}\rangle = (|01\rangle - |10\rangle) / \sqrt{2}$

Please note that the Bell states can be distinguished from one another. All four states are called as maximally entangled states. The last one is called an anti-correlated state. Also note that an EPR pair is in one of the four Bell states.

1.11 QUANTUM FRAGILITY

We now understand that classical information may be encoded into a quantum system. Having an infinite number of states of a qubit has enormous possibilities. We have also seen that a 2-qubit system is very much dazzling. **The point to ponder is that the quantum information is encoded into very**

fragile non-local correlations of different parts of a physical system. Also note that we say that these interactions are 'fragile' because a quantum system interacts continually with its environment and these interactions with the environment destroy the correlations encoded into the quantum system. The internal correlations of a quantum system are transferred into correlations between the quantum systems and the environment. **Thus, the information encoded into the quantum system is lost.**

What can go wrong with quantum information?

1. If we try to measure the state of a qubit in a quantum system then the system collapses.
2. Quantum information cannot be copied (no cloning theorem will be discussed later).
3. Errors like noise errors may be found.
4. **With classical bits we observe bit-flip errors i.e. a 0 becomes a 1 and vice versa.** We expect the same thing to happen to qubits: -

$$|0> \rightarrow |1> \text{and} |1> \rightarrow |0>.$$

5. Also, a qubit may experience **a phase error i.e. the phase may flip** and then

$$|0> \rightarrow |0> \text{and} |1> \rightarrow - |1>.$$

6. **The quantum information is continuous. If the state of the qubit is –**

$$|\psi> = \alpha_0 |0> + \alpha_1 |1>$$

Then, either α_0 or α_1 or both may change by an infinitesimal quantity, ϵ. And then we experience a qubit error of a new type, one we cannot encounter when dealing with classical bits.

1.12 ROTATION OPERATIONS ON THE BLOCK SPHERE

Single qubit operations are defined as the rotations on the block sphere. When a qubit is represented as a spin one-half particle, the Pauli spin matrices, $\sigma = \{\sigma_x, \sigma_y, \sigma_z\}$ will describe the spin rotations on the Block Sphere. Before we derive the rotation matrices, let us firstly discuss matrix exponentiation. If β is a real number and if matrix A is such that $A^2 = I$ then,

$$e^{i\beta A} = \cos(\beta) I + i \sin(\beta) A$$

If σ is a Pauli matrix, then a finite rotation through an angle β about a given vector n on the Block Sphere is defined as a linear operator with matrix representation-

$$R_n(\beta) = \exp(-i (\beta/2)\, n . \sigma)$$

$$= \cos(\beta/2) \mathbf{I} - \mathbf{i} \sin(\beta/2) \mathbf{n}.\sigma$$

where **(n .σ) is the scalar product of the two vectors.** In this equation, $n = (n_x, n_y, n_z)$ and

$$\sigma = \{\sigma_x, \sigma_y, \sigma_z\} \text{ with –}$$

$$\sigma_x = \begin{bmatrix} 0 & 1 \\ 1 & 0 \end{bmatrix}$$

$$\sigma_y = \begin{bmatrix} 0 & -i \\ i & 0 \end{bmatrix}$$

$$\sigma_z = \begin{bmatrix} 1 & 0 \\ 0 & -1 \end{bmatrix}$$

The rotations about the x, y and z axis with the same angle β are denoted as $R_x(\beta)$, $R_y(\beta)$ and $R_z(\beta)$ respectively. And they are computed by observing that (n . σ) becomes [(1, 0, 0) . (σ_x, 0, 0)], [(0, 1, 0) . (0, σ_y, 0)] and [(0, 0, 1). (0, 0,σ_z)] respectively.

Hence, **the final rotations matrices along x, y and z-axis on a block sphere showing a unit vector as a qubit** are as follows: -

I.

$$R_x(\beta) = \cos(\beta/2)\, I - i \sin(\beta/2)\, \sigma_x$$

$$= \begin{bmatrix} \cos(\beta/2) & 0 \\ 0 & \cos(\beta/2) \end{bmatrix} + \begin{bmatrix} 0 & -i\sin(\beta/2) \\ -i\sin(\beta/2) & 0 \end{bmatrix}$$

Therefore, we can say that the rotation of a qubit along x-axis on a block sphere is given by the expression: -

$$R_x(\beta) = \begin{bmatrix} \cos(\beta/2) & -i\sin(\beta/2) \\ -i\sin(\beta/2) & \cos(\beta/2) \end{bmatrix}$$

II.

$$R_y(\beta) = \cos(\beta/2)\, I - i \sin(\beta/2)\, \sigma_y$$

$$= \begin{bmatrix} \cos(\beta/2) & 0 \\ 0 & \cos(\beta/2) \end{bmatrix} + \begin{bmatrix} 0 & -\sin(\beta/2) \\ \sin(\beta/2) & 0 \end{bmatrix}$$

Therefore, we can say that the rotation of a qubit along y-axis on a block sphere is given by the expression: -

$$R_y(\beta) = \begin{bmatrix} \cos(\beta/2) & -\sin(\beta/2) \\ \sin(\beta/2) & \cos(\beta/2) \end{bmatrix}$$

III.

$$R_z(\beta) = \cos(\beta/2)\, I - i \sin(\beta/2)\, \sigma_z$$

$$= \begin{bmatrix} \cos(\beta/2) & 0 \\ 0 & \cos(\beta/2) \end{bmatrix} + \begin{bmatrix} -i\sin(\beta/2) & 0 \\ 0 & i\sin(\beta/2) \end{bmatrix}$$

Therefore, we can say that the rotation of a qubit along z-axis on a block sphere is given by the expression: -

$$R_z(\beta) = \begin{bmatrix} \cos(\beta/2) - i\sin(\beta/2) & 0 \\ 0 & \cos(\beta/2)\, i\sin(\beta/2) \end{bmatrix}$$

$$= \begin{bmatrix} e^{-i\beta/2} & 0 \\ 0 & e^{i\beta/2} \end{bmatrix}$$

Thus, **the composition of two rotations with angles δ and β is: -**

$$R_z(\delta)\, R_x(\beta) = \begin{bmatrix} e^{-i\delta/2}\cos(\beta/2) & -ie^{-i\delta/2}\sin(\beta/2) \\ -ie^{i\delta/2}\sin(\beta/2) & e^{i\delta/2}\cos(\beta/2) \end{bmatrix}$$

Please note that any rotation on the Block Sphere can be reduced to the previous expression for some angles δ and β. Also note that the rotation operations are invertible i.e. a rotation about the x,

y or z axis with an angle β followed by a rotation with an angle –β about the same axis is equivalent to an identity transformation, as it leaves the qubit in the original state. That is,

$$R_x(\beta)\, R_x(-\beta) = I$$
$$R_y(\beta)\, R_y(-\beta) = I$$
$$R_z(\beta)\, R_z(-\beta) = I.$$

1.13 QUANTUM COMPUTER APPLICATIONS

Be it any field of science-Physics, Chemistry or Biology, Quantum has its ramifications everywhere. Some of the applications of Quantum Computing and hence Quantum Computers that work on Quantum Algorithms are as follows:-

1. **Quantum Computers can simulate chemistry:** Researchers and scientists have used Google's Sycamore processor to perform the largest chemistry simulations using **Quantum Computers. For example,** simulating molecular reactions that may result in newer batteries and newer drugs. **Please understand that performing these kinds of simulations becomes exponentially more complex as molecules get larger and Quantum Computers can overcome these challenges.** Researchers at Google Quantum AI, Columbia University, and The University of California used Monte Carlo algorithm and relied on this algorithm designed for quantum physics models of fermions (a class of particles that includes electrons). Such algorithms working on classical computers do not scale well to simulating larger molecules. Also the researchers found that a hybrid approach (classical + quantum) could help this algorithm to overcome this obstacle. Scientists simulated the H4 molecules, molecular nitrogen and solid diamond. These involved as many as 120 orbitals. These are the largest chemistry simulations performed to date with the help of quantum computers. Some of the quantum computing packages capable of performing quantum chemistry simulations on a quantum computer are listed below:-
   - (a) **CHEMIQ** (developed by Origin Quantum in China).
   - (b) **INQUANTO** (by Quantinuum).
   - (c) **Microsoft's quantum chemistry package** that provides a Quantum Chemistry Library for performing quantum chemistry simulations via its cloud known as **Azure Quantum.** It is developed in Q# as a HLL to write the instructions to the quantum computer.
   - (d) **OPENFERMION** is an **open-source chemistry package** for quantum computers. It has been launched by **Google. It is possible to submit various quantum algorithms for quantum chemistry on quantum computers via Google's cloud platform.** Also, Xanadu at Toronto, Canada, created **Pennylane as a cross-platform Quantum Python library capable of performing Quantum Chemistry Simulations on any platform.**
   - (e) **QAMUY:** It is a **quantum computing cloud service** for chemistry (by QunaSys in Japan). It can perform quantum chemical calculations on quantum computers. It provides single-point energy calculations, geometry optimization, molecular dynamics, excited state calculations etc. for molecules and periodic systems. **Right from input till analysis, it is a complete package.**

(f) **QISKIT NATURE:** Developed by IBM Quantum, is the earliest software development kit for quantum computing. It can perform various quantum chemistry simulations. It has a robust collection of quantum algorithms for quantum chemistry. Also they provide open-access to real quantum hardware using a IBM-ID on the IBM Quantum Lab.

(g) **QUBEC:** It is a quantum computing platform particularly designed for applications in the field of chemistry, developed by Qu&Co in Netherlands.

2. **Quantum Computers used to design signed Binary Subtractor using Quantum Gates** (to be discussed shortly in next chapter).
3. **Quantum Computing Optimization Techniques for Network Coding for communication and signal processing.**
4. **New superconducting diodes could improve performance of Quantum Computers and AI.** This diode, developed at University of Minnesota, is more energy-efficient and tunable superconductor diode. This device is more energy efficient as it can process multiple electrical signals at a time, contains a series of gates to control the flow of energy (not available in earlier diodes). **Note that earlier diodes were made of semiconductors but now scientists have made new superconducting diode that has an ability to transfer energy without losing any power.**
5. **The** computing power of quantum machines is still very low. It is in its infancy stage. So, increasing the performance is the main challenge. University of Innsbruck, Austria, presented a new architecture for a Universal Parity quantum computer that overcomes such limitations. **Please note that qubits serve as a computing unit and as a memory at the same time. Also note that all qubits in a quantum computer must be able to interact with each other because the quantum information cannot be copied and it cannot be stored in memory as in the case of a classical computer. After optimization, however, it was shown by them that the physical qubits in this architecture do not represent individual bits but encode the relative coordination between the bits. This means that not all qubits have to interact with each other anymore.** But parity computers can perform operations between two or more qubits on a single qubit.
6. **Quantum Computing in AI field:** It includes many applications like Quantum Game Theory, Quantum algorithms for decision problems, Quantum algorithms for Learning and Quantum Search.
7. **There is a need for light-matter interfaces for the quantum internet, to connect computers together. Sparrow Quantum** is trying to become leader in the market today for light-matter interfaces for commercial quantum technologies. Kurt Stokbro, the CEO of Sparrow Quantum and Peter Lodahl, the chief science officer of Sparrow Quantum quote that **"the qubit quality i.e. the fidelity of the photons that we generate is very high."** Denmark is also a good home, to a burgeoning quantum system. This would naturally help Sparrow Quantum's growth.
8. In another application, scientists created a **biological quantum circuit,** *i.e. quantum entangling of a multi-celled organism.*
9. **Nuclear Quantum Computing:** University of New South Wales explained how entangling an electron with the nuclei of two phosphorous atoms allowed them to control them as qubits without any information loss.

10. Quantum computers can **calculate the molecular energy** also.
11. **Quadratic Unconstrained Binary Optimization (QUBO) is a mathematical problem formulation used in the field of optimization and computational complexity theory.** The purpose of QUBO-problem is **to find the binary variable's values that minimize a quadratic objective function, subject to certain constraints.** The word **'quadratic'** here refers to the quadratic nature of the objective function that as you know involves the square of the variables. **'Unconstrained'** means that there are no explicit constraints on the variables and **'Binary'** indicates that the variables can only take on binary values. Now this QUBO-problem is of great significance in different fields of optimization, machine learning and quantum computing. Many real-world optimization problems like resource allocation, logistics planning and scheduling have been solved using QUBO. **Please note that QUBO-problems have gained attention in the context of quantum computing because they can be efficiently mapped to certain types of quantum hardware like quantum annealers.** We define **quantum annealing as a technique that is used to find the minimum energy state of a physical system that can be applied to solve QUBO-problems. Also note that ability to map QUBO-problems to quantum annealing hardware has led to advancements in solving complex optimization problems using quantum computing techniques.**
12. Microsoft has built their version of a **quantum supercomputer that is a huge machine which can solve certain problems better than classical computers.**
13. Another application of quantum computing comes with the fact that today 'Entanglement' and 'Communication' with Quantum Mechanics has opened up a new field of secure communication.
14. Besides the search and cryptography applications, quantum computers are valuable tools for Quantum AI, Quantum Machine Learning (QML), Quantum Neural Networks (QNN) and Quantum Deep Learning (QDL). Machine learning algorithms perform tasks like image recognition by finding hidden patterns in the data and then creating mathematical models that allow algorithm to recognize data patterns in data sets. Here, success means involving huge amount of data for training. But with QML, the huge range of different states open to quantum particles implies that now we need fewer parameters and lesser training data too.
15. Financial applications like risk management, logistics etc. also have a chance of benefitting from quantum computers.

SUMMARY

In this chapter, we have studied what is Quantum Computing? What are its units of measurement or information storage mechanisms? Quantum computing uses quantum mechanics to perform calculations. Building quantum computer is a challenging task as qubits are highly sensitive to environmental noise. They need complex error-correction techniques. At the intersection of quantum computing and machine learning lays QML or Quantum Machine Learning. Several libraries and platforms facilitate the development of QML algorithms and applications.

The key advantages of quantum computing includes: -

- Parallelism.
- Quantum superposition.

- Quantum entanglement.
- Improved accuracy.
- Security.
- Cryptography.
- Optimization.
- Machine learning.
- Chemistry.
- Finance.
- Weather forecasting.
- Particle physics.

We found that there are three main pillars of quantum computing, namely, **Superposition, Entanglement and Interference.**

At a high level, quantum entanglement is the deep link that can exist between two qubits, no matter the distance that separates them. When dealing with multiple qubits, we cannot simply consider them separately so we must take into account the joint system that will be mathematically described by the tensor product of the individual states. An interesting aspect of quantum systems is that the product states and entangled states are not mutually exclusive categories i.e. a quantum state can evolve from one to the other under the action of certain quantum gates. **Please understand that it is the phenomenon of quantum entanglement that allows quantum computers to perform complex calculations in parallel. Entanglement implies that an alteration in the state of one entangled particle instantaneously affect the state of other particles, no matter how far apart they are.** Hence, an entangled state cannot be factorized as a product of the states of its constituents i.e. it cannot be broken down into separate states for each particle.

Quantum Supercomputers are no more a dream now rather a reality. It is also said by the researchers that they observed a sort of mechanical vibration between two layers of atoms by observing the type of light those atoms emitted when stimulated by a laser. This team of scientists had earlier studied a **quantum-level quasi-particle called as an 'exciton'. Information can be encoded into an exciton and then released in form of a photon** i.e. a tiny particle of energy considered to be the quantum unit of light. **Note here that those quantum properties of each photon emitted like photon's polarization, wavelength etc. can function as a quantum bit of information (or qubits). Also note that because this qubit is carried by a photon, it travels at the speed of light.** In this chapter, the bird's- eye view of having a strong quantum network, we always have a desire to have different new ways of reliably creating, operating, storing and transmitting qubits. **Photons are a natural choice for transmitting this quantum information because optical fibers enable us to transport photons long distances at high speeds with low losses of energy or information.** The scientists moved from 'Photon' to 'Phonon' which is another type of quasi-particle that is the product of atomic vibration, which is similar to breathing. What was actually observed is **that every single photon emitted by an exciton was coupled with one or more phonons.** This was just like climbing a quantum energy ladder up. This was the overarching goal i.e. from photons to excitons and then to phonons. The challenge is compounded by the difficulty in building the quantum hardware itself. Actually, quantum computers can store data in qubits and these qubits can be made using various technologies like superconducting rings, optical traps and photons of light. Also some technologies require cooling to near absolute zero others operate at room temperature only. Qubits are coaxed into superposition states and are also entangled with each other. Running algorithms on a quantum computer involves directing the evolution of these superposition states. The quantum rules used here are not possible on classical machines. Complex computations are possible on quantum computer machines with a huge number of qubits. Also qubits and their interactions must be robust against errors introduced through the effects of thermal vibrations, cosmic rays, electromagnetic interference and other sources of noise. **These disturbances can result in the leakage of some vital information from the processor and this situation is known as decoherence.** Actually, today operational tweaks are ripe for exploration in this field. Drug discovery and materials science applications might require quantum computers that can perform a trillion decoherence –free operations in lesser time.

Scientific findings tell that for very small problem sizes, the classical computer is faster whereas for larger problem sizes, the quantum computer is faster. The need is to invent novel high-speed quantum algorithms.

Quantum computing can process a huge amount of data sets at a much quicker speeds and feed data to AI technologies which can then feed data to AI technologies, which can analyze data to a finer level to find patterns and abnormalities. **Note that with quantum computers we can do more and better advanced analysis and construct machine learning (ML) models.** That is,

Quantum Computing ---→ more and more datasets ---→ AI technology ---→ analyze data ----→ to find patterns

Thus, it makes it so much easier to use more data, allowing data scientists to have a better understanding of the data they are working with. Another team of data scientists found that deep-learning AI technology can accurately quantify the amount of entanglement in a given system. We also know that measuring a quantum state will destroy it. They have developed a technique named as **quantum tomography where multiple copies of the state are made and each is measured. This technique can ensure 100% accuracy.** This team used AI to improve on the precision of estimates of the degree of entanglement of a given system rather than measuring them directly. So, the AI app was taught to study entangled quantum states using data generated by another system that provided numerical data. Then, the AI apps used the resulting data to generate successive estimations of the degree of entanglement that grew more precise with each run. Some proposed quantum machine learning algorithms are like quantum support vector machine (QSVM), quantum principal component analysis (QPCA), quantum k-means. An example of QML is the quantum approximate optimization algorithm (QAOA) which is used to solve the optimization problems. QAOA is a hybrid algorithm that combines classical optimization with quantum operations to find the optimal solution to a problem. Another field gaining momentum in this arena is sparrow based quantum communication, quantum computers on cloud and so on. Some platforms and libraries for QML are as follows: -

- TensorFlow Quantum (TFQ) source: *https://www.tensorflow.org/quantum*
- PennyLane source: *https://pennylane.ai*
- Qiskit Machine Learning source: *https://qiskit.org/ecosystem/machine-learning/*
- Pyquil source: *https://pyquil-docs.rigetti.com/en/stable*
- IBM Q Experience source: *https://quantum-computing.ibm.com/*

TFQ is a library as developed by Google. It helps us to create QML models. It provides a high-level interface for constructing quantum circuits. We will study most of these libraries in next few chapters but for now the discussion of **Pyquil** lies in the point of reference. Actually, Pyquil is **a library for quantum programming in Python.** It was developed by Rigetti Computing. **Forest is a suite of software tools for developing and running quantum applications. It includes Pyquil and other tools for quantum programming as well as a cloud based platform for running quantum simulations and experiments.**

On 22nd December 2023, supercomputer for quantum computing was dedicated to Sir Ramanujan, whose extraordinary contributions led to quantum entropy. It is a scale-up product for corporates with computing power for new multi-disciplinary initiatives based on quantum communication and computing.

MULTIPLE CHOICE QUESTIONS [MCQS]

1. Qubits are essentially data stored in-
   (a) Transition states.
   (b) Quantum states.
   (c) Turing states.
   (d) None of the above.
2. Who proposed a method to test for existence of the proposed hidden variables-
   (a) John Von Neumann.
   (b) John bell.
   (c) Jacobson.
   (d) None of the above.
3. In quantum theory, the Greek letter psi represents-
   (a) The Plank's constant.
   (b) The wave function.
   (c) Entanglement.
   (d) None of the above.
4. Which algorithm is explained in the following question –**"If we have a black box that we send input to and get output from, how we determine if that particular black box contains a constant function or a balanced function?"**
   (a) Simon's algorithm.
   (b) Grover's algorithm.
   (c) Deutsch's algorithm.
   (d) Shor's algorithm.
5. Select the quantum search algorithm-
   (a) Simon's algorithm.
   (b) Grover's algorithm.
   (c) Deutsch's algorithm.
   (d) Shor's algorithm.
6. Which of the following is an invalid qubit state?
   (a) $|0\rangle$
   (b) $|1\rangle$
   (c) $0.64\,|0\rangle + 0.36\,|1\rangle$
   (d) $1/\sqrt{2}\,|0\rangle + 1/\sqrt{2}\,|1\rangle$
7. If 'n' denotes the number of qubits then the number of values that can be stored simultaneously in a quantum computer would be-
   (a) 2n
   (b) n/2
   (c) 2^n
   (d) None of the above.
8. The basic building blocks in a quantum computer are-
   (a) Gates.
   (b) Qiskit.

(c) IBM

(d) None of the above.

9. Which type of error is found in both classical bits as well as in qubits?

(a) Entropy.

(b) Bit-flip errors.

(c) Syntax errors.

(d) Logical errors.

10. Which of the following is false about Bell state?

(a) $1/\sqrt{2}\,|00\rangle + 1/\sqrt{2}\,|11\rangle$

(b) First and second qubits are not entangled.

(c) The qubits are correlated with each other.

(d) Bell state is used in Quantum Teleportation Protocol.

11. A Register that is composed of a number of qubits is known as-

(a) Serial Register.

(b) Quantum Register.

(c) Parallel Register.

(d) None of the above.

12. The state of a quantum register with m-qubits can be represented as a ______ dimensional vector in complex vector space-

(a) 2^m

(b) 2m

(c) m/2

(d) None of the above.

13. A qubit in superposition behaves as if it were in both $|0\rangle$ and $|1\rangle$ states simultaneously.

(a) True.

(b) False.

(c) Partially True.

(d) Partially False.

14. When a qubit in superposition is measured then-

(a) It irreversibly collapses into either 0 or 1 state, thereby destroying the superposition.

(b) It will not destroy superposition state.

(c) More measurements should be made.

(d) None of the above.

15. A linear increase in the number of qubits in a register leads to-

(a) Radial growth in the state space of the register.

(b) Exponential growth in the state space of the register.

(c) Polynomial growth in the state space of the register.

(d) None of the above.

16. All states of a quantum register can be in all of its states at the same time, this allows-

(a) Serial processing.

(b) Parallel processing.

(c) Central processing.

(d) None of the above.

17. The state space of a qubit can be visualized by using an imaginary sphere known as the-

(a) Atmosphere.

(b) Ecosystem

(c) Block sphere.

(d) None of the above.

18. A qubit can be any point of the block sphere-

(a) True.

(b) False.

(c) Partially true.

(d) None of the above.

19. A 4-bit classical register can store one number from 0 to 15 at a time, whereas a 4-qubit quantum register can store-
   (a) All 16 numbers in a superposition state.
   (b) Only 4 numbers in a superposition state.
   (c) Only 10 numbers in a superposition state.
   (d) None of the above.
20. All values in a qubit register can be simultaneously accessed and operated. This allows-
   (a) Truly parallel computation.
   (b) Classical computation.
   (c) Polynomial computation.
   (d) None of the above.
21. The type of computers in which the computational task is represented as the energy of a configuration of subatomic particles, the energy is then anneâled or gradually lowered to arrive at a solution are known as-
   (a) Quantum circuit computers.
   (b) Adiabatic quantum computers.
   (c) Quantum Parallel Computers.
   (d) None of the above.
22. The workhorses of quantum programming are-
   (a) Quantum bits or qubits.
   (b) Bits only.
   (c) Dits.
   (d) None of the above.
23. The tiny bits of a qubit are also known as-
   (a) Qubelets.
   (b) Tablets.
   (c) Platelets.
   (d) None of the above.
24. The radius of the block sphere is-
   (a) 0
   (b) 1
   (c) 2
   (d) 3
25. Block sphere is also known as the-
   (a) Block ball.
   (b) Small ball.
   (c) Big ball.
   (d) None of the above.
26. The states that fill the interior of the Block Sphere are all-
   (a) Mixtures.
   (b) Bits.
   (c) Dits.
   (d) None of the above.
27. A quantum electronic circuit realization of a qubit is named as-
   (a) Quantronium.
   (b) Plutonium.
   (c) Selenium
   (d) None of the above.
28. Which of the following is the latest discovery to form qubits-
   (a) Electron.
   (b) Photon.
   (c) Phonon.
   (d) None of the above.
29. No cloning theorem states that-
   (a) Qubits (unknown quantum state) can't be cloned.
   (b) Qubits can never be created or destroyed.
   (c) Qubits are not fragile.
   (d) None of the above.

30. Electrons have spins whereas photons have-
    (a) Dependent polarizations.
    (b) Independent polarizations.
    (c) No polarizations.
    (d) None of the above.
31. If maximum information is available in a qubit state then the system is said to be in a-
    (a) Pure state.
    (b) Impure state.
    (c) Stable state.
    (d) None of the above.
32. When a qubit is represented as a spin state of an electron, the only arbitrary unitary transformations possible in acting on the state are-
    (a) Revolutions of spin.
    (b) Rotations of the spin.
    (c) Collapsible spin.
    (d) None of the above.
33. The famous cat experiment was performed by-
    (a) Schrodinger.
    (b) Paulli.
    (c) Einstein.
    (d) None of the above.
34. The intersection between quantum computing and machine learning is explored by-
    (a) QML.
    (b) QDL.
    (c) Quantum Algorithms.
    (d) None of the above.
35. Rigetti computing company has developed: -
    (a) PennyLane.
    (b) Pyquil.
    (c) TFQ.
    (d) IBM Q.
36. Measurement-based Quantum Computing (MBQC) is driven by measurements performed on an entangled resource state that is called as-
    (a) Solid state.
    (b) Matter state.
    (c) Cluster state.
    (d) None of the above.
37. Adiabatic Quantum Computing (AQC) as used by D-Wave, uses which method to solve optimization problems-
    (a) Quantum parallelism.
    (b) Quantum annealing.
    (c) Quantum Measurement.
    (d) None of the above.
38. ___________ are the heart of quantum computers-
    (a) Bits.
    (b) Qubits.
    (c) Dits.
    (d) Hits.
39. When quantum information is lost to the environment that disrupts computation, then this is referred to as-
    (a) Coherence.
    (b) Decoherence.
    (c) Fault-tolerance.
    (d) None of the above.
40. For quantum storage, we started with electrons, then we came to photons, then magnetic properties and now we have discovered-
    (a) Phonons.
    (b) Polymers.
    (c) Polyester.
    (d) None of the above.

Answers															
1.	(b)	2.	(b)	3.	(b)	4.	(c)	5.	(b)	6.	(c)	7.	(c)	8.	(a)
9.	(b)	10.	(b)	11.	(b)	12.	(a)	13.	(a)	14.	(a)	15.	(b)	16.	(b)
17.	(c)	18.	(a)	19.	(a)	20.	(a)	21.	(b)	22.	(a)	23.	(a)	24.	(b)
25.	(a)	26.	(a)	27.	(a)	28.	(c)	29.	(a)	30.	(b)	31.	(a)	32.	(b)
33.	(a)	34.	(a)	35.	(b)	36.	(c)	37.	(b)	38.	(b)	39.	(b)	40.	(a)

CONCEPTUAL SHORT QUESTIONS WITH ANSWERS

Q1. What are the differences between quantum circuit and adiabatic computer?

Ans. Basically, there are two types of quantum computers: -

(a) **Quantum Circuit Computers:** These computers are built from a network of quantum gates that take an initial guess of a solution to a computational task and transform it using quantum principles to one that solves the problem.

(b) **Adiabatic Quantum Computers:** In these types of computers, the computational task is represented as **the energy of a configuration of subatomic particles.** Then the **energy is annealed or we can say gradually lowered to arrive at the solution.**

Q2. Although quantum computers are very powerful, even more than supercomputers, still qubits used by them are fragile. What does that mean?

Ans. Quantum states can be destroyed by even the tiniest disturbance like minuscule amounts of heat or radio-wave energy. Therefore, qubits must be manipulated to execute quantum algorithms but must be isolated from the outside world.

Q3. What are the different ways in which quantum computing can be integrated with cloud computing?

Ans. The following are some of the ways of integration of quantum with cloud: -

1. By providing **remote access to quantum computers,** cloud computing can make quantum computing more accessible to a wider range of users like researchers, developers and businesses that may not have the resources or expertise to build and maintain their quantum computing infrastructure.
2. Cloud computing can provide the necessary classical computing resources to support these hybrid calculations. This is known as **hybrid Quantum Classical computing.**
3. **Cloud computing providers can use quantum computing to develop and implement quantum-resistant cryptography, ensuring the security of sensitive data stored in the cloud.**
4. The aggregation of quantum computing, AI and ML algorithms running in the cloud, can help to solve complicated optimization problems with better accuracy. **For instance,** quantum computing can be used to improve the training of machine learning models and makes searching of larger datasets more effectively and efficiently.

5. Cloud computing can provide developers and researchers **to access quantum hardware and other computational resources** which can result in breakthroughs and discoveries. Cloud can support the development of new quantum algorithms and applications.

Q4. What are the challenges that one may face when integrating quantum computing with cloud computing?

Ans. Some of the challenges faced when integrating quantum computing with cloud computing are as follows: -

1. As quantum computing solves very complex problems of the real world, so this complexity can make it difficult for the users to access and use the quantum computing resources in the cloud.
2. The binding together of quantum and cloud computing also create scalability challenges. This is so because it further adds more challenges like the need for high-speed and low latency communications between quantum and classical components, need to manage and allocate resources dynamically.
3. Vulnerability also increases when we combine both quantum and cloud computing as the need is to protect sensitive quantum algorithms and data from unauthorized access or tampering.
4. Interoperability is also a challenge as different platforms may use different technologies and programming models.
5. Although cloud offers cheaper services but with quantum computing on cloud, the cost of accessing quantum computing resources on the cloud can still be high.
6. Quantum computing is still in its infancy stage. So, prediction of whether the future development of quantum computing with cloud can be difficult.

Q5. What are the minimum requirements for using quantum computers on the cloud platform?

Ans. The following are some of the requirements for using quantum computers on the cloud platform:

1. Execution of **quantum algorithms and simulations** need hardware like **quantum processors and quantum simulators. Please note here that this hardware may be provided by cloud computing service providers or may be procured by the user.**
2. **High speed and low latency network connectivity** is needed to support remote access to quantum computing resources on the cloud. This can include both LANs and WANs.
3. **Quantum software like quantum compilers, quantum simulators, quantum programming languages and quantum libraries** are all needed to support the development and execution of quantum algorithms and simulations.
4. **Better security measures** are needed to protect **sensitive quantum algorithms and data from unauthorized access or tampering. For example,** quantum encryption, authentication and access control methods.
5. The combination of quantum computing and cloud computing must be **scalable** too. This may include the ability to **dynamically allocate and manage computational resources.** And also the ability to **support high-performance computations.**

6. **Interoperability** between the quantum and cloud platforms-models and interfaces, is also mandatory.

Q6. Define what is quantum cloud computing? What benefits do they provide?

Ans. **Quantum cloud computing makes quantum computing resources available to organizations, academics and other user resources through cloud technology. Cloud-based quantum computers** function at greater speeds, higher computing power than traditional/ classical/ conventional computers. **Also note that this is so because they apply the principles of quantum physics when solving complex computational problems.**

Q7. What are the different types of quantum computers that exist? What are Universal quantum computers?

Ans. Different types of quantum computers are as follows: -

a. Quantum annealers.

b. Analog quantum simulators.

c. Universal quantum computers.

Quantum annealers are considered to be the least powerful among quantum computers but work well to solve optimization problems.

Analog quantum simulators are powerful systems that can solve physics and biochemistry problems.

Universal quantum computers are the most powerful and widely used type of quantum computer. It is quite difficult to build them. They can potentially access up to 1 million qubits. However, the current technology can only access around 100 to 400 qubits. A universal quantum computer is also known as a Quantum Turing Machine (QTM). **It is defined as an abstract machine capable of seizing all power of quantum computation. This means that it is capable of executing any quantum algorithm.**

Q8. How is quantum computing detriment of the very famous Blockchain technology?

Ans. There are two reasons for it: -

1. Quantum computing can hypothetically be used to gain an unfair advantage over other proof-of-work (PoW) miners. It can dominate blockchain mining.

2. Quantum computing can also decrypt encryption codes used by blockchains. **Please note that this means that quantum computing can enable an attack on a block chain network using cryptography. Also note that however, it is not all doom and gloom for cryptographic systems because quantum cloud computing may also offer an effective solution for protecting and strengthening blockchains from quantum attacks.**

Q9. What is the difference between cloud computing and quantum cloud computing?

Ans. **Quantum cloud computing applies quantum principles to distributed computing, whereas cloud computing uses remote servers to provide distributed computing services.** The need is to refine computing technology and enable more users to access quantum computers through the cloud. **For example, IBM's Osprey quantum computer** features 433 qubits. But the company has plans to scale up to 4000 qubits by 2025.

Q10. How does quantum cloud computing work?

Ans. **The objective is to connect users directly to quantum processors, emulators and simulators. Physical quantum computers are** very complex, making cloud-based access an ideal setup for those who need to harness the power of quantum computing without purchasing their own quantum computer.

As per the latest IBM reports, its own quantum computer hardware is roughly the size of a car that is mainly composed of cooling systems to ensure that the superconducting processor remains at the ultra-cold ideal operating temperatures.

Q11. What is the need of quantum cloud computing on large scale?

Ans. Large-scale quantum cloud computing platforms can be used to solve problems related to optimization in logistics and scheduling of resources in business.

Q12. What is the way of using quantum cloud computing?

Ans. **Quantum algorithms** are created on conventional computers and tested on quantum computers to ensure viability. Cloud quantum computing allows businesses and researchers to leverage the technology to explore various quantum computing applications. Cloud companies will be the first quantum-as-a-service provider.

Q13. Why is quantum annealing also called as adiabatic quantum computation (AQC)? Give an example to explain. Also explain what is energy minimization controversy?

Ans. **Quantum annealing is sometimes called as adiabatic quantum computation (AQC) because annealing is a form of quantum computing that relies in the adiabatic theorem to perform calculations.** Adiabatic theorem was postulated by Max Born and Vladimir Fock in 1928. It states that "**A quantum mechanical system subjected to gradually changing external conditions adapts its functional form but when subjected to rapidly varying conditions there is insufficient time for the functional form to adapt, so the spatial probability density remains unchanged.**" This theorem is better understood by a simple example of a pendulum oscillating in a vertical plane. In this experiment, we know that if the support of the pendulum is moved abruptly, then the mode of oscillation of the pendulum will change. On the other hand, if the support is moved very slowly, the motion of the pendulum relative to the support will remain unchanged. **Please understand that this is the gist of the adiabatic process** i.e. a gradual change in external conditions allows the system to adapt such that it retains its initial character.

Hamiltonian (H) is an important concept in quantum mechanics especially for quantum annealing. In quantum mechanics, **a Hamiltonian is an operator corresponding to the total energy of the system in most of the cases. That is, it is the sum of the kinetic energies of all particles plus the potential energy of the particles associated with the system.** So,

$$H (E_{tot}) = \Sigma KE + \Sigma PE$$

In general **quantum annealing,** can be explained by the following steps: -

S1: Find a potentially complicated Hamiltonian whose ground state describes the solution to the problem in hand.

S2: Prepare a system with a simple Hamiltonian and initialize to the ground state.

S3: Use an adiabatic process to evolve the simple Hamiltonian into the desired complicated Hamiltonian. **By the adiabatic theorem, the system remains in the ground state, so at the end of the state of the system describes the solution to the problem.**

D-wave Systems is the company that is pioneer in this form of quantum computing and D-wave has sold commercially several quantum computers with quite larger number of qubits. **Believe it or not, there is a company in Canada called D-wave Systems selling 2000-qubit computers commercially.** As a matter of fact, a D-Wave computer can only solve quantum annealing problems i.e. problems solvable by the adiabatic theorem.

However, quantum annealing is quite restrictive too. Some of the constraints are as follows: -

1. Platforms like IBM Q use logic gates to control the qubits while quantum annealing computers don't have logic gates. Therefore, they can't fully control the state of the qubits.
2. D-Wave systems claim that their qubits tend to a **minimum energy state. Please note that they can't be controlled via quantum gates but their behavior can be predicted by the adiabatic theorem. That is why; they are good tools for solving energy minimization problems.**
3. Quantum annealing is used basically for the **combinatorial optimization problems where the search space is discrete with a local minimum.** Quantum annealing takes the advantage of the fact that all physical systems tend toward a minimum energy state. **For example,** consider a hot cup of coffee, when you leave it for some time, it starts to cool down until it reaches a temperature equal to the surrounding environment. So, we can say that it tends towards a **minimum energy state.**

Q14. Differentiate between coherence and decoherence. Suggest some good experiment to test Decoherence experimentally.

Ans. 14 As we know that in quantum mechanics, particles are explained by the **wave function. And a definite phase relation between the states is known as coherence. This coherence is mandatory for the functioning of quantum computers.**

However, **please note that when a quantum computer is in contact with its surroundings, coherence decays with time. This process is called as quantum decoherence (H. Dieter Zeh, 1970).** In other words, formally, decoherence is the time that takes for the superposition of states to disappear. This is due to the probabilistic nature of the wave function. It can also be explained as the **loss of information from a system into the environment.** There are some existing methods to extend the coherence time of qubits for use in quantum memory, but those processes are complex and typically involve **flipping or reversing of the spin.** Although that process works to reverse the spectral drift that causes decoherence, it also leads to the loss of whatever information was encoded in the system. Now this new system however, eradicates the need to reverse the spin. **Also note that the new system extends the coherence time of the qubits and also prevents the loss of data.**

And the time it stays in superposition is known as decoherence or qubit longevity. Researchers have now described a method to achieve a 20-fold increase in the coherence times for nuclear spin qubits. Li, at MIT, further reported that one of problems in quantum information is that- *"Nuclear spins are very attractive platforms for quantum sensors, gyroscopes and quantum memory but they have coherence times of the order of 150 microseconds in presence of electronic spins and then the information just disappears."* Researchers have tried and tested many ways to **coax qubits so that they remain in their quantum state for longer times.**

Experiment: In quantum mechanics, we have studied that particles can be in multiple states like not excited v/s excited or in two different locations, at the same time. It is only the act of observation that gives a random value for a particular state. If the excitation is measured by the energy levels of the particle—here low energy level means not excited and high energy means excited, when an electromagnetic wave is sent to the particle at a proper frequency, then the particle will alternate between high and low energy levels. Then, the state of the particle can be measured and averaged producing what is called as **Rabi oscillations. Please note that because the particle is never completely isolated due to atomic collisions, electromagnetic fields or thermal baths, so the superposition will stop and the oscillations will disappear.** Hence, decoherence gives information about the interaction of a quantum object and its environment. This is crucial for quantum computing. **Also note that this means that the higher the decoherence** (i.e. the time it stays in superposition)**, the higher the quality of the qubit will be.**

Note:

1. **Some qubit designs like superconductor loops have a very low longevity and need to be kept at extremely low temperatures (-271° C) to counter this effect.**
2. **Others like trapped ions and diamond vacancies have a very high longevity and can be kept at room temperatures.**

Companies that are working on quantum designs (to be studied in next chapter) face a daunting challenge and are trying to wrestle with qubit longevity.

Q15. What sort of noise can destroy quantum information?

Ans. 15 We say that noise is basically the adversary of the quantum computer. For different quantum architectures, different noise sources are most relevant like magnetic field noise from the environment, control noise from the microwave or laser fields that you apply to control your quantum computer or even cosmic rays that hit your quantum chip and destroy the quantum information.

Q16. Define what are spectator qubits? How are they used?

Ans. 16 **Spectator qubits are co-located in the quantum processor together with the data qubits that are used in the computation.** These bits don't participate in the quantum computation itself i.e. they will not become entangled with the data qubits. Instead of this, they can be used to **monitor noise that would affect the data qubits. And hence, enable longer and more complex quantum computation.** You can use exactly the same qubit type for your data and for your spectator qubits. But just assign them different tasks, either data processing for the data qubits or noise monitoring for the spectator qubits. **Also note that it would be better and useful to use different qubit types for the two tasks in order to make it simpler to control them independently. We don't want the two types to become entangledand also you don't want the control and the measurement of the spectator qubits to cause extra noise on the data qubits.** Two different species of atoms may be used that have different qubit frequencies because it allows us to control them independently.

As explained above, that the spectator qubits are co-located with the data qubits in (QPU), so they can experience **the same noise that the data qubits experience.** So, **perform measurement on the spectator qubits to estimate what that noise is in real-time while a quantum computation is running on the data qubits.** This noise measurement can then be used to adapt the rest of the computation on the data qubits in a manner that corrects for the noise. In nutshell, the quantum information can be stored longer in the data qubits as they are actively shielded from this noise. To achieve this, the noise, the spectator and the data qubit experience need to be correlated.

Q17. Explain the use of quantum technology in agriculture field.

Ans. 17 Quantum technology has emerged as a transformational tool that can revolutionize the farming industry. **Quantum sensing and computing** offer superior detection sensitivities and data processing capabilities compared to the conventional methods. The behavior of a quantum system is defined by quantum mechanics like an atom's energy levels are quantized. These quantum states of atoms or molecules can be electronic, magnetic or vibrational levels. While quantum technology is still sprouting at its nascent stages, it has a power to increase the productivity and efficiency of farms. **As per the latest reports and surveys, it has been found that hybrid machines that mix conventional and quantum processing will be available very soon and this will enhance agricultural capabilities. Also note that the quantum future promises to help farmers achieve the production increases but they need to win the fight for food security.**

Q18. What is Quantum Sensing?

Ans. 18 **When a quantum system is used to detect small changes in a physical quantity, quantum sensing is established.** Any of the already mentioned quantum characteristics can be used for detection—**quantum coherence, quantum entanglement or quantum states can all be used to monitor changes in a physical quantity precisely.** This kind of quantum technology platform needed will depend on the physical parameter that a quantum sensor responds to. For example, trapped ions will make an excellent probe for detecting electric fields as they are charged particles. Also, neutral atom-based quantum sensors can measure gravity very accurately at a given location.

Q19. Show how photosynthesis is a quantum mechanical effect?

Ans. 19 To show that photosynthesis is a quantum mechanical effect only; consider an example of the annual migratory habits of birds as they are tied to quantum entanglement. As another example, there is also evidence that quantum tunneling is associated with how smell is sensed. Plants convert sunlight into energy through the chemical process of photosynthesis.

This conversion process happens at close to 100% efficiency. Current solutions based on quantum mechanics have demonstrated how plants can achieve photosynthesis with high conversion efficiency. Photosynthesis is the synthesis of energy out of light or photons.

Q20. Assume that a flipped coin can be measured as either Heads (H) or Tails (T).

(a) **If the coin is in normalized state $1/\sqrt{10}\,|H\rangle + 3/\sqrt{10}\,|T\rangle$, what is the probability that the coin will be tails?**

(b) **During a flip, the coin is in a state $1/3|H\rangle + 2/3\,|T\rangle$. Is this state normalized?**

(c) **A machine is built to flip coins and put them into a state ½ |H> + √3/2 |T>** when flipped. If 100 coins are flipped, how many coins should land on tails?

(d) **A coin starts in the state 1/√10 |H> + 3/√10 |T>. After measurement is made on the coin, what could be the state of the coin?**

Ans. 20 (a) 9/10 or 90%. The probability is the square of the amplitude.

(b) No. because 1/9 + 4/9 != 1 and Normalization means the total probabilities add up to 1.

(c) 75 coins.

(d) Measurement collapses the superposition onto either |H> or |T>.

Q20. A qubit is prepared in an unknown state. It is then measured with the outcome |0>.

(a) **Which of the following could be its initial state before the measurement:**

|0>, 1/√10 |0> + 3/√10 |1>, ½ |0> + √3/2 |1> and/or 1/√2 (|0> + |1>)?

(b) **If you tried to measure the same qubit a second time, can you narrow down what the initial state was?**

(c) **Another qubit is prepared in the same unkown state. It is measured in the |1> state. What can you say about the initial state now?**

Ans. 20 (a) All of them are possible as they all can produce |0> after measurement.

(b) After measurement, the state in the question is in |0>, since the superposition collapsed. As it is in the |0> state after measurement, if you try to measure the same state again you will always measure |0>. No new information is provided about the state after the collapse to |0>.

(c) If |0> is measured from the unknown state, and a second identical state is prepared and is measured in the |1> state, then you know the unknown state contains some non-zero superposition of both |0> and |1>. For example, it is |ψ> = α |0> + β |1> with α != 0 and β != 0. So, you can rule out |ψ> = |0> as the initial state but all of the other three states given in part-a are still possible. Measurements of many more particles are needed to determine the numerical values of α and β in order to find the exact state, $\begin{bmatrix} 0 \\ 1 \end{bmatrix}$, which is the |1> state.

Q21. What is the matrix product of matrix X = $\begin{bmatrix} 0 & 1 \\ 1 & 0 \end{bmatrix}$ and the |1> state?

Ans. 21 The matrix product is $\begin{bmatrix} 0 \\ 1 \end{bmatrix}$ which is the |0> state.

Q22. Is 1/√2 |00> + 1/√2 |01> an entangled state? If so, show that it cannot be written as a product. If not, what is the individual state of the two qubits?

Ans. 22 No, not entangled. Knowing that the first qubit is 0 does not narrow down whether the second qubit is 0 or 1. Qubit 1 is |0> and Qubit 2 is 1/√2 (|0> + |1>). The combination of the two qubits to form a multi-qubit state gives the state in the question.

Q23. Suppose Alice has one half of an entangled pair and Bob has the other half. When Alice makes a measurement on her qubit, Bob's qubit instantaneously changes its state. Can Alice and Bob use entanglement to transmit information faster than the speed of light? Why or why not?

Ans. 23 No, Alice measures a random value. This automatically changes Bob's state. However, Alice would need to send a classical message to Bob to find out which state Bob measured. Therefore information is still bounded by the classical speed of light. This scenario is consistent with Bell's theorem.

Q24. What is the Hilbert space?

Ans. 24 The linear combination of two or more vectors is another state vector in the same Hilbert space. It describes another state of the system. A physical qubit is a 2-level quantum mechanical system. We can represent a qubit as a 2D complex Hilbert space, C^2. **The state of the qubit at any given time can be represented by a vector in this complex Hilbert space.** The Hilbert space is provided with the inner product which allows us to determine the relative positions of two vectors representing qubit states. To represent two or more qubits, we can tensor product (to be discussed shortly) Hilbert spaces together to represent the combined states of the qubits. **Also note that we have methods to represent separable states where qubits are independent of one another and entangled states; such as a Bell state where we cannot separate the two qubit states.**

Q25. State Max Born's rule.

Ans. 25 Max Born in 1926 gave a rule- **"The modulus squared of the amplitude of a state is the probability of that state resulting after measurement."** If the amplitude is $1/\sqrt{2}$ the probability obtaining the state is $|1/\sqrt{2}|^2 = ½$. Hence, the probability of measuring the light in either the vertical or horizontal polarization state is 50%. **Please note that we chose an amplitude of** $1/\sqrt{2}$ **in order to normalize the states so that the sum of the modulus squared of the amplitudes will equal one.** This enables us to connect the amplitudes to probabilities of measurement with the Born rule.

Q26. How entanglement and superposition are related?

Ans. 26 Entanglement occurs when we have a superposition of states that is not separable.

Q27. In general, we use 2-level qubit systems to build quantum computers. Can we chose other types of computing architectures?

Ans. 27 Yes, we could build a quantum computer with **qutrits which are 3-level systems. Note that we can think of these as having states of 0, 1 or 2 or a superposition of these states.**

Q28. Define what is a qudit, qubit and qurit? Give some examples to explain.

Ans. 28 Qubits and qurits are specific instances of qudits which can be computing units of any number of states. the Siddiqi Lab at UC Berkeley has designed a qutrit-based quantum computer. **Please understand that in a qutrit system, we can represent more states than a qubit system with the same number of computational units.**

For example, a qubit system of say 100 qubits can handle 2^{100} states while a qutrit can handle 3^{100} states. That is, it is the number that is 17 orders of magnitude larger. **Also note that we**

can say that to represent the same number space as a 100 qubit system, we need 63 qutrits approx. ($\log_3(2^{100})$). Thus, it is more difficult to build qutrit systems. That is why, the company giants are working with qubits only, as of now. But each of these systems can run any algorithm that the others can i.e. they can simulate each other. `

Q29. Suggest some checklist to analyze the advances in quantum hardware and the impact of engineering progress in this field.

Ans. 29 Some of the features of checklist are as follows: -

1. If we have a 2-level system comprised of an ensemble of atoms but where the qubits are not individually addressable then this system would fail the Quantum Computing test. We must firstly, ask a question that a QC is whether Turing-complere or Universal. This feature is called as **Universality.**
2. **Fidelity is a measure of the ability for a qubit to remain in coherence through a computation.** The horse race for qubits is on but we must first of all examine the claims made on the fidelity of those qubits.
3. In order to achieve a fault-tolerant platform we must determine the **scalability** of its architecture like Is the architecture scalable to 10^6 qubits and beyond?
4. **Number of Qubits** is another checklist feature. **Please note here that maintaining the simultaneous coherence of larger and larger number of qubits is a technical challenge. Also note that it is important to look at architecture-specific limitations of the qubits,** like nearest-neighbor connections. This is done in order to avoid crosstalks.
5. How many operations we can implement before coherence break downs is referred to a **circuit depth. For instance,** a 100,000 qubit computer would be possible but if it can't implement more than a few operations before losing coherence it is of limited value.
6. We should aim at **limited logical connectivity because more operators (circuits) means more potential for noise and errors.** To achieve low logical connectivity, we may include logical 'swap' operations in our algorithms that will effectively simulate greater connectivity. **Also note that more operators means more potential for noise and errors.**
7. Is the quantum hardware available on **cloud**? No organization will buy a quantum computer but can share its resources and the QC itself on the cloud.

Q30. List some of the applications of Quantum Computing.

Ans. 30 Some of the applications of quantum computing are as follows: -

1. Quantum Computing (QC) is helpful in healthcare and medicine field.
2. QC in banking and finance.
3. QC in drug discovery and research.
4. QC in aviation, travel and logistics.
5. QC in crypto security.
6. QC in space exploration and weather predictions.
7. QC to solve complex optimization problems.
8. QC in chemistry and Agriculture.

9. QC in AI and Machine Learning.
10. QC for optimization of big date.
11. QC for simulation of better battery designs.
12. QC for autonomous vehicles future.
13. QC in education and research field.
14. QC to revolutionize defense and warfare.
15. QC in life science.
16. QC in cyber security and hacking.
17. QC in movies.
18. QC in spiritually.
19. QC in Robotics.
20. QC in nuclear research.
21. QC in sports.
22. QC in traffic optimization.

And many more.

Q31. Show that $1/\sqrt{5}\,|0\rangle + 2i/\sqrt{5}\,|1\rangle$ is a perfectly valid state (where $i^2 = -1$).

Ans. 31 As we know that the modulus of coefficients square should be one. So, we can say that-

$$(1/\sqrt{5})^2 + (2i/\sqrt{5})^2 = 1/5 + |4i^2| / 5 = 1/5 + 4/5 = 5/5 = 1$$

Hence, it is a perfectly valid state.

Q32. What is Quantum Uncertainty Principle?

Ans. 32 The Quantum Uncertainty principle as introduced by Werner Heisenberg states that- **"There is a fundamental limit to how precisely we can simultaneously measure certain pairs of properties of a particle like its position and momentum."** This principle is the heart of many quantum technologies.

Q33. Define what do you mean by quantum energy and quantum fuel?

Ans. 33 Recall the concept of photon from your school days. It was something like this-

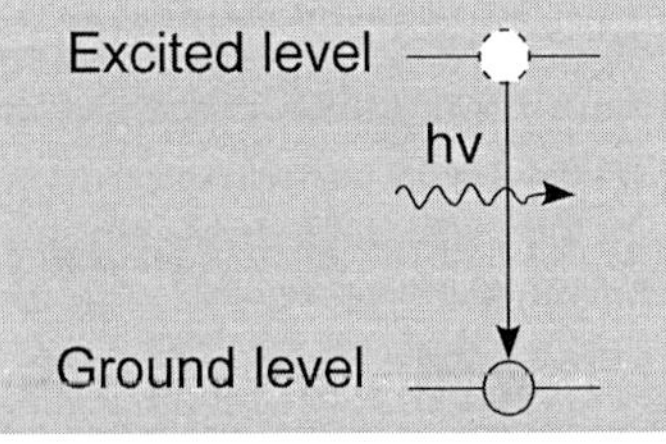

The basic idea of quantum energy is that the things have energy levels that look like steps on a ladder. When they move up and down, they absorb or emit a quantum of energy. If the energy is emitted as light, it is called a **photon.** The energy of a photon is related to its **wavelength** (λ) through the universal constant *h*, called **Planck's constant.** The wavelength of light determines its color i.e. red is about 450 nanometers, while blue light is about 650 nanometers.

Q34. What are the practical limitations of quantum computing?

Ans. 34 The following are some of the limitations of quantum computing-

1. The primary limitation that QC must overcome is the problem of **noise or decoherence.** Quantum systems interact with the external environment via vibrations, temperature fluctuations, and electromagnetic fields, which causes information carried by qubits to decay over time. While the complete isolation of any quantum system is impossible, these interactions can be minimised. The interaction of qubits with the surrounding environment needs to be limited as efficiently as possible in order to allow sufficient time for computation. This can be addressed by quantum error correction, which also allows greater fidelity from quantum computation. According to recent estimates, each functional or "logical" qubit requires more than 1,000 physical qubits to perform state-of the-art error correction.
2. Another limitation that arises is the need for qubits to be **entangled,** i.e., the state of any qubit must be correlated with that of the others. This means the loss of some qubits. Both these limitations lead to a loss of qubits. Therefore, building a fully functioning quantum computer will require billions of qubits, since a large percentage of these will be **consumed** by the system to compensate for entanglement and error correction. **Holevo's theorem states that "the amount of data that can be retrieved from n-qubits cannot be larger than the amount of data that can be retrieved from n bits."** Therefore, most of the data in a collection of qubits cannot be retrieved.
3. Also, the **quantum gates are very slow and error prone.** They rapidly lose data. This, along with the complex measurement process in quantum systems, makes the creation of quantum algorithms quite complex.

Q35. What are the three main reasons for developing quantum computers?

Ans. 35 Three reasons are:

a) To solve exponential problems.

b) For secure communications.

c) For accuracy and approximation.

EXERCISE QUESTIONS

Q1. What are the differences between the following: -

(a) Classical and quantum computing.

(b) Bits and Qubits.

(c) Coherence and decoherence.

Q2. Name the three pillars of quantum computing and explain them.

Q3. Compare and contrast classical superposition and quantum superposition.

Q4. State the law of quantum superposition.

Q5. What does the famous Cat experiment by Schrodinger show?

Q6. What happens when we try to measure the qubit state?

Q7. What is a Block Sphere? What does it show? An arrow on a block sphere indicates what?

Q8. Explain a simple model of quantum computer using a coin that has been flipped in the air.

Q9. How is the phenomenon of superposition useful for quantum computers?

[Hints: The phenomenon of superposition allows quantum computers to perform operations on two bits of information at once with a single qubit. It is possible to create a general purpose Universal Quantum Computer using photons as qubits, beam splitters to create superposition and pieces of glass that slow down the photons along the selected paths.]

Q10. Are the following two-qubit states entangled?

(a) $\sqrt{3}/2\ |00\rangle + \frac{1}{2}\ |11\rangle$

(b) $\frac{1}{2}\ |00\rangle + \frac{1}{2}\ |01\rangle + \frac{1}{2}\ |10\rangle - \frac{1}{2}\ |11\rangle$

Q11. What are the Bell states? Explain.

Q12. Discuss the roles of Max Plank, Einstein, Bohr, Heisenberg, Schrodinger, Born and Feynman in the field of science that led to the development of quantum computing.

Q13. Explain how will you represent rotation operations of the qubits on the block sphere? Derive the final rotations matrices along x, y and z-axis on a block sphere showing a unit vector as a qubit.

Q14. The measurement causes the qubit to change its state. Show the state of the qubit before and after the measurements.

Q15. What is an EPR pair?

Q16. Comment on the fragility of the quantum information.

Q17. Distinguish between the pure states and impure states.

Q18. "The state of a classical bit can be either the north or the south pole of the equator but a qubit can be any point on the block sphere." Justify this statement.

Q19. A qubit can exist in multiple states simultaneously. Explain.

Q20. Write a short note on the Quantum Register.

Q21. What is quantum tunneling?

Q22. What is adiabatic quantum computer?

Q23. "When qubits are un-entangled, a measurement of one of the qubits has absolutely no effect on the other qubit while if the qubits are entangled then the measurement of one will have effect on the other one." Justify this statement.

Q24. $|\psi\rangle = 1/\sqrt{2}\ |00\rangle + 1/\sqrt{2}\ |11\rangle$ is one of the famous Bell states, a highly entangled state of its two qubits. Then-

(a) Write the four equations of the amplitudes. If this Bell state is decomposed as the tensor product of two qubits.

(b) What is the result of measuring the first qubit of $|\psi>$?

(c) What is the result of measuring the second qubit after measuring the first qubit?

Q25. What are the challenges that we face when designing quantum computers?

Q26. What are spectator qubits? How are they different from regular qubits?

Q27. Explain the use of quantum technology in the field of agriculture.

Q28. What is quantum sensing?

Q29. What is quantum coherence?

Q30. Quantum coherence-enabled functionality holds the potential to drive technologies like such as quantum computing, quantum communications, quantum simulation and quantum sensing. Explain this with some examples.

Q31. A Phonon explorer is a software tool to analyze Phonon dispersion. Throw some light on it.

Q32. How is photosynthesis, a quantum mechanical effect?

Q33. How is 'Quantum Gravity' connected to Quantum Computing?

Q34. What are quantum sensors and the applications of quantum sensing?

Q35. Write short notes on the following: -

(a) Future of Quantum Sensing.

(b) Quantum Parallelism.

Q36. What benefits quantum sensors provide in a nuclear power plant?

[Hints: 1. to detect isotopes in nuclear energy plants.

2. to monitor and control the safety of the nuclear power plant due to radiation.

3. to detect early the faulty equipments.

4. are deployed in electricity transmission grids—'smart grids'.

5. to develop smart buildings.]

Q37. Can a Bell state be written as a product state? Why so?

Q38. Is Bell state an entangled state or Not?

Q39. State the BELL'S theorem.

[Hints "According to quantum mechanics, the value of a certain combination of correlations for experiments of two distant systems can be higher than the highest value allowed by any local realistic theory of the type proposed by EPR, in which the local properties of a system determine the result of any experiment on that system."]

Q40. What are the two main types of quantum computers?

Q41. Consider a qubit that is in the following quantum state $|\psi>$:

$$|\psi> = -0.35/n\,|0> + 0.28\,/n\,|1>$$

(a) Calculate n so that $|\psi>$ is a valid quantum state.

(b) Draw the qubit represented by the quantum state $|\psi>$.

Q42. Is this the valid quantum state representation: -

$$0.25\ |0> - 0.75\ |1>.$$

Q43. What is Quantum Machine Learning (QML)?

Q44. What is quantum annealing?

Q45. After electron, photon and other atomic particles, today we talk of another type of quasi-particle known as a phonon. How phonons got originated from photons?

Q46. What is Quantum Deep Learning (QDL)?

Q47. Can qubits be made to remain in their quantum state for longer time? If so, how? Are there any recent advancement in this field?

Q48. How can we achieve quantum speed-ups better than classical or parallel computers?

Q49. For what sort of problems is classical computer faster and for what sort of problems is a quantum computer faster?

Q50. How is the application of quantum computing helpful in the field of data science?

Math Foundation for Quantum Computing

2

2.0 INTRODUCTION

Quantum mechanics is more fundamental than classical mechanics. It works at both microscopic (atomic and subatomic) and macroscopic levels. But quantum mechanics becomes more vital when we talk of particles and systems at microscopic levels. This is so because microscopic level particles move with high velocity. When any two quanta of energy interact, irrespective of their properties, including whether they are particles or antiparticles, massive or massless, fermions, or bosons etc. , the result of that interaction has the potential to inform you about the underlying laws and rules that the system has to obey.

Quantum mechanics represents a mathematical model of the physical world. It can explain the phenomena like the energy spectra of atoms. This classical mechanics will fail to explain. We now study *linear algebra, matrix operations, vector spaces, Hermitian operators, Hilbert spaces, inner products, tensor products and outer products of vectors in a Hilbert space.* In 20th century, John Von Neumann observed that all of the quantum mechanics can be described by linear algebra. **And the vector is one of the central objects of linear algebra.** But understanding of quantum computing requires some knowledge of the properties of complex numbers too.

2.1 MATRIX ALGEBRA- BASIS VECTORS AND ORTHOGONALITY

Linear transformation and a matrix is the same thing. A rectangular array of elements (A) with m rows and n columns is called as a **matrix.** That is,

$$A = \begin{bmatrix} a_{11} & a_{12} \cdots\cdots\cdots & a_{1n} \\ a_{21} & a_{22} \cdots\cdots\cdots & a_{2n} \\ \vdots & \vdots & \vdots \\ a_{m} & a_{m2} \cdots\cdots\cdots & a_{mn} \end{bmatrix}$$

Please note that matrix, A, can be interpreted as a linear map from vector space of dimension n, F^n, to the vector space of dimension m, F^m, equipped with the canonical base. Also note that if n = m, then A is a linear map from F^n to itself.

Now, let the first row of matrix be denoted by: -

$$\alpha_1 = (a_{11}, a_{12}, \dots\dots\dots, a_{1n})$$
$$\alpha_2 = (a_{21}, a_{22}, \dots\dots\dots, a_{2n})$$
$$\vdots$$
$$\vdots$$
$$\alpha_m = (a_{m1}, a_{m2}, \dots\dots\dots, a_{mn})$$

These are the set of vectors spanning a subspace of dimension m of a vector space, V_n (F) and is called as the **row space** of the (m * n) matrix, A. Hence, the basic row operations on the matrix are as follows: -

(a) Interchanging of any two rows.

(b) Multiplication of all elements of a row by a constant, c.

(c) Addition of any multiple of a row to any other row.

We now define some matrices types.

•Two matrices are **row-equivalent** if one is obtained from the other by a finite sequence of row operations.

- When n = m then the **identity matrix,** I = $[a_{ij}]$ is the matrix with a_{ii} =1 and a_{ij} = 0, if i != j. **For instance,** the identity matrix in vector space of dimension 4 is-

$$\mathbf{I_4} = \begin{bmatrix} 1 & 0 & 0 & 0 \\ 0 & 1 & 0 & 0 \\ 0 & 0 & 1 & 0 \\ 0 & 0 & 0 & 1 \end{bmatrix}$$

- **A permutation matrix, P,** is an identity matrix with rows and columns permuted.
- The **determinant** of an (n * n) matrix, A = $[a_{ij}]$ is the polynomial -

$$\det(A) = |A| = \sum \operatorname{sgn}(\phi)\, a(1, 1\phi)\, a(2, 2\phi) \dots\dots\, a(n, n\phi)$$

where ϕ denotes one of n! different permutations of integers 1, 2, ….,n.

if ϕ is an **even permutation, then sgn(ϕ)** = +1.

if ϕ is an **odd permutation, sgn(ϕ)** = -1.

The determinant can be expressed as-

$$\det(A) = A_{i1}a_{i1} + A_{i2}a_{i2} + \dots\dots + A_{in}a_{in}$$

Here, the coefficient A_{ij} of a_{ij} is called the as **cofactor** of a_{ij}. We define **cofactor as a polynomial in the remaining rows of A. It can be described as the partial derivative of A. Also note that the cofactor polynomial contains only entries from an (n – 1) * (n – 1) matrix M_{ij}, also called as a minor, obtained from A by eliminating row i and column j.**

- If we permute two rows of A, then the sign of the determinant |A| changes. **The determinant of the transpose of a matrix is equal to the determinant of the original matrix.** That is,

$$|A^T| = |A|$$

- **If two rows of A are identical** then: -

$$|A| = 0$$

- A square (n * n) matrix is **triangular** if all entries below the diagonal are zero. The determinant of a triangular matrix is the product of its diagonal elements.
- To compute the determinant |A| one should perform elementary row operations on matrix A and reduce it to a **triangular form.**
- **The characteristic polynomial of matrix A is:** -

$$c(\lambda) = \det(A - \lambda I) = |A - \lambda I|.$$

- **The trace of a matrix A is the sum of its diagonal elements:** -

$$Tr(A) = \sum_i a_{ii}$$

- **The trace of an operator A is the trace of A, the matrix representation of A^2.** The trace has the following properties: -
  1. **It is cyclic.** That is, Tr (AB) = Tr (BA).
  2. **Linearity:** That is, Tr (A + B) = Tr (A) + Tr (B) and Tr(cA) = cTr(A) where c is some constant.
  3. **Invariance under the similarity transformation, S:** Tr (SAS^+) = Tr(S^+SA) = Tr(A), where S^+ is Hermitian conjugate or dual of A: $A^+ = (A^*)^T$.

The determinant, the trace and the characteristic polynomial are quantities associated with any linear map from a finite dimensional vector space into itself.

Vector Spaces

We firstly, define a vector space, V. **A vector space, V, is a collection of elements called as vectors, a field F of elements called as scalars and two operations, vector addition and scalar multiplication. A field** is a set of scalars with the property that if a and b belong to F then a+b, a-b, ab and a/b are also in F.

Addition: The addition operation takes any two vectors u and v in V and produces a third vector in V. It is written as u + v in V. The addition operation follows the following **laws:** -

1. **u + v is a vector in V (closure)**
2. **u + v = v + u (commutativity)**
3. **(u + v) + w = u + (v + w) (associativity)**
4. **There is a zero vector 0 in V such that for every u in V, (u + 0) = u (identity)**
5. **For every u in V, there is a vector in V denoted by –u such that u + (-u) = 0 (inverse).**

Multiplication: The scalar multiplication that takes a scalar c in F, a vector **v** in V and produces a new vector written as cv in V that satisfy the following conditions: -

1. **cv is in V (closure)**
2. **c(u + v) = cu + cv (distributivity)**
3. **(c + d) u = cu + du (distributivity)**
4. **c(du) = (cd) u (associativity)**
5. **1(u) = u (identity)**

For example, consider two rows of complex numbers X and Y in a complex vector space C^n:

$$X = (x_1, x_2, x_3 \ldots\ldots, x_n)$$

$$Y = (y_1, y_2, y_3 \ldots\ldots, y_n)$$

Then, **the *addition operation*** can be done **component-wise** as follows:-

$$X + Y = (x_1 + y_1)\ (x_2 + y_2)\ldots\ldots, (x_n + y_n)$$

The *multiplication operation* is done by multiplying each component of X (or Y) by a complex number c:

$$c\ (X) = (cx_1, cx_2, \ldots\ldots, cx_n)$$

It can be easily shown that all of the conditions of the vector space are satisfied. Thus, C^n is indeed a vector space.

Let us now discuss about Basis Set / state vector.

For a vector space, a basis set is a subset of vectors that enables every vector in the vector space to be represented as a unique linear combination of the vectors in this subset. But none of the vectors in the subset can be expressed as a linear combination of the remaining vectors. **Please note that in general, an n-dimensional vector space will have a basis set of n distinct vectors. Also note that if the vectors in the basis are unit vectors, i.e. each has a magnitude 1 and each is perpendicular to others then the basis is called as an orthonormal basis.**

For instance, the unit vectors i, j and k constitute an orthonormal basis for normal 3D vector space. The unit vectors i, j and k are the standard unit vectors: -

$$i = \begin{bmatrix} 1 \\ 0 \\ 0 \end{bmatrix};\quad j = \begin{bmatrix} 0 \\ 1 \\ 0 \end{bmatrix};\ k = \begin{bmatrix} 0 \\ 0 \\ 1 \end{bmatrix}$$

Now any vector can be written as a linear combination of the standard unit vectors: -

$$V = \begin{bmatrix} v_1 \\ v_2 \\ v_3 \end{bmatrix}$$

$$= v_1 \begin{bmatrix} 1 \\ 0 \\ 0 \end{bmatrix} + v_2 \begin{bmatrix} 0 \\ 1 \\ 0 \end{bmatrix} + v_3 \begin{bmatrix} 0 \\ 0 \\ 1 \end{bmatrix}$$

$$= v_1 i + v_2 j + v_3 k$$

Thus, we can say that in a Cartesian 3D space a vector, v is a set of three numbers called as **components (v_x, v_y, v_z). Please note that any vector, v, in this space can be expanded in terms of the three unit vectors i, j, k. Also note that a function called an inner product enables the formation of numbers from vectors.** The inner product of two vectors, u and v, in this space is defined as:-

$$u \cdot v = u_x v_x + u_y v_y + u_z v_z$$

Note that the length also known as the norm of a vector u is $\sqrt{u} \cdot v$

In quantum computing, the vectors are members of a **complex vector space.** A vector space in N dimensions would have N basis vectors and N components. A vector in this space can be represented by:

$$|v> = \begin{bmatrix} v_0 \\ v_1 \\ \vdots \\ v_{N-1} \end{bmatrix}$$

The inner product of two vectors u and v in the complex space is denoted as <u, v>. It is a function that takes u and v as inputs and produces a complex number as the output.

Let the column representation of vectors u and v be-

$$u = \begin{bmatrix} u_0 \\ u_1 \\ \vdots \\ u_{N-1} \end{bmatrix} \text{ and } v = \begin{bmatrix} v_0 \\ v_1 \\ \vdots \\ v_{N-1} \end{bmatrix}$$

Then the inner product is as follows: -

$$<uv> = \begin{bmatrix} u_0 \\ u_1 \\ \vdots \\ u_{N-1} \end{bmatrix} \cdot \begin{bmatrix} v_0 \\ v_1 \\ \vdots \\ v_{N-1} \end{bmatrix}$$

$$= \mathbf{u^* \, v} = \sum\nolimits_{\mathbf{i <- 0 \text{ to } N-1}} (u_i * v_i)$$

Where u^* $(u^*_0, u^*_1, \ldots\ldots\ldots\ldots u^*_{N-1})$ is the **complex conjugate of u.**

For example, the inner product of the quantum states w_1 and w_2 represented by the two column vectors in the complex vector space is derived by taking the **complex conjugate of the first vector w_1 and then multiplying the corresponding components of two vectors and finally summing these products: -**

$$w_1 = \begin{bmatrix} 3+i \\ \\ 4+i \end{bmatrix} \text{ and } w_2 = \begin{bmatrix} 3i \\ \\ 4 \end{bmatrix}$$

That is,

$$<w_1\, w_2> = <w_1 * w_2> = \begin{bmatrix} 3-i \\ \\ 4+i \end{bmatrix} \quad \begin{bmatrix} 3i \\ \\ 4 \end{bmatrix}$$

$$= 19 + 13i$$

Also note that the length (norm) of a vector is derived by taking the square root of the inner product of the vector with itself. Hence, **the length of the vector,** say, for example-

$$\begin{bmatrix} 1-i \\ 2 \end{bmatrix}$$

Then, its length/ norm are calculated as follows: -

$$\sqrt{\begin{bmatrix} <1-i \\ 2 \end{bmatrix} \begin{bmatrix} 1+i \\ 2 \end{bmatrix}}$$

$$= \sqrt{1+1+4} = \sqrt{6}.$$

2.2 DIRAC NOTATION

In quantum physics, a different notation called as **Dirac Notation** is used to represent quantum states. In this notation, the inner product of two vectors u and v is denoted by $\langle u \mid v \rangle$ where the left part $\langle u|$ is called the **bra** and the right part $|v\rangle$ the **ket. Thus, in the Dirac notation or the bra-ket notation, an inner product is denoted by a < > (braket).**

Ket:

A vector v in a complex vector space, V is denoted by a ket-

$$|\mathbf{v}\rangle$$

A ket is analogous to a column vector. Because the vector space is complex, all items in a column vector are complex numbers.

Addition of two kets: The addition of two kets gives another ket. **The addition of kets is commutative as well as associative too.** That is,

$$(|\psi\rangle + |\varphi\rangle) = |\omega\rangle = (|\varphi\rangle + |\psi\rangle)$$

And

$$(|\psi\rangle + |\varphi\rangle) + |\omega\rangle = |\psi\rangle + (|\varphi\rangle + |\omega\rangle)$$

Please note that the set of kets is closed under the addition operation.

Properties of Kets

1. $(c_1 + c_2)\,|u\rangle = c_1\,|u\rangle + c_2\,|u\rangle$
2. $c_1\,(c_2\,|u\rangle) = (c_1\,c_2)\,|u\rangle$
3. $c\,(|u\rangle + |v\rangle) = c\,|u\rangle + c\,|v\rangle$
4. $|1|\,u\rangle = |u\rangle$
5. $|u\rangle + |0\rangle = |u\rangle$

Also note that quantum computing deals exclusively with complex vector space. So, scalar c is also assumed to be complex. The product of a complex number c and a ket $|u\rangle$ can be written in either order i.e.

$$c\,|u\rangle = |u\rangle\,c$$

A ket can also be written as a linear combination of other kets: -

$$|v\rangle = \sum_{i=0 \text{ to } N-1} |v_i\rangle$$

That is,

$$|v\rangle = \begin{bmatrix} v_0 \\ v_1 \\ v_2 \\ \vdots \\ v_{N-1} \end{bmatrix}$$

Also there is a special vector in a vector space, **the null or zero vector.** The zero vector is written as 0 and not as |0>. Thus,

$$|u\rangle + 0 = |u\rangle$$
$$0\,|u\rangle = 0$$

Bra:

In linear algebra, both column vectors and row vectors are used. Dirac Notation provides a symbol called a **bra to represent a row vector.** The bras corresponding to kets |0> and |1> are-

$$\langle 0| = (1\ 0)$$
$$\langle 1| = (0\ 1)$$

Remember that in a complex vector space, V, for every ket there is a unique bra. Also remember that the bra corresponding to the ket is obtained by taking the conjugate transpose of the ket and vice versa. A bra <u| acting on a vector, v turns it into a complex number, c. And can be written as follows: -

$$\langle u\,|: v) \rightarrow c$$

For example, if v is written in the ket notation then

$$\langle u\,|\,(|v\rangle) = c$$
$$\text{Or } \langle u\,|\,v\rangle = c$$

This indicates that <u| can be combined with any ket vector |v> to get the complex number c. In such a situation, the notation <u| needs to be written as (<u|) where any ket vector could be placed in the **blank spot.** The quantity <u| can be considered as a function that assigns to every vector in V a complex number. **This tpe of function is called as a linear functional. Similarly, a bra vector can be interpreted s an operator that acts on a ket vector to produce a complex number.** Hence, the bras corresponding to the kets |1> and |0> are the **conjugate transpose of the kets:**

$$\langle 1| = [0\ 1]$$
$$\langle 0| = [1\ 0]$$

Bras are useful in computing probability amplitudes.

For instance, as we know that the general state of a qubit is $|\psi\rangle = \alpha\,|0\rangle + \beta\,|1\rangle$. Then, the probability of a qubit being in state |1> can be determined by combining the general qubit state with the bra <1| as follows: -

$$\langle 1\,|\,|\psi\rangle = \langle 1\,|\psi\rangle$$
$$= \langle 1\,|\,(\alpha\,|0\rangle + \beta\,|1\rangle)$$

$$= \alpha <1|\ |0> + \beta <1|\ |1>$$

$$= \alpha\begin{bmatrix}0\ 1\end{bmatrix}\begin{bmatrix}1\\0\end{bmatrix} + \beta\begin{bmatrix}0\ 1\end{bmatrix}\begin{bmatrix}0\\1\end{bmatrix}$$

$$= \alpha.\ 0 + \beta\ .1$$

$$= \beta$$

Please note that the quantity <1 | |ψ> can be interpreted as the probability amplitude for being in state |1>. Similarly, <0 |ψ> is the probability amplitude for being in state |0>. Also note that <0|1> and <1|0> are both equal to zero and are known as orthogonal states. The amplitudes <0|0> and <1|1> are both equal to one.

In general, for any quantum state, |ψ>, the amplitude <ψ | ψ> = 1. This can be proved also, as follows:

To prove: $<\psi\ |\ \psi> = 1.$

Proof: Since $|\psi> = \alpha\ |0> + \beta\ |1>$, the dual or bra associated with it is-

$$|\psi> = \alpha^*\ |0> + \beta^*\ |1>$$

Thus, the amplitude <ψ | ψ> can be computed as-

$$<\psi\ |\ \psi> = (\alpha^* <0| + \beta^* <1|)\ (\alpha\ |0> + \beta\ |1>)$$

$$= \alpha^*\ \alpha <0\ |\ 0> + \alpha^* \beta <0\ |\ 1> + \beta^* \alpha <1\ |\ 0> + \beta^* \beta <1\ |\ 1>$$

As <0|1> = 0 and <1|0> = 0. Also both <0|0> and <1|1> are equal to 1. Thus,

$$<\psi\ |\ \psi> = |\alpha^2| + |\beta^2| = 1.$$

Hence, proved.

Similarly, the sum of two bras can be derived as follows: -

$$(<c_1\ | + <c_2\ |)\ |v> = <c_1|\ (|v>) + <c_2|\ (v>)$$

Rules followed by Bras and kets are as follows: -

1. $<v\ |\ au> = a<v\ |\ u>$ (where a is some constant)
2. $<av\ |\ u> = a^* <v\ |\ u>$
3. $<v\ |\ u>^* = <uv>$
4. $<u\ | + <v| = <u + v|$

Please note the order changes in which the bras and the kets are expressed based on how they are used as operators. For example, <v | w> != <w | v>.

Scalars, that is, complex numbers, however, can be moved through the expressions. **For example,**

$$|v> <v\ |\ w> <w| = <v\ |w> v> <w\ |$$

Since <v |w> is a complex number.

2.3 INNER PRODUCT AND HILBERT SPACES

The inner product of two vectors u and v in the complex space is denoted by <uv>. It generates a complex number as the output.

Properties that inner product must satisfy are as follows: -

1. **Linearity:** (<a| (w | b> + v |c>) = w <a | b> + v <a | c>
2. **Symmetry:** (u | v) = (v | u)*
3. **Positivity:** <u | u> ≥ 0 for |u> ! = 0.

The vector space V, with an inner product is called **as an inner product space.** In quantum physics, a unit vector in a Hilbert Space is associated with a physical system. **A Hilbert space is a complex vector space with an inner product.** As the inner product between two vectors results in a complex number, the Dirac notation for the inner product of the vectors |u> and |v> in a complex vector space is denoted by: -

$$\langle u \mid v \rangle = c$$

Where, **c is a complex number. The term <u | v> is called as a bracket.** Also note that <u | v> = <v | u>*. A vector |u> is normalized if-

$$(|u\rangle, |u\rangle) = 1$$

If for two vectors (|u>, |v>) = 0 then the vectors (|u> and |v> are **orthogonal.**

2.4 MATRICES AND TENSORS

Matrices: We usually talk of two things-

(a) Orthogonal vectors.

(b) Orthogonal matrices.

Orthogonal vectors: The vectors x and y are said to be orthogonal vectors if and only of x . y = 0. That is, inner product of these vectors is zero. **A non-empty set of mutually orthogonal non-zero vector is called as an orthogonal set of vectors.**

Orthonormal vectors: The vectors x and y for which x . y = 0 and |x| = 1, |y| = 1 are called as orthonormal vectors. If x, y are any vectors and x.y = 0 the x/|x|, y/|y| are orthonormal. In general, say $x_1, x_2......, x_m$ be m vectors in R^n. then **this set of vectors forms an orthonormal system of vectors, if-**

$$x_i \cdot x_j = x^T{}_i\, x_j = \begin{cases} 0, i\,! = j \\ 1, i = j. \end{cases}$$

Let us now define an orthogonal matrix and its properties.

Orthogonal matrix: A real matrix, A is called an orthogonal matrix if A is non-singular and its transpose is the same as it's inverse. That is, $A^T = A^{-1}$ or $A^TA = AA^T = I$.

Properties of orthogonal matrices are as follows: -

1. *The product of two or more orthogonal matrices is orthogonal.*
2. *The inverse and the transpose of an orthogonal matrix are orthogonal.*
3. *The determinant of an orthogonal matrix has the value +1 or -1.*
4. *The Eigen values of an orthogonal matrix are real or complex conjugates in pairs and have absolute value 1.*

Tensors: The knowledge of tensor is very vital to understand the core concepts of quantum programming—**superposition and entanglement.** The state of a single quantum bit can be represented as a unit/ column vector in a 2D vector space, C^2. **But quantum information processing systems use multiple qubits. And the joint state of such a system can only be expressed using a new vector space that takes into account the interaction among the qubits. This vector space is generated by using a special operation known as a tensor product or Kronecker product or direct product.** This tensor product is denoted by

Combines the smaller vector spaces of the individual qubits and forms a bigger space. **The elements of the bigger vector space are identified as tensors. For example,** the tensor product of two 2D vectors,

$$U = \begin{bmatrix} x_1 \\ y_1 \end{bmatrix} \text{ and } V = \begin{bmatrix} x_2 \\ y_2 \end{bmatrix}$$

is computed as follows:-

$$U \otimes V = \begin{bmatrix} x_1 \\ y_1 \end{bmatrix} \otimes \begin{bmatrix} x_2 \\ y_2 \end{bmatrix}$$

tensor product

$$= \begin{bmatrix} x_1 \begin{bmatrix} x_2 \\ y_2 \end{bmatrix} \\ y_1 \begin{bmatrix} x_2 \\ y_2 \end{bmatrix} \end{bmatrix} = \begin{bmatrix} x_1x_2 \\ x_1y_2 \\ y_1x_2 \\ y_1y_2 \end{bmatrix}$$

But we also know that the vector representation of single qubit states |0> and |1> are –

$$|0> = \begin{bmatrix} 1 \\ 0 \end{bmatrix} \text{ And } |1> = \begin{bmatrix} 0 \\ 1 \end{bmatrix}$$

Using these vector representations and the definition of the tensor product, the 2-qubit states can be represented as follows: -

$$|00> = \begin{bmatrix} 1 \\ 0 \\ 0 \\ 0 \end{bmatrix} ; \quad |01> = \begin{bmatrix} 0 \\ 1 \\ 0 \\ 0 \end{bmatrix}$$

Some basic properties of tensor products: -

1. If A and B are operators on m and n dimensional vectors respectively then A $\otimes$ B is an operator on n * m dimensional vector.

2. The product of any scalar, s, with tensor product $A \otimes B$ is equal to –

$$s(A \otimes B) = (sA) \otimes B = A \otimes (sB).$$

3. $$(A \otimes B)^* = (A^* \otimes B^*).$$

4. If A is an (m * n) matrix and B an (p * q) matrix then their tensor product is (mp * nq) matrix.
5. If A, B, C and D are matrices then-

   (a) $$A \otimes (B + C) = (A \otimes B) + (A \otimes C)$$

   (b) $$A \otimes (B \otimes C) = (A \otimes B) \otimes C$$

   This means that the derivative of a tensor product is independent of the order of evaluation. Therefore, it is an **associative operation.**

   (c) $$(A \otimes B)(C \otimes D) = (AC) \otimes (BD)$$

   That is, the distribution law holds.

6. If A, B are matrices and U, V and W are vectors then we say-

   (a) $$(A \otimes B)(U \otimes V) = AU \otimes BW$$

   (b) $$(U + V) \otimes W = U \otimes W + V \otimes W$$

   (c) $$U \otimes (V + W) = U \otimes V + U \otimes W$$

7. If s and t are scalars, U and V are vectors then-

$$sU \otimes tV = st(U \otimes V)$$

2.5 UNITARY OPERATORS AND PROJECTORS

An operator represented by an (n * n) matrix A is unitary if it produces an identity matrix when multiplied by its conjugate transpose. That is,

$$AA^+ = I$$

In other words, A is a unitary matrix if its conjugate transpose is equal to its inverse i.e.

$$A^+ = A^{-1}$$

For example, the following is **a unitary matrix-**

$$A = ½\begin{bmatrix} 1+i & 1-i \\ 1-i & 1+i \end{bmatrix}$$

The **conjugate transpose** of the matrix is-

$$A^+ = ½\begin{bmatrix} 1-i & 1+i \\ 1+i & 1-i \end{bmatrix}$$

So, we want to prove that $AA^+ = I$.

Now,

$$AA^+ = A=¼\begin{bmatrix} (1+i)(1-i)+(1-i)(1+i) & (1+i)(1+i)+(1-i)(1-i) \\ (1-i)(1-i)+(1+i)(1+i) & (1-i)(1+i)+(1+i)(1-i) \end{bmatrix}$$

$$= \frac{1}{4}\begin{bmatrix} 2+2 & 2-2 \\ 2-2 & 2+2 \end{bmatrix}$$

$$= \frac{1}{4}\begin{bmatrix} 4 & 0 \\ 0 & 4 \end{bmatrix}$$

$$= \begin{bmatrix} 1 & 0 \\ 0 & 1 \end{bmatrix}$$

$$= I$$

Hence, proved.

Some properties of Unitary Operators-

1. A **unitary operator preserves the inner product of any two vectors,** u and v in the vector space, V.
2. **The operator is invertible. Please note that the matrix corresponding to the operator is invertible if and only if the matrix is not singular. The determinant of a singular matrix is zero.**
3. The **eigen functions are orthonormal and are complete too.**
4. **Eigen values need not be real.**

Let us now study about the Projection operator.

Projection Operator:

It is an operator that helps in the measurement process and is known as the **projection operator or a projector.** As we know that **any state vector has a unitary length. The outer product of any state vector with itself is a projection operator.** That is,

$$|\psi_a\rangle\langle\psi_a| = P\psi_a$$

Property of a projection operator are-

1. $$(P\psi_a)^2 = |\psi_a\rangle\langle\psi_a|\psi_a\rangle\langle\psi_a| = |\psi_a\rangle\langle\psi_a| = \mathbf{P}\,\psi_a$$
2. **It is Hermitian, i.e.** $\mathbf{P} = \mathbf{P^{+}}$.
3. **A projection operator is equal to its own square.**
4. **Two projectors P_i and P_j are orthogonal if, for every state in the Hilbert space-**

   $$P_i P_j |\psi_a\rangle = 0 \qquad \text{where } 0 \le i, j \le n\text{-}1.$$

   This condition is also written as follows: -

   $$P_i P_j = 0.$$

   Assume the expansion of an arbitrary ket $|\varphi\rangle$ in a basis $(v_0, v_1, v_2,\ldots\ldots)$ as follows: -

   $$|\varphi\rangle = \sum_{i=0 \text{ to } n} c_i |v_i\rangle$$

   Now suppose that the linear operator $\langle v_1|v_1\rangle$ is applied to vector $|\varphi\rangle$ then this will pick up the vector's projection in the $|v_1\rangle$ direction as follows:

   $$|v_1\rangle\langle v_1|\varphi\rangle$$

Also note that if the vectors are orthonormal, the operator $|v_0> < v_0| + |v_1> < v_1|$ projects the vector onto the 2D subspace defined by $|v_1>$ and $|v_2>$ as below-

$$|v_0> < v_0 |\varphi> + |v_1> < v_1 |\varphi>$$

In general, this sum may be extended to the sum over all the basis vectors as follows: -

$$|v_0> < v_0 |\varphi> + |v_1> < v_1 |\varphi> + \ldots\ldots |v_{n-1}> < v_{n-1} |\varphi>$$

5. **If an operator composed of the sum of all the single projection operators for a given set of orthonormal basis states acts on a vector,** v_i, **the resulting vector is given by: -**

$$|\varphi> = \sum_{i=0 \text{ to } n-1} <v_i \varphi> v_i >$$
$$= \sum_{i=0 \text{ to } n-1} <v_i> < v_i \ \varphi>$$
$$= \sum_{i=0 \text{ to } n-1} |v_i> < v_i | \ |\varphi>$$

Thus, we can write as follows-

$$\sum_{i=0 \text{ to } n-1} |v_i> < v_i | = I$$

where I is an identity operator. This is also more formally known as **the completeness relation for the chosen orthonormal basis. Please understand that it indicates that the sum of the projections of a vector in all possible directions returns the original. The set** $|v_i> < v_i|$ **acts as an operator in the direction** $|v_i>$ and **is called as the projection operator,** P_v. **Also note that-**

$$P^2_v = P_v P_v = |v> <v| |v> <v| = |v> <v| = P_v$$

2.6 EIGEN VALUES AND EIGEN VECTORS

We have already studied some basic laws that connect this physical world and quantum mechanics. Some of them are as follows: -

1. Every physical system has an associated complex vector space with an inner product / Hilbert space called as the **state space of the system. A unit vector that represents the physical system in the state space is known as the state vector.** It contains the complete information about the system.
2. All **measureable properties or observables** of a physical system are represented by **Hermitian operators** that are acting in the **system's state space. Please understand that any measurement performed on a quantum system involves some interaction between the system and the observer.** Thus, when an observable is measured obtaining a certain outcome λ, then **the measurement leaves the system in a state that is an Eigen vector of the operator with Eigen value,** λ.
3. The probability of measuring an observable with Eigen value, λ, **in a quantum state is-**

   $$\textbf{prob}(\lambda) = |<a | \lambda>|^2$$

   where $|a>$ is an Eigen vector of the corresponding Hermitian operator with Eigen value λ.
4. Measurements in systems having **the same state vector may not result in the same outcomes.** Only the probabilities of various outcomes can be known.
5. **The expectation value of a measurable quantity Q is defined as the average of values that is likely to be obtained if Q is measured on a large number systems having the same state vector**

$|u\rangle$. The expectation value is given by-

$$\langle u| Q | u\rangle$$

provided $\langle u | u\rangle = 1.$

6. **The state space of a composite physical system is the tensor product of the state spaces of the component systems.**
7. **The evolution of a quantum system in time is described by a unitary transformation.**
8. Eigen values are a special set of scalars associated with a linear system of equations i.e. matrix equation, sometimes also known as the **characteristic roots, characteristic values, proper values or latent roots.** Mathematically, consider a column vector and call it v. Also consider an (n *n) matrix and call it A. then consider some scalar, λ. **If, it is true that $Av = \lambda v$ then we say that v is an Eigen vector of the matrix A and that λ is an Eigen value of the matrix A.** In matrix notation, we can write as $(A - \lambda I)\, x = 0$; where λ is a **scalar,** I is an **identity matrix of order n, x is a solution vector.**
9. The word 'Eigen' is a German word meaning *'specific', 'proper' or 'particular'.* **We also define an Eigen vector of some linear transformation, T, is a vector that when T is applied to it does not change direction, it only changes scale.** It changes scale by a **scalar value λ, the Eigen value.** Thus, we can write that-

   $$T(v) = \lambda v$$

   In point no. 8, the matrix A is now replaced with the transformation, T. This not only shows what are Eigen vectors and values but it also specifies that a matrix, when applied to a vector will transform that vector. **Note that the matrix itself is an operation on the vector.** These transformations are needed in the next chapter also when we study about the quantum circuits with quantum gates.
10. The **sum of the Eigen values** of a matrix, A is equal to the **trace of the matrix A.**
11. **The product of the Eigen values of a matrix A is equal to the determinant of A. Also note that matrix, A is singular if and only if at least one of its Eigen values is zero.**
12. **A square matrix, A of order n has always n linearly independent Eigen vectors when its Eigen values are distinct. The matrix A may also have n linearly independent Eigen vectors even when some Eigen values are repeated.**
13. **The problem of determining the Eigen values and Eigen vectors of a matrix is called an Eigenvalue problem.**
14. The set of the Eigen values is called as **the spectrum of A.**
15. If A is a square matrix, A and A^T **have the same Eigen values, since a determinant can be expanded by rows or columns.**
16. The Eigen values of an upper triangular, lower triangular or diagonal matrix are the **main diagonal entries.**
17. If $\lambda_1, \lambda_2, \ldots, \lambda_n$ are the Eigen values of A, then the Eigen values of: -
    (a) kA are $k\lambda_1\, k\lambda_2, \ldots\, k\lambda_n$.
    (b) A^m are $\lambda^m{}_1, \lambda^m{}_2, \ldots, \lambda^m{}_n$.
    (c) A^{-1} (if it exists) are $1/\lambda_1, 1/\lambda_2, \ldots, 1/\lambda_n$.

18. $A - kI$ has the Eigen value $\lambda_1 - k, \ldots\ldots \lambda_n - k$, for any scalar k.
19. $(A - kI)^{-1}$ has the Eigen value $1/(\lambda_1 - k), \ldots\ldots, 1/(\lambda_n - k)$.
20. A real matrix, A, may have complex Eigen values i.e. **if $\alpha + i\beta$ is an Eigen value then its conjugate $\alpha - i\beta$ is also an Eigen value.**
21. **The Eigen values of a symmetric matrix are real.**
22. **The Eigen values of a skew-symmetric matrix are pure imaginary or zero.**
23. **The Eigen vector corresponding to Eigen value is not unique.**

Before we discuss further, let us solve some problems on Eigen vectors.

Example 1: Find the Eigen values and Eigen vectors of the matrix $\begin{bmatrix} 5 & 4 \\ 1 & 2 \end{bmatrix}$

Solution 1: The **characteristic equation is $|A - \lambda I| = 0$.**

$$\begin{vmatrix} 5-\lambda & 4 \\ 1 & 2-\lambda \end{vmatrix} = \mathbf{0}$$

Or $\lambda^2 - 7\lambda + 6 = 0$

So, $\lambda = 6, 1.$

Thus, the **Eigen values** are 6 and 1.

Let us now find out the **Eigen vectors** now.

If x, y are the components of an Eigen vector corresponding to the Eigen value, λ, then

$$|\mathbf{A} - \lambda\mathbf{I}|\,\mathbf{X} = \begin{bmatrix} 5-\lambda & 4 \\ 1 & 2-\lambda \end{bmatrix}\begin{bmatrix} x \\ y \end{bmatrix} = \mathbf{0}$$

Case-1: When $\lambda = \mathbf{6}$, the above equation becomes-

$$\begin{bmatrix} -1 & 4 \\ 1 & -4 \end{bmatrix}\begin{bmatrix} x \\ y \end{bmatrix} = 0$$

So, $-x + 4y = 0$

Or $x/4 = y/1$ gives the Eigen vector (4, 1)

Case-2: When $\lambda = \mathbf{1}$, the above equation becomes-

$$\begin{bmatrix} 4 & 4 \\ 1 & 1 \end{bmatrix}\begin{bmatrix} x \\ y \end{bmatrix} = 0$$

So, $x + y = 0$

Or $x = -y$

Or $x/1 = y/-1$ gives the Eigen vector (1, -1).

Thus, the Eigen vectors are (4, 1) and (1, -1).

Example 2: Let A = $\begin{bmatrix} 1 & 1 & -1 \\ 1 & 3 & 4 \\ 7 & -5 & 2 \end{bmatrix}$ **Determine whether or not-**

(a) The rows of A are orthogonal.

(b) A is an orthogonal matrix.

(c) The columns of A are orthogonal.

(d) Normalizing each row of matrix A and find matrix B.

(e) Is B an orthogonal matrix?

(f) Are the columns of matrix B orthogonal?

Solution 2: Let us solve each of these parts now-

(a) Yes, since $(1, 1, -1) . (1, 3, 4) = (1)(1) + (1)(3) + (-1)(4) = 0$

$(1, 3, 4) . (7, -5, 2) = 7 - 15 + 8 = 0$

And $(1, 1, -1) . (7, -5, 2) = 7 - 5 - 2 = 0.$

(b) No, since the rows of A are not unit vector.

$|(1, 1, -1)| = \sqrt{1^2 + 1^2 + (-1)^2} = \sqrt{3}.$

(c) No, for example,

$(1, 1, 7) . (1, 3, -5) = 1 + 3 - 35 = -31 != 0.$

(d) $|(1, 1, -1)| = \sqrt{1 + 1 + 1} = \sqrt{3},$

$|(1, 3, 4)| = \sqrt{1 + 9 + 16} = \sqrt{26}$

$|(7, -5, 2)| = \sqrt{49 + 25 + 4} = \sqrt{78}.$

Hence, $\mathbf{B} = \begin{bmatrix} 1/\sqrt{3} & 1/\sqrt{3} & -1/\sqrt{3} \\ 1/\sqrt{26} & 3/\sqrt{26} & 4/\sqrt{26} \\ 7/\sqrt{78} & -5/\sqrt{78} & 2/\sqrt{78} \end{bmatrix}$

(e) Yes, since rows of matrix B are still orthogonal and are now unit vectors.

(f) Yes, since the rows of matrix B form an orthogonal set of vectors, the columns of B must automatically form an orthogonal set.

SUMMARY

Every classical computer or a non-quantum computer can be best described by quantum mechanics. This is so because quantum mechanics is the basis of the physical universe. In this chapter, we have studied Dirac's notation, linear algebra and other methods to cover the key concepts of quantum mechanics. **According to the principles of quantum mechanics, systems are set to a definite state only once they are measured.** Before measurement, a system is in an indefinite state (qubits) but it collapses to a determinate state (0 or 1) after measurement. Also we have seen that what are orthogonal vectors and matrices and orthonormal vectors and matrices. The chapter also discusses about orthonormal vectors and matrices.

MULTIPLE CHOICE QUESTIONS [MCQS] WITH ANSWERS

1. What is one of the central objects of linear algebra?
   (a) Scalar.
   (b) Vector.
   (c) Length.
   (d) None of the above.
2. The multiplication of a vector by a number /scalar is also called as a scalar because-
   (a) It scales the vector.
   (b) It reduces the vector.
   (c) It adds two vectors.
   (d) None of the above.
3. In quantum mechanics, we use-
   (a) Simple numbers.
   (b) Complex numbers.
   (c) Real numbers.
   (d) All of the above.
4. A superposition of states can be represented as a linear combination of vectors representing their states-
   (a) False.
   (b) True.
   (c) Partly true.
   (d) None of the above.
5. When one of the vectors is the zero vector, then we use the term-
   (a) Orthogonal.
   (b) Perpendicular.
   (c) Both 'a' and 'b'.
   (d) None of the above.
6. The process of changing a complex number into its conjugate is known as-
   (a) Concatenating.
   (b) Merging.
   (c) Conjugating.
   (d) Sorting.
7. The complex conjugate or simply the conjugate of the number z = (a+bi) is-
   (a) a-bi
   (b) a/bi
   (c) a * bi
   (d) None of the above.
8. The tensor product of a column vector with a row vector yields a-
   (a) Vector.
   (b) Scalar.
   (c) Matrix.
   (d) None of the above.
9. The tensor product of two column vectors yields another-
   (a) Row vector.
   (b) Column vector.
   (c) Scalar.
   (d) None of the above.
10. The tensor product of (a * b) matrix with a (c * d) matrix is a-
    (a) (a . c) * (b. d) matrix.
    (b) (a . b) * (c. d) matrix.
    (c) (b . c) * (c. d) matrix.
    (d) (a . b) * (b. d) matrix.
11. The operation "A injects into B" shows which property of functions-
    (a) Productivity.
    (b) Injectivity.
    (c) Subjectvity.
    (d) Multiplicity.
12. A space of vectors is known as-
    (a) Solar space.
    (b) Center space.
    (c) Vector space.
    (d) None of the above.

13. The number of vectors for any basis for V is known as-
    (a) Area of Vector space, V.
    (b) Dimension of Vector space, V.
    (c) Probability of Vector space, V.
    (d) None of the above.
14. In Dirac's notation, we say that the two vectors, u and v are orthogonal iff-
    (a) $\langle u|v\rangle = 1$.
    (b) $\langle u|v\rangle = 0$.
    (c) $\langle u|v\rangle = ½$.
    (d) $\langle u|v\rangle = \sqrt{1/2}$.
15. A linear transformation and a matrix are the same thing-
    (a) True.
    (b) False
    (c) Partially true.
    (d) Partially false.
16. In general, the Eigen value associated to an Eigen vector v is the scalar λ appearing in the definition of an Eigen vector-
    (a) $T v = \lambda v$.
    (b) $v = T \lambda v$.
    (c) $T = v \lambda v$.
    (d) None of the above.
17. Collectively, the Eigen vectors and Eigen values of a transformation is known as its-
    (a) Eigen space.
    (b) Eigen stuff.
    (c) Eigen vector.
    (d) None of the above.
18. The Eigen stuff is sometimes called as the-
    (a) The Eigen system of transformation.
    (b) The Cartesian system.
    (c) The coordinate system.
    (d) None of the above.
19. A linear operator is referred to as Hermitian iff-
    (a) It is equal to its transpose.
    (b) It is equal to the operator.
    (c) It is equal to its conjugate transpose.
    (d) None of the above.
20. Unit vectors remain unit vectors even after an application of a unitary matrix-
    (a) True.
    (b) False.
    (c) Partially true.
    (d) None of the above.
21. Qubit can be represented as a 2D complex-
    (a) Hilbert space.
    (b) Aerospace.
    (c) Vector space.
    (d) None of the above.
22. A collection of n-qubits is known as a-
    (a) Parallel register.
    (b) Serial register.
    (c) Quantum register.
    (d) None of the above.
23. The dimension of the tensor product of n-dimensional Hilbert spaces is-
    (a) 2n.
    (b) n^2.
    (c) 2^n.
    (d) n/2.
24. Bras always come before-
    (a) nets.
    (b) kets.
    (c) sets.
    (d) None of the above.

Answers															
1.	(b)	2.	(a)	3.	(b)	4.	(b)	5.	(a)	6.	(c)	7.	(a)	8.	(c)
9.	(b)	10.	(a)	11.	(b)	12.	(c)	13.	(b)	14.	(b)	15.	(a)	16.	(a)
17.	(b)	18.	(a)	19.	(c)	20.	(a)	21.	(a)	22.	(c)	23.	(c)	24.	(b)

CONCEPTUAL SHORT QUESTIONS WITH ANSWERS

Q1. What is the relationship between quantum computing and linear algebra?

Ans. 1 The following are the points of relationship: -

1. A **qubit** can be represented by a 2D complex Hilbert space.
2. The **state of the qubit** is represented by a vector in the Hilbert space.
3. The vectors representing the states of the qubit have a norm of 1.
4. **The quantum register consisting of n-qubits is a 2^n dimensional complex Hilbert space composed of the n-fold tensor product of the 2D Hilbert spaces representing the qubits.**
5. **A computational basis vector** of the space represents a **definite computational state of the qubit.**
6. **A superposition of states is a linear combination of the computational basis vectors.**
7. **Quantum logic gates** (to be discussed shortly), are **unitary operators** which act on the state space.
8. **Because unitary operators preserve the norm of the vectors they act on, states are transformed to new states and not to just any vector in the space. That is why; we can build quantum circuits using unitary operators.**

Q2. Give two differences between a classical and quantum computer.

Ans. 2 The following are the points of differences: -

1. The operations in a quantum computer are reversible.
2. The input data in a quantum computer is maintained in a given operation.

Q3. For the superposition state-

$$3/5\,|0\rangle + 4/5\,|1\rangle$$

Here, what is more likely to be observed-- |1> or |0>?

Ans. 3 The numbers 3/5 and 4/5 in the linear combination above are called as **coefficients or amplitudes**, in the superposition of the states |0> and |1>. The **square of their absolute values, $|3/5|^2$ and $|4/5|^2$ are the probabilities of observing each of states, |0> and |1>, on measurement.** Hence, in this case, |1> is more likely to be observed than |0>. **Also note that in quantum mechanics, we use complex numbers as the amplitudes and not the real numbers.**

Q4. List the equivalent formulations of invertibility.

Ans. 4 The following are equivalent for a linear transformation, T: -

1. Determinant (T) = 0.
2. T is not invertible.
3. The rows of the matrix representing T are linearly dependent.
4. The columns of the matrix representing T are linearly dependent.

Q5. Explain the following statement-"The tensor product of Hilbert spaces is another Hilbert space."

Ans.5 A qubit can be represented as a 2D complex Hilbert space. A qubit is denoted with letter, H (Hilbert). A qubit is represented by a vector space, also called as a Hilbert space. For instance, the vectors |0> and |1> are states in a 2D Hilbert space/ state space, H, which represents 1 qubit. So, |0> and |1> are an orthonormal basis for H. in quantum mechanics field, **every state is a superposition of these two states. A collection of n-qubits is named as a quantum register and denote it as follows: -**

$$\underbrace{H \otimes H \otimes \ldots\ldots \otimes H}_{\text{n-times}}$$

Thus, the statement, **"The tensor product of Hilbert spaces is another Hilbert space."** Although, it will have a greater dimension now.

Q6. Differentiate between a quantum superposition and a classical superposition.

Ans. 6 A **superposition of a classical membrane vibration state** with itself results in a different state with twice the magnitude of the original oscillation. But please note that there is no physical characterization of a quantum state which corresponds to the magnitude of a classical classification. Consider a classical state with amplitude of oscillation zero everywhere corresponding to a membrane at rest. **Also note that no equivalent state exists for a quantum system due to the fact that a zero ket vector does not represent a valid state.**

Q7. What is a symmetric matrix? List some of its properties.

Ans. 7 **A square-matrix is symmetric if it is equal to its transpose.** That is, an (n * n) matrix A is symmetric if $A = A^T$ such a matrix is symmetric about its main diagonal.

Properties of symmetric matrices

1. **The transpose of a symmetric matrix, A is also symmetric.**
2. **The product of a symmetric matrix A and a scalar c,** i.e. cA is also symmetric.
3. **The inverse of the transpose of a symmetric matrix A is equal to the inverse of the matrix-**

$$(A^T)` = A`$$

4. **If A and B are two symmetric matrices and $(A+B)^T = A^T + B^T = A + B$ then (A + B) is a symmetric matrix.**
5. **The product of two symmetric matrices is also symmetric if the two matrices commute** i.e. AB = BA.

Q8. What are orthogonal matrices? List some of its properties.

Ans. 8 **A square- matrix is called orthogonal if the transpose of the matrix; A is equal to its inverse.** That is, if

$$A^T = A^{-1}$$

$$A^T A = I$$

Then the matrices are orthogonal.

Properties of orthogonal matrices

1. **The inner product of any two row vectors or any two column vectors is equal to zero.**
2. **Identity matrices are orthogonal.**

3. **The product of an orthogonal matrix and its transpose matrix is equal to the identity matrix of the same order.**
4. **The product of two orthogonal matrices is also orthogonal.**
5. **An orthogonal matrix is always a symmetric matrix.**

Q9. How are Hermitian operators related to Eigen values? What are the properties of Hermitian operators?

Ans. 9 A class of operators of special importance are the **Hermitian operators because the Eigen values of a Hermitian operator are the possible values of the observables. Please understand that this means that the measured values are real number and not the complex numbers.** Quantum mechanics says that the operators that are equal to their ad-joints are called as **Hermitian or self-adjoint. To put it in a proper light,** we say that an operator A is Hermitian if and only if it satisfies the following equation: -

$$A^+ = A$$

For example, we derive the adjoint of the given matrix representing a linear operator and determine whether it is Hermitian or not?

$$A = \begin{bmatrix} 3 & 3+i & 2 \\ 3-i & 3 & i \\ 2 & -i & 1 \end{bmatrix}$$

The complex conjugate of matrix A is A* and is as follows: -

$$A^* = \begin{bmatrix} 3 & 3-i & 2 \\ 3+i & 3 & i \\ 2 & i & 1 \end{bmatrix}$$

Then, A* is transposed which gives us-

$$A^+ = \begin{bmatrix} 3 & 3+i & 2 \\ 3-i & 3 & i \\ 2 & -i & 1 \end{bmatrix} = A$$

As $A = A^+$ so, the matrix is Hermitian.

Also note that every entry in A^+ is equal to the complex conjugate of the entry symmetrically located with respect to the diagonal of the matrix.

Properties of Hermitian operators

1. **They are complex analogue of symmetric matrices. To put it in a proper light, the diagonal entries of a Hermitian matrix must be real since the conjugation process must not change these entries.** Moreover, each entry and its image across the diagonal must be complex conjugates.
2. **The expectation value of a Hermitian operator is real on any state.** However, it is also true that any operator whose expectation value is real for all states must be Hermitian.
3. **The Eigen values of Hermitian operators are real.**

Q10. What are Unitary operators? List some of its properties.

Ans. 10 An operator represented by an (n * n) matrix A is unitary if it produces an identity matrix when multiplied by its conjugate transpose: -

$$AA^{+} = I$$

That is, A is a unitary matrix if its conjugate transpose is equal to its inverse: -

$$A^{+} = A^{-1}$$

Properties of Unitary operators

1. **A unitary operator preserves the inner product of any two vectors u and V in the vector space, V.**
2. **The operator is invertible. Also note that the matrix corresponding to the operator is invertible if and only if the matrix is not singular. The determinant of a singular matrix is zero.**
3. **The Eigen functions are orthonormal and they are complete.**
4. **Eigen values may not be real.**

Q11. Define computational basis.

Ans. 11 Every vector space has an infinite number of orthonormal basis. Practically speaking, a basis set that is easy to work with is selected rather than any particular one. **This basis is called as the computational basis.** This basis set need not be unique, the number of the base vectors contained in the set is invariant. In a quantum state, +/- basis is a **complete orthonormal basis. That is why, any qubit state can be represented using the basis states +/-. The +/- basis is also called as Hadamard basis or the diagonal basis.**

Q12. Who is the father of quantum mechanics? What was his contribution?

Ans. 12 Max Planck (1900) is known as the father of quantum mechanics. He suggested that heat and light come in units that can't be divided and this he called as the **"energy quanta".** His idea came from his efforts to solve the black-body radiation experiments where a body that completely absorbs all radiation/heat inside it has a cavity that allows some radiation to escape. **Please note that as the heat increases inside the box, the frequency of radiation reaches ranges visible to the human eye, thereby glowing at different colors.** He said, that **the energy of one quantum is-**

$$E = h\nu = E_2 - E_1$$

Where h is the Planck's constant and ν is the frequency.

Planck observed that the radiations are emitted or absorbed by black bodies **discontinuously and not continuously.** Later, he introduced the term **"quantum" which means small bundle or packet of energy. He proposed that energy of radiation is atomistic and that it is released in discrete portions or small portions called as quanta.** The energy of an electromagnetic wave is directly proportional to its frequency. **Please note, in above equation that higher is the**

frequency of radiation, greater is the energy associated with it. Also note that he said that when a system /body gains or loses energy, it must do so in terms of some definite whole number multiple of small discrete amounts known as Quanta. This means that the energy of a body can increase or decrease by 1, 2, 3, 4....n quantum but never by 1.5, 1.6, 1.8 10.8 etc.

Max Planck used the **second law of thermodynamics (also known as entropy) to derive a formula for the experimental results derived from the black-body radiation problem.** That is,

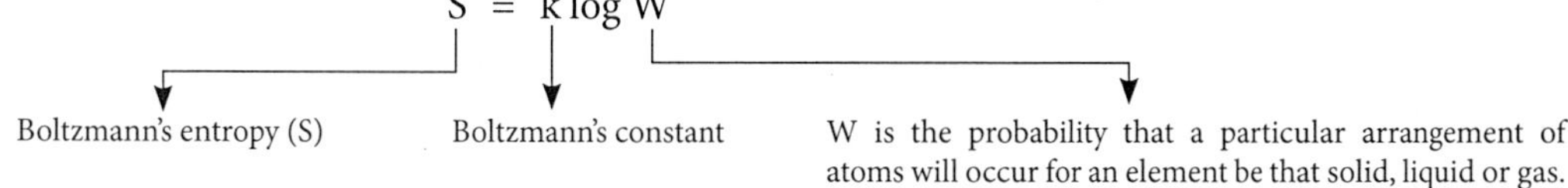

Using Boltzmann's statistical method wanted that the chunks decrease to zero over time. That is why; he gave this equation, which he called as **energy quanta.**

Q13. **Say,**

$$|a\rangle = \begin{bmatrix} 3 \\ 1 \end{bmatrix}$$

$$|b\rangle = \begin{bmatrix} 1 \\ 2 \end{bmatrix}$$

$$|c\rangle = \begin{bmatrix} -2 \\ 6 \end{bmatrix}$$

Compute <a | b> and <a | c>.

Ans. 13 Now,

$$\langle a | b\rangle = [3 \quad 1] \begin{bmatrix} 1 \\ 2 \end{bmatrix} = 3 + 2 = 5 \text{ (we multiply bra by ket>}$$

Bra Ket

$$\langle a | c\rangle = [3 \quad 1] \begin{bmatrix} -2 \\ 6 \end{bmatrix} = -6 + 6 = 0 \text{ (we multiply bra by ket>}$$

Bra Ket

As <a | b>!= 0, so, now we know that |a> and |b> are **not orthogonal.** Similarly, because <a | c> = 0 thus, |a> and |c> are **orthogonal.**

Q14. **What do you mean by orthonormal bases?**

Ans. 14 The word **"orthonormal"** has two parts: ortho from orthogonal and normal from normalized, which simply means **unit.** Say, we are working with 2D kets, then an orthonormal basis will consist of a set of two unit kets that are orthogonal to one another. **In general, if we are working with n-dimensional kets, an orthonormal basis consists of a set of n unit kets that are mutually orthogonal to one another.**

Q15. **What are Unitary matrices? Why are they significant?**

Ans. 15 The matrices with complex entries that correspond to **orthogonal matrices are called Unitary. A matrix M is unitary if M^+ M is the identity matrix, where M^+ means first transpose of M, then take the conjugate of all the entries. Also note that real numbers are a subset of the complex numbers, so all orthogonal matrices are unitary.**

Q16. **What happens when the qubits are unentangled or entangled?**

Ans. 16 **When qubits are unentangled, a measurement of one of the qubits has absolutely no effect on the other qubit.** On the other hand, **if qubits are entangled, the measurement of one will have an effect on the other one.**

Q17. **Define super-liminal communication.**

Ans. 17 **Super-luminal communication is the types of communication that is faster than the speed of light.**

Q18. **What is spontaneous parametric data-conversion?**

Ans 18 A process in which a laser beam sends photons through a special crystal, then most of the photons just pass through but some photons split into two. **But please remember that the energy and the momentum must be conserved in this case i.e. the total energy and momentum of the two resulting photons must equal the energy and momentum of the initial photon. Also note that the laws of conservation promise that the state describing the polarization of the two photons is entangled.**

Q19. **Given the following quantum measurements-**

$$|\psi\rangle = -4/10\,|00\rangle - 4\sqrt{3}/10\,|01\rangle + 3/10\,|10\rangle + 3\sqrt{3}/10\,|11\rangle$$

Compute the probabilities and resultant states to measure two-qubit states 00, 01, 10 and 11. (ψ) is the qubit state.

Ans. 19 The following table shows that-

Measurement	Probability	Resultant state
00	$\lvert -4/10\rvert^2 = 16/100 = 16\%$	$\lvert\psi\rangle = \lvert 00\rangle$
01	$\lvert -4\sqrt{3}/10\rvert^2 = 48/100 = 48\%$	$\lvert\psi\rangle = \lvert 01\rangle$
10	$\lvert 3/10\rvert^2 = 9/100 = 9\%$	$\lvert\psi\rangle = \lvert 10\rangle$
11	$\lvert 3\sqrt{3}/10\rvert^2 = 27/100 = 27\%$	$\lvert\psi\rangle = \lvert 11\rangle$

Hence, the probabilities and the resultant states to measure two-qubit states 00, 01, 10 and 11 are 16%, 48%, 9% and 27%

EXERCISE QUESTIONS

Q1. Define the following: -

(a) Linearly dependent vectors.

(b) Non-Linearly dependent vectors.

(c) Basis of a vector space.

(d) Dimensions of a vector space.

(e) Smallest subset.

[Hint: The smallest subset is the subset with the smallest cardinality.]

Q2. What is a Hilbert space? Define separable Hilbert spaces.

Q3. What are Eigen vectors and Eigen values? Explain with an example.

Q4. Distinguish between classical superposition and quantum superposition.

Q5. What is a Hermitian operator?

Q6. What is projection operator? Explain with an example.

Q7. When are two projectors said to be orthogonal?

Q8. What are rotation operators?

Q9. For an (m * m) matrix A show that-

$$(A^+)^+ = A$$

Q10. Show that $|+\rangle = 1/\sqrt{2}\,(|0\rangle + |1\rangle)$ and $|-\rangle = 1/\sqrt{2}\,(|0\rangle - |1\rangle)$ form an orthonormal basis in H_2. Construct the projectors P_+ and P_- corresponding to these basis vectors.

Q11. What is the trace of a Pauli matrix?

Q12. What do you say about the following quantum state-

$$|\Psi\rangle = \cos(\theta/2)\,|0\rangle + \sin(\theta/2)\,e^{i\phi}\,|1\rangle$$

Is it pure or mixed type?

Q13. What will be the correct form of the state $|0+\rangle$ in the computational basis, if you are given that-

$$|0\rangle = (1, 0)^T \text{ and}$$

$$|+\rangle = 1/\sqrt{2}\,(|0\rangle + |1\rangle) = 1/\sqrt{2}\,(1. 1)^T)$$

Q14. What is an Eigen-value problem? List some of the properties of Eigen values.

Q15. Define the following terms: -

(a) Unit vector.

(b) Orthogonal vectors.

(c) Orthonormal vectors.

(d) Orthonormal system of vectors.

Q16. Find the Eigen values and Eigen vectors of the following matrix-

$$A = \begin{bmatrix} 1 & 1 & 3 \\ 1 & 5 & 1 \\ 3 & 1 & 1 \end{bmatrix}$$

Q17. Prove that the following matrix is orthogonal-

$$A = \begin{bmatrix} -2/3 & 1/3 & 2/3 \\ 2/3 & 2/3 & 1/3 \\ 1/3 & -2/3 & 2/3 \end{bmatrix}$$

3 Quantum Circuits Design

3.0 INTRODUCTION

Gates are the basic building blocks in a quantum computer. Quantum gates are different from the classical gates in the sense that quantum gates operate on all of the possible states of the qubit simultaneously. In the circuit model of quantum computing, the basic circuit is a **quantum logic gate. Please recall that many of the digital gates used in classical computing are not reversible.** As we know that a gate transforms its input to its output according to the rules hardwired into the truth table. **But please remember that a quantum gate transforms the state of a quantum system into a new state. And the state transformations performed by the quantum gates and circuits are expressed by Hermitian operators. Such a matrix describing the state transformation is called as a transfer matrix. Also note that the matrices characterizing quantum gates are unitary and that the transformations performed by these gates are reversible.** Recall that a unitary transformation corresponds to a length-preserving and information preserving rotation in a vector space. **To put it in a proper light, the length preserving requirement ensures that the total probability of the set of states is always equal to one.**

The point to ponder is that a quantum gate has an equal number of qubits (1, 2 or 3) at the input and at the output. However, in each case, the input and output states are expressed by vectors in a Hilbert space with the corresponding number of dimensions; H_2 for a 1-qubit gate, H_4 for a 2-qubit gate, H_8 for a 3-qubit gate, **Please note that the input/output state of a n-qubit quantum gate is calculated as the tensor product of the corresponding state vectors of the individual I/O qubits.**

As an example, the input state of a 2-qubit gate is $|\varphi\rangle \otimes |\psi\rangle$ if the state vectors of the 2-input qubits are $|\varphi\rangle \otimes |\psi\rangle$. Therefore, the **orthonormal basis used for the analysis of a quantum gate** comprises of–

(a) 2 vectors in H_2, $|0\rangle$ and $|1\rangle$.

(b) 4 vectors in H_4, $|00\rangle$, $|01\rangle$, $|10\rangle$ and $|11\rangle$.

(c) 8 vectors in H_8, $|000\rangle$, $|001\rangle$, $|011\rangle$, $|100\rangle$, $|101\rangle$, $|110\rangle$ and $|111\rangle$.

And that the Eigen values corresponding to these Eigen vectors represent the result of the measurement of the quantum system's state.

The **steps that are followed when using a quantum gate** are as follows:–

1. *Start with an informal description of the transformation performed by the gate.*
2. *From this informal description, we construct the truth table.*
3. *Then, the matrix corresponding to the quantum operator, is used.*
4. *We construct the Eigen vectors in a specific orthonormal basis.*
5. *Then, we construct the projectors reflecting the transformation of the input performed by the quantum gate.*

In general, if |V> is the initial state of a quantum system applied as input to the gate performing a state transformation described by the operator, G, with a matrix representation G = $[g_{ij}]$, then the resulting state |W> of the quantum system is expressed as:–

$$|W> \;=\; G\,|V>.$$

In quantum circuits, mathematically gates are represented as **transformational matrices or linear operators that must be unitary. Please note that this is the required condition because the norm of the system wave function must be equal to 1 at all times.** Actually, unitary transformations preserve the norm. Each unitary transformation, U, has an inverse transformation U^{-1} = U, where U^{+} is the conjugate of U. **That is why, quantum calculations are reversible.**

How to do that?

All these calculations are performed by applying a succession of these unitary matrices on **single or multi-qubit systems.** A single qubit is represented as a (2 * 1) matrix i.e.

$$1 \text{ qubit } = \begin{pmatrix} 0 \\ 1 \end{pmatrix} \text{ or } \begin{pmatrix} 1 \\ 0 \end{pmatrix}$$

$$\text{Now,}\quad \begin{matrix} \\ R_0 \\ R_1 \end{matrix} \begin{pmatrix} C_0 \\ 0 \\ 1 \end{pmatrix}_{(2*1)}$$

Similarly, 2 qubits as a (4 * 1) matrix and 3 qubits as (8 * 1) matrix. **Also note that if a gate acts on a single qubit then it is called as a single-qubit gate, 2 qubit gate and a 3 qubit gate.** Every unitary operator is valid single qubit gate.

3.1 DISTRIBUTED QUANTUM COMPUTING

Distributed quantum computing is a special type of application of quantum networking. It is not only for data communication but also for **coordinating computation.** As we know that the quantum processors are linked through some quantum network. This permits the constituent processors to exchange qubits between them. **To put it in a proper light, we can say that this is creating quantum cluster computing too.** This is scalable too as is the case with classical computer clusters. It also aids in combating decoherence. **Please note that as the quantum processors grow more and more complex, decoherence is more difficult to control. Also note that having smaller quantum processors that share data makes controlling each processor's coherence more manageable.**

3.2 QUBIT DESIGN METHODS

Before we discuss about quantum gates, let us see what are the different qubit design methods? When we talk about qubit design, only companies with huge financials (money) can jump into the race. According to Popkin, the most common methods of qubit design are as follows:-

I. **Superconducting Loops:** Recall those school days, when we were taught that when an electric current passes through a conductor, some energy is lost in the form of heat and light. This is called as **resistance.** It depends on the type of material like some metals like Copper or Gold are good conductors of electricity and thus have low resistance. **Please note that the colder the material is, the better conductor of electricity it becomes. Also note that the lower the temperature gets, the lower the resistance.** No matter how cold gold or copper gets, it will always show a level of resistance. On the other hand, Mercury is different i.e. when cooling down Mercury to 4.2 degrees Kelvin (above absolute zero), its resistance becomes zero. This has resulted in the discovery of superconductor, a material that has zero electrical resistance at very low temperatures. Also some more other superconducting materials have been found like aluminum, gallium, niobium etc. that show zero resistance at a critical temperature. **The point to ponder is that in superconductors electricity flows without any loss, so a current in a closed loop can flow forever.** Actually, this fact has been proved experimentally by researchers that they were able to maintain electricity flowing over superconducting rings for many years. A superconducting qubit is typically a tiny loop or line of metal that behaves like an atom which in itself is a quantum object. **To put it in a proper light, the two states of the qubit correspond to two energy states of this artificial atom—its lowest energy state (ground state) and the next one up. The states are initiated and controlled using microwave pulses. Superconducting qubits** can be manufactured with existing technologies used to make transistors. The qubit processor is as wide as the thickness of a finger-nail. Although superconducting qubits are small and inexpensive yet the hardware needed to operate them is neither. **The point to ponder is that to behave like an atom, a superconducting qubit must be cooled to a few hundredths of a degree above absolute zero i.e. -273 degrees Celcius.** Now doing this requires **a dilution refrigerator** (a machine bigger than our refrigerators at home). Now this dilution refrigerator is costlier to buy and complex to operate. Also, **at least two wires and other hardware are needed for every qubit.**

Principle: In a qubit made of a superconductor loop, a current oscillates back and forth around a loop. A microwave is injected which excites the current into a superposition of states. (see fig. 3.1).

Google's largest functioning computer has 53 superconducting qubits whereas IBMhas 433. Google's qubits are made of aluminium while IBM uses a mix of aluminium and niobium.

Advantages and disadvantages of this design are as follows:-

Advantages:

1. Low error levels; 99.4% logic success rates are observed.
2. It is fast and is built on existing materials. Superconducting qubits allow for fast gate operations. This makes it possible to do faster quantum computations.

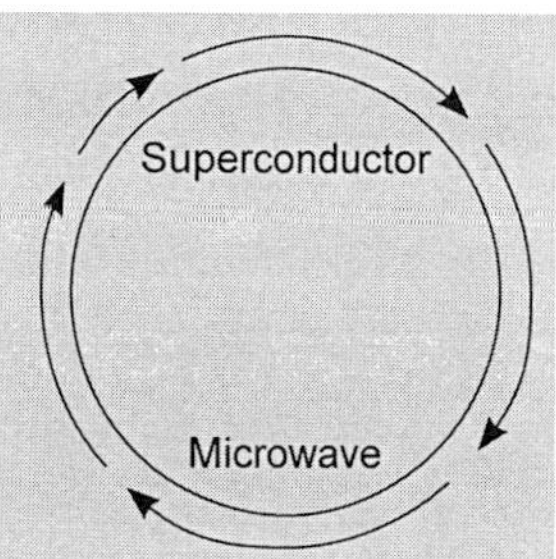

Fig.3.1: A Superconductor loop qubit

3. Decent number of entangled qubits (9), that is capable of performing a 2-qubit operation.
4. ICs allow for the potential to scale up the number of qubits.

Disadvantages:

1. Low longevity (0.00005s). This is the minimum amount of time a superposition of states can be kept.
2. It must be kept as a very cold temperature, at a super frosty, –271° C.
3. Superconducting qubits are sensitive to environmental noise and decoherence. This limits qubit coherence times.
4 Interactions between qubits and their neighbouring qubits can lead to errors.

Applications: This design is used by IBM's cloud platform Q Experience. It is also used by Google and a private venture called Quantum Circuits Inc. (QCI) that manufactures a practical quantum computer based on superconductors.

Superconducting qubits are at the forefront of quantum computing research. Companies like IBM, IonQ, D-wave, Google, Rigetti etc. are in this field. These qubits are constructed from superconducting materials that exhibit zero electrical resistance at extremely low temperatures. Superconducting qubits are manipulated by sending microwave pulses through circuit elements known as **Josephson junctions.**

II. **Trapped Ions: An ion trap is a technique for controlling quantum states in a qubit.** It uses a combination of electric or magnetic fields to capture charged ion particles in a system isolated from the external environment. Lasers are applied to couple qubit states for single operations or coupling between the internal states and the external motional states for entanglement. It is therefore, now possible to dream of a large-scale universal quantum computing by scaling with **arrays of ion traps. This technique is also capable of building large entangles states via photonically connected networks of remotely entangled ion chains. Such computers are called as trapped ion quantum computers.** These computers offer excellent coherence. Many company giants like IonQ located in Maryland, USA, Quantinuum, Honeywell etc. are in this field. Trapped-ion qubit is a charged atom or molecule that behaves like a tiny bar magnet. The two states of the ion correspond to two orientations of this magnet (up and down).

Principle: In this technique, ions are confined using electromagnetic fields and manipulated using laser pulses. Please note here that the internal energy levels of ions serve as qubits.

Advantages:

1. Researchers claim that trapped ions can hold **entanglement for up to 1000s** which is large as compared to superconductor loops, which so it for about 0.00005 secs.
2. **Better success rates** (99.9%) than superconductors (99.4%).
3. Highest number of entangled qubits capable **of performing a 2-qubit operation**.
4. **Longer coherence times** because ions are externally isolated. This helps in error correction.
5. **Laser manipulations** enable high-fidelity gate operations.

Disadvantages:

1. **Slow operations as it requires lot of lasers.**

2. **Scalability** is a challenge here as manipulating multiple ions and to maintain qubit interaction presents scalability issues. Each chip can contain at most a few tens of ions without the interactions among them becoming too complex to control. So, reaching millions of qubits will require moving ions between modules.
3. Better technology of lasers is required to **control ions.**
4. Chips in **multiple vacuum chambers** will also be needed to be connected to reach the million-qubit target.

Applications: Alpine Quantum Technologies has a computer with 24 qubits, IonQ has 29 qubits and Quantinuum has 32 qubits. They use two yetterbium ions. AQT uses calcium ions. Each of these company's trapped-ion computer contains same elements—a computing chip, a cylindrical vacuum chamber, lasers and a light detector. The chip houses the ions and traps using electric fields in the voids between its tiny printed circuits. The laser shoots through the windows of the vaccum chamber, cooling the ions and operating the qubits. The emptiness of the space around an ion qubit means that its state (0 or 1 or both) is relatively unimpacted by state-destroying air particles. **This is the reason that it can retain its quantum information for minutes to hours** (while superconducting qubit was only a few hundred microseconds). In this technique, there is a long life for quantum data storage. **But please note that this can be problematic for performing complex calculations because the property that gives the qubit good data storage abilities makes it difficult to control interactions among the qubits.** Therefore, calculations on this system take more time.

III. **Silicon Quantum dots:** As we know that Intel, who is the juggernaut of CPUs manufacturing, is implementing this design. In this technique, electrons are confined vertically to the ground state of a quantum gallium arsenide (GaAs) well, forming a 2D electron gas (2DEG). A 2DEG electron gas is free to move in two dimensions. But is tightly confined in the third. **Please note that this tight confinement leads to quantized energy levels for motion in the third direction which may be great interest in quantum-based structures.** 2DEG are currently found on transistors made from semiconductors. They also exhibit quantum effects like the Hall effect, in which a 2D electron conductance becomes quantized at low temperatures and strong magnetic fields.

Advantages:

1. It is stable as is built on existing semiconductor materials.
2. Better longevity than superconductor loops at 0.03secs.

Disadvantages:

1. Lower number of entangled qubits (i.e. 2) capable of performing a 2-qubit operation.
2. Lower success rates than superconductor loops or trapped ions but still high at 99%

IV. **Topological Qubits:** Topological qubits seek to eliminate error levels features of quantum computers. Errors are due to the probabilistic nature of quantum mechanics. They are described by the **longevity or the duration of qubit entanglement. A** topological qubit uses **2D- quasi-particles called as anyons,** whose paths pass around one another to form braids in a 3D space-time. These braids form the logic gates that make up the computer. Microsoft and Bell Labs are the giants that are supporting this design now.

Advantages:

1. Stable and error-free.
2. Longevity doesn't apply.

Disadvantages:

1. Still in its infancy stages.

V. **Diamond Vacancies: Diamond vacancies are the locations in the diamond's crystal lattice where there should be a carbon atom but there isn't one.** Diamond vacancies try to use nanometer–scale atomic defects in diamond materials to function as **qubits. Note that it has been found that using atomic force microscopy that the surface of natural diamonds shows several types of defects. This defect of vacancy along with a Nitrogen atom adds an electron to a diamond lattice. The electron spin can be thus controlled with a laser.** According to Researchers, diamond vacancies solve perennial problems of reading information out of qubits in a simple way. **Please note that diamonds are natural light emitters and hence, the light particles emitted by diamond vacancies preserve the superposition of states. Thus, they can move information between quantum computing devices. Also note that there is no need of cooling as it works well at room temperatures.** Researchers are developing processes for blasting the diamond beams of electrons to produce more vacancies.

Advantages:

1. High longevity (10s).
2. High success rates (99.2%).
3. Decent number of entangled qubits (6) capable of performing a 2-qubit operation.
4. Qubits operate at room temperature.

Disadvantages:

1. Quite small number of vacancies in surface material (only 2%). That is, only 2% of the surface of the diamond has them.
2. Difficult to entangle.

Operating qubits is not that much difficult as is the correction of errors that pop up as quantum computations progress. **An error occurs when the state of a qubit is altered by some influence outside of those used to run the computer** like heat, radiation from space etc.

VI. **Linear Optical Quantum Computers:** These types of quantum computers are being researched by many company giants like AEGIQ, PsiQuantum, Xandu etc. **Please note that these computers leverage photons as qubits.** These photons can be manipulated using beam splitters, wave-plates and other optical elements.

Advantages:

1. **Computations are faster as photons travel at the speed of light,** thereby enabling high-speed gate operations.
2. **Lower decoherence is found because photons interact minimally with their environments** which **reduces decoherence effects too.**

Disadvantages:

1. Photon interactions are probabilistic that makes error correction and its detection quite complex. **This is called as non-determinism.**
2. Generating strong photon-photon interactions for logic gates is also challenging task. This is called as **non-linearity**.

VII. **Quantum Dot Quantum Computers: Quantum dot qubits use nanoscale semiconductor structures to trap and manipulate individual electrons that are serving as qubits.** Many company giants like AEGIQ, Fujitsu, Toshiba etc. are using this concept.

Advantages:

1. They can be **integrated** into existing semiconductor technology.
2. They can achieve **high-fidelity gate operations.**

Disadvantages:

1. These computers can be susceptible to environmental noise that may result in **decoherence.**
2. Controlling **multiple quantum dots** for large-scale computations poses challenges.

VIII. **Color Center (NV) Quantum Computers: Color center qubits use defects in diamond crystals known as color centers, to host qubits.** Company giants like Quantum Brilliance, Diatope, Quantum Diamond Tech, Nvision, Element Six, Q-ctrl etc. are the major players in this field.

Advantages:

1. **Longer coherence times** can make them suitable for error correction.
2. Diamond fabrication techniques allow for **better scalability.**

Disadvantages:

1. **Qubit initialization and its information reading** can be challenging in these types of computers.
2. **Coupling of qubits** is also difficult i.e. ensuring interactions between distant qubits is complex.

IX. **Neutral Atom Quantum Computers: Neural atom qubits** use **arrays of neutral atoms to create qubits.** Note that these qubits are manipulated using lasers. Scalability is less of a problem for these **neutral-atom qubit.** Company giants like PASQUAL, ATOM COMPUTING, COLDQUANTA, QUERA COMPUTING etc. are working on it. QuEra has a quantum computer with 256 neutral rubidium atoms.

A neutral atom quantum computer is like a **charged-atom but lighter.** *To make the light traps, researchers shine a laser through lens above a chamber containing neutral atoms. The lens split the incoming beam into a multitude of light spots, each of which can hold an atom in place.* **Please note that the same splitting occurs for other laser beams which are used to operate the qubits.** Today, scientists have created arrays of two to 1,000 neutral-atom qubits.

Advantages:

1. Neutral-atom qubits also have longer lifetime. They can retain their information for tens of seconds. **Also note that isolated neutral-atoms have a long coherence time, so higher coherence is seen.**

2. **Better scalability- optical lattices enable** the creation of arrays of neutral atom qubits.
3. Easy to make neutral-atom qubits,

Disadvantages:

1. Precisely controlling individual neutral atoms is complex.
2. Ensuring interactions between neighbouring qubits while maintaining coherence is difficult.
3. Speed is also an issue. They can perform a few calculations per second as compared to trapped-ion quantum computers. But it is 1000 times slower than a super-conducting qubit system. Performing a complex calculation requires hitting the atom with a properly timed sequence of laser pulses.

Some other approaches for Qubit design are also being explored in order to expand the Quantum spectrum. They are as follows: -

- **Electron on Helium Qubits:** Electrons are trapped on the surface of superfluid Helium, which acts as a substrate for qubits.
- **Cavity Quantum Electrodynamics:** Qubits are coupled to photons in high-quality cavities. This provides **strong qubit-photon interactions.**
- **Magnetic molecules / Molecular Spins:** Molecules with unpaired electrons serve as qubits due to their inherent magnetic properties.
- **Nuclear Magnetic Resonance (NMR):** NMR uses nuclear spins in molecules as qubits. This has applications in both **quantum computing and quantum simulation.**

3.3 OPERATION ON QUBITS—TYPES OF GATES, MEASUREMENT GATE

We have been studying about classical logic gates right from our school days. AND, OR NOT, EX-OR, EX-NOR, NAND, NOR gates are very common. **Also we have studied that NAND gates are universal. This means that any logic function can be expressed using only NAND Boolean operations.** So, we can construct a logic circuit using only NAND gates. **Please note that XOR gate is not universal gate.** It does not change the parity of its input. **A binary string has odd parity if it has an odd number of 1s and has even parity if it has an even number of 1s. If the input has odd parity and the input string is 01 (or x = 1 and y = 0 and then the input string is 10). So does the output. It is 1 if the input has even parity, so does the output, it is 0.**

All classical logic states are irreversible or non-invertible. **Also note that this means that knowing the output we cannot determine the input for all possible combinations of input values. For instance,** knowing that the output of NAND gate is 0, we cannot predict its input. But also recall that the NOT gate is reversible and two cascaded NOT gates recover the input of the first one. **To put it in a proper light, the irreversibility of classical gates means that there is an irretrievable loss of information.**

On the other hand, quantum gates are classified under two categories: -

(a) Single qubit gates.

(b) Multi-qubit gates.

Let us discuss them one by one.

I. Single Qubit Gates: A one-qubit gate is a black box that transforms an input qubit i.e. $|\psi\rangle = \alpha_0 |0\rangle + \alpha_1 |1\rangle$ **into an output qubit** $|\varphi\rangle = \alpha'_0 |0\rangle + \alpha'_1 |1\rangle$. Diagrammatically,

Mathematically, a gate G is represented by a (2 * 2) transfer matrix with complex entries g_{ij} with i, j ϵ {1, 2}:–

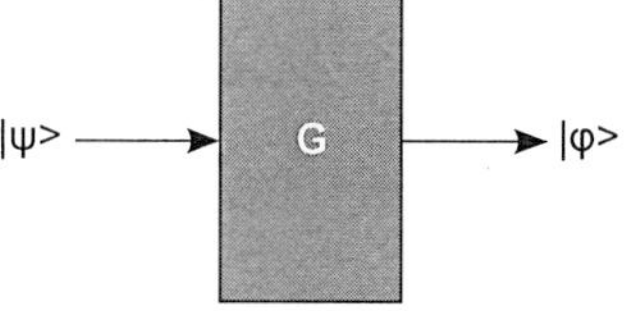

Fig.3.2: Single Qubit Gate

$$G = \begin{pmatrix} g_{11} & g_{12} \\ g_{21} & g_{22} \end{pmatrix}$$

Keeping in mind that **the normalization condition requires that** $|\alpha_0|^2 + |\alpha_1|^2 = 1$ and based on the same lines $|\alpha'_0|^2 + |\alpha'_1|^2 = 1$. **Please note that this requires that G must be a unitary matrix** i.e. $G^+G = I$, where G^+ is the adjoint of G, a matrix obtained from G by first converting G^T, the transpose of G and then taking the complex conjugate, g^*_{ij}, of each matrix element (or by first taking the complex conjugate of each element) and then transposing the matrix. That is, the transpose of matrix, G will be G^T and is given by–

$$G^T = \begin{pmatrix} g_{11} & g_{21} \\ g_{12} & g_{22} \end{pmatrix}$$

It implies that–

$$G^+ = \begin{pmatrix} g^*_{11} & g^*_{21} \\ g^*_{12} & g^*_{22} \end{pmatrix}$$

Now the condition for G to be unitary is that $G^+G = I$, i.e.

$$G^+G = \begin{pmatrix} g^*_{11} g_{11} + g^*_{21} g_{12} & g^*_{11} g_{21} + g^*_{21} g_{22} \\ g^*_{12} g_{11} + g^*_{22} g_{12} & g^*_{12} g_{21} + g^*_{22} g_{22} \end{pmatrix} = \mathbf{I}$$

where I is a (2 * 2) identity matrix. **The point to ponder is that G is invertible and its inverse, G^+ is also unitary. Also understand that this implies that a quantum gate with a unitary transfer matrix can always be inverted. This also proves that quantum gates are reversible whereas classical gates are irreversible.**

Given the transfer matrix of a quantum gate, G, and the input and output qubits represented as column vectors, the transformation performed by the gate is given by the equation–

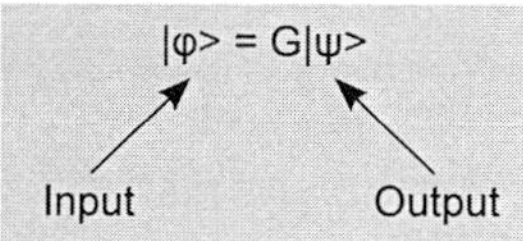

For a single-qubit gate, this equation can also be written as follows:–

$$\begin{pmatrix} \alpha^*_0 \\ \alpha^*_1 \end{pmatrix} = \begin{pmatrix} g_{11} & g_{12} \\ g_{21} & g_{22} \end{pmatrix} \begin{pmatrix} \alpha^*_0 \\ \alpha^*_1 \end{pmatrix}$$

Therefore, $\alpha'_0 = g_{11}\,\alpha_0 + g_{12}\,\alpha_1$ and $\alpha'_1 = g_{21}\,\alpha_0 + g_{22}\,\alpha_1$

Some important one-qubit gates and their transfer matrices are discussed below.

1. **The I, identity gate:** It leaves a qubit unchanged i.e.

$$I = \begin{pmatrix} 1 & 0 \\ 0 & 1 \end{pmatrix}$$

2. **X or NOT gate:** It **transposes the components** of a qubit as follows:–

$$X = \sigma_x = \begin{pmatrix} 0 & 1 \\ 1 & 0 \end{pmatrix}$$

3. **Y gate:** It **multiplies** the input qubit by i and **flips the two components** of the qubit as follows:–

$$Y = \sigma_y = \begin{pmatrix} 0 & -i \\ i & 0 \end{pmatrix}$$

4. **Z gate:** It changes the phase i.e. flips the sign of a qubit:–

$$Z = \sigma_z = \begin{pmatrix} 1 & 0 \\ 0 & -1 \end{pmatrix}$$

5. **The Hadamard gate, H:–**

$$H = 1/\sqrt{2} \begin{pmatrix} 1 & 1 \\ 1 & -1 \end{pmatrix}$$

Also note that the transfer matrices of the first four gates, namely, I, X, Y and Z are the identity matrix, I and the Pauli matrices (discussed next) $\sigma_x, \sigma_y, \sigma_z$ **respectively.** Keeping in mind, the black-box concept, the output vectors of these gates i.e. $|\varphi\rangle$, for the given input $|\psi\rangle = \alpha_0 |0\rangle + \alpha_1 |1\rangle$ are as follows:–

$$|\varphi\rangle = I|\psi\rangle = \begin{pmatrix} 1 & 0 \\ 0 & 1 \end{pmatrix}\begin{pmatrix} \alpha_0 \\ \alpha_1 \end{pmatrix} = \begin{pmatrix} \alpha_0 \\ \alpha_1 \end{pmatrix}$$

or $$|\varphi\rangle = \alpha_0 |0\rangle + \alpha_1 |1\rangle.$$

Similarly,

$$|\varphi\rangle = \sigma_x |\psi\rangle = \begin{pmatrix} 0 & 1 \\ 1 & 0 \end{pmatrix}\begin{pmatrix} \alpha_0 \\ \alpha_1 \end{pmatrix} = \begin{pmatrix} \alpha_1 \\ \alpha_0 \end{pmatrix}$$

or $$|\varphi\rangle = \alpha_1 |0\rangle + \alpha_0 |1\rangle.$$

Also, $$|\varphi\rangle = \sigma_y |\psi\rangle = \begin{pmatrix} 0 & -i \\ i & 0 \end{pmatrix}\begin{pmatrix} \alpha_0 \\ \alpha_1 \end{pmatrix} = i = \begin{pmatrix} -\alpha_1 \\ \alpha_0 \end{pmatrix}$$

or $$|\varphi\rangle = -i\alpha_1 |0\rangle + i\alpha_0 |1\rangle.$$

And finally,

$$|\varphi\rangle = \sigma_z |\psi\rangle = \begin{pmatrix} 1 & 0 \\ 0 & -1 \end{pmatrix}\begin{pmatrix} \alpha_0 \\ \alpha_1 \end{pmatrix} = \begin{pmatrix} \alpha_0 \\ -\alpha_1 \end{pmatrix}$$

or $$|\varphi\rangle = \alpha_0 |0\rangle - \alpha_1 |1\rangle.$$

Also note that–

$$|\varphi> = H|\psi> = 1/\sqrt{2}\begin{pmatrix}1 & 1\\ 1 & -1\end{pmatrix}\begin{pmatrix}\alpha_0\\ \alpha_1\end{pmatrix}$$

or

$$|\varphi> = \alpha_0/\sqrt{2}\ (|0> + |1>) + \alpha_1/\sqrt{2}\ (|0> - |1>).$$

Please note that the Hadamard gate, H, when applied to a pure state, |0> or |1> creates a superposition state i.e.

$$H|0> = 1/\sqrt{2}\ (|0> + |1>)$$

and

$$H|1> = 1/\sqrt{2}\ (|0> - |1>)$$

Also note that it means that the transformation of a qubit |x>, with x = 0 or x = 1, carried out by a Hadamard gate can be written as follows:–

$$|x> = 1/\sqrt{2}\ (|0> + (-1)^x|1>)$$

The point to ponder is that single gate operations correspond to rotations and reflections on the Block sphere.

1. **Pauli's Gate: Pauli gate** is the **quantum analog of the classic NOT gate. It rotates** the qubit 180 degrees in the X-axis. If you observe the block sphere again,

   You will observe that **X-axis points outside the screen** (arrow is outward). In 1945 Wolfgang Ernst Pauli, developed the very famous **Pauli's exclusion principle which states that "no two electrons can exist in the same quantum state."** He was greatly admired by Einstein, Bohr and Heisenberg for his work.

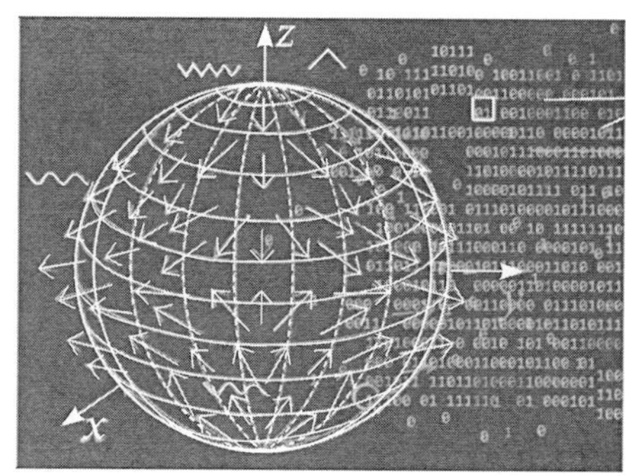

   The Rotation Gates: Y, Z

   Rotation gates over the Y and Z axis are known as the Pauli Y and Pauli Z gates respectively. The following points you must ponder–

   - Pauli Y gate acts on a single qubit. It rotates around the Y-axis of the Block sphere by Π radians (180 degrees). It maps |0> to i|1> and |1> to –i|0>.
   - Pauli Z gate acts on a single qubit. It rotates around the Z-axis of the Block sphere by Π radians (180 degrees). It leaves the basis state |0> unchanged and maps |1> to –i|1>.

   The following table shows the Pauli's gate–

Name	Matrix	Circuit symbol
Pauli X, X, NOT, bit flip, σ_x	$\begin{pmatrix}0 & 1\\ 1 & 0\end{pmatrix}$	–[X]– –⊕–
Pauli Y, Y, σ_y	$\begin{pmatrix}0 & -i\\ i & 0\end{pmatrix}$	–[Y]–
Pauli Z, Z, phase flip, σ_z	$\begin{pmatrix}1 & 0\\ 0 & -1\end{pmatrix}$	q –[z]–

The Pauli gate rotates the qubit 180 degrees in x, y or z axis. For instance, in figure 3.3, one possibility is shown.

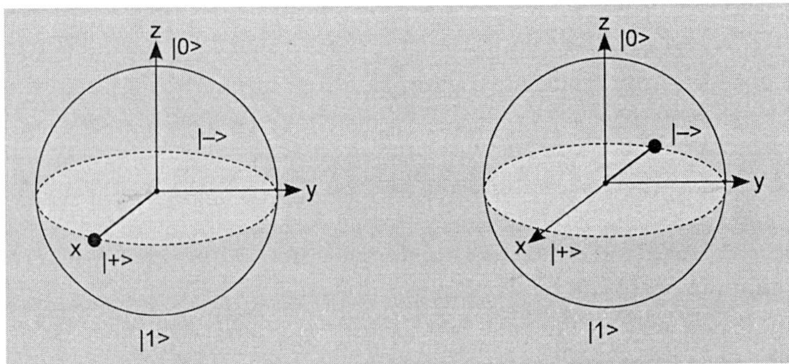

Fig.3.3: Pauli gate rotates the qubit 180 degrees

2. **Hadamard gate: It changes the base state of a qubit from |0> to (|0> + |1>)/ $\sqrt{2}$ and |1> to (|0> – |1>)/ $\sqrt{2}$; by making the probabilities of both basis states equal.** It is made of two rotations, ∏ around Z-axis and followed by ∏/2 about Y-axis. The representation of Hadamard gates is as follows:–

$$H = 1/\sqrt{2}\begin{pmatrix}1 & 1\\ 1 & -1\end{pmatrix}$$

The resultant states of a Hadamard transform are as follows:–

|+> and |–> which are equal to (**|0> + |1>)/ $\sqrt{2}$ and |1> and (|0> – |1>)/ $\sqrt{2}$.** So, H|0> = |+>, H|1> = |–>, H|+> = |0>, H|–> = |1>.

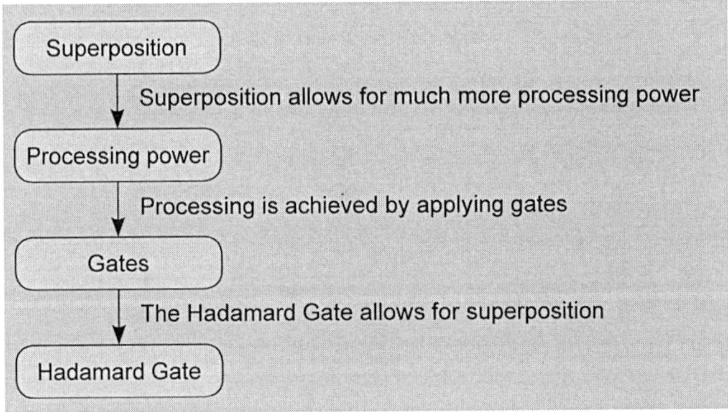

Fig.3.4: Role of Hadamard gate

Please note here that H is certainly a unitary matrix, HH^{*} = I. Also note that Hadamard transform is used in the Entanglement circuit, so the output that qubit value has, decides the output of the second qubit, where the two qubits are joined using a CNOT gate which contributes to the entanglement phenomenon.

The Hadamard gate acts on a **single qubit. It is the combination of two rotations:–**

1. ∏ over the X-axis.

2. Π/2 over the Y-axis.

The Hadamard gate is the quantum equivalent of the Hadamard matrix, a square whose entries are either + 1 or −1 and whose rows are mutually orthogonal. **The point to ponder is that the Hadamard transform is useful in data encryption and many other signal processing and data compression algorithms.** The role of Hadamard gate is shown in the flowchart of figure 3.4.

II. Multi-Qubit Gates: The gates that act on more than one qubit are called as Multi-qubit gates. These gates promote information exchange between qubits.

1. **CNOT gate:** This is a controlled NOT gate which is just like classical NOT gate but it includes two qubits unlike the conventional one. It has a **control qubit and a target qubit** (to be discussed shortly). It is a gate with two inputs and two outputs and named as CNOT or Controlled-NOT gate. One of the inputs is called as the **control input** and the other one is called as the **target input.** Similarly, the first output is called as the **control** and the second is called as the **target. The classical equivalent of a quantum CNOT gate is the XOR gate** i.e. its output is the sum modulo two, $\oplus$ **of its two inputs. For a classical CNOT gate, the target output is equal to the target input if the control input is 0 and flipped if the controlled input is 1**.

   Flipping a classical bit means complementing it, transforming it to a i.e. if a = 0, it becomes 1 and vice versa. On the other hand, **flipping a qubit** $|\psi\rangle = \alpha_0 |0\rangle + \alpha_1 |1\rangle$ **results in** $|\varphi\rangle = \alpha_1 |0\rangle + \alpha_0 |1\rangle$, where the projections on the two basis vectors are swapped.

   Similarly, a quantum CNOT gate has two inputs **i.e. the control input is a qubit in state** $|\psi\rangle$ **and the target input is a qubit in state** $|\varphi\rangle$.

   Operation of CNOT Quantum gate: The **control input** is transferred directly to the **control output of the gate. The target output is equal to the target input** if the control input is $|0\rangle$ and it is flipped if the control input is $|1\rangle$. **Note that the input and the output qubits of a CNOT quantum gate can be represented as vectors in a 4D Hilbert space,** H_4**. Also note that the two qubits applied to the input of the CNOT gate are a control qubit** $|\psi\rangle$ **and a target qubit** $|\varphi\rangle$. That is,

   $$|\psi\rangle = \alpha_0 |0\rangle + \alpha_1 |1\rangle$$

   and

   $$|\varphi\rangle = \beta_0 |0\rangle + \beta_1 |1\rangle$$

   The input vector of the quantum CNOT gate is as follows:–

   $$|V_{CNOT}\rangle = |\psi\rangle \otimes |\varphi\rangle = \begin{pmatrix} \alpha_0 \\ \alpha_1 \end{pmatrix} \otimes \begin{pmatrix} \beta_0 \\ \beta_1 \end{pmatrix} = \begin{pmatrix} \alpha_0\beta_0 \\ \alpha_0\beta_1 \\ \alpha_1\beta_0 \\ \alpha_1\beta_1 \end{pmatrix} \quad ...(1)$$

   tensor product

   Figure 3.7 (a and b) compares a classical CNOT gate and a quantum CNOT gate. In 3.7 (a), x is the control input and y is the target input. This control input may be 0 or 1. Two outputs are also shown. x remains as x while y becomes $x \oplus y$ where is $\oplus$ **addition modulo 2. Also note here that the target output is equal to the target input if the control input is 0 and**

it is flipped if the control input is 1. On the other hand, in figure 3.7 (b), **also a quantum CNOT gate has two inputs, the control input is a qubit in state |x> and the target input is a qubit in state |y>.**

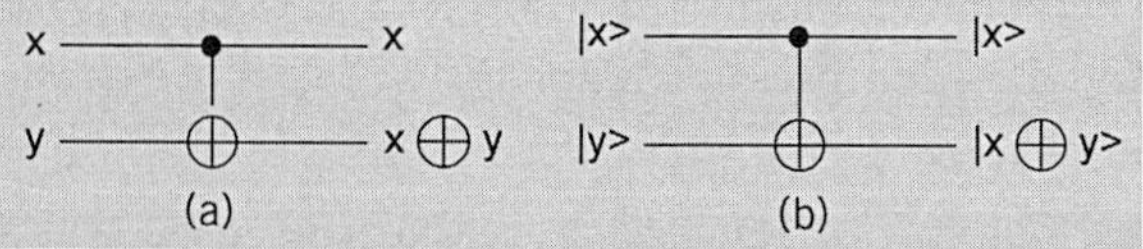

Fig.3.7 (a) and (b): Compares a classical CNOT gate and a quantum CNOT gate.

Please note here that if the control qubit is one then the gate will flip the target qubit. Controlled gates act on 2 or more qubits where 1 or more qubits act as a control for some operation. For instance, the controlled NOT gate (CNOT or cX) acts on 2 qubits. It performs the NOT operation on the 2nd qubit only when the first qubit is |1> and otherwise leaves it unchanged.

$$\textbf{CNOT} = \textbf{cX} = \begin{pmatrix} 1 & 0 & 0 & 0 \\ 0 & 1 & 0 & 0 \\ 0 & 0 & 0 & 1 \\ 0 & 0 & 1 & 0 \end{pmatrix}$$

We shall be discussing this in detail a bit later.

2. **CZ gate (controlled Z):** It is similar to the CNOT gate but does perform Z on the target qubit.
3. **CY gate (controlled Y):** This is similar to the CNOT gate but does perform Y on the target qubit.
4. **Toffoli gate (CCNOT gate):** This is a 3-qubit gate which is similar to a CNOT gate but has two control bits and one target qubit. This is also called as **Deutsch**, $D^{(\Pi/2)}$ **gate** which flips the 3rd qubit only if the first two qubits are |1>.

   (we shall be discussing these gates in detail shortly).
5. **Swap Gate:** This gate swaps the two qubits in these basis states, |00>, |01>, |10> |11>.

$$\textbf{Swap} = \begin{pmatrix} \mathbf{1} & \mathbf{0} & \mathbf{0} & \mathbf{0} \\ \mathbf{0} & \mathbf{0} & \mathbf{1} & \mathbf{0} \\ \mathbf{0} & \mathbf{1} & \mathbf{0} & \mathbf{0} \\ \mathbf{0} & \mathbf{0} & \mathbf{0} & \mathbf{1} \end{pmatrix}$$

Its matrix representation is–

Swapping |01>:

$$\textbf{Measurement Gate} = \begin{pmatrix} 1 & 0 & 0 & 0 \\ 0 & 0 & 1 & 0 \\ 0 & 1 & 0 & 0 \\ 0 & 0 & 0 & 1 \end{pmatrix} \begin{pmatrix} 0 \\ 1 \\ 0 \\ 0 \end{pmatrix} |01\rangle = \begin{pmatrix} 0 \\ 0 \\ 1 \\ 0 \end{pmatrix} |10\rangle$$

As already explained that if you try to measure this quantum state of a qubit, then it alters its state i.e. the state collapses to either 0 or 1 state which contradicts the principle of superposition. Entanglement is one way of qubit manipulation while another method is manipulation via quantum gates. **The measurement gate takes a qubit in a superposition of states as input and splits either a 0 or 1. Also note that the output is not random.** There is a probability of a 0 or 1 as output which depends on the state the qubit is originally in. **To put it in a proper light, the measurement gate should be the last step on a quantum circuit because if we do it in the middle stage then the whole system collapses to either 0 or 1.** This also defeats the parallelism achieved by the superposition of the states. It is shown in figure 3.5.

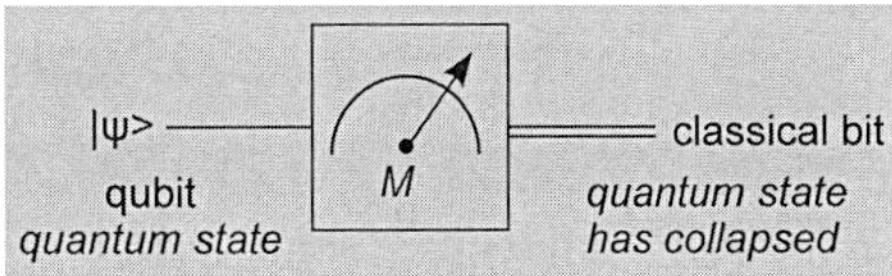

Fig.3.5: The Measurement Gate with its output probability

Swap Gate: The swap gate takes 2 qubits and swaps its states. It is shown in figure 3.6.

The initial state, |ϕ> is input on the first line while it becomes output at the bottom circuit line. While the output |ψ> becomes input on the second wire. Thus, a **swap operation** is performed.

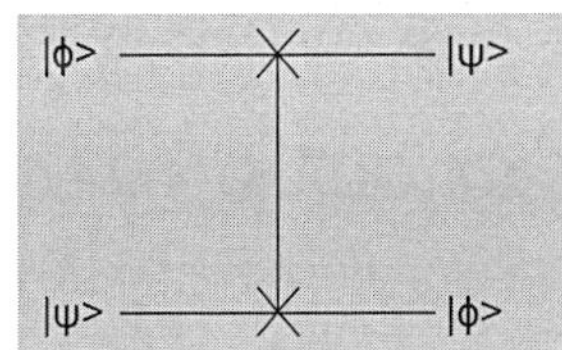

Fig.3.6: The Swap Gate with its output

3.4 REVERSIBLE LOGIC GATES

I was told when studying Digital Systems that loss of energy is a major problem in the digital circuits. In classical gates, energy dissipation results due to information loss. As per the Landauer observations, the loss of each bit of information leads to at least–

$$kT \log (2) = E_{released} \text{ (heat)}$$

This shows the amount of energy released in form of heat, where k is the Boltzman's constant, T is the temperature at which the computation is performed. In any computer, this heat is significant. **Please note that such a system carries out many millions of operations per second. It's because of this that it becomes hot in a short amount of time. Also note that the loss of information and the resulting heat generation can be avoided by replacing classical gates with reversible gates.** So, we can say that–

- Classical gates → irreversible, lose information.
- Quantum gates → reversible, don't lose information.

In reversible quantum gates, it is possible to determine bits on the inputs of the gate from the outputs of the gate. **Classical gates are irreversible i.e.** all possible input combinations in such a gate are mapped to one of the two possible outputs 0 and 1. **For example,** consider the following AND gate truth table–

X	Y	Z
0	0	0
0	1	0

X	Y	Z
1	0	0
1	1	1

Here, when x = 0 and y = 1 then z = 0 i.e. **the information on y-line is lost in output. In an AND gate,** for example, a complete knowledge about the input can't be determined from the output, hence **the operation of the AND gate is not reversible. Note that the NOT gate is an exception. In general, because in classical gates, a 2 bit input maps into a 1-bit output, so 1 bit of information is lost on every operation and it is not recoverable. This is the reason as to why classical gates are not-reversible.** On the other hand, quantum reversible gates do not lose information. **To put it in a proper light, a reversible gate must have exactly the same number of inputs and outputs that allows the input value to be uniquely determined from the output value and vice versa. That is why, a NOT gate with a single input and a single output is reversible.** Bennett reports that **any computing system can be made reversible by replacing each classical gate in the system with its reversible equivalent.**

3.5 QUANTUM LOGIC GATES AND CIRCUIT– X GATE, Y GATE, Z GATE, NOT GATE, √NOT, HAMDARD GATE, PHASE GATE, T GATE, REVERSIBLE LOGIC, CNOT GATE, CONTROLLED-U GATE

Quantum computers manipulate qubits using quantum gates. The gates are applied to the qubits and the states of the qubits change depending on which gate is applied. On block sphere, the gate provides instructions for rotating the qubit's arrow around the sphere. Also understand that a quantum algorithm has to be implemented on a quantum computer using quantum gates. After running a quantum algorithm, the result is retrieved by measuring the qubit's state. The hardware implementation of quantum gates depends on how the qubit and the quantum computer have been implemented. **For instance,** one can have a qubit based on spin. Then the gates can be implemented using an external magnetic field to change the spin and hence the qubit state.

When the **qubit is in superposition of all basis states,** then **the superposition also flips.** The following points are worth mentioning:–

1. **Classical computers** use **classical logic gates** to operate on **classical bits.** Based on similar lines, computation on a quantum computer is caused by **coding quantum logic gates to act on qubits. This coding can be done by using QISKIT tool, IBMQ tool etc.**
2. Some common **single-qubit gates** include the X, Z and H gates (discussed below).
3. **Each quantum gate** can be mathematically represented as **a unitary matrix which acts on qubits.**

Let us now study in detail these different types of basic quantum logic gates one by one.

I. **X-Gate/NOT gate:** It is also known as a **bit flip gate.** It is the quantum equivalent of a classical NOT gate. That is, if |X> is the input to an X gate then the output of the gate is |X'>. As already mentioned that because the states of a qubit |0> and |1> are represented by the column vectors as–

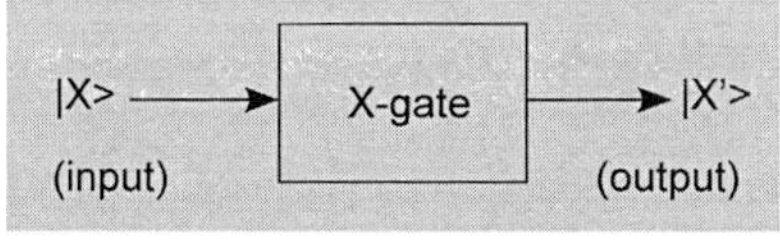

$\begin{pmatrix}1\\0\end{pmatrix}$ and $\begin{pmatrix}0\\1\end{pmatrix}$ respectively.

Hence, we get–

$$X|0> = \begin{pmatrix}0 & 1\\1 & 0\end{pmatrix}\begin{pmatrix}1\\0\end{pmatrix} = \begin{pmatrix}0\\1\end{pmatrix} = |1> \qquad \text{(i.e. } 0 \to 1)$$

Similarly,

$$X|1> = \begin{pmatrix}0 & 1\\1 & 0\end{pmatrix}\begin{pmatrix}0\\1\end{pmatrix} = \begin{pmatrix}1\\0\end{pmatrix} = |0> \qquad \text{(i.e. } 1 \to 0)$$

Please note that the X-gate is also known as a bit flip gate as it inverts each input bit. The matrix for the X gate is–

$$\mathbf{X} = \begin{pmatrix}0 & 1\\1 & 0\end{pmatrix}$$

Also note that this matrix is same as that of a Pauli's matrix, σ_x. That is why it is called as X gate.

What happens if two X gates are connected/ cascaded in series to form a quantum circuit?

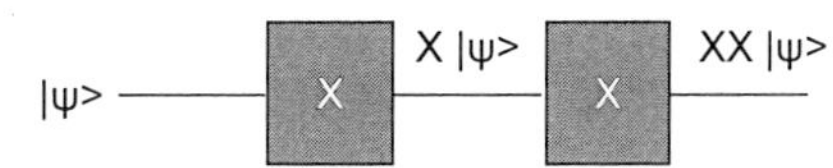

The line in this quantum circuit is called as a **quantum wire.** It basically represents a **single qubit.** An input at the input of the 1st X gate is transformed to X |ψ> and the 2nd gate acts on it to form XX |ψ>. **This is also known as cascading of X-gates.** Now let us replace each X by its matrix representation, which obviously results in an **identity matrix, I.** that is,

$$X.X = \begin{pmatrix}0 & 1\\1 & 0\end{pmatrix}\begin{pmatrix}0 & 1\\1 & 0\end{pmatrix} = \begin{pmatrix}1 & 0\\0 & 1\end{pmatrix} - I$$

In nutshell, we say that two NOT gates in series is basically equivalent to a quantum wire i.e. nothing happens and the output is the same as the original input.

The matrix representation of the state of a superposed qubit, α |0> + β |1> is as given below:

$$\begin{pmatrix}\alpha\\\beta\end{pmatrix}$$

Hence, **if a superposed qubit goes through an X gate,** then the result will be–

$$\begin{pmatrix}0 & 1\\1 & 0\end{pmatrix}\begin{pmatrix}\alpha\\\beta\end{pmatrix} = \begin{pmatrix}\beta\\\alpha\end{pmatrix} = \alpha|1> + \beta|0>$$

The point to ponder is that the X gate 'negates' the computational basis states |0> and |1> correctly. It can't correctly negate an arbitrary superposition state.

II. Y gate: This gate is represented by the Pauli matrix, σ_y. It maps |0> to i |1> and |1> to –i |0>. So,

$$Y = \begin{pmatrix} 0 & -i \\ i & 0 \end{pmatrix}$$

$$Y|0> \begin{pmatrix} 0 & -i \\ i & 0 \end{pmatrix}\begin{pmatrix} 1 \\ 0 \end{pmatrix} = \begin{pmatrix} 0 \\ i \end{pmatrix} = i|1> \qquad \text{(i.e. } |0> \rightarrow i\,|\,1>)$$

$$Y|1> \begin{pmatrix} 0 & -i \\ i & 0 \end{pmatrix}\begin{pmatrix} 0 \\ 1 \end{pmatrix} = \begin{pmatrix} -i \\ 0 \end{pmatrix} = -i|0> \qquad \text{(i.e. } |1> \rightarrow -i\,|\,0>)$$

Thus, the matrix, Y, defines the transformation as below:–

$$Y(\alpha|0> + \beta|1>) = \alpha Y|0> + \beta Y|1> = i\alpha|1> - i\beta|0>$$

III. Z gate/Phase Flip gate: It is also called as a **phase flip gate.** This gate maps the **input |k> to (–1)^k |k>.** So, we can say that for an input |0>, the output of the Z gate is not changed i.e. it is also |0> and for an input |1> the output is –|1>. That is,

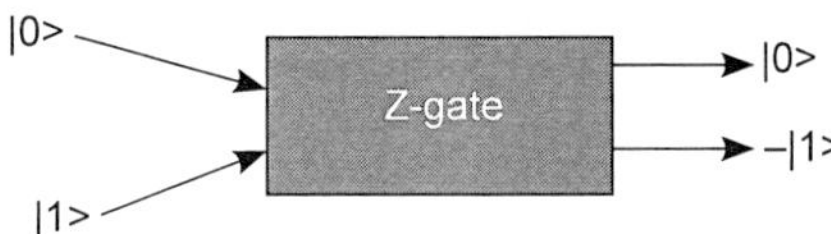

Thus, from the above discussion, we can write the Z-gate matrix as follows:–

$$Z = \begin{pmatrix} 1 & 0 \\ 0 & -1 \end{pmatrix}$$

Please note that this is similar matrix as that of the Pauli matrix, σ_z. Also the mapping of |0> and |1> using the matrix for the Z-gate is shown below:–

For input $\quad$ **|0>, Z|0>** $= \begin{pmatrix} 1 & 0 \\ 0 & -1 \end{pmatrix}\begin{pmatrix} 1 \\ 0 \end{pmatrix} = \begin{pmatrix} 1 \\ 0 \end{pmatrix} =$ **|0>** $\quad$ (as it is the output)

For input $\quad$ **|1>, Z|1>** $= \begin{pmatrix} 1 & 0 \\ 0 & -1 \end{pmatrix}\begin{pmatrix} 0 \\ 1 \end{pmatrix} = \begin{pmatrix} 0 \\ -1 \end{pmatrix} =$ **–|1>** $\quad$ (as it is the output)

Therefore, the matrix Z defines the transformation–

$$Z(\alpha|0> + \beta|1>) = \alpha Z|0> + \beta Z|1> = \alpha|0> - \beta|1>$$

$$\begin{pmatrix} 1 & 0 \\ 0 & -1 \end{pmatrix}\begin{pmatrix} \alpha \\ \beta \end{pmatrix} = \begin{pmatrix} \alpha \\ -\beta \end{pmatrix} = \alpha|1> + \beta|0>$$

Please understand that this is the reason as to why this transformation is also called as phase-flip transformation. The Z-gate leaves a |0> state unchanged but flips the sign of the |1> state to – |1>. That is, shown on the next page.

Also note that this is equivalent to changing the qubit from a |+> state to a |–> state.

α|0> + β|1> ⟶ Z-gate ⟶ α|0> – β|1>

IV. √NOT (Square Root of NOT) Gate: We define square-root NOT gate now. **A square-root NOT gate is a 1-qubit gate that is designed to implement the following expression:–**

√NOT . √NOT = √NOT

Please note that there is no such operation in classical logic. √NOT gate is a better example of how a gate can exist even though Boolean Algebra can't be used to describe its operational working.

The matrix representation of a **√NOT gate can be represented as follows: -**

$$\sqrt{NOT} = 1/\sqrt{2}\begin{vmatrix}1 & -1\\1 & 1\end{vmatrix}$$

Two cases arise:

Case-1: When a |0> is applied to a √NOT gate, the output is–

$$\sqrt{NOT}\,|0> = 1/\sqrt{2}\begin{vmatrix}1 & -1\\1 & 1\end{vmatrix}\begin{vmatrix}1\\0\end{vmatrix} = 1/\sqrt{2}\begin{vmatrix}1\\1\end{vmatrix}$$

$$= 1/\sqrt{2}\left(\begin{vmatrix}1\\0\end{vmatrix}+\begin{vmatrix}0\\1\end{vmatrix}\right) = 1/\sqrt{2} = (|0> + |1>)$$

Case-2: When a|1> is applied to a √NOT gate, the output is–

$$\sqrt{NOT}\,|1> = 1/\sqrt{2}\begin{vmatrix}1 & -1\\1 & 1\end{vmatrix}\begin{vmatrix}0\\1\end{vmatrix} = 1/\sqrt{2}\begin{vmatrix}-1\\1\end{vmatrix}$$

$$= 1/\sqrt{2}\left(\begin{vmatrix}0\\1\end{vmatrix}-\begin{vmatrix}1\\0\end{vmatrix}\right) = 1/\sqrt{2}\ (|1> - |0>)$$

Conclusions:

1. When a qubit in state |0> or state |1> is applied to a **√NOT gate** then it leaves the qubit in an equal superposition of states |0> and |1>.
2. If the output is applied to another **√NOT gate, a superposition of |0> and |1> states will be the input to the second √NOT gate since the unmeasured output of the first gate can't be assigned any definite value.**
3. **The output of the second gate when two √NOT gates are connected in series can be derived from the unmeasured output states of √NOT |0> and √NOT |1>.**
4. **When the output of the first √NOT gate is 1/ $\sqrt{2}$ (|0> + |1>), then the output of the second √NOT gate will be |1>.**
5. Similarly, **when the output of the first √NOT gate is 1/ $\sqrt{2}$ (|1> – |0>), then the output of the second √NOT gate will be |0>.**

6. The quantum NOT gate operates exactly like its classical counterpart.
7. If the NOT gate is implemented using two unknown gates in series then these two gates can be assumed to be performing as **√NOT gates.**
8. So, the logic operation of the NOT gate is written as–

$$\sqrt{\text{NOT}} \,.\, \sqrt{\text{NOT}} = \text{NOT}$$

This is not possible in classical NOT gates. **Thus, we can say that √NOT gate is a truly non-classical gate.**

V. The Hadamard gate (to cause superposition)

If a qubit starts in a definite |0> or |1> state, the Hadamard gate puts each into a superposition of |0> and |1> states. **Please understand that by applying the Hadamard gate to a single qubit creates a superposition state of both |0> and |1>.** Recall that measurement collapses this superposition. It means that **only one classical state can be observed and all other quantum information is lost. Also note that this measurement collapse is the reason as to why a qubit's state can't be duplicated. And this is known as no-cloning theorem of quantum computing.** Once a superposition state is measured, it fundamentally changes into one of the basis states. Hence, it can't be duplicated.

We say that the Hadamard gate is a truly quantum gate. Hadamard gate is **self-inverse gate.** It maps |m> to–

$$H|m> = 1/\sqrt{2}\ \Sigma_{k=0,1}\,(-1)^{mk}\,|k> = (|0> + (-1)^m\,|1>)\,/\,\sqrt{2} \qquad ...(1)$$

The effect of the Hadamard gate on the computational basis states |0> and |1> are as follows: (assume m = 0 and 1 respectively)

$$H|0> = H\begin{pmatrix}1\\0\end{pmatrix} = (0> + (-1)^0\,|1>)/\sqrt{2} \text{ (from (1))}$$

$$= (0> + |1>)/\sqrt{2} = |+> \qquad ...(2)$$

$$H|1> = H\begin{pmatrix}0\\1\end{pmatrix} = (0> + (-1)^1\,|1>)\,/\,\sqrt{2} \text{ (from (1))}$$

$$= (0> - |1>)\,/\,\sqrt{2} = |-> \qquad ...(3)$$

That is why, the matrix for the Hadamard gate is given by–

$$H = 1/\sqrt{2}\begin{vmatrix}1 & 1\\1 & -1\end{vmatrix}$$

The point to ponder is that a Hadamard gate converts a |0> state and a |1> to a superposition state of |0> and |1>. Also the point to ponder is that when the superposed qubit is measured, there is an equal probability of it being in the state |1> or |0>. A Hadamard gate acts on a superposed state α |0> + β |1> linearly as follows:–

$$H(\alpha|0> + \beta|1>) = H\alpha|0> + H\beta|1> = \alpha H|0> + \beta H|1>$$

$$= \alpha.(|0> + |1>)/\sqrt{2} + \beta.(|0> - |1>)/\sqrt{2} \text{ (from 2 and 3)}$$

$$= \alpha + \beta/\sqrt{2}\ |0> + \alpha - \beta/\sqrt{2}\ |1>$$

Also note that a quantum register of size, n, not only stores an individual string but also all possible combinations of n-qubit at the same time. For instance, a 2-qubit register can store |01> or |10> at any time i.e.

$$|01> = |0> \otimes |1>$$

And

$$|11> = |1> \otimes |1>$$

tensor product

But a 2-qubit register can also store both the strings simultaneously. This is achieved by putting the 1st qubit to a superposition of |0> and |1> instead of just |0> or |1> and can be done by applying the qubit to a Hadamard gate.

Let us generalize this.

Principle: This can be extended to all qubits in a quantum register of size, n, by first preparing each qubit in the state |0> and then applying the Hadamard gate to each of the n- qubits in parallel. This is shown in figure 3.7.

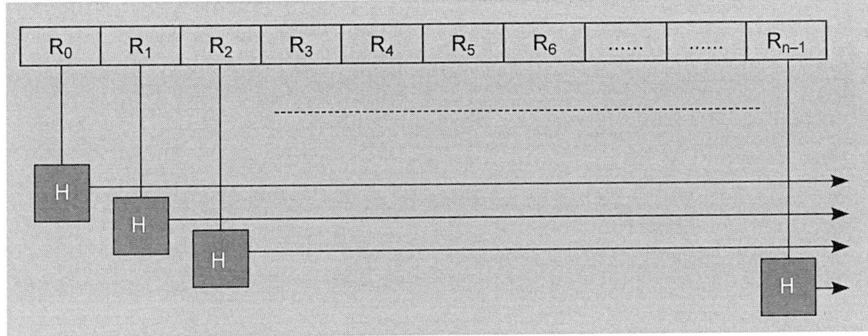

Fig.3.7: A Generalized view of applying Hadamard gates to n-qubit register

Please note that the resulting state of the register is an n-qubit superposition containing 2^n component states. Also note that these states are all possible bit strings corresponding to n-qubits. That is,

$$H|0> \otimes H|0> \otimes \ldots \otimes H|0> = 1/\sqrt{2}^{\,n} \Sigma_{k=0 \text{ to } 2^{n-1}} |k>$$

Before we discuss further, let us solve some examples based on quantum gates now.

Example 1: Say, a right spin $1/\sqrt{2}$ (|0> + |1>) is sent through a Hadamard gate that creates a superposition of |+> and |-> given by $1/\sqrt{2}$ (|+> + |->). Now, perform a basis change to prove that this is equivalent to producing a |0> state.

Solution 1: Now,

$$1/\sqrt{2}\ (|+> + |->) = 1/\sqrt{2}\,(1/\sqrt{2}\,|0> + 1/\sqrt{2}\ |1>) + 1/\sqrt{2}\ (1/\sqrt{2}\,|0> - 1/\sqrt{2}\ |1>)$$

$$= ½\,|0> + ½\,|1> + ½\,|0> - ½\,|1 = |0>.$$

Example 2: Prove that by applying the Hadamard gate twice to a |0> state qubit recovers its original state. What do you infer from that?

Solution 2: As we know that–

$$H|0> = 1/\sqrt{2} \begin{pmatrix} 1 & 1 \\ 1 & -1 \end{pmatrix} \begin{pmatrix} 1 \\ 0 \end{pmatrix} = 1/\sqrt{2} \begin{pmatrix} 1 \\ 1 \end{pmatrix}$$

Using matrix multiplication, we can say that–

$$H\,H|0> \;=\; ½\begin{pmatrix}1 & 1\\ 1 & -1\end{pmatrix}\begin{pmatrix}1\\ 1\end{pmatrix} = \begin{pmatrix}1\\ 0\end{pmatrix}$$

From this proof, we infer that all quantum gates are reversible as a consequence of the unitary matrix condition. As a natural choice, the gates must be unitary so that the probabilities always add up to 1. Also note that multiplying any unitary matrix by its conjugate transpose will return the identity matrix i.e. reverses the gate to get the original state by $UU^+ = U^+U = I$. **The Hadamard matrix is self-unitary** i.e. it is its own conjugate transpose, $U = U^+$.

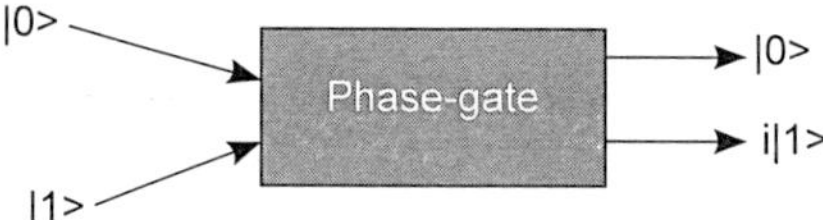

Example 4: Can you show the effects of X, H and Z gates in form of a flowchart or a transition diagram?

Solution 4: The following transition diagram shows the effects of X, H and Z gates (see fig. 3.8)–

VI. The Phase gate: This gate converts a |0> into |0> and a |1> into i|1>. That is,

It can be represented by the following matrix:–

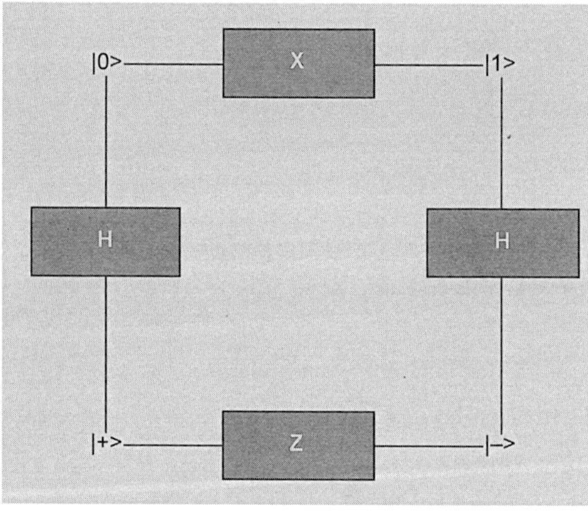

Fig.3.8: Effects of X, H and Z-gates

$$S\,|0> \;=\; \begin{pmatrix}1 & 0\\ 0 & i\end{pmatrix}$$

Thus, the mappings of |0> and |1> using the matrix for the S gate is shown below:–

$$S\,|0> \;=\; \begin{pmatrix}1 & 0\\ 0 & i\end{pmatrix}\begin{pmatrix}1\\ 0\end{pmatrix} = \begin{pmatrix}1\\ 0\end{pmatrix} = |0>$$

$$S\,|1> \;=\; \begin{pmatrix}1 & 0\\ 0 & i\end{pmatrix}\begin{pmatrix}0\\ 1\end{pmatrix} = \begin{pmatrix}0\\ -i\end{pmatrix} = i\,|1>$$

Hence, the matrix, S, defines the transformation as follows:–

$$S(\alpha|0> + \beta|1>) = \alpha S|0> + \beta S|1> = \alpha|0> + i\beta|1>$$

Please note that a Z gate can be obtained by connecting two S-gates in series, i.e.

$$S^2 = \begin{pmatrix} 1 & 0 \\ 0 & i \end{pmatrix}\begin{pmatrix} 1 & 0 \\ 0 & i \end{pmatrix} = \begin{pmatrix} 1 & 0 \\ 0 & -1 \end{pmatrix} = Z$$

VII. T-gate (or Π /8 gate): The matrix for the T-gate (also known as Π/8 gate) is given by–

$$T = \begin{pmatrix} 1 & 0 \\ 0 & \exp(i\Pi/4) \end{pmatrix} = \begin{pmatrix} 1 & 0 \\ 0 & (1+i)\sqrt{2} \end{pmatrix}$$

That is,

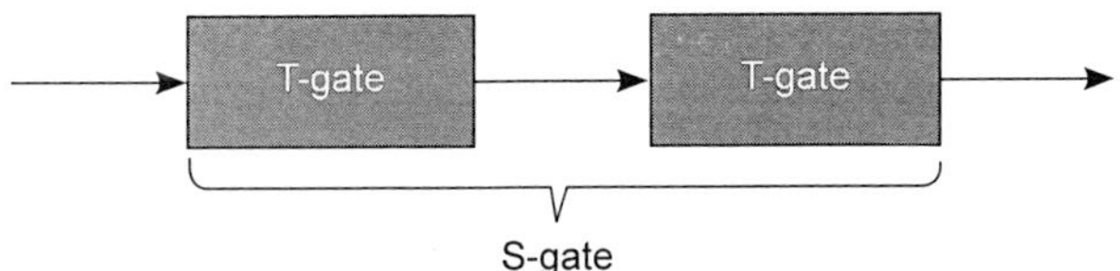

Please note that an S-gate can be formed by connecting two T-gates in series and hence we can write that–

$$T^2 = \begin{pmatrix} 1 & 0 \\ 0 & (1+i)\sqrt{2} \end{pmatrix}\begin{pmatrix} 1 & 0 \\ 0 & (1+i)\sqrt{2} \end{pmatrix}$$

$$= \begin{pmatrix} 1 & 0 \\ 0 & i \end{pmatrix} = S$$

Hence proved.

Let us now discuss the quantum gates that work on two qubits.

I. **CNOT gate/Reversible Ex-OR:** The gates as discussed above act on s single qubit. But also there are quantum gates that perform logic operations on multiple qubits. This controlled NOT gate (CNOT) gate is a multi-qubit state. This gate can be used do generate **entanglement.** The CNOT gate takes in two qubits—a control qubit and a target qubit and outputs two qubits. The CNOT gate can be represented by figure- 3.9 (in tabular form).

In fig. 3.9, **|x> is the control input while |y> is the target input.** The dependence of output x XOR y, on the control |x> is shown by a vertical line from |x> to one of the inputs of the EX-OR gate while the other input of the gate is driven by the target input, |y>. **The control qubit remains the same while the target obeys the following laws:–**

Law-1: If the control qubit is |0> then leave the target qubit alone.

Law-2: If the control qubit is |1> then on the target qubit flip |0> → |1> and |1> → |0>.

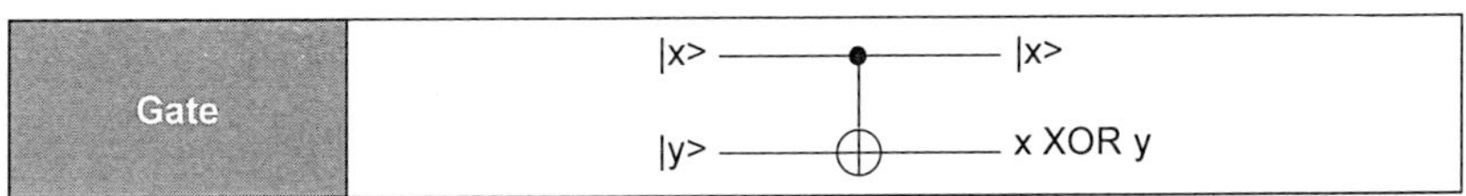

Matrix	CNot = $\begin{bmatrix} 1 & 0 & 0 & 0 \\ 0 & 1 & 0 & 0 \\ 0 & 0 & 0 & 1 \\ 0 & 0 & 1 & 0 \end{bmatrix}$
Reversibility	$\begin{bmatrix} 1 & 0 & 0 & 0 \\ 0 & 1 & 0 & 0 \\ 0 & 0 & 0 & 1 \\ 0 & 0 & 1 & 0 \end{bmatrix} \times \begin{bmatrix} 1 & 0 & 0 & 0 \\ 0 & 1 & 0 & 0 \\ 0 & 0 & 0 & 1 \\ 0 & 0 & 1 & 0 \end{bmatrix} = \begin{bmatrix} 1 & 0 & 0 & 0 \\ 0 & 1 & 0 & 0 \\ 0 & 0 & 1 & 0 \\ 0 & 0 & 0 & 1 \end{bmatrix} = 1$
Example	Let $\|x> = \begin{bmatrix} 0 \\ 1 \end{bmatrix}$ and $\|y> = \begin{bmatrix} 1 \\ 0 \end{bmatrix}$ $\|x> \oplus \|y> = \begin{bmatrix} 0 \\ 1 \end{bmatrix} \oplus \begin{bmatrix} 1 \\ 0 \end{bmatrix} = \begin{bmatrix} 0 \\ 0 \\ 1 \\ 0 \end{bmatrix}$ $\begin{bmatrix} 1 & 0 & 0 & 0 \\ 0 & 1 & 0 & 0 \\ 0 & 0 & 0 & 1 \\ 0 & 0 & 1 & 0 \end{bmatrix} \times \begin{bmatrix} 0 \\ 0 \\ 1 \\ 0 \end{bmatrix} - \begin{bmatrix} 0 \\ 0 \\ 0 \\ 1 \end{bmatrix} - \begin{bmatrix} 0 \\ 1 \end{bmatrix} \oplus \begin{bmatrix} 0 \\ 1 \end{bmatrix}$

Fig.3.9: Various Properties of CNOT gate

Before		After	
Control bit	**Target bit**	**Control bit**	**Target bit**
|0>	|0>	|0>	|0>
|0>	|1>	|0>	|1>
|1>	|0>	|1>	|1>
|1>	|1>	|1>	|0>

This truth-table show that if you plug-in the "Before" values into this circuit then it will produce the "After" values.

Let us analyse its truth-table now, see figure-3.9(b)

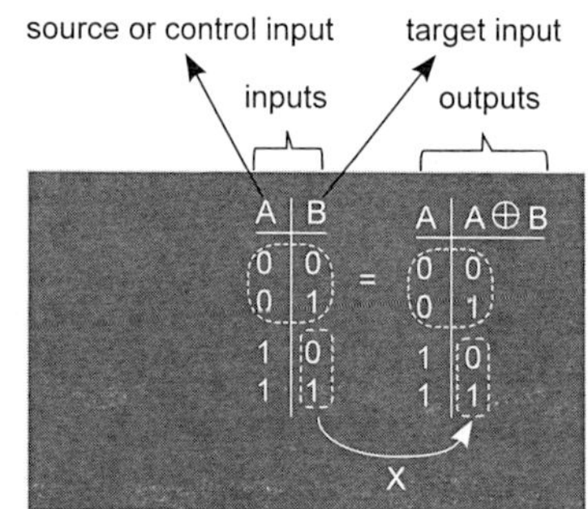

Fig.3.9(b)

From the truth table, we observe that output A = A, i.e. x takes the value of sources. The source is also called as the **control input** and it controls the application of the NOT operation on the target input. The output, B = A $\oplus$ B i.e. B is inverse of target B when source is 1 else B (output) = B (input). **Please note that whether B (output) gets the inverted value of the target B or is controlled by source, A. This is the reason as to why CNOT gate is also known as a controlled NOT gate.**

Also we observe from the truth table that in CNOT gate the inputs can be uniquely determined from the output that verifies the reversibility of the gate.

That is,

$$A_{output} = A_{input}$$
$$B_{output} = A \oplus B$$
$$\text{And B} = B' \text{ when a} = 1$$
$$\text{else } B_{output} = B_{input} \text{ when a} = 0$$

AB \ AB	00	01	10	11
00	1	0	0	0
01	0	1	0	0
10	0	0	0	1
11	0	0	1	0

It can be represented by a matrix too.

Working: If the target qubit is |0> and the control qubit is either |0> or |1> then the target takes the value of the control qubit i.e. **it becomes a copy of the control qubit but the control qubit itself doesn't change. But please note that a superposition in the control qubit results in the entanglement of the control and target qubits.**

Say, the control input is |1> and the target input is |0>. In this case, the combined state of the control and the target inputs is as follows:–

$$= 1/\sqrt{2}\ (|1> + |0>)\ |0> = 1/\sqrt{2}\ (|10> + |00>)$$

Also note that the combined state is a superposition of states |10> and |00>. However, when the control input of the CNOT gate is a superposition of |0> and |1> i.e. α |1> + β |0> and the target qubit |0>, the output of the gate is an **entangled state that is a superposition of the output states of the two individual inputs 1/√2 |10> and 1/√2 |00>.**

Hence, the combined output state of the CNOT gate is as follows:–

$$(1/\sqrt{2}\ |10> + 1/\sqrt{2}\ |00>)$$

Because for a CNOT gate–

$$|00> \rightarrow |00>, |10> \rightarrow |11>$$

So, the combined output state is as follows:–

$$1/\sqrt{2}\ |11> \text{ and } 1/\sqrt{2}\ |00>$$

To put it in a proper light, this output state can't be separated as a product of two single states unlike the combined input state. As a natural choice, the output state is entangled.

II. **Controlled-U Gate:** The CNOT gate can be extended also so that it works on 2-qubits based on a single control qubit. Assume that U is a single qubit gate that can be represented with a unitary matrix as follows:–

$$U = \begin{vmatrix} u_{00} & u_{01} \\ u_{10} & u_{11} \end{vmatrix}$$

Now the controlled-U gate can operate on 2-qubits in such a way that the first qubit serves as a control line. A controlled-U gate is as shown in figure 3.10

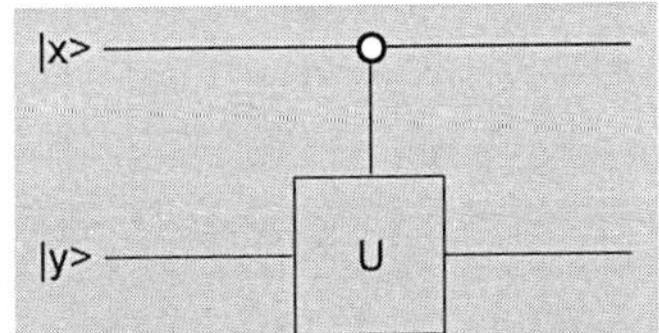

Fig.3.10: A Controlled-U gate

Here, when |x> =0, output is also |0> and |y> is |y> but when |x> = 1, then the output is |Uy>.

Thus, |0x> → |0x> and |1x> → |1, Uy>.

Hence, the input-to-output mapping of this gate can be

represented as follows:–

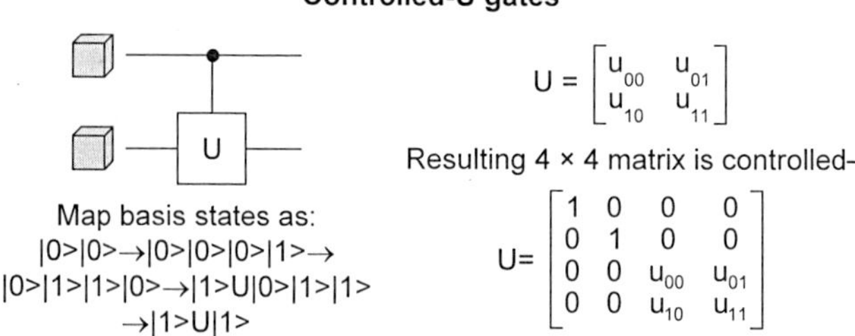

This supports the fact that the controlled version of a U-gate matrix can be obtained by substituting the lower 2*2 sub-matrix of a 4*4 identity matrix with a single qubit matrix of the chosen gate. This implies that if U is a Pauli matrix X, Y or Z then the resulting controlled gates is identified as **controlled-X, controlled-X and controlled-X gates respectively.** These are shown in figs. 3.11 (a), (b) and (c).

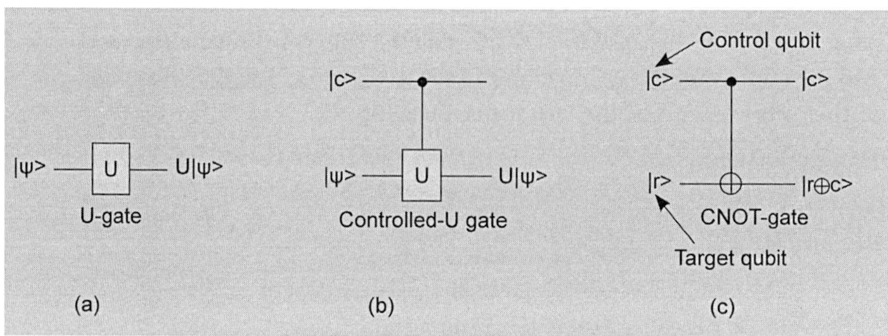

Fig.3.11: A Controlled-U gate

In general, a generalized controlled-U gate is also shown in fig. 3.12

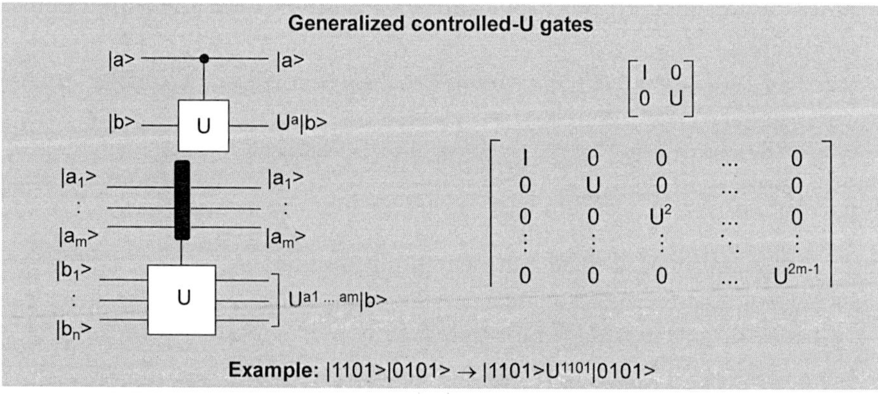

Fig. 3.12: Generalized Controlled-U gate

3.6 UNIVERSAL SETS OF QUANTUM GATES

It has been observed that 3-input or 3-output reversible logic gates are very much useful for classical reversible computation. There are two gates namely, **Fredkin gate and Toffoli gates are universal gates for irreversible computation. A universal gate is the one that allows the building of a circuit corresponding to any Boolean function.** Recall that in classical digital circuits, both NAND and NOR gates have been called as Universal gates. similarly, both **Fredkin gate and Toffoli gates** can be shown to function as NAND gates.

3.7 REVERSIBLE GATES—FREDKIN GATE, TOFFOLI GATE, PERES GATE

Let us now discuss the Reversible Gates—Fredkin Gate, Toffoli Gate, Peres Gate one by one.

I. **Fredkin Gate/CSWAP gate/cS gate:** Fredkin gate is a classical computational circuit. It was invented by Edward Fredkin. It is a **universal gate meaning that any logical or arithmetical operation can be performed entirely from these gates.** However, **the quantum version of the Fredkin gate is a 3-qubit gate that performs a controlled swap.** 3-qubit quantum gates have 3 inputs a, b and c and 3 outputs as a', b' and c'. **Note that 1 or 2 of the inputs are named as control qubits and are transferred directly to the output. The other inputs are named as target qubits.** Many multi-valued quantum circuit gates implementation use swap-based and NOT-based gates. **Please note that SWAP and NOT GATES are basic primitives in quantum world** from which many other gates have been built like two-valued controlled NOT gate/ Feynman gate, two-valued controlled-controlled NOT gate / Toffoli gate, two-valued controlled-swap gate/ Fredkin gate and their multi-valued variants.

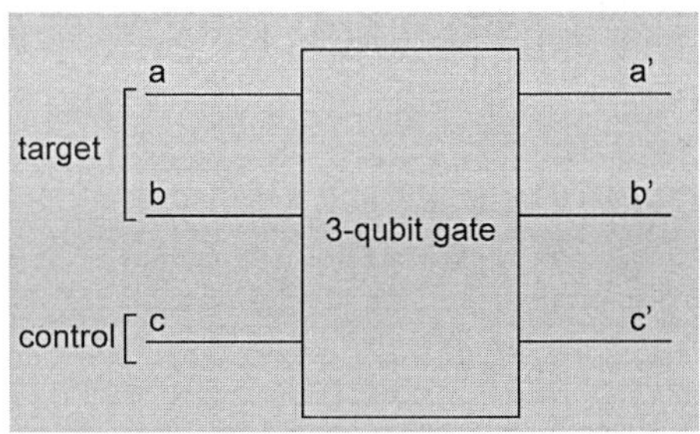

Fig.3.13: Fredkin gate with three inputs and three outputs

It is shown in figure- 3.13

Case-a: When c=0, then the inputs appear at the output, a' = a and b' = b (see fig. 3.13 (a))

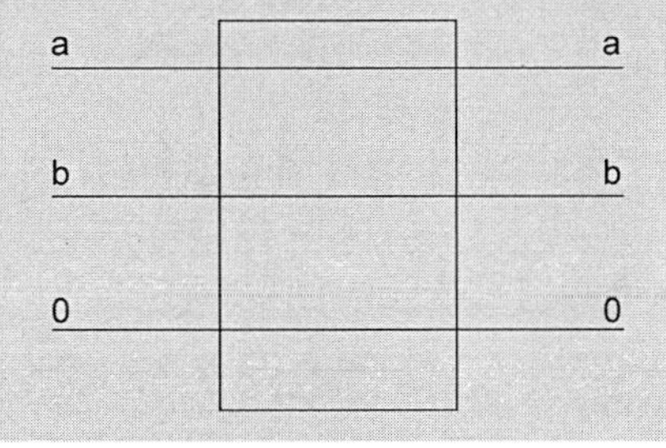

The truth table for this case-a is–

Input			Output		
a	b	c	a'	b'	c'
0	0	0	0	0	0
0	1	0	0	1	0
1	0	0	1	0	0
1	1	0	1	1	0

Case-b: when c=1, the inputs are swapped, a' = b and b' = a (see fig. 3.13 (b))

The truth table for this case is–

Input Output					
a	b	c	a'	b'	c'
0	0	1	0	0	1
0	1	1	1	0	1
1	0	1	0	1	1
1	1	1	1	1	1

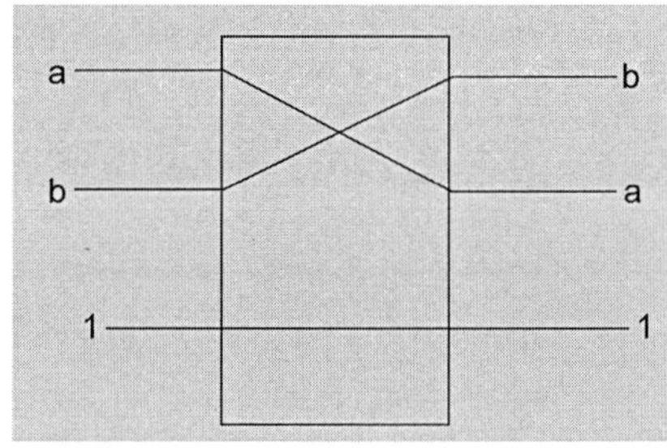

Case-c: The full table of Fredkin gate (see fig. 3.13 (c))

The full truth table of Fredkin gate is–

Input			Output		
a	b	c	a'	b'	c'
0	0	**0**	0	0	0
0	1	**0**	0	1	0
1	0	**0**	1	0	0
1	1	**0**	1	1	0
0	0	1	0	0	1
0	1	1	1	0	1
1	0	1	0	1	1
1	1	1	1	1	1

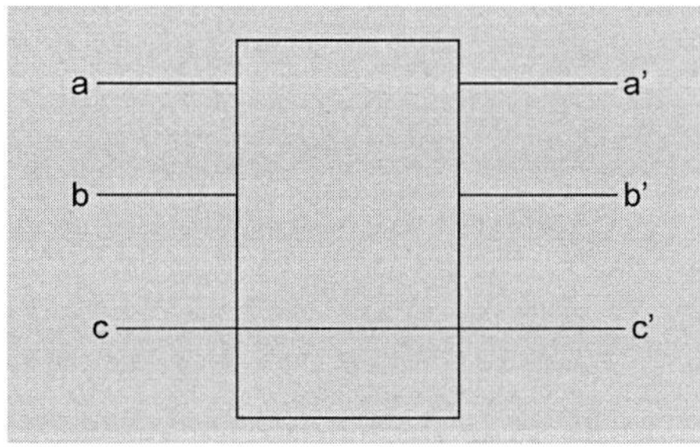

Working of Fredkin gate:

When a = 0 then a' = bc and b' = bc then the **Fredkin gate becomes an AND gate.**

And when a = 1 and b = 0 then we have–

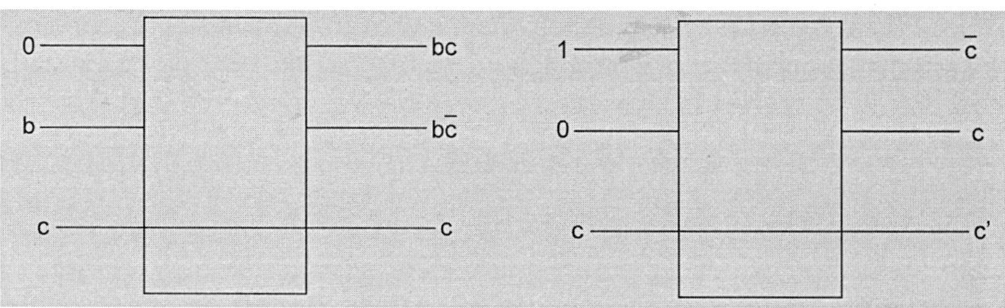

(a) Fredkin gate becomes an AND gate **(b)** Fredkin gate becomes a NOT gate

Fig. 3.14

Now, when a = 1 and b = 0 then a' = c' and b' = c. **Thus, we find that when a = 1 and b = 0 then the Fredkin gate becomes a NOT gate.**

Explanation: First of all, we should know that there are quantum Fredkin gates which are reversible just as we have classical ones that perform similar functions but are not reversible. Here, we have used the classical form of this gate to construct the truth table. Also the Booelan functions are derived based on its inputs and outputs. If we see the classical Fredkin gates then we find that it has two target inputs, 'a' and 'b' and a control input, 'c'. Also it has three outputs, a', b' and c'. **Please understand that the input of the Fredkin gate determines the output based on the following rules:–**

1. **The control input, c is transferred directly to the output, c' = c.**
2. **When c = 0, the two target inputs are transferred without modification to the output i.e. a' = a and b' = b. The truth table for this case has four entries, one for each possible combination of values of 'a' and 'b'.**
3. **When c = 1, the two target inputs are swapped i.e. a' = b and b' = a.**

The Boolean equations relating the output and the input of the Fredkin gate can be obtained from the truth tables of the circuit, as above. **Also note that the full truth table of the Fredkin gate is obtained by concatenating the truth tables for the two circuits.** The Boolean functions for the output of the Fredkin gate have been derived using the rules as above. Each output is a logical sum consisting of 4 terms, one for every entry when the desired output is true. Each term is the logical product of the corresponding inputs taken either directly or negated. The output expressions are as follows:–

$$a' = \overline{ac} + bc$$
$$b' = \overline{bc} + ac$$
$$c' = \overline{ac} + ac = c\,(\overline{a} + a) = c.$$

That is why the output, c' = c.

To put it in a proper light, we can confirm that the control input is transferred directly to the output. This gate is universal as well as conservative because in a conservative gate the number of 0s and 1s remain constant as signals pass through from the input to the output of the gate. Therefore, there is no loss of information.

Now, we are in a position to study quantum Fredkin gate.

Quantum Fredkin gate: A system of 3 qubits requires an 8-dimensional complex vector space with a basis consisting of 8 vectors as follows:–

$$|000>$$
$$|001>$$
$$|010>$$
$$|011>$$
$$|100>$$
$$|101>$$
$$|110>$$
$$|111>$$

Let us now compute the individual basis vectors. We note that the tensor product of the 3 single-qubit state vectors is as follows:–

$$\begin{pmatrix} a \\ b \end{pmatrix} \otimes \begin{pmatrix} c \\ d \end{pmatrix} \otimes \begin{pmatrix} e \\ f \end{pmatrix} = \begin{pmatrix} ac \\ ad \\ bc \\ bd \end{pmatrix} \otimes \begin{pmatrix} e \\ f \end{pmatrix} = \begin{pmatrix} ace \\ acf \\ cde \\ cdf \\ bce \\ bcf \\ bde \\ bdf \end{pmatrix}$$

Here, the basis vectors in H_2 are as follows:–

$$|0> = \begin{pmatrix} 1 \\ 0 \end{pmatrix} \qquad |1> = \begin{pmatrix} 0 \\ 1 \end{pmatrix}$$

Hence, the matrix representation of the gate is as follows:–

abc \ a'b'c'	000	001	110	011	100	101	110	111
000	1	0	0	0	0	0	0	0
001	0	1	0	0	0	0	0	0
010	0	0	1	0	0	0	0	0
011	0	0	0	1	0	0	0	0
100	0	0	0	0	1	0	0	0
101	0	0	0	0	0	0	1	0
110	0	0	0	0	0	1	0	0
111	0	0	0	0	0	0	0	1

Each of the basis vectors in H_8 is a tensor product of three basis vectors in H_2. **For example,**

$$|000> = \begin{pmatrix}1\\0\\0\\0\\0\\0\\0\\0\end{pmatrix} \qquad |001> = \begin{pmatrix}0\\1\\0\\0\\0\\0\\0\\0\end{pmatrix} \qquad |010> = \begin{pmatrix}0\\0\\1\\0\\0\\0\\0\\0\end{pmatrix} \qquad |011> = \begin{pmatrix}0\\0\\0\\1\\0\\0\\0\\0\end{pmatrix}$$

$$|100> = \begin{pmatrix}0\\0\\0\\0\\1\\0\\0\\0\end{pmatrix} \qquad |101> = \begin{pmatrix}0\\0\\0\\0\\0\\1\\0\\0\end{pmatrix} \qquad |110> = \begin{pmatrix}0\\0\\0\\0\\0\\0\\1\\0\end{pmatrix} \qquad |111> = \begin{pmatrix}0\\0\\0\\0\\0\\0\\0\\1\end{pmatrix}$$

The point to ponder is that each basis vector in H_8 is a column vector with a single 1 in the row corresponding to the binary representation of the corresponding integer plus 1. For instance, |000> has a single 1 in row-1 (i.e. 1 = 0 + 1), **|011> has a single 1 in row-4** (i.e. 4 = 3 + 1), **|101> has a single 1 in row-6** (i.e. 6 = 5 + 1). This goes on. If we add the eight terms, then we get the final Fredkin matrix (as above). In H_8, the input state of a Fredkin gate, is a **superposition of the basis vectors with complex coefficients.**

Properties of Fredkin gate

1. **Fredkin gate is reversible, i.e.** if we know a', b' and c' then we can determine a, b and c.

   let us see how?

   We can express a, b, c as functions of a', b' and c'. Using the final truth-table of Fredkin (as above), we obtain the following expressions:–

$$\begin{aligned}
a &= a'\overline{b'c'} + a'b'\overline{c'} + \overline{a'}b'c' + a''b''c \\
&= a'\overline{c'}\,(\overline{b'} + b') + b'c'(\overline{a'} + a') = a'\overline{c'} + b'c'. \\
b &= \overline{a'}b'\overline{c'} + a'b'\overline{c'} + a'\overline{b'}c' + a'b'c' \\
&= b'\overline{c'}\,(\overline{a'} + a'') + a'c'(\overline{b'} + b') = b'\overline{c'} + a'c'. \\
c &= \overline{a'b'}c' + a'\overline{b'}c' + \overline{a'}b'c' + a'b'c' = \overline{b'}c''\,(\overline{a'} + a') + b'c'(\overline{a'} + a') \\
&= \overline{b'}c' + b'c' = c'.
\end{aligned}$$

2. **If we apply two consecutive Fredkin gates with (a, b, c) as input and (a', b',c') as output for the first and (a',b',c') as input and (a", b", c") as output for the second gate then the output of the second gate is the same as the input of the first one.** That is, a" = a, b" =b, c" = c. **We observe from the truth-table once again, that the Fredkin gate conserves the number of 1s at its input. That is why, it is also called as a conservative logic gate.** (This is analogous to the laws of conservation of mass, energy and momentum, as in physics).

3. **Fredkin gate is Universal gate** i.e. it can simulate both AND and NOT gates. Consider again fig. 3.14 (a) with a = 0. In this scenario,

$$a' = bc \quad \text{and} \quad b' = \overline{bc}$$

Please note here that the output of the Fredkin gate is similar to the output of an AND gate as we can see that the product of b and c corresponds to the Boolean AND.

Based on similar lines, we can prove that the Fredkin gate can simulate a NOT gate too. Consider again the scenario in fig. 3.14 (b) with a = 1 and b = 0. We observe that–

$$a' = \overline{c} \quad \text{and} \quad b' = c$$

Please note here that the output of the Fredkin gate is similar to the output of a NOT gate as we can see that the output, a' corresponds to the Boolean NOT. Also note that in figures 3.13 (a), (b) and (c), we observe that two copies of the input, c are generated and can be used as a FANOUT gate. Another observation is that the Fredkin gate can perform a switching function called as "crossover" when it swaps its two inputs.

II. **Toffoli Gate/ Controlled-Controlled-NOT Gate:** The Toffoli gate has **two control inputs, 'a' and 'b' and one target input, 'c'** (recall that Fredkin gate had only one control input). The outputs of Toffili gates are as follows:–

A' = a, B' = b and c'. **The point to remember is that the Toffoli gate is a universal gate and is reversible too.** It is shown in fig. 3.15 along with its truth-table, circuit symbol and matrix.

Toffoli Gate (CCNOT)

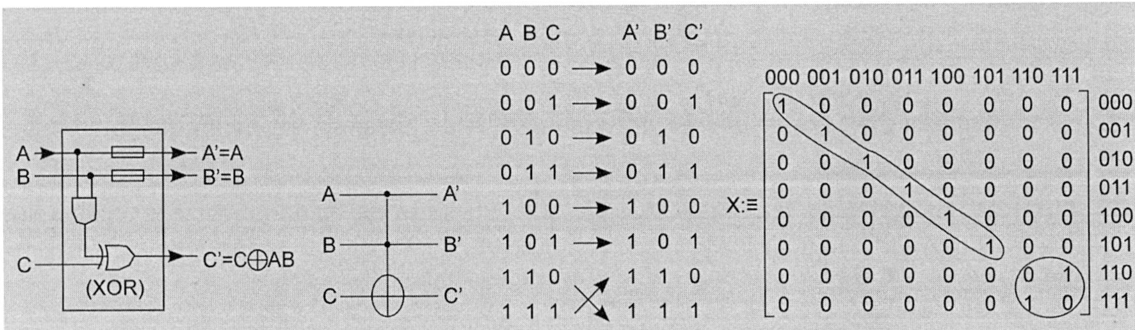

Fig.3.15: Toffoli gate with its symbol, circuit, truth-table and matrix

Actually, there are both classical and quantum variants of a Toffoli gate. However, the truth-table and the transfer matrix of classical and quantum Toffoli gates are same. Fig. 3.15 shows the classical Toffoli gate and its truth table with its matrix.

Working of classical Toffoli gate: The Toffoli gate has three inputs, two control inputs, A and B and a target, C. **If both of the control bits (or qubits) are 1 then C is flipped else its state is**

unchanged. The truth table of the classical Toffoli gate reflects the functional description, C' = C for the first six entries and C' = $\overline{C}$ for the last two, when A = B = 1. That is,

A	B	C	A'	B'	C'	
0	0	0	0	0	0	C' = C for 1st six entries
0	0	1	0	0	1	
0	1	0	0	1	0	
0	1	1	0	1	1	
1	0	0	1	0	0	
1	0	1	1	0	1	
1	1	0	1	1	1	C' = $\overline{C}$ for last two entries
1	1	1	1	1	0	

From the truth-table we observe that C' = C $\oplus$ (A AND B). But from the definition of addition modulo two ($\oplus$) it follows immediately that for any binary variable A, $1 \oplus A = \overline{A}$ and $0 \oplus A = A$.

If C = 1 then C' = A NAND B.

If C = 0 then C' = A AND B.

Please note that this implies that the Toffoli gate implements both NAND and AND functions. This is shown in fig. 3.16.

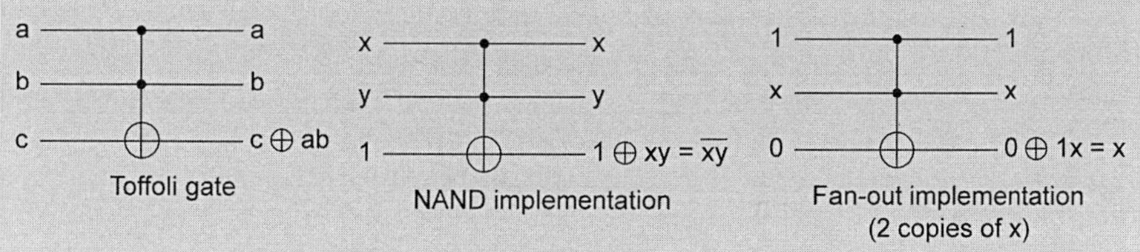

Fig.3.16: Classical Toffoli gate can be used to implement a NAND gate when c = 1 as then c' = 1 $\oplus$ (a AND b) = NOT (a and b). But if c = 0 then c' = a AND b. Also shown in this fig. is a quantum Toffoli gate that performs a FANOUT function.

The third part of the fig. 3.16 shows a FAN-OUT circuit. When a = 1 and c = 0, the target output c' = c $\oplus$ (a AND b) = 0 $\oplus$ b = b. Thus, **the 2nd control input bit is replicated.**

Working of quantum Toffoli gate: Assume that the three input qubits corresponding to a, b and c are as follows:–

$|\psi\rangle = \alpha_0 |0\rangle + \alpha_1 |1\rangle \qquad |\psi\rangle = \beta_0 |0\rangle + \beta_1 |1\rangle \qquad |\zeta\rangle = \gamma_0 |0\rangle + \gamma_1 |1\rangle$.

Then the input state is given by the tensor product of the three qubits as follows:–

$$|V_{Toffoli}\rangle = |\psi\rangle \otimes |\varphi\rangle \otimes |\zeta\rangle$$

Now, if we substitute the expressions for the 3-qubits and carry out the vector multiplication, we get:–

$$|V_{Toffoli}\rangle = \alpha_0\beta_0\gamma_0 |000\rangle + \alpha_0\beta_0 \gamma_1 |001\rangle + \alpha_0\beta_1 \gamma_0 |010\rangle + \alpha_0\beta_1 \gamma_1 |011\rangle + \alpha_1\beta_0 \gamma_0 |100\rangle + \alpha_1\beta_0\gamma_1 |101\rangle + \alpha_1\beta_1 \gamma_0 |110\rangle + \alpha_1\beta_1 \gamma_1 |111\rangle.$$

Therefore, the **vector describing the input state** is:–

$$|V_{Toffoli}> = \begin{pmatrix}\alpha_0\\ \alpha_1\end{pmatrix} \otimes \begin{pmatrix}\beta_0\\ \beta_1\end{pmatrix} \otimes \begin{pmatrix}\gamma_0\\ \gamma_1\end{pmatrix} = \begin{pmatrix}\alpha_0\beta_0\\ a_0\beta_1\\ \alpha_1\beta_0\\ \alpha_1\beta_1\end{pmatrix} \otimes \begin{pmatrix}\gamma_0\\ \gamma_1\end{pmatrix} = \begin{pmatrix}\alpha_0\beta_0\gamma_0\\ \alpha_0\beta_0\gamma_1\\ \alpha_0\beta_1\gamma_0\\ \alpha_0\beta_1\gamma_1\\ \alpha_1\beta_0\gamma_0\\ \alpha_1\beta_0\gamma_1\\ \alpha_1\beta_1\gamma_0\\ \alpha_1\beta_1\gamma_1\end{pmatrix}$$

Also we observe that the truth table of the Toffoli gate clearly shows that the quantum circuit maps its input to the output as follows:–

$|000> \rightarrow |000>$ $\quad |001> \rightarrow |001>$ $\quad |010> \rightarrow |010>$ $\quad |011> \rightarrow |011>$

$|100> \rightarrow |100>$ $\quad |101> \rightarrow |101>$ $\quad |110> \rightarrow |111>$ $\quad |111> \rightarrow |110>$

Hence,

$$G_{Toffoli} = |000><000| + |001><001| + |010><010| + |011><011| + |100><100| + |101><101| + |110><111| + |111><110|.$$

As we know that the transfer matrix of Toffoli gate is–

$$X := \begin{array}{c} \begin{array}{cccccccc} 000 & 001 & 010 & 011 & 100 & 101 & 110 & 111 \end{array} \\ \left[\begin{array}{cccccccc} 1 & 0 & 0 & 0 & 0 & 0 & 0 & 0\\ 0 & 1 & 0 & 0 & 0 & 0 & 0 & 0\\ 0 & 0 & 1 & 0 & 0 & 0 & 0 & 0\\ 0 & 0 & 0 & 1 & 0 & 0 & 0 & 0\\ 0 & 0 & 0 & 0 & 1 & 0 & 0 & 0\\ 0 & 0 & 0 & 0 & 0 & 1 & 0 & 0\\ 0 & 0 & 0 & 0 & 0 & 0 & 0 & 1\\ 0 & 0 & 0 & 0 & 0 & 0 & 1 & 0 \end{array}\right] \end{array} \begin{array}{c} \\ 000\\ 001\\ 010\\ 011\\ 100\\ 101\\ 110\\ 111 \end{array}$$

This is $G_{Toffoli}$. The output of the Toffoli gate is given by:–

$$|W_{Toffoli}> = G_{Toffoli}\,|V_{Toffoli}>$$

Or

$$|W_{Toffoli}> = \begin{bmatrix} 1 & 0 & 0 & 0 & 0 & 0 & 0 & 0\\ 0 & 1 & 0 & 0 & 0 & 0 & 0 & 0\\ 0 & 0 & 1 & 0 & 0 & 0 & 0 & 0\\ 0 & 0 & 0 & 1 & 0 & 0 & 0 & 0\\ 0 & 0 & 0 & 0 & 1 & 0 & 0 & 0\\ 0 & 0 & 0 & 0 & 0 & 1 & 0 & 0\\ 0 & 0 & 0 & 0 & 0 & 0 & 0 & 1\\ 0 & 0 & 0 & 0 & 0 & 0 & 1 & 0 \end{bmatrix} \begin{pmatrix}\alpha_0\beta_0\gamma_0\\ \alpha_0\beta_0\gamma_1\\ \alpha_0\beta_1\gamma_0\\ \alpha_0\beta_1\gamma_1\\ \alpha_1\beta_0\gamma_0\\ \alpha_1\beta_0\gamma_1\\ \alpha_1\beta_1\gamma_0\\ \alpha_1\beta_1\gamma_1\end{pmatrix} = \begin{pmatrix}\alpha_0\beta_0\gamma_0\\ \alpha_0\beta_0\gamma_1\\ \alpha_0\beta_1\gamma_0\\ \alpha_0\beta_1\gamma_1\\ \alpha_1\beta_0\gamma_0\\ \alpha_1\beta_0\gamma_1\\ \alpha_1\beta_1\gamma_1\\ \alpha_1\beta_1\gamma_0\end{pmatrix}$$

III. **Peres Gate:** It is the modified form of the Toffoli gate only. The classical block diagram, its equivalent Quantum diagram and its truth-table for the three inputs: A, B and C as well as the outputs P, Q and R is as follows:–

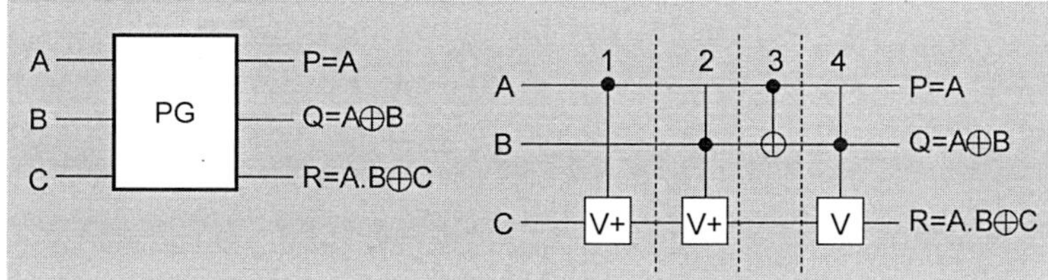

(a) Peres Gate **(b)** Quantum implementation of the Peres Gate

Inputs			Outputs		
A	B	C	P	Q	R
0	0	0	0	0	0
0	0	1	0	0	1
0	1	0	0	1	0
0	1	1	0	1	1
1	0	0	1	1	0
1	0	1	1	1	1
1	1	0	1	0	1
1	1	1	1	0	0

Fig.3.17: Symbol, Quantum Peres gate, truth–table of Peres gate

From the truth table we observe that the mapping from input to output is as follows:–

$000 \rightarrow 000$ $001 \rightarrow 001$

$010 \rightarrow 010$ $011 \rightarrow 011$

$100 \rightarrow 110$ $101 \rightarrow 111$

$110 \rightarrow 101$ $111 \rightarrow 100$

The matrix for Peres showing inputs and outputs is as follows:–

$$\begin{pmatrix} 1 & 0 & 0 & 0 & 0 & 0 & 0 & 0 \\ 0 & 1 & 0 & 0 & 0 & 0 & 0 & 0 \\ 0 & 0 & 1 & 0 & 0 & 0 & 0 & 0 \\ 0 & 0 & 0 & 1 & 0 & 0 & 0 & 0 \\ 0 & 0 & 0 & 0 & 0 & 0 & 1 & 0 \\ 0 & 0 & 0 & 0 & 0 & 0 & 0 & 1 \\ 0 & 0 & 0 & 0 & 0 & 1 & 0 & 0 \\ 0 & 0 & 0 & 0 & 1 & 0 & 0 & 0 \end{pmatrix}$$

The circuitry of Peres circuit is as follows:–

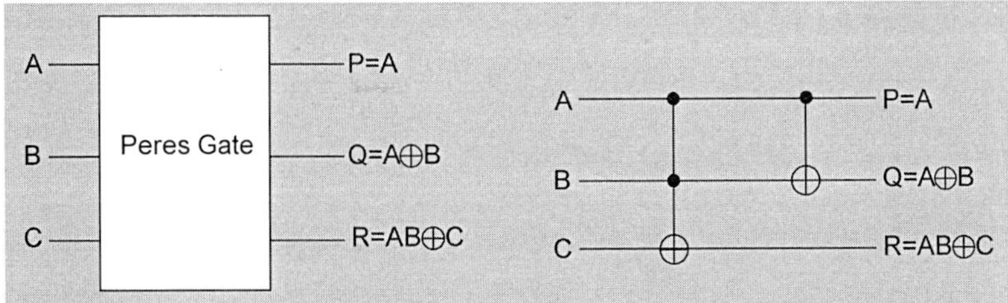

Fig.3.18: Peres gate Equations

That is,

$$P = A$$
$$Q = A \oplus B$$
$$R = AB \oplus C$$

Note: The Fredkin gate, Toffoli gate and the Peres gate discussed in this section are all reversible gates.

Before we discuss further, let us summarize the gates so studied in tabular format.

Gate name	# Qubits	Circuit Symbol	Unitary Matrix	Description
Hadamard	1	$-\boxed{H}-$	$\frac{1}{\sqrt{2}}\begin{bmatrix}1 & 1\\1 & -1\end{bmatrix}$	Transforms a basis state into an even superposition of the two basis states.
T	1	$-\boxed{T}-$	$\begin{bmatrix}1 & 0\\0 & e^{i\pi/4}\end{bmatrix}$	Adds a relative phase shift of π/4 between contributing basis states. Sometimes called a π/8 gate, because diagonal elements can be witten as $e^{-i\pi/8}$ and $e^{i\pi/8}$.
CNOT	2		$\begin{bmatrix}1&0&0&0\\0&1&0&0\\0&0&0&1\\0&0&1&0\end{bmatrix}$	Controlled-not; reversible analogue to classical XOR gate. The input connected to the solid dot is passed through to make the operation reversible.
Toffoli (CCNOT)	3		$\begin{bmatrix}1&0&0&0&0&0&0&0\\0&1&0&0&0&0&0&0\\0&0&1&0&0&0&0&0\\0&0&0&1&0&0&0&0\\0&0&0&0&1&0&0&0\\0&0&0&0&0&1&0&0\\0&0&0&0&0&0&0&1\\0&0&0&0&0&0&1&0\end{bmatrix}$	Controlled-controlled-not; a three-qubit gate that switches the third bit for states where the first two bits are 1 (that is, switches $\|110\rangle$ to $\|111\|$) and vice versa).

Pauli-Z	1	─[Z]─	$\begin{bmatrix} 1 & 0 \\ 0 & -1 \end{bmatrix}$	Adds a relative phase shift of π between contributing basis states. Maps |0> to –|1> itself and |1> to –|1>. Sometimes called a "phase flip."
Z-Rotation	1	─[RZ(θ)]─	$\begin{bmatrix} e^{-i\theta/2} & 0 \\ 0 & e^{i\theta/2} \end{bmatrix}$	Adds a relative phase shift of (or rotates state vector about x-axis by) θ.
NOT	1	─⊕─	$\begin{bmatrix} 0 & 1 \\ 1 & 0 \end{bmatrix}$	Analogous to classical NOT gate; switches |0> to |1> and vice versa.

Also some of the quantum gates studied are as follows:–

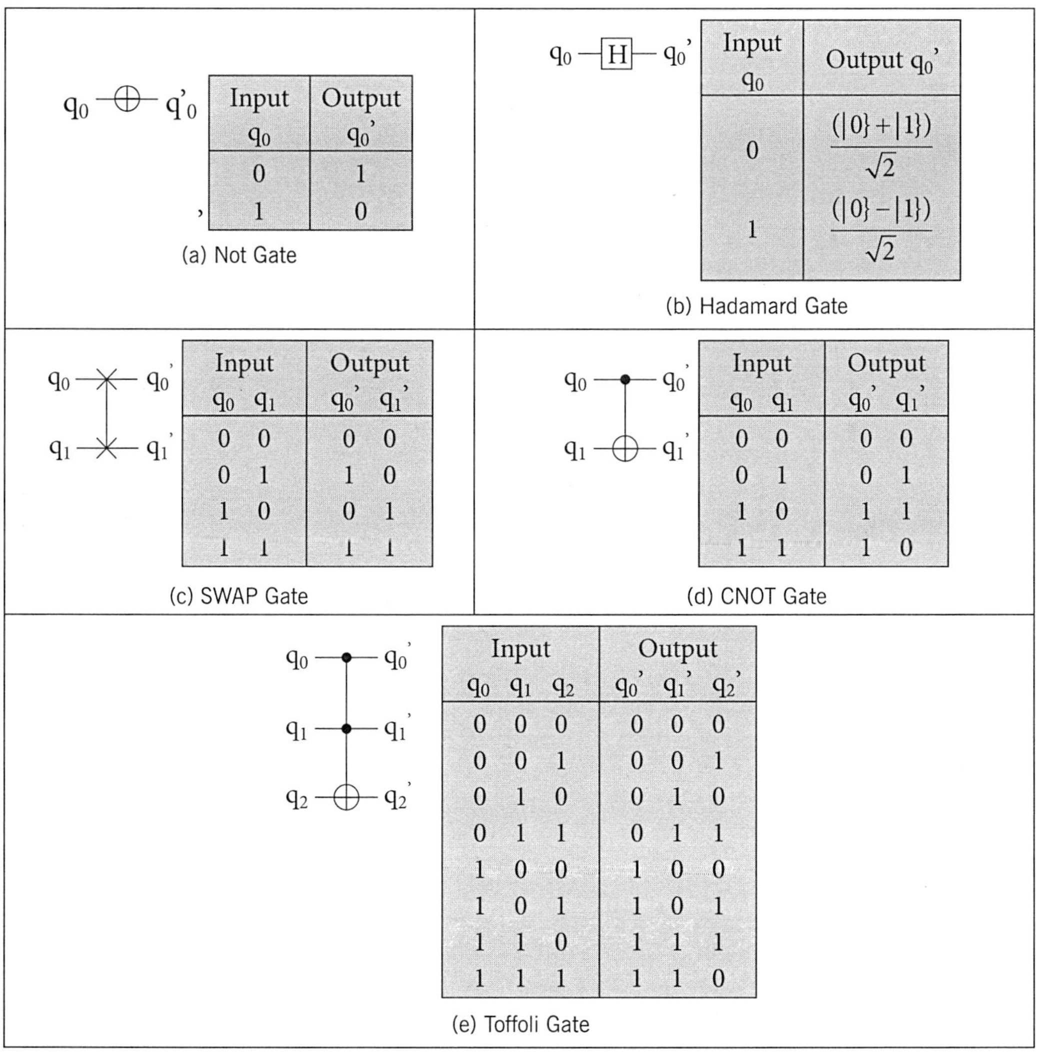

Input q_0	Output q_0'
0	1
1	0

(a) Not Gate

Input q_0	Output q_0'
0	$\frac{(\|0\}+\|1\})}{\sqrt{2}}$
1	$\frac{(\|0\}-\|1\})}{\sqrt{2}}$

(b) Hadamard Gate

Input q_0 q_1	Output q_0' q_1'
0 0	0 0
0 1	1 0
1 0	0 1
1 1	1 1

(c) SWAP Gate

Input q_0 q_1	Output q_0' q_1'
0 0	0 0
0 1	0 1
1 0	1 1
1 1	1 0

(d) CNOT Gate

Input q_0 q_1 q_2	Output q_0' q_1' q_2'
0 0 0	0 0 0
0 0 1	0 0 1
0 1 0	0 1 0
0 1 1	0 1 1
1 0 0	1 0 0
1 0 1	1 0 1
1 1 0	1 1 1
1 1 1	1 1 0

(e) Toffoli Gate

3.8 NO CLONING THEOREM AND ITS PROOFS

The transformations that are carried by quantum circuits are **unitary. As a result, unknown quantum states can't be copied (or cloned).** Before we discuss no cloning theorem and its proof, let us ponder on two observations made so far:–

1. A gate performs a linear transformation of its input vector |V> into an output vector |W> = G |V> with G the transfer matrix of the gate.
2. The transformations performed by matrices can be represented by linear operators.

No Cloning Theorem

- There is no unitary transform that allows us to copy a qubit
  - → Proof: Suppose U is a copying matrix: U|c0> = |cc> for all states |c>
  - → Then,

$$\text{if } |c\rangle = \frac{1}{\sqrt{2}}(|0\rangle + |1\rangle),\ U|c\rangle = \frac{1}{\sqrt{2}}(|00\rangle + |11\rangle)$$

$$\text{but } U|c\rangle = |cc\rangle = \frac{1}{2}(|00\rangle + |01\rangle + |10\rangle + |11\rangle) \neq \frac{1}{\sqrt{2}}(|00\rangle + |11\rangle)$$

- Illustration: Copy a bit using CNOT...yields an entangled state!

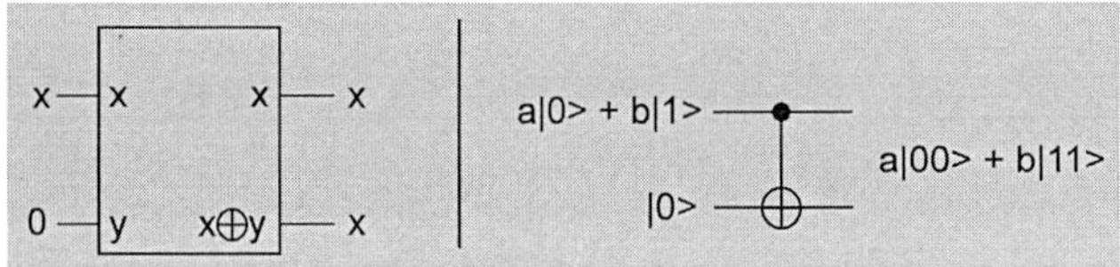

Classical and quantum circuits to copy an unknown bit

Quantum No Cloning Theorem

(Wooters & Zurek 1982)

An unknown quantum state cannot be cloned.

→ Impossible to generate copies unless state already known.

Proof: Suppose U_C is unitary cloning operator

$$U_C(|\alpha\rangle|0\rangle) = |\alpha\rangle|\alpha\rangle$$
$$U_C(|\beta\rangle|0\rangle) = |\beta\rangle|\beta\rangle$$

But if

$$|\gamma\rangle = \frac{1}{\sqrt{2}}(|\alpha\rangle + |\beta\rangle)$$

$$U_C(|\gamma\rangle|0\rangle) = \frac{1}{\sqrt{2}}(|\alpha\rangle|\alpha\rangle + |\beta\rangle|\beta\rangle \neq |\gamma\rangle|\gamma\rangle)$$

Conclude no operator U_C exists

Proof by Contradiction

Say, G is a unitary transformation corresponding to the unitary matrix, G, of a two-input gate that allows us to replicate an input qubit. Furthermore, assume that $|\psi>$ and $|\varphi>$ are two orthogonal quantum states of two qubits. Now, we apply each one of them at **the first input of the gate independently while the second qubit input is |0>.** Also assume that the gate clones its input, so it implies that–

$$G(|\psi> \otimes |0>) = |\psi> \otimes |\psi>$$

In condensed form, we can write as follows:–

$$G(|\psi>0>) = |\psi\psi> \quad ...(1)$$

Also, we find that–

$$G(|\varphi> \otimes |0>) = |\varphi> \otimes |\varphi>$$

Or we can write:–

$$G(|\varphi 0>) = |\varphi\varphi> \quad ...(2)$$

To put it in a proper light, equation-1, equation-2 simply state that when the 2nd input qubit is |0> then the state of the quantum system at the output of the gate is composed of two replicas of the first qubit i.e. $|\psi>$ for the first case and $|\varphi>$ for the second case. **Also note that the input and output states are represented by the vectors in H_4 obtained by taking the tensor product of the two vectors describing the state of the two qubits at the input respectively** (the output of the gate).

Conclusions: We observe that there is no linear operation that reliability clones unknown quantum states. It is possible to clone known states after a measurement has been performed. **Please understand that before the measurement of a quantum system in an unknown state, the outcome of the measurement is uncertain. After the measurement, the outcome is the projection of the state on one of the basis vectors.** Hence, it is well-determined.

Summarization: In nutshell, non-orthogonal pure quantum states $\{|\psi_i>\}$ can't be cloned. This simply means that no physical system that carries out the transformation $|\psi> \rightarrow |\psi_i> | \psi_i>$ may exist.

Before we discuss further, we solve some problems on quantum circuits now.

Example 1: Design a 2-bit adder circuit using reversible quantum gates.

Solution 1: Let us design a two bit adder step-by-step:

Gates used: Toffoli gate, a CNOT gate.

Circuit diagram:

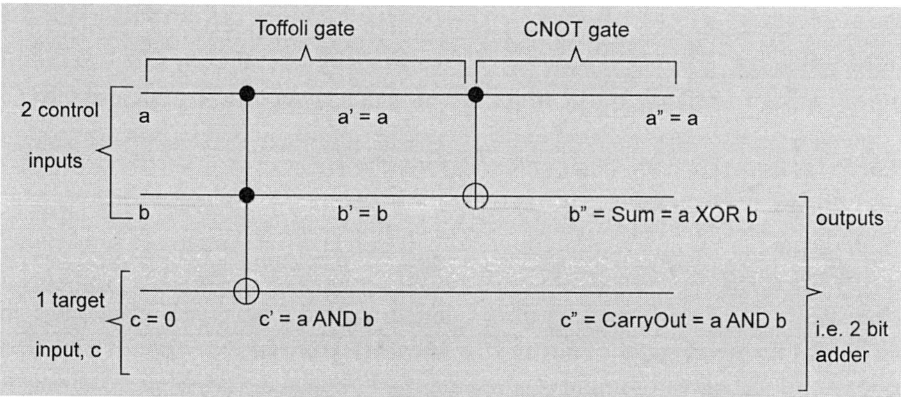

Fig.3.19: 2-bit adder using Toffoli and CNOT Reversible gates

As shown in figure-3.19, there are two control inputs to the Toffoli gate, a and b and its target input c = 0. **The target output of the Toffoli gate is** (remember that c = 0) **as follows:–**

$$c' = c \oplus (a \text{ AND } b) = a \text{ AND } b$$

Please note that this state propagates to the output and thus we can write–

$$c' = a \text{ AND } b$$

Then a" = a' = a as the control input of the CNOT propagates to its output unchanged. Last but not the least, b' = b and this becomes the target input of the CNOT gate. **Also note that the target output of the CNOT gate is as follows:–**

$$b'' = a' \text{ XOR } b' = a \text{ XOR } b$$

Finally, we conclude that the two outputs of the circuit are the Sum and the CarryOut of the two inputs, 'a' and 'b'.

Example 2: Design a quantum circuit for swapping of two qubits.

Solution 2: Let us design a circuit for swapping of two qubits step-by-step:

Gates used: 3 CNOT gate.

Circuit diagram: CNOT gate.

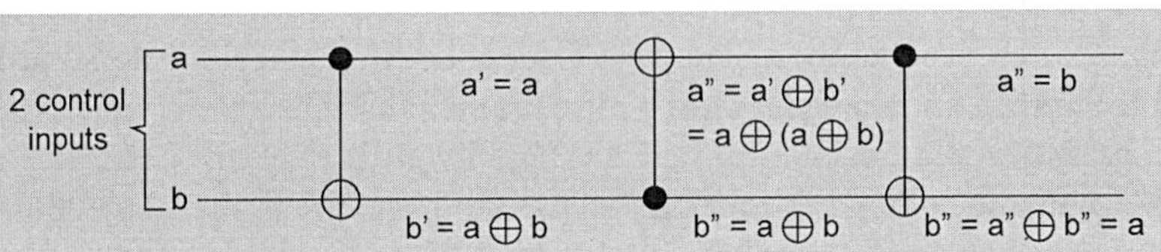

Fig.3.20: 2-bit swapper using Three CNOT Reversible gates

As shown in figure-3.20, there are 3 CNOT gates. Given Booelan variables, a and b, we observe that–

$$a \oplus (a \oplus b) = (a \oplus a) \oplus b = b$$

and

$$b \oplus (a \oplus b) = (b \oplus b) \oplus a = a$$

Please note that $(a \oplus a) = 0$ and $(0 \oplus b) = b$. In order to prove that the two inputs are swapped, we find out the output of each stage. **The inputs to the 2nd stage are** a' = a and b' = $a \oplus b$. **The inputs to the 3rd stage** are a" = $a \oplus (a \oplus b)$ = b and b" = $a \oplus b$. **Also note that the outputs of the 3rd stage are a''' = b and b''' = $b \oplus (a \oplus b)$ = a. Thus, we can say that the circuit swaps its two inputs.**

Example 3: Design a full one qubit adder circuit using reversible Toffoli and CNOT quantum gates.

Solution 3: Let us design a full one-qubit adder step-by-step:

Gates used: Toffoli gate, a CNOT gate.

Circuit diagram: Let us now rig the circuit with Toffoli and CNOT gates to implement a full one-bit adder. It is shown in fig. 3.21 as follows:–

Working: firstly, we see that the first three qubits from the top, i.e. |c> = |CarryIn>, |x> and |y> are **the control qubits on all gates. That is why they are transferred without any change to the output.** Now, we only will have to compute expressions for |Sum> and |CarryOut>. To make the working simple, let us drop the **ket notations** and denote the **qubit vector |x> simply as x. If we call s_1 and s_2** as the results of CNOT transformations at stages marked as 1 and 2 (see fig. 3.21) then we can write the following expressions:–

$$\begin{aligned} s_1 &= c \oplus 0 = c \\ s_2 &= s_1 \oplus x = c \oplus x \\ \text{Sum} &= s_2 \oplus y = (c \oplus x) \oplus y \end{aligned}$$

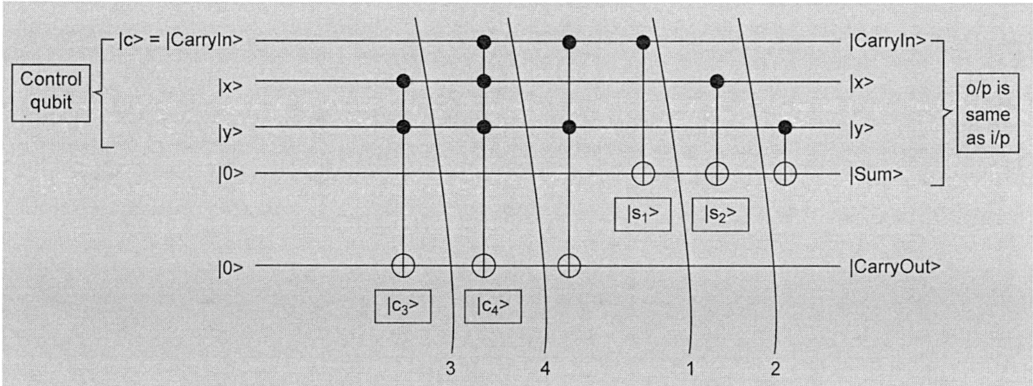

Fig.3.21: Full one-qubit adder using reversible Toffoli and CNOT gates

To put it in a proper light, we say that we can show that–

$$(\mathbf{c} \oplus \mathbf{x}) \oplus \mathbf{y} = \mathbf{xyc} + \overline{\mathbf{xyc}} + \overline{\mathbf{yxc}} + \overline{\mathbf{cxy}}$$

We can prove this equation by using the fact that $x \oplus y = xy' + x'y$ and the de Morgan's laws–

$$\overline{x + y} = \overline{xy} \qquad \text{and} \qquad \overline{xy} = \overline{x} + \overline{y}.$$

We call c_3 and c_4, the results of the transformations performed by the Toffolli gates at stages marked as 3 and 4 in fig. 3.21. We find that–

$$\begin{aligned} c_3 &= 0 \oplus (xy) = xy \\ c_4 &= c_3 \oplus (cx) = (xy) \oplus (cx) \\ \text{CarryOut} &= c_4 \oplus (cy) = (xy) \oplus (cx) \oplus (cy) \end{aligned}$$

Also it can be proved that–

$$(xy) \oplus (cx) \oplus (cy) = xyc + \overline{x}yc + x\overline{y}c + xy\overline{c}$$

Example 4: Consider a three-qubit gate with a CNOT gate as follows:–

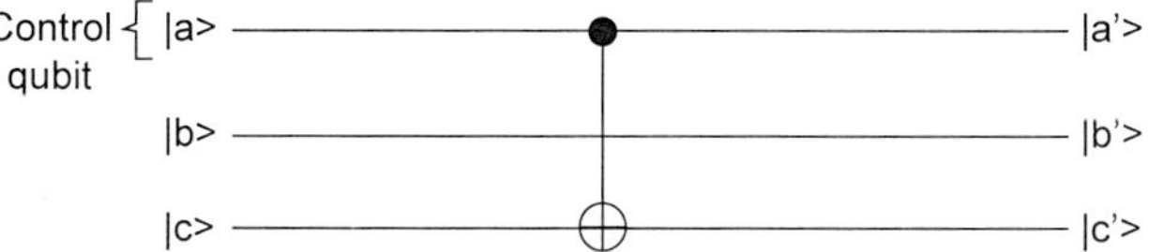

Compute its transfer matrix.

Solution 4: From the figure given in question, we find that–

- a' = a, b' = b and c' = depends on 'a'.

- The top most qubit |a> is the control qubit of a CNOT gate. So, it is transferred to the output unchanged i.e. |a'> = |a>.
- The 2nd qubit is not affected, i.e. |b'> = |b>.
- The 3rd qubit is flipped when |a> = |1> and left unchanged if |a> = |0>. That is,

$$c' = c \text{ if } a = 0$$
$$c' = \bar{c} \text{ if } a = 1$$

Therefore, the truth table of this circuit is as follows:–

	a	b	c	a'	b'	c'	
a = 0	0	0	0	0	0	0	c' = c if a = 0
	0	0	1	0	0	1	
	0	1	0	0	1	0	
	0	1	1	0	1	1	
a = 1	1	0	0	1	0	1	c' = c if a = 1
	1	0	1	1	0	0	
	1	1	0	1	1	1	
	1	1	1	1	1	0	

Please understand that this means that the quantum circuit maps its input to the output as follows:–

|000> → |000> |001> → |001>

|010> → |010> |011> → |011>

|100> → |101> |101> → |100>

|110> → |111> |111> → |110>

3.9 EFFICIENCY IN APPROXIMATING UNITARY TRANSFORMATION

As already studied, that single-qubit transformation must be unitary to preserve the norm. **Please remember that the state of a qubit can be represented as a unit vector on the Block sphere. Also recall that when we apply a transformation to a qubit, the corresponding vector on the Block sphere is also transformed.** We are interested in the rotations with an angle θ about x, y and z axis. The three rotations are performed respectively by the following operators obtained by the exponentiation of the σ_x, σ_y and σ_z Pauli matrices. Also we have seen that the rotation matrices satisfy the following properties:–

$$R_y(\theta_1)\, R_y(\theta_2) = R_y(\theta_1 + \theta_2)$$
$$R_z(\theta_1)\, R_z(\theta_2) = R_z(\theta_1 + \theta_2)$$
$$\sigma_x\, R_y(\theta)\, \sigma_x = R_y(-\theta)$$
$$\sigma_x\, R_z(\theta)\, \sigma_x = R_z(-\theta)$$

3.10 IMPLEMENTING MEASUREMENTS WITH QUANTUM GATES

The process of randomly selecting a qubit, collapsing the qubit by getting rid of the other qubit in the quantum state and recording the state of the selected qubit as a binary bit is called measuring a qubit.

Suppose you are given a qubit in state, $|\psi> = \alpha\,|0> + \beta\,|1>$ and a measurement apparatus. Now, you are asked to compute, α and β coefficients, i.e. to compute the quantum state. This is not quite possible. **As a natural choice, the principles of quantum mechanics state that the quantum state of a system is not directly observable.** So, what we can do is to guess approximate information about α and β. **This process is called as measurement in the computational basis.**

- **Quantum measurement circuit**
  - **Converts qubit state $|\psi> = \alpha|0> + \beta|1>$ into a bit M**
    - Resuit - 0 with probability α^2, 1 with probability β^2

Thus, we see from Fig. 3.22 that the measurement process splits the probabilities of the classical bits 0 and 1 equal to the absolute values of the coefficients α and β squared. Practically speaking, we can imagine this process taking place by observing a physical photon, phonon, atom or electron with a measurement apparatus. **That is why; measurement is also regarded as a quantum gate. Please understand that measurement disturbs the quantum system state giving a classical bit outcome. Also note that after the process, the coefficients α and β are destroyed. This means that we can't store large amount of information in a qubit.**

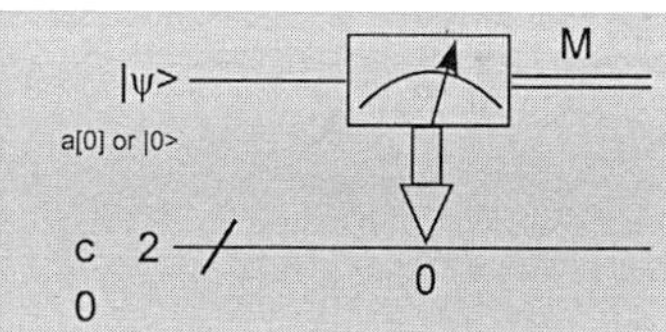

Fig.3.22: Measurement of a Quantum State

Normalization of the quantum state: Given a measurement in a computational basis,

$\alpha\,|0> + \beta\,|1>$, **the probability of the classical bit 0 and 1 must add to 1**. That is,

Probability (0) + Probability (1) $= |\alpha^2| + |\beta^2| = 1$

To put it in a proper light, this means that the length of the quantum state vector must be 1 (normalized). This comes from a fact that measurement probabilities add to 1.

3.11 GENERAL QUANTUM CIRCUIT

We need a quantum circuit to be able to execute a unitary transformation, G depending on the state of a single qubit. We need to address the flow of control in the quantum circuits so as to enable us to implement 'if-then-else' constructs. **Please note that the CNOT gate is one of the gates in this family of quantum circuits that allows us to control the target qubit depending on the value of the control qubit.**

Control qubits are represented as shaded circles whereas the **target qubits** are open circles (or boxes) as in figure 3.23.

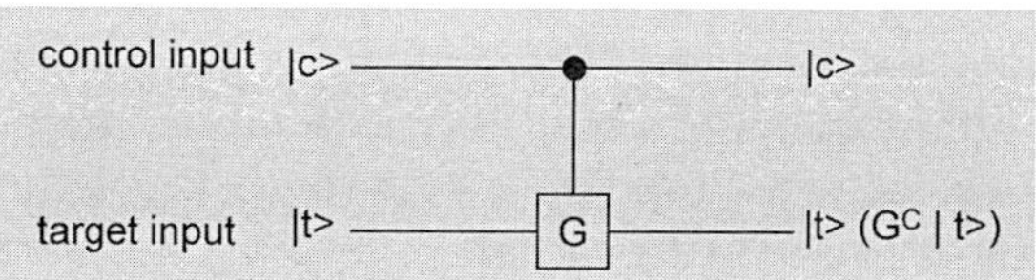

Fig.3.23: A Generic Quantum Circuit

Working of Generic Quantum Circuit: A controlled-G operation is shown in the generic model of figure 3.23. Two cases arise:

Case 1: When the control qubit is |c> = |0>, then the target qubit is transferred directly to the output.

Case 2: When the control qubit is |c> = |1>, then the transformation described by G is applied to the target qubit.

3.11.1 Single-qubit controlled operations

The Controlled-Z Operation: As already studied, that the Z gate flips the sign of the projection of a qubit on |1>. Figure-3.24(a) shows a quantum circuit for the controlled-Z operation. So, it maps:–

$|0> \rightarrow |0>$ and $|1> \rightarrow -|1>$.

Hence, we say that the controlled-Z gate maps its input to the output as follows:–

$|00> \rightarrow |00>$ $|01> \rightarrow |01>$ $|10> \rightarrow |10>$ $|11> \rightarrow -|11>$

Also the transfer matrix of the controlled-Z circuit of figure 3.24(a) is as follows:–

$$G_{\text{controlled-Z}} = |00><00| + |01><01| + |10><10| - |11><11|$$

$$= \begin{bmatrix} 1 & 0 & 0 & 0 \\ 0 & 1 & 0 & 0 \\ 0 & 0 & 1 & 0 \\ 0 & 0 & 0 & -1 \end{bmatrix}$$

Or

$$G_{\text{controlled-Z}} = \begin{pmatrix} I_2 & 0 \\ 0 & \sigma_z \end{pmatrix}$$

Please note that if we change the roles of the control and the target qubits i.e. reverse them **then also it will have an identical behavior.** This is shown in figure-3.24(b).

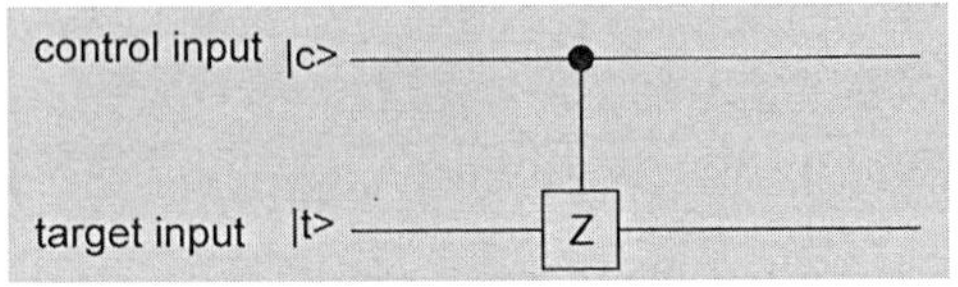

(a): Original Quantum Circuit for the controlled-z operation

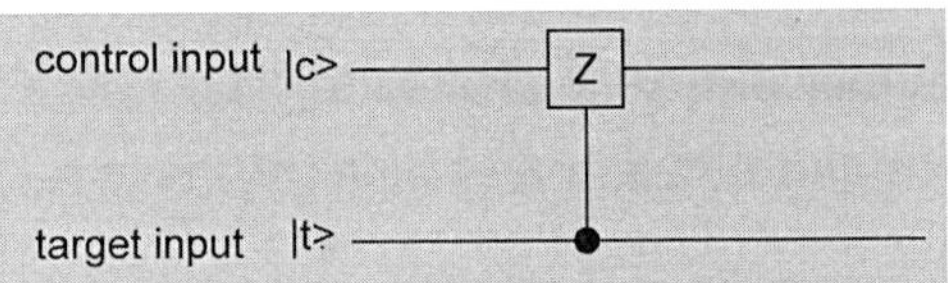

(b): Circuit when the roles of the control and target qubits are reversed

Fig.3.24

We can see that the controlled-Z gate maps its input to the output exactly like the one in figure 3.24 (a) and (b). Hence, we can say that the two circuits are equivalent.

Also note that the roles of the control qubit and the target qubit can be reversed by an approximate change of basis. It is shown in figure- 3.25

Explanation: The circuit of fig. 3.25(a) consists up of three stages. There are two ways of finding out the output of a **multi-stage quantum circuit. Firstly, we may analyze out the transformations applied to each qubit, at each stage.** This technique works for the 1st qubit of the circuit as shown in fig. 3.25(a). **The first qubit–**

$$|\psi> = \alpha_0 |0> + \alpha_1 |1> = \begin{pmatrix} \alpha_0 \\ \alpha_1 \end{pmatrix} \text{ is}$$

is applied to the input of a Hadamard gate and its state is transformed by **the 1st stage of the circuit** to:-

$$|\psi_1\rangle \;=\; H\,|\psi\rangle = 1/\sqrt{2}\begin{pmatrix}1 & 0\\ 0 & -1\end{pmatrix}\begin{pmatrix}\alpha_0\\ \alpha_1\end{pmatrix} = 1/\sqrt{2}\begin{pmatrix}\alpha_0+\alpha_1\\ \alpha_0-\alpha_1\end{pmatrix}$$

The 2nd stage does not alter the state of the 1st qubit because it acts as the control qubit of a CNOT gate. So, we can say that–

$$|\psi_2\rangle \;=\; |\,\psi_1\rangle \;\ldots\text{is } \psi_2$$

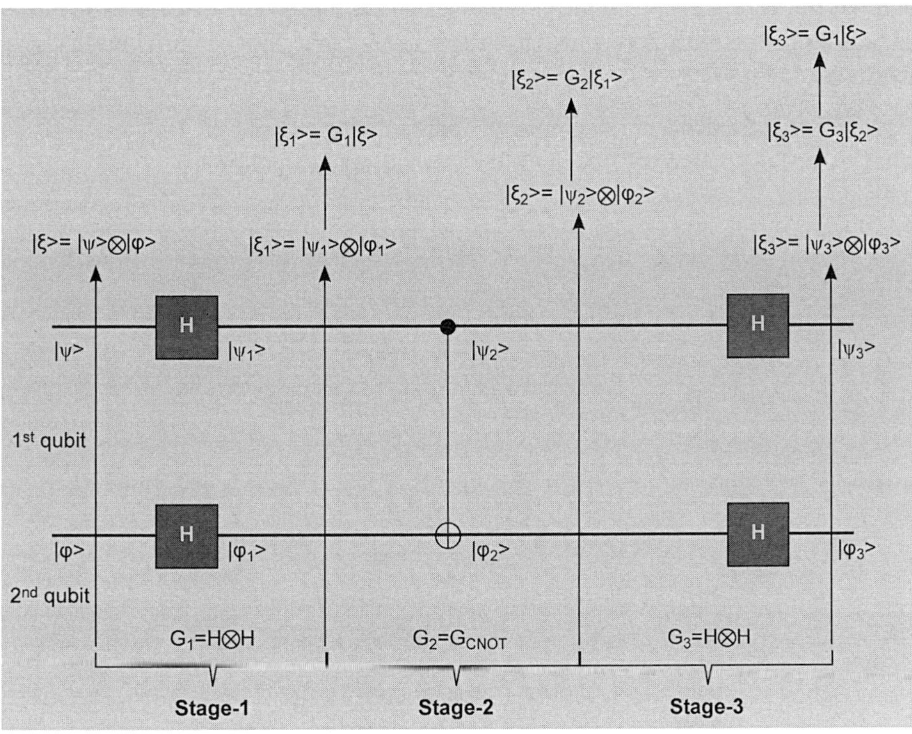

Fig.3.25(a): Circuit showing way of the basis of control and target qubits being changed by a pair of Hadamard gates

The 3rd stage transforms the state of the first qubit as given below:-

$$|\psi_3\rangle \;=\; \mathbf{H}\,|\psi_2\rangle = \mathbf{1/\sqrt{2}}\begin{pmatrix}1 & 0\\ 0 & -1\end{pmatrix}\;\mathbf{1/\sqrt{2}}\begin{pmatrix}\alpha_0+\alpha_1\\ \alpha_0-\alpha_1\end{pmatrix}$$

$$= \tfrac{1}{2}\begin{pmatrix}\alpha_0+\alpha_1+(\alpha_0-\alpha_1)\\ \alpha_0-\alpha_1-(\alpha_0-\alpha_1)\end{pmatrix} = \begin{pmatrix}\alpha_0\\ \alpha_1\end{pmatrix}$$

So, we can say that–

$$|\psi_3\rangle \;=\; |\,\psi\rangle \qquad \ldots\text{is } \psi_3$$

Please note that this method cannot be applied when the state of 1 qubit is affected by the state of other qubits, because in the case of the 2nd qubit–

$$|\varphi\rangle = \beta_0 |0\rangle + \beta_1 |1\rangle = \begin{pmatrix} \beta_0 \\ \beta_1 \end{pmatrix}$$

For the 1st stage, we can calculate–

$$|\varphi_1\rangle = \mathbf{H}\,|\psi\rangle = 1/\sqrt{2} \begin{pmatrix} 1 & 1 \\ 1 & -1 \end{pmatrix} \begin{pmatrix} \beta_0 \\ \beta_1 \end{pmatrix} = 1\sqrt{2} \begin{pmatrix} \beta_0 + \beta_1 \\ \beta_0 - \beta_1 \end{pmatrix}$$

For the 2nd stage, we can say that the state of the target qubit $|\varphi_2\rangle$depends on the value of the control qubit. **To put it in a proper light, the more general method to calculate the output state of a multi-stage quantum circuit is to construct the transfer matrices of individual stages and then to multiply them.**

Let us now write the equations for these three stages of figure 3.25 (a).

For the 1st stage of the circuit (see fig. 3.25a), we can write as follows:–

$$G_1 = H \otimes H = 1/\sqrt{2} \begin{pmatrix} 1 & 1 \\ 1 & -1 \end{pmatrix} \otimes 1/\sqrt{2} \begin{pmatrix} 1 & 1 \\ 1 & -1 \end{pmatrix}$$

$$= \tfrac{1}{2} \begin{pmatrix} 1 & 1 & 1 & 1 \\ 1 & -1 & 1 & -1 \\ 1 & 1 & -1 & -1 \\ 1 & -1 & -1 & 1 \end{pmatrix}$$

A reversed CNOT gate equivalent to the circuit of fig. 3.25 (a) is as follows:–

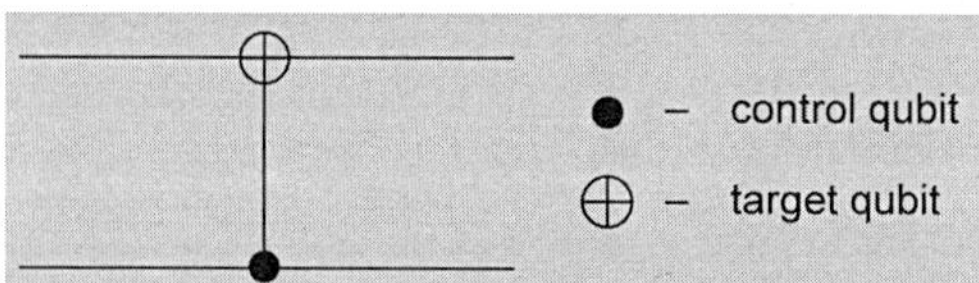

Fig.3.25(b): Reversed CNOT gate equivalent to circuit of fig. 3.25 (a).

The 2nd stage is a CNOT gate, so,

$$G_2 = G_{CNOT}$$

Now **the transfer matrix of the 1st two stages is–**

$$G_2\,G_1 = \begin{pmatrix} 1 & 0 & 0 & 0 \\ 0 & 1 & 0 & 0 \\ 0 & 0 & 0 & 1 \\ 0 & 0 & 1 & 0 \end{pmatrix} \tfrac{1}{2} \begin{pmatrix} 1 & 1 & 1 & 1 \\ 1 & -1 & 1 & -1 \\ 1 & 1 & -1 & -1 \\ 1 & -1 & -1 & 1 \end{pmatrix}$$

$$= \tfrac{1}{2} \begin{pmatrix} 1 & 1 & 1 & 1 \\ 1 & -1 & 1 & -1 \\ 1 & -1 & -1 & 1 \\ 1 & 1 & -1 & -1 \end{pmatrix}$$

Similarly, for the 3rd stage, the transfer matrix is–

$$G_3 = H \otimes H = ½ \begin{pmatrix} 1 & 1 & 1 & 1 \\ 1 & -1 & 1 & -1 \\ 1 & 1 & -1 & -1 \\ 1 & -1 & -1 & 1 \end{pmatrix}$$

Finally, the transfer matrix of the entire circuit, G_a is as follows:–

$$G_a = G_3 G_2 G_1 = ¼ \begin{pmatrix} 1 & 1 & 1 & 1 \\ 1 & -1 & 1 & -1 \\ 1 & -1 & -1 & 1 \\ 1 & 1 & -1 & -1 \end{pmatrix} \begin{pmatrix} 1 & 1 & 1 & 1 \\ 1 & -1 & 1 & -1 \\ 1 & -1 & -1 & 1 \\ 1 & 1 & -1 & -1 \end{pmatrix}$$

$$= ¼ \begin{pmatrix} 4 & 0 & 0 & 0 \\ 0 & 0 & 0 & 4 \\ 0 & 0 & 4 & 0 \\ 0 & 4 & 0 & 0 \end{pmatrix}$$

Or we can say that–

$$G_a = \begin{pmatrix} 1 & 0 & 0 & 0 \\ 0 & 0 & 0 & 1 \\ 0 & 0 & 1 & 0 \\ 0 & 1 & 0 & 0 \end{pmatrix}$$

Actually, we can explore the state of the entire circuit, described by vectors in H_4. The input state is–

$$|\xi> = |\psi> \otimes |\varphi> = \begin{pmatrix} \alpha_0 \\ \alpha_1 \end{pmatrix} \otimes \begin{pmatrix} \beta_0 \\ \beta_1 \end{pmatrix} = \begin{pmatrix} \alpha_0\beta_0 \\ \alpha_0\beta_1 \\ \alpha_1\beta_0 \\ \alpha_1\beta_1 \end{pmatrix}$$

Therefore, the state of the 2-qubit system after the 1st stage is as follows:–

$$|\xi_1> = |\psi_1> \otimes |\varphi_1> = 1/\sqrt{2} \begin{pmatrix} \alpha_0 + \alpha_1 \\ \alpha_0 - \alpha_1 \end{pmatrix} \otimes 1/\sqrt{2} \begin{pmatrix} \beta_0 + \beta_1 \\ \beta_0 - \beta_1 \end{pmatrix}$$

or we can write it as–

$$|\xi_1> = ½ \begin{pmatrix} (\alpha_0 + \alpha_1)(\beta_0 + \beta_1) \\ (\alpha_0 + \alpha_1)(\beta_0 - \beta_1) \\ (\alpha_0 - \alpha_1)(\beta_0 + \beta_1) \\ (\alpha_0 - \alpha_1)(\beta_0 - \beta_1) \end{pmatrix}$$

But we know that–

$$|\xi_1\rangle \;=\; G_1\,|\xi\rangle = \tfrac{1}{2}\begin{pmatrix} 1 & 1 & 1 & 1 \\ 1 & -1 & 1 & -1 \\ 1 & 1 & -1 & -1 \\ 1 & -1 & -1 & 1 \end{pmatrix}\begin{pmatrix} \alpha_0\beta_0 \\ \alpha_0\beta_1 \\ \alpha_1\beta_0 \\ \alpha_1\beta_1 \end{pmatrix}$$

Or we can write–

$$|\xi_1\rangle \;=\; \tfrac{1}{2}\begin{pmatrix} (\alpha_0(\beta_0+\beta_1)+(\alpha_1(\beta_0+\beta_1)) \\ (\alpha_0(\beta_0-\beta_1)+(\alpha_1(\beta_0-\beta_1)) \\ (\alpha_0(\beta_0+\beta_1)-(\alpha_1(\beta_0+\beta_1)) \\ (\alpha_0(\beta_0-\beta_1)-(\alpha_1(\beta_0-\beta_1)) \end{pmatrix}$$

Also note that this expression coincides with the expression for $|\xi_1\rangle$ as derived earlier.

Similarly, we can also determine the state of the 2-qubit system after the 2nd and 3rd stage i.e.

$$|\xi_2\rangle \;=\; G_2\,|\xi_1\rangle \qquad\qquad |\xi_3\rangle = G_3\,|\xi_2\rangle$$

What after the 3rd stage? In general, the state after the 3rd stage can also be computed knowing the transfer matrix of the entire circuit, G_a and the input state, $|\xi\rangle$ as follows:–

$$|\xi_3\rangle \;=\; \mathbf{G_a}\,|\xi\rangle$$

Let us now analyze the circuit of fig. 3.25(b). This circuit performs the following **mappings:**

|00> → |00> |01> → |11> |10> → |10> |11> → |01>

Its transfer matrix is as follows:–

$$\mathbf{G_b} \;=\; |00\rangle \rightarrow |00\rangle + |01\rangle \rightarrow |11\rangle + |10\rangle \rightarrow |10\rangle + |11\rangle \rightarrow |01\rangle$$

Or we can write–

$$G_b \;=\; \begin{pmatrix} 1000 \\ 0000 \\ 0000 \\ 0000 \end{pmatrix} + \begin{pmatrix} 0000 \\ 0001 \\ 0000 \\ 0000 \end{pmatrix} + \begin{pmatrix} 0000 \\ 0000 \\ 0010 \\ 0000 \end{pmatrix} + \begin{pmatrix} 1000 \\ 0000 \\ 0000 \\ 0100 \end{pmatrix}$$

Thus, we can finally say that–

$$G_b \;=\; \begin{bmatrix} 1 & 0 & 0 & 0 \\ 0 & 0 & 0 & 1 \\ 0 & 0 & 1 & 0 \\ 0 & 1 & 0 & 0 \end{bmatrix}$$

and $\qquad G_a \;=\; G_b.$

Hence, this proves that both of the circuits in fig. 3.25(a) and (b) are **equivalent.**

The Controlled-H Operation: The quantum circuit for **the Controlled-H Operation** is shown in figure 3.26.

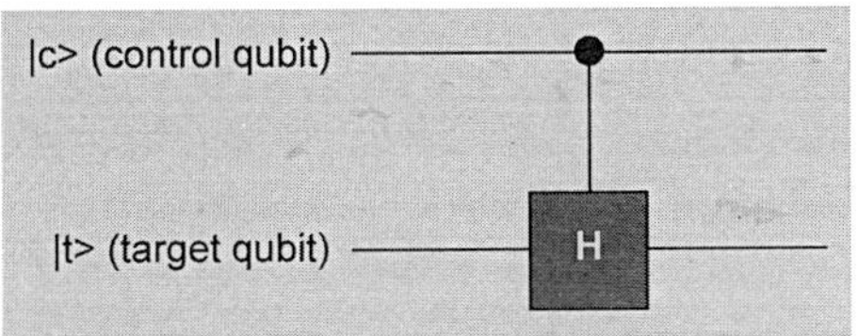

Fig.3.26: Quantum circuit for the controlled-H operation

Working: Here, |c> is the **control qubit** and |t> is the **target qubit.** The working of this quantum circuit is very simple–

if |c> = |0>, **then target qubit, |t> is not changed;**

if |c> = **|1>, then target qubit is set to superposition state;**

if |t> = **|0> then it becomes** $1/\sqrt{2}$ **(|0> + |1>);**

if |t> = **|1> then it becomes** $1/\sqrt{2}$ **(|0> - |1>);**

Also note that the controlled-H gate maps its input to the output as given below:–

|00> → |00>

|01> → |01>

|10> → $1/\sqrt{2}$ **(|10> + |11>)]**

|11> → $1/\sqrt{2}$ **(|10> – |11>)**

The transfer matrix of the circuit of fig. 3.26 is as follows:–

$$G_{controlled\text{-}H} = |00\rangle\langle 00| + |01\rangle\langle 01| + 1/\sqrt{2}\,|10\rangle(\langle 10| + \langle 11|) + 1/\sqrt{2}\,|11\rangle(\langle 10| - \langle 11|).$$

Thus, we can write now–

$$G_{controlled\text{-}H} = \begin{pmatrix} 1 & 0 & 0 & 0 \\ 0 & 1 & 0 & 0 \\ 0 & 0 & 1/\sqrt{2} & 1/\sqrt{2} \\ 0 & 0 & 1/\sqrt{2} & -1/\sqrt{2} \end{pmatrix} = \begin{pmatrix} I_2 & 0 \\ 0 & H \end{pmatrix}$$

The Controlled-R_k Operation:

As we know that the R_k matrix of rotation is given by–

$$R_k = \begin{pmatrix} 1 & 0 \\ 0 & e^{2}\Pi^{i}/2^{k} \end{pmatrix}$$

Let us now draw a **quantum circuit for the controlled- R_k operation.** It is shown in figure-3.37.

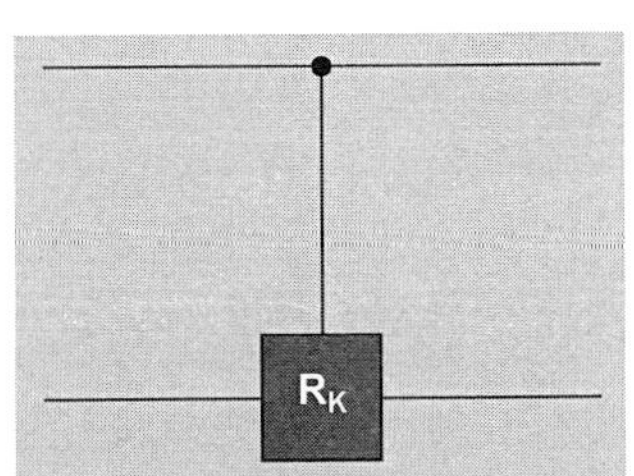

Fig.3.37: Quantum circuit for controlled-R_k operation

The controlled- R_k gate maps its input to the output as follows:–

|00> → |00> |01> → |01>

|10> → |10> |11> → $e^{2\Pi i/2^k}$|11>.

Also note that the transfer matrix of the circuit of fig. 3.37 is as follows:–

$$G_{controlled\text{-}Rk} = |00\rangle\langle 00| + |01\rangle\langle 01| + |10\rangle\langle 10| + e^{2\Pi i/2^k}|11\rangle\langle 11|.$$

Thus, we can write this equation as follows:–

$$G_{controlled\text{-}Rk} = \begin{pmatrix} 1 & 0 & 0 & 0 \\ 0 & 1 & 0 & 0 \\ 0 & 0 & 1 & 0 \\ 0 & 0 & 0 & e^{2}\Pi^{i}/2^{k} \end{pmatrix}$$

The Controlled-P Operation: First of all we draw the quantum circuit for **The Controlled-P Operation and its equivalent phase shift circuit,** as in figure- 3.38(a) and (b).

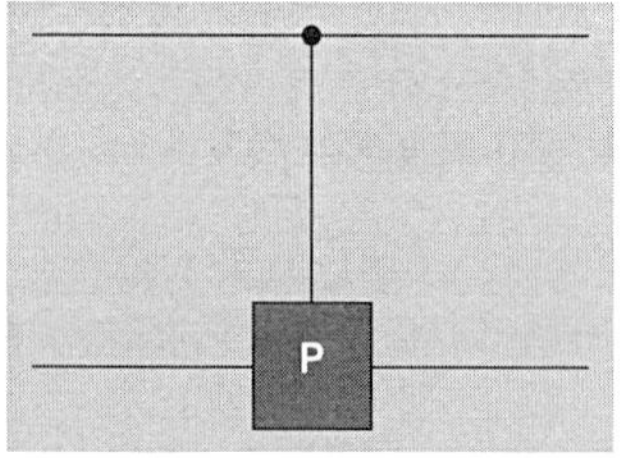

(a) Quantum circuit for controlled-P operation

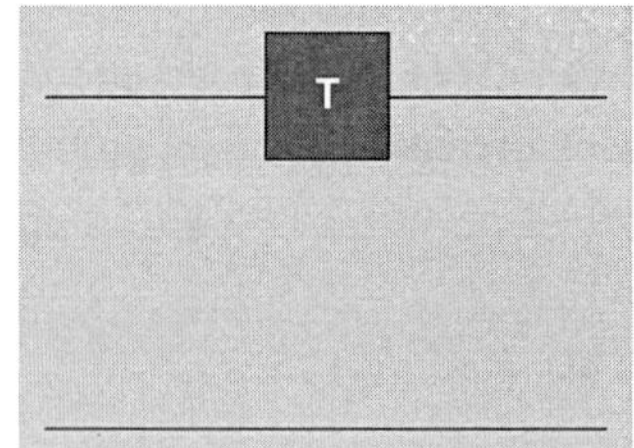

(b) Equivalent phase shift Quantum circuit for controlled- P operation

Fig. 3.38

If $\mathbf{P}_\alpha$ **is a phase shift and** $\mathbf{T}_\alpha$ **is a phase transformation** then we can write–

$$P_\alpha = \begin{pmatrix} e^{i\alpha} & 0 \\ 0 & e^{i\alpha} \end{pmatrix}$$

And

$$T_\alpha = \begin{pmatrix} 1 & 0 \\ 0 & e^{i\alpha} \end{pmatrix}$$

The point to ponder is that the quantum circuit of fig. 3.38 (a) i.e. a controlled-P circuit, performs the following transformations on its input qubits:–

$|00\rangle \rightarrow |00\rangle$ $\quad |01\rangle \rightarrow |01\rangle$ $\quad |10\rangle \rightarrow e^{i\alpha}|10\rangle$ $\quad |11\rangle \rightarrow e^{i\alpha}|11\rangle$

Also note that the transfer matrix of the controlled-P gate quantum circuit is as follows:

$$G_{controlled\text{-}P} = |00\rangle\langle 00| + |01\rangle\langle 01| + e^{i\alpha}|10\rangle\langle 10| + e^{i\alpha}|11\rangle\langle 11|.$$

Thus, we can write this equation as follows:–

$$G_{controlled\text{-}P} = \begin{pmatrix} 1 & 0 & 0 & 0 \\ 0 & 1 & 0 & 0 \\ 0 & 0 & e^{i\alpha} & 0 \\ 0 & 0 & 0 & e^{i\alpha} \end{pmatrix}$$

On the other hand, **the transfer matrix of quantum circuit of fig. 3.38 (b)** is as follows:–

$$G_{T\alpha} = T_\alpha \otimes I = \begin{pmatrix} 1 & 0 \\ 0 & e^{i\alpha} \end{pmatrix} \otimes \begin{pmatrix} 1 & 0 \\ 0 & 1 \end{pmatrix} = \begin{pmatrix} 1 & 0 & 0 & 0 \\ 0 & 1 & 0 & 0 \\ 0 & 0 & e^{i\alpha} & 0 \\ 0 & 0 & 0 & e^{i\alpha} \end{pmatrix}$$

This transfer matrix is same as $G_{controlled\text{-}P}$, the transfer matrix of the circuit in fig. 3.38 (a). **Thus, we can say that the two circuits are equivalent.**

Now consider a generic single qubit controlled gate with matrix, U (see fig. 3.39 (a)).

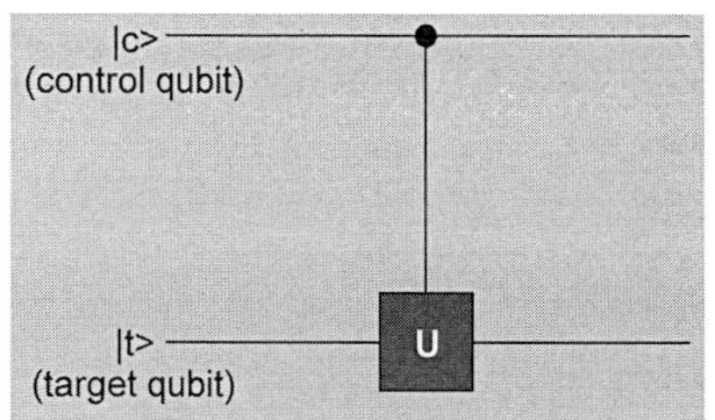

(a) Generic single qubit controlled gate with matrix, U = Aσx Bσx C.

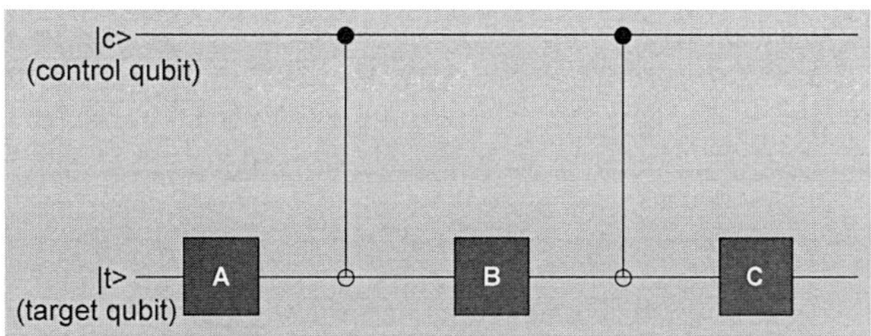

(b) A circuit simulating the generic single qubit controlled gate as in 3.39 (a).

Fig. 3.39

Also fig. 3.39 (b) simulates the general 1-qubit controlled gate as shown in fig. 3.39 (a) wherein A, B and C are the rotation matrices, as defined earlier.

Working: Two cases arise:

Case-1: when the control qubit is |c> = |0>, then the target qubit becomes–

$$|t> \rightarrow ABC\,|t> = I\,|t> = |t>$$

Case-2: when the control qubit is |c> = |1>, then the target qubit becomes–

$$|t> \rightarrow A\,\sigma_x\,B\,\sigma_x\,C\,|t> = U\,|t>$$

This is so because ABC = I and U = A σ_x B σ_x C according to the last proposition done.

3.11.2 Multiple-qubit controlled operations

Problem: Consider a circuit performing a unitary transformation, U, with n control qubits as $|c_0>, |c_1>, |c_2> ..., |c_{n-1}>$ and k target qubits as $|t_0>|t_1>|t_2> ... |t_{k-1}>$ at the input. We need to design an n-qubit controlled, single target qubit unitary function quantum circuit. Then, we need to design an n-qubit controlled, k-target qubit quantum circuit. Use unitary transformation, U, and apply it to the k target qubits.

Solution: Let us draw its circuit diagram first.

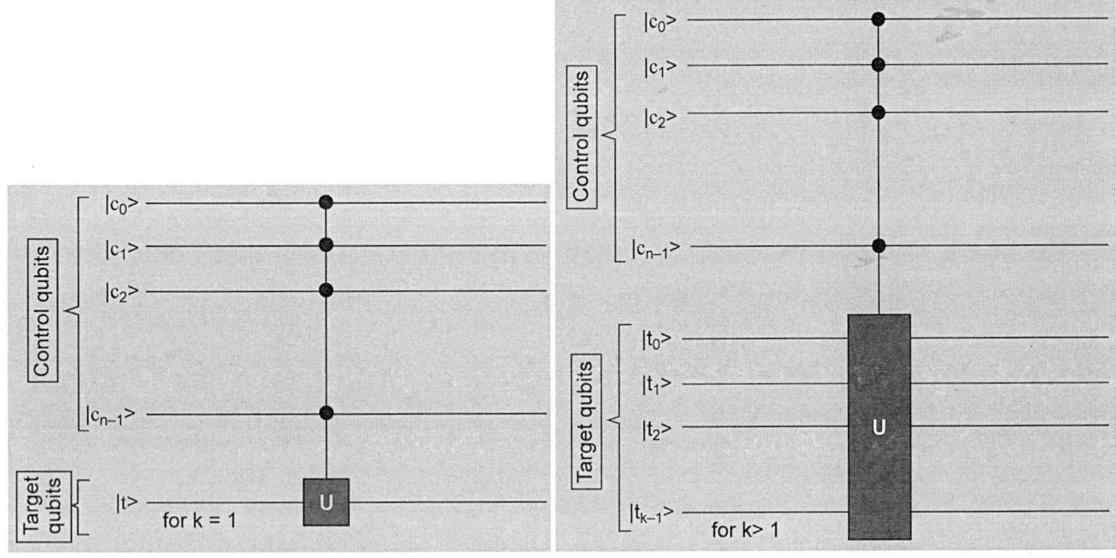

(a) An n-qubit controlled, single target qubit unitary function quantum circuit

(b) An n-qubit controlled, k-target qubit quantum circuit, Unitary transformation, U, is applied to k-target qubits

Fig. 3.40

Also shown in fig. 3.40 (b) is an n-qubit controlled, k-target qubit quantum circuit. The Unitary transformation, u, is applied to the k target qubits.

Explanations: Figure 3.40 (a) shows the case when k = 1. For n = 2, the unitary operator, U, has a matrix, U given by–

$$U = \begin{pmatrix} u_{00} & u_{01} \\ u_{10} & u_{11} \end{pmatrix}$$

When all controlled qubits of the circuit in Fig. 3.40 (a) are set to 1, we apply the transformation to the target qubit, $|t\rangle = \alpha_0\,|0\rangle + \alpha_1\,|1\rangle$.

When the logical product, AND, of all control qubits is not 1, we transfer directly the qubits to the output of the circuit.

Using **Feynman's notation,** we define the **operator for this quantum circuit acting upon (n + 1) qubits with n control qubits,** $|c_0\rangle, |c_1\rangle, |c_2\rangle, \ldots, |c_{n-1}\rangle$ and **one target qubit** $|t\rangle$ as follows:–

(formal definition)

$$\Lambda_n(U)\,(|c_0\, c_1 \ldots\ldots C_{n-1} t\rangle = \begin{cases} |c_0 c_1 c_2 \ldots c_{n-1} t\rangle & \text{if } \mathbf{\Lambda}_{j=0 \text{ to } n-1}(c_j) = 0 \\ \alpha_0\,|c_0 c_1 c_2 \ldots c_{n-2} 0\rangle + \alpha_1\,|c_0 c_1 c_2 \ldots c_{n-1} 1\rangle & \text{if } \mathbf{\Lambda}_{j=0 \text{ to } n-1}(c_j) = 1 \end{cases}$$

Please note that the notation if $\Lambda_{j=0 \text{ to } n-1}(c_j) = 1$ **means that** c_0 **AND** c_1 **AND** $c_2 \ldots\ldots c_{n-2}$ **AND** c_{n-1} **= 1. Also note that the transfer matrix of the circuit is as follows:**

$$\begin{pmatrix} 1 & 0... & 0 & 0 & 0 \\ 0 & 1 & 0 & 0 & 0 \\ \hline 0 & 0... & 1 & 0 & 0 \\ 0 & 0... & 0 & u_{00} & u_{01} \\ 0 & 0... & 0 & u_{10} & u_{11} \end{pmatrix}$$

Figure 3.40 (b) shows the case when k > 1 target qubits. To put it in a proper light, an alternative notation for multiple-qubit controlled operation is $C^n (U_k)$ where n is the number of control qubits and k is the number of target qubits. Now, the Unitary transformation, U_k is applied to the target qubits when the control condition is satisfied.

Say, $U^{c0\,c1\,...\,cn-1} | t_1 t_2 ... t_k>$ represents that the transformation U is applied to the target qubits only if the logical product of $c_0\ c_1\ ...\ c_{n-1}$ **is equal to one. Therefore, the transformation is–**

$C^n (U_k) | c_0\ c_1 ... c_{n-1} > | t_0\ t_1 ... t_{k-1}> = | c_0\ c_1 ... c_{n-1}> U^{c0\,c1\,...\,cn-1} | t_1\ t_2 ... t_k>$.

To further understand the multiple-qubit controlled operations, we construct a quantum circuit using **Toffoli gates, with n = 6 control qubits labeled as** $| c_1>$, $| c_2>$,$| c_3>$, $| c_4>$,$| c_5>$ and $| c_6>$ and **one target qubit as |t>.** We draw now a general circuit that can be **used for any number, n, of control qubits. Also, this circuit has an additional (n – 1) work qubits as $|w_1>$, $|w_2>$,$|w_3>$,$|w_4>$, and $|w_5>$ initially in state |0>. At the end of the computation, the work qubits are returned to state |0>.** (see fig. 3.41).

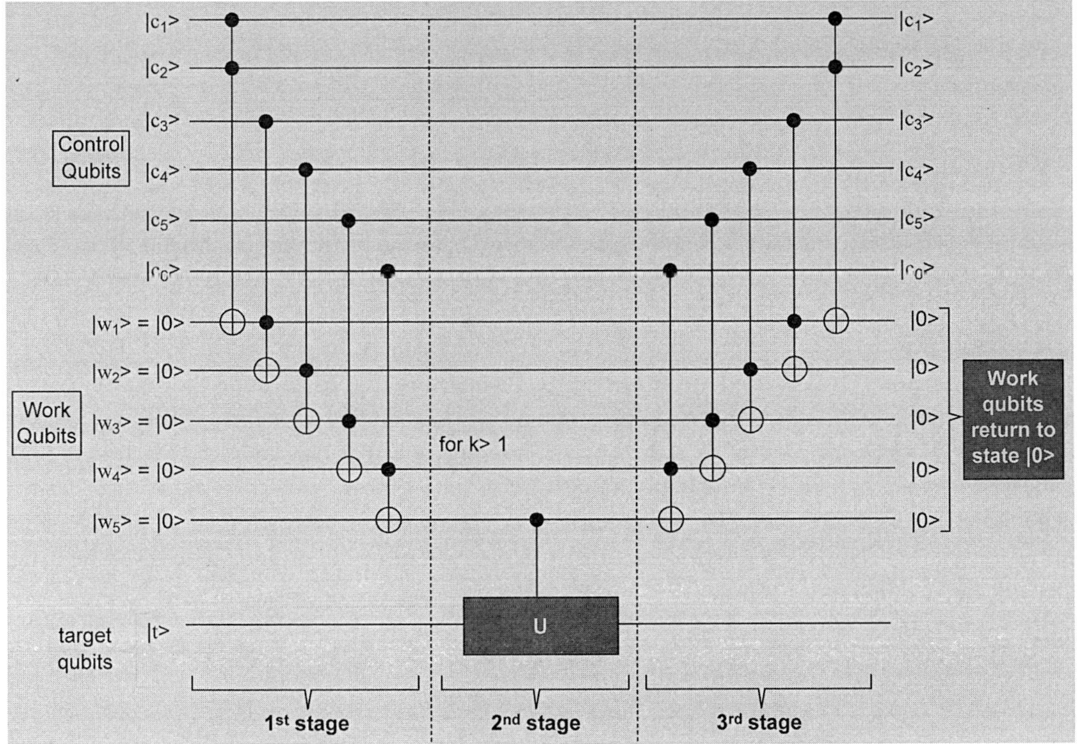

Fig.3.41: 6-qubit controlled circuit with 5 work qubits and one target qubit subjected to Unitary transformation, U and implemented with Toffoli gates.

Working: Let us understand this circuit stage-by-stage.

Stage-1: 1st stage produces the logical product, AND of all the 6 control qubits in one of the work qubits in, $|w_5>$.

Stage-2: 2nd stage performs a single qubit U-controlled transformation of the target qubit.

Stage-3: 3rd stage (final stage) returns all work qubits i.e. $|w_1>$, $|w_2>$, $|w_3>$,$|w_4>$ and $|w_5>$ **to their original state, $|0>$.**

Let us verify the 1st stage. We observe that the 1st Toffoli gate from left ANDs **$|c_1>$ and $|c_2>$ and changes the state of $|w_1>$ from $|0>$ to $|c_1\ c_2>$. The next Toffoli gate changes the state of $|w_2>$ from $|0>$ to $|c_1\ c_2\ c_3>$ and so on. The point to ponder is that we are only interested in Reversible Quantum circuits. Hence we should return the work qubits to their original state.**

Let us now show that the last work qubit, $|w_5>$, is set to $|0>$. The 1st Toffoli gate of the 3rd stage of the circuit (see fig. 3.41) performs the following operations:

$|w_5>$ AND [($|c_1>$ AND $|c_2>$ ... AND $|c_6>$) AND ($|c_1>$ AND $|c_2>$ ... AND $|c_6>$)] = $|w_5>$

Before we discuss further, let us solve some examples now.

Example 1: In the quantum circuit of fig. 1, the control qubit is in a superposition of $|0>$ and $|1>$.

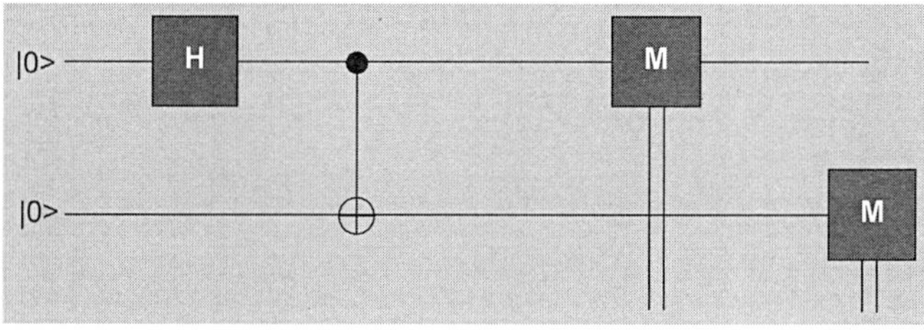

What is the effect of a CNOT gate?

Solution 1: From the circuit, we find that **before the CNOT operation** (in ket notation), the control qubit is in the $1/\sqrt{2}\ |0> + 1/v\ |1>$ state, while the target qubit is in the $|0>$ state. Hence, the 2-qubit input state is $1/\sqrt{2}\ |00> + 1/\sqrt{2}\ |01>$. **Applying the rules for the CNOT,** the 1st state $|00>$ does not change as the control qubit is $|0>$. However, for the 2nd state $|01>$, **the control qubit is $|1>$ and so the target qubit is flips from $|0>$ to $|1>$.** The **result** of the CNOT gate is the state $1/\sqrt{2}\ |00> + 1/\sqrt{2}\ |11>$. **This is a special state and is called as the Bell state. Please note that the 2-qubits are entangled after the CNOT.** This state can't be written as the product of two separate qubits. As with the single-qubit gates, the CNOT gate operates on all states in the superposition. For e.g. the CNOT gate acts on the four basis states of a 2-qubit system simultaneously. **Also note that the quantum algorithms leverage this parallelism to ensure speed improvements over classical computers.** Furthermore, as with all quantum gates, **the CNOT is reversible meaning the operation can be undone which can be used to figure out the original qubit states.**

Example 2: Predict the state produced by these quantum circuits:-

(a)

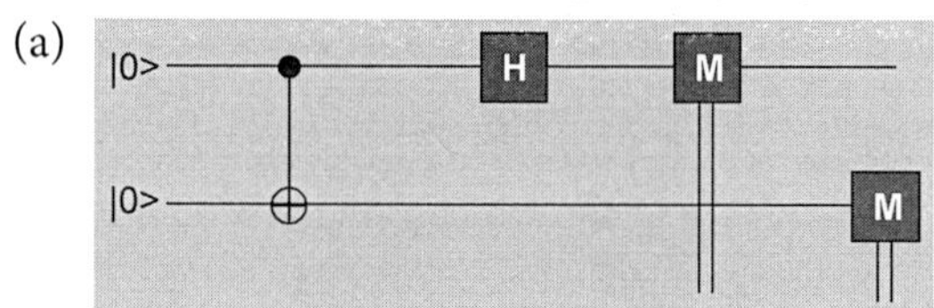

(b)

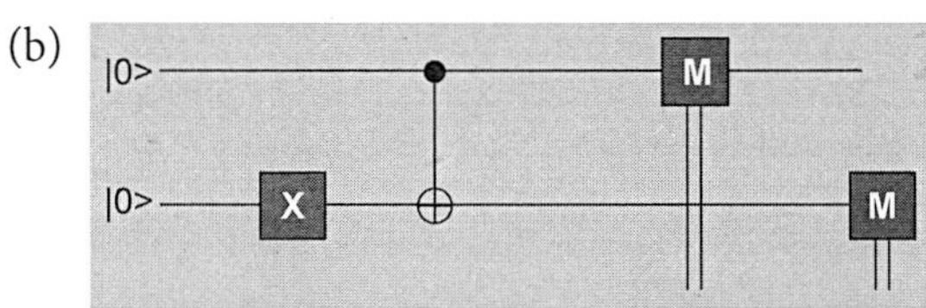

(c)

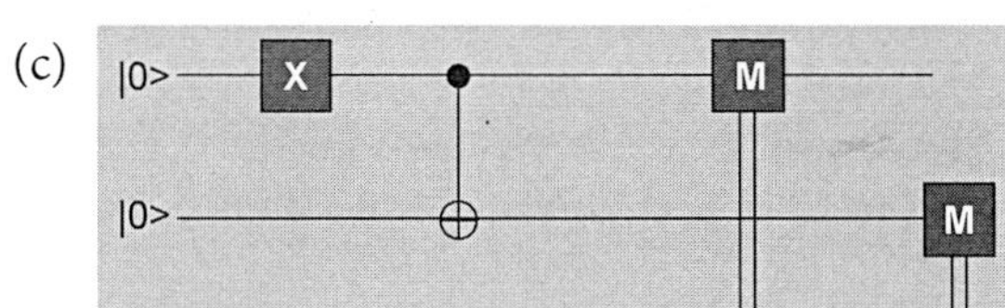

(d)

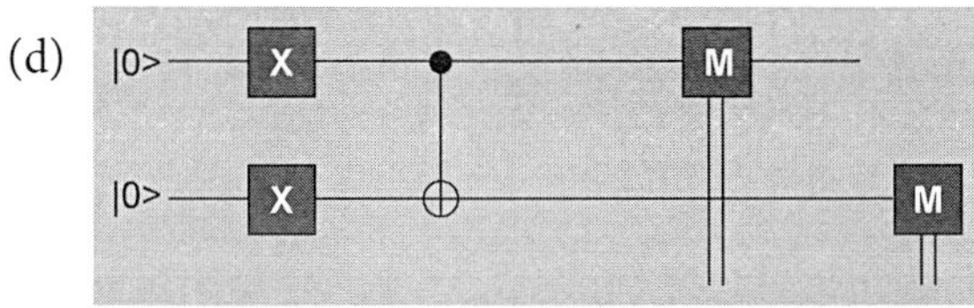

Solution 2: We have to observe that which qubit is the control qubit.

(a) |01> (b) |10> (c) |11> (d) |01>

Example 3: Predict the state produced by these quantum circuits:–

(a)

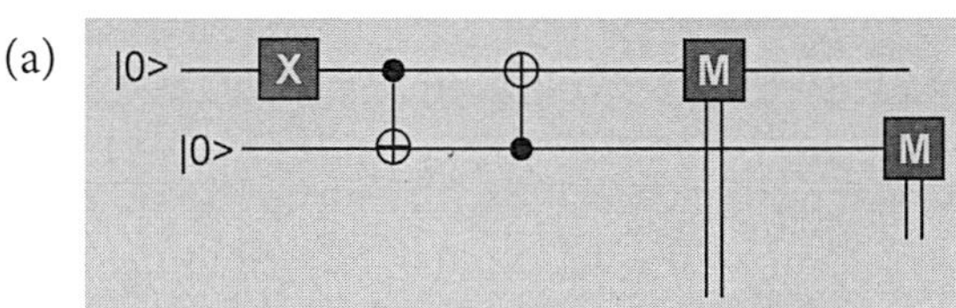

(b)

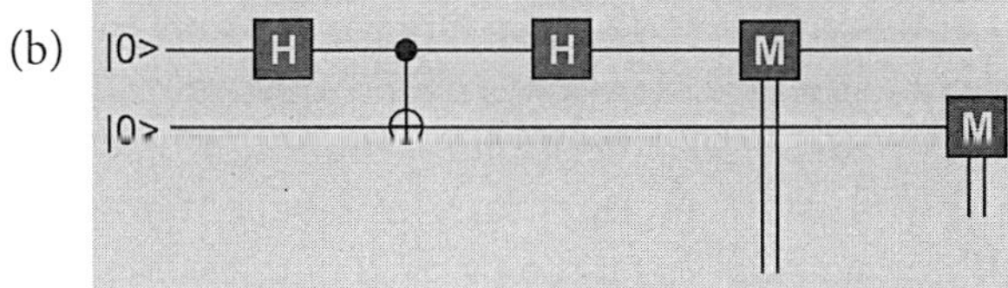

Solution 3: Let us consider the quantum circuit of fig. a first:

(a) Here, **the state changes from the start to the end after every gate as follows:–**

|00> → |01> → |11> → |10>.

(b) Based on these guidelines, the circuit of fig. b gives–

$|00\rangle \ |0\rangle \ (1/\sqrt{2}\ |0\rangle + 1/\sqrt{2}\ |1\rangle) \rightarrow 1/\sqrt{2}\ (|00\rangle + |11\rangle) \rightarrow 1/\sqrt{2}\ |0\rangle\ (1/\sqrt{2}\ |0\rangle + 1/\sqrt{2}\ |1\rangle) + 1/\sqrt{2}\ |1\rangle\ (1/\sqrt{2}\ |0\rangle - 1/\sqrt{2}\ |1\rangle) = \frac{1}{2}(|00\rangle + |01\rangle + |10\rangle - |11\rangle)$.

Example 4: Apply matrix multiplication to show how applying an X–gate flips:

(a) A qubit in the |0> state.

(b) A qubit in the general $|\psi\rangle = \alpha\ |0\rangle + \beta\ |1\rangle$ state.

Solution 4:

(a) $$X|0> = \begin{pmatrix} 0 & 1 \\ 1 & 0 \end{pmatrix} \begin{pmatrix} 1 \\ 0 \end{pmatrix} = \begin{pmatrix} 0 \\ 1 \end{pmatrix} = |1>$$

(b) $$X|\psi> = \begin{pmatrix} 0 & 1 \\ 1 & 0 \end{pmatrix} \begin{pmatrix} \alpha \\ \beta \end{pmatrix} = \begin{pmatrix} \beta \\ \alpha \end{pmatrix} = \beta\,|0> + \alpha\,|1>$$

Example 5: A |0> qubit is passed through a Hadamard gate. We measure the qubit state as |1>. Which of the following choices best describes the result if we perform a measurement on the qubit a second time without reintializing?

(a) |0> **(b) |1>** **(c) 50% chance of |0> or |1>.**

Solution 5: The superposition will collapse into a |1> state after the measurement. Hence, option –b is the right choice.

Example 6: What is a unitary matrix?

Solution 6: Each quantum gate can be mathematically represented as a unitary matrix which acts on qubits.

3.12 PROGRAMMING MODEL FOR A QUANTUM COMPUTING PROGRAM

As we know that classical computers process data by retrieving information from a hard disk and then processing it with digital logic circuits. On the other hand, quantum computers process data by bombarding the information containing molecule with short pulses of radiation. **This process of processing data by bombarding the information containing molecule with short pulses of radiation is called as Bombardment and an algorithmic operation on the data contained within the molecule is represented by a Bombardment Cycle.** When the algorithm terminates, the quantum state of the molecule is measured, a process which itself biases the end result. This intonation is due to a fundamental uncertain nature of quantum mechanics. **Please note that to solve this problem, quantum computing algorithms are run multiple times. And the weighted average of the output asymptotically approaches the correct answer. Also note that because the quantum mechanical phenomena are inherently probabilistic rather than deterministic, a well-defined answer on the 1st try is not possible.**

There are several tools to build and analyze quantum circuits too. **For example, QISKIT by IBM, OCEAN by D-WAVE** etc. But let us see the programming model that is followed by IBM in QISKIT tool.

The programmer's model of Quantum Computing is as follows:–

(a) **Input** of a N-qubit quantum computer is a vector of dimension N containing classic bits 0 and 1.

(b) **Quantum program** (or circuit) is a ($2^n * 2^n$) **unitary matrix** of complex numbers $Q \in C^{2n} * C^{2n}$) that operates on the input to generate the output.

(c) **Output** of a N-qubit computer is also a vector of dimension, N, containing classical bits 0 and 1.

Steps to be followed for quantum programming:–

S1: Create a **quantum program.**

S2: Create **one or more qubits and classical registers to measure the qubits.**

S3: Create a circuit which groups the **qubits in a logical execution unit.**

S4: Apply **quantum gates on the qubits** to achieve a desired result.

S5: **Measure the qubits into the classical register** to collect a final result.

S6: **Compile the program.** This step creates a JSON representation of the program in a specific format that will be explained a bit later.

S7: **Run the simulator or real quantum device.**

S8: Fetch the results.

The output of a quantum circuit is not **deterministic** like our classical computers. **This is so because the probabilities of each output for a given input depend on the program (unitary matrix) it went through.** So, we need to **design the quantum circuit** in such a way that it gives better answers. Then, we calculate the **error bound** for our circuit-based on its design and then determine how many times we have to run the experiment to reach the desired accuracy.

How to derive the probability of each output of a quantum circuit from the input and the circuit?

First of all, we take the classic input vector of dimension, N of 0's and 1's and convert it to a **quantum state vector,** $\overrightarrow{q_{in}}$ of dimension 2^n i.e.,

$$\overrightarrow{q_{in}} \in C^{2n}$$

Then, we multiply it by the program matrix that has a dimension of $(2^n * 2^n)$!

Also note that this initial transformation also transforms the discrete zeroes and ones into complex numbers.

For example, in a 3-qubit quantum computer, the quantum state vector has dimension $2^3 = 8$. The following representation shows all 8 possible conversions from the classic input to the quantum state vector. That is,

000 → 1000 0000 == (1.0, 0.0, 0.0, 0.0, 0.0, 0.0, 0.0, 0.0)

001 → 0100 0000 == (0.0, 1.0, 0.0, 0.0, 0.0, 0.0, 0.0, 0.0)

010 → 0010 0000 == (0.0, 0.0, 1.0, 0.0, 0.0, 0.0, 0.0, 0.0)

011 → 0001 0000 == (0.0, 0.0, 0.0, 1.0, 0.0, 0.0, 0.0, 0.0)

100 → 0000 1000 == (0.0, 0.0, 0.0, 0.0, 1.0, 0.0, 0.0, 0.0)

101 → 0000 0100 == (0.0, 0.0, 0.0, 0.0, 0.0, 1.0, 0.0, 0.0)

110 → 1000 0010 == (0.0, 0.0, 0.0, 0.0, 0.0, 0.0, 1.0, 0.0)

111 → 0000 0001 == (0.0, 0.0, 0.0, 0.0, 0.0, 0.0, 0.0, 1.0)

The points to ponder from this example and the final conclusions are as follows:-

(a) **If the classic input is 000,** then we are sure that all 3 bits are 0. Therefore, the probability of all three 0's is 1.0 and all other possible combinations have 0 probability.

(b) **If the classic input is 001,** then we are certain that bit one and two are 0 and bit three is 1. The probability of that is 1.0 and all others are zero.

Finally, we have our **quantum state vector,** we just multiply it by the unitary matrix, Q, of the quantum circuit and obtain the 2^n dimensional output quantum state vector, $\overrightarrow{q_{out}}$ i.e.,

$$\overrightarrow{q_{out}} = Q\,\overrightarrow{q_{in}}$$

Last but not the least, **the probability of each classical outcome of the measurement is proportional to the square of the length of each entry in the quantum vector** (similar to Schrodinger equation).

For e.g.2: Suppose that the 3 qubit output were–

$$\overrightarrow{q_{out}} = \begin{pmatrix} \sqrt{3}/2 \\ 0.0 \\ \frac{1}{2} \\ 0.0 \\ 0.0 \\ 0.0 \\ 0.0 \\ 0.0 \end{pmatrix}$$

Then, the probability of the 1st and 3rd possible outcomes would be the length of each component squared:–

$$|\sqrt{3}/2|^2 = (\sqrt{3})^2/2 = 3/4 \qquad (\text{as } 3/4 * 100 = 75\%)$$
$$|1^2/2|^2 = 1^2/2 = 1/4 \qquad (\text{as } 1/4 * 100 = 25\%)$$

i.e. 75% for the first and 25% for the 3rd outcomes.

For input–

(a) 1st outcome means 000; all output bits are zero.

(b) 3rd outcome means, 010; 1st and 3rd bits are zero but the 2nd one is 1.

Note: All other outcomes have probability = 0 and hence can't occur e.g. 001 is impossible.

Please keep in mind that the quantum state vector can also contain complex numbers as we are doing quantum mechanics but we just take their magnitude in that case. For e.g. the following quantum state would lead the same probabilities as the previous one–

$$|(1 + \sqrt{2}i)/2|^2 = (1^2 + \sqrt{2}^2)/2^2 = 3/4$$
$$|i/2|^2 = 1^2/2^2 = 1/4$$

Also note the following points from this quantum state vector:–

1. **The input quantum state** is just a **simple state** where we are certain of the values of each classic input bit.
2. The matrix has to be **unitary** as the total probability of all possible outcomes must be 1.0
3. This is true for the input matrix and unitary matrices have the probability of maintaining that property after multiplication.
4. A Quantum Circuit is capable of rapidly doing a unitary matrix multiplication of a huge 2^N sized matrix. To achieve this, we encode our algorithm in that matrix multiplication, considering the probabilistic interpretation of the output. So, we have a better chance of obtaining that **speed-up.**

To put it in a proper light, we can say that at the level of the programmer's model of Quantum Circuits we saw that making a quantum circuit actually comes down to designing one by unitary

matrix only. Currently, the quantum programmers use **quantum logic gates. Also note that these gates are needed to map the matrix to real quantum hardware and all quantum hardware designs so far.** You manipulate a small number of qubits at a time (say, 2) and add more and more such operations (i.e. a modular approach). **The point to ponder is that there are quantum compilers** to increase the portability of the quantum programs. **It is worth mentioning that the programs manually crafted for a specific hardware will be more efficient.** This situation is analogous to what classical digital circuit programmers will do by using smaller logic gates to design more complex circuits rather than directly creating one big, complex and monolithic circuit. Commonly constructed quantum gates with 1, 2 or 3 qubits, as input, is very common. **Please note here that the gates themselves are just unitary matrices that operate on the input qubits and produce the same number of output qubits.**

We are in a position to solve an example now.

Example 1: The matrix for the quantum CNOT gate, which takes 2 qubits as input is–

$$\begin{pmatrix} 1 & 0 & 0 & 0 \\ 0 & 1 & 0 & 0 \\ 0 & 0 & 0 & 1 \\ 0 & 0 & 1 & 0 \end{pmatrix}$$

If we have a 2-qubit gate but an input with more qubits (say, 3 qubits) then what does the 2-qubit gate (4 * 4 matrix) do for the final 3-qubit matrix (8 *8)? In other words, how do we scale quantum gates up to match the total number of qubits?

Solution 1: We just extend the matrix in a way such that the partial measurement of the original small gate qubits leaves all other qubits unaffected. **Classical computers rely on processor registers or memory states all the time.** On the other hand, **quantum programmers can use the classic languages to help describe their quantum programs more easily.** This is done in IBM's QISKIT toolkit wherein you write a Python program that makes QISKIT Library calls that describe the quantum program.

3.13 STEPS PERFORMED ON A CLASSICAL COMPUTER

The basic duty of any processor is to fetch, decode and execute instructions as long as it is powered on. That is,

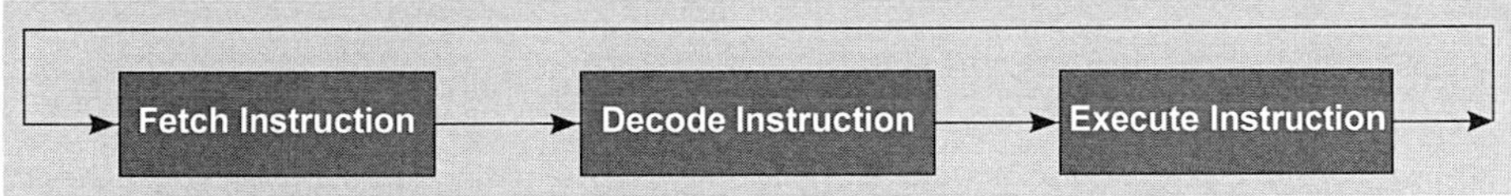

The combination of these three steps is known as an instruction cycle.

The **instruction cycle of a classical computer** follows the following steps: -

S1: Instruction is fetched.

S2: Instruction is decoded.

S3: Operand is fetched.

S4: Instruction is executed.

S5: Store the result.

When you write a computer program to implement an algorithm on a conventional computer, you choose any high-level language like Python, Scala, Julia, Java and so on. Your program will contain some branching statements, for loops, variables etc. so, computer programs are just a sequence of bit-level operations. **Please note that the classical computers are build from Boolean logic gates whereas the quantum computers work on quantum gates and circuits using quantum mechanics principles.**

3.14 STEPS PERFORMED ON A QUANTUM COMPUTER

Steps to be followed for quantum programming: -

S1: Create a **quantum program.**

S2: Create **one or more qubits and classical registers to measure the qubits.**

S3: Create a circuit which groups the **qubits in a logical execution unit.**

S4: Apply **quantum gates on the qubits** to achieve a desired result.

S5: **Measure the qubits into the classical register** to collect a final result.

S6: **Compile the program.** This step creates a JSON representation of the program in a specific format that will be explained a bit later.

S7: **Run the simulator or real quantum device.**

S8: Fetch the results.

The output of a quantum circuit is not **deterministic** like our classical computers. **This is so because the probabilities of each output for a given input depend on the program (unitary matrix) it went through.** So, we need to **design the quantum circuit** in such a way that it gives better answers. Then, we calculate the **error bound** for our circuit-based on its design and then determine how many times we have to run the experiment to reach the desired accuracy.

Let us now create a single qubit, 1 classic register to measure the qubit and then we apply the Pauli X gate (bit flip) n the qubit and finally measure its value.

We write a Python code and use Composer circuit for the same.

```
#################################
Line no. 2      import sys
Line no. 3      import qiskit
Line no. 4      import logging
Line no. 5      from qiskit import Quantum Program
                # Main sub
                def main( ):
                # create a program
Line no. 11     qp = Quantum Program( )
                #create 1 qubit
Line no. 14     quantum_r = qp.create_quantum_register("qr", 1)
                #create 1 classical register
Line no. 17     classical_r = qp.create_classical _register("cr", 1)
                #create a circuit
```

```
Line no. 20    qp.create_circuit("Circuit", [quantum_r], [classical_r])
               # get the circuit by name
               circuit = qp.get_circuit('Circuit')
               # enable logging
Line no 26     qp.enable_logs(logging.DEBUG);
               # Pauli X gate to qubit 1 in the Quantum Register "qr"
Line no. 29    circuit.x(quantum_r[0])
               #measure gate from qubit 0 to classical bit 0
Line no. 32    circuit.measure(quantum_r[0], classical_r[0])
               #backend simulator
Line no. 35    backend = 'local_qasm_simulator'
Line no. 37    #Group of circuits to execute
               circuits = ['Circuit']
               # compile your program
               qobj = qp.compile(circuits, backend)
Line no. 41    # run in simulator
               result = qp.run(qobj, timeout = 240)
               #show result counts
               print (str(result.get_counts('Circuit')))
##########################################################
# Linux :main( )
# windows
if _name_ = = '_main_':
main( )
freeze_support( )
```

Explanation:

Lines 2-5: import the required libraries (like #include files in C/C++): sys(system), qiskit(quantum classes), logging (for debugging) and Quantum Program (the foundation class for all programs.

Line 11: creates a **QuantumProgram. Note that this is the access point to all operations.**

Line 14: In order to create a qubit list, use the quantum program create_quantum_register(NAME, SIZE) system call where NAME is the name of the register list and SIZE is the number of qubits.

Line 17: For each qubit, create a classical register to perform measurement using the system call create_classical_register(NAME, SIZE).

Line 20: Then, **create a circuit with system call create_circuit(NAME, QUANTUM_SET, CLASSIC_SET) where** NAME is the name of the circuit, QUANTUM_SET is a list of qubits and CLASSIC_SET is the list of classic registers. **Also understand that a circuit is a logical unit that holds all qubits and classical registers.**

Line 26: Enable debugging with the system call enable_logs(LEVEL) where LEVEL can be one of logging.DEBUG, logging.INFO etc.

Line 32: Next, **run the qubits through quantum gates and perform measurements on the qubits to collect results. Please note that in this case we apply Pauli X gate which flips the qubit from its ground state |0> to |1>.**

Lines 37–41: Finally, **compile the program and run the simulator (or real device).** In this case, we run in the local Python simulator (local_qasm_simulator).

As every program does, we now **wrap the program in the main function and then call it** with–

if _name_ = = '_main_':

main( )

freeze_support( ) #this line will freeze program to produce executable.

Please note that this is required in Windows because QISKIT executes the program using asynchronous tasks (executors) and when the task fires, the sub-process will execute the main module at startup. Also note that that is why you need to protect the main code to avoid creating sub-processes recursively.

Now, we run the program.

OUTPUT:

INFO: qiskit._jobprocessor: <qiskit._result.Result.Result Object at 0x 000000000D99F470>

{'1': 1024}

Hence, the result is the JSON document {'1' : 1024} where 1 is the **measurement of the qubit** (recall that we use X-gate to flip the bit) and 1024 is the number of iterations of that result. **Also note that the probability of this result is calculated by dividing the number of the result iterations (1024) by the total number of iterations of the program (1024).** So, in this case–

$$P = 1024/1024 = 1$$

Note: Quantum computers are probabilistic machines so all measurements come attached with a probability for that specific result.

Programmers can execute this program on IBM's Q Experience Composer. Composer is an excellent tool to construct simple quantum circuits, execute them and analyze their results.

We shall study more about composer a bit later.

3.15 QUANTUM PARALLELISM AND THE DEUTSCH'S PROBLEM

Traditional/ classical/ conventional computers are able to compute the values of the function, f(x) for a given input, x, in a single time step. Say, x is a binary string of length, n. We now have two extreme choices for computing the value of the function, f(x) for the 2^n possible values of the argument, x as follows:

Choice-1: Use a single copy of the circuit repeatedly and obtain all the values of the function after 2^n time steps.

Choice-2: Use 2^n copies of the circuit each with a different input, x, and obtain all values in a single time step.

On the other hand, quantum circuits have a unique ability to perform the function as explained above i.e. to compute the values of the function, f, for all possible values of the input, x, in a single step and with a single copy of the circuit. **This property of the quantum logic circuits is known as Quantum Parallelism. Note that it can be traced back to the superposition principle and to entanglement. As a natural choice, the state of a quantum system is a superposition of the basis states of the corresponding Hilbert space.**

We start with |x>, a single qubit with two possible values, |0> and |1>. The possible values of the function are |f(x)> = |0> or |f(x)> = |1>. **The point to ponder is that we want to construct a circuit whose output is a superposition of |f(0)> and |f(1)>.** As already studied, that given a function f(x) we can construct a quantum circuit consisting of Fredkin gates only that can transform two qubits, |x> and |y> into |x (y ⊕ f(x))> as shown in figure 3.42 (a). **Please note that the function f(x) is hardwired into the circuit.**

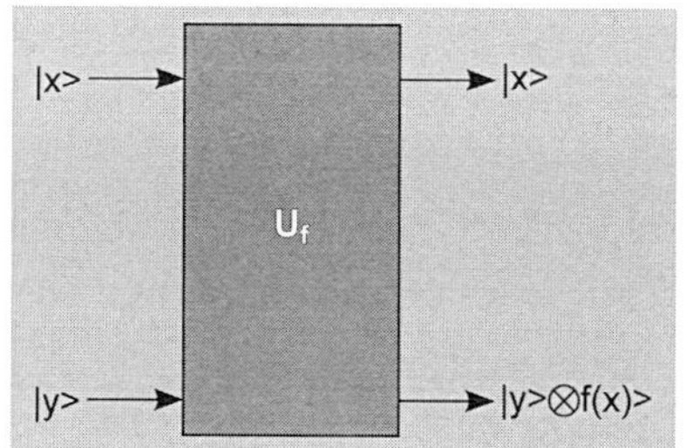

(a) A reversible quantum circuit transforms |xy> → |x(y ⊕ f(x))>

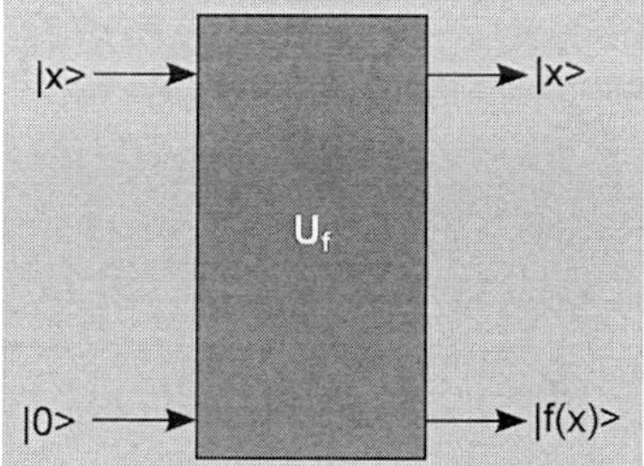

(b) same circuit as in (a) except here |y> = |0>

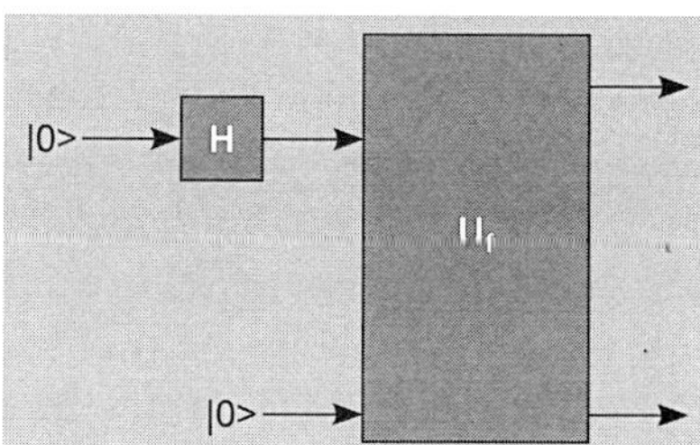

(c) First qubit is in superposition state due to presence of Hadamard gate

Fig.3.42

In fig. 3.42 (b), if the 2nd qubit is set to |0>, then the transformation carried out by the circuit is–

|x 0> → |x f(x)>

Please note that this notation shows that the input is the tensor product of the two vectors representing the states |x> and |0> and that this state is transformed into a state represented by the tensor product of the vectors |x> and |f(x)>. Also note that an equivalent representation using ket vectors is–

|x> |0> → |x> |f(x)>

Now consider figure 3.42 (c). Here, the qubit in state |0> is applied first to a Hadamard gate and the output of the Hadamard gate, $(|0> + |1>)/\sqrt{2}$ is then applied to the circuit of fig. 3.42 (c). The two output qubits of the circuit are–

$$(|0> + |1>)/\sqrt{2})$$

And $$f((|0> + |1>)/\sqrt{2}) = (|f(0)> + | f(1)>)/\sqrt{2}$$

Keep in mind that the output state of the quantum system is obtained as the tensor product of these two vectors as follows:

$$(|0\ f(0)> + |0\ f(1)> + |1\ f(0)> + |1\ f(1)>)/2$$

Thus, the output state contains the information about | f(0)> and |f(1)>. This property of the quantum circuits is known as quantum parallelism. And that this result can be extended to an input consisting of, say, m qubits. Now we need **a quantum circuit to transform an m-dimensional vector |x> into |f(x)>.** Furthermore, as analogy, **the m-qubits have to be applied in a superposition state using m Hadamard gates. Such a circuit transforming the m-qubits is a quantum gate array** It is shown in figure-3.43.

Fig. 3.34 shows a quantum gate array characterized by a linear transformation (U_f).

Inputs to this gate array: |x> ϵ $H_2{}^m$ that is a 2^m – dimensional vector acting as a **control input. The 2nd input is |y> ϵ $H_2{}^k$** that is a 2^k – dimensional vector acting as a **work or ancilla qubit.**

Outputs from this gate array: |x> and |y $\oplus$ f(x)> ϵ $H_2{}^n$ with n = (m + k).

Please note that when |y> = |0>, the 2nd output becomes |y $\oplus$ f(x)> = **|f(x)>.** Assume that the input vector |x> is in superposition state. Also assume that it can be expressed as a linear combination of 2^m vectors forming an orthogonal basis in $H_2{}^m$. **The gate array performs a linear transformation.** So, now onwards, the transformation is applied to all basis vectors used to express the **input superposition simultaneously.** And that it generates a **superposition of results.** In other words, the values of the function, f(x), for the 2^m possible values of its argument, x, are computed simultaneously. **The point to ponder is that quantum computers can provide an exponential increase of computational space for a linear increase in physical space. Also note that quantum parallelism permits us to construct the entire truth table of a quantum gate array having 2^n entries in a single time step.** On the other hand, in a classical system, **we can compute the truth table in one time step with 2^n gate arrays running in parallel or we can say that we need 2^n time steps with a single gate array.**

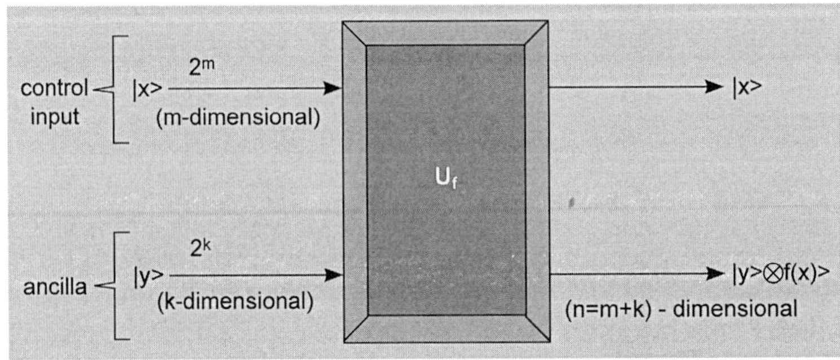

Fig.3.43: Shows the transformation, Uf: |xy> → |x(y $\oplus$ f(x))> performed by Quantum Gate Array

Actually, we need some level of **algorithmic complexity to exploit the quantum parallelism.** We **start with n-qubits, each in state |0>.** Then we apply a Walsh-Hadamard Transform. Also we have already studied that **each qubit is transformed by a Hadamard gate and that the Hadamard gate transforms |0> as below:-**

$$H : |0> \rightarrow (|0> + |1>)/\sqrt{2}$$

That is, |0> is transformed into a superposition state now with the application of Hadamard gate. Thus, we can write that–

$$(H \otimes H \ldots \otimes H) \mid 00 \ldots 0> \;=\; (|0> + |1>) \otimes (|0> + |1>) \ldots (|0> + |1>)/(\sqrt{2})^n$$
$$= 1/\sqrt{2}^n \, \Sigma_{j = 0 \text{ to } 2}{}^{n-1} \, |j>$$

Now, **the output of the gate array when we add a k-bit register to the superposition state of integers in the range 0 to $2^n - 1$ with n = m + k is as follows:-**

$$U_f \, (1/\sqrt{2}^n \, \Sigma(_{x = 0 \text{ to } 2}{}^n - 1) \, |x\, 0>) \;=\; 1/\sqrt{2}^n \, \Sigma \, (_{x = 0 \text{ to } 2}{}^n - 1) \, U_f \, |x\, 0>)$$
$$= 1/c^n \, \Sigma \, (_{x = 0 \text{ to } 2}{}^n - 1) \, |x \, f(x)>$$

Hence, when we measure the output of the quantum gate array we can only observe one value.

Before we go further, let us solve a very popular problem of Quantum Parallelism i.e. The Deutsch's Problem.

Example 1: (Deutsch's Problem): "Consider a black box characterized by a transfer function that maps a single input bit, x into an output, f(x). The transformation performed by the black box, f(x), is a general function and might not be invertible. We assume that it takes the same amount of time, T, to carry out each of the four possible mappings performed by the transfer function, f(x) of the black box–

$$f(0) = 0, f(0) = 1, f(1) = 0 \text{ and } f(1) = 1$$

and it takes no time to compare the results. The problem posed by David Deutsch is to distinguish if f(0) = f(1) or f(0) ≠ f(1)."

Solution 1: This problem can be solved on a classical computer and/or on a quantum computer. Two cases arise:-

Case-1: When using a classical computer, one way is to compute **sequentially** f(0) and f(1) and then compare the results, **for a total time 2T.** This is shown in figure 3.44(a). A **classical parallel solution** is also shown in figure 3.44(b).

A parallel solution is–

A **classical parallel solution is shown in figure 3.44 (b)** wherein we have two replicas of the circuit. **We feed 0 as input to one of the replicas of the black box and 1 to the other.** There, we **compare the partial results.** Now, we obtain the answer after time, T, but we need two copies of the system rather than one. This is actually, classical parallelism example.

Case-2: Now we consider a quantum computer with a transfer function, U_f that takes as input two qubits |x> (control) and |y> (target) and two outputs as |x> and |y ⊕ f(x)>. We have an option of selecting the states of the two qubits |x> and |y>.

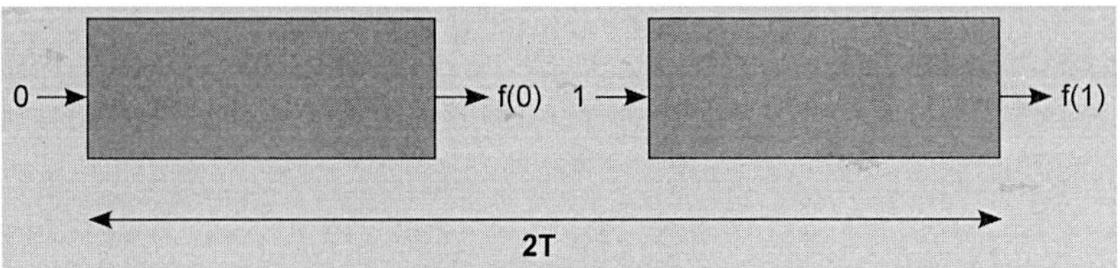

(a) A Sequential Solution to Deutsch's problem using a single copy of a classical circuit to compute f(x)

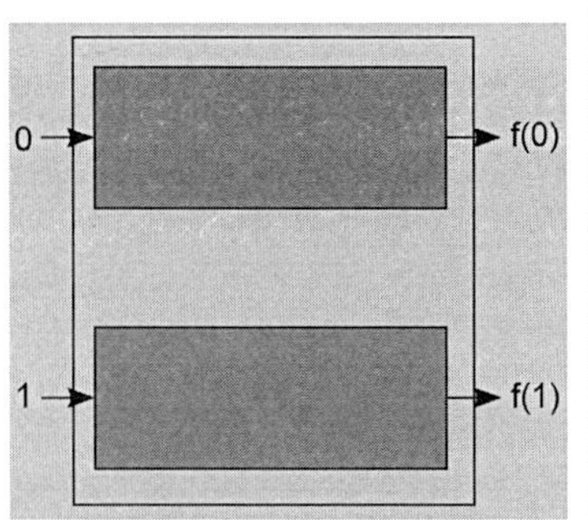

(b) A Parallel Solution to Deutsch's problem using a two copies of classical circuit to compute f(x)

2-qubits
(Control qubit) |x>
|x>=1/√2 |0>+1/√2 |1>
(target qubit) |y>
|y> = |0>
U_f
T
Outputs
|x>
|y⊕f(x)>
|ψ>

(c) Quantum black box with a transfer function, U_f; evaluates to f(0) and f(1) simultaneously.

Fig.3.44

Note that we now have a choice of selecting 1st qubit in the state |x> = (|0> + |1>)/$\sqrt{2}$ and the 2nd qubit in the state |y> = (|0> – |1>)/$\sqrt{2}$ and the 2nd qubit in the state |y> = (|0> – |1>)/$\sqrt{2}$. This is shown in figure 3.44(c).

We prove that the 1st output qubit of the circuit is |f(0) ⊕ f(1)>. Therefore, when f(0) = f(1) this qubit is |0> (as 0 ⊕ 0 = 0 and 1 ⊕ 0 = 1). When f(0) ≠ f(1) then this qubit is |1> (as 0 ⊕ 1 = 1 and 1 ⊕ 0 = 1).

Solution to Deutsch's problem: In order to compute the output state of this circuit, we need to consider the four stages of this circuit. We also examine the four vectors, $|\xi_0>$, $|\xi_1>$,$|\xi_2>$ and $|\xi_3>$ describing the state of the system at each stage. This is shown in figure 3.45.

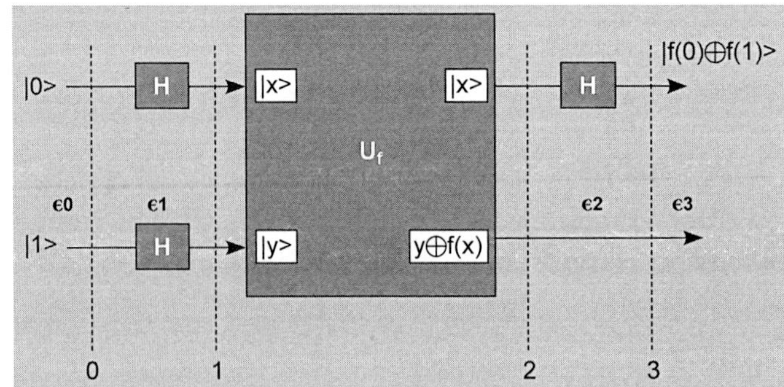

Fig.3.45: Quantum circuit to solve Deutsch's problem

The **first output qubit** of the circuit is $|f(0) \oplus f(1)>$. Hence, if $f(0) = f(1)$ then this qubit is $|0>$ and if $f(0) \neq f(1)$ then this qubit is $|1>$. **The input state is $|\xi_0>$, the state after the Hadamard gate is $|\xi_1>$, the output state of the circuit implementing U_f is $|\xi_2>$ and the output state of the circuit is $|\xi_3>$.**

The **input vector is** as given below:-

$$|\xi_0> = |01> = \begin{pmatrix}1\\0\end{pmatrix} \otimes \begin{pmatrix}0\\1\end{pmatrix} = \begin{pmatrix}0\\1\\0\\0\end{pmatrix}$$

The **transfer matrix of the 1st stage is–**

$$G_1 = H \otimes H = 1/\sqrt{2}\begin{pmatrix}1 & 1\\1 & -1\end{pmatrix} \otimes 1/\sqrt{2}\begin{pmatrix}1 & 1\\1 & -1\end{pmatrix} = 1/2\begin{pmatrix}1 & 1 & 1 & 1\\1 & -1 & 1 & -1\\1 & 1 & -1 & -1\\1 & -1 & -1 & 1\end{pmatrix}$$

Therefore, we can write–

$$|\xi_1> = G_1\,|\xi_0> = 1/2\begin{pmatrix}1 & 1 & 1 & 1\\1 & -1 & 1 & -1\\1 & 1 & -1 & -1\\1 & -1 & -1 & 1\end{pmatrix}\begin{pmatrix}0\\1\\0\\0\end{pmatrix} = 1/2\begin{pmatrix}1\\-1\\1\\-1\end{pmatrix}$$

Or we can rewrite it as follows:-

$$|\xi_1> = \tfrac{1}{2}\,(|00> - |01> + |10> - |11>)$$
$$= [(|0> + |1>)/\sqrt{2}]\,[(|0> - |1>)/\sqrt{2}]$$

The **2 qubits applied to the input of the black box** are as follows:-

$$|x> = (|0> + |1>)/\sqrt{2} \quad \text{and} \quad |y> = (|0> - |1>)/\sqrt{2}$$

But we know that $\quad |0 \oplus f(x)> = |f(x)>$

So, we can write now–

$$|y \oplus f(x)> = (|f(x)> - |1 \oplus f(x)>)/\sqrt{2}$$

But $|1 \oplus f(x)>$ is equal to $|0>$ when $f(x) = 1$ and it is equal to $|1>$ when $f(x) = 0$.

$$|y \oplus f(x)> = \begin{cases} (|0> - |1>)/\sqrt{2} & \text{if } f(x) = 0 \\ -(|0> - |1>)/\sqrt{2} & \text{if } f(x) = 1 \end{cases}$$

Hence, we can write that–

$$|y \oplus f(x)> = (-1)^{f(x)}\,(|0> - |1>)/\sqrt{2}$$

Please note that when $f(0) = f(1)$, the state of the 2 output qubits of the black box,

$|x\rangle \otimes |y \oplus f(x)\rangle$ is as follows:

$$|\xi_2\rangle = \begin{cases} (|0\rangle + |1\rangle/\sqrt{2})(|0\rangle - |1\rangle/\sqrt{2}) \rightarrow 1/2\begin{pmatrix} 1 \\ -1 \\ 1 \\ -1 \end{pmatrix} & \text{if } f(0) = f(1) = 0 \\ -(|0\rangle + |1\rangle/\sqrt{2})(|0\rangle - |1\rangle/\sqrt{2}) \rightarrow -1/2\begin{pmatrix} 1 \\ -1 \\ 1 \\ -1 \end{pmatrix} & \text{if } f(0) = f(1) = 0 \end{cases}$$

The students can also prove that if $f(0) \neq f(1)$, then the output of the black box is as given below:–

$$|\xi_2\rangle = \begin{cases} (|0\rangle - |1\rangle/\sqrt{2})(|0\rangle - |1\rangle/\sqrt{2}) \rightarrow 1/2\begin{pmatrix} 1 \\ -1 \\ -1 \\ 1 \end{pmatrix} & \text{if } f(0) = 0 \text{ and } f(1) = 1 \\ -(|0\rangle - |1\rangle/\sqrt{2})(|0\rangle - |1\rangle/\sqrt{2}) \rightarrow -1/2\begin{pmatrix} 1 \\ -1 \\ -1 \\ 1 \end{pmatrix} & \text{if } f(0) = 1 \text{ and } f(1) = 0 \end{cases}$$

We can now combine these two results and so we get–

$$|\xi_2\rangle = \begin{cases} \pm(|0\rangle + |1\rangle/\sqrt{2})(|0\rangle - |1\rangle/\sqrt{2}) \rightarrow \pm 1/2\begin{pmatrix} 1 \\ -1 \\ 1 \\ -1 \end{pmatrix} & \text{if } f(0) = f(1) \\ \pm(|0\rangle - |1\rangle/\sqrt{2})(|0\rangle - |1\rangle/\sqrt{2}) \rightarrow \pm 1/2\begin{pmatrix} 1 \\ -1 \\ -1 \\ 1 \end{pmatrix} & \text{if } f(0) \neq f(1) \end{cases}$$

Similarly, we now derive the **transfer matrix 3rd stage of the quantum circuit** of figure 3.45 as follows:–

$$\mathbf{G_3 = H \otimes I} = 1/\sqrt{2}\begin{pmatrix} 1 & 1 \\ 1 & -1 \end{pmatrix} \otimes \begin{pmatrix} 1 & 0 \\ 0 & 1 \end{pmatrix} = 1/2\begin{pmatrix} 1 & 0 & 1 & 0 \\ 0 & 1 & 0 & 1 \\ 1 & 0 & -1 & 0 \\ 0 & 1 & 0 & -1 \end{pmatrix}$$

Now two cases arise–

Case-1: If f(0) = f(1), then we can say–

$$|\xi_3> = \pm 1/\sqrt{2}\begin{pmatrix} 1 & 0 & 1 & 0 \\ 0 & 1 & 0 & 1 \\ 1 & 0 & -1 & 0 \\ 0 & 1 & 0 & -1 \end{pmatrix} 1/2 \begin{pmatrix} 1 \\ -1 \\ 1 \\ -1 \end{pmatrix} = \pm 1/\sqrt{2}\begin{pmatrix} 1 \\ -1 \\ 0 \\ 0 \end{pmatrix}$$

$$= \pm |0> |0> - |1>/\sqrt{2}$$

Case-2: If f(0) ≠ f(1), then we can say–

$$|\xi_3> = \pm 1/\sqrt{2}\begin{pmatrix} 1 & 0 & 1 & 0 \\ 0 & 1 & 0 & 1 \\ 1 & 0 & -1 & 0 \\ 0 & 1 & 0 & -1 \end{pmatrix} 1/2 \begin{pmatrix} 1 \\ -1 \\ -1 \\ 1 \end{pmatrix} = \pm 1/\sqrt{2}\begin{pmatrix} 0 \\ 0 \\ 1 \\ -1 \end{pmatrix}$$

$$= + |1> (|0> - |1>/\sqrt{2})$$

Conclusions and Results:

On observing **the 1st output qubit of the quantum circuit, we conclude that f(0) = f(1) when the qubit is |0> and f(0) ≠ f(1) when the qubit is |1>.** In nutshell,

$$f(0) \oplus f(1) = \begin{cases} 0 & \text{if} \quad f(0) = f(1) \\ 1 & \text{if} \quad f(0) \neq f(1) \end{cases}$$

Hence, in final form we can re-write $|\xi_3>$ as–

$$|\xi_3> = \pm |f(0) \oplus f(1)> (|0> - |1>/\sqrt{2})$$

Also note that by measuring the 1st output qubit of the circuit we are able to determine $f(0) \oplus f(1)$ after performing a single evaluation of the function, f(x).

Quantum parallelism allows us to evaluate a function for many different values of the inputs simultaneously. Say, we have a function, f(x) where x takes in n number of different values. By developing a suitable unitary transform, one can evaluate f(x) for all possible values of x simultaneously using a quantum computer. **The point to ponder is that many quantum algorithms leverage quantum parallelism.**

Consider figure-3.44(c) again. It shows quantum parallelism. Now say, we want to evaluate a function, f(x) that has a binary domain and range i.e.

$$f: X \in \{0, 1\} \rightarrow \{0, 1\}$$

As seen in figure 3.44(c), an easier way to evaluate the function is to start with an equal superposition state–

$|x> = 1/\sqrt{2}\ |0> + 1/\sqrt{2}\ |1>$ as the input data and a qubit initialized to the state |y> = |0> as the target qubit. **Please understand that with a suitable unitary gate, U_f, we transform this joint state |x, y> to $|x, y \oplus f(x)>$ where $\oplus$ denotes modulo 2 addition.** The **output state** after applying the unitary gate, U_f can be expanded as follows:

$$|\psi\rangle = |x, y \oplus f(x)\rangle = |x, f(x)\rangle = 1/\sqrt{2}\,|0, f(0)\rangle + 1/\sqrt{2}\,|1, f(1)\rangle$$

Also note that the state in this equation is a useful state where we have as components both f(0) and f(1) entangled with their corresponding inputs. This looks as if we have evaluated the function at once over its entire domain by creating a superposition state for all values in its domain. **This phenomenon of evaluating the function at once over its entire domain by creating a superposition state for all values in its domain is called as quantum parallelism.**

How do we get the function evaluations from this superposition state, $|\psi\rangle$?

As already studied, to be able **to extract any information from a given state, we need to perform measurement.** Also we have studied that if we make the data qubit to be 0, we **collapse the state** to $|0, f(0)\rangle$. Now if we make a measurement for the 2nd qubit, **we are sure to get the values of f(0) as measurement with 100% certainty.** Similarly, **if we measure the 1st qubit to be 1 on the 2nd qubit, we are sure to measure the value of f(1).**

We can also generalize this approach to a function with multiple input values in its domain. Suppose we have a function with $N = 2^n$ values in its domain such that–

$$f: X \in \{0, 1, 2, ..., 2^n - 1\} \rightarrow \{0, 1\}$$

To put it in a proper light, we can create an equal superposition state of all 2^n values as the computational basis states by using Hadamard gates on a system of n qubits. As an example to explain this, we start with 2 qubits initially at the $|0\rangle$ state, as shown in figure 3.46 (a).

So, on applying Hadamard gate on each of them, we get:

$$H^{\otimes 2}: |00\rangle \rightarrow H|0\rangle \otimes H|0\rangle = (H|0\rangle)^{\otimes 2} = (1/\sqrt{2}\,|0\rangle + 1/\sqrt{2}\,|1\rangle)^{\otimes 2} \quad ...(1)$$

This shows **Hadamard gate on 2 qubits.**

In general, we can also show Hadamard gate on n qubits. See fig 3.46 (b).

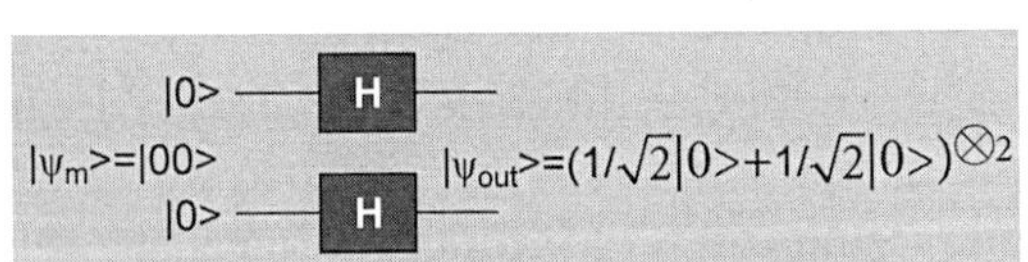

(a) Hadamard Gate on 2 qubits

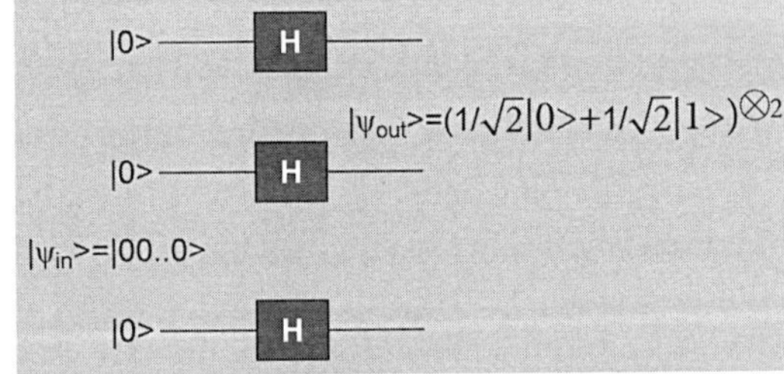

(b) Hadamard Gate on n qubits

Fig. 3.46

Next, we expand the state in equation-1 as follows:

$$(1/\sqrt{2}\,|0\rangle + 1/\sqrt{2}\,|1\rangle)^{\otimes 2} = (1/\sqrt{2}\,|0\rangle + 1/\sqrt{2}\,|1\rangle) \otimes (1/\sqrt{2}\,|0\rangle + 1/\sqrt{2}\,|1\rangle)$$
$$= \tfrac{1}{2}\,(|00\rangle + |01\rangle + |10\rangle + |11\rangle)$$

Conclusions: By using Hadamard gates on 2 qubits that are initialized at $|0\rangle$ state, we could get an **equal superposition of 4 computational basis states.** Also, we can denote a **binary string** representation of **the computational basis states** in terms of its integer representation as given below:

$$\tfrac{1}{2}\,(|00\rangle + |01\rangle + |10\rangle + |11\rangle) = \tfrac{1}{2}\,(|0\rangle + |1\rangle + |2\rangle + |3\rangle)$$

Let us now make it general, that is, **instead of 2 qubits, if we start with n qubits** initialized at |0> state then **by applying the Hadamard transform on each of the qubits, we will get the following superposition state–**

$$(1/\sqrt{2}\,|0> + 1/\sqrt{2}\,|1>)^{\otimes n} = 1/2^{n/2}\,\Sigma(x_{n-1} {=} 0 \text{ to } 1) \cdots \Sigma(x_1 {=} 0 \text{ to } 1)\,\Sigma(x_0 {=} 0 \text{ to } 1)|x_{n-1}, \ldots, x_1, x_0>$$

Where $x_0, x_1, \ldots x_{n-1}$ represent the values of the qubits in an **n–dimensional computational basis state.** The equation given above can be simplified by treating the binary string as an integer number based on the following expression:–

$$x = x_{n-1}2^{n-1} \ldots + x_1 2^1 + x_0 2^0$$

Note that this also reduces the expression for the superposition of states as given below:

$$(1/\sqrt{2}\,|0> + 1/\sqrt{2}\,|1>^{\otimes n} = 1/2^{n/2}\,\Sigma_{\,(x\,=\,0 \text{ to }} 2^n - 1)\,|x> \qquad \ldots(2)$$

Substituting the state in equation-2 as the **input data through the unitary gate, U_f for quantum parallelism, the output** that we get is given by the expression–

$$|\psi> = 1/2^{n/2}\,\Sigma_{(x=0 \text{ to }} 2^n - 1)\,|x, f(x)>$$

The point to ponder is that by using n-qubits, we can have a function evaluated for 2^n inputs in its domain, quickly. As a natural choice, in order to get the function values, we will have to make measurements on the state |ψ> and each measurement would yield the input, x and its corresponding function value, f(x).

3.16 QUANTUM INTERFERENCE

As already studied, in quantum computing and its algorithms, the main objective is to bias the probability distribution given by the state of a quantum system to favor one or more outcomes.

For example, the Hadamard gate, H, transforming the state |ψ> = 1/√2 |0> – 1/√2 |1> to the state |1> is a good example of quantum interference. The application of a Hadamard gate to an arbitrary qubit is an example of **quantum interference.**

Please understand that the Hadamard transform works on each of the basis states in |ψ>. It transforms the state |0> to the superposition state 1/√2 |0> + 1/√2 |1> and the basis state |1> to 1/√2 |0> – 1/√2 |1> as follows:–

$$\begin{aligned} H\,|\psi> &= 1/\sqrt{2}\,H\,|0> - 1/\sqrt{2}\,H\,|1> \\ &= 1/\sqrt{2}\,1/\sqrt{2}\,(|0> + |1>) - 1/\sqrt{2}\,1/\sqrt{2}\,(|0> - |1>) \end{aligned}$$

From these equations, it is crystal clear that it looks as if each basis state in |ψ> is transformed by H to a superposition of all its basis states. **In nutshell, the superposition state pertaining to 1/√2 H |0> and 1/√2 H |1> interferes in such a way that the probability amplitudes of the |0> state undergoes destructive interference, whereas that of |1> undergoes constructive interference to the output state |1>** as follows:

$$\begin{aligned} H\,|\psi> &= 1/\sqrt{2}\,1/\sqrt{2}\,(|0> + |1>) - 1/\sqrt{2}\,1/\sqrt{2}\,(|0> - |1>) \\ &= \tfrac{1}{2}\underbrace{(1 - 1)}_{\text{Desctructive -Interference}}|0> + \tfrac{1}{2}\underbrace{(1 + 1)}_{\text{Constructive -Interference}}|1> \end{aligned}$$

$$= 1/2\;0\,|0> + \tfrac{1}{2}\,2\,|1> = |1>$$

Conclusions: The qubit in state $|\psi\rangle = 1/\sqrt{2}\,|0\rangle - 1/\sqrt{2}\,|1\rangle$ has a 50 – 50 chance of showing up as either of the two computation basis states 0 or 1 on measurement. **However, please note that by applying the Hadamard transform, we take the benefit of interference in such a way that it biases the new state $|\psi_{new}\rangle = H\,|\psi\rangle$ to the output state 1 with 100% probability.**

We are in a position to solve some examples now.

Example 1: Draw a quantum circuit that implements the Deutsch-Jozsa algorithm. Also explain its working step-by-step.

Solution 1: The following steps are followed:–

S1: Get two qubits and put them into a |0> 1> product state. The circuit is shown in figure 3.47 below–

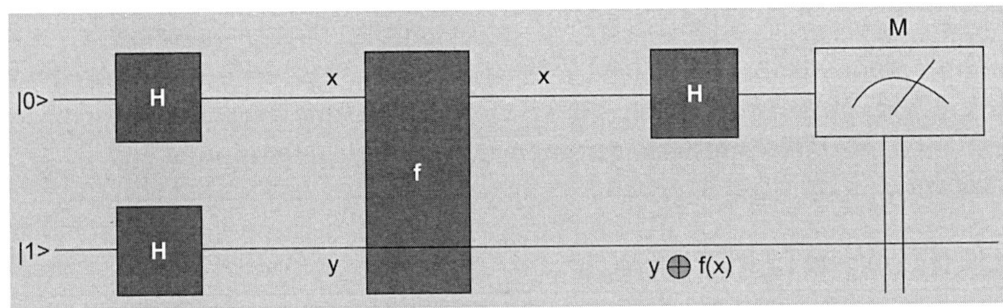

Fig.3.47: Quantum circuit for The Deutsch-Jozsa algorithm

The generic function, f(x), is shown in box with f inside it. The labels below or above the lines indicate how the function is implemented.

S2: Operate on each qubit with the Hadamard gate. Follow the rules of the Hadamard gate. The two qubit state is now as follows:

$$\frac{1}{2}\,(|0\rangle + |1\rangle)\,(|0\rangle - |1\rangle) \qquad ...(1)$$

As explained earlier, in quantum computing, modular arithmetic with **mod 2** is defined as follows:–

$$f(0) \oplus f(1) = 0 \qquad \text{if } f(0) + f(1) = 0, 2, 4, 6 \ldots$$

$$f(0) \oplus f(1) = 1 \qquad \text{if } f(0) + f(1) = 1, 3, 5, \ldots$$

Please note that the circle with a plus inside $\oplus$ denotes this modular arithmetic "mod 2" operation. Also note that the $\oplus$ operation outputs the remainder of dividing a number x by the number 2.

For instance,

if $f(0) = 0$ and $f(1) = 1$ then $f(0) \oplus f(1) = 1$ whereas if $f(0) = 1$ and $f(1) = 1$ then $f(0) \oplus f(1) = 0$

In quantum computing ecosystem, the function f(x) is implemented by–

$$|x\rangle\,|y\rangle \xrightarrow{f} |x\rangle\,|y\rangle \oplus f(x) \qquad ...(2)$$

For example, say $f(0) = 1$ then $|0\rangle\,|1\rangle \xrightarrow{f} |0\rangle\,|1\ f(0)\rangle = |0\rangle\,|0\rangle$. This is mandatory to ensure that the function operation is **unitary.**

S3: Next we apply the function f(x) using the rule (as in equation-2). After performing the arithmetic, the two qubit state can be re-arranged as follows:

$$\tfrac{1}{2}\, [|0> (|0 \oplus f(0)> - |1 \oplus f(0)>)] + |1> [|0> \oplus f(1)> - |1 \oplus f(1)>)]$$

To put it in a proper light, the effect of f(x) on the state, it is important to note that if $f(0) = 0$ then $|0 \oplus f(0)> - |1 \oplus f(0)> = |0> - |1>$. Also note that if $f(0) = 1$ then $|0 \oplus f(0)> - |1 \oplus f(0)> = - |0> + |1>$.

Note: A similar formula is required for f(1) case too.

S4: Now, we throw away the 2nd qubit. We just keep the first qubit and make sure that it is normalized correctly. The 1st qubit is as follows:–

$$1/\sqrt{2}\, (|0> + (-1)^{(f(0) + f(1))} |1>) \qquad ...(3)$$

Why we need the 2nd qubit? The reason for using the 2nd qubit is to perform the gate operations and collect the like-terms which ensures that the algorithm works. Also note that this 2nd qubit is called as an ancilla qubit because it is not measured. This is shown in fig 3.47 as the lack of the measurement operator in the 2nd qubit line.

S5: Applying a Hadamard gate to the qubit state that is in equation-3, we produce

$$\tfrac{1}{2}\, [(1 + (-1)^{(f(0) + f(1))}] |0> + [1 - (-1)^{(f(0) + f(1))}) |1>)]$$

S6: Measure the qubit: *If f(x) is constant then the state in equation of step-5 reduces to |0> while if f(x) is balanced then the state reduces to |1>.*

Results and conclusions: In nutshell, this algorithm proves that a single measurement of |0> or |1> depicts whether the function is **constant or balanced. Also this algorithm extends to functions that take in any number of inputs. Please note that this is good as only one single measurement can tell you whether a function of any size is constant or balanced. Also note that for a classical computer to perform the same task, it would need to measure each of the inputs that is exponentially slower.**

Example 2: Consider a function with two inputs such that f(x) = 1. Show that the Deutsch-Jozsa algorithm works in this case by generating the vector |y> = |00> as the final output.

Solution 2: The initial input state will be $|\psi_{in}> = |0> |0> |1>$. Apply Hadamard gates to this state and we get–

$$|\psi'> = 1/2\sqrt{2}\, (|000> - |001> + |010> - |011> + |100> - |101> + |110> - |111>$$

Then we apply U_f to the system and we get–

$$|\psi''> = 1/2\sqrt{2}\, (|001> - |000> + |011> - |010> + |101> - |100> + |111> - |110>$$

The final step is to apply $H^{\otimes 2}$ to the first two qubits. So, we now get–

$$|\psi_{out}> = 1/2\sqrt{2}\, \{[(|0> + |1>)/\sqrt{2}]\, [(|0> + |1>)/\sqrt{2}]\, |1> - [(|0> + |1>)/\sqrt{2}\, ([|0> + |1>)/\sqrt{2})\, |0> + [(|0> + |1>)/\sqrt{2}\, (|0> - |1>)/\sqrt{2}]\, |1> - [(|0> + |1>)/\sqrt{2}]\, [(|0> - |1>)/\sqrt{2}]\, |0> + [(|0> - |1>)/\sqrt{2}]\, [(|0> + |1>)/\sqrt{2}]\, |1> - [(|0> - |1>)/\sqrt{2}]\, [(|0> + |1>)/\sqrt{2}]\, |0> + [(|0> - |1>)/\sqrt{2}]\, [(|0> - |1>)/\sqrt{2}]\, |1> - [(|0> - |1>)/\sqrt{2}]\, [(|0> - |1>)/\sqrt{2}]\, |0>]$$

Next, we expand all these terms and we get–

$$|\psi_{out}\rangle = 1/4\sqrt{2}\ [(|00\rangle + |01\rangle + |10\rangle + |11\rangle)\ |1\rangle - (|00\rangle + |01\rangle + |10\rangle + |11\rangle)\ |0\rangle + (|00\rangle - |01\rangle + |10\rangle - |11\rangle)\ |1\rangle - (|00\rangle - |01\rangle + |10\rangle - |11\rangle)\ |0\rangle + (|00\rangle + |01\rangle - |10\rangle - |11\rangle)\ |1\rangle - (|00\rangle + |01\rangle - |10\rangle - |11\rangle)\ |0\rangle + (|00\rangle - |01\rangle - |10\rangle + |11\rangle)\ |1\rangle - (|00\rangle - |01\rangle - |10\rangle + |11\rangle)\ |0\rangle]$$

We now want to factor these terms to put them in the form with the **3rd qubit as ($|0\rangle - |1\rangle/\sqrt{2}$).** So, we will get–

$$|\psi_{out}\rangle = 1/4\ [-(|00\rangle + |01\rangle + |10\rangle + |11\rangle)\ (|0\rangle - |1\rangle/\sqrt{2}) - (|00\rangle - |01\rangle + |10\rangle - |11\rangle)\ (|0\rangle - |1\rangle/\sqrt{2}) - (|00\rangle + |01\rangle - |10\rangle - |11\rangle)\ (|0\rangle - |1\rangle/\sqrt{2}) - (|00\rangle - |01\rangle - |10\rangle + |11\rangle)\ (|0\rangle - |1\rangle/\sqrt{2})]$$

Hence, we can conclude that–

$$|\psi_{out}\rangle = -|00\rangle\ [|0\rangle - |1\rangle/\sqrt{2}]$$

The point to ponder is that the measurement on the first two qubits gives 00 and that this confirms that this is a **constant function.** On the other hand, if the measurement returns 10 then we say that the function is **balanced.**

Example 3: Determine what happens when we compute H $|\psi\rangle$ for $|\psi\rangle = \alpha\ |0\rangle + \beta\ |1\rangle$.

Solution 3: We know that H $|\psi\rangle$ for qubit, $|\psi\rangle = \alpha\ |0\rangle + \beta\ |1\rangle$ will be–

$$H\ |\psi\rangle = [\alpha + \beta/\sqrt{2}]\ |0\rangle + [\alpha - \beta/\sqrt{2}]\ |1\rangle$$

Please note that the probability to find $|1\rangle$ has been changed as follows:–

$$\beta \rightarrow \alpha - \beta/\sqrt{2}$$

Observing at the state and so we can write–

$$|\psi\rangle = |0\rangle + |1\rangle/\sqrt{2}$$

Example 4: When we develop quantum algorithms, interference and parallelism play a fundamental role. Also we know that the Hadamard gate transforms $|\psi\rangle \rightarrow |0\rangle$. This is a manifestation of quantum interference i.e. the addition of probability amplitudes. What are the two types of interference you encountered? Explain in brief.

Solution 4: Actually, there are two types of interference–

(a) Positive interference: the probability amplitudes add **constructively to increase.**

(b) Negative interference: the probability amplitudes add **destructively to decrease.**

Quantum interference plays a vital role in the development of quantum algorithms. **Please note that this means that quantum interference allows us to gain information about a function f(x) that depends on evaluating the function at many values of x.** That is, interference allows us to deduce certain **global properties** of the function.

Example 5: What happens if we apply the Hadamard transform to the state

$$|\psi\rangle = [|0\rangle + (-1)^x\ |1\rangle]/\sqrt{2} \qquad \text{(where } x \in \{0, 1\}\text{)}.$$

Solution 5: We know that–

$$H\ |\psi\rangle = \alpha\ H|0\rangle + \beta\ H\ |1\rangle = \alpha\ [|0\rangle + |1\rangle/\sqrt{2}] + \beta\ [|0\rangle - |1\rangle/\sqrt{2}]$$

$$= [\alpha + \beta/\sqrt{2}]\ |0> + [\alpha - \beta/\sqrt{2}]\ |1>$$

The result is–

$$H\ |\psi> \ = \ [1+ (-1)^x/2]\ |0> + [1 - (-1)^x/2]\ |1>$$

Case-1: if x = 0, this means that–

$$H\ [|0> + |1>/\sqrt{2}] \ = \ |0>$$

Case-2: if x = 1, this means that–

$$H\ [|0> - |1>/\sqrt{2}] \ = \ |1>$$

With the Hadamard transformation of the state, we observe–

(a) **Positive interference with regard to the basis state |0>. Note that the 2 amplitudes add to increase the probability of finding 0 on measurement.** Here, it goes to unity meaning that we are certain to find 0.

(b) **Negative interference** wherein the terms |1> and |–1> cancel.

The point to ponder is that we move from a state where there was a 50% chance of finding 1 on measurement to one where there is no chance of finding 1 on measurement.

Example 6: What role does quantum interference play in the development of quantum algorithms?

Solution 6: Quantum interference provides us information about a function; f(x) that depends on evaluating the function at many values of x. **In nutshell, quantum interference allows us to deduce certain global properties of the function.**

Example 7: Say, we have an identity function as follows:

$$f(x) = \begin{cases} 0 & \text{if } x = 0 \\ 1 & \text{if } x = 1 \end{cases}$$

And constant functions as f(x) = 0, f(x) = 1

And the bit-flip functions as follows:

$$f(x) = \begin{cases} 1 & \text{if } x = 0 \\ 0 & \text{if } x = 1 \end{cases}$$

Why are the identity and the bit-flip functions called as balanced? What is the global property?

Solution 7: The identity and the bit-flip functions are called as balanced functions because **the outputs are opposite for half the inputs.** So, a function on a single bit can be **constant or balanced. Note that whether a function on a single bit is constant or balanced is a global property.**

Example 8: From the given table, find out which of the functions are constant and which are balanced?

f_1	f_2	f_3	f_4
$f_1(0) = 0$	$f_2(0) = 0$	$f_3(0) = 1$	$f_4(0) = 1$
$f_1(1) = 0$	$f_2(1) = 1$	$f_3(1) = 0$	$f_4(1) = 1$

Solution 8: From the table, we observe that there are only 4 possible single qubit functions. The functions f_1 and f_4 are **constant.** On the other hand, the functions **f_2 and f_3** are balanced.

Example 9: Suppose you run a classical algorithm and you find that f(0) = 1 then can you guess whether the function is constant or balanced?

Solution 9: No, we can't say as it could be either a balanced function f_3 or the constant function f_4. A classical computer would have to evaluate both f(0) and f(1) to find out the answer.

Example 10: Define the following–

(a) Quantum parallelism. **(b) De-coherence.**

(c) Results of quantum computations.

Solution 10: The following are there definitions–

(a) **Quantum Parallelism:** Quantum computers can perform a function operation on all qubits simultaneously. This is known as **quantum parallelism.**

(b) **De-coherence: It has been observed that the more qubits you add, the more likely it is that the qubits will interact accidently with the environment. This, however, destroys the system's quantum properties through a process known as de-coherence.**

(c) **Results of quantum computations:** Getting the results from the quantum computations requires measuring the qubits. But too many measurements could spoil the quantum advantage.

Example 11: Answer the following questions–

(a) How many different classical pieces of information can be represented by 8 classical bits?

(b) What about a quantum computer with 8 qubits?

(c) What advantage does the quantum computer have over the classical computer?

Solution 11:

(a) Both the classical and quantum computer can represent $2^8 = 256$ classical bits of information.

(b) Both the classical and quantum computer can represent $2^8 = 256$ classical bits of information.

(c) The quantum computer can create a superposition of up to 256 possibilities and do a computation on all of them. But a measurement will be only one classical value.

Example 12: What is an Oracle in Deutsch-Jozsa algorithm? What is black box? Show the role of oracle in this algorithm.

Solution 12: Deutsch-Jozsa algorithm is the simplest and first algorithm as invented by David Deutsch and Richard Josza. A conventional computer takes (2n – 1) evaluations when compared to a quantum computer that can do it in 1 shot. It basically takes n inputs and gives one bit value as the output. **Please note that the point here is not whether the output is 0 or 1. Rather it is about a function, f. It is about deciding whether the function is constant or balanced.** Another term used is **Oracle** which performs an XOR operation. This problem is called as **black box.**

The steps of Deutsch-Jozsa algorithm are as follows:–

S1: We need to take **n-qubits where (n – 1) are in the state |0> which will be the upper states and the last one is in the state |1> which will be the lower state.**

S2: Apply **Hadamard transform** on all n-qubits.

S3: Then apply the **Oracle on the upper and lower state** where it performs **XOR.**

S4: Next, **re-apply the Hadamard transform to all the upper states.**

S5: Lastly, **measure all of the qubits.**

The point to ponder is that after measuring the answer qubit if it turns out to be 0, then the function is constant else it is balanced. Also note that here constant means the function will output the same value independent of the input whereas balanced means the function generates half of a bunch of 0s and another half of 1s.

Example 13: What are systolic arrays? What role do they have in quantum computers?

Solution 13: The word systolic has been borrowed from the medical field just as the heart pumps the blood, information is pumped through a systolic array in various directions and at regular intervals. In 2D systolic arrays, information is pumped from left to right and from top to bottom. The information meets at internal nodes where processing occurs. The same information passes onward i.e. left to right or downward.

As we know that in quantum computing, all system states can occur at the same time. So, all of the paths of the tree in quantum computing occur in parallel. It is only after measurement that a single path will be observed as the whole system's superimposed state will collapse into that single state. Each path in the tree of quantum computation is a single computation and hence a massive computational parallelism occurs with large number of calculations performed simultaneously. Here, the path with the highest probability has the highest probability to be measured.

3.17 TOPOLOGICAL QUANTUM COMPUTING

The process of reconstructing the state for a source of a quantum system by measurements on the system is known as Quantum state tomography. In quantum process tomography, the states are known but the quantum dynamics of the system is unknown. **Please understand that the objective is to characterize the process by probing it with quantum states.** The dynamics of a quantum system is explained by a completely positive linear map as follows:–

$$\in(\rho) = \Sigma_I A_i \rho A^+_i$$

where $\Sigma_i A_i A^+_i = I$ will ensure that the map preserves the trace. **This is called as Krauss's form.**

Ancilla-assisted quantum process tomography is of interest to us.

We are in a position to solve an example now.

Example 1: Consider the density matrix–

$$\rho = \frac{1}{2}(I_2 + r.\sigma)$$

where $r.\sigma = r_1.\sigma_1 + r_2.\sigma_2 + r_3.\sigma_3$ and $r^2 \leq 1$. Consider the four normalized vectors a_1, a_2, a_3, a_4 in R^3 as–

$$a_1 = 1/\sqrt{3}\begin{pmatrix}1\\1\\1\end{pmatrix} \quad a_2 = 1/\sqrt{3}\begin{pmatrix}1\\-1\\-1\end{pmatrix} \quad a_3 = 1\,1/\sqrt{3}\begin{pmatrix}-1\\1\\-1\end{pmatrix} \quad a_4 = 1/\sqrt{3}\begin{pmatrix}-1\\-1\\1\end{pmatrix}$$

such that–

$$\mathbf{a_j^T\, a_k = 4/3\, \delta_{jk} - 1/3} = \begin{cases} 1 \text{ for } j = k \\ -1/3 \text{ for } j \neq k \end{cases}$$

We are given that–

$$\mathbf{\Sigma_{(j=1 \text{ to } 4)}\, a_j = 0 \quad \text{and} \quad 3/4\, \Sigma_{(j=1 \text{ to } 4)}\, a_j\, a^T{}_j = I_3}$$

Such a quartet of vectors consists of the vectors pointing from the center of a cube to non-adjacent corners. These four vectors can be viewed as the normal vectors for the faces of the tetrahedron that is defined by the other four corners of the cube. Owing to the conditions the four vectors are normalized. Each such quartets of a_j's defines a positive operator-valued measure for minimal four-state tomography owing to–

$$\mathbf{\Sigma_{(j=1 \text{ to } 4)}\, P_j = I_2, \qquad P_j = 1/4\, (I_2 + a_j \,.\, \sigma)}$$

(a) Show that $p_j = \langle P_j \rangle = tr\,(P_j\rho) = 1/4\,(1 + a_j \,.\, r)$.

(b) Given p_j for $j = 1, 2, 3, 4$ find the density matrix, ρ.

Solution 1: (a) As we know that $tr\,(\sigma_1) = tr\,(\sigma_2) = tr\,(\sigma_3) = 0$; so we have–

$$\langle P_j \rangle = tr\,(P_j\rho) = 1/8\, tr\,((I_2 + a_j \,.\, \sigma)\,(I_2 + r\,.\sigma)) = 1/8\, tr\,((I_2 + a_j.\sigma + r.\sigma + (a_j.\sigma)\,(r.\sigma))$$
$$= 1/8\, tr\,(I_2 + (a_j.\sigma) + r.\sigma\,)) = 1/8\, tr\,(I_2 + a_j.r)\, I_2) = 1/4\,(1 + a_j.r)$$

(b) Because

$$I_3\, r = 3/4\, [\Sigma_{(j=1 \text{ to } 4)}\, \mathbf{a_j\, a^T{}_j}]\, \mathbf{r}$$

The vector r is obtained as follows:–

$$r = 3/4\, \Sigma_{(j=1 \text{ to } 4)}\, (a_j \,.\, r)\, a_j = 3\, \Sigma_{(j=1 \text{ to } 4)}\, 1/4\,(1 + a_j \,.\, r)\, a_j = 3\, \Sigma_{(j=1 \text{ to } 4)}\, p_j\, a_j.$$

where we used $\Sigma_{(j=1 \text{ to } 4)}\, \mathbf{a_j = 0}$. From $a_j \,.\, \sigma = 4P_j - I_2$ and substituting r from above yields the density matrix as follows:–

$$\rho = 6\, \Sigma_{(j=1 \text{ to } 4)}\, p_j\, P_j - I_2 = \Sigma_{(j=1 \text{ to } 4)} \langle P_j \rangle\, (6P_j - I_2) = 1/2\,(I_2 + r \,.\, \sigma)$$

It is concluded that p_j is restricted to the range $0 \le p_j \le 1/2$ and the probabilities p_j obey the inequalities–

$$1/4 \le \Sigma_{(j=1 \text{ to } 4)}\, p^2{}_j = (3 + r^2)/12 \le 1/3$$

The **upper bound is reached by all pure states,** $\rho = \rho^2$ and $r^2 = 1$.

The **lower bound is reached for the completely mixed state,** $\rho = 1/3\, I_2$ and $r^2 = 0$.

3.18 TELEPORTATION AND SUPERDENSE CODING

Many computer scientists were arguing on the topic like "can we transport quantum states?" After many years, scientists gave the term **teleportation that is defined as the instantaneous transport of matter from one location to another.** Actually, classical data processing operations destroy entanglement but quantum operations can create it, preserve it and use it for many tasks like transmission of classical data (quantum superdense coding) or intact quantum states (teleportation) from the sender to the receiver. Thus, **we define quantum teleportation as the transmission of quantum information using a classical channel and entanglement.** It depicts the use of entanglement as a communication resource. To put it in a proper light, quantum teleportation is the disembodied transport of an unknown quantum state from one place to another.

Basic idea: Two distinct operators i.e. Alice at a sending station and Bob at the receiving station will share an entangled quantum bipartite state and exploit its non-local character as a quantum resource.

Quantum teleportation is an application based on the Entanglement phenomenon where qubits can be transported through larger distances without any medium in between the receivers. **The point to remember is that we may not be able to transport macroscopic objects like people but we can transport qubits over a particular distance by entangling them and transmitting the state of the original qubit's state using the entanglement phenomenon. Also remember that entanglement occurs when the qubits are forced to hold mutually exclusive states.** Hence, the observer will be able to determine the state of a qubit if the state of its entangled qubit is known.

Quantum Teleportation steps–

Step-1: Identify the **desired qubit** that has to be teleported.

Step-2: Create a **classical channel that can transmit two qubits and an EPR entangled pair is generated.**

Step-3: Then, each of these **qubits that are entangled is transported to two different locations.**

Step-4: Bell's measurement is performed on one of the qubits and information is obtained. Then the state of another qubit is manipulated accordingly.

No-teleportation theorem states that-"A random quantum state can't be converted into a sequence of traditional classical bits and neither can they be used to reconstruct the original state."

To put it in a proper light, we can say that it is an extension of no-cloning theorem. It implies that if you can convert a qubit into a series of classical bits, then it would be easy to copy the qubit which is against the quantum laws and this will result in the destruction of the original state. Hence, a qubit can't be copied as a series of classical bits.

Quantum teleportation is used to replace the state of one qubit with that of another over a long distance without the qubits directly interacting with each other, it works only at the level of individual quantum particles like photons, electrons etc. On the other hand, **superdense coding is the process in which two classical bits of information are transmitted by sending just one quantum bit. The objective of quantum teleportation is to transfer the unknown sate information of the first/source qubit without measuring the second/destination qubit.** This avoids the disturbance of the first qubit. **Please note that the second qubit does not receive a copy of the quantum state of the first qubit as it is impossible to produces an exact copy of an arbitrary quantum state** (as per no-cloning theorem). So, the second qubit does not receive the copy of the state information of the first hence, the original state of the first is teleported to it. **Also note that the process is not faster than light and a pair of entangled states has to be distributed before time.**

Actually, quantum teleportation is a process that is closely related to superdense coding. Its formal definition is, "**quantum teleportation is the process by which the state of a qubit (ψ) can be transmitted from one location to another with the help of classical communication and a Bell pair.**" It is the method of transmitting quantum states between a sender and a receiver without using any communication channel.

Workflow of Quantum Teleportation

Let us draw its overall workflow diagram.

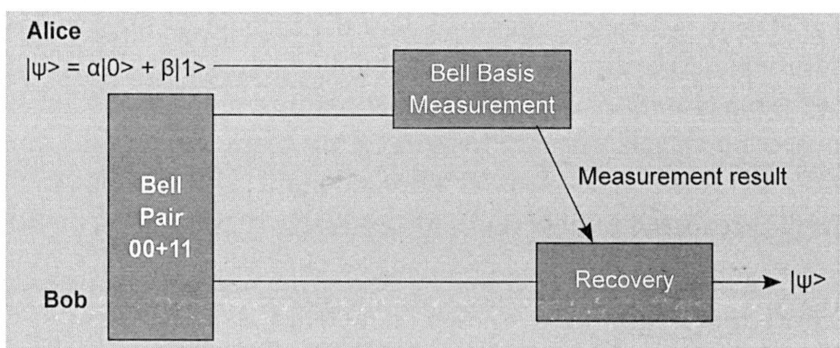

Working:

S1: Alice and Bob start by sharing a Bell Pair of entangled qubits. One goes to Alice and the other goes to Bob at separate remote locations. Imagine that the Bell Pair is prepared by a 3rd party (Eve).

S2: Alice prepares her qubit to be teleported in state $|\psi\rangle = \alpha|0\rangle + \beta|1\rangle$. Then she performs a Bell basis measurement of her qubit and the entangled qubit from the Bell pair provided by Eve. Then, Alice sends the measurement result by classical means to Bob.

S3: At this junction, there is a posterior state for Bob's qubit as a function of the measurement performed by Alice. This is the main point to understand the procedure. **Note that both share an entangled qubit.** So, we will see how Bob, by applying a suitable quantum gate, can recover the original state ψ created by Alice.

To understand this, let us look at Bob's posterior state at the moment of Alice's measurement before the recovery operation. To do this, we write the joined states of the 3 qubits involved in the process. Also note that the ket notation is ignored for simplicity.

Given Alice's state as $|\psi\rangle = \alpha|0\rangle + \beta|1\rangle$, if we **combine it with the shared entangled qubit** from the Bell pair provided by Eve, i.e. [Alice state ($|\psi\rangle$) + [shared entangled qubit], we get the following:-

$$(\alpha 0 + \beta 1)\,(00 + 11) = \alpha 000 + \alpha 011 + \beta 100 + \beta 111 \qquad ...(1)$$

Next we must write the **state of the first 2 qubits using the Bell basis states** as follows:

$$B0 = 00 + 11 \qquad 00 = B0 - B1$$

$$B1 = 10 + 01 \qquad 01 = B1 - B3$$

$$B2 = 00 - 11 \qquad 10 = B1 - B3$$

$$B3 = 10 - 01 \qquad 11 = B0 - B2$$

So, equation-1 becomes–

$$(\alpha 0 + \beta 1)\,(00 + 11) = B0\,(\alpha 0 + \beta 1) + B1\,(\alpha 1 + \beta 0) + B2\,(\alpha 0 - \beta 1) + B3\,(-\alpha 1 + \beta 0) \qquad ...(2)$$

Equation-2 shows the states for the 3 qubits after Alice performs her measurement. Bob knows how to recover Alice's ψ by looking at the posterior state of the qubits in equation-2 i.e. the states within the parenthesis. The following table shows this–

Bell State	Posterior State	Bob's Recovery Operation
B0	$\alpha 0 + \beta 1$	Ψ
B1	$\alpha 1 + \beta 0$	X_ψ
B2	$\alpha 0 - \beta 1$	$Z\psi$
B3	$-\alpha 1 + \beta 0$	$ZX\psi$

Table: Quantum Teleportation Recovery

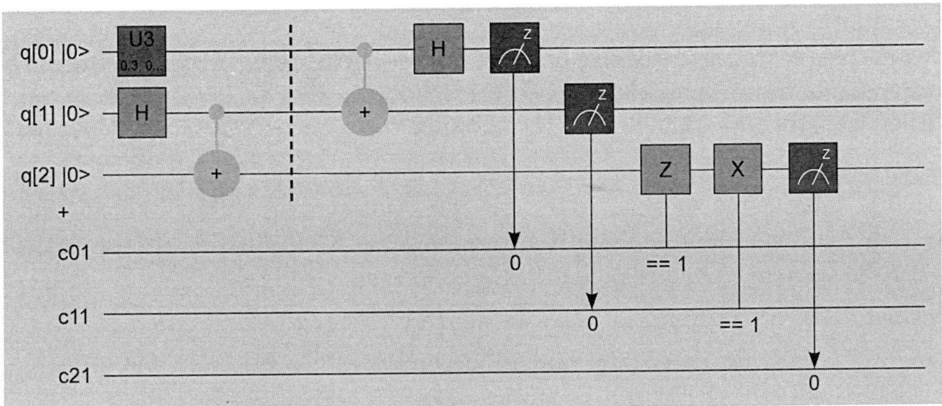

Fig.3.48: Quantum Teleportation Circuit Diagram

In nutshell, this **quantum teleportation protocol provides the means to recover the state ψ of any qubit by sharing an entangled Bell Pair between two remote parties.** Hence, it is named as **teleportation.**

Let us now study the quantum teleportation circuit.

Step-by-step explanation:

1. The **gates to the left of the dotted line represent the Bell Pair** prepared by the 3rd party (Eve) i.e. qubits 1 and 2.
2. **Alice prepares her qubit (0) to a given state, ψ.** The actual value of ψ is irrelevant as it will be recovered by Bob at the final stage of the process. Alice receives qubit[1] from Eve and qubit[2] goes to Bob.
3. **Alice performs a measurement on her qubits [0, 1]** (as shown to the right of the dotted line) and sends the results by classical means to Bob.
4. Bob applies the recovery rules to his qubit(2) as mentioned earlier depending on the outcomes sent by Alice. Finally, after a measurement of qubit[2], Bob recovers the state ψ, originally created by Alice. **Please note that this is made possible by the fact that Alice and Bob share an entangled pair of qubits which makes the whole thing work.**

Results:

1. Bob qubit's state will be $|\psi\rangle_B = \alpha|0\rangle_B + \beta|1\rangle_B$ and the Alice's qubit state will be undefined, thereby not violating the no-cloning theorem.

2. **Please understand that as no information is being physically moved so there is no transfer of energy.**
3. **Also understand that the classical bits don't know about the teleportation completely, hence, if an eaves dropper tries to interfere, Alice might interact with Bob using entanglement.**

Applications of Quantum Teleportation

Some real-time applications of quantum teleportation are as follows:

1. **Quantum internet** is a reliable network that connects devices to a remote quantum computer that can perform operations much faster than a classical computer.
2. **Quantum cryptography** involves more than two parties in which quantum teleportation is possible and successful between any 2 parties with the aid of the 3rd party. This can be named as a **reliable tripartite quantum protocol. Just remember that, there can be no bipartite entanglement in the tripartite entangled state.**
3. Alice is able to transfer the quantum state and not the actual particle and to send only the classical information to Bob. **Note that the transfer of quantum information happens instantly although Bob needs to first receive classical information regarding the result of Alice's measurement before validating his own result.**

Mathematical interpretation:

We are in a position to dissect and explore the process explained above and to understand the transformations of quantum states involved in teleportation. Also we have already seen earlier that there are **many entangled states of two particles.** Now let us assume that the particles in the possession of Alice and Bob ('particle 1' and 'particle 2') are in **maximally entangled state** as follows:

$$|\beta_{00}> \;=\; |00> + |11>/2$$

And that 'particle 3' (i.e. Eve) is in state–

$$|c> \;=\; \alpha_0\,|0> + \alpha_1\,|1> \text{ with } |\alpha_0|^2 + |\,\alpha_1\,|^2 = 1$$

The joint state of 'particle 3 (eve)' and 'particle 1 (Alice)' is $|\xi>$ and is a vector in H_8 because 'particle 1' is entangled with 'particle 2'. That is,

$$|\xi> \;=\; |c> \otimes |\beta_{00}> = \begin{pmatrix}\alpha_0\\ \alpha_1\end{pmatrix} \otimes 1/\sqrt{2}\begin{pmatrix}1\\0\\0\\1\end{pmatrix} = 1/\sqrt{2}\begin{pmatrix}\alpha_0\\0\\0\\\alpha_0\\\alpha_1\\0\\0\\\alpha_1\end{pmatrix}$$

or we can write it as–

$$|\xi> \;=\; \mathbf{1/\sqrt{2}\,(\alpha_0\,|\,000> + (\alpha_0\,|\,011> + \alpha_1\,|\,100> + \alpha_1\,|\,111>)}$$

When Alice performs a joint measurement of her qubits, she gets one of the four equally probable results i.e. |00> or |01> or |10> or |11>. We have already studied that the measurement forces the pair of qubits to one of the four basis states and transforms quantum information into classical one. Then, she sends Bob the result of her measurement– 00, 01, 10 or 11, over a classical communication channel. **Please note that the measurement performed by Alice forces the qubit in Bob's possession to change to one of four states as follows:**

1. $|\eta_{00}\rangle = \alpha_0 |0\rangle + \alpha_1 |1\rangle$ when the result is 00. 2. $|\eta_{01}\rangle = \alpha_0 |1\rangle + \alpha_1 |0\rangle$ when the result is 01.

3. $|\eta_{10}\rangle = \alpha_0 |0\rangle - \alpha_1 |1\rangle$ when the result is 10. 4 $|\eta_{11}\rangle = \alpha_0 |1\rangle - \alpha_1 |0\rangle$ when the result is 11.

Now, Bob applies to his qubit the transformations performed by one-qubit gates depending on the string received from Alice as per the following table–

String received by Bob	Gate applied by Bob	Qubit in Bob's possession becomes
00	I	$I|\eta_{00}\rangle = |c\rangle$
01	X	$X|\eta_{01}\rangle = |c\rangle$
10	Z	$Z|\eta_{10}\rangle = |c\rangle$
11	Y	$Y|\eta_{11}\rangle = |c\rangle$

Note that the qubit in Bob's possession is in the same state as the original qubit of Eve's. As explained earlier, the state of Eve's qubit has been altered and hence the no-cloning theorem is not violated. **Also note that the new state obtained as a result of the transformation of the original state of 'particle 1' and 'particle 3' can be written as–**

$$|\xi\rangle = (H \otimes I \otimes I)(G_{CNOT} \otimes I)(|\xi\rangle)$$

Let us now discuss about super dense coding.

Super Dense Coding (SDC) is a data transfer protocol that demonstrates better information processing capabilities of a quantum system. It is a simple procedure that allows for transferring 2 classical bits of information to another party using a single qubit. The superdense coding protocol is shown in fig. 3.49. *It is a technique used to send two qubits on a single qubit between two points when they*

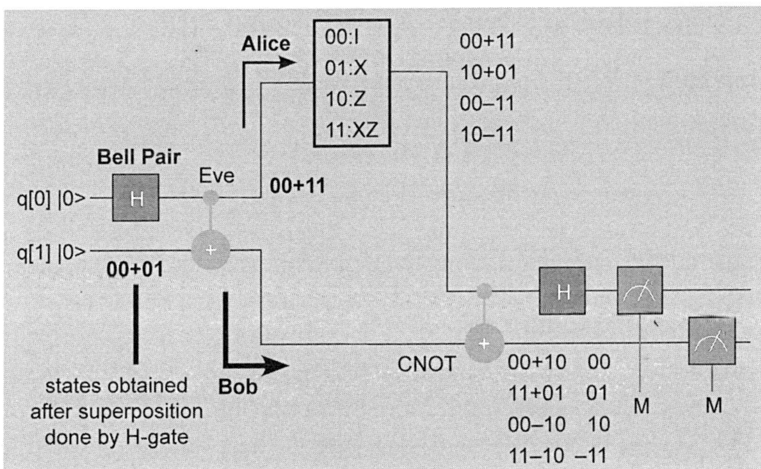

Fig.3.49: Super dense coding protocol

are already connected by a pair of entangled photons. This communication protocol was given by Charles Bennett and Stephen Wiesner in 1992. But it was experimented by Klaus Mattle, Harald Weinfurter et. al The initial entanglement preceding the transmission of the two bits in the qubits avoids violating Holevo's theorem that set of qubits can't carry more information than the equivalent number of classical bits.

Let us now see this process of SDC step-by-step:–

Step-1: The process starts with a **3rd party (Eve) generating a Bell Pair** (see fig. 3.49). Eve starts with 2 qubits in the basis state |0>. She applies **a Hadamard gate to the 1st qubit to create superposition.** Then it applies **a CNOT gate using the 1st qubit as the control (dot) and the 2nd as the target (+).** That is,

$$\text{Hadamard Gate (H)} \xrightarrow{\text{causes}} \text{superposition}$$

$$\text{CNOT gate} \xrightarrow{\text{causes}} \text{entangles both qubits}$$

This results in the states as shown in table below–

Gate	Outcome states of q_0 and q_1	Meaning
H	|00> → |00> + |10> (after superposition)	When H gate is applied to the 1st qubit, it enters **superposition.** So, we get the states 00 + 10 where the 2nd qubit remains as 0. **Also note that the square root (2) from the Hadamard matrix has been omitted for simplicity.**
CNOT	|00> + |10> → |00> + |11> (after entanglement)	The CNOT gate **entangles both qubits.** It flips the target (+) if the control (.) is 1, else it leaves intact. So, we flip the 2nd qubit if the 1st is 1 resulting in 00 + 11.

Step-2: The 1st qubit (i.e. |00> + |10>) is sent to Alice and the **2nd qubit** to Bob. **Please note that Alice and Bob may be in remote places. The objective of this protocol is for Alice to send 2 classical bits of information to Bob using her qubit.** But before she does it, she needs to apply a set of **quantum rules or gates** to her qubit depending on the 2-bits of information she wants to send. The encoding rules for SDC are as follows:

Rules	Outcome states (after SDC encoding)
00: I (Identity gate)	I(00 + 11) = 00 + 11
01: X (flip gate)	X(00 + 11) = 10 + 01
10: Z	Z(00 + 11) = 00 – 11
11: ZX	ZX(00 + 11) = 10 – 11

Step-3: If she sends a 00, she does nothing to her qubit (applies the identity gate). **If she sends a 01** then she applies the X gate (or bit flip). For a 10, she applies the Z-gate. **Please note that the Z-gate flips the sign/ phase of the qubit if the qubit is 1.** So, Z|0> = |0> and Z|1> = – |1>. Finally, **if she sends 11,** then she applies gates XZ to her qubit. Then Alice sends her qubit to Bob for the final step in the process.

Step-4: Bob receives Alice's qubit (qubit 0) and uses his qubit to reverse the process of the Bell state created by Eve. That is, he applies **the CNOT gate to the 1st qubit followed by the Hadamard gate (H)** and finally performs **a measurement in both qubits to extract the 2 classical bits encoded in Alice's qubit.** This is shown in table–

Gate	Outcome States	Details
CNOT	00 + 10 11 + 01 00 – 10 11 – 10	We start with Alice's states from step-2: 00 + 11 10 + 01 00 – 11 10 – 11 **Note: The CNOT gate flips the 2nd qubit if the first is 1 resulting in the states in column #2.**
H	00 01 10 –11	Applying the Hadamard to the 1st qubit in the last row results in the outcomes in column 2. When Bob performs measurements in the computational basis states, he ends up with 4 possible outcomes with probability 1 each. These outcomes match what Alice meant to send in step-2, column-1. **Also note that the last outcome has a negative sign. As the probability is computed as the amplitude squared, -1 becomes 1 which is correct.**

Before we discuss further, let us solve an example on SDC now.

Example 1: A W state is a 3-qubit state of the form–

$$|W_n\rangle = 1/\sqrt{(2+2n)}\,(|100\rangle + \sqrt{n}e^{i\gamma}|010\rangle + \sqrt{(n+1)}\,e^{i\delta}|001\rangle)$$

Consider the particular case of $|W_1\rangle = ½\,(|100\rangle + \sqrt{2}\,|001\rangle)$. Show that if Alice takes qubit 1 and Bob takes qubits 2 and 3, Alice can perform a local unitary operation and send Bob her qubit, which results in the transmission of 2 classical bits to Bob.

Solution 1: If Alice does nothing to her qubit, then when she sends Bob the 1st qubit he has the state–

$$|W_1\rangle = ½\,(|100\rangle + |010\rangle + \sqrt{2}\,|001\rangle) = |\psi_{00}\rangle$$

in his possession. Now suppose that Alice applies the X gate. The state becomes–

$$X \otimes I \otimes I\,|W_1\rangle = ½\,(|000\rangle + |110\rangle + \sqrt{2}\,|101\rangle) = |\psi_{01}\rangle$$

If instead Alice applies iY, we will get–

$$iY \otimes I \otimes I\,|W_1\rangle = ½\,(-|100\rangle + |010\rangle + \sqrt{2}\,|001\rangle) = |\psi_{10}\rangle$$

Suppose Alice applies the Z-gate then it gives–

$$Z \otimes I \otimes I\,|W_1\rangle = ½\,(|000\rangle - |110\rangle - \sqrt{2}\,|101\rangle) = |\psi_{11}\rangle$$

Please note that these states are orthogonal.

For example,

$$|\psi_{00}|\,\psi_{01}\rangle = ¼\,(|100\rangle + |010\rangle + \sqrt{2}\,|001\rangle).(|000\rangle + |110\rangle + \sqrt{2}\,|101\rangle)$$

$$= ¼\,(\langle 1|0\rangle \langle 0|0\rangle \langle 0|0\rangle + \langle 0|1\rangle \langle 1|1\rangle \langle 0|0\rangle + 2$$

$$(\langle 0|1\rangle \langle 0|0\rangle \langle 1|1\rangle) = 0$$

Also note that this means that after Alice sends Bob the 1st qubit, he can distinguish among the states by making a 3-qubit projective measurement. With an acceptable coding protocol, Bob can recover the two classical bits 00, 01, 10 and 11 when he obtains the measurement result $|\psi_{00}\rangle$, $|\psi_{01}\rangle$, $|\psi_{10}\rangle$, or $|\psi_{11}\rangle$ respectively.

SUMMARY

Once you have a particular computation in mind, the next query is how to design a quantum circuit that achieves it. To do this, you need to specify what quantum gates are to be used and how they have to be "wired" together. A set of quantum gates and their associated wiring diagram defines a quantum circuit. **Note that the transformation of inputs to outputs of such circuits must be unitary because for it to be realizable quantum, the circuit must cause the quantum state i.e. the input to the circuit to evolve to evolve in accordance with Schrodinger's equation. This Schrodinger's equation always shows that an isolated quantum system will undergo a unitary evolution.** In nutshell, for a hypothetical circuit to have any chance of being realizable quantum mechanically, it has to implement a unitary transformation on its input. **Also note that this means that the quantum gates that make the circuit must themselves be unitary. The point to ponder is that unitary implies reversibility.** This means that the outputs of any quantum gate can be inferred, uniquely from its inputs and vice versa. In this chapter, we flesh out each of these steps.

MULTIPLE CHOICE QUESTIONS [MCQS]

1. Bits work on either 0 or 1 but quantum computers can work on–
   (a) Only 0. (b) Only 1.
   (c) Both 0 and 1 simultaneously. (d) None of the above.
2. Digital circuits use digital gates whereas quantum circuits use–
   (a) Vacuum tubes. (b) Quantum gates. (c) Transistors. (d) None of the above.
3. The matrices characterizing quantum gates are–
   (a) Unitary. (b) Ternary. (c) Binary. (d) None of the above.
4. The transformations performed by these gates are–
   (a) Non-reversible. (b) Reversible. (c) Linear. (d) None of the above.
5. A quantum gate has ________ number of qubits (1 2 or 3) at the input and at the output–
   (a) Different. (b) Equal. (c) Parallel. (d) None of the above.
6. **A** topological qubit uses 2D-quasi-particles called as–
   (a) Anyons. (b) Cations. (c) Anions. (d) None of the above.
7. Light particles emitted by diamond vacancies preserve the superposition of states. This helps them to–
   (a) To move information between quantum computing devices. (b) To shine.
   (c) To be used in ornaments. (d) None of the above.
8. ________ gates operate on a single qubit and leaves the basis state $|0\rangle$ unchanged but maps the basis state $|1\rangle$ to $e^{i\varphi}|\rangle$
   (a) Hadamard gates. (b) Phase shift gates. (c) Pauli gates. (d) Toffoli gates.
9. ________ states that "the probability density of finding a particle at a particular point is proportional to the square of the magnitude of the particle's wave function at that point"
   (a) Hilbert space. (b) Hilbert rule.
   (c) Schrodinger equation. (d) Born's rule.

10. ________ states that "the circuits that consist of only gates from the normalizer of the qubit Pauli group can be perfectly simulated in polynomial time on a probabilistic classic computer"

(a) Schrodinger's equation. (b) Gottesman-Knill Theorem.
(c) Born's rule. (d) Phase shifting.

11. XX, YY and ZZ gates are collectively named as–

(a) Ising gate. (b) Pauli's gate. (c) CNOT gate. (d) None of the above.

12. If Alice and Bob have a single qubit each, which they entangle, it is possible for Alice to teleport the information encoded in a 3rd unknown qubit into the–

(a) Alice's qubit. (b) Bob's qubit. (c) Eve's qubit. (d) All of the above.

13. Quantum teleportation sends quantum information by using the ______ and ______ properties of quantum mechanics–

(a) De-coherence and coding. (b) Entanglement and measurement.
(c) Superposition and interference. (d) None of the above.

14. Quantum teleportation will–

(a) Destroy the qubit to be teleported. (b) Will not destroy qubit to be teleported.
(c) Makes qubit fragile. (d) None of the above.

15. Quantum teleportation will transfer the information contained within qubit without knowing the information being transferred–

(a) True. (b) False. (c) Partially true. (d) None of the above.

16. No cloning theorem says that you can't clone a qubit. Then at what during teleportation does the unknown qubit collapses into a definite state–

(a) Once it is received. (b) Once it is measured after Hadamard gate.
(c) Once it is sent. (d) None of the above.

17. If Bob knows that his qubit is in $b|0\rangle + a|1\rangle$ state, which gate would he use to change it back into the original needed $a|0\rangle + b|1\rangle$ state?

(a) X (b) Z (c) X then Z (d) CNOT gate.

18. If Bob knows that his qubit is in $a|1\rangle - b|0\rangle$ state, which gate would he use to change it back into the original needed $a|0\rangle + b|1\rangle$ state?

(a) X (b) Z (c) X then Z (d) CNOT gate.

19. The phenomenon of evaluating the function at once over its entire domain by creating a superposition state for all values in its domain is called as–

(a) Quantum parallelism. (b) Quantum supremacy.
(c) Quantum Superposition. (d) All of the above.

20. In the figure shown below, M refers to–

(a) Multiplexing. (b) Modulation.
(c) Measurement. (d) None of the above.

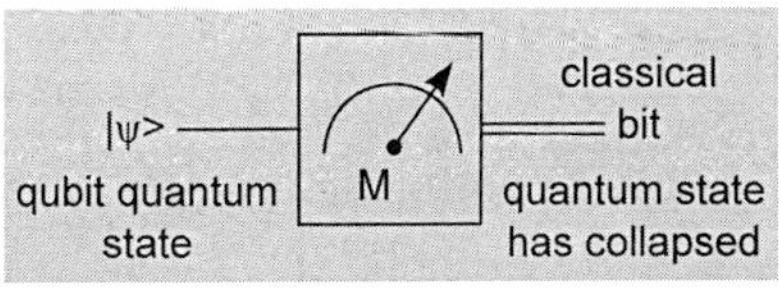

$|\psi\rangle$
qubit quantum state
M
classical bit
quantum state has collapsed

21. SDC refers to–

(a) Software Development Cycle. (b) Super Dense Coding.
(c) Simple Data Coding. (d) None of the above.

22. **Quantum cryptography** involves more than two parties in which quantum teleportation is possible and successful between any 2 parties with the aid of the 3rd party. This can be named as a–
   (a) Reliable tripartite quantum protocol. (b) TCP/IP protocol.
   (c) Random Forest protocol. (d) None of the above.
23. "A random quantum state can't be converted into a sequence of traditional classical bits and neither can they be used to reconstruct the original state." This is known as–
   (a) No-teleportation theorem. (b) No-cloning theorem.
   (c) No-hazard theorem. (d) None of the above.
24. Tools to build and analyze quantum circuits are–
   (a) QISKIT by IBM, OCEAN by D-WAVE. (b) Rational Rose by IBM.
   (c) Intellij. (d) None of the above.
25. The process of reconstructing the state for a source of a quantum system by measurements on the system is known as–
   (a) Quantum state tomography. (b) Quantum cryptography.
   (c) Quantum holography. (d) None of the above.
26. Which of the following is NOT correct about Quantum Teleportation Protocol (QTP)?
   (a) QTP uses Bell state.
   (b) In QTP, state of qubit is teleported from one place (source) to the other place (Destination).
   (c) Two classical bits are required to be sent from source to destination.
   (d) Source and destination must be on the Earth only.
27. During teleportation, the Block sphere components of Alice and Bob's qubit are identical. This shows that–
   (a) Qubit has been teleported from Alice to Bob.
   (b) Super Dense Coding has been achieved.
   (c) Entanglement has been achieved.
   (d) Both 'a' and 'b'.
28. Teleportation can't work faster than light because–
   (a) Still there is a need to maintain a classical communication link during teleportation.
   (b) No need of classical communication link.
   (c) Teleportation is inherently slower.
   (d) None of the above.
29. ________ describes the state of a quantum system.
   (a) No-teleportation theorem. (b) No-cloning theorem.
   (c) The trace. (d) A density matrix.
30. An abstract machine that can be visualized as a black box that produces some result is known as a–
   (a) Oracle. (b) Stub.
   (c) Driver. (d) None of the above.

Answers															
1.	(c)	2.	(b)	3.	(a)	4.	(b)	5.	(b)	6.	(a)	7.	(a)	8.	(b)
9.	(d)	10.	(b)	11.	(a)	12.	(b)	13.	(b)	14.	(b)	15.	(a)	16.	(b)
17.	(a)	18.	(a)	19.	(a)	20.	(c)	21.	(b)	22.	(a)	23.	(a)	24.	(a)
25.	(a)	26.	(d)	27.	(d)	28.	(a)	29.	(d)	30.	(a)				

CONCEPTUAL SHORT QUESTIONS WITH ANSWERS

Q1. What are the steps performed on a classical computer? Compare and contrast the steps of quantum computers too.

Ans. 1 The following **steps are performed on a classical computer–**

S1: Input data is provided that is stored in form of 0s and 1s.

S2: Processing is done using combinational logic circuits comprising of AND, OR and NOT gates. These gates are the building blocks of the digital logic circuits.

S3: Memory storage has to be done either in RAM or ROM.

S4: The control unit manages the control flow and keeps track of the current instruction to be executed.

S5: Using algorithms and data structures.

S6: The output is then generated in form of data or results.

S7: During program execution, errors or exceptions may occur and the computer must be able to handle those errors.

The following **steps are performed on a quantum computer–**

S1: Qubit initialization is the first step in preparing the quantum computer for the subsequent computation.

S2: A quantum circuit is then rigged. Quantum gates are used. These gates may be single-qubit gates, operating on individual qubits or multi-qubit gates acting on 2 or more qubits simultaneously.

S3: Superposition and entanglement are the pillars of quantum computing. Quantum computers exploit these principles to work.

S4: Quantum Algorithms leverage the unique properties of qubits and quantum operations to solve problems more efficiently than classical algorithms. For example, Shor's algorithm for factoring large numbers, Grover's search algorithm and quantum phase estimation. **Please note that these algorithms take the advantage of quantum mechanics to provide significant speedups over their classical counterparts.**

S5: Measurement of the qubits is the next step. It has been observed if you try to measure qubits then their superposition state collapses into classical bits (0 or 1). The solution to this problem is to **scan the qubit indirectly with the help of entangled particles.**

S6: Error correction and Noise mitigation is the next step. As we know that quantum computers are inherently susceptible to noise and errors due to their fragile qubit states, so this step is must.

Quantum error correction techniques, redundant qubits and error correcting codes are used to improve the accuracy and reliability of quantum programs.

S7: Hybrid Quantum–classical computing may be done wherein the quantum algorithms are designed to work in conjunction with classical algorithms. In such a scenario, a quantum computer solves a specific sub-problem and a classical computer handles the remaining tasks. **Also note that these hybrid classical-quantum computers can harness the strengths of both types of computing resources and thus provides powerful solutions to complex problems.**

Q2. What can you say about the following–

(a) Classical-to-quantum data conversion.

(b) Quantum-to-classical data conversion.

Ans. 2 (a) **Classical-to-quantum data conversion:** In order to transfer data from classical bits to quantum qubits, classical information must be encoded into quantum states. This process typically involves initializing qubits in the $|0>$ state and then applying a series of quantum gates to create the desired quantum states that represent the classical data. **For instance, the classical bit 0 can be represented by the qubit state $|0>$ while a classical bit 1 can be represented by the qubit states $|1>$.**

(b) **Quantum-to-classical data conversion:** If you want to convert the quantum information back to the classical data then quantum measurements are performed on the qubits. And these measurements collapse the qubit states into classical bit vales of either 0 or 1. **The flesh out of this is that the measurement process is probabilistic and the outcomes are determined by the amplitudes of the qubit states. Also note that the resulting classical bit values can then be used by the classical computers for further processing or output generation.**

Q3. What is the three-qubit teleportation protocol? Also give its mathematical description.

Ans. 3 The **protocol** is as follows–

Step-1: Alice and Bob meet up and make a qubit each, which we call as qubit #2 and #3. The point to ponder is that at this point, the 2 qubits are completely independent. We may think of the qubits as two different balls that don't contain any information about the other. Then, Alice and Bob decide to **entangle their qubits** by causing an interaction between the qubits like applying a CNOT gate. *You may think of entanglement as Alice writing some information on Bob's ball that only she knows how to read. And Bob writing information on Alice's ball that only he knows how to read.* For Bob to read Alice's information on his ball, Alice needs to send him a classical message describing how to understand it and vice-versa. They don't tell each other how to read the information. One possible entangled state **called as the Bell-state, that they decide to create is–**

$$1/\sqrt{2}\,|00> + 1/\sqrt{2}\,|11>$$

Alice takes her qubit and walks away. Bob takes his and walks in a different direction. This situation is like this–

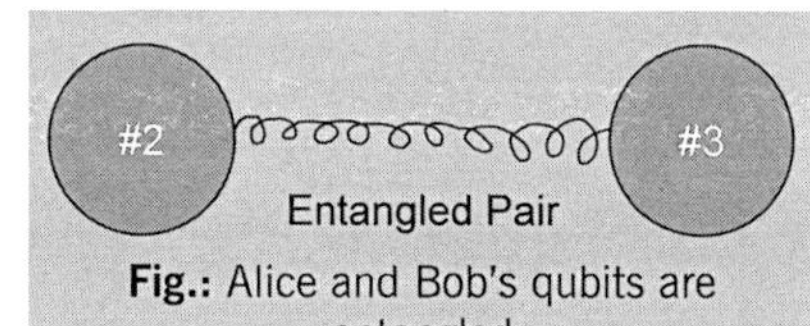

Fig.: Alice and Bob's qubits are entangled

Step-2: Now **Alice obtains a 3rd qubit in an unknown state (qubit #1) that she wants to transfer to Bob.** She can only communicate with him classically by email or phone and it would take too long to physically bring the qubit to Bob. Now the situation is like this–

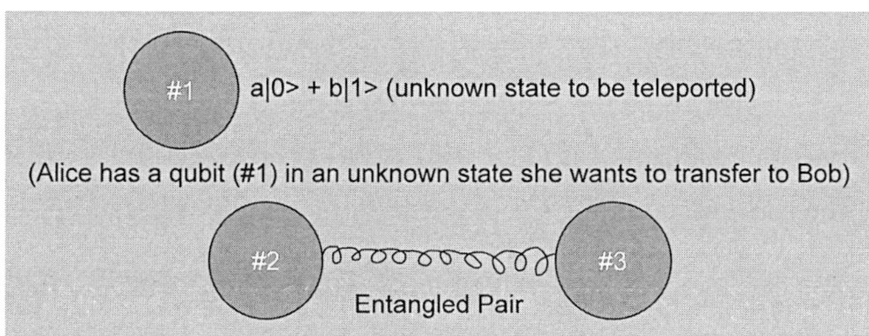

Step-3: Alice passes (interacts) **her two qubits (qubits #1 and #2) using a CNOT gate and measures the qubit she originally had (qubit #2).** Then she sends the **unknown qubit to be teleported** (i.e. qubit #1) **through a Hadamard gate** and **afterwards measures the output. Please recall that the Hadamard gate is used to create a superposition of states.** This situation is like shown below.

The point to ponder is that because Alice's original qubit (qubit #2) **was entangled with Bob's, the CNOT interaction with qubit #1 immediately changes the state of Bob's qubit.**

Mathematical Interpretation:

Input(s):

Qubit #1 is the qubit to be teleported;

Qubit #2 and #3 are the entangled pair shared by Alice and Bob.

Fig.: Alice passes her 2 qubits through a CNOT gate

In ket notation, the three qubit state is written in the order |#1 #2 #3>. Many other ways of writing them in ket notation exist but the order of the qubits is kept unchanged. **For example, if qubit #1 = |0>, qubit #2 = |1> and qubit #3 = |1> then they can be written as |0> |1> |1> = |011> = |0> |11> = |01> |1>.** This is many a times useful as we can then show if the gate ia acting on a single qubit.

From step-1 and step-2 we have that Alice and Bob's qubits in the Bell state, that is, $1/\sqrt{2}$ (|00> + |11>). Qubit #1 is in an unknown state a|0> + b|1>. In step-3, the three qubits need to be written together in ket notation by multiplying the qubit to be teleported by the entangled Bell state. The product is as follows:–

$$[a|0> + b|1>]\ [1/\sqrt{2}\ |00> + 1/\sqrt{2}\ |11>] = 1/\sqrt{2}\ [a|000> + a|011> + b|100> + b|111>] \qquad ...(1)$$

Next, we apply a CNOT gate using the first qubit in this equation-1 as the **control** and the second as the **target. Remember that the target (qubit #2) changes state only if the control is |1>.** After applying the CNOT gate the three-qubit state is–

$$1/\sqrt{2}\ [a|000> + a|011> + b|110> + b|101>] \qquad ...(2)$$

Next we apply a Hadamard gate to qubit #1 in equation-2. **Please understand that the Hadamard gate changes the states as follows:–**

The state |0> → $(1/\sqrt{2})$ (|0> + |1>) and |1> → $(1/\sqrt{2})$ (|0> – |1>). Hence, the three-qubit state is as follows:

½ [a (|0> + |1>) |00> + a (|0> + |1>) |11> + b (|0> – |1>) |10> + b (|0> – |1>) |01>)] ...(3)

In the next step, we distribute the product of qubits throughout equation-3 to find–

½ [a (|000> + a|100> + a|011> + a|111> + b|010>) – b|110> + b |001> – b|101] ...(4)

Last but not the least, we combine the like terms of equation-4 based on the first two qubits to get–

½ [|00> (a |0> + b|1>) +|10> (a(|0> – b |1>) + |01> (a|1> + b |0>) + |11> (a |1> – b(|0>)] ...(5)

Please note that the qubit #1 and qubit #2 belong to Alice. Also note that the state of Bob's qubit #3 has changed by applying the CNOT and Hadamard gates to Alice's qubits. From equation-5, we observe that Bob's qubit is currently in one of the four possible superposition states. That is,

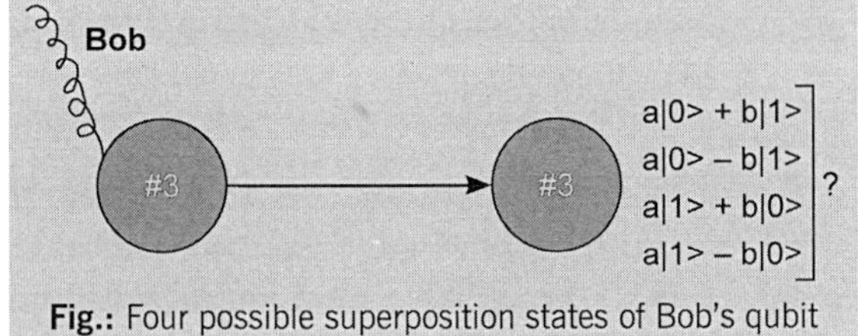

Fig.: Four possible superposition states of Bob's qubit

The four possible superposition states of Bob's qubit depend on Alice's original qubit #2 through the initial entanglement in step-1 as well as depending on the unknown qubit #1to be teleported from the CNOT gate in step-3. **Please note that we need to measure the state of Alice's qubit #2 and qubit #1 to find out the way Bob's qubit depends on these two. Also note that Bob has not done anything with his qubit at this stage.**

Step-4: Alice now sends the two classical bits of information from the measurements to Bob by email or phone. As per equation-5, her measurements can be 00, 10, 01 or 11. Each has 25% probability.

Depending on the measurement obtained by Alice, Bob can recover the original state of the teleported qubit i.e., a|0> + b|1> by using a combination of X or Z gates. This is shown in figure below. At this stage, **the qubit has been successfully teleported from Alice to Bob. This ends the teleportation protocol.**

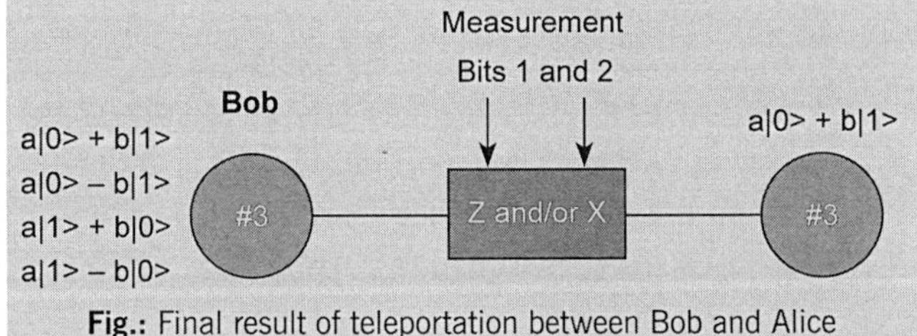

Fig.: Final result of teleportation between Bob and Alice

Conclusions: In this teleportation process, the original qubit #1 that has to be teleported does not remain in its original quantum state i.e. a|0> + b|1>. **This is so because Alice performs a measurement on it during the teleportation protocol. As a result, there is no copy of qubit #1 existing at any time. So, teleportation does not contradict the no-cloning theorem. Also understand that neither Alice nor Bob know what qubit #1's coefficients a or b are at any point in the process. All they know is that qubit #1 has been teleported from Alice to Bob.**

Q4. Suppose that f(00) = f(01) = 0, f(10) = f(11) = 1. Apply Deutsch-Josza algorithm and show that at least one of the first two qubits ends up as a 1.

Ans. 4 The input state is again $|\psi_{in}\rangle = |0\rangle\,|0\rangle\,|1\rangle$, and on applying Hadamard gate we get–

$$|\psi'\rangle = 1/2\sqrt{2}\,(|000\rangle - |001\rangle + |010\rangle - |011\rangle + |100\rangle - |101\rangle + |110\rangle - |111\rangle)$$

We apply U_f to the system, so we get–

$$|\psi''\rangle = 1/2\sqrt{2}\,(|000\rangle - |001\rangle + |010\rangle + |011\rangle + |101\rangle - |100\rangle + |111\rangle - |110\rangle)$$

Applying Hadamard gates to the first two inputs gives–

$$\begin{aligned}|\psi_{out}\rangle = {} & ¼\,[(|0\rangle + |1\rangle/\sqrt{2})\,(|0\rangle + |1\rangle/\sqrt{2})\,|0\rangle - (|0\rangle + |1\rangle/\sqrt{2})\,(|0\rangle + |1\rangle/\sqrt{2})\,|1\rangle \\ & + (|0\rangle + |1\rangle/\sqrt{2})\,(|0\rangle - |1\rangle/\sqrt{2})\,|0\rangle + (|0\rangle + |1\rangle/\sqrt{2})\,(|0\rangle - |1\rangle/\sqrt{2})\,|1\rangle \\ & + (|0\rangle - |1\rangle/\sqrt{2})\,(|0\rangle + |1\rangle/\sqrt{2})\,|1\rangle - (|0\rangle - |1\rangle/\sqrt{2})\,(|0\rangle + |1\rangle/\sqrt{2})\,|0\rangle \\ & + (|0\rangle - |1/\sqrt{2})\,(|0\rangle - |1\rangle/\sqrt{2})\,|1\rangle - (|0\rangle - |1\rangle/\sqrt{2})\,(|0\rangle - |1\rangle/\sqrt{2})\,|0\rangle]\end{aligned}$$

Again we expand this result and we get–

$$\begin{aligned}|\psi_{out}\rangle = {} & 1/4\sqrt{2}\,[(|00\rangle + |01\rangle - |10\rangle - |11\rangle)\,|1\rangle + (|00\rangle + |01\rangle + |10\rangle + |11\rangle)\,|0\rangle \\ & - (|00\rangle + |01\rangle + |10\rangle + |11\rangle)\,|1\rangle + (|00\rangle - |01\rangle + |10\rangle - |11\rangle)\,|0\rangle + (|00\rangle \\ & - |01\rangle + |10\rangle - |11\rangle)\,|1\rangle - (|00\rangle + |01\rangle - |10\rangle - |11\rangle)\,|0\rangle + (|00\rangle - |01\rangle \\ & - |10\rangle + |11\rangle)\,|1\rangle - (|00\rangle - |01\rangle - |10\rangle + |11\rangle)\,|0\rangle]\end{aligned}$$

We rearrange this equation as follows–

$$\begin{aligned}|\psi_{out}\rangle = {} & ¼\,[(|00\rangle + |01\rangle + |10\rangle + |11\rangle)\,(|0\rangle - |1\rangle/\sqrt{2}) + (|00\rangle - |01\rangle + |10\rangle - |11\rangle) \\ & (|0\rangle - |1\rangle/\sqrt{2}) - (|00\rangle + |01\rangle - |10\rangle - |11\rangle)\,(|0\rangle - |1\rangle/\sqrt{2}) - (|00\rangle - |01\rangle \\ & - |10\rangle + |11\rangle)\,(|0\rangle - |1\rangle/\sqrt{2})\end{aligned}$$

Hence, we observe that–

$$|\psi_{out}\rangle = |10\rangle\,(|0\rangle - |1\rangle/\sqrt{2})$$

Results: Measurement on the first two qubits returns 10 because at least one qubit was 1. **This shows that the function is balanced.**

Q5. List down some quantum effects.

Ans. 5 Some quantum effects are as follows:

(a) Superposition.

(b) Rotating qubits.

(c) Canceling qubit combinations.

(d) Entangling qubits.

(e) Back-to-back H gates for restoring qubit to its original state.

Q6. Deutsch's algorithm has three parts. What are they?

Ans. 6 Deutsch's algorithm has 3 parts as follows:

(a) **Incorporate** the function, F.

(b) **Embed** the function, F in a quantum circuit.

(c) **Collapse and measure** the top qubit only. A 0 indicates a constant function and a 1 points to a balanced function.

Q7. Explain the Deutsch oracle circuit. What will be the actual computation cost of the Deutsch oracle?

Ans. 7 The first quantum algorithm was **Deutsch oracle.** And its generalization to an arbitrary number of qubits was done by **Deutsch and Jozsa.** The circuit for the original bi-qubit oracle is as follows:

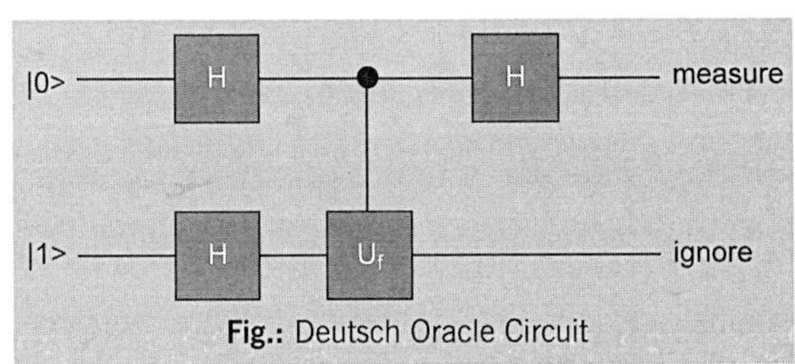

Fig.: Deutsch Oracle Circuit

It is crystal clear from the figure that the two boxes labeled as H represent the **Hadamard rotations. Please understand that its role is to rotate the qubit's polarization sideways** i.e. Hadamard gates rotate qubits sideways. The polarization is expected to be up or down initially. That is,

$$H|0> = 1/\sqrt{2}\ (|0 + |1>) \quad ...(1)$$

$$H|1> = 1/\sqrt{2}\ (|0 - |1>) \quad ...(2)$$

Also understand that when applied again, it restores the original polarization because H^2 = 1. The point to ponder is that this will not actually happen in this circuit because the controlled U_f gate couples both qubits. Therefore, something is going to happen to the top qubit between the two applications of H. Here, U_f is defined as follows–

$$U_f|x>|y> = |x>|y \oplus f(x)> \quad ...(3)$$

where $\oplus$ is a modulo-2 addition. It is controlled by f(x) NOT gate rather than controlled by X-NOT gate. **But please remember that if f(x) = x, then it is a normal controlled-NOT gate.**

Here, f(x) is an arbitrary function of the top qubit state that maps |0, 1} onto {0, 1}. Also, {0, 1} is a small universe. Hence, f(x) can be one of the only two things: either **constant or balanced. The latter means that it is either f(0) = 0 and f(1) = 1, or f(0) =1 and f(1) = 0. Also note that this circuit is called as an oracle because it answers a question: Is this function balanced?** The oracle says "yes" or "no" as the case may be.

What will be the actual computation cost of the Deutsch oracle?

In simple case of f(x) = 0, we end up with two pulses only for the whole algorithm—namely the two Hadamard operations that the top qubit is subjected to. On the other hand, in the complex case when f(x) = 1, the total number of gates is 11. **This means that we may have to perform up to 11 atomic operations on the two qubits in order to find out our answer,** whereas classically this calculation requires only two operations i.e. f(0) and f(1). A classical oracle would require 2^n measurements, one for each value of the argument to ascertain that f is constant. Say for n = 512, this converts to $1.34 * 10^{154}$ versus 512 measurements only. The oracle lets us determine whether the function is constant or balanced. For this, we have to measure all output lines on the top. If we find |0> on every line, the function is constant else it is balanced.

Q8. What is the source of the quantum computer's power?

Ans. 8 The source of the quantum computer's power is **the ability to run operations simultaneously on 2^n different values.** Although supercomputers can perform tasks parallel, deploying tens of thousands of CPUs sometimes. We may never be able to put together $1.34 * 10^{154}$ CPUs to match quantum computers.

Q9. State Deustsch-Jozsa problem.

Ans. 9 Deustsch-Jozsa problem is–

Given: For any combination of inputs, you are told what the function returns but not the function, F itself.

Determine: Whether the function, F is constant or balanced.

Q10. To comprehend the idea of qubit, throw some light on IBMs quantum computer.

Ans. 10 Qubits can be realized in different ways. In case of the quantum computer placed in cloud by IBM, qubits are realized using Josephson junction. **Note that the superconducting qubits used in the IBM architecture are known as Transmon qubits.** Different topologies of quantum computer are available. They can be accessed freely through the Internet. **For example,** IBMQX2, IBMQX4 and IBMQX5. IBMQX2 and IBMQX4 are **five-qubit quantum computers** whereas IBMQX5 is a **16 qubit quantum computer. Please note that in these computers we are not allowed to implement any arbitrary gate and that we have to select from a library of gates which is comprised of the gates from Clifford group and T gate.** The interactions between the qubits are not the same for all choices of two qubits. **Also note that the interaction between the qubits is stronger when a qubit having higher frequency is selected as the control qubit and qubit having lower frequency is chosen as the target.** To put it in a proper light, we can say that **the frequencies of the qubits determine the directions in which CNOT gates can be applied directly.**

Being superconductivity-based quantum computers, all of these IBMQX* series work at a very low temperature. As a natural choice, the operating temperatures for IBMQX2 and IBMQX4 are 0.0178K and 0.021K, respectively.

Q11. How are EPR pairs and Bell states related?

Ans. 11 An EPR pair refers to entangled pairs. **Please note that an EPR pair can be in one of the four states called as Bell states. These states form a normal basis–**

$|\beta_{00}\rangle = (|00\rangle + |11\rangle)/\sqrt{2}$ $\quad$ $|\beta_{01}\rangle = (|01\rangle + |10\rangle)/\sqrt{2}$

$|\beta_{10}\rangle = (|00\rangle - |11\rangle)/\sqrt{2}$ $\quad$ $|\beta_{11}\rangle = (|01\rangle - |10\rangle)/\sqrt{2}$

Also note that the four Bell states are the states of maximum entanglement between the two particles. And that any one of them can be transformed into any other by a purely local rotation of one of the particles. The last state in the above equations i.e. β_{11} is usually called as the **anti-correlated state.**

Q12. Construct a quantum circuit to create Bell states. Also derive the output equations of the first and the second stage of the circuit.

Ans. 12 The circuit below shows the quantum circuit to create Bell states–

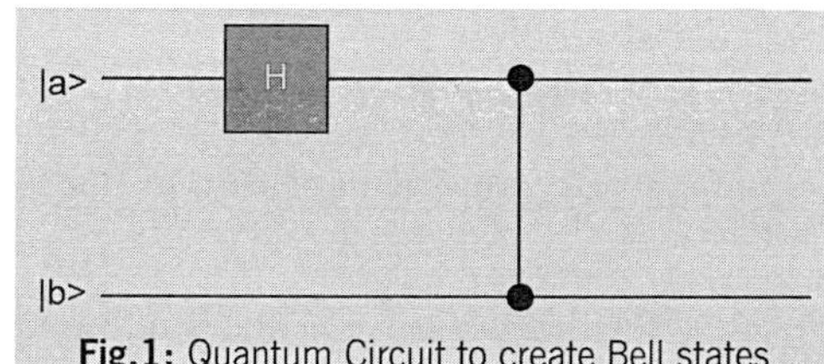

Fig.1: Quantum Circuit to create Bell states

This circuit takes as input two particles in pure states |0> and |1> and creates a pair of entangled particles. The circuit consists of a CNOT gate with a Hadamard gate on its control input. **To put it in a proper light, the truth table of the this circuit is constructed and is as follows:**

In	Out
$\|00>$	$(\|00> + \|11>) / \sqrt{2} = \|\beta_{00}>$
$\|01>$	$(\|01> + \|10>) / \sqrt{2} = \|\beta_{01}>$
$\|10>$	$(\|00> - \|11>) / \sqrt{2} = \|\beta_{10}>$
$\|11>$	$(\|01> - \|10>) / \sqrt{2} = \|\beta_{11}>$

Operation of circuit: Let us understand this circuit stage by stage now.

Stage-1: In this stage, two input qubits are transformed separately. The first qubit, |a>, is applied to the input of a Hadamard gate, H. It produces an output state |a'>. The second qubit, |b> is applied to the input of an identity gate, I, and produces an output |b'> = |b>.

Stage-2: In 2nd stage, we can see a CNOT gate with input state |V> and output state |W>. Hence,

$$|V> \ = \ |a'> \otimes |b'>$$

And

$$|W> \ = \ G_{CNOT} \, |V>.$$

Therefore, the output of the circuit is as follows:–

$$|W> \ = \ G_{CNOT} \, |V> = G_{CNOT} \, (|a'> \otimes |b'>)$$

To recall it again, we say that the output of the Hadamard gate with $|\psi> = \alpha_0 \, |0> + \alpha_1 \, |1>$ as input is–

$$(\alpha_0/\sqrt{2}) \, (|0> + |1>) + (\alpha_1/\sqrt{2}) \, (|0> - |1>)$$

Before we derive the output of the first and the second stage of the circuit, let us draw the circuit diagram with 2-stages now.

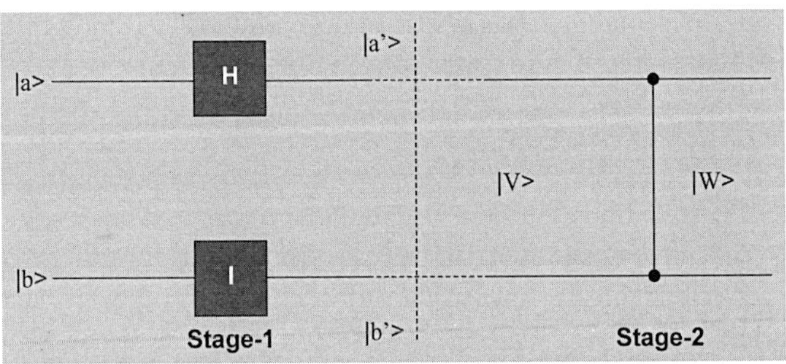

Fig.: Two stages of the circuit in fig.-1 showing I gate for the second qubit in the first stage

We are now in a position to derive the equations for these 2 stages.

There are 4 possible cases depending on the input qubits i.e. |a> and |b>.

Case-1: when |a> = |0> and |b> = |0>

$$|a'\rangle = (|0\rangle + |1\rangle)/\sqrt{2};\ |b'\rangle = |0\rangle$$

The **input state is** as follows:

$$|V\rangle = 1/\sqrt{2}\begin{pmatrix}1\\1\end{pmatrix} \otimes \begin{pmatrix}1\\0\end{pmatrix} = 1/\sqrt{2}\begin{pmatrix}1\\0\\1\\0\end{pmatrix}$$

The **output state** is as follows:

$$|W\rangle = G_{CNOT}|V\rangle = \begin{pmatrix}1&0&0&0\\0&1&0&0\\0&0&0&1\\0&0&1&0\end{pmatrix} 1/\sqrt{2}\begin{pmatrix}1\\0\\1\\0\end{pmatrix} = 1/\sqrt{2}\begin{pmatrix}1\\0\\0\\0\end{pmatrix} = |\beta_{00}\rangle$$

Case-2: when $|a\rangle = |0\rangle$ and $|b\rangle = |1\rangle$

$$|a'\rangle = (|0\rangle + |1\rangle)/\sqrt{2};\ |b'\rangle = |1\rangle$$

The **input state is** as follows:

$$|V\rangle = 1/\sqrt{2}\begin{pmatrix}1\\1\end{pmatrix} \otimes \begin{pmatrix}0\\1\end{pmatrix} = 1/\sqrt{2}\begin{pmatrix}0\\1\\0\\1\end{pmatrix}$$

The **output state** is as follows:

$$|W\rangle = G_{CNOT}|V\rangle = \begin{pmatrix}1&0&0&0\\0&1&0&0\\0&0&0&1\\0&0&1&0\end{pmatrix} 1/\sqrt{2}\begin{pmatrix}0\\1\\0\\0\end{pmatrix} = 1/\sqrt{2}\begin{pmatrix}0\\1\\1\\0\end{pmatrix} = |\beta_{01}\rangle$$

Case-3: when $|a\rangle = |1\rangle$ and $|b\rangle = |0\rangle$

$$|a'\rangle = (|0\rangle - |1\rangle)/\sqrt{2};\ |b'\rangle = |0\rangle$$

The **input state is** as follows:

$$|V\rangle = 1/\sqrt{2}\begin{pmatrix}1\\-1\end{pmatrix} \otimes \begin{pmatrix}1\\0\end{pmatrix} = 1/\sqrt{2}\begin{pmatrix}1\\0\\-1\\0\end{pmatrix}$$

The **output state** is as follows:

$$|W\rangle = G_{CNOT}|V\rangle = \begin{pmatrix}1&0&0&0\\0&1&0&0\\0&0&0&1\\0&0&1&0\end{pmatrix} 1/\sqrt{2}\begin{pmatrix}1\\0\\-1\\0\end{pmatrix} = 1/\sqrt{2}\begin{pmatrix}1\\0\\0\\-1\end{pmatrix} = |\beta_{10}\rangle$$

Case-4: when |a> = |1> and |b> = |1>

$$|a'> = (|0> - |1>)/\sqrt{2};\ |b'> = |1>$$

The **input state is** as follows:

$$|V> = 1/\sqrt{2}\begin{pmatrix}1\\-1\end{pmatrix} \otimes \begin{pmatrix}0\\1\end{pmatrix} = 1/\sqrt{2}\begin{pmatrix}0\\1\\0\\-1\end{pmatrix}$$

The **output state** is as follows:

$$|W> = G_{CNOT}\,|V> = \begin{pmatrix}1&0&0&0\\0&1&0&0\\0&0&0&1\\0&0&1&0\end{pmatrix} 1/\sqrt{2}\begin{pmatrix}0\\1\\0\\-1\end{pmatrix} = 1/\sqrt{2}\begin{pmatrix}0\\1\\-1\\0\end{pmatrix} = |\beta_{11}>$$

Hence, we have derived the equations for the **output of the quantum circuit that is used to create entangled particles from the particles in pure states.**

Q13. What is the necessary but not a sufficient condition for reversibility?

Ans. 13 A quantum computer consists of **input quantum wires** and **output quantum wires as conduits** for qubits and quantum circuits that are **further made of quantum gates. Please understand that the number of input and output bits of a classical gate may differ while a quantum gate maps q-input qubits into precisely q-output qubits.** This is the necessary but not a sufficient condition for reversibility.

Q14. Explain Teleportation with respect to quantum information theory.

Ans. 14 In teleportation process, we scan out part of the information from object-A, which we wish to teleport, while causing the remaining, unscanned, part of information to pass via Einstein-Podolsky-Rosen effect, into another object-C, which has never been in contact with A. Later, we apply to C, a treatment depending on the scanned-out information, to get C into exactly the same state as A was in before it was scanned.

Q14. What is the hidden variable theory?

Ans. 14 In a hidden variable theory, there is a variable or variables that determine the real polarization angle of photons. These variables have definite values from the moment of photons are formed. They determine what the result of the polarization measurement will be.

Q15. What is local realism?

Ans. 15 There are 2 assumptions that are followed in Gedanken experiment. These 2 assumptions are together called as **local realism.** They are as follows:

1. **Locality:** Measurements of different physical properties of different objects, carried out by different individuals, at distinct locations, can't influence each other.
2. **Realism:** Physical properties are independent of observations.

Q16. State and explain Landauer's principle.

Ans. 16 **There are 2 basis of Landauer's principle- one is energy consumption and the other is entropy.** Let us state them one by one now.

Law based on energy consumption: "When a computer erases a bit of information, the amount of energy dissipated into the environment is at least $k_B T \ln 2$". (where k_B is Boltzmann's constant and T is the temperature of the environment).

Law based on entropy: "When a computer erases a bit of information, the entropy of the environment increases by at least $k_B \ln 2$ with k_B as Boltzmann's constant."

Explanation: Landauer's principle traces the energy consumption in a computation to the need to erase information. He provides only a **lower bound on the energy consumption.** Just to recall that logic circuits in microprocessors need 500 $k_B T \ln 2$ in energy for each logic operation. A result of Landauer's principle is that- **"No strictly positive lower bound on energy consumption exists for a reversible computer, then in principle we can compute without any energy loss."**

According to Landauer's principle, the entropy of the entire system increases as a result of erasing information. The fact that erasing information requires consumption of energy is in strict agreement with the second law of thermodynamics. **Please note that erasing information reduces our knowledge about the state of a system that leads to an increase of the entropy. Also note that we need to consume energy to compensate for the increase of the entropy.**

Q17. What is adiabatic switching and hot-clocking?

Ans. 17 **Adiabatic switching** is the term that refers to a switching device that does not produce heat. A scheme in which the energy is saved by varying the power supply voltages is known as **hot-clocking.**

Q18. A rotation matrix by an angle γ is given below–

$$R(\gamma) = \begin{pmatrix} \cos\gamma & -\sin\gamma \\ \sin\gamma & \cos\gamma \end{pmatrix}$$

Describe the action of this operator on a qubit $|\psi\rangle = \cos\theta\, |0\rangle + \sin\theta |1\rangle$.

Ans. 18 The rotation matrix will act on the state as follows:

$$R(\gamma) \mid \psi\rangle = \begin{pmatrix} \cos\gamma & -\sin\gamma \\ \sin\gamma & \cos\gamma \end{pmatrix} \begin{pmatrix} \cos\theta \\ \sin\theta \end{pmatrix} = \begin{pmatrix} \cos\gamma\cos\theta - \sin\gamma\sin\theta \\ \sin\gamma\cos\theta + \cos\gamma\sin\theta \end{pmatrix}$$

But the basic formulas of trigonometry are as follows–

$$\cos(\alpha + \beta) = \cos\alpha \cos\beta - \sin\alpha \sin\beta$$

$$\sin(\alpha + \beta) = \sin\alpha \cos\beta + \cos\alpha \sin\beta$$

So, the rotated state can be written as-

$$|\psi'\rangle = \begin{pmatrix} \cos(\gamma + \theta) \\ \sin(\gamma + \theta) \end{pmatrix} = \cos(\gamma + \theta)\, |0\rangle + \sin(\gamma + \theta)\, |1\rangle$$

Recall again the block sphere. The rotation operator has rotated the state vector relative to the z-axis by an angle γ. **To put it in a proper light, we can say that the rotation operator has**

altered the relative length of each probability amplitude. Please note that if the original qubit is measured, the probability that we will find the system in the state |0> is given by $\cos^2\theta$ whereas the probability that we will find the system in state |1> is given by $\sin^2\theta$. Also note that if we rotate the state before measurement, then these probabilities are changed to $\cos^2(\gamma + \theta)$ and $\sin^2(\gamma + \theta)$ respectively.

Q19. Explain the following terms:

(a) Quantum sensors.

(b) Quantum imaging.

(c) Quantum metrology.

Ans. 19 (a) Quantum sensors: Entangled particles can be used to create highly sensitive and precise sensors. **For example,** entangled photons can be used in interferometry to measure small displacements and rotations with extreme accuracy. This has some potential applications in the emerging areas like geodesy, gravitational wave detection and basic physics experiments

(b) **Quantum imaging:** Entangled photons can be used to create images with better resolution and lower noise than classical light sources. Quantum imaging techniques have potential applications in medical imaging, microscopy and remote sensing.

(c) **Quantum metrology:** Quantum entanglement can be explored to get more precise measurements of physical quantities like time frequency and distance. This has applications in many fields like atomic clocks, global positioning systems (GPS) and the calibration or other measurement devices.

Q20. With a suitable diagram, explain the quantum computing layers and compare it with classical computing layers.

Ans. 20 The following figure compares different quantum computing architectural layers with that of classical computing layers:

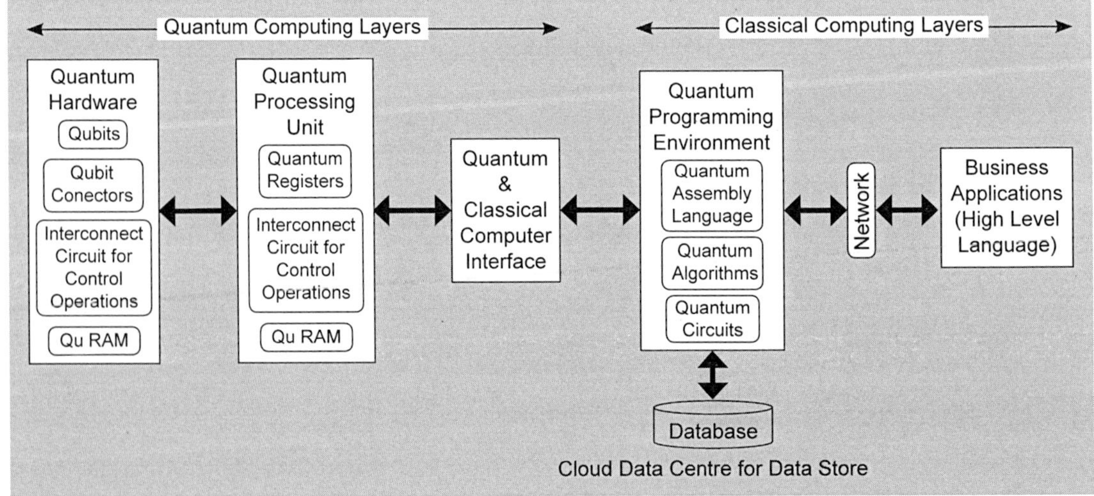

EXERCISE QUESTIONS

Q1. A **Gray code/mirror reflection code** of length n, G_n, is a sequence of binary numbers such that adjacent members of the list differ exactly in one position. Gray codes can also be defined recursively as follows:

$$G_1 = \{0, 1\} \qquad G_n = \{0G_{n-1}, 1G_{n-1}\}$$

For instance,

$$G_2 = \{00, 01, 11, 10\}.$$

(a) Construct $G_3 = \{g_0, g_1, g_2, g_3, g_4, g_5, g_6, g_7\}$.

(b) Construct the operator U_{GRAY} performing the circular transformations as follows:

$$|g_i> \rightarrow |\, g_{i+1}>$$
$$|g_{i+1}> \rightarrow |\, g_{i+2}>$$
$$\vdots$$
$$\vdots$$
$$|g_{i-1}> \rightarrow |\, g_i>.$$

Q2. Prove the relation as given below between the Toffoli gate, CNOT gate and I gates:

$$G_{TOFFOLI} = |0><0| \otimes I + |1><1| \otimes G_{NOT}$$

Q3. Design a full one-qubit adder constructed with Toffoli and CNOT gates. Display the values of the individual qubits at every stage of the circuit.

Q4. Construct the transfer matrix of the quantum circuit given below:

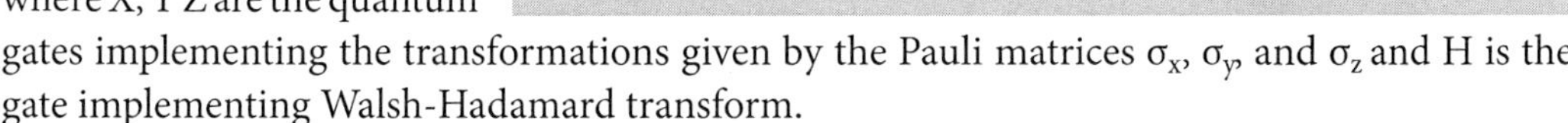

where X, Y Z are the quantum gates implementing the transformations given by the Pauli matrices σ_x, σ_y, and σ_z and H is the gate implementing Walsh-Hadamard transform.

Q5. Prove that the transfer matrices of the X, Z and H gates are unitary. Also verify these outputs.

Q6. Explain the steps performed on classical computers.

Q7. Explain the steps performed on quantum computers.

Q8. Explain the programming model for a quantum computing program.

Q9. Explain the Bell State operations on qubits.

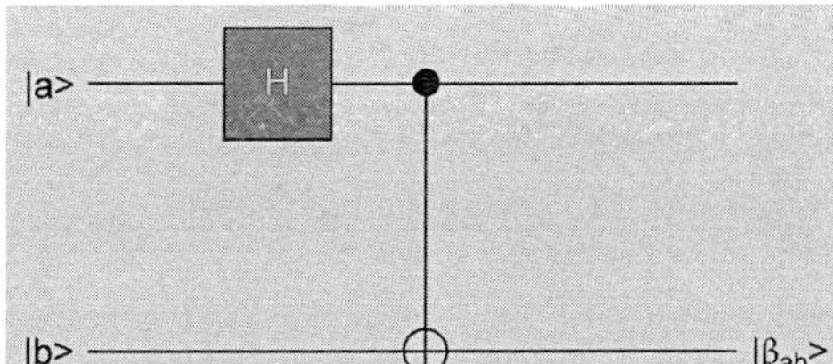

Q10. What do you mean by moving data between bits and qubits?

Q11. A Hadamard gate is applied to the qubit $|\psi> = \cos\theta\ |0> + e^{i\varphi} \sin\theta\ |1>$ and subsequently a measurement is made. What is the probability that this measurement finds the system in the state $|1>$?

Q12. Describe a circuit that will generate the Bell states.

[**Hints:** The diagram for a quantum circuit that creates Bell states is–

Time moves from left to right with wires used to represent the passage of time where the state is left alone. First of all, we apply a Hadamard gate to the qubit, $|a>$, to generate a superposition state. Then this is used as the control bit in a CN gate. The result is the Bell state, $|\beta_{ab}>$.]

Q13. Try to find out whether the controlled NOT gate can act as a cloning machine. Check whether can it clone the state $a|0> - b|1>$? Assume that the superposition state given by $a|0> - b|1>$ is used as the control qubit and that the target qubit is given by $|1>$. Then also consider the case where the target qubit is $|0>$. Can you think of any specific states that the CN gate might clone?

Q14. What is gate decomposition? Explain with an example.

Q15. Show that the following circuits are equivalent–

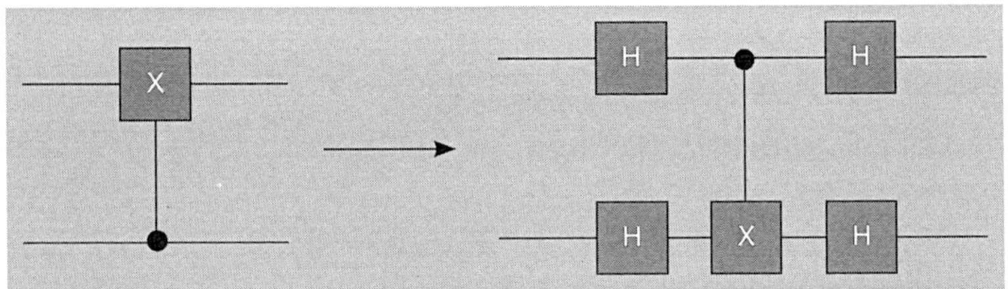

Q16. Consider a function with two inputs such that $f(x) = 1$. Explicitly show that the Deutsch-Jozsa algorithm works in this case by generating the vector $|y> = |00>$ as the final output.

Q17. The GHZ state is the three-qubit state given by–

$$|GHZ> = (|000> + |111>) / \sqrt{2}$$

Suppose that Alice takes the first qubit and Bob takes qubits 2 and 3. Show that this scenario can be used for superdense coding.

Q18. Explain the superdense coding protocol.

Q19. Draw a circuit diagram of quantum teleportation. Explain all steps followed.

Q20. Explain the following–

(a) Cancelling circuit.

(b) Splitting qubits.

(c) Tagging.

Q21. Explain the step-by-step analysis of Deutsch-Jozsa oracle.

Q22. Write short notes on–

(a) Quantum state tomography.

(b) Reversible gates.

(c) CCNOT gates.

(d) Toffoli gate.

(e) Topological quantum computer.

Q23. The Feynman gate is a 2 input/2 output gate given by–

$$x'_1 = x_1$$
$$x'_2 = x_1 \oplus x_2$$

(i) Give the **truth table** for the Feynman gate.

(ii) Show that **copying** can be implemented using the Feynman gate.

(iii) Show that the **complement** can be implemented using the Feynman gate.

(iv) Is the Feynman gate **invertible**?

Q24. The Fredkin gate $F(x_1, x_2, x_3)$ has 3 inputs (x_1, x_2, x_3) and three outputs $(y_1, y_2\ y_3)$. It maps Boolean patterns–

$$(x_1, x_2, x_3) \rightarrow (x_1, x_3, x_2)$$

If and only if $x_1 = 1$, else it passes the Boolean pattern unchanged. Draw its truth-table.

Q26. The Toffoli gate $T(x_1, x_2, x_3)$ has 3 inputs (x_1, x_2, x_3) and three outputs $(y_1, y_2\ y_3)$. It maps Boolean patterns–

$$(x_1, x_2, x_3) \rightarrow (x_1, x_2, x_3 \oplus (x_1 . x_2))$$

If and only if $x_1 = 1$, else it passes the Boolean pattern unchanged. Draw its truth-table.

Q27. What is superluminal communication? Explain with an example.

Q28. State and prove no-cloning theorem.

Q29. What is the basic key idea behind superdense coding?

Q30. In CNOT gate, the rule is that the second qubit undergoes NOT if and only if the first qubit is in state |1>. Explain this with its equations.

Q31. What is Square Root of NOT gate? What happens when we connect two SRNOT gates serially? Show that a deterministic NOT gate is obtained by connecting two SRNOT gates serially.

Q32. "Classical computing is deterministic whereas quantum computing is probabilistic computing." Justify this statement.

Q33. Show how a (4 * 4) Toffoli gate be constructed using (3 * 3) Toffoli gates.

Q34. Analyze the following Peres full adder circuit:

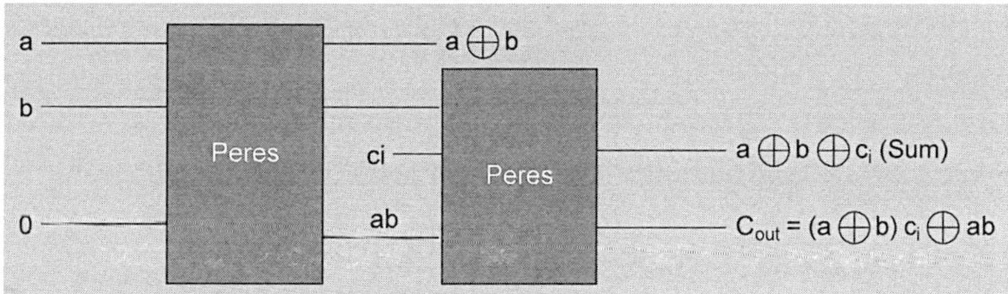

Q35. Prove that AND gate is a non-linear gate.

Q36. Prove that all reversible gates with 2 inputs and 2 outputs are linear.

Q37. What is the difference between the elementary transformation in the classical case and that of quantum case?

[**Hints:** Elementary transformation in the classical case is a map from B^n to B^n which alters and depends on a small number of bits and the remaining bits are not used. On the other hand, elementary transformation in the quantum case means the tensor product of an arbitrary unitary operator acting on a small number of qubits and the identity operator acting on the remaining qubits.]

Q38. Define what is an oracle/ black box.

[**Hint:**

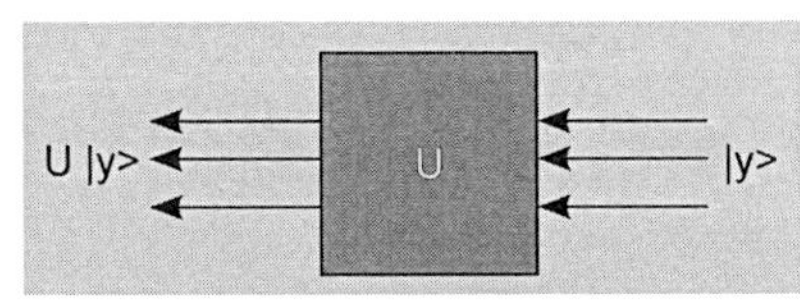

A quantum computer can query the oracle by sending y so that different values of y may form superpositions and the oracle will return superpositions accordingly. The oracle can encode the answer into a phase factor. Our oracle/black box is defined as an operator U acting by the rule as follows–

$$U\,|y> \;=\; \begin{cases} |y> & \text{if } A(y)=0, \\ -|y> & \text{if } A(y)=1.] \end{cases}$$

Q39. What is a Parameterized quantum circuit? Explain.

Q40. Define the following–

(a) Ancillary input.

(b) Garbage output.

(c) Quantum cost.

Q41. A scientist runs a quantum algorithm on a quantum computer. It includes 11,000 repeated shots of the same circuit design. The cost to execute this task includes a per-task charge of Rs. 80, plus 10,000 shots at a per-shot price of Rs. 0.750. What are the total cost charges?

Q42. Design a novel signed binary adder using quantum gates.

Q43. Design a novel signed binary subtractor using quantum gates.

Q44. Design a novel carry look-ahead adder using quantum gates.

Q45. Design a novel signed binary multiplier using quantum gates.

Q46. Design a novel squarer using quantum gates.

Q47. Design a novel exponential calculator using quantum gates.

Q48. Design a circuit to add three qubits (Full Adder). Show the circuit. Also draw its truth-table. Is there any other way of doing it?

Q49. Why is reversible logic a good solution in quantum computers?

Q50. Give an overview of basic quantum gates used for arithmetic computations.

Q51. Can you create a Java applet with a GUI that displays a qubit on the Block Sphere. The program requires as input the values of the complex coefficients α_0 and α_1 of the state vector,

$$\Psi = \alpha_0\,|0> + \alpha_1\,|1>.$$

When the user clicks on the link to the object stored on the web server, a GUI form should be displayed allowing the user to enter the mandatory data. Verify that $|\alpha_0|^2 + |\alpha_1|^2 = 1$. Also carry out the required computations and then download the applet.

Q52. A quantum programmer runs a quantum algorithm on the Rigetti quantum computer. This task includes 10,000 reported shots of the same circuit design. The cost to execute this task includes a per task charge of \$0.30 plus 10,000 shots at a per shot price of \$0.00035. Find the total charges?

[Hints: Task charges = 1 task × \$0.30/task

= \$0.30

Shot charges = 10000 shots × \$0.00035/shot

= \$3.50

Total charges = \$3.80 (\$0.30 + \$3.50)]

Quantum Algorithms

4

4.0 INTRODUCTION

An algorithm is a step-by-step procedure to solve a given problem. Just as there are classical algorithms, similarly we have quantum algorithms. These algorithms are used to solve complex problems easily. Today, even quantum computers and supercomputers are being used together, so the algorithms have to be modified accordingly. Algorithm is a pedantic topic. Algorithms must be precise, complete, unambiguous, and consistent and so on. Although the term algorithm is too anemic yet we say that an algorithm must be reliable and should produce correct output. **Please note that now we can define that a quantum algorithm is a finite sequence of well-defined instructions to solve a problem or a class of problems that are executed on qubits and quantum gates. Also note that these algorithms are just like classical algorithms except that they have at least a portion that is dependent on calculations using quantum computing. The point to ponder is that many quantum algorithms actually have a substantial part of the algorithm that can be executed in a classical computing manner, but with only a portion being executed in qubits.**

In this chapter, we will focus on three classes of quantum algorithms-

- Algorithms to find the **periodicity** of a function.
- **Search** algorithms.
- Algorithms for **simulation** of quantum systems.

According to Peter Shor, the quantum algorithms will offer a better speed-up over their classical counterparts into 3 categories:

(a) **Class-1:** Algorithms that find the periodicity of a function using Fourier Transforms. In this class, **Simon's algorithm, Shor's algorithm and Hallgren's algorithms** are included to solve various problems like factoring and computation of discrete algorithms, solving Bell's equation respectively.

(b) **Class-2:** Search algorithms that can perform an exhaustive search of N-items in $\sqrt{N}$ time. **Grover's search algorithm** falls under this class.

(c) **Class-3:** Algorithms for simulating quantum systems like **Feynman's approach. Please note that this is potentially a large class of algorithm but not many algorithms have been yet developed.** But the work is still in its infancy stage.

Also note that the quantum algorithms must rely on the superposition states for a better speed-up. Peter Shor quotes that if we assume that no polynomial time quantum algorithms exist for solving NP-hard problems, then the class of problems we have to search for is neither NP-hard nor P. The current challenge in the development of quantum simulation algorithms is to identify physical simulations requiring a small number of qubits (a number less than 100 qubits). Such a simulation would require a small number of quantum gates.

In this chapter, we will be studying 4 main quantum algorithms:-

(a) Shor's algorithm (by Peter Shor in 1994).

(b) Grover's algorithm (by Lov Grover in 1996).

(c) Deutsch's algorithm (by David Deutsch in 1985).

(d) Deutsch-Jozsa algorithm (by both David Deutsch and Richard Jozsa in 1992).

4.1 BASIC TECHNIQUES EXPLOITED BY QUANTUM ALGORITHMS—PROBABILISTIC VERSUS QUANTUM ALGORITHM

Quantum algorithms are computational procedures that leverage the unique properties of quantum mechanics like superposition, entanglement and quantum parallelism, to solve problems more efficiently than classical algorithms. Let us understand the basic techniques as exploited by different quantum algorithms versus classical algorithms.

The probabilistic search algorithms will assume a certain probability distribution over the state space of a system. That is, instead of knowing with certainty that at time, t, the system is in state j, we now know the probability distribution p (t). so, we can compute $p_j(t)$, the probability of the system being in state j at time, t. Hence, the system is defined now by a **state probability vector** as follows-

$$P(t) = (p_1(t), p_2(t), \ldots..p_j(t), \ldots)$$

Please note that the evolution of the system in time is obtained by multiplying the state probability vector with the state transition matrix. If we know P (t) at time, t = 0, then we can calculate P (t) for any t.

On the other hand, a quantum system is characterized by a state probability vector but this characterization is incomplete as we also need to know the amplitude of each state. **Also note that the amplitude is a complex number characterized by its magnitude and phase. The point to ponder is that the probability of a state is equal to the square of the absolute value of the amplitude of that state.** However, this phase does not have any analogy for classical probabilistic algorithms. In order to understand this, we consider two possible states of a qubit as follows:-

$$|\varphi_0\rangle = (|0\rangle + |1\rangle) / \sqrt{2}$$

$$|\varphi_1\rangle = (|0\rangle - |1\rangle) / \sqrt{2}$$

To put it in a proper light, the probabilities of observing the two basis states, $|0\rangle$ and $|1\rangle$ are the same for $|\varphi_0\rangle$ and $|\varphi_1\rangle$.

$$p_0 = p_1 = |+ 1/\sqrt{2}|^2 = ½$$

The amplitude of $|\varphi_1\rangle$ in state $|1\rangle$ is $-1/\sqrt{2}$ which means that its **phase is inverted.** For a coin tossing problem, $|0\rangle$ and $|1\rangle$ are the **basis states and $|\varphi_0\rangle$ and $|\varphi_1\rangle$ are obtained after tossing. In quantum**

algorithms, to flip a fair coin means to apply the Walsh-Hadamard transform, H, to the two basis states-

$$|\varphi_0\rangle = H\,|0\rangle$$
$$|\varphi_1\rangle = H\,|1\rangle$$

where
$$H = 1/\sqrt{2}\begin{bmatrix} 1 & 1 \\ 1 & -1 \end{bmatrix}$$

Here, **both of the states $|\varphi_0\rangle$ and $|\varphi_1\rangle$ have the same probability distribution i.e. ½ and ½ but the amplitude vectors for the two states are different i.e. $(1/\sqrt{2}, 1/\sqrt{2})$ and $(1/\sqrt{2}, -1/\sqrt{2})$, respectively. Also note that if we apply Walsh-Hadamard transform, H, to the state $|\varphi_0\rangle$, the system then ends up in the state $|0\rangle$ while H applied to the state $|\varphi_1\rangle$ leads to the state $|1\rangle$.**

Using these approaches, we shall be studying the following algorithms (table 4.1) in this chapter.

Table-4.1: Various Quantum algorithms.

Algorithm	Purpose	Problem type	Quantum speed-up	Main features
Shor's algorithm	• Factoring large numbers. • Finding discrete logarithms.	• Integer factorization. • Discrete logarithm.	Exponential.	Uses Quantum Fourier Transform (QFT). Polynomial time complexity compared to classical algorithms.
Grover's Algorithm	Unstructured search.	Unstructured search.	Quadratic.	Uses Grover's operator (i.e. diffusion operator). Applicable to a wide range of problems with an unsorted database.
Deutsch's algorithm	Determining if a function is balanced or is constant.	Oracle-based problem.	Polynomial.	First quantum algorithm to show speed-up. Uses Hadamard gates for equal superposition of basis states.
Deutsch-Jozsa algorithm	Determining if a function is balanced or is constant for n-bit input.	Oracle-based problem.	Polynomial.	A generalized version of Deutsch's algorithm for n-bit input. Solves a problem in a single query while classical algorithms need $(2^{n-1} + 1)$ queries.

4.2 QUANTUM FOURIER TRANSFORM (QFT) AND QUANTUM PHASE ESTIMATION (QPE)

QFT **is a process of linear mapping of fundamental algebraic structures.** It was invented by Don CopperSmith in 1994 (USA). The classical computers, FFT can be implemented in O (M log M) steps where M is the length of the input. But quantum computers can implement the FFT exponentially faster in O ($\log^2$ M) time. **The point to ponder is that how can an algorithm take time less than M. Please note that we can encode the input in a superposition of just m = log M qubits. This superposition consists of 2^m amplitude values.** So, we will write the superposition as follows:

$$|\alpha> = \Sigma_{(j=0 \text{ to } M-1)} \alpha_j |j>$$

Where α_i is the amplitude of the m-bit binary string corresponding to the number, i.

Also note that the |j> notation is really another way of writing a vector where the index of each entry of the vector is written out explicitly in the special bracket symbol.

To take the flesh out of it, we find that starting from this input superposition |α>, the Quantum Fourier Transform (QFT) manipulates it appropriately in m = log M stages. At each stage, the superposition evolves so that it encodes the intermediate results at the same stage of classical FFT. This can be achieved with m quantum operations per stage. Finally, after m such stages and $m^2 = \log^2$ M elementary operations, we obtain the superposition |β> that corresponds to the desired output of the QFT. We know that QFT provides an amazing speed. **The point to ponder is that the classical FFT algorithm outputs the M complex numbers β_0, ..., β_{M-1}.** On the other hand, **QFT just prepares a superposition as follows-**

$$|\beta> = \Sigma_{(j=0 \text{ to } M-1)} \beta_j |j>$$

Algorithm (Quantum Fourier Transform):

Input: A superposition of m = log M qubits, $|\alpha> = \Sigma_{(j=0 \text{ to } M-1)} \alpha_j |j>$.

Method: Using O (m^2) = O ($\log^2$ M) quantum operations perform the quantum FFT to obtain the superposition $|\beta> = \Sigma_{(j=0 \text{ to } M-1)} \beta_j |j>$.

Output: A random m-bit number j i.e. $0 \leq j \leq M-1$, from the probability distribution

$$\Pr[j] = |\beta_j|^2.$$

As already studied, a quantum circuit takes some number, n, of qubits as input and outputs the same number of qubits. In quantum circuits these n-qubits are carried by n- wires going from left to right. And a quantum circuit consists of the application of a sequence of elementary quantum gates to single qubits and pairs of qubits.

Two basic functionalities of quantum circuits to use when designing quantum algorithms are as follows: -

1. **Quantum Fourier Transform (QFT).**
2. **Classical Functions.**

QFT-based quantum circuits take n-qubits as input in some state |α> and the output state |β> that results from applying the QFT to |α>.

Classical functions, assume a function f with n- input bits and m-output bits. Say, we have a classical circuit that outputs f(x). Then, there is a quantum circuit that on input consisting of an n-bit string x padded with m 0's, outputs x and f(x). It can be shown that two recursive classical circuits can be emulated by a single quantum circuit.

Recall from the theory of supercomputers that the gates in the classical FFT circuit after recursive calls to $FFT_{M/2}$, the wires pair up j with M/2 +j. Now, we need to add and subtract these two quantities to obtain the jth and the $(m/2 +j)^{th}$ outputs respectively.

Now the point to ponder is that how can a quantum circuit achieve the result of these M classical gates? This is done as follows:

We just need to perform **the Hadamard gate on the first qubit. Also recall that for every possible configuration of the remaining (m – 1) qubits x, this pairs up the strings 0x and 1x.** So, translating this from binary means that we are pairing up x and M/2 +x. Furthermore, the result of the Hadamard gate is that for each such pair, **the amplitudes are replaced by the sum and difference that is normalized by 1/ √2,** respectively. However, the phase that must be applied to the $(M/2 + j)^{th}$ wire for each j requires more attention. **Please note that the phase of ω^j must be applied only if the first qubit is 1.** Now if j is represented by the (m – 1) bits $j_1, \ldots, j_{m-1}$, then $\omega^j = \Pi_{(l = 1 \text{ to } m-1)} \omega^{2jl}$. Thus, the phase ω^j can be applied by applying for the lth wire, for each l, a phase of ω^{2l} if the lth qubit is a 1 and the 1st qubit is a 1. This thing can also be done by another 2-qubit quantum gate i.e the controlled phase gate. it leaves the two qubits unchanged unless they are both 1.

Analysis of QFT:

The number of quantum gates is given by the formula: -

$$\mathbf{S(m) = S(m-1) + O(m) = O(m^2).}$$

So, QFT on inputs of size $M = 2^m$ will take $O(m^2) = O(\log^2 M)$ quantum operations.

QFT is a basic building block for very popular algorithm named as Shor's algorithm. **A quantum computer can perform Discrete Quantum Fourier Transform in $O(n^2)$ time using Hadamard gates and some phse shift gates.** On the other hand, classical computer does it in $O(n2^n)$, where quantum computer shows the exponential growth in time complexity.

Some points to remember before we explain QFT:

1. It **maps one vector to another.**
2. In **classical sense,** a Fourier Transform maps Vector, $X = (x_0, x_1, \ldots\ldots x_{N-1})$ to vector, $Y = ((y_0, y_1, \ldots\ldots y_{N-1})$ using the formula give below:

$$y_k = 1/\sqrt{N} \sum_{(n=0 \text{ to } N-1)} x_n \, \omega^{-kn}{}_N$$

where $k = 0, 1, 2, \ldots.., N-1.$

On the other hand, in quantum ecosystem, there is only a minute change that a QFT acts on quantum gates too. **Consider a basis state |x>, applying QFT on it** will result in the following operation-

QFT: $$|x\rangle \rightarrow 1/\sqrt{N} \sum_{(k = 0 \text{ to } N-1)} \omega^{xk}{}_N |k\rangle$$

Before we discuss further, let us see what are phase shift gates? They are single qubit gates that impact state |1> and will map it to $e^{i\theta}|1\rangle$. It shifts the phase of a vector in block sphere. **Please note that even swap gate and Z-gate are sometimes represented using this phase gates where** $\varphi = \Pi / 2$ and $\varphi = \Pi$ respectively. Its matrix representation is as follows:

$$R_\varphi = \begin{bmatrix} 1 & 0 \\ 0 & e^{i\theta} \end{bmatrix}$$

Also note here that the 1st column is the case of basis state, |0> and the 2nd one is for state |1> where it multiplies with e $^{i\theta}$. Tensor product is applied to all possible states of a qubit.

Mathematical Interpretation:

QFT is effectively a change of basis from the computational basis to a Fourier basis. **For e.g.**

1 qubit: States in computational basis are |0> and |1>.

States in Fourier basis are |+> and |- >

Recall that on a block sphere, north pole refers to qubit |0> while at south pole it refers to |1>.

And that we are going from basis on the two poles of the block sphere to a basis on the equatorial plane.

Next we will study two things on how to build a quantum circuit that applies QFT.

(a) Show QFT mathematically.

(b) Show circuit to implement QFT expression.

I. Show QFT mathematically:

As n qubits = 2^n basis states. Define N = 2^n. Then,

|x~> = QFT |x>

Fourier basis (↑ |x~>) Computational basis (↑ |x>)

$$= 1 / \sqrt{N} \sum_{(y = 0 \text{ to } N-1)} e^{2\Pi_{ixy} / N} |y>$$

(analogous to inverse discrete Fourier transform)

For e.g. 1-qubit case [=> N = 2]

$$|0^{\sim}> = 1 / \sqrt{2} \sum_{(y = 0 \text{ to } 1)} e^{2\Pi_{i(0).y} / 2} |y>$$
$$= 1/ \sqrt{2} \sum_{(y = 0 \text{ to } 1)} |y>$$
$$= 1 / \sqrt{2} (|0> + |1>)$$

Similarly,

$$|1^{\sim}> = 1 / \sqrt{2} \sum_{(y = 0 \text{ to } 1)} e^{2\Pi_{i(1).y} / 2} |y>$$
$$= 1/ \sqrt{2}\, e^{2\Pi_{i(0).y} / 2} |0> + e^{2\Pi_{i(1).y} / 2} |1>$$
$$= 1 / \sqrt{2} (|0> + (-1) |1>)$$
$$= 1 / \sqrt{2} (|0> - |1>)$$

Note: For multiple qubits. Say, n = 3,

$$|x^{\sim}> = 1 / \sqrt{8} \sum_{(y = 0 \text{ to } 7)} e^{2\Pi_{ixy} / 2^3} |y>$$

For example 1,

$$|y> = |4> \Leftrightarrow |100>$$

$$4 = 2^2(1) + 2^1(0) + 2^0(0)$$

$$4/2^3 = [2^2(1) + 2^1(0) + 2^0(0)] / 2^3$$

$|x\sim\rangle = 1/\sqrt{N}\sum_{(y=0 \text{ to } N-1)} e^{2\Pi_{ixy}/N}|y\rangle$ $\quad y = [y_1 y_2 y_3 \ldots y_n]$

$= 2^{n-1} y_1 + \ldots + 2^{m-n} y_n$

$$=1/\sqrt{N}\underbrace{\sum_{(y_1=0 \text{ to } 1)}\sum_{(y_2=0 \text{ to } 1)}\ldots\sum_{(y_n=0 \text{ to } 1)}}\, e^{2\Pi_{ix}/N\sum_{(k=1 \text{ to } n)} y_k 2^{n-k}}|y_k\rangle$$

$$= 1/\sqrt{N} \quad \sum_{(y_1, y_2, \ldots, y_k} \bigotimes_{(k=1 \text{ to } n)} e^{2\Pi_{ix}/N\ 2^{n-k}\ y_k}|y_k\rangle$$

$$= 1/\sqrt{N} \bigotimes_{(k=1 \text{ to } n)} |0\rangle + e^{2\Pi_{ix}/N\ 2^{n-k}}|1\rangle$$

$$= 1/\sqrt{N} \bigotimes_{(k=1 \text{ to } n)} |0\rangle + e^{2\Pi_{ix} 2^{-k}}|1\rangle$$

For $\quad k = 1$ term: $|0\rangle + e^{2\Pi_{ix/2}}|1\rangle$

For $\quad k = 2$ term: $|0\rangle + e^{2\Pi_{ix/4}}|1\rangle$

[Note: $\quad \mathbf{x = [x_1 x_2 x_3 \ldots x_n]}$

$\mathbf{x/2 = 0.\, x_1 x_2 x_3 \ldots x_{n-1}}$

$\mathbf{x/4 = 0\,0\, x_1 x_2 x_3 \ldots x_{n-2}}$ **]**

Final Form is:

$$\mathbf{1/\sqrt{N}\,(|0\rangle + e^{2\Pi ix/2}|1\rangle) \otimes (|0\rangle + e^{2\Pi ix/4}|1\rangle) \otimes \ldots\ldots (|0\rangle + e^{2\Pi ix/2^n}|1\rangle)}$$

i.e. we went from $|\mathbf{x_1 x_2 \ldots x_n}\rangle$ **to** ⟶ (the above)

For example 2:

$$n = 3 \text{ qubits} \Rightarrow N = 2^3 = 8$$

$$|x\rangle = |5\rangle$$

QFT $\quad |x\rangle = 1/\sqrt{8}\,(|0\rangle + e^{2\Pi i\,5/2}|1\rangle) \otimes (|0\rangle + e^{2\Pi i\,5/4}|1\rangle) \otimes (|0\rangle + e^{2\Pi i\,5/8}|1\rangle)$

NOTE: $\quad \mathbf{2\Pi i\,(5/2) = 2\Pi i\,(2^2/2 + 1/2)}$

$\mathbf{= 2\Pi i\,(2 + 1/2)}$

Since, $\quad \mathbf{e^{2\Pi i Z} = 1 \text{ for any integer } Z,}$

$\mathbf{e^{2\Pi i\,(5/2)} = e^{2\Pi i\,(2+1/2)} = e^{2\Pi i\,(1/2)} = e^{\Pi i} = -1}$ **]**

Having solved these examples, let us now discuss further on QFT.

$$|x\sim\rangle = 1/\sqrt{N}\sum_{(y=0 \text{ to } N-1)} e^{2\Pi ixy/N}|y\rangle$$

$$= 1/\sqrt{N}\sum_{(y=0 \text{ to } N-1)} e^{2\Pi ixy/_{2^n}}|y\rangle$$

Let us write $\quad y = \sum_{(k=1)} {}^{y}{}_{k}{}^{2n-k} \quad (y = y_1 \ldots\ldots y_n = 2^{n-1} y_1 + \ldots\ldots + 2^0 y_n)$

Then $\quad y/2^n = \sum_{(k=1 \text{ to } n)} {}^{y}{}_{k}{}^{2k}$

And we get-

$$|x\sim\rangle = 1/\sqrt{N}\sum_{(y=0 \text{ to } N-1)} e^{2\Pi ix}{}_{(k=1 \text{ to } n)}\, y_k/2^k \quad |y_1 y_2 \ldots y_n\rangle$$

$$= 1/\sqrt{N}\sum_{(y=0 \text{ to } N-1)}\prod_{(k=1 \text{ to } n)} e^{2\Pi ix}\, y_k/2^k \quad |y_1 y_2 \ldots y_n\rangle$$

Recall that-

$$\sum_{(y=0 \text{ to } N-1)} = \sum y_{1=0 \text{ to } 1} \sum y_{2=0 \text{ to } 1} \ldots\ldots \sum y_{n=0 \text{ to } 1}$$

$$\downarrow$$

$$|x^{\sim}\rangle = 1/\sqrt{N}\,(|0\rangle + e^{2\Pi ix/2}|1\rangle) \otimes (|0\rangle + e^{2\Pi ix/4}|1\rangle) \otimes \ldots\ldots (|0\rangle + e^{2\Pi ix/2^n}|1\rangle)$$

The point to ponder is that we went from-

$$|x\rangle = |x_1\rangle \otimes |x_2\rangle \otimes \ldots\ldots \otimes |x_n\rangle \text{ to}$$

$$|x^{\sim}\rangle = 1/\sqrt{N}\,(|0\rangle + e^{2\Pi ix/2}|1\rangle) \otimes (|0\rangle + e^{2\Pi ix/4}|1\rangle) \otimes \ldots\ldots (|0\rangle + e^{2\Pi ix/2^n}|1\rangle).$$

Hence, Proved.

II. Show circuit to implement QFT expression.

Please note that we went from-

(a) $|x\rangle = |x_1\rangle \otimes |x_2\rangle \otimes \ldots\ldots \otimes |x_n\rangle$ **to**
$|x^{\sim}\rangle = 1/\sqrt{N}\,(|0\rangle + e^{2\Pi ix/2}|1\rangle) \otimes (|0\rangle + e^{2\Pi ix/4}|1\rangle) \otimes \ldots\ldots (|0\rangle + e^{2\Pi ix/2^n}|1\rangle).$

(b) Each qubit went from $|x_k\rangle$ **to** $|0\rangle + e^{2\Pi ix/2^k}|1\rangle).$

Two observations:

1. $|x^{\sim}\rangle$ contains terms like $|00\ldots\ldots00\rangle$ $e^{2\Pi ix/2^n}|00\ldots\ldots01\rangle)$ $e^{2\Pi ix/2^{n-1}}|00\ldots\ldots10\rangle)$ $e^{2\Pi ix/2^1}|10\ldots\ldots00\rangle)$	2. e $|1111\ldots.1111\rangle$ $e^{2\Pi ix/2^1}\, e^{2\Pi ix/2^2}\, e^{2\Pi ix/2^3} \ldots e^{2\Pi ix/2^n}$ Hints: • Phase is qubit-dependent. • Need to add up more components with more "1"s

Now, 2 ingredients are required:

(1)

$$H|x_k\rangle = \begin{cases} (x_k = 0)\ (|0\rangle + |1\rangle)/\sqrt{2} \\ (x_k = 1)\ (|0\rangle - |1\rangle)/\sqrt{2} \end{cases}$$

$$= (|0\rangle + e^{\Pi ix_k}|1\rangle)/\sqrt{2}$$

$$= e^{2\Pi ix_k}/2$$

(2)

$$UROT_k|x_j\rangle = e^{2\Pi i}/2^k\,|x_j\rangle$$

$$\Rightarrow UROT_k = \begin{bmatrix} 1 & 0 \\ 0 & e^{2\Pi}i\ /2^k \end{bmatrix}$$

Applies phase $e^{2\Pi}i/2^k$

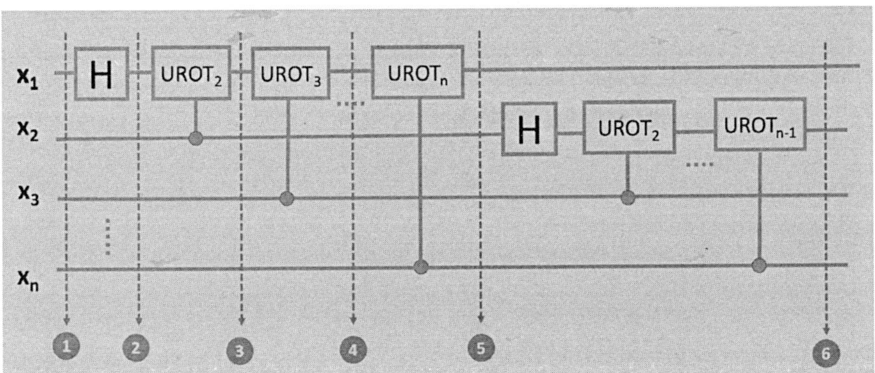

Building the QFT circuit

- Step 1 : $|x_1x_2...x_n\rangle$
- Step 2 : $[|0\rangle + e^{\frac{2i\pi}{2^1}x_1}|1\rangle] \otimes |x_2x_3...x_n\rangle$
- Step 3 : $[|0\rangle + e^{\frac{2i\pi}{2^2}x_2}e^{\frac{2i\pi}{2^1}x_1}|1\rangle] \otimes |x_2x_3...x_n\rangle$
- Step 4 : $[|0\rangle + e^{\frac{2i\pi}{2^3}x_3}e^{\frac{2i\pi}{2^2}x_2}e^{\frac{2i\pi}{2^1}x_1}|1\rangle] \otimes |x_2x_3...x_n\rangle$
- Step 5 : $[|0\rangle + e^{\frac{2i\pi}{2^n}x_n}...e^{\frac{2i\pi}{2^2}x_2}e^{\frac{2i\pi}{2^1}x_1}|1\rangle] \otimes |x_2x_3...x_n\rangle$

$$= [|0\rangle + e^{(\frac{2i\pi}{2^n}x_n+\frac{2i\pi}{2^{n-1}}x_{n-1}+...+\frac{2i\pi}{2^2}x_2+\frac{2i\pi}{2^1}x_1)}|1\rangle] \otimes |x_2x_3...x_n\rangle$$

$$e^{(\frac{2i\pi}{2^n}x_n+\frac{2i\pi}{2^{n-1}}x_{n-1}+...+\frac{2i\pi}{2^2}x_2+\frac{2i\pi}{2^1}x_1)} = e^{2i\pi(\frac{x_n}{2^n}+\frac{x_{n-1}}{2^{n-1}}+...+\frac{x_1}{2^1})}$$

and

$$x = 2^0x_n + 2^1x_{n-1} + ... + 2^{n-1}x_1 \Leftrightarrow \frac{x}{2^n} = \frac{x_n}{2^n} + \frac{x_{n-1}}{2^{n-1}} + \quad + \frac{x_1}{2^1}$$

so Step 5 is : $(|0\rangle + e^{\frac{2i\pi x}{2^n}}|1\rangle) \otimes |x_2x_3...x_n\rangle$, then :

- Step 6 : $(|0\rangle + e^{\frac{2i\pi x}{2^n}}|1\rangle) \otimes (|0\rangle + e^{\frac{2i\pi x}{2^{n-1}}}|1\rangle)|x_3x_4...x_n\rangle$
- Step '7' : $(|0\rangle + e^{\frac{2i\pi x}{2^n}}|1\rangle) \otimes (|0\rangle + e^{\frac{2i\pi x}{2^{n-1}}}|1\rangle) \otimes (|0\rangle + e^{\frac{2i\pi x}{2^{n-2}}}|1\rangle)|x_4x_5...x_n\rangle$
- Step 'final' : $(|0\rangle + e^{\frac{2i\pi x}{2^n}}|1\rangle) \otimes (|0\rangle + e^{\frac{2i\pi x}{2^{n-1}}}|1\rangle) \otimes ... \otimes (|0\rangle + e^{\frac{2i\pi x}{2^1}}|1\rangle)$

This is the reversed order from derived-form, but OK otherwise.

Let us discuss about Quantum Phase Estimation (QPE) now.

Problem: Recall that a unitary matrix has eigen values of the form $e^{i\theta}$ and that it has eigen vectors that form an orthonormal basis as follows:

$$U|\psi\rangle = e^{i\theta_\psi}|\psi\rangle$$

Can we extract θ_ψ given the ability to prepare $|\psi\rangle$?

Solution: Yes. Use QPE.

Why should we care about it?

(a) Hamiltonian evolution operator is unitary.

(b) Implications for quantum simulations.

So, the QPE trick is-

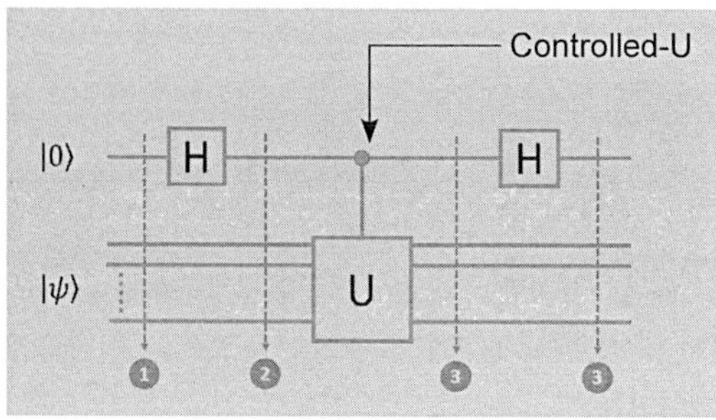

Let us again see this step-by-step.

- Step 1 : $|0\rangle\,|\psi\rangle$
- Step 2 : $\frac{1}{\sqrt{2}}(|0\rangle\,|\psi\rangle + |1\rangle\,|\psi\rangle)$
- Step 3 : $\frac{1}{\sqrt{2}}(|0\rangle\,|\psi\rangle + |1\rangle\,U|\psi\rangle) = \frac{1}{\sqrt{2}}(|0\rangle\,|\psi\rangle + |1\rangle\,e^{i\theta_\psi}\,|\psi\rangle) = \frac{1}{\sqrt{2}}(|0\rangle\,|\psi\rangle + e^{i\theta_\psi}\,|1\rangle\,|\psi\rangle)$
- Step 4 : $\frac{1}{\sqrt{2}}(\frac{1}{\sqrt{2}}(|0\rangle + |1\rangle)\,|\psi\rangle + e^{i\theta_\psi}\,\frac{1}{\sqrt{2}}(|0\rangle - |1\rangle)\ |\psi\rangle)$

$$= \frac{1}{2}(|0\rangle + |1\rangle)\,|\psi\rangle + e^{i\theta_\psi}(|0\rangle - |1\rangle)\ |\psi\rangle)$$

$$= \frac{1}{2}(|0\rangle\,(1 + e^{i\theta_\psi}) + |1\rangle\,(1 - e^{i\theta_\psi}))\,|\psi\rangle$$

Measuring qubit 0 : $P(|0\rangle) = |\frac{1+e^{i\theta_\psi}}{2}|^2 = \cos^2(\frac{\theta_\psi}{2})$; $P(|1\rangle) = |\frac{1-e^{i\theta_\psi}}{2}|^2 = \sin^2(\frac{\theta_\psi}{2})$
Not easy to measure θ_ψ for relatively small angles :

For $\theta_\psi = 1^\circ$: $P(|0\rangle) = 0.9999$ and $P(|1\rangle) = 7.615 \times 10^{-5}$

For $\theta_\psi = 10^\circ$: $P(|0\rangle) = 0.9924$ and $P(|1\rangle) = 7.596 \times 10^{-4}$
Measuring the phase on one qubit yields low precision.

Measure qubit 0:

prob. $|1 + e^{i\theta\psi}/2|^2$ => measure 0
prob. $|1 - e^{i\theta\psi}/2|^2$ => measure 1
} almost ½ each but with small shift.

if $\theta_\psi > 0$, prob[0] $= \cos^2(\theta_\psi / 2)$
prob[1] $= \sin^2(\theta_\psi / 2)$.

Please understand that to measure θ precisely using this bit of information, we need to do lots of measurements. For example,

θ_ψ = 1° => prob[0], prob[1] = {0.9999, 7.615 * 10^{-5}}

θ_ψ = 10° => prob[0], prob[1] = {0.9924, 0.007596}

Also note that this is not a good idea to try to measure with such a low precision.

Better solution is: Use multiple qubits to measure phase.

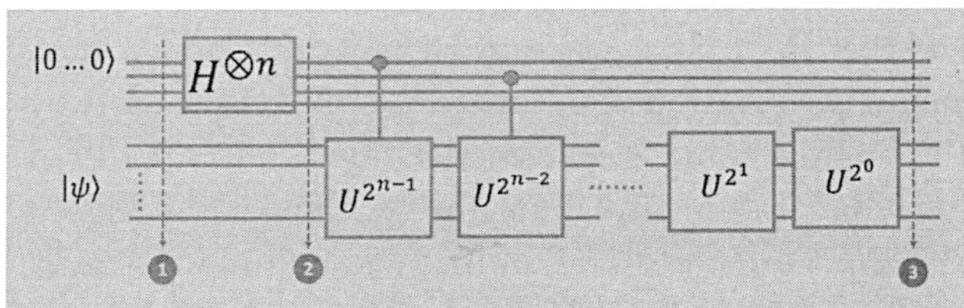

Hint: [Better solution = use multiple qubits to extract the phase.]

Step-1: $|0\rangle^{\otimes n}|\psi\rangle$

Step-2: $1/(\sqrt{2})^n\,(|0\rangle + |1\rangle)^{\otimes n}|\psi\rangle$

Before discussing further, please note that-

$$U2^x|\psi\rangle = U2^{x-1}U|\psi\rangle$$
$$= U2^{x-1}e^{i\theta\psi}|\psi\rangle$$

Step-3: $(1/\sqrt{2})^n\,(|0\rangle + e^{i\theta\psi 2^{n-1}}|1\rangle) \otimes (|0\rangle + e^{i\theta\psi 2^{n-2}}|1\rangle) \otimes \ldots\ldots\ (|0\rangle + e^{i\theta\psi 2^0}|1\rangle)$

Remember QFT form:

$|\tilde{x}\rangle = 1/\sqrt{N}\,(|0\rangle + e^{2\Pi ix/2}|1\rangle) \otimes (|0\rangle + e^{2\pi ix/4}|1\rangle) \otimes \ldots\ldots\ (|0\rangle + e^{2\pi ix/2^n}|1\rangle)$.

Please note that this is the same form but it changes $\theta_\psi \rightarrow$ to $2\pi\,\theta_\psi / 2^n$. So, we will get access to θ when applying QFT^{-1} on ancilla register.

Also note that the measurement should yield $2^n * (1/2^n)\,\theta$.

The complete summary of QFT is as follows: -

Quantum Fourier Transform

$$QFT:|j\rangle \rightarrow \frac{1}{\sqrt{2}}\sum_{k=0}^{N-1} e^{2\pi ijk/N}|k\rangle$$

$$QFT_n:|x\rangle \rightarrow \frac{1}{\sqrt{2^n}}\sum_{y=0}^{2^n-1} e^{2\pi ixy}|y\rangle$$

$$\rightarrow \frac{1}{\sqrt{2^n}}\sum_{y1=0}^{1}\cdots\sum_{y_n=0}^{1} e^{2\pi ix\left(\sum_{i=1}^{2^n} yt2^{-1}\right)}|y_1 \cdot y_2 \cdot, \cdots y_n\rangle$$

$$\rightarrow \frac{1}{\sqrt{2^n}}\sum_{y1=0}^{1}\cdots\sum_{y_n=0}^{1}\bigotimes_{i=1}^{n} e^{2\pi ixyt2^{-1}}|yt\rangle$$

$$\rightarrow \frac{1}{\sqrt{2^n}}\bigotimes_{i=1}^{n}\left[\sum_{yt=0}^{1} e^{2\pi ixyt2^{-1}}|yt\rangle\right]$$

$$\rightarrow \frac{1}{\sqrt{2^n}}\bigotimes_{i=1}^{n}\left[\sum_{yt=0}^{1}|0\rangle + e^{2\pi ix^{-1}}|1\rangle\right]$$

$$\frac{\left(|0\rangle + e^{2\pi i0\cdot x_n}|1\rangle\right)\left(|0\rangle + e^{2\pi i0\cdot x_{n-1}x_n}|1\rangle\right)\cdots\left(|0\rangle + e^{2\pi i0\cdot x_1x_2\cdots x_n}|1\rangle\right)}{\sqrt{2^n}}$$

$\longrightarrow$ **Basis States - Level**

$$QFT:|j\rangle \rightarrow \frac{1}{\sqrt{N}}\sum_{k=0}^{N-1} e^{2\pi ijk/N}|k\rangle$$

$\longrightarrow$ **Qubit - Level**

$$\frac{1}{\sqrt{N}}\sum_{y=0}^{2^{n-1}} e^{2\pi ixy}|y\rangle \rightarrow \frac{1}{\sqrt{2^2}}\sum_{y=0}^{2^{2-1}} e^{2\pi i(0..x_1..x_2)y}|y\rangle$$

$\longrightarrow$ **2,3 - Qubit Level**

$$\frac{1}{\sqrt{N}}\sum_{y=0}^{2^{n-1}} e^{2\pi ixy}|y\rangle \rightarrow \frac{1}{\sqrt{2^3}}\sum_{y=0}^{2^{3-1}} e^{2\pi i(0..x_2x_3)y}|y\rangle$$

$\longrightarrow$ **n - Qubit Level**

$$QFT_n:|x\rangle \rightarrow \frac{1}{\sqrt{2^n}}\sum_{y=0}^{2^{n-1}} e^{2\pi ixy}|y\rangle = \frac{\left(|0 + e^{2\pi i(0\times x_n)}|1\rangle\right)}{\sqrt{2}} \otimes \frac{\left(|0\rangle + e^{2\pi i(0\times x_{n-1}x_n)}|1\rangle\right)}{\sqrt{2}}$$

$$\cdots \otimes \frac{\left(|0\rangle + e^{2\pi i(0\cdot x_2\cdots x_n)}|1\rangle\right)}{\sqrt{2}} \otimes \frac{\left(|0\rangle + e^{2\pi i(0\cdot x_1\cdots x_n)}|1\rangle\right)}{\sqrt{2}}$$

4.3 AMPLITUDE AMPLIFICATION

Amplitude amplification **is a gate combination** that is frequently connected to the phase kickback mechanism (discussed in next section 4.4). **The process of amplifying one** particular **amplitude of**

the computational state vector of the control qubits, that are submitted to an oracle function, at the expense of all other amplitudes is known as amplitude amplification. It can replace the classical Monte Carlo simulations too. At Fermi Lab, a researcher in 2021 demonstrated a method to create an amplitude amplification working on a non-Boolean oracle. In 2016, Low and Chuang developed a technique named as **Qubitization that enables the creation of optimized amplitude amplification techniques.** This led to the development of the singular value transformation algorithm (QSVT) that brings an exponential speed-up by applying polynomial transformations to the singular values of a block of a unitary. It is similar to SVD (Singular Value Decomposition) of matrices to find the values in their diagonal matrix. It can also be used in QML techniques as well as with quantum least squares fitting algorithms. Many quantum digital processing techniques can avoid using a QFT and can provide better speed-ups for low-pass and high-pass signal filters.

Even Grover's search algorithm (to be discussed shortly) that is used to search unstructured data uses a trick called as **amplitude amplification that elevates the output from the unstructured mess.**

Steps for Amplitude Amplification

Step-1: For amplitude amplification to happen, there should be a uniform superposition of states i.e. $|s\rangle = H^{\otimes n}|0\rangle^n$.

Step-2: We have to pick up the King from the group of people using oracle. Amplitude amplification stretches the amplitude of the king, therefore, reducing the amplitudes of other items. Now the final measurement will result in the right answer i.e. the king. So, we apply oracle reflection to the king. This converts the amplitude of the king to **negative.**

Step-3: After the unitary transformation, U_w, in step-1 above, without any relaxation, apply another unitary transform U_s which will do not negate it more but instead **it will amplify it three times and decreases the amplitudes of other items. This is so because the secondary unitary transform that we have applied will flip the entire average amplitude which was decreased by negating the amplitude of the king due to the unitary transformation in step-2.**

Step-4: Now repeat steps-2 and step-3 nearly $\sqrt{N}$ times.

Note: In scenario of multiple search algorithms, repeat the above steps-2 and 3 $\sqrt{N/M}$ times.

4.4 PHASE KICK-BACK ALGORITHM

Phase kickback is the phenomenon that distinguishes quantum computation from classical computation. **It refers to the fact that controlled operations have effects on their controls as well as targets that effect corresponding phase operations.**

For example,

When a controlled NOT gate's target qubit is in the state $1/\sqrt{2}$ ($|0\rangle - |1\rangle$then the effect of controlled NOT gate is similar to the effect of applying a Pauli Z gate to the controlled NOT's control qubit. Many algorithms use this mechanism like Bernstein-Vazirani algorithm (to be discussed in next section) and in Quantum Phase Estimation algorithm.

Phase kickback actually provides a valid reason also for why qubits will be disturbed by measurements?

As already studied, that a measurement is an operation that flips a classical bit (the result) with the flip being controlled by a quantum bit (the qubit being measured). **The point to ponder is that this creates kickback from the bit to the qubit which randomizes the qubit's phase.**

Phase kickback is a powerful quantum phenomenon that uses entanglement properties to allow for the transfer of phase information from a target register to a control qubit. It plays a significant role in the design of many quantum algorithms.

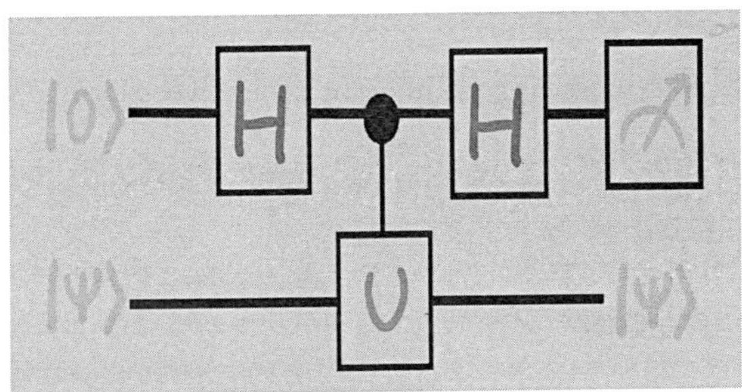

Fig.4.1: QFT circuit Diagram

In a phase kickback circuit, an ancilla qubit is prepared in a superposition state using a Hadamard gate and it acts as a control qubit for a controlled unitary gate applied to the target register. When the target register is in an eigenstate of the unitary gate, the corresponding eigenvalue's phase is "kicked back" to the control qubit. A subsequent Hadamard gate on the ancilla qubit enables the extraction of the phase information through measurement.

In Deutsch-Jozsa algorithm, lies a point of reference that by applying the unitary transform on the target qubit in superposition, we will get the function value, f(x), to show up in the global phase. **This phenomenon is known as the phase kickback trick.**

The role of oracle is to change the phase of the item found in the computational basis state vector, x. Please understand that instead of sending the phase to the ancilla qubit, y, it is applied to the result found in the source, x qubits. This is due to the phase kickback mechanism. For example, it has been used in the famous Grover's algorithm (to be discussed shortly).

To understand this mechanism, with an example of a two-qubit phase kickback circuit now.

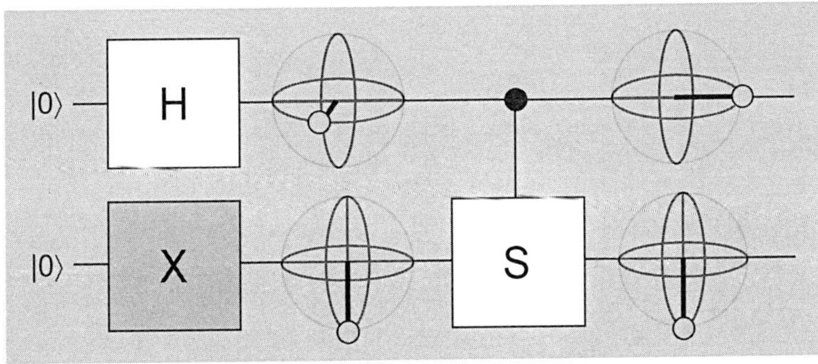

Fig.4.2: 2-qubit phase kickback circuit

Please note that a control-phase ends up modifying the phase of the control qubit instead of the phase of the target qubit. *This is perfectly valid and it works as after the X-gate being applied to the target qubit, the qubit state becomes an eigenvector of the control-S operation that is executed afterwards.* **Also note that it is not changed by a phase rotation.** Because a control-phase changes the global phase of both qubits, the phase modification can only happen on the control qubit. Inspite of the fact, that the entanglement created by the control-S gate, the qubits remains separable. In general, when the target qubit |ψ> is an eigen vector of the unitary, U (here, a S gate), the target qubit doesn't change after the control-U gate. Recall that U |ψ> = $e^{i\varphi}$ |ψ>. The control qubit also changes. One of its computational state vector amplitudes gets multiplied by the eigenvalue of the eigenvector of U.

4.5 QUANTUM PHASE ESTIMATION (QPE)

QPE was proposed by Alexei Kitaev (in 1995).

Quantum Phase Estimation (QPE) uses quantum Fourier Transform (QFT) and QPE itself is the core component of many complex algorithms like period finding and factoring of numbers. These two problems are complex to be solved by the classical computers. QPE algorithm tries to estimate the **eigenvalue** given the **eigenvector** of a unitary transform. **Please recall that the Eigen values of a unitary matrix are of unit norm. Also note that for a known unitary matrix, U, if we have an eigenvector |u> and a corresponding eigenvalue of $e^{-2\Pi i\varphi}$, then the objective of QPE is to estimate the phase, φ.**

QPE is an algorithm that is used to find the phase of an eigenvector of a unitary operator, U. This operator can be implemented as an oracle function that is applied to a quantum state |ψ> i.e. decomposed in n controlled- unitaries operating on m-qubits from |ψ>. We are looking for a phase angle θ according to U |ψ> = $e^{2\Pi i\theta}$|ψ>. Actually, this algorithm is based on the inverse QFT. *Practically speaking, the QPE can estimate the angle θ with a precision ϵ with executing U for 0(1/ϵ) times.* **This means a high probability within an error, ϵ). The angle θ is encoded over n-classical bits at the exit of the inverse QFT.**

QPE is the cornerstone of quantum chemistry quantum algorithms to find the ground state of a quantum many-body system. It has its applications in quantum linear algebra and quantum random walks. QPE is also used in the period finding part of Shor's algorithm. Because it uses QFT so this algorithm requires high-fidelity qubits.

Before we discuss further, let us solve some examples now.

Example-1: Design a three-qubit QFT circuit.

Solution 1: Consider the case when N = 2^3. Let us determine the transfer matrix, of the circuit.

We know that-

$$e^{i\theta} = \cos\theta + i\sin\theta$$

$$\cos(2k+1)\Pi/2 = 0$$

$$\sin(2k+1)\Pi/2 = 1$$

and

$$e^{i\Pi/2} = i$$

$$e^{i\Pi/4} = \sqrt{i}.$$

If we denote $\omega = \sqrt{i}$ we observe that $\omega^2 = i$ and $\omega^4 = -1$. We can then write-

$$R_2 = \begin{bmatrix} 1 & 0 \\ 0 & e^{i2}\Pi / 2^2 \end{bmatrix} = \begin{bmatrix} 1 & 0 \\ 0 & \omega^2 \end{bmatrix}$$

$$R_3 = \begin{bmatrix} 1 & 0 \\ 0 & e^{i2}\Pi / 2^3 \end{bmatrix} = \begin{bmatrix} 1 & 0 \\ 0 & \omega \end{bmatrix}$$

So, the transfer matrix of a **controlled-R_2 gate** is based on the derivation done earlier. Therefore, we have that-

$$G_{\text{controlled-R2}} = \begin{bmatrix} 1 & 0 & 0 & 0 \\ 0 & 1 & 0 & 0 \\ 0 & 0 & 1 & 0 \\ 0 & 0 & 0 & e^{i2}\Pi / 2^2 \end{bmatrix}$$

$$= \begin{bmatrix} 1 & 0 & 0 & 0 \\ 0 & 1 & 0 & 0 \\ 0 & 0 & 1 & 0 \\ 0 & 0 & 0 & \omega^2 \end{bmatrix}$$

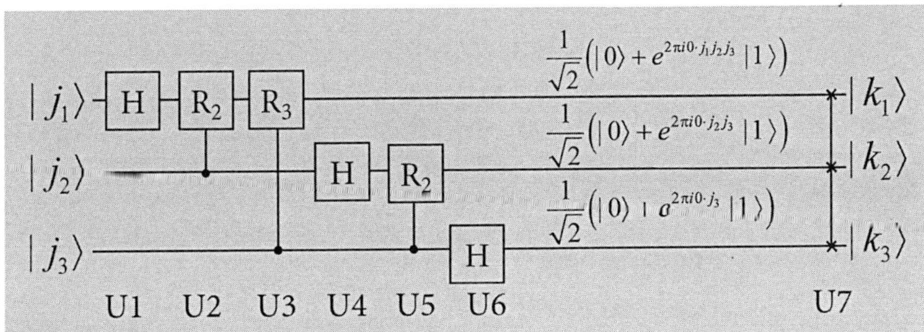

Fig.4.3: QFT circuit for $N = 2^3$ consisting of 6-stages with transfer matrix of individual stages are U_1, U_2, U_3, U_4, U_5 and U_6.

Explanation of circuit: From figure-4.3 we observe that the circuit consists of 6 stages. We calculate the transfer matrix of each stage. We denote a (2 * 2) identity matrix as I. The (4 * 4) identity matrix is denoted as I_4.

For 1st stage,

$$G_1 = H \otimes I \otimes I = 1/\sqrt{2} \begin{bmatrix} 1 & 1 \\ 1 & -1 \end{bmatrix} \otimes \begin{bmatrix} 1 & 0 \\ 0 & 1 \end{bmatrix} \otimes \begin{bmatrix} 1 & 0 \\ 0 & 1 \end{bmatrix}$$

Or we can write-

$$G_1 = 1/\sqrt{2}\begin{bmatrix}1 & 0 & 1 & 0\\ 0 & 1 & 0 & 1\\ 0 & 0 & -1 & 0\\ 0 & 1 & 0 & -1\end{bmatrix} \otimes \begin{bmatrix}1 & 0\\ 0 & 1\end{bmatrix}$$

$$G_1 = 1/\sqrt{2}\begin{bmatrix}I_4 & I_4\\ I_4 & -I_4\end{bmatrix}$$

and

$$I_4 = \begin{bmatrix}1 & 0 & 0 & 0\\ 0 & 1 & 0 & 0\\ 0 & 0 & 1 & 0\\ 0 & 0 & 0 & 1\end{bmatrix}$$

For 2nd stage,

$$G_2 = G_{\text{controlled-}} R_2 \otimes I = \begin{bmatrix}1 & 0 & 0 & 0\\ 0 & 1 & 0 & 0\\ 0 & 0 & 1 & 0\\ 0 & 0 & 0 & \omega^2\end{bmatrix} \otimes \begin{bmatrix}1 & 0\\ 0 & 1\end{bmatrix}$$

$$= \begin{bmatrix}I_4 & 0\\ 0 & M_{(2,4)}\end{bmatrix}$$

where

$$M_{(2,4)} = \begin{bmatrix}1 & 0 & 0 & 0\\ 0 & 1 & 0 & 0\\ 0 & 0 & \omega^2 & 0\\ 0 & 0 & 0 & \omega^2\end{bmatrix}$$

For 3rd stage,

From the circuit of figure-4.3, it is observed that this circuit performs the following mappings-

$|000> \rightarrow |000>$

$|001> \rightarrow |001>$

$|010> \rightarrow |010>$

$|011> \rightarrow |011>$

$|100> \rightarrow |100>$

$|101> \rightarrow \omega\,|101>$

$|110> \rightarrow |110>$

$|111> \rightarrow \omega\,|111>$

Hence, the transfer matrix of this 3rd stage is as follows:

$$G_3 = \begin{bmatrix} I_4 & 0 \\ 0 & M_{(3,4)} \end{bmatrix}$$

Where

$$M_{(3,4)} = \begin{bmatrix} 1 & 0 & 0 & 0 \\ 0 & \omega & 0 & 0 \\ 0 & 0 & 1 & 0 \\ 0 & 0 & 0 & \omega \end{bmatrix}$$

Similarly, **the transfer matrix of the 4th stage is-**

$$G_4 = I \otimes H \otimes I = 1/\sqrt{2} \begin{bmatrix} 1 & 0 \\ 0 & 1 \end{bmatrix} \otimes \begin{bmatrix} 1 & 1 \\ 1 & -1 \end{bmatrix} \otimes \begin{bmatrix} 1 & 0 \\ 0 & 1 \end{bmatrix}$$

Or we can say that-

$$G_4 = 1/\sqrt{2} \begin{bmatrix} 1 & 1 & 0 & 0 \\ 1 & -1 & 0 & 0 \\ 0 & 0 & 1 & 1 \\ 0 & 0 & 1 & -1 \end{bmatrix} \otimes \begin{bmatrix} 1 & 0 \\ 0 & 1 \end{bmatrix}$$

Therefore, the **transfer matrix of the 4th stage is-**

$$G_4 = \begin{bmatrix} M_{(4,4)} & 0 \\ 0 & M_{(4,4)} \end{bmatrix}$$

Where,

$$M_{(4,4)} = \begin{bmatrix} 1 & 0 & 1 & 0 \\ 0 & 1 & 0 & 1 \\ 1 & 0 & -1 & 0 \\ 0 & 1 & 0 & -1 \end{bmatrix}$$

Similarly, **the transfer matrix of the 5th stage is-**

$$G_5 = I \otimes G_{controlled\text{-}} R_2 = \begin{bmatrix} 1 & 0 \\ 0 & 1 \end{bmatrix} \otimes \begin{bmatrix} 1 & 0 & 0 & 0 \\ 0 & 1 & 0 & 0 \\ 0 & 0 & 1 & 0 \\ 0 & 0 & 0 & \omega^2 \end{bmatrix}$$

$$= \begin{bmatrix} M_{(5,4)} & 0 \\ 0 & M_{(5,4)} \end{bmatrix}$$

Where $M_{(5,4)} = G_{controlled\text{-}} R_2$.

And the **final last stage will be-**

$$G_6 = I \otimes I \otimes H = I \otimes H = 1/\sqrt{2} \begin{bmatrix} 1 & 0 & 0 & 0 \\ 0 & 1 & 0 & 0 \\ 0 & 0 & 1 & 0 \\ 0 & 0 & 0 & 1 \end{bmatrix} \otimes \begin{bmatrix} 1 & 1 \\ 1 & -1 \end{bmatrix}$$

$$= 1/\sqrt{2} \begin{bmatrix} M_{(6,4)} & 0 \\ 0 & M_{(6,4)} \end{bmatrix}$$

Where

$$M_{(6,4)} = \begin{bmatrix} 1 & 1 & 0 & 0 \\ 1 & -1 & 0 & 0 \\ 0 & 0 & 1 & 1 \\ 0 & 0 & 1 & -1 \end{bmatrix}$$

So, **the transfer matrix of the circuit** of fig. 4.3 is:

$$QFT_3 = 1/(\sqrt{2})^3 \begin{bmatrix} 1 & 1 & 1 & 1 & 1 & 1 & 1 & 1 \\ 1 & \omega^1 & \omega^2 & \omega^3 & \omega^4 & \omega^5 & \omega^6 & \omega^7 \\ 1 & \omega^2 & \omega^4 & \omega^6 & 1 & \omega^2 & \omega^4 & \omega^6 \\ 1 & \omega^3 & \omega^6 & \omega^1 & \omega^4 & \omega^7 & \omega^2 & \omega^5 \\ 1 & \omega^4 & 1 & \omega^4 & 1 & \omega^4 & 1 & \omega^4 \\ 1 & \omega^5 & \omega^2 & \omega^7 & \omega^4 & \omega^1 & \omega^6 & \omega^3 \\ 1 & \omega^6 & \omega^4 & \omega^2 & 1 & \omega^6 & \omega^4 & \omega^2 \\ 1 & \omega^7 & \omega^6 & \omega^5 & \omega^4 & \omega^3 & \omega^2 & \omega^1 \end{bmatrix}$$

So, we can also find the matrices G_1, G_2, G_3, G_4, G_5 and G_6. **But please note that an input $|v\rangle$ to the circuit above gets transformed to $G_1|v\rangle$ and then to $G_2G_1|v\rangle$ etc. Also note that after passing through 6 stages, it becomes-**

$$|w\rangle = G_6G_5G_4G_3G_2G_1|v\rangle = G_t|v\rangle$$

Where G_t is given by-

$$G_t = G_6G_5G_4G_3G_2G_1$$

We can also verify the expression for $GQFT_3$ directly from the definition of the QFT. In our example, n = 3 and the three input qubits are as follows:

$$|\alpha\rangle = \alpha_0|0\rangle + \alpha_1|1\rangle, |\beta\rangle = \beta_0|0\rangle + \beta_1|1\rangle \text{ and } |\gamma\rangle = \gamma_0|0\rangle + \gamma_1|1\rangle$$

So, the initial state of the system is as follows:

$$|v\rangle = |\alpha\rangle \otimes |\beta\rangle \otimes |\gamma\rangle$$

If the input state is:

$$|v\rangle = v_0 |000\rangle + v_1 |001\rangle + v_2 |010\rangle + v_3 |011\rangle + v_4 |100\rangle + v_5 |101\rangle + v_6 |110\rangle + v_7 |111\rangle$$

Then its transform is as follows:

$$|w\rangle = 1/(\sqrt{2})^3 (\omega_0 |000\rangle + \omega_1 |001\rangle + \omega_2 |010\rangle + \omega_3 |011\rangle + \omega_4 |100\rangle + \omega_5 |101\rangle + \omega_6 |110\rangle + \omega_7 |111\rangle).$$

Where,

$$\omega_0 = v_0 + v_1 + v_2 + v_3 + v_4 + v_5 + v_6 + v_7$$

$$\omega_1 = (v_0 - v_4) + (v_1 - v_5)\, \omega^1 + (v_2 - v_6)\, \omega^2 + (v_3 - v_7)\, \omega^3$$

$$\omega_2 = (v_0 - v_2 + v_4 - v_6) + (v_1 - v_3 + v_5 - v_7)\, \omega^2$$

$$\omega_3 = (v_0 - v_4) + (v_3 - v_7)\, \omega^1 - (v_2 - v_6)\, \omega^2 + (v_1 - v_5)\, \omega^3$$

$$\omega_4 = v_0 - v_1 + v_2 - v_3 + v_4 - v_5 + v_6 - v_7$$

$$\omega_5 = (v_0 - v_4) - (v_1 - v_5)\, \omega^1 + (v_2 - v_6)\, \omega^2 - (v_3 - v_7)\, \omega^3$$

$$\omega_6 = (v_0 - v_2 + v_4 - v_6) - (v_1 - v_3 + v_5 - v_7)\, \omega^2$$

$$\omega_7 = (v_0 - v_4) - (v_3 - v_7)\, \omega^1 - (v_2 - v_6)\, \omega^2 + (v_1 - v_5)\, \omega^3$$

Example-2: QFT of any periodic superposition with period k is an array that is everywhere zero, except at indices that are multiples of M/k and all these k non-zero coefficients have equal absolute values. So, if we sample the output, we will get an index that is a multiple of M/k and each of the k such indices will occur with probability 1/k.

Say, the vector $|\alpha\rangle = (\alpha_0, \alpha_1, \ldots\ldots, \alpha_{M-1})$ **is a periodic function k and with no offset (i.e. the non-zero terms are** $\alpha_0, \alpha_k, \alpha_{2k}, \ldots$**). Hence,**

$$|\alpha\rangle = \sum_{(j=0 \text{ to } M/k-1)} \sqrt{k/M}\, |jk\rangle$$

Show that its Fourier transform $|\beta\rangle = (\beta_0, \beta_1, \ldots\ldots, \beta_{M-1})$ **is also periodic with period M/k and no offset.**

Solution 2: Suppose that the input to the QFT, $|\alpha\rangle = (\alpha_0, \alpha_1, \ldots\ldots, \alpha_{M-1})$ is such that $\alpha_i = \alpha_j$ when i= j mod k, where k is a particular integer that divides M. That is, the array, α consists of M/k repetitions of some sequence $(\alpha_0, \alpha_1, \ldots\ldots, \alpha_{k-1})$ of length k. Also suppose that exactly one of the k numbers $(\alpha_0, \alpha_1, \ldots\ldots, \alpha_{k-1})$ is non-zero, say α_j. Then, we can say that $|\alpha\rangle$ is periodic with period k and offset j. this gives us an important conclusion that if the input vector is periodic, we can use QFT sampling to compute its period.

Rule: If the input to QFT sampling is periodic with period k, for some k that divides M. Then, the output will be a multiple of M/k and it is equally likely to be any of the k multiples of M/k.

The point to ponder is that by repeating the sampling a few times and then taking the GCD of all indices returned, we will get the number M/k with a very high probability and then from it the period k of the input.

Proof: In the input vector, the coefficient α_l is $\sqrt{k/M}$ if k divides l and is zero otherwise. Substituting this in the formula for the jth coefficient of $|\beta>$:

$$\beta_j = 1/\sqrt{M} \sum_{(l=0 \text{ to } M-1)} \omega^{jl} \alpha_l = \sqrt{k} / M \sum_{(l=0 \text{ to } M/k-1)} \omega^{jik}.$$

The summation is a geometric series, $1 + \omega^{jk} + \omega^{2jk} + \omega^{3jk} + \ldots\ldots$, containing M/k terms and with ratio ω^{jk}. Remember that, ω is a complex Mth root of unity.

Two cases arise:

Case-1: If the ratio is exactly 1.

Case-2: If the ratio is not 1.

Case-1: If the ratio is exactly 1, that happens if jk = 0 mod M then the sum of the series is simply the number of terms.

Case-2: If the ratio is not 1, we can apply the usual formula for geometric series to find that the sum is as follows:

$$1 - \omega^{jk(M/k)} / (1 - \omega^{jk}) = (1 - \omega^{Mj}) / (1 - \omega^{jk}) = 0$$

Hence, β_j is $1/\sqrt{k}$ if M divides jk and is zero otherwise.

In general, we can assume the original superposition to be periodic with period k but with some offset, l < k as follows:

$$|\alpha> = \sum_{(j=0 \text{ to } M/k-1)} \sqrt{k/M}\, |jk + l>.$$

Then, the Fourier Transform, $|\beta>$ will have non-zero amplitudes precisely at multiples of M/k.

4.6 QUANTUM WALKS

Quantum walks are more beneficial than classical random walks. **In case of classical random walks,** a particle starts out in some initial position / vertex on a graph, G = (V, E) and walks to neighboring vertices in a probabilistic manner. The final probability distribution of finding the particle at a given vertex, V is desired. **For example,** 1D walk on a line is an example of classical random walk. These walks are implemented be generating pseudo-random numbers at each step. The particle's position is updated, at each iteration according to the outcome of random number generator. On the other hand, **Quantum random walk is a** random walk that utilizes the quantum evolution based on **a Hamiltonian graph.** At the end of the random walk, we get the **probability amplitude vector** pertaining to vertices of the graph.

Let us tabulate the differences between the two.

Classical Random Walk	Quantum Random Walk
1. In this type of walk, the walker moves to one of the vertices with some probability.	1. Quantum random walks are based on the probability amplitudes.
2. Classical random walks converge to any limiting distribution.	2. Quantum random walks do not converge to any limiting distribution.
3. Superposition and interference causes drastic difference between the quantum and classical random walk.	3. Superposition and interference causes drastic difference between the quantum and classical random walk.

Classical Random Walk	Quantum Random Walk
4. Quantum random walks do not spread faster than classical random walk.	4. Quantum random walks spread faster than classical random walk.
5. Classical random walks don't have faster **hitting times (h_{AB}) that is defined as the expected time it takes for the walker starting at vertex A to reach vertex B for the first time.**	5. Quantum random walks have faster **hitting times (h_{AB}) that is defined as the expected time it takes for the walker starting at vertex A to reach vertex B for the first time.**

In case of quantum random walk, the Hamiltonian graph, H_G is generally an **adjacency matrix.** Many a times, it is desired to add the identity matrix, I, so that each vertex of the graph has an edge to itself. **Such a graph is known as a complete graph.** In this scenario, the Hamiltonian graph, is given by-

$$H_G = A + I$$

Please understand that once we have the Hamiltonian graph, we can use a suitable number of qubits to define a quantum system. For example, say if we have N vertices in the graph, then we can have a quantum system of $n = \log_2 (N)$ qubits. Then the quantum system of n-qubits is obtained using the Schrodinger's equation. That is,

$$H_G |\psi (t)>$$

Also understand that the state $|\psi (t)>$ would contain the probability amplitudes of each vertex in the graph at time, t.

4.7 MAJOR ALGORITHMS

According to Peter Shor, the quantum algorithms will offer a better speed-up over their classical counterparts into 3 categories:

(d) **Class-1:** Algorithms that find the periodicity of a function using Fourier Transforms. In this class, **Simon's algorithm, Shor's algorithm and Hallgren's algorithms** are included to solve various problems like factoring and computation of discrete algorithms, solving Bell's equation respectively.

(e) **Class-2:** Search algorithms that can perform an exhaustive search of N-items in $\sqrt{N}$ time. **Grover's search algorithm** falls under this class.

(f) **Class-3:** Algorithms for simulating quantum systems like **Feynman's approach. Please note that this is potentially a large class of algorithm but not many algorithms have been yet developed.** But the work is still in its infancy stage.

Also note that the quantum algorithms must rely on the superposition states for a better speed-up. Peter Shor quotes that if we assume that no polynomial time quantum algorithms exist for solving NP-hard problems, then the class of problems we have to search for is neither NP-hard nor P. The current challenge in the development of quantum simulation algorithms is to identify physical simulations requiring a small number of qubits (a number less than 100 qubits). Such a simulation would require a small number of quantum gates.

In this chapter, we will be studying 4 main quantum algorithms:-

(e) Shor's algorithm (by Peter Shor in 1994).

(f) Grover's algorithm (by Lov Grover in 1996).

(g) Deutsch's algorithm (by David Deutsch in 1985).

(h) Deutsch-Jozsa algorithm (by both David Deutsch and Richard Jozsa in 1992).

4.8 SHOR'S ALGORITHM

Peter Shor (1994) found a polynomial time algorithm for the factorization of n-bit numbers on computers. It finds prime factors for an integer, N. It is a quantum algorithm. It can be used to hack the RSA encryption with the aid of few classical lines of code. It needs more qubits than those exist currently. A quantum computer can also hack a 2048 bit RSA encryption. **Please understand that the Shor's algorithm gives exponential speed-up over common classical algorithm for factoring. Also note that because of the usage of QFT and a method called Modular Exponentiation which is used to find the remainder when a variable is raised to the exponent power and divided by a positive integer.** This simplifies the hardest task that stops a classical computer to factor prime numbers. Also recall that the decoherence and errors cause issues. Even then IBM was successful to a factor 15 to 3 * 5 in 2001.

This algorithm can be classified in 2 parts: **a classical part that is executed on a classical computer and a quantum part which takes the help of a quantum computer.** In classical way, we should go on guessing one number at a time and check if it works. **To put it in a proper light, even Shor's algorithm starts with a random guess of a number.**

Principle: Shor's algorithm reduces the factorization problem to the problem of finding the period of a function but uses quantum parallelism to find a superposition of all values of the function in one step. The algorithm, then, computes the QFT of the function that sets the amplitudes into multiples of the fundamental frequency (f = 1/ T). **Now to factor an integer, Shor's algorithm measures the period of the function.**

Workflow: The integer factorization problem reduces to another problem i.e. **order finding, which in turn requires phase estimation which further requires QFT.** This can be shown as follows (see figure-4.4):

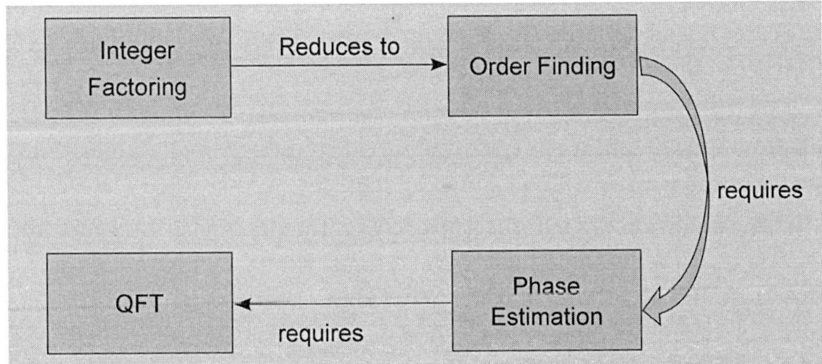

Fig.4.4: Symbiotic association between Integer Factorization, order finding, phase estimation and QFT

This symbiotic association is quite complicated. It is clear from fig. 4.4 that the integer factorization problem is reduced to order finding problem. So, we must construct an algorithm that allows us to determine the prime factors of N based on the process to find the order of integers x mod N for x < N. **But please understand that for this to happen efficiently, we have to choose carefully the integers,** **x** as we can't simply try all x < N. Now, comes the phase estimation step. **Recall that phase estimation refers to the algorithm that allows us to estimate the Eigen value associated with an Eigen vector of a unitary operator.** Keep in mind that this phase estimation technique is the core heart of several algorithms in quantum computing. Furthermore, Quantum Fourier Transform (QFT) is also used by the phase estimation algorithm.

Let us now write the very famous Shor's algorithm now.

Even Shor's algorithm starts with a random guess of a number. Let that random number be r. But it will then try to find two numbers $r^{p/2} + 1$ **because it is obvious that $r^p = m.N + 1$ is true.** This can be rewritten as follows: -

$$r^{p/2} + 1, r^{p/2} - 1 = m. N$$

Steps of Shor's algorithm

Step-1: Take a value, x and raise it to the power of r i.e. r^x and find out how much bigger it is than m.N which should give a result of the power raised and the excess amount to m.N i.e.

$|x, r^x - m.N>$. **The point to ponder is that a quantum computer will not do this by taking one number at a time. Instead it puts r^x in a superposition state in which x = 1, 2, 3, ... at the same time.**

Step-2: At this 2nd stage, it not only calculates the gap for one r^x at a time. Instead it uses **superposition** to calculate $|x, r^x - m.N>$ where x = 1, 2, 3... at the same time. This is the usefulness of a quantum computer.

Step-3: If $r^x = m.N + 1$ then there should be a condition where $r^{x+p} = m_1 .N + 1$. **These values maintain a frequency. Its frequency can be computed by inversing a period,** using QFT.

Step-4: Note that QFT can now perform **destructive interference and can give us that one value of p. Please note that if p is even, and then substitute it in** $r^{p/2} + 1$ **to get the factors.**

Step-5: **Also note that if p is odd then** start again from **guessing a random number.**

Shor's algorithm gives exponential speed-up for integer factorization using a quantum computer. Traditional asymmetric cryptography depends on the very common problem of factoring large primes. Peter Shor in his famous paper on 'Polynomial-Time Algorithms for Prime Factorization and Discrete Logarithms on a Quantum Computer' proposed a **quantum factorization method.** He suggests to find the **period/ order of an element**, a, in the multiplicative group modulo N i.e. the least positive integer such that-

$$x^r \equiv 1 \pmod N$$

where N is the number to factor and r is the period of **x module N.**

Basic idea (behind Shor algorithm): G. L. Miller (1976) postulated that using randomization, factorization can be reduced to finding the period of an element **a modulo N.**

Actually, Shor divide his algorithm in three stages out of which two are performed by a classical computer in polynomial time as follows:

1. **Input preparation:** It is done in a classical computer in polynomial time, log (n).
2. **Finding the period, r, of the element a, such that $a^r \equiv 1$ (mod N)** via a quantum circuit. **Please note that according to Shor, it takes O $((\log n)^2 (\log \log n) (\log \log \log n))$ steps on a quantum computer.**
3. **Postprocessing:** It is done in a classical computer in a polynomial time log (n).

Let us now compare the time complexities for common factorization algorithms in a tabular form.

Table-1: Time complexities for common factorization algorithms

Algorithm	Time Complexity
Peter Shor's algorithm	$(\log n)^2 (\log \log n) (\log \log \log n)$
Number Field Sieve	$\exp[c(\log n)^{1/3} (\log \log n)^{2/3}]$
Quadratic Sieve	$\exp(\sqrt{\ln n \ln \ln n})$

The point to ponder is that this Shor's algorithm has a polynomial time complexity that is better than the exponential time by the Number Field Sieve (i.e. the fastest known method for factorization in a classical computer). As a natural choice, researchers have shown that **Shor's algorithm could factor a 200 digit integer in few minutes. Also note that such a manoeuvre will shake the foundation of current asymmetric cryptography used to generate the encryption keys for all sort of web communications.**

Please note the following points regarding Shor Algorithm:

1. **Symmetric cryptography is very much resistant to quantum computation and hence to Shor's algorithm.**
2. **This algorithm can be easily implemented and simulated in a classical system using the Python library: ProjecQ.**
3. **Period finding is the basic building block of this Shor's algorithm.**
4. **By using a modular approach, this problem is reduced to finding a period, r, of the function $f(x) = a^x$ mod N.** That is,

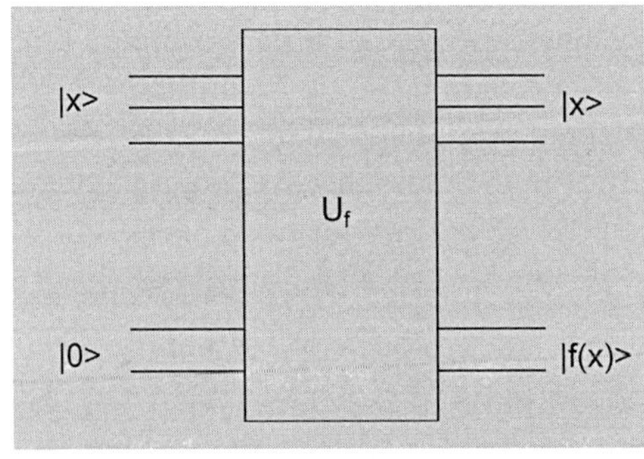

$$U_f = \Sigma_{(x = \text{to } M-1)} |x\rangle |f(x)\rangle$$

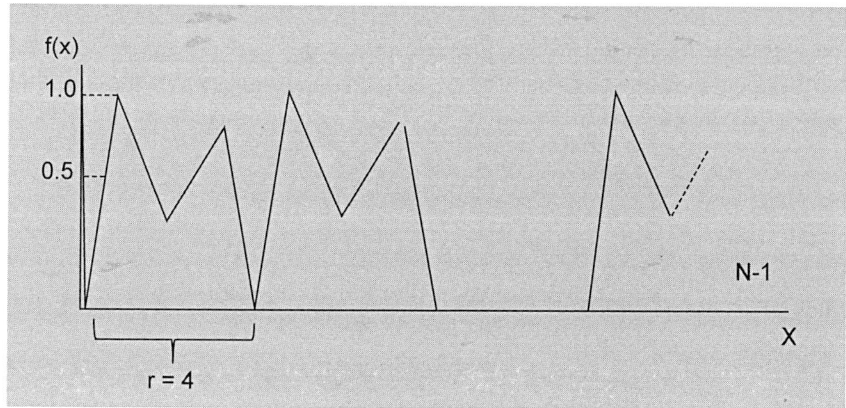

Measure $|f(x)\rangle \rightarrow \Sigma_{(x=0 \text{ to } M-1)} \alpha_x |x\rangle$

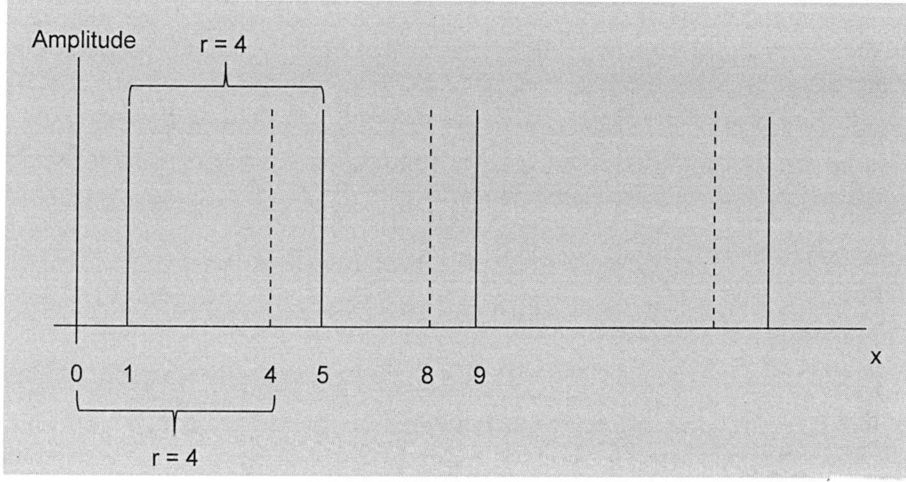

Fig.4.5: Periodic function f(x) with period r = 4

From figure-4.5, it is clear that it is an example of a periodic function f(x) with r = 4.

To take the flesh out of it, that the algorithm works properly, we say that f(x) must meet the following three conditions:

Condition-1: f(x) is one-to-one on each period i.e. the values of f(x) must not repeat. In figure-4.5, we see that these values are represented by the vertices of each line per period.

Condition-2: For any given M, or the number of periods, r must divide M. For instance, given M = 1000 and period, r = 4 we find that M/r = 1000/4 = 250.

Condition-3: M divided by r must be greater than r, i.e. $M > r^2$.

Working: Shor's algorithm **transforms f(x) into a quantum circuit, U_f** where the inputs are in **superposition. Also note that if we measure the 2nd register in U_f, we may see the values for the amplitudes-**

$$\Sigma_{(x=0 \text{ to } M-1)} \alpha_x |x\rangle$$

This is also shown in figure 4.5. **Also we observe from the figure 4.5 that the amplitudes are exactly four units apart which is the period we are looking for.** In this case, we get periodic superpositions with r = 4. What needs to be done with these periodic superpositions? Shor relies on another trick for this and it is QFT (as discussed earlier).

Working:

(1) **Problem:** Factoring a number, N = pq, where p, q are prime and large is classically difficult, $O(\exp[c.n^{1/3} (\log n)^{2/3}])$.

(2) **How modular arithmetic works?**

$$5/3 = \text{quotient} = 1, \text{remainder} = 2$$

$$5 \equiv 2 \pmod 3$$

x		1	2	3	4	5	6	7	8	9	
x	≡	1	2	0	1	2	0	1	2	0	(mod 3)

Note: $x \equiv 0 \pmod 3 \Rightarrow$ x is a multiple of 3.

$x \equiv 1 \pmod 3 \Rightarrow$ x is 1 + some multiple of 3.

In general,

$$x \equiv y \pmod 3 \Rightarrow x = 3k + y \text{ for some } k \in Z.$$

Also note that the periodicity of modular arithmetic is-

$$x \equiv y \pmod N \text{ means } y \in \{0, 1, 2, \ldots\ldots, N\}$$

For e.g. $x \equiv y \pmod 3$ means $y \in \{0, 1, 2\}$.

(3) **Solution:**

begin algorithm:

(1) pick "a" coprime (≡ gcd (a, N) = 1) with N = pq. (if unsure, check quickly if coprime).

(2) find the "order" r of the function $a^r \pmod N$.

≡ smallest r such that $a^r \equiv 1 \pmod N$.

(3) If r is even,

$$x \equiv a^{r/2} \pmod N.$$

$$\text{if } x + 1 \equiv 0 \pmod N \text{ then}$$

$$\{p, q\} = \{\gcd(x+1, N), \gcd(x-1, N)\}$$

else: find another "a".

(4) **Example: factoring 15**

$$15 = [1111] = 4 \text{ bits}$$

Coprime: pick a = 13

x = 0 1 2 3 4 5 6 7

$13^x \pmod{15}$ = 1, 13, 4, 7, 1, 13, 4, 7

Smallest r > 0 such that $13^r \equiv 1 \pmod{15}$ is r = 4.

Given $r = 4,$

$x \equiv 13^{4/2} \text{ (mod 15)} \equiv 4 \text{ (mod 15)}$

$x+1 = 5 \equiv 0 \text{ (mod 15)}$

$\{p, q\} = \{4-1, 4+1\} = \{3, 5\}$

The first thing we must do is **order finding.** Let x and N be positive integers with no common factors such that x < N. Then the order of x is the smallest positive integer r such that-

$$\mathbf{x^r = 1 \bmod N}$$

We should be able to compute mod N. Let us take an example for this. Firstly, x and N can't have any common factors because their GCD is 1. Say, we assume that x = 5 and N = 44. To find $\mathbf{x^r = a \bmod N}$**,** we calculate $\mathbf{x^r}$ **and subtract N till we get the last integer greater than 0. Please note that the first two cases are less than N = 44, so we don't do anything** i.e.

$$5^1 = 5.\ 5^2 = 25$$

Now since $5^3 = 125$, **also note that (44) (2) = 88 and 125 – 88 = 37. Therefore, we have-**

$$\mathbf{5^3 = 37 \text{ (mod 44)}}$$

Next, $5^4 = 625$. We have (14) (44) = 616, so we have-

$$\mathbf{5^4 = 9 \text{ (mod 44)}}$$

Finally, $5^5 = 3125$. This gives that 71 * 44 = 3124, which is 1 less than $5^5 = 3125$.

This is now the point where we stop. Hence, we get-

$$\mathbf{5^5 = 1 \text{ (mod 44)}}$$

The order of 5 is 5.

The point to ponder is that this process of finding the powers, $x^r = 1$ (mod N) is very much cumbersome. Also with large numbers, it will slow down even the best computers as then the time required will be exponential in log N.

Then what is the solution? Using a quantum algorithm based on phase estimation.

To solve the problem of order finding, we consider the unitary operator as follows:

$$U_x|y\rangle = \begin{cases} |xy \bmod N\rangle & 0 \le y \le N-1 \\ |y\rangle & N \le y \le 2^L - 1 \end{cases}$$

Where $L = \lceil \log N \rceil$. The eigen-states of U_x are as follows:

$$|u_t\rangle = 1/\sqrt{r}\ \Sigma_{(k=0 \text{ to } r-1)} \exp[-2\Pi ikt / r]\ |x^k \bmod N\rangle$$

Also the eigen-values are given by-

$$U_x|u_t\rangle = e^{2\Pi i(t/r)}|u_t\rangle$$

Please understand that we can apply the phase estimation algorithm to these states to estimate the phase t/r and hence to find an estimate of the order. Also understand that the order-finding algorithm begins by considering a superposition of these eigen-states. This implies that the eigen-states sum to |1>. So, we start now the order finding with the input state-

$$|\psi_{in}\rangle = |1\rangle = 1/\sqrt{r}\ \Sigma_{(t=0 \text{ to } r-1)}|u_t\rangle$$

To take the flesh out of it, we can calculate the quantity x^k mod N using quantum parallelism. Also the period r/t that gives us the order, r is found by the phase estimation process. Measurement gives an estimate of a random t/r for $0 \leq t \leq r-1$. And to obtain the exact value, continued fractions are applied. Simply put, we use order finding to find the factors of some odd integer, N. This can be written in form of a pesudocode-

Input: odd integer, N.

Repeat

Randomly select x ϵ {2, ……, N-1} a ϵ {2,….., N V 1}

d = gcd (x, N)

if d >= 2 then u = d, v = N/d

else

Find the order r such that $x^r = 1$ mod N

$y = x^{r/2} - 1$ mod N

d = gcd (y, N)

if d >= 2 then u = d, v = N/d

until find u, v.

Let us solve an example now.

Shor's Algorithm Example

$$n = 10, \quad N = 2^{10} = 1024, \quad \sqrt{n} = 32$$

Suppose we run shor's algorithm, we get y = 139

$$\frac{y}{N} = \frac{139}{1024}$$

We want to search some fraction $\frac{k}{r}$ near it within

$$\frac{k}{r} = \frac{1}{1024}, \quad r < \sqrt{n} = 32$$

$$= \frac{1}{\frac{1024}{139}} = \frac{1}{7+\frac{51}{139}} = \frac{1}{7+\frac{1}{\frac{139}{\sqrt{1}}}} = \frac{1}{7+\frac{1}{2+\frac{37}{51}}} = \cdots$$

Contime we get, $\frac{3}{22}, \frac{8}{55}$ $55 > \sqrt{n} = 32$ does not meat $r < \sqrt{n}$

$\frac{3}{22}$ is not dose enough.

$$\frac{3}{32} - \frac{139}{1024} = 0.00062 \geq 0.00049 = \frac{1}{2048}$$

So, the |y> we mesured might not be a good "|y>"

Shor's algorithm uses 2 main subroutines-

- A reduction of the factoring problem to the period-finding problem.
- A QFT-based algorithm for solving the period-finding problem.

The period finding problem involves determining the period of a function that repeats its values in regular intervals. Shor's algorithm efficiently solves the period-finding problem using quantum computing only, which then allows for the extraction of the factors of the composite number. **From the above algorithm, it is clear that the Shor's algorithm begins by choosing a random integer, 'a', that is smaller than the composite number 'N' to be factored. The GCD of 'a' and 'N' is then computed.**

If the GCD is not equal to 1, it means that a non-trivial factor has been found.

But if the GCD is 1, Shor's algorithm proceeds to find the period 'r' of the function, f(x) = a^x mod N. The period 'r' is the smallest positive integer for which a^r mod N = 1.

Quantum Circuit:

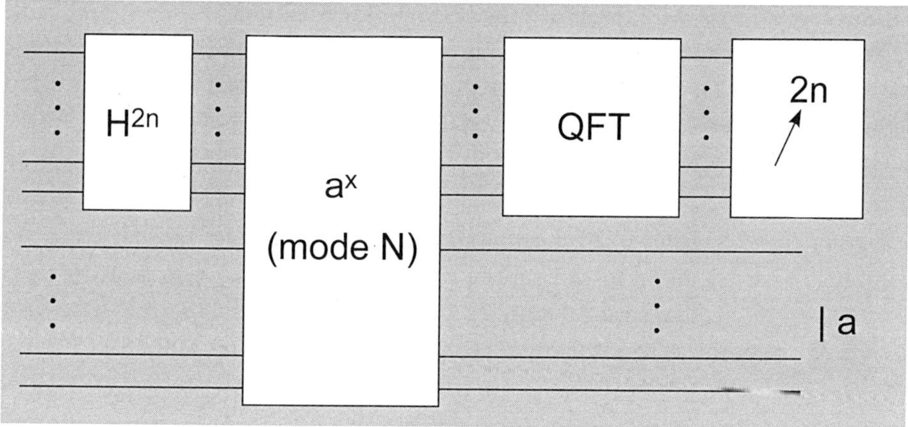

Fig.4.6: Shor's Algorithm Quantum Circuit

The algorithm utilizes a quantum circuit with **two quantum registers. The 1st register holds the input while the 2nd register holds the output of the function,** f(x). **After initializing the qubits, Hadamard gates are applied to create a superposition of all possible input values in the 1st register. Then the function,** f(x) **is applied as an oracle, computing the output for all possible inputs simultaneously. Next, QFT is applied to the 1st register and a measurement is performed. The result of this measurement is used to find out an estimate of the period 'r' using classical techniques like continued fractions.**

Once the period 'r' has been determined, the factors of the composite number 'N' can be extracted.

If 'r' is an odd number, the algorithm is restarted with a new random value of 'a'.

If 'r' is an even number, the factors can be found by computing the GCD of $a^{r/2} + 1$, $a^{r/2} - 1$ and 'N'.

If either of these values yields a non-trivial factor i.e. a factor other than 1 or 'N', the algorithm is successful.

Please remember the following points regarding the Shor's algorithm: -

1. Shor's algorithm demonstrates the power of quantum computing in problem solving that are complex.
2. A real-life application of Shor's algorithm is in **cryptography.** Many cryptographic algorithms are based on the fact that it is computationally difficult to factor large integers. Shor's algorithm can factor such integers more efficiently using quantum computers. **For example,** commonly used RSA public key cryptography faces a difficulty of factoring large integers to keep messages secure. **Please note that if a quantum computer can efficiently factor large integers, then the security of RSA is at stake (compromised). Also note that a quantum computer with running Shor's algorithm has the potential to revolutionize cryptography.** It may threaten the security of many existing cryptographic systems. Also it presents a chance of the development of new quantum-safe cryptography schemes that are not vulnerable to Shor's algorithm.
3. The **core** of Shor's algorithm for factoring a large integer is **a quantum method for computing the period, r of the function: $f_{x,n}$ (a) = x^a mod n, that is exponentially** more efficient than any classical method. **Please note that this is vital because the result from number theory tells us that once we know r, we can obtain the factors of n from gcd($x^{r/2}$ -1, n) and gcd($x^{r/2}$ +1, n).** We know that computing the GCD is simpler. Hence, Shor's hybrid algorithm that uses **a fast quantum method for calculating the period and a fast classical method for calculating the factors** from the period is very much **efficient.**
4. **Working of Shor's algorithm:** The objective is to find the period of the function $f_{x,n}$(a). To do this, we create a single quantum memory register that we partition into two parts called as Register-1 and Register-2. **Also understand that the complete register consists of a chain of qubits, so we are going to use a more compact notation for representing its contents.** If Register-1 is holding the (base 10) number, 'a' and Register-2 is holding the (base 10 number), 'b' then we represent the state of the complete register as |a, b>.
5. **In Register-1, we create a superposition** of the integers a = 0, 1, 2, 3,...... that will become the arguments of the function $f_{x,n}$ (a).
6. Then, we compute in quantum parallel, $f_{x,n}$ (a) evaluated on each input, a and place the result in Register-2.
7. **This creates a superposition** (in Register-2) of the function evaluations $f_{x,n}$ (a) in the time it takes to compute just one such function evaluation classically.
8. Next, we measure the state of Register-2. **The point to ponder is that this collapses the superposition stored in Register-2 and we get some answer, k** (say). **Also this means that there was some value of 'a' such that x^a mod n = k.**
9. Of the bat we know that this process of measuring the state of Register-2 has a serious side-effect on the state i.e. the contents of Register-1. **Remember that Register-1 and Register-2 are two parts of a single quantum register.**
10. **By observing the contents of Register-2, we basically change the contents of Register-1 to be a superposition of just those values of 'a', such that x^a mod n = k.**

11. Now the values stored in Register-1 are of the form {a, a+r, a + 2r, K} encoded as a superposition of states of the form ω |a> + ω |a + r> + ω |a + 2r> +K. **Please note that at this point of time, the amplitudes with which each state appears are all equal.**

12. Next we compute the discrete Fourier transform of the contents of Register-1and put the result back into Register-1.

13. **Note that because Register-1contains a periodic function so its Fourier transform will be peaked up at multiples of the inverse period, 1/r.**

14. **Fourier transforms map functions in the time domain to the functions in the frequency domain.** The frequency is the inverse of the period.

15. **This simply means that the Fourier transform of the superposition stored in Register-1 will be some new superposition. But now the amplitudes with which various states appear are no longer equal.**

16. **The point to ponder is that states corresponding to integer multiples of the inverse period and those close to them, appear with greater amplitudes than those that don't correspond to integer multiples of the inverse periods.**

17. Therefore, if you now measure the state i.e. read the contents of Register-1, you will most likely see a result that is close to some multiple of the inverse period.

18. **Repeat this process then you will rapidly get enough samples of integer multiples of the inverse period to be able to determine the period unambiguously.**

In nutshell, we can say that the Shor's algorithm for finding the period of $f_{x,n}(a) = x^a \bmod n$ relies on quantum parallelism to create a superposition of values of the periodic function, $f_{x,n}(a)$ on measurement to project out a periodic function in Register-1 and upon a discrete Fourier transform to bring the desired interference effect between **solutions** i.e. integer multiples of the inverse period and **non-solutions** i.e. numbers that are not integer multiples of the inverse period. So, now we have with us the period. Hence, the factors of n are found from $\gcd(x^{r/2} - 1, n)$ and $\gcd(x^{r/2} + 1, n)$. **Recall that, as in a true classical case, the method will find non-trivial factors of n provided r is even and $x^{r/2} \equiv +/- 1 \bmod n$. The constraint that q should have small prime factors is there to ensure that it is physically possible to implement Shor's algorithm in a quantum circuit that is small in comparison to n.** Also the final step in Shor's algorithm uses '**continued fraction expansion**'. This is truly a classical computation. The continued fraction expansion is used to identify what multiple of the inverse period, r, is obtained. This continued fraction is given by the expression-

$$x = [a_0, a_1, k, a_N]$$

Note that a truncated continued fraction is called as a convergent. Also note that the nth convergent is given by-

$$[a_0, a_1, k, a_n]$$

Let us now state the theorem on continued fractions.

Theorem on Continued Fractions: "If p/q is any rational number satisfying $|p/q - x| < 1/2q^2$ then p/q is a convergent of the continued fraction. Also the convergent is such that gcd(p, q) = 1."

We can use this theorem to find the closest rational to the terms λ/r and thus find the period, r.

4.9 GROVER'S SEARCH ALGORITHM

In 1996, **Lov Grover developed a search algorithm** that is popularly named as Grover's algorithm. To understand it in a simple way, just assume some unsorted data store that has N entries. So, given these N elements, the **worst-case scenario for classical queries** is that it will take N queries. The **average case will be N/2.** But Grover's algorithm will work in √N, which is naturally better than its classical counterpart. To achieve this, using Grover's algorithm on N-elements, we must perform a small step. That is, there must be an N-dimensional state space which is provided by **log2N qubits. This space we call it as state space and is denoted by H.**

Grover's algorithm is an **unstructured search quantum procedure to find the entry of n bits on a digital haystack of N elements. Please understand that the Grover's algorithm provides a significant speed-up of O(√N) steps. Also note that when we have millions of entries then the square-root of 10^{12} is much faster than 10^{12}.**

Say, we want to search for an element, x, using Grover's algorithm. The steps in form of a pseudo-code for this are as follows:

Step-1: Prepare the input, given f:{0, 1, 2,….., N-1} →{0,1}. **To put it in a proper light, we note that the size of the input is 2^n where n is the number of bits and N is the number of steps or size of haystack.** The main objective is to find x such that f(x) = 1.

Step-2: Apply a **basis superposition to all qubits in the input using H-gates.**

Step-3: Perform a **phase inversion** on the **input qubits.**

Step-4: Perform an **inversion about the mean on the input.**

Step-5: Repeat steps-3 and step-4 at least √N times. **Note that there is a high probability that 'x' data-item will be found at this point.**

What is phase inversion and inversion about the mean?

Step-1: (Phase Inversion)

This is the first step in the algorithm. It must be performed in a **superposition of all states in the haystack. Please note that if the element that we are searching for is where f(x′) = 1, then the superposition can be expressed as Σα |x>.** So, what phase inversion means is as given below-

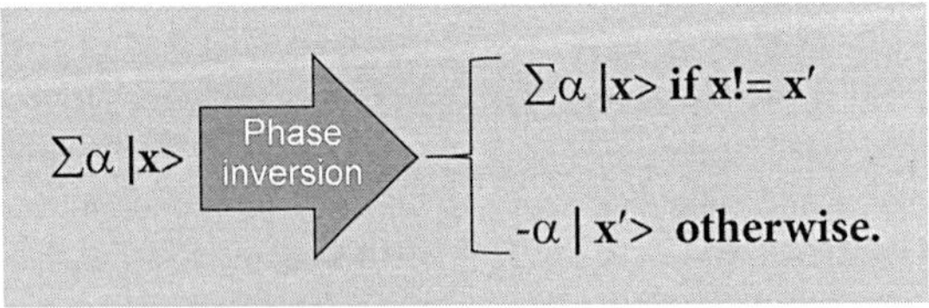

It implies that if a given x is not the element we are looking for (x != x′), **then it leaves the superposition intact else it inverts the phase** i.e. the sign of the complex coefficient, α of the qubit. In nutshell, we can say that the amplitude of x′ gets inverted and the rest remains the same.

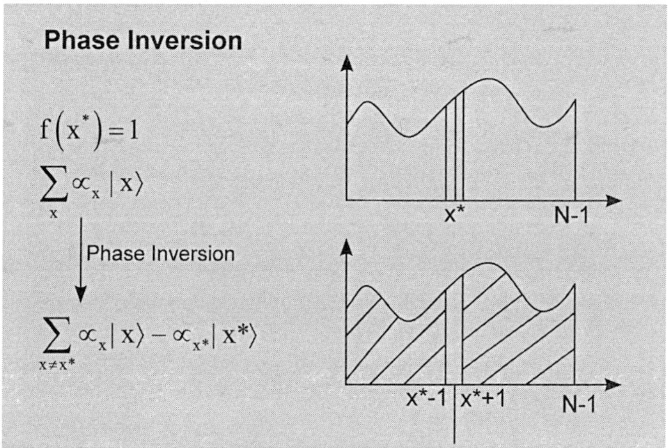

Fig.4.7: Phase Inversion

Step-2: (Inversion about mean)

Given the previous superposition as $\Sigma\alpha$ **|x>, the expression definition of the mean,** μ, as the average value of the amplitudes as follows:

$$M = \Sigma_{(x=0 \text{ to } N-1)} \alpha_x / N$$

Now **flip the amplitudes about this mean.** That is,

$$\alpha_x \rightarrow (2\mu - \alpha_x)$$

$$\Sigma \alpha_x |x> \rightarrow \Sigma (2\mu - \alpha_x) |x>$$

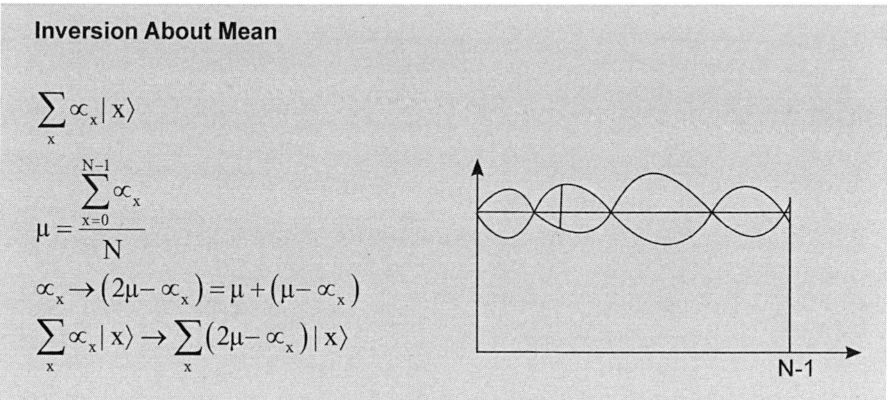

Fig.4.8: Inversion about Mean

In fig. 4.8, the superposition state of the qubits as defined by the wave function, ψ, is shown. **Please observe here that the mean (μ) of this function is shown as the horizontal line in the chart. Also note that this 'inversion about the mean' does is it mirrors the wave function, ψ, over the mean, μ, resulting in a mirror wave.** This is shown by a dotted line. **The point to ponder is that it this is equivalent to rotating the waves over the axis, μ.**

Figure-4.9 (a) to (d) shows a single Grover's iteration.

Fig.4.9: (a): Superposition

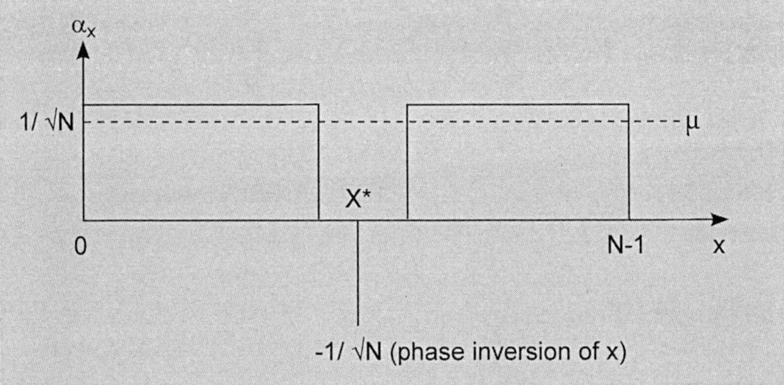

Fig. 4.9 (b): Phase Inversion

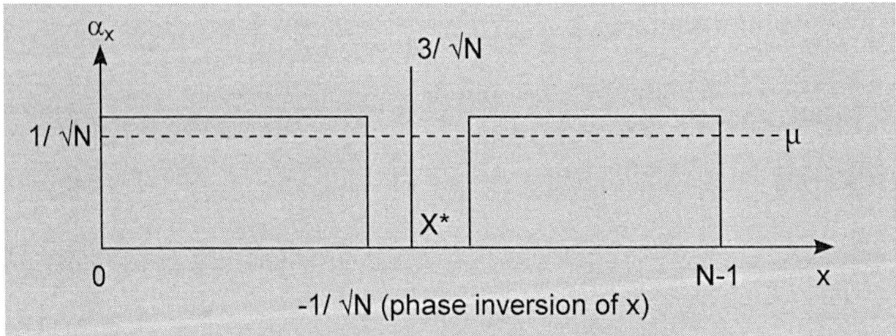

Fig. 4.9 (c): Inversion about mean

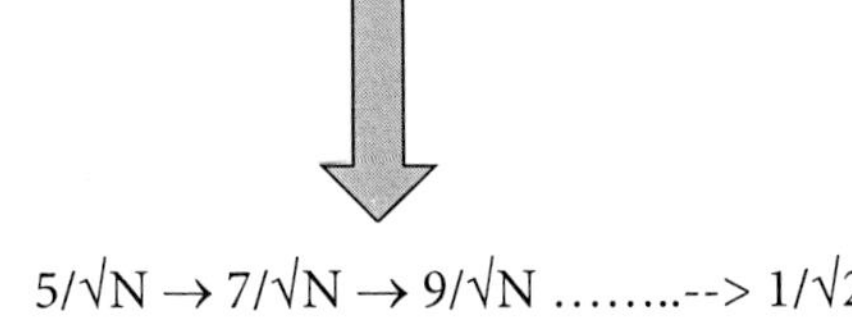

Fig. 4.9 (d): Amplitude increase after √N steps

Please note the following points from the figures 4.9 (a) to (d): -

1. **The superposition of all qubits puts all amplitudes at $1/\sqrt{N}$.**

2. A phase inversion puts the amplitude for x^* at $-1/\sqrt{N}$. **Also note that this has the effect of lowering slightly the value of the mean,** μ, and is shown by the dotted line in figure 4.9 (b).
3. The point to ponder is that after the inversion about the mean, the mean amplitude drops a little but x^* goes high, as much as $2/\sqrt{N}$ above the mean, μ.
4. **Repeat** this sequence. The amplitude of x^* increases by about $2/\sqrt{N}$ and in approx. $\sqrt{N}$ steps, **the amplitude becomes $1/\sqrt{2}$.**
5. Now, if we **measure our qubits, the probability of finding x^*** (i.e. the element we are looking for) is **the square of the amplitude i.e. $(1/\sqrt{2})^2 = ½$.**
6. Finally, we are **successful** in **searching out the element x^* in approx.. $\sqrt{N}$ steps.**

This is the single iteration of **Grover's algorithm.**

Grover's algorithm uses a quantum circuit with a set of qubits that are initialized to |0> state. This algorithm consists of 2 main things-

(a) **Oracle:** That marks the target item.

(b) **Diffusion operator:** It amplifies the probability amplitude of the marked item.

This process of repeatedly applying the oracle and the diffusion operator in an iterative way is known as a Grover's iteration. In nutshell, the probability of measuring the target item becomes vital that allows the algorithm to find the target item with high probability in $O(\sqrt{N})$ steps. Actually, oracle is a black box function designed to recognize the target item in the database. **Please understand that when applied to the quantum state, the oracle flips the sign of the amplitude of the target item's quantum state without affecting the other states. Also understand that the oracle encodes the problem-specific information into the quantum system that enables the Grover's algorithm to locate the target item.** On the other hand, the **diffusion operator or Grover's operator is applied after the oracle to amplify the marked target item's amplitude while supressing the other item's amplitudes.** This diffusion operator is constructed by performing a series of operations i.e. applying Hadamard gates to all qubits, using a conditional phase shift and applying Hadamard gates again. **And this sequence of operations inverts the amplitudes of the quantum states about their average, amplifying the amplitude of the target state.** Quantum circuit for one- iteration of the Grover's algorithm is shown in figure- 4.10.

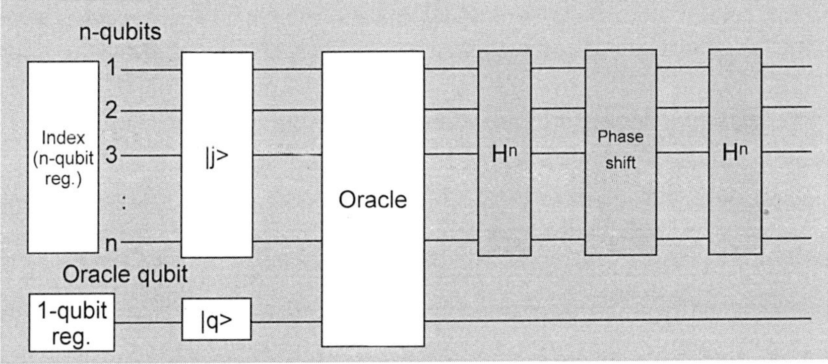

Fig.4.10: Quantum circuit for 1-iteration of Grover's algorithm.

In quantum circuit of fig. 4.10, a n-qubit register is used to specify the index of an item, |j>. A 1-qubit register is required for the oracle qubit, |q>. The n qubits produced by the oracle are applied to a circuit consisting of n Hadamard gates. The equal superposition state resulting from the H^n circuit is processed by a phase shift circuit. This is followed by again a circuit consisting of n Hadamard gates. **Please note that the phase shift leaves |j> unchanged when f (j) = 0 and transforms |j> →- |j> when f(j) > 0.** The oracle performs the transformation |j> → $(-1)^{f(j)}$ |j>. **Also note that the work qubits used by the oracle for intermediate results are omitted.**

Quantum circuit for Grover's Algorithm:

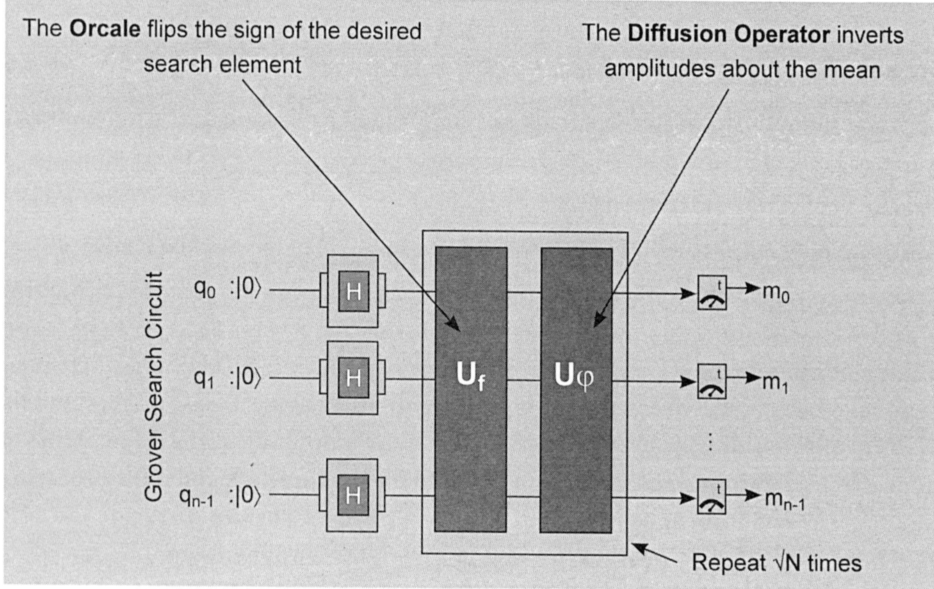

Fig.4.11: Quantum Circuit for Grover's Algorithm

Applications of Grover's Algorithm

1. **Grover's** algorithm can search a database of unstructured data more efficiently than its classical counterparts. The most well-known application of Grover's algorithm is searching an unsorted database. Classical algorithms take linear time to search through N items, whereas Grover's algorithm requires only about √N iterations. This quadratic speedup becomes increasingly valuable as dataset sizes grow. Efficient database search has implications for information retrieval, data analysis, and optimization. This can be beneficial in areas like **data mining, machine learning, deep learning and AI.**

2. It can be used to solve **optimization problems** like finding the shortest path between two points in a network or minimizing the energy of a physical system.

3. It can be used to solve some **specific cryptographic problems** also like finding the Hash function or breaking some symmetric key encryption algorithms. While classical brute-force attacks on symmetric keys would take 2^n operations (where n is the key length), Grover's algorithm reduces this to about $2^{(n/2)}$ operations.

4. It can be used to **speed-up some machine learning algorithms** like nearest neighbour search or clustering.
5. It can be used to solve some **combinatorial optimization problems** like Traveling Salesman Problem (TSP) or graph coloring.
6. Grover's algorithm has applications in simulating quantum systems. It can be used to search for specific quantum states within a complex system, aiding in tasks like quantum chemistry simulations and material science.
7. Grover's algorithm's principles of **amplitude amplification and quantum interference** have found applications in quantum machine learning (QML) algorithms. Quantum-enhanced search capabilities can be incorporated into various machine-learning tasks, potentially leading to improved optimization and pattern recognition.

Limitations of Grover's algorithm:

1. Grover's algorithm's speedup is dependent on the ability to construct an oracle that can mark the target item. In some cases, designing such an oracle can be complex and resource-intensive, potentially reducing the practical advantage gained from the algorithm. So, oracle's complexity is an issue.
2. The algorithm assumes a single solution to the search problem. If there are multiple valid solutions, Grover's algorithm doesn't guarantee finding the optimal one. The probability of finding a valid solution increases with the number of iterations, but it's not guaranteed to be found within a specific number of steps.
3. While Grover's algorithm showcases the potential of quantum computing, its practical implementation requires stable and error-corrected quantum hardware. Quantum systems are prone to noise, errors, and decoherence, which can affect the algorithm's performance.
4. Grover's algorithm is specialized for search problems and doesn't provide a general exponential speedup like some other quantum algorithms, such as Shor's algorithm for factoring large numbers.
5. Grover's algorithm's impact will be realized more once such quantum computers become more accessible and capable of handling complex computations.

We are in a position to solve an example on Grover's algorithm now.

Example-1: Design a quantum circuit for H_4 when the cardinality of the search space $|s| = 4$.

Solution 1: We need to design a quantum circuit that performs the initial Walsh-Hadamard transforms and one iteration of Grover's algorithm when the cardinality for the search space $|H| = 4$. Therefore, the indexes can only be 00, 01, 10, 11. The top two qubits are initially in state |0> and the third is in state |1>. So, we draw its circuit now.

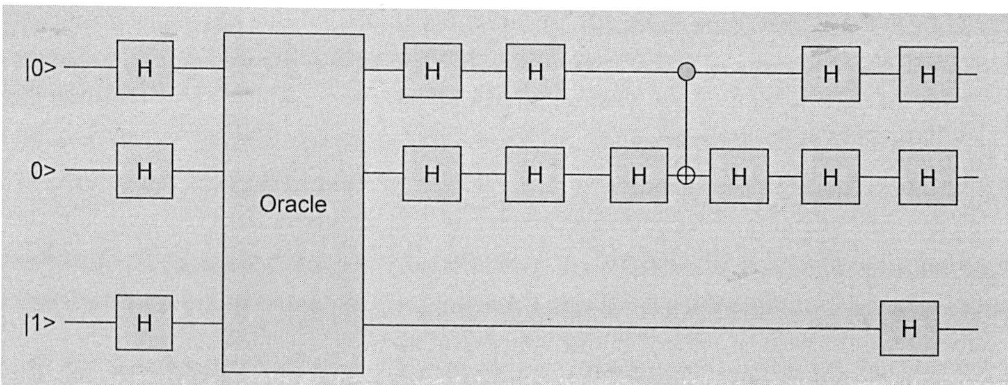

Example-2: Show that Grover's algorithm is faster than classical search algorithms.

Solution 2: As we know that the Grover's algorithm is a quantum search algorithm. It searches in O(√N) steps only. So, the saving is huge. **For example,** if a data base contains $3 * 10^8$ items, then Grover's algorithm will find the pointed item / key in about 17,321 steps on average. If it takes 1 sec per iteration, our search will take about 5 hrs. Now, to search through the entire database of $3 * 10^8$ items in classical way (like linear or binary searches) at the same rate of 1 item per second, would take one person 43 years. Assuming 8 hours of work per day, 5 days per week, 48 weeks per year and 4 weeks leave.

Example-3: Consider a simple database of 8 items. One of these items possesses the unique property we're searching for. In classical computing, it would take an average of 4 tries to find the item. However, with Grover's algorithm, the solution can be found in just a single step. Show this in a stepwise manner.

Solution-3:

1. Start with **all qubits in a superposition** i.e. $|s\rangle = (|0\rangle + |1\rangle + |2\rangle + \ldots + |7\rangle) / \sqrt{8}$.
2. Apply the **oracle gate:** This gate marks the correct item. If, for instance, the correct item is $|3\rangle$, the oracle would multiply the amplitude of $|3\rangle$ by -1.
3. Apply the **Grover diffusion operator:** This operator amplifies the amplitude of the marked item(s) and reduces the amplitude of the others.
4. Repeating steps 2 and 3 multiple times **amplifies the probability of measuring the marked item(s).**
5. **Measurement collapses the quantum state,** revealing the marked item(s).

Geometrical Interpretation of Grover's algorithm:

Let us assume that |b> represent the state corresponding to a uniform superposition of all solutions to the search problem and |ψ> shows the initial state. Then, we say that the Grover's iteration is a rotation in the 2D space that spans from |b> and |ψ>. This is shown in figure below.

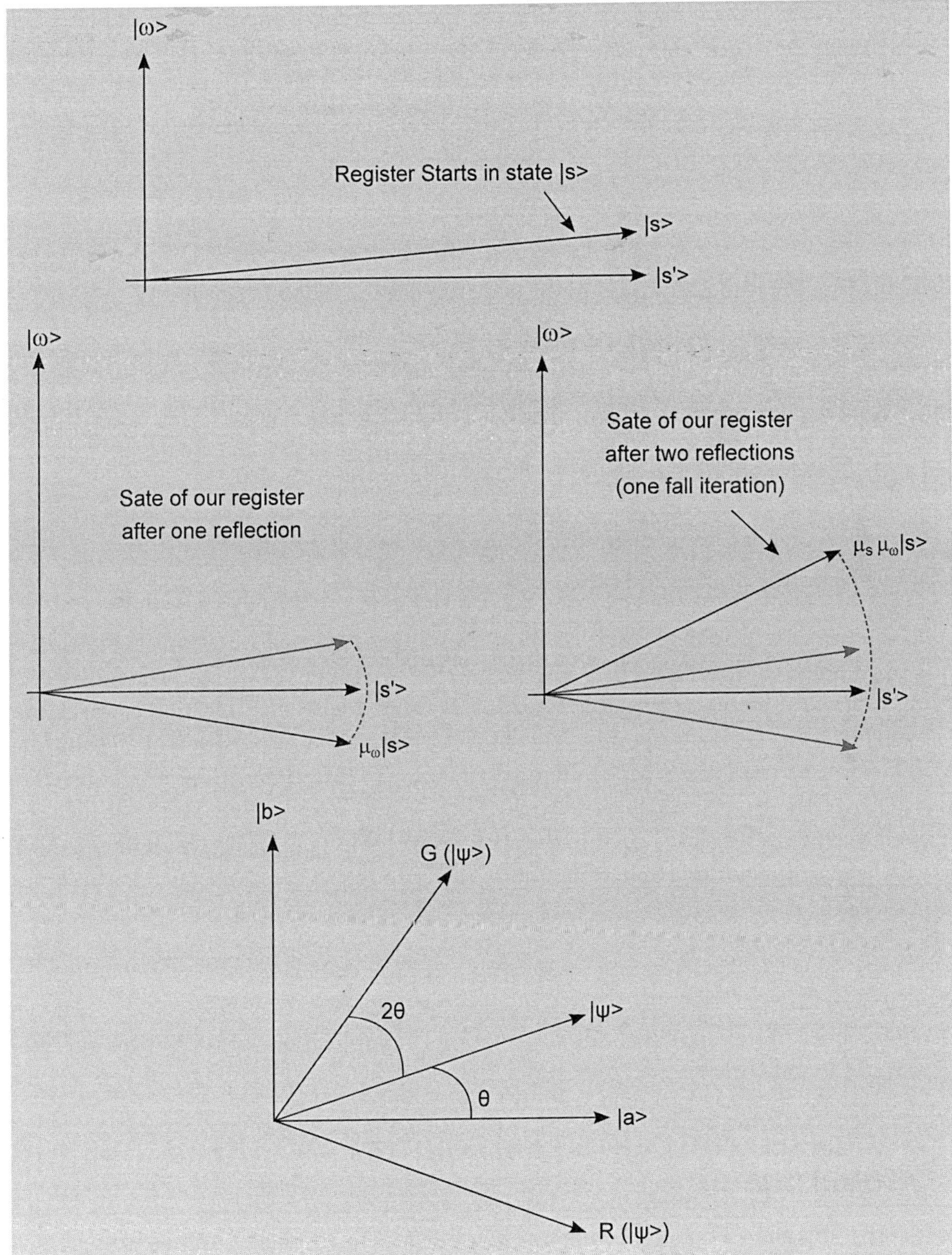

A reflection about |a> transforms the original state |ψ> into R (|ψ>) = $f_{|\psi>}$. Then, this state is transformed into G (|ψ>) by a reflection about |ψ>. These two transformations are equivalent to a rotation of the original state |ψ> with an angle 2θ. **Please note that the state vectors |a>, |b>, |ψ>, R(|ψ>) and G(|ψ>) are of unit length.** This is the graphical representation of one-iteration of Grover's search algorithm.

Recall that $N = 2^n$ is the number of elements in the search space and M is the number of elements which satisfy the query. Then, this graph shows the transformations of the vector, $|\psi>$. The initial state $|\psi>$ is in the space spanned by $|a>$ and $|b>$. It can be expressed as follows-

$$|\psi> = \alpha_0 |a> + \alpha_1 |b> = \sqrt{(N - M/N)}\, |a> + \sqrt{(M/N)}\, |b>$$

Hence, we can denote-

$$\alpha_0 = \cos\theta/2 = \sqrt{(N - M/N)} = \sqrt{(1 - M/N)}$$
$$\alpha_1 = \sin\theta/2 = \sqrt{(M/N)}$$

Also note that the transformation of the state $|\psi>$ has the following property-

$$f_{|\psi>} = f(\alpha_0 \,|\, a> + \alpha_1 \,|\, b>) = \alpha_0 |a> - \alpha_1 |a>$$

The point to ponder is that for any number, m, of Grover's iterations, the resulting state G^m $|\psi>$ remains in the plane spanned by $|a>$ and $|b>$. **The product of two reflections is a rotation.** It is also possible to compute the rotation angle between the original vector $|\psi>$ and G ($|\psi>$) i.e. the vector obtained after the two composite reflections. Also seen in this figure is that-

$$G\,|\psi> = \cos 3\theta/2\, |a> + \sin 3\theta/2\, |b>$$

After m Grover iterations,

$$G^m |\psi> = \cos[(2m + 1)/2\, \theta]\, |a> + \sin[(2m + 1)/2\, \theta]\, |b>$$

Conclusions: This graphical interpretation shows that repeated iterations bring the resulting vector, G^m $|\psi>$ closer and closer to $|b>$. **Therefore, this produces with high probability one of the outcomes superposed by $|b>$. The state vector $|\psi>$ is rotated with one iteration towards the vector $|b>$ by an angle θ using Grover's operator, G, which represents a superposition of all solutions to the search problem. It behaves like $\sqrt{(M/N)}$. In nutshell, only O ($\sqrt{M/N}$) iterations are required to rotate $|\psi>$ close to $|b>$. This also proves the efficiency of this Grover's algorithm. The basic idea is that the Grover operator rotates the state $|\psi'>$ into the state we are looking for $|x'>$. This it does in small steps and thus we have to apply it multiple times** say, m times. In such a case, the equations become-

$$G^m |x'> = \cos m\theta\, |x'> - \sin m\theta |\psi'>$$

(where $|x'>$ is the input that we want to search)

$$G^m |\psi'> = \sin m\theta\, |x'> + \cos m\theta\, |\psi'>$$

Also it has been observed that about $\sqrt{2^n}$ rotations or applications of the Grover operator, G are desired to find the state $|x'>$.

4.10 SIMPLIFIED THE DEUTSCH ALGORITHM AND THE DEUTSCH-JOZSA ALGORITHM

Quantum algorithms allow a quantum computer to evaluate a function, f(x), for many different values of x simultaneously. This happens to be the fundamental feature of these quantum algorithms. Deutsch was the first person to show that quantum computers are much faster than traditional/classical computers. Suppose that there is a function that map {0, 1} into {0, 1}. If it is known that f(x) is either **constant (0 or 1 for all values of x) or balanced (0 for exactly half for all possible x and 1 for the other half), then the problem is to decide of what type it is. All of** the possible function mappings of a function {0, 1} to {0, 1} are as follows-

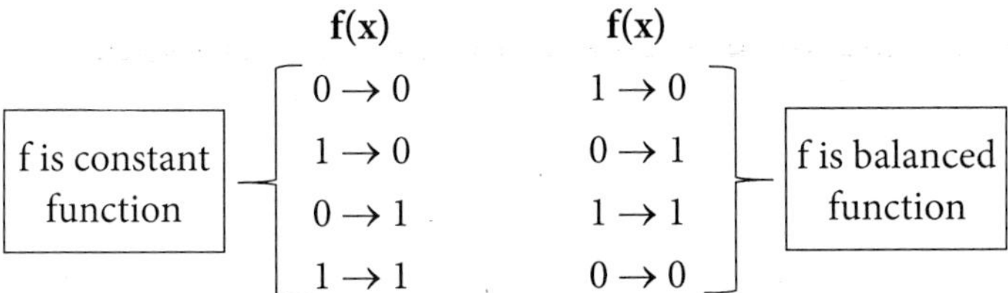

Now assume that this function is implemented inside a **black box /oracle. Please note that on the left column, the function produces a constant value of 0 or 1 for the inputs. Hence, f is a constant function.** On the other hand, **on the right hand side column, for one half of the inputs, the function produces 0 and for the other half it produces 1. Now, we say that the function is a balanced function.** But Deutsch's algorithm (father of quantum computing) does not check the values of f(0) and f(1) separately, rather it finds out the value of f simultaneously for x = 0 and x = 1. According to him, a function f(x) is **balanced** if the value of f(x=0)   f(x=1) = 1. On the other hand, the function is **constant** if f(x=0) = f(x=1).

Quantum circuit for the Deutsch's algorithm has already been explained in previous chapter.

Let us now discuss about Deutsch-Jozsa algorithm next.

Deutsch-Jozsa algorithm

Working principle: Deutsch-Jozsa algorithm works on a single input bit where f: (0, 1) → (0, 1). In general, Deutsch-Jozsa algorithm can act on an n-bit function as-

$$f: (0, 1)^n \rightarrow (0, 1)$$

Also note that in the worst case scenario, the function in an oracle needs to be called $2^{n-1}+1$ times to check whether it is balanced or a constant function.

It is really surprising. How will you pass n bits with a value of 0 or 1 to the function to see if an output of 0 or 1 is obtained? **This process of passing n bits to the function is called a query.** The goal is to give information to understand the behaviour of the output. The device's output is usually 0 if you don't execute enough queries. The probability dictates that the output will be zero for a finite number of inputs.

How many times do we query the function to obtain the result? By result, we mean a long chain of 0 and 1, but the probability of receiving 0 and 1 leads to the conclusion of "constant" or "balanced" behaviour. Start with the classical approach and the best case. You need only two queries. Why?

- In the first call, you pass the value 0 to the function and receive the value 0; it's written like this: f(0) = 0
- In the second call, you pass the value 1 to the function and receive the value 1; the corresponding mathematical equation is f(1) = 1

Please note that the number of inputs is finite, so we will not query the function to infinity. Also note that the results are statistical, meaning that you have an output probability of obtaining 0 or 1. Getting 1 once doesn't mean that the function has an equal distribution.

The function is balanced i.e. it's the best case (f(1) = 0 and f(0) = 1). In the worst case scenario, we need to test half of the possibilities plus one. By balanced we mean **half of the function has the values**

0s and the other 1s. So, you will need to test half of the input plus one. 2^n represents all the possibilities, so half of them are written $2^{n-1}$and you need one more test. Hence, $2^{(n-1)} + 1$ tests.

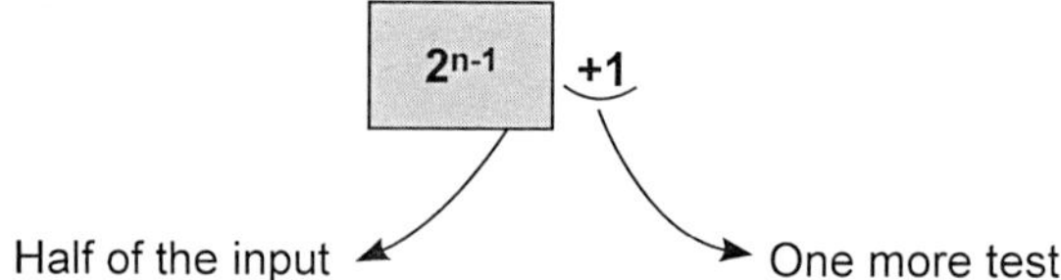

This shows the representation of half of the space in the worst classical case to test the balance of a finite input space to the classical function (oracle).

Case study: Imagine you have a 4-bit string in input. This means 2^4 possibilities (=16). You will test 8 combinations plus one, so 9 evaluations. In the same way, we can compute the probability that the function is balanced.

$$P(x) = 1 - \frac{1}{2^{x-1}}$$

with $1 < x < 2^{(n-1)}$.

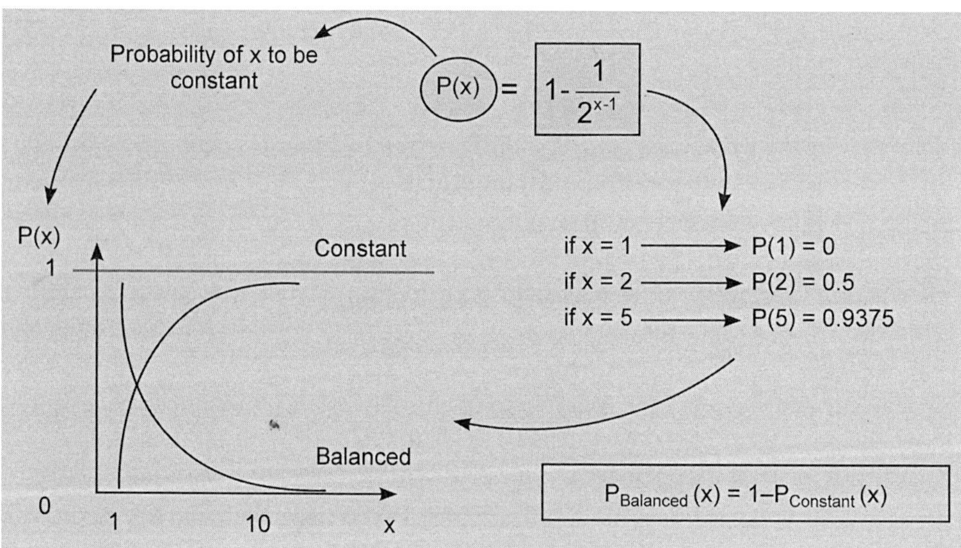

Fig.4.12: Evolution of the probabilities.

The point to ponder is that the more queries you do, the higher the probability that the function is constant.

The worst or best case has the same value with Deutsch-Jozsa's quantum algorithm. A unique query is required to find if the function is balanced or constant.

As already studied, that a quantum computer accesses some form of parallelism when using qubits. The quantum layer estimates all the possibilities at once. Deutsch Jozsa's algorithm uses this property with a specific component called an **oracle**. An oracle is a **black-box** operation. The oracle will evaluate all possible input variations in one query to output an aggregate result.

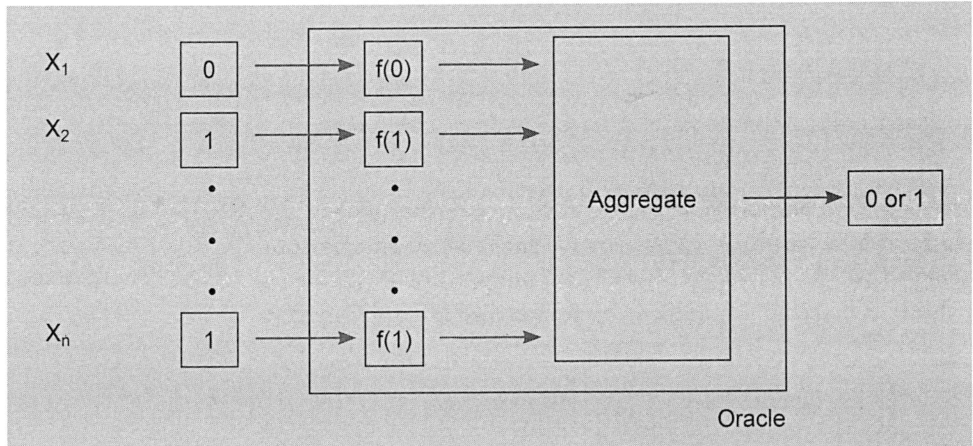

Fig.4.13: An oracle for Deutsch Jozsa's algorithm.

Let us see its time complexity in terms of Big O notation Here, you have an **exponential gain** which is a quantum advantage. The classical approach needs $2^{(n-1)} + 1$calls; against 1 for the quantum algorithm. **And this difference in time complexity is 2^n and it's called exponential optimization.**

What are these oracles? In the arena of quantum algorithms, **oracles are black-box operations.** They provide an algorithm (like a classical function) as an input to another algorithm. To take the flesh out of it, **Oracles are like masks with different properties that will help you simulate the physical effect you want to solve.** An oracle will act on qubits to output a transformation. The formulation is written like this: O |x> = |f(x)> where *O* is the oracle and *x* a **state vector** of the qubits $x = \{x_0, x_1, ..., x_n\}$ with *n* the number of inputs).

The main advantage of Oracle is allowing the user to focus on the quantum techniques to analyze the function rather than the function itself. But there is a vital drawback to the black-box. **The output size can be different from the input size, which would break the reversibility rule. It's essential to ensure that your oracle can be reversible.**

Oracle in the context of Deutsch-Jozsa's algorithm, in the constant case, i.e. **the input is equal to the output.** The **transformation** corresponds to a multiplication of the identity matrix and the input as follows:

$$\text{Input x I} = \text{Output} = \text{Input}$$

On the other hand, in the balanced case, the oracle's output will be half 0s and half 1s.

Quantum circuit for Deutsch-Jozsa

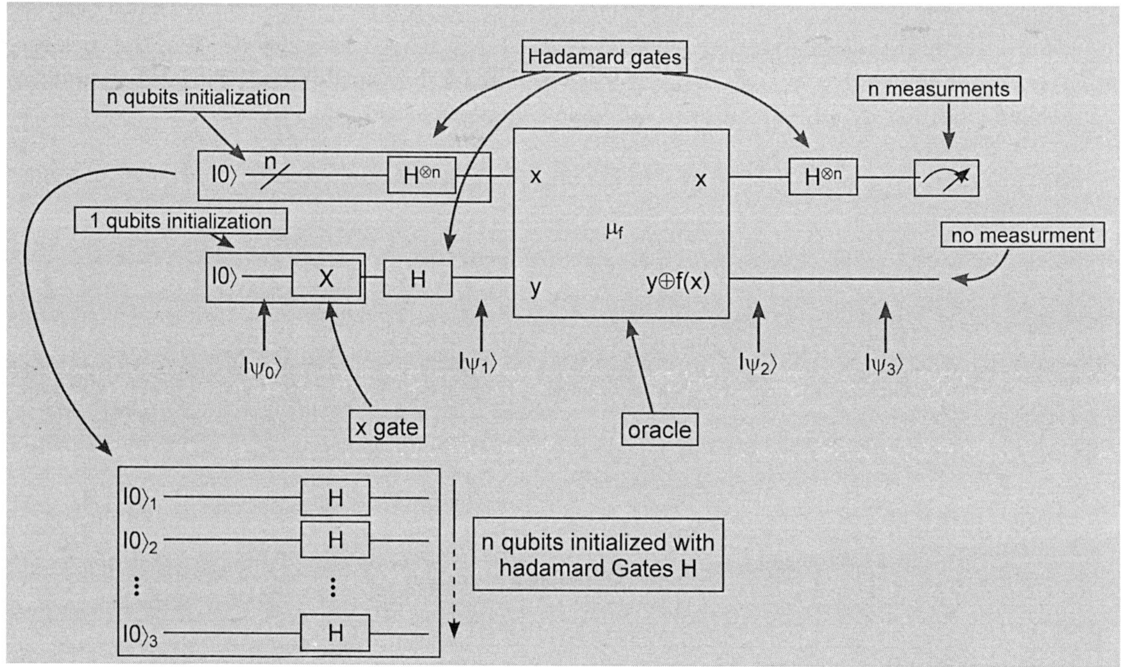

Fig.4.14: A General Quantum circuit for Deutsch-Jozsa problem with n-qubits initialized.

Note that |ψ_x> are the different phases of the quantum algorithm. In this circuit, the n-qubits are initialized to zero and split by an H gate. The bottom qubit is initialized to |1>. Then, these (n+1) qubits are passed to the U_f block. Lastly, the top n-qubits are split again by H gates and then measured.

When you start a quantum circuit, you initialize the circuit at the state 0. This is the |ψ_0> step. Each qubit will have the state 0 or the column vector (1, 0). **Please note that this quantum circuit is a generalized model because you can create a quantum circuit with *n*** qubits. You also need one qubit with the initialization at state 1; the X quantum gate does this. The X-gate performs a bit flip operation; it inverts the state, passing from 0 to 1.

Every qubit is put in a superposition 0 and 1 states. These states are then passed to the oracle. We query the oracle with a superposition state.

The quantum circuit for this Deutsch-Jozsa algorithm has already been discussed in 2nd chapter of this book.

We are in a position to solve some problems on Deutsch-Jozsa algorithm now.

Example-1: Consider a simple two-bit input that result in function *f(x)* being balanced. The following are all the possible inputs and outputs of *f*:

$$\mathbf{f(0,0) = 0}$$
$$\mathbf{f(0,1) = 1}$$
$$\mathbf{f(1,0) = 1}$$
$$\mathbf{f(1,1) = 0}$$

(are the possibilities of f)

The oracle for *g(x)* that takes in a 2-bit input will be:

$$U_f \mid x_1, x_0\rangle = (-1)^{f(x_1,x_0)} \mid x\rangle$$

In the oracle, x0 and **x1** represent the first and second inputs of *f* respectively. **Check if the oracle is correct?**

Solution-1: Implement the oracle into the quantum register using the steps listed below:

1. **Initialize the two qubits in the first register to 0 and the qubit in the second register to 1.** Mathematically, it can be expressed as the equation below. The subscripts 0, 1, and 2 are used to denote each qubit, with a subscript of 01 representing qubits 0 and 1.

$$\mid \psi_0\rangle = \mid 00\rangle_{01} \otimes \mid 1\rangle_2$$

2. **Add a Hadamard gate for each qubit,** which would enable the qubits to be in a superposition state.

$$\mid \psi_1\rangle = \frac{1}{2}(\mid 00\rangle + \mid 01\rangle + \mid 10\rangle + \mid 11\rangle)_{01} \otimes \frac{1}{\sqrt{2}}(\mid 0\rangle - \mid 1\rangle)_2$$

Truth Table of the Hadamard Gate is as follows:

Input Qubit	Output Qubit
$\mid 0\rangle$	$\frac{1}{\sqrt{2}}(\mid 0\rangle + \mid 1\rangle)$
$\mid 1\rangle$	$\frac{1}{\sqrt{2}}(\mid 0\rangle - \mid 1\rangle)$
$\frac{1}{\sqrt{2}}(\mid 0\rangle + \mid 1\rangle)$	$\mid 0\rangle$
$\frac{1}{\sqrt{2}}(\mid 0\rangle - \mid 1\rangle)$	$\mid 1\rangle$

This shows the mapping Ket 0 to Ket +, Ket 1 to Ket -, and vice versa.

Note here that the Hadamard Gate is its own inverse. Applying the Hadamard Gate to state-0 brings it to a superposition which we'll call '+' due to the plus sign in the middle. Applying the Hadamard Gate to state + brings it back to 0. Similarly, applying the Hadamard gate twice transforms 1 to '-', which then transforms back into 1.

3. Implement the oracle function into this equation now.

$$\begin{aligned}\mid \psi_2\rangle = \frac{1}{2\sqrt{2}}\Big[&\mid 00\rangle_{01} \otimes (\mid 0 \oplus 0 \oplus 0\rangle - \mid 1 \oplus 0 \oplus 0\rangle)_2 \\ &+ \mid 01\rangle_{01} \otimes (\mid 0 \oplus 0 \oplus 1\rangle - \mid 1 \oplus 0 \oplus 1\rangle)_2 \\ &+ \mid 10\rangle_{01} \otimes (\mid 0 \oplus 1 \oplus 0\rangle - \mid 1 \oplus 1 \oplus 0\rangle)_2 \\ &+ \mid 11\rangle_{01} \otimes (\mid 0 \oplus 1 \oplus 1\rangle - \mid 1 \oplus 1 \oplus 1\rangle)_2\Big]\end{aligned}$$

4. Simplify the expression above. The expression now becomes:

$$|\psi_2\rangle = \frac{1}{2\sqrt{2}}\Big[|00\rangle_{01} \otimes (|0\oplus 0\oplus 0\rangle - |1\oplus 0\oplus 0\rangle)_2$$
$$+|01\rangle_{01} \otimes (|0\oplus 0\oplus 1\rangle - |1\oplus 0\oplus 1\rangle)_2$$
$$+|10\rangle_{01} \otimes (|0\oplus 1\oplus 0\rangle - |1\oplus 1\oplus 0\rangle)_2$$
$$+|11\rangle_{01} \otimes (|0\oplus 1\oplus 1\rangle - |1\oplus 1\oplus 1\rangle)_2\Big]$$

5. For the two qubits on the first register, apply a Hadamard gate.

$$|\psi_3\rangle = |1\rangle_0 \otimes |1\rangle_1 \otimes (|0\rangle - |1\rangle)_2$$

6. Now, measure the two qubits and the outcome will be a non-zero state of 11, showing that *f* is **balanced**.

4.11 SIMON'S ALGORITHM

Daniel Simon's statement is as follows- **"It takes f: {0, 1}^{n} → {0, 1}^{n} as input, 2 sets of n-qubits. Assume there is a secret number s** ∊ {0, 1}^{n} **so that f(x) = f(x ⊕ s). Now, we need to build a quantum circuit and iterate it n-1 times to find n-bit linearly independent strings i.e.** $y_1, y_1, \ldots\ldots, y_{n-1}$ ∊ {0, 1}^{n} ." That is,

$$\left.\begin{array}{l} y_1 \cdot s = 0 \\ y_1 \cdot s = 0 \\ \vdots \\ \vdots \\ y_{n-1} \cdot s = 0 \end{array}\right\}$$

Please note that these are the n-1, n-bit equations, where

$$y_1 \cdot s = y_1^{(1)} \cdot s_1 + \ldots\ldots y_n^{(1)} \cdot s_n$$

With classical/traditional computer, there will be at most, in worst case scenario, $s^{n-1} + 1$ function evaluations.

Steps of Simon's algorithm-

S1: Initialize **two n-qubit registers** to the **zero state.**

S2: Apply a **Hadamard transform (H)** to the **first register.**

S3: Apply the **query function (F).** This **query function acts on both quantum registers.**

S4: Measure the second register (M).

S5: Apply a **Hadamard transform to the first register.**

So, for the Simon's algorithm the quantum circuit may be drawn as follows-

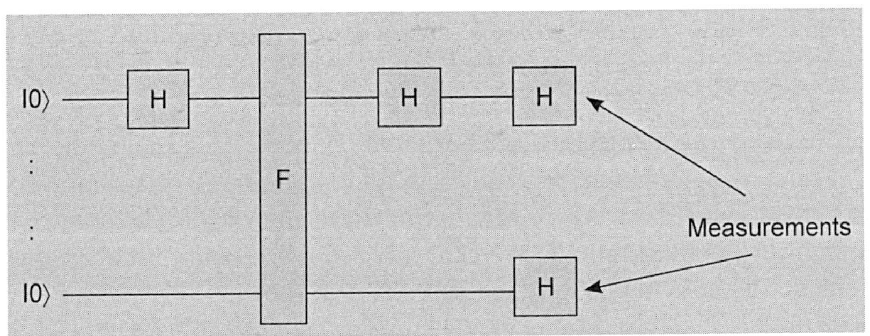

Fig.4.15: Simon's algorithm quantum circuit

Mathematical Interpretation-

1. As a first step, it will **put the first set of n-qubits in a superposition state with Hadamard transform.** That is,

$$|\psi\rangle = (H^{\otimes n} |0^n\rangle) \otimes |0^n\rangle = [\textstyle\sum_{x \in \{0,1\}^n} 1/\sqrt{2^n}\, |x\rangle] \otimes |0^n\rangle.$$

2. Apply the **oracle** that we have studied in DJ algorithm earlier, **without phase shifts.** This gives us-

$$|\psi\rangle' = 1/2^{n/2} \textstyle\sum_{x \in \{0,1\}^n} (|x\rangle \otimes |f(x)\rangle).$$

3. Last but not the least, we apply the **Hadamard transform to the n-qubits again,** which will result in-

$$|\psi\rangle^n = 1/2^n \textstyle\sum_{x \in \{0,1\}^n} [\sum_{y \in \{0,1\}^n} ((-1)^{x.y} |y\rangle \otimes |f(x)\rangle)]$$

where $$H^{\otimes n} |x\rangle = 1/\sqrt{2^n} \textstyle\sum_{y \in \{0,1\}^n} ((-1)^{x.y} |y\rangle$$

4. Finally, as we do, measure it. Actually, There are 2 types of outputs for this algorithm: -

Output-1: $x \oplus y = 0^n$ where f is a one-to-one function. **Please understand that this is the case where probabilities ($1/2^n$) of n-bit string are uniformly distributed.**

Output-2: $x \oplus y = s$ **and** $s \neq 0^n$, which will give a resultant as follows-

$$p_y = |1/2^n \textstyle\sum_{z \in A} ((-1)^{x_1 .y} (1 + (-1)^{y.s}) |z\rangle) |^2$$

Now, two cases arise-

Case-1: If y.s is an odd number then it turns out to be zero which is a no result outcome.

Case-2: If y.s is an even number then-

$$p_y = |1/2^n \textstyle\sum_{x \in \{0,1\}^n} ((-1)^{x.y} |f(x)\rangle) |^2 = \begin{cases} 1/2^{n-1} & \text{if y.s is even} \\ 0 & \text{if y.s is odd} \end{cases}$$

Simon tried to demonstrate the ability to determine the periodicity of a function exponentially faster on a quantum computer compared to a classical one. His problem considers an oracle that implements a function mapping an n-bit string to an m-bit string-

$$f: \{0,1\}^n \rightarrow \{0,1\}^m$$

Where m>= n and it is assured that f is a 1:1 type function or 2:1 type function with non-zero period, $s \in \{0,1\}^n$ such that for all x, x_0 we have $f(x) = f(x_0)$ if and only if $x_0 = x \oplus s$ where $\oplus$ corresponds to addition modulo-2. **Please remember that when we use addition modulo-2, we equate 2 with 0. For example, $1 \oplus 1 = 0$ and we can say that 'the sum of 1 and 1 mpdulo-2 is 0'.** Now, the problem is to determine the type of function f and if it is 2:1, to find the period, s. The scenario is similar to Deutsch's problem only i.e. we are given an oracle, a black box function where you can find the output for specific inputs but not the underlying function. The issue is to find out if this black box process ever sends two different inputs to the same output. **Also note that in these algorithms we don't find out what the underlying function in the black box is. We can only see the relation between the input and the output, from outside the box.** Actually, Simon succeeded in showing that we can solve this problem to find the periodicity of a function exponentially faster on a quantum computer as compared to the traditional/ classical computer. This point was then used by Shor to develop his algorithm on factoring.

4.12 OSSS TOOLKITS FOR IMPLEMENTING QUANTUM PROGRAMS

OSS toolkits means open source software tools for quantum programming. They allow researchers, developers, academicians to explore, learn and experiment with quantum algorithms and protocols. Some of the OSS toolkits for implementing quantum programs are as follows:

1. **Forest by Rigetti Computing.**
2. **Qiskit by IBM.**
3. **Q# by Microsoft.**
4. **Cirq by Google AI Quantum.**
5. **ProjectQ.**
6. **PennyLane.**
7. **StrawBerry fields by Xanadu**
8. **Ocean by D-Wave systems.**

Let us discuss them one by one now.

1. **Forest** is a suite of tools developed by Rigetti Computing. It is used for designing and running quantum programs on their quantum processors. It includes the Quil programming language with a Python library called as pyQuil and a QVM (Quantum Virtual Machine) for simulating quantum circuits. (Visit: *https://www.rigetti.com/forest*).
2. **Qiskit** is an open-source framework developed by IBM for working with quantum computers at the level of circuits, algorithms and applications. It allows users to design and run quantum computing experiments on IBM's cloud-based quantum devices. (Visit: *https://qiskit.org*).
3. **Q#** is a domain-specific programming language for quantum computing. It has been developed by Microsoft. The Quantum Development Kit (QDK) includes the Q# language, a quantum simulator and many other tools for quantum computing development. (Visit: *https://docs.microsoft.com/en-us/quantum*).
4. **Cirq (Google AI quantum)** is a Python library developed by Google for creating, editing and invoking Noisy Intermediate Scale Quantum (NISQ) circuits. (Visit: https://github.com/quantumlib/Cirq).

5. **ProjectQ** is an open-source software framework for quantum computing that allows users to implement quantum algorithms using a high-level, hardware programming language. It can be interfaced with different hardware platforms and simulators. (Visit: *https://projectq.ch*).
6. **PennyLane** is a cross-platform Python library for QML, automatic differentiation and optimization of hybrid quantum-classical computations. It is developed so as to work with different quantum computing frameworks like Qiskit, Cirq and ProjectQ. (Visit: https://pennylane.ai).
7. **Strawberry Fields** is a full-stack Python library for designing, simulating and optimizing continuous-variable quantum optical circuits. It is integrated with their photonic quantum computing platform. (Visit: *https://strawberryfields.ai*).
8. **Ocean** is a D-wave software development kit (SDK) for solving complex optimization problems using their quantum annealing processors. It is a library by D-wave. It also mentions Quantum-as-a-Service (QaaS) on cloud platform that is also known as **Quantum Cloud.** It provides us a Python-based interface to work with D-wave quantum hardware. (Visit: *https://docs.ocean.dwavesys.com/en/stable*).

Please understand that these toolkits act as a foundation for developing quantum computing applications. Also understand that they help to bridge the gap between quantum hardware and software.

We can compare them in a tabular form as follows-

Table-4.1: Different vendors and libraries for Quantum Programming.

Features	Forest	Qiskit	Q#
High-level language used	Python (PyQuil)	Python	Q# with C# or Python host.
Main focus	Superconducting qubits	Superconducting qubits	Topological qubits.
Uses Gates	Universal gate set	Universal gate set	Universal gate set
Simulator used	Quantum Virtual Machine (QVM)	Qiskit Aer	QuantumSimulator
Noise simulation	Yes	Yes	Yes
Hardware used	Rigetti Quantum Processors (QPU)	IBM Quantum Processors	Not available.
Quantum Volume Support	Yes	Yes	Yes
Libraries used	pyQuil, Grove	Qiskit Aqua, Qiskit Ignis	Q# libraries, Quantum Katas.
Integration	AWS Braket	Quantum Azure	Quantum Azure
Documentation	Good	Excellent	Excellent
Ecosystem	Growing	Large	Growing.

Other types of frameworks, tools, simulators:

1. **Quantum Programming Studio** is a web-based GUI designed to allow users to construct quantum algorithms. You can get the results by simulating directly in the browser or by executing on real quantum computers.
2. **Quantum Computer Emulator (QCE)** is a software emulator that emulates different types of hardware designs of quantum computers. It provides an environment to debug and execute quantum algorithms under realistic experimental conditions. QCE has both GUI and the simulator itself.
3. **SimQubit** is also a GUI-based quantum circuit simulator that allows editing of quantum circuits.
4. **Qubit101** is a user-friendly quantum circuit editor as well as simulator. This tool helps users to create, modify and save quantum circuits. The supported platforms include Rigetti Forest, IBM Qiskit, Google Cirq and Tensor Flow, MS Quantum Development Kit, Amazon Braket etc.
5. **Google's Cirq , is** used for crafting and optimizing quantum circuits. It is a very powerful tool in quantum programmer's arsenal that offers specialized features tailored to the unique challenges posed by quantum computing. It allows developers to simulate and analyse noise models. **Quantum virtual machines in Cirq enable simulations on classical hardware that facilitates robust testing and debugging.**
6. **TornadoQSim** is a **quantum circuit emulator.** It is written in Java.
7. **QuEST** (Quantum Exact Simulation Tool) is a quantum emulator written in C and C++.
8. **Many quantum languages have also been developed** like QCL i.e. Quantum Computation Language, Q Language (used for programming quantum gates like Hadamard, CNOT, SWAP, QFT), QFC AND QPL, QML, qGCL (Quantum Guarded Command Language), ProjectQ, QuTiP (Quantum Toolbox in Python), QNET, Silq, Quipper, QWire,Qubiter, Scaffold, Qumin, lambda calculus by Quantum languages, MCBeth, eQASM, QIRO, Qunity, TWIST, ScaleQC, BQSKit, Yao.jl (a package for the Julia language used for creating quantum circuits), Quirk, QX Quantum Computer Simulator, Qrack, Psitrum, Sandbox AQ, SimQubit and so on.

4.13 IBM'S QUANTUM EXPERIENCE

IBM's provides an open source SDK for working with quantum computers at the level of pulses, circuits and application modules. This kit is QISKIT. QISKIT stands for Quantum Information Science Kit that is a quantum computing dev library created by IBM in 2017. The QISKIT library is a flexible framework for programming quantum computers.

Some of the main features of Qiskit are as follows:

1. It is an open-source quantum computing framework developed by IBM to create, simulate and run quantum circuits on the actual quantum hardware.
2. To use this tool, you need Python 3.6 or higher, knowledge of Jupyter Notebook environment.
3. To install Qiskit, simply run the following command in your terminal or command prompt- **pip install qiskit.**
4. After installation is complete, we can now create a simple quantum circuit.

5. It has 4 main components-
   (a) **Qiskit Terra:** This provides all essential components for building quantum circuits. Terra happens to be the heart of Qiskit. Terra allows users to define and manipulate quantum circuits with ease.
   (b) **Qiskit Aer:** You can develop noise models for simulating realistic noisy simulations that can occur in real quantum computing devices using Aer tools. Aer also provides a C++ simulator framework. It is a high performance simulator designed for accurate quantum circuit simulations. This component is active during the development phase that allows developers to test and debug quantum algorithms before deploying them on actual quantum hardware. It supports many types of noise models that enhances the fidelity of simulations.
   (c) **Qiskit Ignis:** This is a framework for analyzing and minimizing noise in quantum ciruit. It addresses the challenge of noisy quantum processors. It enables developers to optimize the performance of quantum algorithms in presence of noise, thus contributing to a practical quantum computing.
   (d) **Qiskit Agua:** This contains cross-domain algorithms and logic to run these algorithms on a quantum real device or simulator. It includes functionalities tailored for chemistry, finance and optimization. Qiskit Aqua extends Qiskit's capabilities into domain-specific libraries for quantum applications.
6. Qiskit seamlessly integrates with IBM's cloud-based quantum processors that allow developers to execute their quantum algorithms on real quantum hardware. **Please understand that this integration facilitates a bridge between simulation and practical implementation.**
7. In nutshell, as quantum computing continues to evolve, Qiskit remains at the forefront, adapting to technological advancements and expanding its capabilities. **To take the flesh out of it, Qiskit continues to be a cornerstone for those navigating the quantum landscape, empowering them to explore, experiment and innovate in the ecosystem of quantum computing.**

Let us write a simple program in Qiskit now.

```
# import the Qiskit package
import qiskit
# create a quantum register with one qubit
qreg = qiskit.QuantumRegister (1, name = 'qreg')
# create a classical register with one qubit
creg = qiskit. ClassicalRegister (1, name = 'creg')
#create a quantum circuit with the above registers
circ = qiskit. QuantumCircuit (qreg, creg)
#Add a NOT operation on the qubit
circ.x (qreg [0])
# Add a measurement on the qubit
circ.measure (qreg, creg)
# Print the circuit
```

```
print (circ.draw ( ))
# get a backend to run
backend = qiskit.BasicAer. get_backend("qasm_simulator")
# Execure the circuit on the backend and get measurements results
job = qiskit.execute(circ, backend, shots = 5)
result = job.result( )
# Print the measurement results
print (result.get_counts( ))
```

Explanation: After importing the Qiskit library, the program declares a quantum and classical register with one qubit, which it then uses to create a circuit. This program is in close resemblance with that in Cirq. This is because they have different syntaxes. Then, we perform NOT and measurement steps to the circuit which is finally printed out by drawing the circuit. **Please note that Qiskit has the ability to draw and save circuits as files too.** That is,

circ.draw (filename = "qiskit-circuit", output = "latex")

And now we get the following circuit-

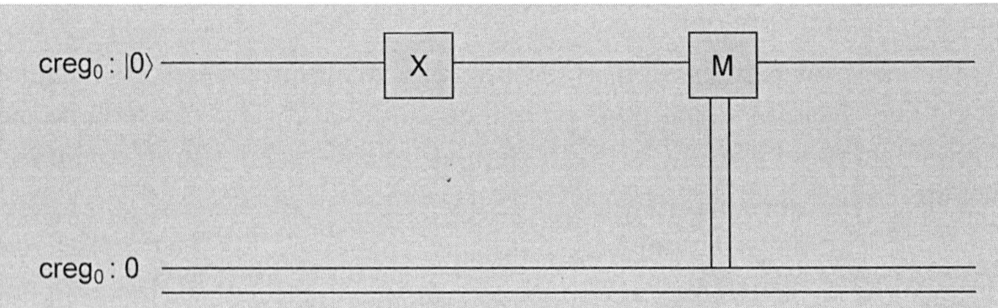

After the printing of this circuit, a backend is declared for executing the quantum circuit. Finally, the measurement count is printed as output. A sample output may be-

{'1' : 5}

Also note that in Qiskit, the measurement outcomes are stored in dictionaries as key-value pairs where keys are bit string and values are the number of times each bit string was measured. The output, here, shows that the only bit string present in the measurement is 1.

Thus, we have discussed one IBM's quantum toolkit.

You can also get access to IBM Q systems. To start using the IBM quantum computer, first of all register yourself and thus create a login and password. To do this, **please follow the following steps:**

S1: **Open the website of IBM Q Experience** i.e. *https://quantum* experience.ng.bluemix.net/qx/experience.

S2: Depending on the web-browser used by you either a "sign in" popup window will open automatically or click on "sign in" button on the top right corner which will opena new tab.

S3: An account will be created after filling all required fields.

In this scenario, your email id will be your login id and the password is of your choice. This finishes registration. Now go to the website and sign-in. at the top-right corner you will see your name as entered during the registration process. After sign-in,

(a) **Click on the "Composer" tab and select a topology that you wish to use for your experiment.**

(b) **Select suitable gates and create your quantum circuit.**

(c) **Either run or simulate the circuit that you have designed in the previous step. To do so, click on the corresponding tabs i.e. either click on "Run tab" or on "Simulate tab". Please note that higher is the number of shots, the more units are required to run the IBM quantum computer**

4.14 MICROSOFT Q (Q#)

The Microsoft Quantum Development Kit (QDK) represents a comprehensive and integrated set of tools that are designed to empower developers in the realm of quantum computing. When anchored by Q# programming language, this kit combines a versatile programming language, a robust development environment and powerful simulators to facilitate quantum algorithm development. Some of the features of Q# are as follows-

1. Core to the QDK is Q# which is a domain-specific programming language tailored for expressing quantum algorithms. Q# seamlessly integrates with classical languages like C# and F#, thereby allowing **developers to create hybrid quantum-classical applications** with ease. Its **high-level abstractions simplify quantum circuit design.**
2. QDK comes equipped with **quantum simulators** that enable efficient testing of the quantum code. Using them developers can **simulate the behavior of quantum algorithms on classical hardware.** So, they can help in **refinement of quantum solutions** before deploying them on **actual quantum processors.**
3. QDK includes a rich set of **quantum libraries and code samples** that accelerates the **learning curve** for developers venturing into the quantum landscape.
4. As quantum computing ecosystem **evolves,** so does the MS QDK. It is the forefront of quantum development frameworks.
5. **Quipper,** is another player in the quantum computing landscape that provides a **functional and scalable programming language** designed for quantum algorithms. Quipper embraces the principles of functional programming to provide **a structured approach to quantum circuit design.** Quipper, help developers to express the quantum algorithms in a modular way. This functional approach improves the code readability and maintainability too.
6. **Quipper** provides a **modular and scalable architecture.** Today quantum circuits can be designed in a hierarchical manner.
7. **Quipper,** comes equipped with an extensive library of quantum gates. **Please note that this library simplifies the process of designing quantum circuits that allows the developers to leverage a broad range of quantum gates seamlessly. Also note that the library is an essential resource for quantum information scientists and researchers working on many quantum algorithms.**

8. **QuTip** stands for Quantum Toolbox in python. It is also an open-source software suite designed for research in quantum computing field.
9. **QuTip is built on Python.** Its Python-like syntax and integration with other scientific computing libraries contribute to a seamless and user-friendly experience.

4.15 RIGETTI PYQUIL (QPU/QVM)

Rigetti **PyQuil is a Python library for quantum computing** using the Quantum Instruction Language (Quil). Some pre-requisites to use it are-

(a) Python 3.6 or later.

(b) Knowledge of Jupyter notebook.

To install **PyQuil and its dependencies, you may run the following command in your terminal or command prompt:**

pip install pyquil

This installs **PyQuil.** We are now in a position to write a simple quantum program. To simulate the quantum program locally, we can use **Rigetti's Quantum Virtual Machine (QVM).** Firstly, check that you must have installed and installed **the Forest SDK which includes the QVM and Quilc compiler.** You can follow the instructions provided in the official documentation-

http://pyquil-docs.rigetti.com/en/stable/start.html#installing-the-forest-sdk

In next step, start the QVM and Quilc in two separate terminal or command prompt windows:

```
qvm –S
bash
copy code
quilc –S
```

In order to execute the quantum program on a real Quantum Processor/ QPU, you need to sign for access to Rigetti Quantum Cloud Services. You will get an API key. Save it. Now you can run the code on a QPU.

SUMMARY

Quantum computers use quantum algorithms that rest on three pillars- superposition, entanglement and quantum parallelism, to solve complex problems in a better way. Qubits are the basic units of information. Many quantum algorithms like Shor's, Grover's, Deutsch's algorithm, Deutsch's –Jozsa algorithm have been discussed in this chapter.

This chapter gives a deep dive into quantum algorithms. By leveraging the strange properties of quantum physics, they can solve some complex problems exponentially faster than classical/traditional computers. **Note that this quantum advantage comes from specialized algorithms that tap into the unique capabilities of quantum systems.** This chapter explores some of the key quantum algorithms powering this computing revolution. For instance, say you have a database with a million of entries (500,000 entries). You want to search for a person's number. Now your conventional/classical/ traditional computer will have to scan each entry one by one to find the right number. Then, it may have to check 5000,000 entries on average before finding the correct entry. But a quantum computer using Grover's algorithm can search the database at a very fast speed. **This is so because it checks all entries simultaneously in parallel. This feat is impossible for classical machines. Also note that quantum parallelism provides enormous efficiency gains that gives the Grover's algorithm a quadratic speedup.** *It is observed that instead of 500,000 checks, it only needs about 1000 checks to find the right entry.* This is naturally an astounding 500x speed improvement !!!

MULTIPLE CHOICE QUESTIONS [MCQS] WITH ANSWERS

1. A finite sequence of well-defined instructions to solve a problem or a class of problems that are executed on qubits and quantum gates is known as-
   (a) Classical algorithm.
   (b) Quantum algorithm.
   (c) Parallel algorithm.
   (d) None of the above.
2. The process of linear mapping of fundamental algebraic structures is known as-
   (a) Quantum Fourier Transform (QFT).
   (b) Quantum Phase Estimation (QPE).
   (c) Quantum Parallelism.
   (d) None of the above.
3. A technique that enables the creation of optimized amplitude amplification techniques is known as-
   (a) Quantization.
   (b) Superposition.
   (c) Qubitization.
   (d) None of the above.
4. It refers to the fact that controlled operations have effects on their controls as well as targets that effect corresponding phase operations is known as-
   (a) Phase Kick-Back Algorithm.
   (b) Simon's algorithm.
   (c) Bernstein algorithm.
   (d) None of the above.
5. A polynomial time algorithm for the factorization of n-bit numbers on quantum computers was given in 1994 by-
   (a) Peter Shor.
   (b) David Deutsch.
   (c) Alan Turing.
   (d) None of the above.
6. Masks with different properties that will help you simulate the physical effect you want to solve are known as-
   (a) Gates.
   (b) Oracles.
   (c) Dbase.
   (d) None of the above.
7. A software emulator that emulates different types of hardware designs of quantum computers is-
   (a) Quantum Computer Emulator (QCE).
   (b) QISKIT
   (c) Q#
   (d) None of the above.
8. OSS toolkits means open source software tools for quantum programming. They allow researchers, developers, academicians to explore, learn and experiment with quantum algorithms and protocols. Which of the following is an OSS toolkit?

(a) MICROSOFT Q#
(b) Python.
(c) Java.
(d) None of the above.

9. To install Qiskit, simply run the following command in your terminal or command prompt-
(a) pip install qiskit.
(b) pop install qiskit.
(c) pre install qiskit.
(d) None of the above.

10. **SimQubit** is a-
(a) Text-based quantum circuit simulator.
(b) GUI-based quantum circuit simulator.
(c) Web-based quantum circuit simulator.
(d) None of the above.

11. Prof. David Deutsch was from-
(a) University of Oxford.
(b) Cambridge University.
(c) GGSIPU.
(d) Delhi University.

12. The quantum black box is an abstract machine that can be viewed as a black box that produces some result and is also known as a-
(a) Database.
(b) Data structure.
(c) Oracle.
(d) None of the above.

13. Shor's algorithm itself contains two parts- one is purely classical and the other part is-
(a) Quantum.
(b) Exponential.
(c) Linear.
(d) None of the above.

14. If two numbers are congruent modulo n, then the difference between a and b will be some-
(a) Divisor of n.
(b) Multiple of n.
(c) Factor of n.
(d) None of the above.

15. The time complexity in the Grover's algorithm for database search is reduced to-
(a) N^2.
(b) N/2
(c) $\sqrt{N}$
(d) None of the above.

16. Hadamard gates as used in the Deutsch-Jozsa algorithm are-
(a) For superposition.
(b) For phase shift.
(c) For rotations
(d) None of the above.

17. The part of Shor's algorithm that is quantum-
(a) The period-finding portion.
(b) The congruence portion.
(c) The modulus portion.
(d) All of it.

18. The wrapping of data and functions together into a single unit is known as-
(a) Abstraction.
(b) Data hiding.
(c) Polymorphism.
(d) Encapsulation.

19. In Q#, what data type represents the result of a projective measurement onto the eigenspaces of a quantum operator with eigen values +/- 1 ?
(a) EigenReturn.
(b) Return.
(c) Result.
(d) EigenResult.

20. Pauli gates are found in which namespace-
    (a) Microsoft. Quantum. Intrinsic
    (b) Microsoft. Quantum. Canon
    (c) Microsoft. Quantum. Gates
    (d) None of the above.
21. In QDK, R-operation is used to-
    (a) Rotate about x or y or z axis.
    (b) Reset a qubit.
    (c) Reset a given gate.
    (d) Rotate about a given Pauli axis.
22. A basic feature of many quantum algorithms is that-
    (a) All are quite slow.
    (b) They allow a quantum computer to evaluate a function f(x) for many different values of x simultaneously.
    (c) Don't use classical computation at all.
    (d) None of the above.
23. Oracle is not a valid quantum gate because-
    (a) Oracle is not unitary or reversible.
    (b) Oracle is a company.
    (c) Oracle is a SQL-based language.
    (d) None of the above.
24. Grover's algorithm requires an oracle that maps an input $(0, 1)^n$ to-
    (a) (0, 0).
    (b) (0, 1).
    (c) (1, 1).
    (d) None of the above.
25. The extra bit that is added is known as-
    (a) Qubit.
    (b) Sign bit.
    (c) Ancilla bit.
    (d) None of the above.
26. The number of times your algorithm will run on a simulator is known as-
    (a) Shots.
    (b) Knots.
    (c) Slots.
    (d) None of the above.
27. More shots can give rise to more-
    (a) Accurate results.
    (b) Less accurate results.
    (c) No results.
    (d) None of the above.
28. An oracle performs-
    (a) NOR operation.
    (b) Ex-XOR operation.
    (c) XOR operation.
    (d) None of the above.
29. In which year was the first quantum computer with 2 –qubits was created?
    (a) 1997.
    (b) 1998.
    (c) 1999.
    (d) 2000.
30. The study of the computational complexity of the problems with respect to quantum computers is known as-
    (a) Quantum complexity theory.
    (b) Data complexity theory.
    (c) Time complexity theory.
    (d) None of the above.
31. The U in the Deutsch-Jozsa algorithm is also referred to as what?
    (a) Black box.
    (b) Delphi.
    (c) Conversion.
    (d) Hadamard gate.
32. What is the correct Big-O notation for the time component of Shor's factoring?
    (a) $O((\log n)^3)$
    (b) $O((\log n)^2)$
    (c) $O((\log n)) * 3$
    (d) $O((\log n)^3)$

33. When evaluating a function using the Deutsch-Jozsa algorithm, which state is defined by all 0s?
    (a) Balanced.
    (b) Constant.
    (c) Superpositioned.
    (d) Void.

34. The Deutsch-Jozsa algorithm allows for _______ reduction in processing time/function analysis-
    (a) Logarithmic.
    (b) Exponential.
    (c) n(0)
    (d) Linear.

35. Quantum-as-a-Service (QaaS) on cloud platform is also known as-
    (a) Quantum Cloud.
    (b) Quantum Race.
    (c) Quantum kit.
    (d) None of the above.

Answers													
1.	(b)	2.	(a)	3.	(c)	4.	(a)	5.	(a)	6.	(b)	7.	(a)
8.	(a)	9.	(a)	10.	(b)	11.	(a)	12.	(c)	13.	(a)	14.	(c)
15.	(c)	16.	(a)	17.	(a)	18.	(d)	19.	(c)	20.	(a)	21.	(d)
22.	(b)	23.	(a)	24.	(b)	25.	(c)	26.	(a)	27.	(a)	28.	(c)
29.	(b)	30.	(a)	31.	(a)	32.	(a)	33.	(b)	34.	(d)	35.	(a)

CONCEPTUAL SHORT QUESTIONS WITH ANSWERS

Q1. What do you understand by the tagging and canceling effects?

Ans. 1 Those **qubit values** that meet the constraints, they are **rotated or tagged.** This is done to distinguish them from those that are not feasible. In quantum ecosystem, the tagging phase is called the **Oracle. Oracle** is a function that decides whether a given state of 0s and 1s qualifies as a solution for the Boolean Logic Expressions. **And this canceling phase is called as reflection and amplification. Please note here that the mathematics of canceling circuit can also be interpreted as reflecting the amplitudes along a suitable axis that has the effect of reducing the non-optimal amplitudes and also amplifying those that satisfy the constraints.**

Q2. Can you explain the high-level steps (abstraction) in Grover's algorithm?

Ans. 2 The following diagram shows the high-level steps (abstraction) in the Grover's algorithm:

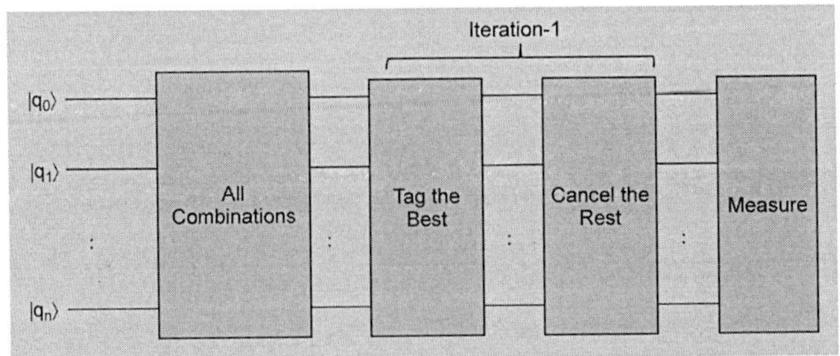

Q3. How can you say that the Grover's algorithm is a massively parallel computation?

Ans. 3 In nutshell, Grover's algorithm is the result of the following quantum effects-

1. Superposition to generate all 2^n combinations of n-qubits.
2. Rotating qubits in order to tag optimal qubit combinations in a mega-qubit and also to cancel or eliminate the non-optimal qubit combinations from the mega-qubit.

The point to ponder is that because of the very nature of quantum mechanics, the qubit combinations within the mega-qubit are acted on simultaneously by the quantum gates. So, we can say that the Grover's algorithm is a massively parallel computation.

Q4. Can you just state the Deutsch-Jozsa algorithm?

Ans. 4 The statement is-

Given: For any combination of inputs, you are told what the function returns but not the function, F itself.

To determine: Whether the function, F is constant or balanced.

Q5. What are the three main steps of Deutsch algorithm?

Ans. 5 Actually, **Deutsch algorithm** has three main steps/parts:

1. **Incorporate** the function, F.
2. **Embed** the function, F in a quantum circuit.
3. **Collapse and measure** the top qubit only. **Recall that a 0 indicates a constant function and a 1 points to a balanced function.**

Q6. Deutsch algorithm works on 2 main principles. What are they?

Ans. 6

1. By putting bits in a superposition state, the quantum computers can implicitly go through all cases simultaneously.
2. Back-to-back H gates restore the mega-qubit to its original state.

Q7. Explain Deutsch simple algorithm for the function, F that works on a single qubit only.

Ans. 7 Let us first of all recall that either the function, F is constant or it is balanced.

Function, F is constant:

A constant function returns the same value for both states of the qubit. For instance, the following is a function F (|x>) that always returns a |0> i.e.

F (|0>) = |0>
F (|1>) = |0>

Function, F is Balanced:

A balanced function F (|x>) will return |0> for one state and |1> for the other. For instance,

F (|0>) = |0>
F (|1>) = |1>

To start with the **Deutsch algorithm** assumes that the **function, F could be incorporated in a quantum circuit** as follows:

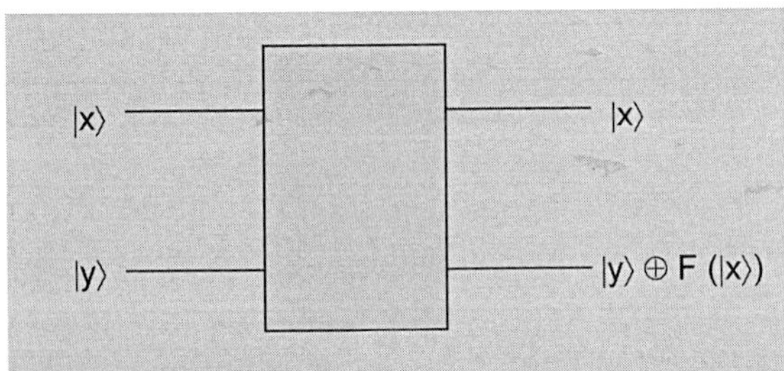

where $\oplus$ is an Exclusive-OR operator. Note that the |x> and |y> qubits on the left are the inputs to the block, U_f. **Please observe that the top qubit on the right hand side of the block U_f is unchanged by the block.** On the other hand, **the bottom qubit has its state changed to** |y> $\oplus$ F (|x>).

Two cases arise:

Case-1: F is a constant function.

Case-2: F is a balanced function.

Case-1: if F is a constant function, F(|x>) = 0 then the truth-table that relates inputs and outputs for the U_f block will work as follows for the set of inputs as |x> and |y>: -

Inputs		Outputs	
|x>	|y>	F(|x>)	|y> $\oplus$ F(|x>)
|0>	|0>	|0>	|0>
|0>	|1>	|0>	|1>
|1>	|0>	|0>	|0>
|1>	|1>	|0>	|1>

Now, to find out the gates for U_f corresponding to this truth-table, let us work out its matrix for these inputs; -

Input: |x> = |0> |y> = |0>

For these inputs, the outputs |x> and |y> $\otimes$ F (|x>), can be written as a 2-qubit quantum state as-

$$|00> \rightarrow |00>$$

We can write this as a state vector too-

$$\begin{bmatrix} 1 \\ 0 \\ 0 \\ 0 \end{bmatrix}$$

Note that this vector becomes the 1st column of the matrix, U_f.

Similarly, for the 2nd input, we have-

Input: |x> = |0> |y> = |1>

For these inputs, the outputs |x> and |y> $\oplus$ F (|x>), can be written as a 2-qubit quantum state as-

|01> → |01>

We can write this as a state vector too-

$$\begin{bmatrix} 0 \\ 1 \\ 0 \\ 0 \end{bmatrix}$$

Note that this vector becomes the 2nd column of the matrix, U_f.

Similarly, for the 3rd input, we have-

Input: |x> = |1> |y> = |0>

For these inputs, the outputs |x> and |y> F (|x>), can be written as a 2-qubit quantum state as-

|10> → |10>

We can write this as a state vector too-

$$\begin{bmatrix} 0 \\ 0 \\ 1 \\ 0 \end{bmatrix}$$

Note that this vector becomes the 3rd column of the matrix, U_f.

Finally, for the 4th input, we have-

Input: |x> = |1> |y> = |1>

For these inputs, the outputs |x> and |y> ⊕ F (|x>), can be written as a 2-qubit quantum state as-

|11> → |11>

We can write this as a state vector too-

$$\begin{bmatrix} 0 \\ 0 \\ 0 \\ 1 \end{bmatrix}$$

Note that this vector becomes the 4th column of the matrix, U_f.

Thus, the matrix A_{Uf} for the U_f block is-

$$A_{Uf} = \begin{bmatrix} 1 & 0 & 0 & 0 \\ 0 & 1 & 0 & 0 \\ 0 & 0 & 1 & 0 \\ 0 & 0 & 0 & 1 \end{bmatrix}$$

You can see that this is an **identity matrix. This means that the block U_f doesn't affect the states passed to it.** That is,

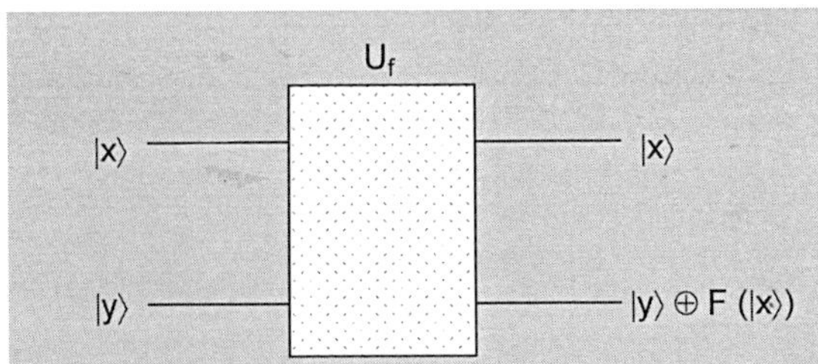

where ⊕ is an Exclusive-OR operator. Note that the |x> and |y> qubits on the left are the inputs to the block, U_f.

Now, consider case-2.

Case-2: if F is a balanced function, F (|0>) = 0 and F (|1>) =1 (as defined earlier too) then the truth-table for U_f block will be-

Inputs		**Outputs**	
|x>	|y>	F(|x>)	|y> ⊕ F(|x>)
|0>	|0>	|0>	|0>
|0>	|1>	|0>	|1>
|1>	|0>	|1>	|1>
|1>	|1>	|1>	|0>

Now, if we follow the same steps as above to calculate the matrix for the constant function, we can similarly compute the **matrix corresponding to the preceding truth-table for the balanced function** as follows: -

$$A_{Uf} = \begin{bmatrix} 1 & 0 & 0 & 0 \\ 0 & 1 & 0 & 0 \\ 0 & 0 & 0 & 1 \\ 0 & 0 & 1 & 0 \end{bmatrix}$$

Please note here that the 1st two columns are the identity columns. This means that when the top qubit, |x> is |0>, the output qubits, |x> and |y> ⊕ F (|x>) are also unchanged. On the other hand, from the 3rd and 4th columns, when the top qubit is |1>, the bottom qubit's state is switched from what it was passed. That is to say that this matrix is that of the Controlled-NOT (CNOT) gate as shown below:

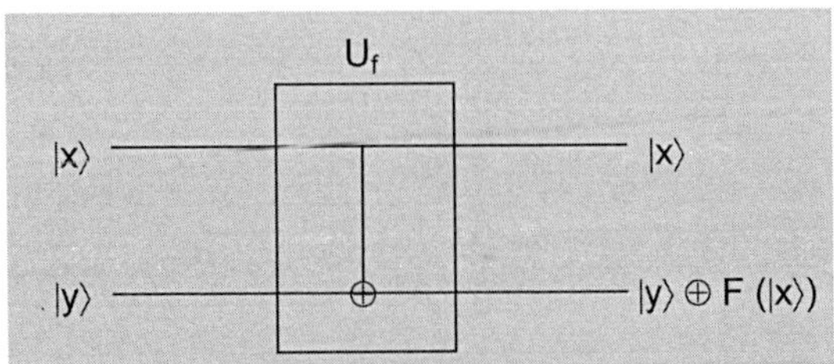

After working out the **circuit block U_f** for different types of **constant and balanced functions,** Deutsch then **embedded** it as shown below: -

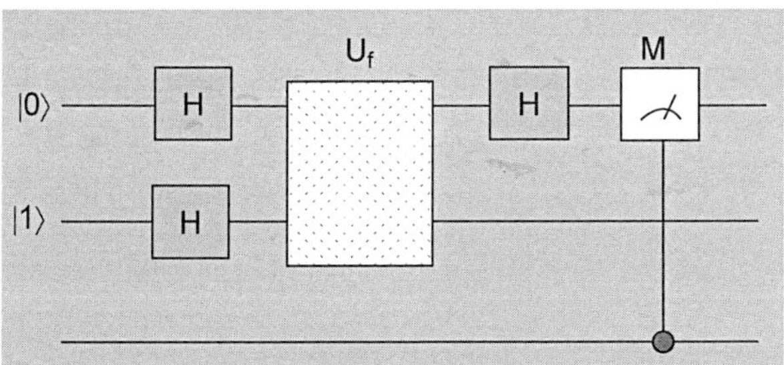

Please note here that only the top qubit is measured. It has been found that you just need to measure it to determine the nature of the function. **Also note that measuring the top qubit in this Deutsch's circuit gives a different result for a constant versus a balanced function.** When the top qubit is measured-

- A |0> indicates that the function, F is constant.
- A |1> indicates that the function, F is balanced.

This implies that whatever the function |F> is, ket is the single measurement of the top qubit that will tell you it's type.

For a single qubit function, this algorithm shows how to **embed the function within a circuit that tells you determine the type of function from one measurement only.** To put it in a proper light, the Deutsch-jozsa algorithm is flexible and elastic as this idea can be extended to functions of many qubits. **For instance,** for a 5-qubit function, F ($|q_0>$, $|q_1>$,$|q_2>$,$|q_3>$,$|q_4>$, the possibilities are: -

(a) **The function is constant and returns a |0> for all 2^5 or 32 states.**

(b) **The function is constant and returns a |1> for all 2^5 or 32 states.**

(c) **The function is balanced and returns a |0> for half the states and |1> for the other half.**

Using a classical/ traditional computer for this function (in worst case), you will need **(16 + 1) = 17 samples** to establish its type – **constant or balanced.** On the other hand, with this Deutsch-Jozsa circuit, you need **only one measurement.**

Q8. How can you say that the computational complexity of Deutsch-Jozsa algorithm is better than that of a classical computer?

Ans. 8 Although we need just one measurement for Deutsch-Jozsa algorithm for a single qubit function and for multiple-qubit function yet we didn't sample the function directly. In fact, the circuit was made of several gates. **Please note that the number of gates increases in linear proportion to the number of qubits while the number of cases to sample in a classical algorithm increases exponentially. So, we can say that the computational complexity of Deutsch-Jozsa algorithm is better than that of a classical computer.**

Q9. What is a diffusion operator in Grover's algorithm?

Ans. 9 In Grover's circuit, a uniform superposition state is obtained by using the Hadamard gates. This is then queried by the oracle gate that flips the amplitude of the x' item (to search) and leaves everything else unchanged. The amplitude of x' is increased next by incorporating a new gate that functions as what is known as the Grover Diffusion operator, D_f. This is shown in the circuit diagram below:

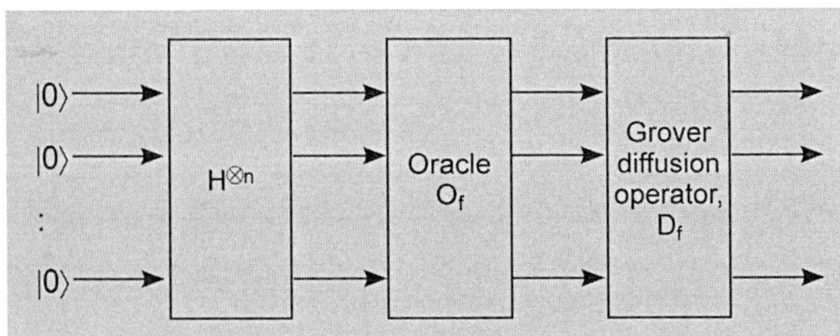

Q10. What do you understand by the amplitude in superposition? Give an example.

Ans. 10 The amplitudes may be understood as lines that are perpendicular to an axis. **Please note that the length of a line is proportional to the amplitude it represents. For instance,** the equal superposition of states resulting from the first Hadamard transformation looks like this-

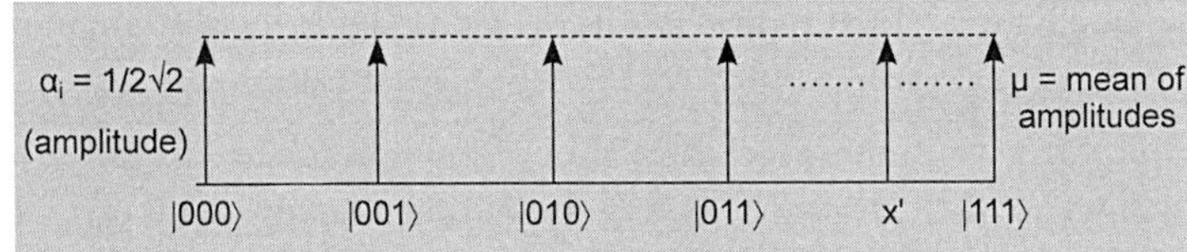

In this diagram, the states (bit strings) are labeled as {000, 001, ...111} and x' is the unknown marked state. **Also note that the uniform amplitudes of all the n-bit strings indicate that x' at this stage can't be distinguished from the other strings.** Next, the superposition state is fed to the oracle, G_f.

Q11. What is the need of creating superposition in quantum algorithms?

Ans. 11 The real art of constructing quantum algorithms is being able to manipulate this superposition so that when we make measurements we get a useful answer.

Q12. How it is that possible that Deutsch-Jozsa algorithm requires only one question to the oracle?

Ans. 12 Say, you are given a function of n variables. There will be 2^n possible input strings. In the best case, we can obtain the answer with only 2 questions to the oracle. But in the worst case, it will take $2^{n-1} + 1$ question. Because (n-1) appears as an exponent, so the function is exponential. In the worst case, it needs an exponential number of inquiries to the oracle. But **Deutsch-Jozsa algorithm** is a quantum algorithm that only needs one question to the oracle. So, the speed-up is substantial.

Q13. What was the need of Berstein Vazirani algorithm?

Ans. 13 If there are n bits, then it takes n-steps for a classical computer to guess that string. On the other hand, a quantum computer can do it in only one shot using this Berstein Vazirani algorithm. This is done in one step but let us write this Berstein Vazirani algorithm now-

Step-1: Apply **Hadamard transform to n-qubit state** $|0\rangle^{\otimes n}$. That is,

$$1/\sqrt{2^n} \sum_{(x = 0 \text{ to } 2^n)} |x\rangle$$

Step-2: Next we apply CNOT gate on the qubits that when applied, the oracle will turn the superposition into the following-

$$1/\sqrt{2^n} \sum_{(x = 0 \text{ to } 2^n)} (-1)^{f(x)} |x>$$

Please note that here oracle means a function, f(x), which performs the dot product, x.s where s is the secret string. Also note that if the dot product is 1, this will flip the state, x.

Step-3: Lastly, **reapply Hadamard transform** to the n-qubit state which will convert |-> to |1> and |+> to |0>.

The point to ponder is that here Hadamard transform puts the qubits in superposition which means no more small steps now.

Q14. Give some classification of quantum algorithms.

Ans. 14 Quantum algorithms may be classified as follows-

1. **Algebraic applications-** linear system, matrix element group representation, subgroup isomorphism etc.
2. **Number theoretic applications-** Shor's factoring algorithm.
3. **Quantum simulations-** Schrodinger equation simulation, transverse model simulation etc.
4. **Learning applications-** Quantum Principal Component Analysis (QPCA), Quantum Support Vector Machine (QSVM) etc.
5. **Inverse function computations-** Grover's algorithm, Berstein Vazirani algorithm.
6. **Quantum utilities-** state preparation, quantum tomography, quantum error correction.
7. **Graph applications-** Approximate quantum algorithms, Quantum Random Walk, Minimum spanning tree, maximum flow etc.

Q15. How quantum algorithms work?

Ans. 15 As we know that the main physiognomies of the quantum ecosystem are- superposition, entanglement and interference. This makes it possible to solve certain problems that used to take exponential time in classical algorithms, in a faster way. Actually, using superposition and interference, a function, f(x) can be assessed concurrently for all values of x. This is called as **quantum parallelism.** The last stage of quantum processing is the **measurement step.** The point to remember is that any quantum computation process ends with system measurement. The following figure shows this

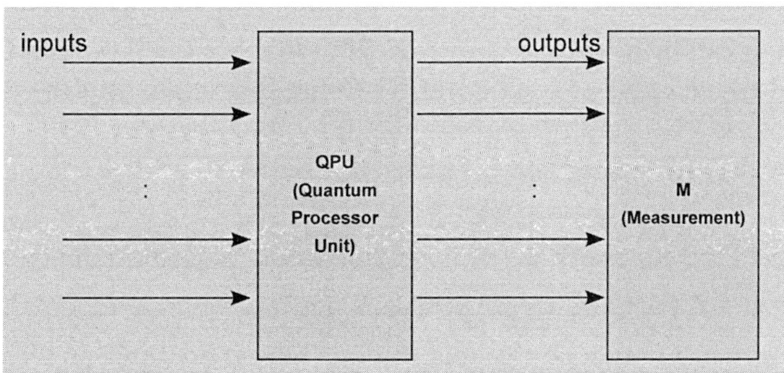

Q16. Comment on the computational complexity in quantum computing.

Ans. 16 The table below shows the class of computational complexity-

Class	Informal Definition
(1) P	This class of problems can be resolved by a deterministic traditional computer in polynomial time.
(2) BPP	This class of polynomials can be resolved by a probabilistic classical computer in polynomial time.
(3) BQP	This class of polynomials can be resolved by a quantum computer in polynomial time.
(4) NP	This class of polynomials can be resolved by a deterministic classical computer in polynomial time.
(5) QMA	Answers can be checked by a quantum computer in polynomial time.

If a problem is unproven to be comprehensive for a complexity class, then it means that it is one of the toughest problems within that class. It means that it is limited inside that class. Say, problems in P as like decision problems that can be solved on polynomial time by a deterministic Turing machine. Then, the equivalent for space efficiency, the group of decision problems that can be resolved by a Turing machine using polynomial space is raised to PSPACE. On the other hand, NP problems are those that need a non-deterministic Turing machine to be resolved. Hence, the exponential time needed on the 'deterministic machine' is not practical.

Another vital complexity class named BPP (Bounded-error Probabilistic Polynomial-time) labels the decision problems that can be solved in polynomial time by a probabilistic time by a probabilistic Turing machine. **Also understand that Probabilistic machines are those with the ability to flip coins to make arbitrary decisions. Also note that quantum computation shows a number of novel complexity classes to the polynomial grouping.** The greatest complexity class Bounded-error Quantum Polynomial-time (BQP). Talking more deeply, BQP is the quantum postponement of BPP. BQP is basically the class of decision problems that can be resolved in polynomial time. This can be done with naturally probabilistic quantum Turing machine. **The point to ponder is that unlike BPP, it is said that $P \subset BQP$. This means that quantum computers are accomplished by resolving some problems in polynomial time that can't be resolved by a classical Turing machine.**

Shor's algorithm shows that factoring is in complexity class P for a quantum computer.

Q17. What do you mean by factoring an integer, N? What are the three conditions if an integer, say p, is said to be a proper fraction of N? Using this logic, find the order of 11 modulo 21 and 5 modulo 21. Using these concepts, draw the flowchart/ write an algorithm of the factorization algorithm based on the order finding. Also write a program to carry out this computation. What do you conclude?

Ans. 17 In order to factor an integer, N, we write N as a product of prime numbers as follows-

$$N = p * q_1 * q_2 .... * q_n$$

Now, **the integer, p is said to be a proper fraction of N if the three conditions are satisfied:-**

Condition-1: another integer q exists such that N = pq.

Condition-2: $p \neq 1$.

Condition-3: $p \neq N$.

It is quite trivial to factor a small integer. The proper factors of 14 are p = 2 and q = 7 while the proper factors of 39 are p = 3 and q = 13. **Please note that the problem becomes more and more complex as the integer to be factored becomes larger and larger.**

Given two integer's r and N, the order of r modulo N is the smallest integer k such that $r^k = 1$ mod N with two additional conditions:-

1. $r^1 \neq 1$ mod N.
2. $(r^{k-1} + r^{k-2} + \ldots\ldots.. + r^2 + r + 1) \neq 1$ mod N.

Graphical interpretation: Now, on computing the order, k modulo N of an integer, q ($q^k = 1$ mod N) can be represented graphically as a cycle of length k-1 as shown in the diagram below-

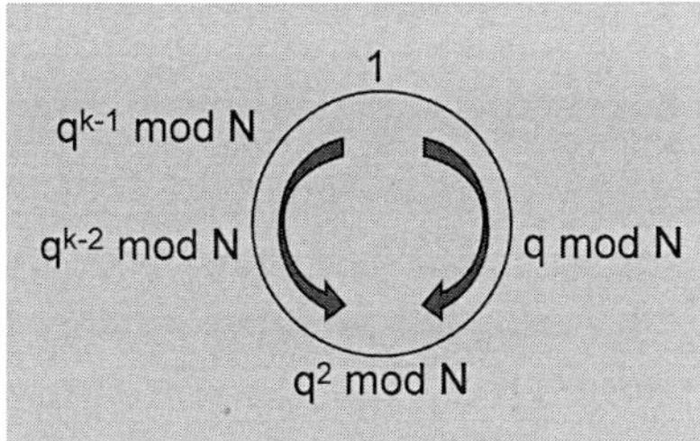

This diagram shows the calculation of the order, k for an integer q such that ($q^k = 1$ mod N) can be represented graphically too, as a cycle of length (k-1).

Example-1: Compute the order of 11 modulo 21. This means that we need to compute the smallest integer, such that $11^k = 1$ mod 21. We start with k = 2 and continue with k = 3, 4, 5, 6. That is,

$$k = 2 - 11^2 = 121 = 5 * 21 + 16 \rightarrow 11^2 = 16 \text{ mod } 21$$

$$k = 3 - 11^3 = 11 * 11^2 = 11 * 16 \text{ mod } 21 = 176 \text{ mod } 21$$

$$= 8 \text{ mod } 21 \rightarrow 11^3 = 8 \text{ mod } 21$$

$$k = 4 - 11^4 = 11 * 11^3 = 11 * 8 \text{ mod } 21 = 88 \text{ mod } 21$$

$$= 4 \text{ mod } 21 \rightarrow 11^4 = 4 \text{ mod } 21$$

$$k = 5 - 11^5 = 11 * 11^4 = 11 * 4 \text{ mod } 21 = 44 \text{ mod } 21$$

$$= 2 \text{ mod } 21 \rightarrow 11^5 = 2 \text{ mod } 21$$

$$k = 6 - 11^6 = 11 * 11^5 = 11 * 2 \text{ mod } 21 = 22 \text{ mod } 21$$

$$= 1 \text{ mod } 21 \rightarrow 11^6 = 1 \text{ mod } 21$$

So, the order of 11 mod 21 is k = 6. **Please note that the length of the cycle is k -1 = 5.** It is shown in figure below-

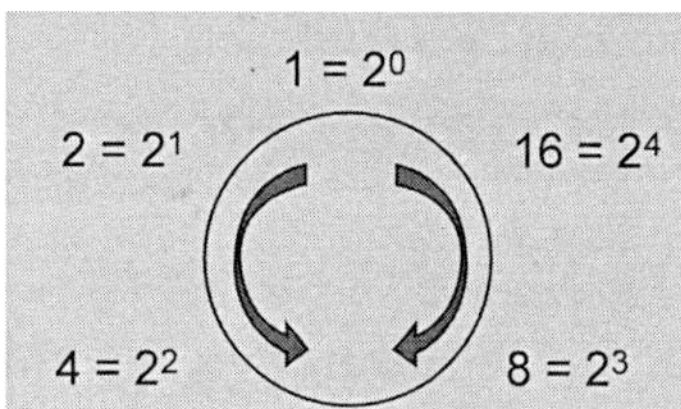

Also note that the order of 5 modulo 21 is also k = 6. Let us prove that.

$5^1 = 5 \bmod 21$ $\rightarrow 5^1 = 5 \bmod 21$

$5^2 = 25 = 1 * 21 + 4$ $\rightarrow 5^2 = 4 \bmod 21$

$5^3 = 125 = (5 * 21 + 20) \bmod 21$ $\rightarrow 5^3 = 20 \bmod 21$

$5^4 = 5 * 5^3 = 5 * 20 \bmod 21 = 100 \bmod 21 = 4 * 21 + 16$ $\rightarrow 5^4 = 16 \bmod 21$

$5^5 = 5 * 5^4 = 5 * 16 \bmod 21 = 80 \bmod 21 = 3 * 21 + 17$ $\rightarrow 5^5 = 17 \bmod 21$

$5^6 = 5 * 5^5 = 5 * 17 \bmod 21 = 85 \bmod 21 = 4 * 21 + 1$ $\rightarrow 5^6 = 1 \bmod 21$

To put it in a proper light, r^k (k has a wide range of values), is quite expensive. The point to ponder is that we only need several powers of r to compute r^k for any value of k. As a natural choice, we can denote any integer, k as-

$$k = k_{m-1} 2^{m-1} + k_{m-2} 2^{m-2} + \ldots k_i 2^i + k_1 2^1 + k_0$$

with $k_i = \{0, 1\}, 0 \leq i \leq m-1$. Then, we can say that-

$$r^k = r^{k_{m-1} 2^{m-1}} * r^{k_{m-2} 2^{m-2}} * \ldots r^{k_2 2^2} * r^{k_1 2^1} * r^{k_0}$$

Actually, to calculate r^k we require at most (m – 1) exponentiations-

$$r^{2^1}, r^{2^2}, r^{2^3}, \ldots, r^{2^{m-1}}$$

For example, say we want to calculate 17^{29}, then we can write as follows-

$$29 = 16 + 8 + 4 + 1 = 2^4 + 2^3 + 2^2 + 2^1 + 2^0$$

Therefore, we can say that-

$$179 = 17^{16} * 17^8 * 17^4 * 17^1$$

Let us now write an algorithm of this factorization algorithm based on the order finding. Consider that N = 21 and q = 11 that produces 3 as a proper factor of 21.

S1: Factor integer N (N = 21).

S2: Choose an integer q < N such that gcd (q, N) = 1 (q = 11).

S3: Find the order k of q modulo N (k = 6).

S4: Check if k is even?

S5: If, no then go to s2 again.

S6: If yes, compute m = k/2 and r = q^m mod N (m = 3, r = 8).

S7: check if r = 1 or r = N?

S8: If yes, then go to s2 again.

S9: If no, then we get the factors of N are gcd(r-1, N) or gcd(r+1, N); (gcd(7, 21) = 3).

Program:

```
power = 1;
for (int i =0; i < m-1; i++) {
        if (r^k_i = = 1) {
                power = power * r^(2^i) mod N
        }
}
```

Please understand that the condition $r^k = 1$ mod N implies that $r^k - 1$ is divisible by N. This means that an integer m exists such that-

$$r^k - 1 = (r-1)\, r^{k-1} + r^{k-2} + \ldots + r^2 + r + 1) = mN$$

Also understand that this equation shows that either (r – 1) or ($r^{k-1} + r^{k-2} + \ldots + r^2 + r + 1$) share a common factor with N. If we assume that r-1 is such a factor or shares a common factor with N. Then we can show that the GCD of N and r-1 is indeed a proper factor of N, namely, gcd(N, r-1) ≠ 1 and gcd(N, r-1) ≠ N.

Two cases arise:

Case-1: if r-1 < N, then the common factor of r-1 and N can't be N.

Case-2: if r-1 >= N, then gcd(N, r-1) could be N if r-1 is a multiple of N. But r-1 is not a multiple of N due to the condition $r^1 \neq 1$ mod N that can also be written as (r-1) ≠ 0 mod N.

Hence, gcd(N, r-1) is a proper factor of N. Many efficient algorithms to find the gcd of two integer numbers already exist.

Conclusions: In nutshell, we can say that the problem of finding the factors of N is reduced to the problem of order finding.

For example, say, N is neither even nor the power of a prime. Here, we are looking for an integer, r with the property that $r^2 - 1$ is a multiple of N but neither r-1 nor r+1 are multiples of N i.e. r ≠ 1 mod N and r ≠ -1 mod N. when N = 21, a possible choice for r is r=8. Now, we can say that $r^2 - 1 = 64 - 1 = 63 = 3 * 21$. **Please note that we expect that r-1 = 8-1 = 7 is a proper factor of N =21. When q=5, we again find that k=6.** So, r = 5^6 mod 21 = 20, r-1 = 19 and r+1 = 21. **Also note here that 21 is a factor but not a proper factor of 21. To take the flesh out of it, we observe that when k = 2m, the condition $q^k = 1$ mod N implies that the factors of N are either gcd(r-1, N) or gcd(r+1, N) with r = q^m mod N.**

As a natural choice, $q^{2m} = 1$ mod N = $q^{2m} - 1 = (q^m - 1)(q^m + 1)$ must be divisible by N.

In the example taken here, the order of (11 mod 21) is k=6. But 6 = 2 * 3. So, m=3 and r = (q^m mod N) = 11^3 mod 21 = 8. Then, r-1 = 8-1 = 7 and p = gcd(r-1, N) = gcd(7,21) = 7 < 21 is a factor of N = 21.

The point to ponder is that the core heart to the efficiency of this algorithm is the selection of q.

Q18. How can you demonstrate the periodicity of x^a mod n. Assume that input, a may be 0, 1, M, r, r+1, M, 2r, 2r+1, M.

Ans. 18 The following table summarizes the periodicity for different values on the input, a and its simplification-

Input (a)	Calling $f_{x,n}$ (a)	Simplifies to-
0	x^0 mod n	1
1	x^1 mod n	x
M	M	M
r	x^r mod n	1
r+1	x^{r+1} mod n	x
M	M	M
2r	x^{2r} mod n	1
2r+1	x^{2r+1} mod n	x
M	M	M

Q19. What is an adiabatic algorithm?

Ans. 19 According to the adiabatic algorithm, a quantum systems remains in its lowest energy state named as the **ground state. In adiabatic transformation, the system is gradually distorted from a preliminary Hamiltonian to a final Hamiltonian. An important condition in this theorem is the energy gap among the ground state and the excited state.**

Q20. What do you mean by Topological- Quantum-Field-Theory model?

Ans. 20 This model named as **Topological- Quantum-Field-Theory** (TQFT) for quantum computing is being stressed by Microsoft today. It defines topological states of the matter. This model was simulated on a standard quantum computer. Its merit lies in its high acceptance to errors. It is accommodating several global topological properties.

Q21. Can you feed the Fourier sampling results to Euclid's GCD?

Ans. 21 If we run Fourier sampling multiple times, then we will get random multiples of M/r.

For example, we may get 25, 75, 50 etc. now if we apply Euclid's greatest common divisor (gcd) to our random outputs then by dividing M by the gcd, we will get the period r. Therefore, we say-

$$r = M/\ \gcd(25, 50, 75....) = 100/25 = 4$$

This is the outline for period finding using a quantum circuit. Let us consider an example now. Let us factor the number, N = 21. We know that there are 2 very basic and efficient operations on which we can rely-

(a) Modular arithmetic i.e. a = b (mod N). like 3 = 15 (mod 12).

(b) Greatest common divisor, gcd (a, b). like gcd (15, 21) = 3.

Thus, for N=21, we need to solve the equation $x^2 \equiv 1 \pmod{21}$. **Please note that this means that find the non-trivial square root x such that-**

(a) N divides (x+1) (x-1).

(b) N does not divide (x+1) (x-1).

(c) Lastly, recover a prime factor by applying gcd(N, x+1).

Now, to find the non-trivial factor for N = 21, we pick a random, x. For instance, given N=21, choose x = 2. So, we get-

$$2^0 \equiv 1 \pmod{21}$$
$$2^1 \equiv 2 \pmod{21}$$
$$2^2 \equiv 4 \pmod{21}$$
$$2^3 \equiv 8 \pmod{21}$$
$$2^4 \equiv 16 \pmod{21}$$
$$2^5 \equiv 11 \pmod{21}$$
$$2^6 \equiv 1 \pmod{21}$$

So, we get the **period, r = 6.**

Here, $2^6 \equiv 2^{(3)2}$. Hence, $2^3 = 8$ is a non-trivial factor such that 21 divide (8 + 1) (8-1). Finally, we recover a factor with gcd(N, x+1) = gcd(21, 9) =3. In general, **pick an element, x at random. Then, loop it through $x^0, x^1, \ldots x^r \equiv$ mod N.** Now, r may be even, chance, i.e. $(\mathbf{x^{r/2}})^2 \equiv \mathbf{1 \pmod N}$. Hence, we now have a **non-trivial square root of 1 mod N.** However, it has been shown that the probability that we get lucky of r being even is ½. On the other hand, if we are unlucky then we must repeat the procedure again.

EXERCISE QUESTIONS

Q1. What are the differences between the classical algorithms and quantum algorithms?

Q2. Explain Deutsch-Jozsa algorithm with the help of a neat diagram.

Q3. What is an Oracle? Why is it used?

Q4. Throw some light on the major contributions by IBM in the field of quantum computing.

Q5. Explain Shor's algorithm with the help of a neat diagram.

Q6. Write short notes on-

(a) Quantum superposition.

(b) Quantum parallelism.

Q7. List some features of the IBM quantum experience.

Q8. Compare and contrast the quantum tools like Forest, Qiskit and Q#.

Q9. What are the conditions of the Deutsch Problem?

Q10. Explain in details the working of Grover's algorithm. Also explain the role of oracle and the Grover diffusion operator. What are its benefits?

Q11. What are the differences between QFT and QPE?

Q12. Explain Bernstein-Vazirani algorithm.

Q13. Write Simon's algorithm.

Q14. What do you mean by quantum period-finding function?

Q15. Try to find the state |10> using the Grover's algorithm.

Q16. Compute the order of 10 mod 15.

Q17. Suppose u, v and w are three integers. Prove that-

(a) u.w = gcd (u, w) . lcm (u,v) if u,v $\geq$ 0.

(b) gcd[(u, v) . w] = gcd(u . w, v . w) if w $\geq$ 0.

Q18. What are the different classes of quantum algorithms? Give examples.

Q19. Explain in stages showing a quantum circuit for solving Deutsch's problem.

Q20. Explain with a neat diagram a three-qubit QFT.

Q21. Explain how superposition and interference allows the Deutsch-Jozsa algorithm to beat the classical algorithm?

Q22. Explain how quantum algorithms work?

Q23. What is an adiabatic algorithm?

Q24. Show how quantum gate works in presence of Grover's algorithm?

Q25. What do you mean by quantum simulation?

Q26. "Grover's algorithm works on amplitude amplification trick". Support this statement.

Q27. What are the steps followed in quantum phase algorithm?

Q28. Suppose there is a function, f(x) with two inputs such that f(x) = 1. Prove that the Deutsch-Jozsa algorithm works in this case by generating the vector |y> = |00> as the final output.

Q29. What do you mean by the Tagging and the Canceling effects in quantum field?

Q30. Grover's algorithm is the result of some quantum effects. What are they?

Q31. What do you mean by the splitting of qubits?

Q32. Deutsch's algorithm has three steps. What are they?

Q33. Discuss some applications of Grover's algorithm.

Q34. Name some quantum computing software platforms.

[**Hint:** Cirq from Googlw, Rigetti, PyQuil, QISKIT, ProjectQ, MS Q#].

Q35. Consider a balanced function, F (|x>) defined as follows-

$$F(|0\rangle) = |1\rangle$$
$$F(|1\rangle) = |0\rangle$$

Now, answer the following questions-

(a) Construct the truth-table for U_f.

(b) Draw Deutsch's circuit with gates that represent U_f.

(c) Now suppose that the function, F (|x>) is constant that always returns a |1>. Repeat parts-a and b for this case too.

Q36. What is the main crux of Shor's algorithm for factoring a large integer?

Q37. Shor's algorithm sometimes fail. Is this true?

[**Hint:** Shor's algorithm is probabilistic and hence it does not always return a non-trivial factor].

Q38. How many pieces of information can a five qubit quantum computer process in parallel?

Q39. The Deutsch-Jozsa algorithm can solve a toy problem on a quantum computer faster than a classical computer can. Explain how is this possible?

[**Hint:** This algorithm shows a single measurement of |0> or |1> that further shows whether the function is constant or balanced. This algorithm simply extends to functions that take in any number of inputs. This is attractive as only one measurement can tell us whether a function of any size is constant or balanced. On a classical/traditional computer, it will have to measure each of the inputs and that is exponentially slower.]

Q40. Give geometrical interpretation of Grover's algorithm.

Q41. Explain the process of period finding with neat waveforms as used by the Shor's algorithm.

Q42. Can you comment on the time complexities of common factorization algorithms like Shor's, Number Field Sieve and Quadratic Sieve?

Q43. How can you challenge asymmetric cryptography with quantum factorization?

Q44. Explain Fourier sampling with neat waveforms.

Q45. List some local and remote simulators for IBM Q Experience.

Q46. The QISKIT development library consists of four core modules that are distributed across the quantum computing stack. What are they? Explain.

Q47. All modules except Aqua is not installed automatically. Then, what is the solution?

[**Hint:** Aqua module can be installed separately and requires a working installation of the core Qiskit library].

Q48. How is programming in qiskit different from that of Cirq?

[**Hint:** Qiskit program declares a quantum and a classical register with one qubit whereas in Cirq a classical register is never explicitly created and qubits are only referred to in a circuit when operations are added].

Q49. Suppose that if $f(0) \neq f(1)$, then what will be the output of the black box in Deutsch's problem?

Q50. Construct a quantum circuit to perform QFT on 2 qubits. Also calculate its transfer matrix.

Q51. Suppose that the set of moduli $\{m_1, m_2, \ldots, m_r\}$ have no common factors. We can represent the integer, a as $a = (a_1, a_2, \ldots, a_{r-1}, a_r)$ using its residues as follows-

$$a_1 = a \bmod m_1,\ a_2 = a \bmod m_2,\ \ldots,\ a_r = a \bmod m_r$$

Show that if we have two integers a and b with the internal representation as-

$a = (a_1, a_2, \ldots, a_{r-1}, a_r)$ and $b = (b_1, b_2, \ldots, b_{r-1}, b_r)$ then the following equations are true-

(a)
$$a + b = (a_1, a_2, \ldots, a_{r-1}, a_r) + (b_1, b_2, \ldots, b_{r-1}, b_r)$$
$$= ((a_1 + b_1) \bmod m_1, (a_2 + b_2) \bmod m_2, \ldots, (a_{r-1} + b_{r-1}) \bmod m_{r-1}, (a_r + b_r) \bmod m_r)).$$

(b)
$$a - b = (a_1, a_2, \ldots, a_{r-1}, a_r) - (b_1, b_2, \ldots, b_{r-1}, b_r)$$
$$= ((a_1 - b_1) \bmod m_1, (a_2 - b_2) \bmod m_2, \ldots, (a_{r-1} - b_{r-1}) \bmod m_{r-1}, (a_r - b_r) \bmod m_r)).$$

(c) $a.b = (a_1, a_2,\ldots, a_{r-1}, a_r) . (b_1, b_2,\ldots, b_{r-1}, b_r)$
$= ((a_1 . b_1) \bmod m_1, (a_2 . b_2) \bmod m_2,\ldots\ldots, (a_{r-1} . b_{r-1}) \bmod m_{r-1}, (a_r . b_r) \bmod m_r))$.

[**Hint:** a mod m_i = b mod m_i if and only if a = = b.]

Q52. Explain Simon's algorithm for phase estimation.

Q53. Write a C++/Java/ Python program to simulate Shor's algorithm.

Q54. Write a C++/Java/ Python program to simulate to simulate Grover's quantum search algorithm.

Q55. Write a C++/Java/ Python program to simulate Simon's algorithm.

Q56. What are the four steps that constitute to one Grover's iteration?

Q57. Explain a quantum circuit for computing f(x) modulo 2^m.

Q58. Draw a flowchart for the quantum search algorithm.

Q59. QFT is simply a function that transforms between two bases, that is,

|state in computational basis> QFT |State in Fourier basis>

Write a QFT for 3 qubit system and 6 qubit system.

Q60. Suppose there is a function with two inputs such that f(x) = 1. Prove that the Deutsch-Jozsa algorithm works in this scenario by generating the vector |y> = |00> as the final output.

Q61. To find out the factors of 9, will this sequence of [3^n (mod 9)] help us or Not? Give reasons to explain.

Q62. Find out the values of [2^n (mod 2q)] where n and q are integers.

Q63. Find out the periods of the sequence [3^n (mod 10)].

Q64. Find out the values of [kn (mod n)] where k and n are integers.

Q65. Find out the period of the sequence [13^n (mod 15)]. Reuse this result to factor 15 now.

[Hints: Resulting sequence is 13, 4, 7, 1, 13, 4, 7, 1,..... and has the period 4. It implies that for some finite integer, k, [(13^2 + 1) (13^2 - 1)] = 168 * 170 = k15. The gcd of the related integer pairs gives the results, gcd(168, 15) = 3 and gcd(170, 15) = 5.

Computational Lower Bound Complexity for Quantum Circuits

5

5.0 INTRODUCTION

We usually talk about two terms- computability and complexity. **Computability is related to the computational problems that the computer can or can't do.** On the other hand, the term **complexity is related to the how efficiently the problem can be solved.** Complexity refers to the space and the time complexity of the problem in hand. It is an important consideration for real world computing. A problem that has been solved theoretically does not mean that it can be solved practically too. **Please note that if the running time of the computer is too long or the memory requirements are too much then a feasible computation can still lie beyond the reach of any practicable computer.** It is important to distinguish between polynomially growing costs-*that are tractable and exponentially growing costs that are intractable.* **Also note that the exponential growth will always exceed polynomial growth regardless of the order of the polynomial. For example,** multiplication and factoring show the differences between the two. **The point to ponder is that it is relatively easy to multiply two large numbers together to get their product but it is very difficult to do the opposite i.e. to find the factors of a composite number. For instance,**

$$1234 * 2425 = ? \text{ (is easy)}$$
$$? * ? = 2992450 \text{ (is hard)}$$

In binary bits, if the numbers being multiplied have L bits then multiplication can be done in a time proportional to L^2, a polynomial in L, for factoring, The best known classical algorithm is **Multiple Polynomial Quadratic Sieve for numbers** involving for about 100 to 150 decimal digits, **the Number Field Sieve for numbers** involving more than roughly 110 decimal digits. In nutshell, **the running time of these algorithms grows sub-exponentially but super-polynomially in L, the number of bits needed to specify the number to be factored, N.** Hence, $L \approx \log_2 N$. The best factoring algorithms require a time of the order $\exp[L^{1/3} \log(L)^{2/3}]$.

The biggest conundrum today is whether to discard the classical algorithms totally and choose quantum ones or not. It might seem preposterous to believe that there is a theory circumscribing the capabilities of computers. The answer is clear from the subsequent discussions below.

5.1 GENERAL IDEAS

Quantum algorithms are a sequence of commands that are executed by quantum circuits that comprise of quantum gates only. As already studied, a qubit can be an atom, a photon, an ion or any quantum system that contains two states. Formally, a quantum algorithm consists of three basic building blocks as follows:

(a) It can **encode classical or quantum data** into the state of a set of input **qubits.**

(b) An order of **quantum gates functional** to this group of input qubits.

(c) **Measurements** of one or more of the qubits at the stub to get a classical result.

Actually, quantum algorithms rely on superposition states. This provides speedup to quantum algorithms. As a result, you can run the quantum algorithm using quantum parallelism on all possible inputs at the same instant of time. **Note that the true art of constructing these quantum algorithms lies in the fact that we should be able to manipulate these super -positions so as to make measurements more accurate.** One more point that lies in reference is that **not every algorithm is open to a quantum speed-up.** Also we can't say that classical algorithms after speed-up are quantum algorithms.

A general basic idea in computational complexity theory is characterized by the idea that computational problems have a certain level of **hardness. Hardness can be defined as the allocation of resources as required by the computational models to solve certain problems. Please note that computational models and resource limitations have ties to the physical world. Also note that as the size of computers decrease, quantum mechanics also now stresses on creation of new, faster and miniature computers.** In nutshell, quantum complexity theory deals with the hardness of computational problems in terms of quantum computational models.

Complexity classes are a group of computational problems that have similar resource-based complexity. Traditionally, there are **four important classical complexity classes** as given in table- 5.1. Consider a pair $A = (A_1, A_0)$ where A_1 is a set of 'yes' instances, A_0 is a set of 'no' instances.

Table- 5.1: Four Classical Complexity classes.

Complexity Class	Definition
P	A problem is in P if a polynomial time, deterministic Turing machine accepts every string in A_1 and rejects every string in A_0
BPP	A problem is in BPP if a polynomial time, deterministic Turing machine accepts every string in A_1 with at least 2/3 probability and accepts every string in A_0 with at most probability of 1/3.
PP	A problem is in PP if a polynomial time, probabilistic Turing machine accepts every string in A_1 with a greater probability than ½ and every string in A_0 with at most probability of 1/2.
PSPACE	A problem is in PSPACE if a deterministic Turing machine running in polynomial space accepts every string in A_1 and rejects every string in A_0

So, we find that different types of problems are now contained in a multitude of complexity classes.

General flow of a quantum algorithm:

1. As a first step, we prepare the superposition. Here, we make equal superposition of all 2^n states by applying H gates.
2. Then, we encode the problem into these states and put phases on all 2^n states and manipulate it in a high dimensional space.
3. Finally, we apply interference to consolidate the superposition into fewer outcomes containing the solution.

Before we discuss further, let us solve some examples now.

Example 1: A problem can't be solved in polynomial time on a classical computer. Under what additional conditions would this problem be an element of the NP complexity class?

Solution 1: If the solutions to the problem are readily verified on a classical computer then this problem can be an element of the NP complexity class.

Example 2: What do you mean by NP?

Solution 2: NP means Non-deterministic Polynomial which means certain types of Turing machines that are called **non-deterministic Turing machines.**

Example 3: Define query complexity.

Solution 3: The count of number of times that we have to evaluate the function to get our answer is known as the query complexity. The function is also sometimes called as a **black box or oracle.** Hence, instead of saying that we are evaluating the function, we can now say that we are querying the black box or the oracle. *Another point that lies in the reference is that we need not worry about how to write an algorithm that emulates the function and hence we need not calculate the number of steps that function takes to evaluate the input.* We have to only keep track of the number of questions.

Example 4: When is a problem, A, NP-Complete and when is it NP-hard?

Solution 4: A problem, A is said to be **NP-complete** iff-

a) A is in NP.

b) All NP problems are polynomial-time reducible to A.

If we only know (b) and not necessarily (a) then we say A is **NP-hard.**

5.2 POLYNOMIAL REPRESENTATIONS

Researchers today classify computational problems based on its difficulty to solve. One of the methods of distinguishing is based on classes of problems that can or can't be solved in polynomial time.

Classical/traditional complexity classes:

Please understand that the problems that can be solved in polynomial time are deemed 'tractable' and are put together into the class "P". On the other hand, **problems that can't be solved in polynomial time are usually deemed 'intractable' and may be in one of the several classes.** The polynomial or exponential distinction is a better indicator of difficulty. This is about P class. Next is another class named as NP. Several algorithms now try to find the partial solutions and then extend them into bigger partial problems that lead to a full solution. This is similar to divide-and-conquer technique. **Also understand that if a partial solution is not further extendable then the algorithm has to back**

up and try another alternative way. The point to ponder is that the number of computational steps required by a deterministic algorithm in order to guarantee that it will find the solution even if the problem size is exponential. In this case, that type of problem is intractable. Many such problems also have the feature that once a candidate solution is found then its correctness can be tested efficiently in **polynomial time.** So, if you could the guess the right solution, then the problem can be solved efficiently. In nutshell, such a possibility means that there is an efficient **non-deterministic algorithm for solving the problem.** Researchers put all such problems into a complexity class named as NP i.e. **nondeterministic polynomial time.** Now the issue is whether P= NP or not? Till date no one knows.

An important property: "A problem in the subclass can be converted into another problem in the class by the action of some polynomial time algorithm." As a result, the class of problems is called as **NP-complete because they are in NP and consist of a complete set of problems mappable into one another in polynomial time.** So, we find that either all NP-complete problems are tractable or none of them are. They stand or fall together. Researchers quote that there are about 1000 distinct NP-complete problems known today. Many real world problems like scheduling, route planning and matching fall under this category.

Let us tabulate our classical complexity classes now. (See table 5.2).

Table- 5.2: Four Classical Complexity classes with examples.

Classical complexity classes	Meaning	Examples
P or PTIME	Polynomial-time. In worst case, running time of algorithm is a polynomial (in the size of input). All problems in P are tractable.	Multiplication.
NP	Non-deterministic-polynomial time. A candidate answer can be checked for correctness in polynomial time.	Factoring composite integers.
NP-complete	Subset of problems in NP that can be mapped into one another in polynomial time. If only one of the problems is in this class is shown to be tractable then they must all be tractable.	Scheduling problem, Satisfiability problem, TSP (Traveling Salesman Problem)
ZPP	Can be solved with certainty by PTMs (Probabilistic Turing Machines) in average case polynomial time.	
BPP	Can be solved in polynomial time by PTMs with probability > 2/3. Probability of success can be made closer to 1 by iterating the algorithm a certain number of times.	Problems in BPP are tractable.

NP-complete problems are not the hardest problems out of all. Several algorithms exist with their running times as double, triply, quadruply exponential in the size of the input. That is, their running times grow as 2^N. For example, Presburger arithmetic is double exponential, in best case. The challenge now is that how can a quantum computer solve an NP-complete problem more efficiently than a traditional/ classical computer.

Let us now discuss about the Quantum complexity classes.

Quantum complexity classes:

To put everything in a proper light, we can say that quantum Turing machines are quantum mechanical generalizations of the probabilistic Turing machines. So, the quantum complexity classes resemble the probabilistic complexity classes. **Note that there is a trade-off between the certainty if your answer being correct versus the certainty of the answer being available within a certain time bound.** That is why; the classical classes P, ZPP and BPP become the quantum classes QP, ZQP and BQP. **This means that a problem can be solved with certainty in worst-case polynomial time, with certainty in average-case polynomial time and with probability greater than 2/3 in worst-case polynomial time by a Quantum Turing Machine (QTM).**

Let us now tabulate and compare some new quantum complexity classes and classical complexity classes. (See table-5.3).

Table- 5.3: New Quantum Complexity classes with their relationships to classical ones.

Quantum class	Computational problems class	Relations with classical complexity classes
QP	Problems can be solved with certainty, in worst case polynomial time by a quantum computer.	$P \subset QP$. Quantum computer can solve more problems in worst-case polynomial time than can a traditional/classical computer.
BQP	Problems can be solved in worst case polynomial time by a quantum computer with probability > 2/3 i.e. the probability of error is bounded, so the "B' in "BQP'.	$BPP \subset BQP \subset PSPACE$ i.e. it is not known whether QTMs are more powerful than PTMs. Peter Shor proved factoring is in BQP.
ZQP	Problems can be solved with zero error probability in expected polynomial time by a quantum computer.	$ZPP \subset ZQP$.

From table 5.3, we observe that-

1. QP is the class of problems that can be solved with certainty on a quantum computer in polynomial time.
2. P is the set of problems that can be solved with certainty on a classical/traditional in polynomial time.
3. As the class QP contains the class P, this implies that there are more problems that can be solved efficiently by a quantum computer as compared to a classical computer.
4. Deutsch and Jozsa showed a problem that was not equivalent to a function evaluation and for this a QTM was exponentially faster than a classical Deterministic Turing Machine (DTM).

The race between the cat and mouse continues, to find the problem for which the QTM beats a DTM and a PTM. Later, Bernstein and Vazirani explored on the computational power of a QTM. They also found a problem that defeated both a DTM and A PTM.

Quantum computing is based on a promise to solve so-called intractable problems whose (classical) computing complexity grows exponentially with their size. These can't be solved with classical computing,

The precise levels of complexity of each algorithm are roughly associated with these classes. N log(N) is the complexity of a classical Fourier transform and is nearly linear since N grows much faster than log(N) and log(N)³ is a log level complexity for the Shor algorithm and a QFT.

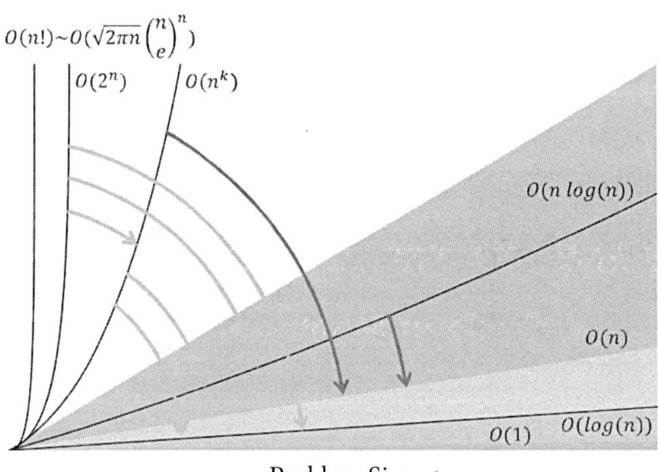

Fig.5.1: Quantum speedup

Graphically, the way computing time grows according to the big O( ) scale of problems is shown in Figure- 5.1. A quantum algorithm's main goal is to move your problem's computation time from the **red zone to the orange, or** better, the **yellow and green zones.**

The starting point is an N which is actually a RSA key size which itself is evaluated in power of 2. A 1024-bit key is 2^{1024}. If we move from 2^{256} to 2^{1024}, the growth of the key size is exponential. With Shor's algorithm, we get an exponential performance gain by going from a square root of 2^{1024} to $\log(2^{1024})$, that is to say 1,024 (in log base 2)! So, the time scale moves from 2^{512} to 1,024, which is a perfectly exponential gain. Deutsch-Jozsa's algorithm has the particularity of traversing all levels of this scale, from an exponential time to a fixed time. We have unfortunately seen that it has no known practical application.

The difference between polynomial and exponential use of computer resources represents the cornerstone of the computational complexity. **For example,** to compute Discrete Fourier Transform (DFT) for a set of n integers or complex numbers requires T(n) time steps with T(n) bounded by a quadratic polynomial. We say that this algorithm is $O\ (n^2)^2$. Also some algorithms are based on a probabilistic approach.

The Bounded-Error Probabilistic Polynomial /time (BPP) group consists of polynomial time algorithms that correctly classify the input string, σ, belongs to the language, L or not. **Also note that we say that the language, L, is in the complexity class, P,** if there is a recognition algorithm that requires a number of steps T (n) **bounded by a polynomial.** Else we can say that **the language requires an exponential time. The point to ponder is that we may get the wrong answers when we run such an algorithm only once.** But if we repeatedly run the algorithm and then take a majority vote, the probability of obtaining the correct answer can be made close to 1 **while maintaining the polynomial running time.**

5.3 QUANTUM CIRCUIT LOWER BOUND

Simon (1994) proved that a quantum computer would resolve any problem exponentially faster than its classical counterpart. **To put it in a proper light, Simon's algorithm has an upper bound of O (n) on a quantum computer.** In nutshell, **the lower bound on the traditional computer is of a greater order than the upper bound on the quantum computer.** So, there is a sparkling display of quantum computers benefit that is crystal clear.

Computational complexity addresses the subject of finding a measure of the difficulty of computational problems. **A complexity class is defined as a collection of languages.** Formally,

"A problem is in TIME [f(n)] if a Turing machines exists that decides if a candidate-string, x, is in the language (i.e. set of strings) **in time O(f(n)), where n is the string length of x."**

To put it in a proper light, **a problem is soluble in polynomial time if it is in TIME (n^q) for some finite, q. Also note that the set of all languages that are in TIME (n^q), for some finite q, comprise the P complexity class. For example,** the decision to discern whether a number is prime or not is a problem in the P complexity class. So, we can say that the complexity class NP includes the problems whose solutions may be readily checked on a classical computer but whose analysis in not soluble in polynomial time on a classical computer. **The point to ponder is that the problem of factoring an integer into its prime factors is a problem in NP complexity class.** When the factor is discovered, it may simply be checked on a classical computer. **Please understand that there is no fast, polynomial time means of solving the factoring problem on a classical computer when it is an NP problem. The class P is a subset of the class NP. Also understand the point that the complexity class, EXP that refers to exponential time, contains all decision problems that may be decided by a Turing machine in exponential time** i.e. in time O ($2n^q$), for a constant q.

Another vital complexity class is PSPACE. Practically speaking, problems included in this class can be solved with resources that are few in spatial size but not in time.

Another complexity class, BPP includes problems that can be solved using randomized algorithms in polynomial time with a bounded error probability.

The complexity class BQP includes all computational problems that can be solved efficiently on a quantum computer. **The fact is that all problems in P can be solved efficiently on a quantum computer.** In general, BQP lies between P and PSPACE. Also, BQP $\subset$ PSPACE and BPP $\subset$ BQ. Thus, we can combine all relations to get-

$$BPP \subset BQ \subset PSPACE, P \subset NP \subset BSPACE \subset EXP$$

In nutshell, we can say that **a problem in class BPP can be solved in the class BQ but not vice-versa.**

Landauer's principle traces the energy consumption in a computation to the need to erase information. He provides only a **lower bound on the energy consumption.** Just to recall that logic circuits in microprocessors need 500 k_B T ln 2 in energy for each logic operation. A result of Landauer's principle is that- **"No strictly positive lower bound on energy consumption exists for a reversible computer, and then in principle we can compute without any energy loss."**

According to Landauer's principle, the entropy of the entire system increases as a result of erasing information. The fact that erasing information requires consumption of energy is in strict agreement with the second law of thermodynamics. **Please note that erasing information reduces our knowledge**

about the state of a system that leads to an increase of the entropy. Also note that we need to consume energy to compensate for the increase of the entropy.

Quantum computers permit us to transcend the well-defined boundary between polynomial and exponential computations. As already explained, that if we are given a quantum circuit that is able to compute in polynomial time, a function f(s), with s as a binary string of length, n then we are able to compute a superposition of all 2^n possible values of the function, f, in **polynomial time with just a single copy of the quantum circuit. That is, it means that only a polynomial effort is needed to compute, f.** On the other hand, if we use a classical/traditional computer for this same problem, then we need **an exponential number of copies of the circuit.**

When we limit circuits to have a bounded fan-in, we need to allow them to have non-constant depth to allow the output to depend on all bits of the input. **Keeping this in mind, we say that the simplest interesting circuit class looks to be the class of bounded fan-in circuits having a size of O (n) and depth of O (log n).**

SUMMARY

In this chapter, we have studied that **the computational complexity theory is based on computational problems.** Also we studied how they are classified on the basis of their difficulty. By difficulty we mean the resources required to solve a problem. Commonly known such problem is P v/s NP problem. P indicates a problem that can be solved in polynomial time. NP problems are the problems for which the answer, if provided, can be verified in polynomial time. But there is no known way to solve the problems in polynomial time. In other words, **P indicates problems that are solvable by a computer in polynomial time while NP are the problems that are not solvable in polynomial time but may be checked in polynomial time.**

The point to ponder is that the P v/s NP problems queries whether every problem whose solution can be quickly verified by a computer can also be quickly solved by a computer. It means that whether P = NP or not? Now, if P ≠ NP then for all NP problems there is a way to solve them in polynomial time and we have not discovered it. Till date, many quantum scientists believe that P does not equal NP but not proven till now.

MULTIPLE CHOICE QUESTIONS [MCQS] WITH ANSWERS

1. Simon's algorithm has an upper bound of __________ on a quantum computer-
   (a) O (1).
   (b) O (n).
   (c) O (n log n).
   (d) None of the above.
2. Bernstein and Vazirani problem can be solved in O (n) time on a classical computer whereas a quantum computer would take-
   (a) O (1).
   (b) O (n^2).
   (c) O (n log n).
   (d) None of the above.
3. A system with a finite number of internal states, a read-write head and a moving tape consisting of individual cells is an abstraction that represents a-
   (a) Parallel machine.
   (b) Service machine.

(c) Turing machine.

(d) None of the above.

04. A Turing Machine in which some transitions are random choices among finitely many alternatives is known as-

(a) Probabilistic Turing Machine (PTM).

(b) Universal Turing Machine (UTM).

(c) Non-deterministic Turing Machine.

(d) None of the above.

5. The quantum model of computation as proposed by David Deutsch is named as-

(a) Quantum Turing machine.

(b) Universal Turing Machine.

(c) Probabilistic Turing Machine.

(d) None of the above.

6. According to the Church-Turing principle-

(a) All computing devices can be quantized.

(b) All computing devices can be simulated by a Turing Machine.

(c) All computing devices can be simulated by a Classical Machine.

(d) All of the above.

7. Problems that can be solved in a reasonable amount of time on a classical computer like O (1), O (log(n)), O(n), O (n log(n)), O(n^2) are examples that are put in class-

(a) P.

(b) NP.

(c) PSPACE.

(d) BPP.

8. O(log(n)) means log(n) is not a polynomial in n but still O(log(n)) is in P because-

(a) It is upper bounded by O (n).

(b) It is upper bounded by O (n log n).

(c) It is upper bounded by O (n^2).

(d) None of the above.

9. PSPACE stands for-

(a) Polynomial Space.

(b) Picture Space.

(c) Paper Space.

(d) None of the above.

10. The energy required to perform a computation scales with the size of problem. This is called as-

(a) Time complexity.

(b) Space complexity.

(c) Energy complexity.

(d) Cyclomatic complexity.

11. The quantum mechanical generalizations of probabilistic Turing machines are known as-

(a) Quantum Turing Machines.

(b) Universal Turing Machines.

(c) Time Turing Machines.

(d) None of the above.

12. According to Deutsch and Jozsa, which was faster-

(a) DTM.

(b) PTM

(c) QTM.

(d) None of the above.

Answers											
1.	(b)	2.	(a)	3.	(c)	4.	(a)	5.	(a)	6.	(b)
7.	(a)	8.	(c)	9.	(a)	10.	(c)	11.	(a)	12.	(c)

CONCEPTUAL SHORT QUESTIONS WITH ANSWERS

Q1. Explain the classical computation as done by a PTM. Also explain when is a computation said to be well-defined? What are Markov Chains?

Ans. 1 The classical computation as done by a PTM may be represented as a **tree where each node corresponds to a state of the PTM. The root of the tree** reflects the staring configuration. Each **level** corresponds to a step of the computation. An **edge** represents a transition from one state to another. **Please note that a state can be reached from a parent state that is located one level up in the tree with a certain probability.** The same state may appear several times at any level of the tree or at different levels. **Please note that the probability of reaching a state appearing multiple times at level i of the tree is the sum total of the probabilities of reaching individual instances of that state. Also note that the probability of reaching an instance of a state of PTM is equal to the product of probabilities assigned to all edges leading from the root to the node corresponding to that state. The point to ponder is that the sum of probabilities of all states at any given level of the tree should be equal to 1.**

Now, a computation is said to be **well-defined** iff the probabilities on the edges from a parent node and the children states don't depend on the position of the node in the tree. These well-defined configurations are also represented as **Markov chains.** This chain has a stochastic matrix related with it whose entries are the transition probabilities between the pairs of states.

Q2. Who proposed the Quantum Turing Machine (QTM)? How is it represented? What is the sufficient condition for a QTM?

Ans. 2 **Quantum Turing Machine (QTM)** was proposed by David Deustch. It is a quantum model of computation. Here, a computation is represented by a **computational tree** where each edge has associated **amplitude i.e. a complex number with a magnitude at most 1. To put it in a proper light, the amplitude associated with a node/ state is the product of the amplitudes of all edges on the path from the root to that node. Remember that the amplitude corresponding to a state appearing multiple times at any level, i, of the tree is the sum of amplitudes of all nodes corresponding to that state at that particular level of the tree. The probability of an instance of a state is the square of the amplitude of the corresponding node. Also the sum of the probabilities of all states at any given level of the tree should be one. For instance,** the probability of a particular final state is the square of the sum of all leaf nodes corresponding to that state. **Note that it is the 'square of the sum' and not 'the sum of the squares.'**

Sufficient condition for a QTM

Actually, the condition that the squares of the amplitudes associated with all edges emerging from a given node sum to unity—is no longer a sufficient condition for a QTM. What we need is that QTM always execute in **unitary steps.** The evolution of a QTM is **unitary and reversible. It means that at each step, the amplitudes of possible states are determined by the amplitude of the current state according to a fixed, local and uniform transformation analogous to a stochastic matrix of a Markov process.**

Q3. State Church-Turing principle and explain it.

Ans. 3 **Church-Turing principle states that "all computing devices can be simulated by a Turing Machine."** This principle means that in order to study computability it is sufficient to restrict ourselves to a single abstract model i.e. the Turing Machine.

Q4. When is a problem said to be intractable? What is a polynomial-time algorithm? Give examples.

Ans. 4 **'Intractable' means that a problem in computer science is intractable if a computer has difficulty in solving it.** On the other hand, **a polynomial-time algorithm is an algorithm whose worst-case complexity is bounded above by a polynomial function of its input size** i.e. if n is the input size, there exists a polynomial p(n) such that-

$$W(n) \in O(p(n))$$

Examples of algorithms with worst-case time complexities with polynomial time are $2n$, $3n^3 + 4n$, $5n + n^{10}$, $n \lg n$.

Examples of algorithms with worst-case time complexities with non-polynomial time are 2^n, $2^{0.01n}$, $2^{\sqrt{n}}$, $n!$

Please note that n lg n is NOT a polynomial in n. Also, however, note that because $n \lg n < n^2$ so it is bounded by a polynomial in n. This means that an algorithm with this much time complexity satisfies the criterion to be called a polynomial-time algorithm. So, now we can say that a problem is called as **intractable in computer science if it is impossible to solve it with a polynomial-time algorithm.**

The point to ponder is that intractability is a property of a problem and it is not a property of any one algorithm for that problem. For a problem to be intractable there must be no polynomial-time algorithm that solves it. As a natural choice, obtaining a non-polynomial time algorithm for a problem does not make it intractable.

For example, the brute-force algorithm for the Chained Matrix Multiplication Problem is a non-polynomial time. Similarly, Divide-and-Conquer algorithm that uses the recursive property is a non-polynomial time. But the dynamic programming algorithm may be $\theta(n^3)$. **Please understand that the problem is not tractable because we can solve it in polynomial time too.**

Q5. How can you say that polynomial time algorithms are much better than algorithms that are not polynomial –time?

Ans. 5 If it takes 1ns (nanosecond) to process basic instructions, then an algorithm with a time complexity of n^3 will process an instance of size 100 in 1 millisecond. On the other hand, an algorithm with a time complexity of 2^n will take billions of years.

For example, if $n = 1{,}000{,}000$ then

$$2^{(0.00001n)} = 1024 \text{ whereas } n^{10} = 10^{60}.$$

Q6. What are the three general categories of the problems as far as intractability is concerned?

Ans. 6 The three categories of problems as far as intractability is concerned are as follows: -

Cat-1: Problems for which polynomial algorithms have been found.

Cat-2: Problems that have been proven to be intractable.

Cat-3: Problems that have not been proven to be intractable but for which polynomial-time algorithms have never been found.

Please note that it has been observed that most of the problems fall into either Cat-1 or Cat-3 only.

Q7. Compare and contrast NP-Hard and NP-Complete problems.

Ans. 7 The following table compares **NP-Hard and NP-Complete problems-**

NP-Hard	NP-Complete
1. NP-hard problem may or may not be in NP.	1. All NP-complete problems are in NP.
2. NP-hard problems can be a benchmark for measuring complexity.	2. NP-c problems can be a benchmark for measuring complexity.
3. It is difficult to solve if NP-hard problems are not in NP.	3. NP-complete is a set of problems where even if one problem of the set is solved then all other problems of that set can be solved efficiently.

Q8. When can you say that a Boolean function, f: $\{0, 1\}^* \rightarrow \{0, 1\}$ is in BQP?

Ans. 8 A Boolean function, f: $\{0, 1\}^* \rightarrow \{0, 1\}$ is in BQP **if there is some polynomial, p: N → N such that f is computable in quantum p (n) time.**

Q9. What will be the best lower bound on circuit size for an NP problem?

Ans. 9 The best lower bound on circuit size for an NP problem **is 5n – o (n).**

Q10. Define what is sensitivity?

Ans. 10 It allows us to prove **lower bounds on the decision tree complexity.**

Q11. Give some examples of NP-complete problems.

Ans. 11 Simulation of complex protein folding, bin packing problem, subset sum problem, Deminer's problem, Graph coloring etc.

Q12. State Deminer's problem.

Ans. 12 The Deminer's problem consists in locating hidden mines in a field with only the number of mines in adjacent areas and the total number of mines in the field as indication, all this without detonating them. This game that runs on windows platform (1989).

Q13. State Rice's theorem.

Ans. 13 Rice's theorem state that no non-trivial property of a program can be decided algorithmically. Please understand that this means that there is no automatic method to detect bugs in a program or to certify that it runs well.

Q14. What do you mean by maximally entangled states? Give an example to explain.

Ans. 14 A Quantum algorithm that handles **maximally entangled states** is also having an exponential speed-up. **Please note that this means that there is a correlation of states between maximum number of qubits in the register until the end of computing.**

For example, consider a register of N qubits. If the algorithm is split into 4 different subspaces of N/4 qubits, we end up managing a space with $4 * 2^{N/4}$ amplitudes or we can say $2^{2+N/4}$. That number is smaller than 2^N, starting with N = 3. For N = 50, the difference is between $2.3 * 10^5$ and 10^{15}.

EXERCISE QUESTIONS

Q1. Explain the paradigm shift from classical to Quantum Turing Machines.

Q2. What are the different classes of quantum algorithms?

Q3. The complexity class P contains all decision problems that can be solved by a deterministic Turing machine using a polynomial amount of computation time or polynomial time. BPP is the class of decision problems solvable by a probabilistic Turing machine in polynomial time with an error probability bounded away from 1/3 for all instances. And the complexity class BQP is the class of decision problems solvable by a quantum computer in polynomial time, with an error probability of at most 1/3 for all instances. Which of the following relations is true?

(a) $P \subset BPP \subset BQP$.

(b) $P \subset BQP \subset BPP$.

(c) $BPPP \subset P \subset BQP$.

(d) None of the above.

Q4. A decision problem may be solved on a Turing machine running in exponential time. To what complexity class does this problem belong?

Q5. Consider a computer that takes

(a) $O(2^n)$ seconds and

(b) $O(3^n)$ seconds; in n-steps of a given process.

Are these respective time intervals polynomial or exponential?

Q6. Write a C/C++/PYTHON/ Java program to design a O (n log n) size straight line program for QFT. Also prove that there exists an algebraic straight line program that uses 7 multiplication gates and computes the matrix multiplication of (2 * 2) matrices. Can you conclude that there is an algebraic straight line program of size $O(n^{2.81})$ for multiplying (n * n) matrices.

Q7. Prove that any function that can be computed by an algebraic circuit of depth d can be computed by an algebraic formula of size $O(2^d)$.

Q8. Comment on the complexity upper and lower bounds of Simon's algorithm.

Q9. Classify different classes of computational complexities.

Q10. Classify quantum algorithms.

Q11. What is Quantum Loading Scheme (QLS)?

Q12. How much time does a quantum algorithm takes for factoring a number, N?

Q13. Compare quantum algorithms based on QFT and on amplitude amplification.

Q14. Explain how O ( ) compares for complexity classes in quantum computing?

Q15. State PCP theorem and explain what it implies?

[Hints: PCP theorem constructs locally testable proof systems i.e. this theorem provides a method to transform every mathematical proof into a form that is checkable by only looking at very few symbols of the proof. Another definition of PCP theorem is that for many NP-complete optimization problems, computing an approximate solution is as hard as computing the exact solution. Hence, it can't be done efficiently until P = NP.]

Quantum Error Correction

6

6.0 INTRODUCTION

In the ever-evolving realm of quantum computing, quantum technology is emerging as a groundbreaking paradigm that promises unparalleled computational power. Today, we stand on the cusp of a quantum computing revolution. Quantum computers reshape the boundaries of what is possible in computation and problem solving. It depends on whether we are dealing with closed quantum systems or open quantum systems. Any interaction of qubits with their environment can corrupt the qubits. By using error correcting codes, it is possible to detect and correct errors in qubits without disturbing their coherence. **Closed quantum systems are those idealized systems that do not interact with the outside world.** Practically speaking, quantum systems interact with the outside environment. Now the problem is that interactions with the environment can introduce noise and cause errors. To solve this problem, we need some kind of error correction. Hence, we need to develop a mathematical formalism to describe quantum systems that interact with the environment. These systems are known as **open systems. Open quantum systems are significant as in an open quantum system; a pure state can evolve into a mixed state.** But we require pure states to do quantum computation. Hence, this type of evolution into mixed states is undesirable.

Quantum error correction tries to achieve fault-tolerant quantum computation by protecting information from errors due to decoherence and other environmental noise. **Please understand that when a quantum computer sets up some qubits, it applies quantum gates to entangle them and manipulate probabilities and then finally measures the output collapsing superposition to a final sequence of 0s or 1s. Also note that this means that you get the entire lot of calculations with your circuits done at the same time.** Finally, you can only measure one output from the entire range of possible solutions. **This process of checking that every possible solution has a probability to be correct and then re-checking it again and again is known as Quantum Error Correction.**

6.1 CLASSICAL ERROR CORRECTION

If two individual bits in a pair are erroneous, like the presence of a double-bit error is indicated. But flipping of two bits simultaneously transforms a valid code word into another valid code word. Hence, the error cannot be detected. **This process of including additional bits to allow the receiver to decide whether the encoded data is corrupt or not is known as error-detection coding and the codes are**

known as error-detecting codes. Please understand that this means that error correction in classical computing systems is concerned with coding methods that promise any errors occurring during the transmission of bits are automatically detected.

As we know that in classical world, error correction is done with redundancy check i.e. by creating copies of data and then assigning probabilities to the possible error conditions and then finally comparing the highest probable condition with the original message to determine if an error has occurred. For example, suppose we have one bit of information as follows:

Table 6.1: Classical error correction for 1 –bit of information

Message	Redundant copies	Error(1)	Error(1,2)
0	0	1	1
	0	0	1
	0	0	0
Probability		(1/3) = 0.33	(1/3) * (1/3) = 0.11

Assume that we have a 1 bit message, 0. We now create three redundant copies for error correction. This is known as **3-bit repetition code.** Further assume that noisy errors are independent and occur with some probability. It is more likely that the error occurs in a single bit and the transmitted message is equal to three 1s but this outcome is less likely. So, we can use this method to correct the message in case of errors in a classical system.

However, this is not possible in quantum computing due to **no-cloning theorem.** As already discussed, **no-cloning theorem states that "it is impossible to create an identical copy of an arbitrary unknown quantum state."** This was postulated by James L. Park in 1970. **The point to ponder is that this no-cloining theorem creates problem for quantum computing as redundant copies of qubits cannot be created for error correction.** In fact, it is possible to spread the information of 1 qubit onto a highly entangled state of several physical qubits. This technique was discovered by Peter Shor with a method of error correcting code by storing the information of 1 qubit onto 9 entangled qubits. But this scheme protects only from errors of a limited form. Many newer techniques of quantum error correction codes have been developed in literature.

Challenges with quantum processing:

1. **No-cloning theorem does not allow copying of qubits.** Hence, a repetition code cannot be designed by duplicating a state many times.
2. A qubit may be in any one of an infinite number of possible superposition states i.e. the linear combination of the states |0> and |1>. So, **different errors on a single qubit may form a combination of errors.** Hence, identification of a specific error becomes infeasible.
3. **It is impossible to measure a qubit to detect an error because measurement of a qubit collapses the superposition state to classical state that makes recovery impossible.**

6.2 FAULT TOLERANCE

The objective of quantum error correction is to move the information stored in a single physical qubit into many qubits. This led to the terms like **physical and logical qubits. Please understand that logical qubits are a group of many physical qubits that contain specific information abiut the physical**

qubits. Also understand that the current ratio of physical qubits to logical qubits is 10^4:1. We can say that the computational power increases only when the number of qubits increases exponentially. **To be further practical, these advancements have improved the fault-tolerance of quantum computers.**

6.3 SHOR'S 3-QUBIT BIT-FLIP CODE

Quantum error correction is mandatory for reliable quantum computing as qubits are susceptible to errors due to their delicate nature and interactions with the environment. The 3-qubit code is the basic starting point for quantum error correction. This method encodes a single logical qubit into three physical ones with the property that it can correct a single bit-flip error in the Pauli X matrix (σ_x). This code is able to correct errors without measuring the state of the original qubit by using 2 extra qubits to extract **syndrome information i.e. information related to possible errors, from the data block without disturbing the original state.** The limitation of this code is that it cannot correct for both bit and phase flips simultaneously. But only a single bit flip. Peter Shor used this method to develop a 9-qubit error correction code.

Shor's 3-qubit code

Today, qubits are the alluring dancers that pirouette through a huge ballet of information processing. **They are the basic building blocks of quantum information that are capable of carrying out remarkable feats of computation that classical bits could not.** One of most popular quantum error codes is the Shor's code as developed by Peter Shor in 1995. **Also note that Shor code can correct one arbitrary error in a qubit by encoding it into 9 qubits. It is a stabilizer code that is a class of quantum error correction codes built upon the laws of stabilizer formalism.**

This error correction code is based on the 3-qubit code and it is capable of correcting bit flips, sign flips or both simultaneously. Shor's code works by encoding 1 single logical qubit into 9 physical qubits using this extra real state to store **syndrome information about the possible errors. Please note that this code can correct errors in a single qubit only.** This code tends to be simpler and it allows for more cooperative circuit structures to the physical limitations of computer architecture. Many other variants also exist as follows:

(a) **Bosonic codes:** These try to store error correction information in **bosonic codes** using the advantage that oscillators have infinitely many energy levels in a single physical system.

(b) **Topological codes:** Given by Alexei Kitaev with the development of his **toric code** for topological error correction. Its structure is defined on a 2D lattice using error chains which define non-trivial topological paths over the code surface.

Therefore, we can say that decoherence and quantum error correction are not making things easy for IT industry that wish to realize the dream of large scale fault-tolerant quantum computers.

Say, there is a qubit in some unknown state-

$$|\varphi\rangle = \alpha|0\rangle + \beta|1\rangle$$

The embedding of this single qubit state, α |0> β |1> as three entangled qubits provides protection from bit-flip errors:

$$(\alpha|0\rangle + \beta|1\rangle)|0\rangle|0\rangle \rightarrow \alpha|000\rangle + \beta|111\rangle$$

But we already know from no-cloning theorem that the following encoding of the unknown qubit cannot be performed-

$$(\alpha|0\rangle + \beta|1\rangle) \otimes (\alpha|0\rangle + \beta|1\rangle) \otimes (\alpha|0\rangle + \beta|1\rangle)$$

That is this **tensor product cannot be done. The 3-qubit code encodes a single logical qubit into three physical qubits** with the property that it can correct a **single-bit flip error.**

Let us now draw a circuitry to encode a single qubit.

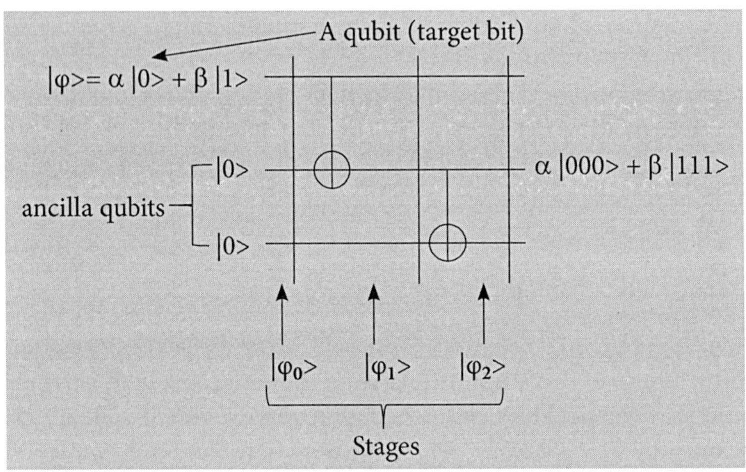

Fig.6.1: Quantum circuit showing encoding of a single qubit.

Working: As shown in figure 6.1, the quantum circuit initializes two ancilla qubits and two CNOT gates. The ancilla qubits are set to 0. The two CNOT gates act upon the ancilla qubits based on the state of the information qubit.

Three inputs to the circuit are: the state $|\psi\rangle$, two ancilla qubits in the state $|00\rangle$.

When the target bit is $|\psi\rangle = |0\rangle$, the ancillary qubits are left unchanged and the output is $|000\rangle$.

When the target bit is $|\psi\rangle = |1\rangle$, the output is $|111\rangle$.

In form of a truth-table, we can write as follows:

Input	**Output**
$|\psi\rangle$	Output
0	$|000\rangle$
1	$|111\rangle$

By superposition principle, the input $|\psi\rangle = |00\rangle = (a|0\rangle + b|1\rangle)|00\rangle$ results in the output-

$$|\psi\rangle_{\text{logical-state}} = a|000\rangle + b|111\rangle \text{ as expected by us.}$$

During phase-1 ($|\varphi_0\rangle$ phase), the inputs to the top CNOT gate are-

$$|\varphi_0\rangle = \alpha|000\rangle + \beta|100\rangle$$

Control input =0, target input = 0 Control input = 1, target input = 0

Here, when the control bit, $|\psi\rangle = |0\rangle$ then the ancillary qubits are left unchanged and the output is $|000\rangle$. But when the control bit, $|\psi\rangle = |1\rangle$ then the output is $|110\rangle$, at stage-1. So,

$$|\varphi_0\rangle = \alpha\,|000\rangle + \beta\,|110\rangle$$

As the top CNOT gate flips from $|10\rangle$ to $|11\rangle$.

During phase-2 ($|\varphi_1\rangle$ phase), the inputs to the lower CNOT gate are-

$$|\varphi_1\rangle = \alpha\,|000\rangle + \beta\,|110\rangle$$

Control input =0, target input = 0 (→ $\alpha\,|000\rangle$)   Control input = 1, target input = 0 (→ $\beta\,|110\rangle$)

Therefore, we have-

$$|\varphi_2\rangle = \alpha\,|000\rangle + \beta\,|111\rangle$$

As the lower CNOT gate flips from $|10\rangle$ to $|11\rangle$.

Conclusions: This circuitry encodes a given qubit, $\alpha\,|0\rangle + \beta\,|1\rangle$ with two other **ancillary qubits into a composite state of three qubits** i.e. $\alpha\,|000\rangle + \beta\,|111\rangle$. **Also note that the qubit state has been repeated only in the computational basis.** Furthermore, the superposition states have redundant encodings but are not repeated. Hence, **no-cloning theorem is not violated.**

6.4 QUANTUM ERROR CORRECTION

Quantum error correction involves the following steps:-

1. Measure all three encoded qubits.
2. Identify the one which differs from the others.
3. Flip back the erroneous qubit.

In the quantum ecosystem, consisting of three qubits, we need to find out whether two qubits are different without measuring their actual values. Practically speaking, this is achieved by using **syndrome measurement that can identify an erroneous qubit from the extracted error syndrome. Also note that the error syndrome indicates whether there is an error and identifies its location.** The error syndrome, say (s_1 s_0) for the 3-qubit system is found out by comparing the parities of qubit-1 and qubit-2. Comparing the parities of qubit-2 and qubit- 3 we get

$$s_1 = \text{qubit-2} \otimes \text{qubit-3}$$
$$s_0 = \text{qubit-1} \otimes \text{qubit-2}$$

Please note that s_1 does not need to know whether the qubit-2 or qubit-3 is equal to 1 or 0 or whether they have equal parity or not. Similarly, s_0 needs to know only if qubit-1 and qubit-2 have equal parity or not. This is also shown in truth-table below:

Table 6.2: Truth-table for error syndromes

s_1	s_0	**Bit –flip Error**
0	0	None
1	0	Qubit-1
1	1	Qubit-2
0	1	Qubit-3

From truth-table, we find that-

1. If qubit-1 and qubit-2 are the same then ancilla z_1 will have value 0.
2. If qubit-2 and qubit-3 are the same then ancilla z_0 will also have value 0.
3. Else the value will be 1 for z_1 and z_0.
4. The two ancillas are actually the error syndrome s_1 and s_0
5. Measurements of the syndrome do not disturb the quantum state.

6.4.1 Bit-Flip Error Correction

Suppose that the quantum channel is transmitting qubits such that a bit is changed from 0 to 1 or vice versa with probability, p. So, the probability that the bit remains unchanged is (1-p). **This type of error in a channel is known as a bit-flip error. Please note that its effect on a qubit is the same as if it has been acted upon by an X operator:**

$$\Psi = \alpha|0\rangle + \beta|1\rangle \xrightarrow{X} \alpha|1\rangle + \beta|0\rangle$$

Bit-flip error = operated by X-operator.

Correction circuit for a single bit-flip error:

As shown in figure 6.1, similarly here also **2 ancilla qubits are** included in the circuit. The **parities** of the qubit-1 and qubit-2 as well as the parity of qubit-2 and qubit-3 are checked using **four CNOT gates.** The **control bits** of these CNOT gates are encoded **qubits** whereas the **target qubits** are the two **ancillary qubits** introduced at the receiving end. **Please note that a pair of CNOT gates is used to check the parity of the 3-qubit data. Before we discuss the working of this circuit, let us draw the circuit for a single bit-flip error now.**

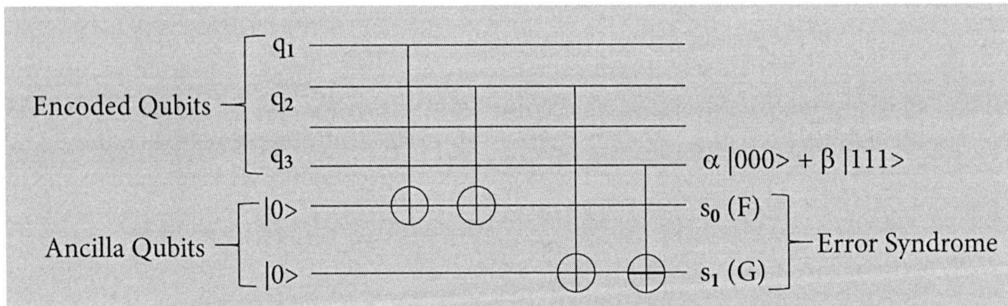

Fig.6.2: Quantum circuit showing encoding of a single qubit.

Working: The working of the circuit of fig. 6.2 is simple. Assume that the encoded data is $(q_1q_2q_3)$ and that F and G be the output state of the first and the second ancilla qubit respectively. From figure 6.2, it is observed that-

$$F = q_1 \oplus q_2$$
$$G = q_2 \oplus q_3$$

Hence, for data $(q_1q_2q_3) = |100\rangle$, the ancilla qubits, $|00\rangle$ will be transformed into $|10\rangle$ and the encoded data now is-

$$(\alpha|100\rangle + \beta|011\rangle)|00\rangle \rightarrow (\alpha|100\rangle + \beta|011\rangle)|10\rangle$$

Please note that the set of 2 ancillary qubits form the syndrome. Also note that the measurement of the two ancilla qubits leads to the identification of a particular qubit among the three that is corrupted else we say all three are error-free. This is shown in table 6.3 below:-

Table 6.3: Ancilla Measurement for Single-bit Flip Errors

State	Operator	Ancilla	Error is in	Comments
α |000> + β |111>	I	|00>	No Error	No error
α |100> + β |011>	X	|10>	qubit-1	Error is in q1
α |010> + β |101>	X	|11>	qubit-2	Error is in q2
α |001> + β |110>	X	|01>	qubit-3	Error is in q3

From this table 6.3, we observe that when an error is detected, an X operator is applied to the erroneous qubit in order to recover from the error. In absence of any error, only an Identity, I, operator is applied because no change in data is necessary. **The point to ponder is that the direct measurement of any of the qubits can be avoided for the error detection because the measurement result of the ancilla qubits is sufficient to detect and identify a qubit flip error. Also note that in a 3-qubit system** (3 qubits; $2^3 = 8$ states) **there can be four pairs of states with each pair having exactly the same ancilla bits** and this shown in table 6.4.

Table 6.4: Ancilla Measurement for Single-bit Flip Errors

3 qubits; $2^3 = 8$ states	State	Ancilla	Error Comments
0	α |000> + β |111>	|00>	No error
1	α |111> + β |000>	|00>	No error
2	α |100> + β |011>	|10>	Error is in q1
3	α |011> + β |100>	|10>	Error is in q1
4	α |010> + β |101>	|11>	Error is in q2
5	α |101> + β |010>	|11>	Error is in q2
6	α |001> + β |110>	|01>	Error is in q3
7	α |110> + β |001>	|01>	Error is in q3

Syndrome bit generator circuit and Parity generation circuit:

First of all, understand that syndrome s_0 corresponds to the even parity of the first two encoded qubits whereas s_1 is the even parity of the last two qubits. The parity generator circuit consists of two pairs of CNOT gates wherein each pair acts as an XOR gate. This is shown in figure 6.3.

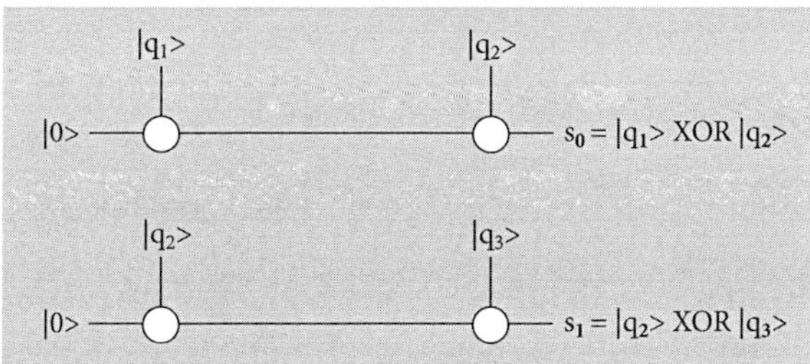

Fig.6.3: Syndrome bit and Parity generator circuit

How a bit-flip error is corrected?

Assume a bit-flip error on the second qubit, q_2 of the entangled qubits | q_1 q_2 q_3>. Therefore, the encoded qubits, α |000> + β |111> will be transformed into-

$$(\alpha\,|000> + \beta\,|111>)\,|00> \rightarrow \alpha\,|010>\,|00> + \beta\,|101>\,|00>)$$
$$= (\alpha\,|010>\,|11> + \beta\,|101>\,|11>)$$
$$= (\alpha\,|010> + \beta\,|101>\,|11>)$$

Please note here that the syndrome will also change from |00> to |11>.

Let us now see the steps need to correct an error (error decoding procedure) as follows:

S1: if the syndrome is 00, there is no error. No action is required.

S2: if the syndrome is 01, 10 or 11 then the erroneous qubit is q_3, q_1 or q_2 respectively.

Now apply X-operation to the qubit identified by the syndrome bits. Herein, the syndrome is 11. So, a bit-flip occurred on qubit q_2 (or 11 in binary). This error can be corrected with a X -operation on the 2nd qubit.

6.4.2 Phase Error Correction

The effect of a **phase flip on a qubit is similar to the application of a Z operator to the qubit:**

$$\Psi = \alpha\,|0> + \beta\,|1 \xrightarrow{Z} \alpha\,|0> - \beta\,|1>$$

Phase-flip error = operated by Z-operator.

A phase-flip error is as follows:

$$|k> \rightarrow (-1)^k\,|\,k> \qquad \text{where } k \in \{0, 1\}$$

This phase-flip error may affect a qubit. This happens when it is transmitted through a channel to the receiver. It can flip the relative phase of |0> and |1>. **Please understand that the sign between |0> and |1> in a quantum state can become inverted when a phase-flip error occurs during transmission.** Hence, a phase-flip error may be represented by the Z matrix too-

$$Z = \begin{bmatrix} 1 & 0 \\ 0 & -1 \end{bmatrix}$$

Also note that the effect of a phase-flip error on a quantum state, |Ψ> can be explained by applying the phase-flip operator Z to |0> and to |1>:

$$Z\,|0> = \begin{bmatrix} 1 & 0 \\ 0 & -1 \end{bmatrix} \begin{bmatrix} 1 \\ 0 \end{bmatrix} = \begin{bmatrix} 1 \\ 0 \end{bmatrix} = |0>$$

$$Z\,|1> = \begin{bmatrix} 1 & 0 \\ 0 & -1 \end{bmatrix} \begin{bmatrix} 0 \\ 1 \end{bmatrix} = \begin{bmatrix} 0 \\ -1 \end{bmatrix} = -|1>$$

Thus, we say that Z maps as follows: -

$$\Psi = \alpha\,|0> + \beta\,|1> \xrightarrow{Z} \alpha\,|0> - \beta\,|1>$$

To take the flesh out of it, we say that there is no method of correcting this kind of error using the 3-qubit code employed for bit-flip errors because the syndrome measurement will produce 00. As a result of this, the error correction operation does nothing and the error is not corrected.

An important point lies in the reference now. If we recall that the two important basis states of a qubit are $|+>$ and $|->$ states-

$$|+> \;=\; (|0> + |1>) / \sqrt{2}$$
$$|-> \;=\; (|0> - |1>) / \sqrt{2}$$

Now, the operator Z, maps $|+>$ to $|->$ and $|->$ to $|+>$ as shown below-

$$|+> \rightarrow |-> \qquad \text{and}$$
$$|-> \rightarrow |+>$$

Therefore,

$$Z|+> \;=\; \begin{bmatrix} 1 & 0 \\ 0 & -1 \end{bmatrix} (|0> + |1> / \sqrt{2})$$

$$= 1/\sqrt{2} \begin{bmatrix} 1 & 0 \\ 0 & -1 \end{bmatrix} (|0> + |1>)$$

$$= 1/\sqrt{2}\,(|0> - |1>) = |->$$

Similarly, we can compute for $Z|->$ also and is shown below-

$$Z|-> \;=\; \begin{bmatrix} 1 & 0 \\ 0 & -1 \end{bmatrix} (|0> - |1> / \sqrt{2})$$

$$= 1/\sqrt{2}\,(|0> + |1>) = |+>$$

In nutshell, a phase-error maps $|+>$ to $|->$ and $|->$ to $|+>$.

6.5 SHOR'S 9-QUBIT CODE

Peter Shor's 9-qubit code (1995) is a **quantum error correction code** that can correct one arbitrary error in a qubit by encoding it into a group of 9 qubits for each logical bit. It can correct X (bit-flip), Z (phase-flip) errors or a combination of both (Y = ZX) on a qubit. It works on the **concept of majority voting.** It assumes that the presence of a single erroneous qubit only. Also it is shown in literature that a quantum code that can correct both bit-flip and phase-flip errors and that it can correct an arbitrary error on a single qubit.

Actually, Shor's code works on 3-qubit repetition code. It encodes a single logical qubit into three physical qubits as-

$$|0_{logical}> \rightarrow |000> \;\text{and}\; |1_{logical}> \rightarrow |111>$$

Then in two steps it encodes a physical qubit:-

S1: Apply phase encoding for the qubit state i.e. $\Psi = \alpha\,|0> + \beta\,|1>$ to guard against phase-flip errors. **Recall that the phase-flip error is similar to the bit-flip error in the basis state $\{ |+>, |-> \}$.** Hence, the qubit state can be encoded as follows:

$$\Psi \;=\; \alpha\,|+> + \beta\,|->$$

Because the qubit state is encoded in the 3-qubit repetition code, hence the following encoding of a qubit is suitable for protection against phase-flip errors:-

$$|0_{logical}> \rightarrow |+++>, |1_{logical}> \rightarrow |--->$$

In nutshell, we can write as follows:-

$$\Psi = \alpha |+> + \beta |-> = |+++> + |--->$$

S2: Encode each of the resulting 3 qubits to prohibit bit-flip errors. The corresponding encoding circuit for 9-qubit code is shown in figure 6.4.

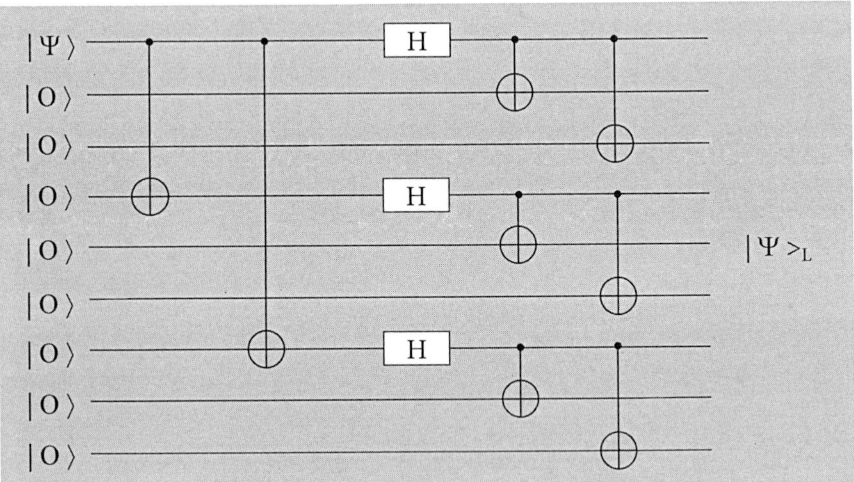

Fig.6.4: Encoding circuitry for 9-qubit code

The CNOT gates on the left (see fig. 6.4) along with the ancillary |0> bits convert the quantum state,

$$\Psi = \alpha |0> + \beta |1> \text{ to } \Psi = \alpha |000> + \beta |111>.$$

Then, the Hadamard gate is applied that transforms this state to-

$$\Psi = \alpha [1/\sqrt{2} (|000> + |111>) . 1/\sqrt{2} (|000> + |111>). 1/\sqrt{2} (|000> + |111>)] + [\beta\, 1/\sqrt{2} (|000> - |111>). 1/\sqrt{2} (|000> - |111>). 1/\sqrt{2} (|000> - |111>)]$$

Please note that each output of the Hadamard gate drives the control inputs of a pair of CNOT gates (see fig. 6.4) **with |0> that feeds the other inputs of the CNOT gates. Also note that the final outputs of the circuit shows that the single qubit state** $\alpha |0> + \beta |1>$ is mapped into a product of 9 **qubits** i.e. it is an extension of 3-qubit repetition code. The basis states for the code are encoded as follows:-

$$|0_{logical}> = [(|000> + |111>) (|000> + |111>) (|000> + |111>)] / 2\sqrt{2}$$
$$|1_{logical}> = [(|000> - |111>) (|000> - |111>) (|000> - |111>)] / 2\sqrt{2}$$

The point to ponder is that the 1st, 4th and 7th qubits are used for the phase-flip code whereas all three blocks of qubits; (1, 2, 3), (4, 5, 6) and (7, 8, 9) are used for the bit-flip code. So, the overall encoded states consist of three blocks each block containing 3 qubits-

[1 2 3]
[4 5 6]
[7 8 9]

Also note that all 9-qubit code words have the structure of a phase-flip code, however, in each of them the (|0> ± |1> part is replaced by (|000> ± |111> i.e bit-flip encoding. **And this type of coding in which there is nesting of one code inside another is called as a concatenated code.** *This idea is very significant in guarding against quantum computer's vulnerability to noise.* Now, single bit-flip or phase-flip errors in any of these blocks can be detected and corrected by using the **error syndromes. Recall that error syndromes for 3-qubit codes are generated by measuring whether or not two qubits are the same or different in standard basis.** In Peter Shor's code, there are 3-qubit codes that form 3 blocks with each block representing an encoding of one such code.

In block 1, the syndrome measurement Z_1Z_2, compares the first and second qubit, if they are same i.e.

$$
\begin{aligned}
Z_1Z_2 &= +1 \quad \text{if the 1}^{\text{st}} \text{ qubit and the 2}^{\text{nd}} \text{ qubit are the same;} \\
&= -1 \quad \text{otherwise.}
\end{aligned}
$$

Similarly, the syndrome measurement Z_2Z_3 compares the 1st and the 3rd qubit in block 1.

$$
\begin{aligned}
Z_2Z_3 &= +1 \quad \text{if the 2}^{\text{nd}} \text{ qubit and the 3}^{\text{rd}} \text{ qubit are the same;} \\
&= -1 \quad \text{otherwise.}
\end{aligned}
$$

Now, if we take all possible combinations of measurement results, then it is possible to find out whether there is a qubit flip-error **in block 1** or not and also its location. This is shown in table-6.5.

Table-6.5: Location of qubit bit-flip error in block-1.

$Z_1Z_2 = +1$	$Z_2Z_3 = +1$	No error.
$Z_1Z_2 = -1$	$Z_2Z_3 = +1$	Qubit 1 has flipped.
$Z_1Z_2 = -1$	$Z_2Z_3 = -1$	Qubit 2 has flipped.
$Z_1Z_2 = +1$	$Z_2Z_3 = -1$	Qubit 3 has flipped.

Similarly, **in block 2,** syndrome measurement Z_4Z_5 compares values of the 4th and 5th qubits and Z_5Z_6 compares the values of 5th and 6th qubits. This is again shown in table-6.6.

Table-6.6: Location of qubit bit-flip error in block-2.

$Z_4Z_5 = +1$	$Z_5Z_6 = +1$	No error.
$Z_4Z_5 = -1$	$Z_5Z_6 = +1$	Qubit 4 has flipped.
$Z_4Z_5 = -1$	$Z_5Z_6 = -1$	Qubit 5 has flipped.
$Z_4Z_5 = +1$	$Z_5Z_6 = -1$	Qubit 6 has flipped.

Similarly, **in block 3,** syndrome measurement Z_7Z_8 compares values of the 7th and 8th qubits and Z_8Z_9 compares the values of 8th and 9th qubits. This is again shown in table-6.7.

Table-6.7: Location of qubit bit-flip error in block-3.

$Z_7Z_8 = +1$	$Z_8Z_9 = +1$	No error.
$Z_7Z_8 = -1$	$Z_8Z_9 = +1$	Qubit 7 has flipped.
$Z_7Z_8 = -1$	$Z_8Z_9 = -1$	Qubit 8 has flipped.
$Z_7Z_8 = +1$	$Z_8Z_9 = -1$	Qubit 9 has flipped.

Example to show the application of Shor's 9-bit coding scheme:

Let us assume that a qubit, α |0> + β |1>, is encoded as α |000> + β |111>. Say, that the 3 qubits are sent via a channel, one at a time. Suppose that a bit-flip error occurs on the 7th qubit (shown in bold face) i.e.

α [(|000> + |111>) (|000> + |111>) (|**1**00> + |**0**11>)]

+ β [(|000> - |111>) (|000> - |111>) (|**1**00> - |**1**11>)] / 2√2

Then, the qubits in the 3 blocks will be as follows: -

Blocks	1	2	3
	000	000	100

To take the flesh out of it, error syndrome measurements can be obtained from the three blocks of qubits, while the 6 observables are derived by comparing the suitable qubits in blocks 1, 2 and 3 as follows:

Z_1Z_2	Z_2Z_3	Z_4Z_5	Z_5Z_6	Z_7Z_8	Z_8Z_9
+1	+1	+1	+1	-1	+1

It is crystal clear that the bit 0 flip error occurred on the 7th qubit i.e. the 1st qubit of the 3rd block as above. The original state can be recovered by applying an X-gate to qubit 7.

Shor's code is based on the principles of stabilizer formalism. It combines two classical error correction codes i.e. the 3-bit repetition code and the 3-bit bit-flip code. Shor's 9-qubit error correction code employs **syndrome measurements** to detect and correct errors. **Shor's method has further rinsed the research work as newer algorithms like Steane code and Surface codes have been developed.**

In nutshell, qubit codes are the intricate choreography that enables the dance of qubits in the quantum realm. They are the foundations on which QEC, encoding and computation rest.

6.6 FAULT TOLERANCE QUANTUM COMPUTATION

Quantum computers are hailed as the ultimate computing system of tomorrow. Still there is a hitch. Inspite of the fact that these are the computers of tomorrow, still errors rapidly creep in.

A new technology now allows operators to dynamically change the layouts of atoms. But all this hinges on shuffling of qubits. Error correction mechanism depends on the ability to shuffle qubits without causing them to fall out of their quantum state. The need is to have more robust qubits called as **hyperfine qubits that have quantum states that last much longer than those of regular qubits. Please understand that this gives them more time to entangle with other qubits and thus create complex quantum states.**

According to the research from Niels Bohr Institute (NBI), a method to use noise to process information has been developed. So, this improves the performance of the quantum computing's qubit. Both NBI and University of Copenhagen together, have developed a better approach that uses **noise to process quantum information. Also note that as a result of this, the performance of the fundamental quantum computing unit of information i.e. qubit, has increased by 700%.**

6.7 SOME NEW QUBIT TOLERANT QUANTUM COMPUTER

The world's first commercial fault-tolerant quantum computer with **logical qubits** is expected to be launched in late 2024. **QuEra** has dramatically reduced the error rate in qubits. This machine uses 256 physical qubits and 10 logical qubits. **Recall that logical and physical qubits that are connected through quantum entanglement mitigate errors in quantum computers by storing the same data in different places. QuEra Computing** company is the quantum computing trailblazer, has a plan that starting in 2024, they will culminate with a system with 100 logical error-corrected qubits this marks down a new era in quantum computing.

In Quantum Error Correction (QEC), the overhead is larger because several physical qubits are required. But the level of error correction is high. QEC is used to achieve fault-tolerant quantum computers that are a long-term goal.

On the other hand, Quantum Error Mitigation (QEM) is a paramount to tap the potential of quantum computing. There are 2 problems-

(a) Qubits available today suffer from noise in the environment that destroys any meaningful computation.

(b) We don't have enough physical qubits to bundle them into **fault-tolerant logical qubits.**

To be further practical, we should try to reduce the impact of noise on the computation. This is known as quantum error mitigation.

The advances made till date has greatly improved the fault tolerance of quantum computers that has opened new doors of the research work in this ecosystem of large-scale quantum computing.

Before delving into more details, it is important to solve an example to deepen your understanding on quantum error correction.

Example 1: Assume a quantum circuit having a controlled NOT gate to corresponding pairs of qubits of the state $|1^{\sim} 0^{\sim}>$ where $|0^{\sim}>$ is a code word for $|0>$ and $|1^{\sim}>$ is a code word for $|1>$ in a quantum error correction code that can correct single qubit errors. To put it in a proper light, the controlled NOT gate is applied to the ith qubit of $|1^{\sim}>$ as control and the ith qubit of $|0^{\sim}>$ as target. Now further suppose that a single qubit error-

$1/\sqrt{2}\ (I_2 + \sigma_1)$ on one of the qubits of $|1^{\sim}>$ occurs before the controlled NOT operation is performed. Can you discuss and interpret the error correction of this scenario?

Solution 1: Suppose the single qubit error occurs on the jth qubit and the encoding $|1^{\sim}>$ and $|0^{\sim}>$ is n qubits long. Therefore the error is-

$$E = 1/\sqrt{2}\left[\bigotimes_{k=1}^{j-1} I_2\right] \otimes \left(I_2 + \sigma_1\right) \otimes \left[\bigotimes_{k=j+1}^{2n} I_2\right]$$

Let us denote the pairwise application of the controlled NOT operation by $U^{\sim}_{CNOT}$. Then, we can say-

$$U^{\sim}_{CNOT}\, E\, |1^{\sim} 0^{\sim}> = U^{\sim}_{CNOT}\, E U^{\sim *}_{CNOT}\, U^{\sim}_{CNOT}\, |1^{\sim} 0^{\sim}>$$

Now the controlled NOT operation is given by-

$$U_{CNOT} = 1/2\,(I_2 + \sigma_3) \otimes I_2 + 1/2\,(I_2 - \sigma_3) \otimes \sigma_1$$

We compute the matrix as follows: -

$$1/\sqrt{2}\, U_{CNOT}\,(I_2 + \sigma_1)\, U^{*}_{CNOT} = 1/\sqrt{2}\,(I_2 \otimes I_2 + \sigma_1 \otimes \sigma_1)$$

Thus, we get the normalized state as-

$$U^{\sim}_{CNOT}\, E\,|1^{\sim}0^{\sim}> = 1/\sqrt{2}$$

$$\left\{ \left(\bigotimes_{k=1}^{2n} I_2 \right) + 1/\sqrt{2} \left(\bigotimes_{k=1}^{j-1} I_2 \right) \otimes \sigma_1 \otimes \left(\bigotimes_{k+j+1}^{n+j-1} I_2 \right) \otimes \sigma_1 \otimes \left(\bigotimes_{k+n+j+1}^{2n} I_2 \right) \right\}$$

$$\times\, U^{\sim}_{CNOT}\,|1^{\sim}\,0^{\sim}>.$$

Conclusions: It is observed that there is a linear combination of no error or a single qubit error in the 1st block of n-qubits and a single qubit error in the 2nd block of n-qubits. Both errors can be independently corrected.

SUMMARY

As studied in classical communication theory, bits are communicated and that the only type of error that can occur is bit-flip. On the other hand, in quantum case, any rotation or phase change in the Hilbert space of the quantum state is an error. **Please understand that this means that there can infinite number of different errors that could occur just for a single qubit. Also note that the measurement to find out the occurrence of the error reduces the error to one compatible with the measurement.** Say, the data is contained in the state $|\psi>$ and the environment is described by the state $|E>$. Then, the initial state of the entire system is described by the tensor product of the states $|\psi> \otimes |E>$, which involves some unitary operation, U.

Error correction involves using multiple physical qubits to represent a single logical bit of data. **To put it in a proper light, the value of those qubits can be compared. So, the system can weed out any that succumb to noise.**

Quantum error correction seeks to achieve fault-tolerant quantum computation by protecting information from errors due to decoherence and other environmental noise.

MULTIPLE CHOICE QUESTIONS [MCQS] WITH ANSWERS

1. In classical communication, a single bit in a group of data can change from 0 to 1 or vice versa. This is known as-
   (a) Single bit error.
   (b) Multi-bit error.
   (c) Phase error.
   (d) None of the above.

2. The method of including additional bits to allow the receiver to decide whether the encoded data is corrupt or not is known as-
   (a) Error syndrome.
   (b) Phase Error.
   (c) Error detecting codes.
   (d) None of the above.

3. The probability of receiving a bit that is different than what was transmitted is known as-
   (a) Random probability.
   (b) Crossover probability.
   (c) Baye's probability.
   (d) None of the above.
4. A repetition code can't be designed by duplicating a state several times-
   (a) True.
   (b) False.
   (c) Partially true.
   (d) None of the above.
5. Bit-flip error on qubit means that it has been acted upon by-
   (a) X-operator.
   (b) Y-operator.
   (c) Z-operator.
   (d) None of the above.
6. Phase-flip error on qubit means that it has been acted upon by-
   (a) X-operator.
   (b) Y-operator.
   (c) Z-operator.
   (d) None of the above.
7. What indicates whether there is an error in a 3-bit quantum system and also it identifies its location-
   (a) Horner's syndrome.
   (b) Error syndrome.
   (c) Belady's syndrome.
   (d) None of the above.
8. Encoding is a process that embeds information into qubits. Quantum encoding is used in different quantum algorithms like-
   (a) Quantum error correction, quantum cryptography and quantum teleportation.
   (b) Quantum phase estimation.
   (c) QFT.
   (d) None of the above.
9. To deal with bit flip and phase flip errors, the error correction schemes that has been developed are named as-
   (a) Calderbank-Shor-Steane or CSS codes.
   (b) CSS style sheets.
   (c) CSA.
   (d) None of the above.
10. A process by which a qubit loses energy to its environment is called as-
    (a) Elimination.
    (b) Dissipation.
    (c) Filtration.
    (d) None of the above.
11. The process of coupling between two initially isolated quantum systems i.e. qubits and its environment, that tends to randomize the relative phases of the possible states of the memory register is known as-
    (a) De-coherence.
    (b) Coherence.
    (c) Interference.
    (d) None of the above.
12. The internal energy levels of ions serve as-
    (a) Bits.
    (b) Qubits.
    (c) Dubits.
    (d) None of the above.

Answers											
1.	(a)	2.	(c)	3.	(b)	4.	(a)	5.	(a)	6.	(c)
7.	(b)	8.	(a)	9.	(a)	10.	(b)	11.	(a)	12.	(b)

CONCEPTUAL SHORT QUESTIONS WITH ANSWERS

Q1. What is the need of quantum error correction?

Ans. We know that qubit interaction with the external environment can produce huge undesirable effects on a qubit. So, there is a need to cope with this unavoidable effect, error correction techniques before we can build a quantum computer. At the same time, no-cloning theorem also does not allow us to duplicate qubits. Hence, there is a need of having a clever error correction policy. For this, we must understand the de-coherence problem first. **De-coherence is the loss of coherence in a quantum system due to interactions with the external environment. Recall that by using qubits, we can model de-coherence by the introduction of a relative phase.** That is,

$$|0> \rightarrow |0>$$

$$\text{and } |1> \rightarrow e^{i\theta} |1>.$$

Hence, an arbitrary qubit, $|\psi> = \alpha |0> + \beta |1>$ is transformed as follows: -

$$|\psi> = \alpha |0> + e^{i\theta} \beta |1>.$$

For example, if $|\psi> = (|0> + |1>) / \sqrt{2}$

The density matrix is transformed as follows:-

$$\rho = ½ \begin{bmatrix} 1 & 1 \\ 1 & 1 \end{bmatrix} \rightarrow 1/2 \begin{bmatrix} 1 & e^{-i\theta} \\ e^{i\theta} & 1 \end{bmatrix}$$

This type of model used for coherence is called as collective dephasing. The point to ponder is that these types of transformations induced by the environment are not desirable. This problem is solvable. **Please understand and remember that an overall global phase** i.e. a phase that multiplies all terms in superposition, **has no effect on the predictions of measurement results. Also understand that a relative phase is a phase that only multiplies a single term in a superposition and does change predictions about possible measurement results.** In nutshell, the implementation of a global phase is irrelevant but the implementation of a relative phase is problematic. In order to solve this problem, we use a mapping, called as a decoherent free subspace. **And this is done with the introduction of logical qubits that are represented as-** $|0_L>$, $|1_L>$. **Also the qubits that we have been using till now are physical qubits. Hence, they are the states of actual physical systems like the energy levels in an atom.** We then introduce decoherence using the collective dephasing model. Because each logical qubit is changed by the same global phase, so an arbitrary logical qubit is unchanged by decoherence. There is no change in the state.

Q2. Explain what is syndrome measurement? Illustrate with the help of an example.

Ans. The application of Pauli's X operator can cause bit flips in a qubit. To correct such errors, usually 2 steps are followed:-

1. Analyze which error occurred.
2. Using a unitary transformation to fix it.

Using the correct unitary operations, we can do the 1st step without damaging the superposition of the logical qubit state.

For instance, say the 2nd qubit was flipped giving-

$$|\psi\rangle = \alpha\,|010\rangle + \beta\,|101\rangle$$

Now to detect the error, we firstly form the product state as follows-

$$(\alpha\,|010\rangle + \beta\,|101\rangle)\,|00\rangle = \alpha\,|010\rangle\,|00\rangle + \beta\,|101\rangle\,|00\rangle \quad \text{........(1)}$$

Please recall that we call these extra bits as ancillary qubits. We pass the entire state through a series of 5 controlled NOT gates. Then, we measure the ancillary qubits at the end. The ancillary qubits will encode the position of the error for the 1st, 2nd, or 3rd qubit as binary 01, 10 or 11. **The result of two ancillary bits is known as the syndrome measurement.**

S1: Pass equation-1 above through the 1st controlled NOT. We take the **1st qubit as the control bit and the 2nd ancillary qubit as the target bit.** So, the state becomes-

$$\alpha\,|010\rangle\,|00\rangle + \beta\,|101\rangle\,|00\rangle \rightarrow \alpha\,|010\rangle\,|00\rangle + \beta\,|101\rangle\,|01\rangle \quad \text{.......(2)}$$

S2: We now pass equation-2 above through a controlled NOT. We take the **2nd qubit as the control bit and the 2nd ancillary bit as the target.** So, the state becomes-

$$\alpha\,|010\rangle\,|00\rangle + \beta\,|101\rangle\,|01\rangle \rightarrow \alpha\,|010\rangle\,|01\rangle + \beta\,|101\rangle\,|01\rangle \quad \text{.......(3)}$$

S3: Now the control qubit is the 2nd qubit while the target is the 1st ancillary. That is,

$$\alpha\,|010\rangle\,|01\rangle + \beta\,|101\rangle\,|01\rangle \rightarrow \alpha\,|010\rangle\,|11\rangle + \beta\,|101\rangle\,|01\rangle \quad \text{.......(4)}$$

S4: Next, we transform equation-4 by passing the state through yet another controlled NOT gate. This time the **control bit is the 3rd qubit and the target is the first ancillary.** So, the state becomes-

$$\alpha\,|010\rangle\,|11\rangle + \beta\,|101\rangle\,|01\rangle \rightarrow \alpha\,|010\rangle\,|11\rangle + \beta\,|101\rangle\,|11\rangle \quad \text{.......(5)}$$

S5: Lastly, we apply one more controlled NOT gate using the 1st ancillary bit as the control bit and the 2nd ancillary bit as the target. This gives us-

$$\alpha\,|010\rangle\,|11\rangle + \beta\,|101\rangle\,|11\rangle \rightarrow \alpha\,|010\rangle\,|10\rangle + \beta\,|101\rangle\,|10\rangle \quad \text{.......(6)}$$

Conclusions: The ancillary qubits are measured that gives 10. Please observe that this implies that the error is in the 2nd qubit. Also, the superposition of the state has been maintained throughout the procedure because the qubits of our state were only used as control bits in the controlled NOT gate. We can fix the error with an X gate by applying it to the qubit which has been flipped. This gives back the original state we can also detect single bit flips using the projection operators. On the other hand, to correct phase flip errors, we can again use a 3-qubit code to encode logical states. This is achieved using the $|+\rangle$ and $|-\rangle$ basis instead of the computational basis.

Q3. Is it possible to convert a phase error to a bit-flip error?

Ans. As we know that $|+\rangle = H(1)$ and $|-\rangle = H(0)$, so **a phase error can be converted to a bit-flip error if the basis is changed from the computational to the Hadamard.** This change can be done **by using the identity H-Z-H.** That is,

$$\text{H-Z-H} = \begin{bmatrix} 1/\sqrt{2} & 1/\sqrt{2} \\ 1/\sqrt{2} & -1/\sqrt{2} \end{bmatrix} \begin{bmatrix} 1 & 0 \\ 0 & -1 \end{bmatrix} \begin{bmatrix} 1/\sqrt{2} & 1/\sqrt{2} \\ 1/\sqrt{2} & -1/\sqrt{2} \end{bmatrix}$$

Solving this matrix equation, we get-

$$= \begin{bmatrix} 1/\sqrt{2} & 1/\sqrt{2} \\ 1/\sqrt{2} & -1/\sqrt{2} \end{bmatrix} \begin{bmatrix} 1 & 0 \\ 0 & -1 \end{bmatrix} \begin{bmatrix} 1/\sqrt{2} & 1/\sqrt{2} \\ 1/\sqrt{2} & -1/\sqrt{2} \end{bmatrix}$$

$$= \begin{bmatrix} 1/\sqrt{2} & -1/\sqrt{2} \\ 1/\sqrt{2} & 1/\sqrt{2} \end{bmatrix} \begin{bmatrix} 1/\sqrt{2} & 1/\sqrt{2} \\ 1/\sqrt{2} & -1/\sqrt{2} \end{bmatrix}$$

$$= \begin{bmatrix} 1 & 0 \\ 0 & -1 \end{bmatrix} = X$$

Thus, we can now say that the identity H-Z-H **converts phase-flip errors to bit errors X. Please note that in a similar way, the H-X-H identity can be used to transform from a bit-flip to a phase-flip error.** This is so because in (|+>, |->) basis, a phase-flip error acts like a bit-flip error. **Also note that the error correcting code for bit-flips can also be used for phase flips only if the basis for each qubit is changed.**

Q4. What are the limitations of Quantum Repetition Codes?

Ans. Some limitations of quantum repetition codes are as follows:-

1. They are not efficient in terms resource usage because they require multiple physical qubits to represent a single logical qubit.
2. These codes are only capable of correcting bit-flip errors that involves a qubit's state flipping from |0> to |1> or vice versa.
3. They cannot correct phase-flip errors or more general types of errors that may occur in quantum systems.
4. Better and advanced quantum error correcting codes like the surface code or Shor's code are capable of correcting a wider range of errors.

Q5. What are the key steps of any quantum error correction circuitry?

Ans. The key steps of any quantum error correction circuitry are as follows:

S1: **Encode** the state, |ψ> as an entangled state of n-qubits.

S2: **Simulate** the introduction of an error in the encoded state to produce a new buggy state of the n-qubits.

S4: **Decode** the buggy state of the entangled qubits.

S5: Determine what error occurred by computing the **error syndrome.**

S6: Given the **error syndrome,** apply a suitable **unitary operator** i.e. rotation to correct the state.

Q6. Why error correction is mandatory for quantum computers?

Ans. As we know that errors due to de-coherence are inevitable in a quantum computer. If no measures are taken and an error of order 1/e is introduced when a gate transforms a quantum state. Then, after O (e) such state transformations, the quantum state becomes so noisy that an incorrect answer is almost certain.

Q7. Why do we need QEC?

Ans. We need QEC due to the following reasons:

1. Superconducting qubits don't work exactly the way they should.
2. Each gate is slightly wrong.
3. Qubits get poked by small external forces.
4. Measurements sometimes lie.

This same is also true for spin qubits, topological qubits, photonic qubits etc.

However, algorithms like Shor, Grover etc. assume that qubits are perfect. Run them with imperfect physical qubits and you will get non-sense out. Instead we need qubits that are flawless incarnations of the idea of quantum information. Such ideal qubits are called as **logical qubits. Please understand that we need to somehow make perfect logical qubits out of noisy physical qubits. Also note that many physical qubits are needed per logical qubit.** Using QEC in algorithms is a long-term goal.

Q8. What is the problem with the repetition code?

Ans. The problem with the repetition code is that it treats z basis states very different to x and y basis states. z-basis states are product states, others are entangled. Also distinguishing encoded z-basis needs a single qubit measurement whereas distinguishing x-basis states needs, d. Also flipping between z-basis states requires d gates but the x basis only takes one.

Q9. Define the following terms-

(a) **Quantum noise.**

(b) **Quantum limit.**

Ans. (a) **Quantum noise:** The objective is to design quantum computers in such a way that even if any interruption occurs, it should be solved in minimal time. External environmental factors can create a disturbance in the functionality. **Please note that this disturbance which disrupts the task execution is called as noise and because it is associated with quantum computing, so it is called as quantum noise.** This noise may be in form of vibrations, industrial noise, thermal noise due to Brownian motion or even fluctuations in power supply and so on. The quantum noise can also occur in form of **Poisson noise or shot noise** which occurs due to discrete nature of the electric charges. Shot noise arises because of the static nature of photoelectrons. **For example,** say we wish to achieve photonic entanglement that will further provide quantum internet within the required mandatory distance. In such a scenario, if any condition like change in polarization due to temperature rise or drop will lead to decoherence and hence the entire setup will be a waste.

(b) **Quantum limit: It is defined as the minimum energy required maintaining error bits in quantum computing** i.e. minimum level of noise during the execution process. **Also note that the need for studying quantum noise is to know the quantum limits of digital transmission.**

Q10. What are the effects of quantum noise?

Ans. The following effects may be seen-

1. Fidelity in the state.
2. Reduced feedback strength i.e. the efficiency of the output is decreased.
3. Complete shutdown of the system.

Q11. Compare error corrections in both classical computers and in quantum computers.

Ans. In traditional/classical computers, error correction is done by 2 methods:-

(a) Guessing the original data.

(b) Retransmission of data that also includes the copying of the original data.

But we know that as per no-cloning theorem we can't create a copy of qubit state. This theorem seems to be an obstacle in error correction techniques.

Problems and challenges faced while error correction in quantum computing-

1. No-cloning theorem is the constraint.
2. Continuous error on a single qubit.
3. Measurement collapses the qubit state.

Solutions to these problems-

1. Although it is not possible to create an identical state but it is quite possible to pass the information of the qubit to the highly entangled qubits i.e. the state of several entangled qubits. This was first discovered by Peter Shor where he showed that by spreading the information one qubit to the highly entangled state of 9 –qubits.
2. To identify, which qubit got affected, we use **syndrome measurement. It is defined as the measurement performed on a computing system to get information about the physical state of the bit and the ways it got affected due to noise that occurred in the system.**
3. After doing syndrome measurement, it can be inferred that the arbitrary noise was due to one or the superposition of the following reasons-

   (a) Bit-flip.

   (b) Phase or sign flip.

   (c) Both bit and phase flip.

Q12. What is QaaS?

Ans. QaaS stands for Quantum-as-a-Service. It means providing access to remote quantum computers, if they are deployed on cloud. This will be at par with AI, ML and DL too. QaaS services work by connecting users directly to Quantum Processing Units (QPUs), quantum emulators and quantum simulators.

Q13. What do you mean by NISQ computers?

Ans. **NISQ** is the short form of "Noisy Intermediate Scale Quantum Computing".

When we talk about quantum computers, we actually mean **fault-tolerant computer devices. Please understand that solving complex problems on quantum computers means several qubits and several qubits needs more and better error correction because most of the**

quantum algorithms are very sensitive to noise. Also note that noise in the quantum circuit gates will limit the power of creating efficient quantum circuits.

Q14. What is crosstalk?

Ans. The interactions between qubits and their neighboring qubits can lead to errors. This leads to crosstalks.

EXERCISE QUESTIONS

Q1. Assume that the environment is in the state as follows-

$$|\varphi_e\rangle = \sqrt{2}/\sqrt{3}\,|0\rangle + 1/\sqrt{3}\,|1\rangle$$

What is the probability that there is a phase flip error on a principal system with density matrix, ρ?

Q2. Explain Shor's three qubit code?

Q3. Explain Shor's nine qubit code?

Q4. Explain the following errors in quantum systems:

(a) Bit-flip errors.

(b) Phase-flip errors.

Q5. Define what is collective de-phasing?

Q6. Distinguish between logical and physical qubits.

Q7. What are CSS codes?

Q8. What is syndrome measurement? Explain with an example.

Q9. Draw a circuitry showing Syndrome bit generator circuit and Parity generation circuit.

Q10. What is bit-flip error correction and phase change error correction in quantum systems?

Q11. Consider the application of the controlled NOT gate to the state $|10\rangle = |1\rangle \otimes |0\rangle$. Suppose that a single qubit error $\sigma_1 \otimes I_2$ occurs before the controlled NOT operation is performed. How many errors does the resulting state have after performing the control NOT operation? Also discuss the case when the error is given by $1/\sqrt{2}\,(I_2 + \sigma_1) \otimes I_2$.

Q12. Why do we use the ancilla qubits for error correction?

Q13. Develop Grover's algorithm using ancilla qubits.

Quantum Cryptography

7

7.0 INTRODUCTION

Due to the exponential growth in the arena of quantum computing, quantum computers have the potential to break traditional cryptographic algorithms. **We can now develop more secure cryptographic systems that are less vulnerable to cyber threats.** Quantum key distribution (QKD) is a method of secure communication that uses the principles of quantum mechanics to generate and distribute secret keys.

There are many types of quantum-inspired cyber security tools being developed that can be used to enhance cyber defense capabilities. **For example,** the Quantum Threat Intelligence Platform (QTIP), developed by the US Department of Defense, uses classical computing to perform advanced threat analysis. By leveraging the power of quantum computing, researchers can develop and test new cryptographic algorithms rapidly and efficiently.

Deep Web and Dark Web are the two terms being used today. **Deep Web** is 95% of the content on the internet which is non-indexable by search engines. It has a peculiar re-routing of connections and multi-layered entry tunnels before reaching the server. But **Dark Web** comprises 5% of the Deep Web. It is underbelly of it. It is the place of secret criminal activities. Dark Web websites are made using cryptographic keys.

7.1 PRINCIPLES OF INFORMATION SECURITY

Information security may be achieved either by **symmetric key cryptography or by public key cryptography.** Let us discuss these two first.

I. **Symmetric key cryptography:** In 1949, Claude Shanon of Bell Labs., USA, published a cryptography method that uses **a single key to encrypt and decrypt** the message. **Please recall that the main use of sharing a secret key is that a large amount of information can be communicated in secret by sharing a small number of key bits** (only 1 key for encryption and decryption). So, we must have secure key formation mechanism. One way is to have a separate pair of keys for each pair of users to enhance security. **But please note that this increases the number of keys rapidly. For instance,** in a group of n-people, the number of keys required will be (n (n – 1)) /2. Hence, this method is one of the biggest challenges.

II. **Public key cryptography:** This method uses separate, mathematically related keys for encryption and decryption. **For instance,** if one person, A, wants to communicate with another person, B, then person A chooses a **private key first. This key is not disclosed to anyone. Then, A and B exchange their public keys.** To send a message to B, A first encrypts the message with public key and then transmits it to B. B uses his private key to extract the corresponding plain text from the encrypted message. **Also note that a public key system in a group of n-people requires 2n keys i.e. n-public and n-private keys. The point to ponder is that, the need for a sender and the receiver to share secret keys using some secure channel is eliminated. All communications involve only public keys and a private key is never transmitted or shared.**

III. **Private key cryptography:** In this method, the secrecy of the key depends on the key itself. That is, how much secure key you have chosen. But the problem is that it needs sharing of a secret between the two parties. **The point to ponder is that now the hacker can copy the secret key during its exchange.** This is a serious security threat. In nutshell, this private key cryptography depends solely on the secrecy of the key.

Conclusions: Public key cryptography does not have a key distribution problem. **To take the flesh out of it, we say that its security relies on the fact that determining the factors of a number that is the product of two very large prime numbers is NOT computationally feasible.** On the other hand, it has been proved by Peter Shor that a **quantum computer can derive the prime factors of very large numbers in polynomial time.** It has been rightly said that public key cryptography will become insecure if quantum computing becomes a reality. And this has happened too. **Before delving into more details, just note that quantum cryptography avoids all these issues by encrypting the shared key using a series of photons.** That is,

$$\text{Quantum cryptography} \xrightarrow{\text{Encryption}} (\text{shared key + series of photons})$$

7.2 ONE-TIME PAD/ RANDOM KEY ENCRYPTION

It is also known as **Random key encryption.** This scheme was proposed by Vernam and is also known as Vernam Cipher. It encrypts data using a random key. **Please understand that the term "one-time pad" shows that the key is used one time and never used again.** Some of the salient features of this type of encryption are-

1. Assume that in this type of communication- the **sender is Alice, receiver is Bob and Eve is the intruder** (data thief).
2. The key must have the same number of bits as the data to be transmitted.
3. It must also consist of completely random bits that are kept secret from everyone except the sender and the receiver.
4. The keys are used only once as indicated above.
5. Both the sender and the receiver must destroy their keys after use.

Principle of operation:

(a) Encryption by Alice:

$$c_i = d_i + k_i \quad i=1, 2, 3\ldots\ldots$$

where d_i are data bits; k_i are key bits; c_i are encrypted data bits.

(b) Decryption by Bob:

$$d_i = c_i + k_i \quad i=1, 2, 3.......$$

Please understand that Alice (sender) encrypts the data that she sends to Bob by EX-ORing it with randomly generated key bits. Also note that Bob receives the encrypted data by EX-ORing the received data with the same key bits.

For example,

Assume that the key bits are as follows:

(100010000101100)

The problem with this approach is that here the sender and the receiver must somehow exchange the secret key bits that they use. **For instance,**

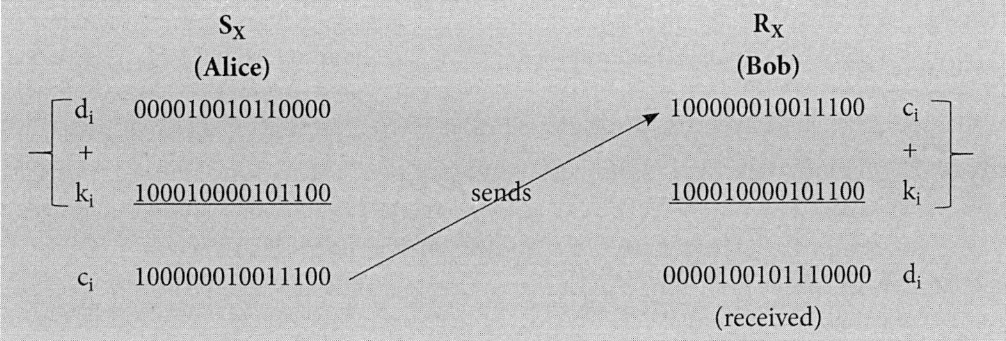

7.3 PUBLIC KEY CRYPTOGRAPHY

In **public key cryptographic system,** 2 separate keys are used i.e. **a public key and a private key. Public key is public and is made accessible to anybody.** On the other hand, **the private key is kept secret.** The entire process of encryption and decryption is shown in figure 7.1.

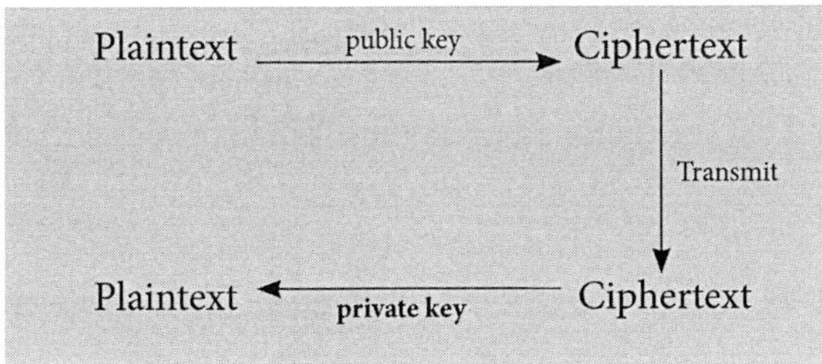

Fig.7.1: A Public key Cryptographic System

Public key cryptographic system, uses a special case of one-way function known as a **trapdoor or one-way function. Please note that a function, f(x), is considered to be a one-way function, if it is easy to calculate the function f(x) = y for any input x. Also note that the opposite i.e. computing x from f(x) is more complex unless some piece of information, the trapdoor is known.**

For example, calculating 5 * 15 = 75 is much faster than finding the prime factors of 75. But the problem can be easily solved if some additional information is given like 5 is prime factor of 75.

The point to ponder is that unlike in symmetric encryption, the 2 keys in public cryptography behave differently. That is, the public key is **the only key that can encrypt data to be sent.** A public key is freely available to anyone who wants to use it. These keys can be distributed as email attachments or through a public key chain server that stores a large number of public keys. **Although any one can have access to the public key, the encrypted data can only be decrypted by a party who knows the corresponding private key. To take the flesh out of it, the distribution of the private key is avoided because this prevents any hacker to use the key. And even if the public key falls in the hands of unauthorized persons, it is impossible to derive the decryption key from the encryption key because it is computationally infeasible.**

Working of public key cryptographic system:

Actually, the process of using public key cryptography is simple. To send a message, **the sender (Alice) obtains a copy of receiver (Bob) public key either by email or from a key chain server that stores a large number of public keys. Then, the resulting encrypted message is sent to Bob who uses his/her shared private key to restore the original message.**

Advantages of public key cryptographic system:

It does not require any **initial secure exchange of secret keys** for encrypting a message. But is requires far **longer keys** to offer the same level of protection as symmetric encryption.

Another new technique known as **elliptic curve cryptography can also be as much secure as is symmetric encryption using similar key lengths.**

7.4 RSA CODING SCHEME

RSA stands for three scientists names—**R**ivest, **S**hamir and **A**delman. It is a **public key cryptographic system.**

Working: It works by generating public and private keys, for this it chooses two large prime numbers, p and q and making N = p.q. Then, a random positive integer, e, is chosen such that it is relatively prime to (p-1) (q-1); where e is called as the **encryption constant.** Then, a decryption constant, d, is derived such that e.d = 1 mod (p-1) (q-1). The public key is (N, e) and the private key is d. **However, note that although N is revealed to all yet the factors p and q of N are kept secret. Another point to note is that if a hacker can factor N to find p and q then he can use e of the public key to derive the private key, d from the expression e.d = 1 mod (p-1) (q-1).**

Steps of RSA algorithm

S1: generate two large prime numbers, p and q and let n = pq.

S2: Let $\varphi = (p-1)(q-1)$.

S3: Choose another number, e which is relatively prime to φ; two numbers a and b that have no common factors other than 1 are said to be **co-prime or relatively prime.**

S4: Select e, $1 < e < \varphi$ such that $\gcd(e, \varphi) = 1$; gcd of 2 integers, a and b is the largest integer that divides both numbers.

S5: Find d, such that $de \equiv 1 \bmod \varphi$. **Note that the notation "a ≡ b (mod n)" means a is congruent to b** i.e. a and b have the same remainder when divided by n.

S6: **(Encryption)** Compute $c = m^e \bmod n$, where m is message block represented as a number $0 < m < n-1$ and c is the encrypted message.

S7: **(Decryption)** Compute $m = c^d \bmod n$.

Better algorithm than this one, for factoring very large numbers efficiently, was proposed by Peter Shor that has already been discussed.

Before we discuss further, let us solve an example on RSA now.

Example 1: Assume that p =3, q = 11. Show that how we would encrypt and decrypt a message m = 6 using RSA algorithm?

Solution 1: We know that the product $n = p * q = 3 * 11 = 33$.

Next, we create a quotient, $\Phi = (3 - 1)(11 - 1) = 2 * 10 = 20$.

Let $e > 1$ such that e and $\Phi = 20$ have no common factors except 1. The smallest number that satisfies this criterion is $e = 3$.

To find d, we use the following equation-

$$de = 1 + x\Phi \qquad \text{(where d is a natural number)}$$

or

$$d = (1 + 20x)/3$$

The smallest value is $x = 1$ which gives us-

$$d = (1 + 20)/3 = 21/3 = 7$$

Hence, the encrypted message that is transmitted for m=6 is as follows: -

$$c = m^e \bmod n = 6^3 \bmod 33 = 18.$$

Alice transmits this signal to Bob who holds a private key d = 7. He decrypts the message using-

$$m = c^d \bmod n = 18^7 \bmod 33 = 6.$$

7.5 QUANTUM CRYPTOGRAPHY

In physics, we have studied that quantum theory says that light is an electromagnetic wave. It is made up of lot of particles called as photons. Each photon has a specific packet of energy, $E = hf$ and a wavelength c/f. **Please recall that light has a pair of electric and magnetic fields that are perpendicular to each other. Also note that if the electric field component of a beam of light vibrates along a single direction like vertical direction then the beam of light is said to be polarized in that direction.** Also we have studied that; polarized photons can be created by passing a normal beam of light through a filter set for a specific angle of polarization. What is observed is that a photon incident on the filter will pass through it or it will be blocked. Also if the photon emerges it will be aligned to the angle of the filter irrespective of its initial polarization angle.

Heisenberg's uncertainty principle shows that certain pairs of properties, called as non-commutating properties, are related in a way that it is impossible to measure these simultaneously. Such pairs are called as conjugates pairs. We also know that photons can be polarized in 2 bases i.e. rectilinear or diagonal. Also a filter allows the transmission of a photon through it if and only if the polarization of the photon is aligned with the filter. **In rectilinear mode,** photons with only horizontal or vertical polarizations pass through the polarizing filter. On the other hand, **in diagonal mode**, only photons with polarization that are at an angle of +45° or -45° to the horizontal axis can pass through the polarizing filter. **In nutshell, in the rectilinear mode, the orientations | and – represent 0° and 90° respectively. in diagonal mode, orientations \ and / represent** +45° and +45° respectively. **Please note here that the rectilinear and diagonal polarizations constitute such a conjugate pair of non-commuting properties. Also note that a filter with** 0° / 90° orientation can correctly detect a rectilinearly polarized photon and a filter with +45° / -45° orientation detect a diagonally polarized photon. **The point to ponder is that if a diagonally polarized filter is used to detect a rectilinearly polarized photon or vice versa then the outcome will be random with equal probabilities and that the photon will lose all information of its previous state.**

Quantum communications works on the fact that information can be encoded as the polarization of photons i.e. the orientation of a photon's oscillation. An oscillation in one direction can be thought of as 0 and in another as 1. There are 2 sets of polarizations that are commonly used—rectilinear and diagonal.in order to receive the data, polarization of the filter must match that of the photons. **Please understand that the property that quantum communication exploits is that in order to receive correct information, photons have to be measured using the correct filter polarization i.e.** the same polarization that the information was transmitted with. If ta receiver is in rectilinear polarization and a diagonally polarized photon is sent then a completely random result will appear at the receiver. So, the information can be sent in such a way so as to make it impossible for a hacker to attack.

Methodology of working:

S1: The **sender transmits information** to the receiver using **random polarizations.**

S2: The **receiver detects this information**, also at random polarizations and **records it.**

S3: Then the **sender informs the receiver of the polarizations** that he used over a **public channel.**

S4: The **receiver and the sender compare a random selection** of the information that was received **at the correct polarization.**

S5: If a **hacker/eavesdropper has intercepted and forwarded the information, the receiver and the sender will be alerted, as a higher percentage of errors than expected will be present.**

S6: If a hacker has been detected, the **whole process has to be repeated.**

7.6 QUANTUM KEY DISTRIBUTION (QKD)

Encryption is the art of encoding messages. This is very much useful to protect your WhatsApp messages as well as securing of top secret data. **Encryption relies on the idea of keys.** But if you want to decrypt some data that say, I have encrypted then you must somehow know the key. But how can I do this? This is where QKD is used.

In private key cryptography, the distribution of keys is a major weakness. However, **quantum cryptography** removes and overcomes this drawback by providing a secure way of sharing a **random key between two separate parties.** Another benefit of quantum keys is that the sender and the receiver can easily verify whether the key has been tampered with or not. **Please note here that QKD is not a technique for encryption and decryption of data rather it allows secure distribution of private keys.**

The name quantum cryptography only tells that it is a form of cryptography that is based on the **laws of quantum mechanics. It promises unconditional security.** Quantum cryptography is possible because-

(a) The polarizations of photons can't be simultaneously measured in incompatible bases (like rectilinear or diagonal).

(b) The polarization of a single photon can't be obtained.

(c) It is not possible for a hacker to access a message between Alice and Bob without changing its meaning.

(d) No-cloning theorem that says that it is impossible to create a duplicate/copy state of a quantum state.

Conclusions: Symmetric keys along with Quantum Key Distribution can promise a secure generation and transmission of the private keys. That is,

Symmetric Keys + QKD → More secure communications

Also note that QKD is secure against new attacking strategies and against determined eavesdropping.

QKD solves the problem of how Alice and Bob can share a key between them without anyone else being able to find the key. So, what is happening is as follows: -

S1: Alice sends a qubit-

Alice starts by **randomly generating a bit which is either 0 or 1.** This will be the **first bit of her secret key.** Then, she generates a **second random bit. Please note that this will tell her how to encode the first bit in a qubit for Bob. Also note that if the 2nd bit is 0 then she sends the 1st bit to Bob as a qubit as follows: -**

$$0 \rightarrow |0\rangle$$
$$1 \rightarrow |1\rangle$$

This is called as using **the Z basis.**

The point to ponder is that if the 2nd bit is 1 then she sends the first bit to Bob as a qubit as follows:-

$$0 \rightarrow |+\rangle = (|0\rangle + |1\rangle) / \sqrt{2}$$
$$1 \rightarrow |-\rangle = (|0\rangle - |1\rangle) / \sqrt{2}$$

This is called as using **the X basis. Alice makes note of her two bits and then sends her qubit to Bob.**

S2: Bob receives a qubit-

This actually means that Bob receives a qubit in one of the 4 states:-

$$|0\rangle, |1\rangle, |+\rangle, |-\rangle$$

Then Bob generates a random bit himself. **If it is 0 then he will measure in the Z basis else if it is 1 then he will measure in the X basis.** Practically speaking, if he picks a different basis to the one Alice used to encode the bit then he may get a wrong answer.

For instance, if he measures $|+\rangle$ in the Z basis then because-

$$|+\rangle = (|0\rangle + |1\rangle) / \sqrt{2}$$

He will get 0, 50% of the time and 1, 50% of the time. And if he measures |0> in the X basis then because-

$$|0> = (|0> + |1>) / \sqrt{2} + (|0> - |1>) / \sqrt{2} = (|+> + |->) / \sqrt{2}$$

Then, he will get +50% of the time and -50% of the time.

S3: Getting the key

Alice and Bob repeat this process many times (n times). Alice then tells Bob and anyone else which basis she used to encode her bit like her 2nd random bit. Then Bob will check which basis he measured in like which random bit he generated. If they match then he keeps that result, if he does not, he gets rid of it. And he announces which one hs had to get rid of.

Finally, they are left with m bits where m < n.

7.7 BB84

BB stands for Bennet and Basard (1984), who proposed a quantum key distribution (QKD) protocol. Named as BB84, this protocol allows a sender (Alice) to send photons to a receiver (Bob). **Please note that Alice and Bob communicate using a one-way quantum channel and a two-way public channel.**

Three principles used in BB84 QKD are as follows:-

1. **The no-cloning theorem that states that quantum states can't be copied.** This means that **Eve cannot tap a quantum communication channel,** copy the quantum states used to create the key for himself and sends the original message down the line to Bob.
2. **Measurements results in state collapse,** as already studied. **Please note that the basic aspect of QKD is that different bases will be used to create a bit string.** As already studied, that when we make measurements in one of the given bases, we are actually causing state collapse such that measurements in the other basis are completely random. **Also note that this means that extracting some information about the state disturbs the state of the system.**
3. **Measurements are irreversible.**

Alice has a source of single photons and two polarizing filters i.e. one rectilinear and one diagonal. This is shown in figure- 7.2.

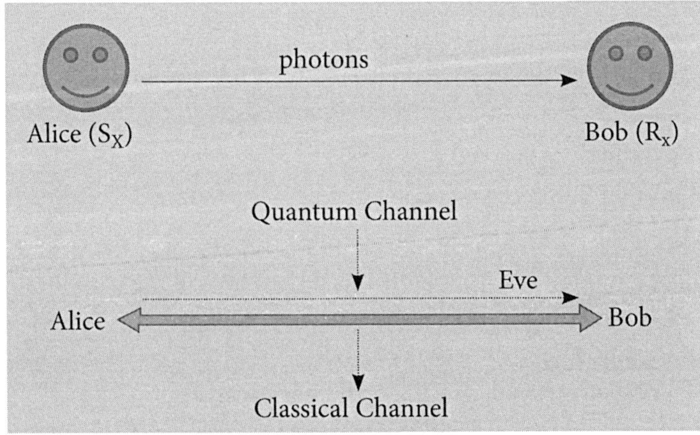

Fig.7.2: A QKD System workings

Working: The quantum channel used here is vulnerable to any possible manipulation from an eaves dropper. Alice and Bob must ensure that the hacker/ eavesdropper, usually assumed as Eve, cannot tap on the quantum channel and listen to exchanges over the classical channel. **Please recall that a photon has three types of spins** i.e. horizontal, vertical and diagonal. **Also note that an unpolarized photon has all of the three spin states at the same time.** By passing it through a polarization filter, a photon can be polarized to let through only a particular spin. All of the unwanted types are chopped off. **The point to ponder is that single photons can't be copied because the linearity of quantum mechanics does not allow cloning of unknown states.**

What BB84 Protocol is Implemented?

This protocol can be implemented using polarized single photons. Alice can transmit single photons randomly in either a rectilinear or diagonal basis. **Note that in each of this basis, one orientation of the photon is used to represent the logic value 0 and the other one to represent 1.** *To be further practical, this is accepted by Alice and Bob before the key formation begins.*

Practically speaking, in quantum cryptography ecosystem, a qubit is represented by the polarization state of a photon. Also note that the polarization state of a randomly polarized photon is a superposition of any pair of orthogonal states like Horizontal (H) and vertical (V) polarization, +45° and -45° diagonal polarization. Therefore, the polarization of a photon can be modeled by a qubit. So, now the state of the qubit is shown as below:

$$
\begin{aligned}
|\psi\rangle &= a\,|H\rangle + b\,|V\rangle \\
&= c\,|{+45°}\rangle + d\,|{-45°}\rangle
\end{aligned}
$$

where a, b, c and d are complex numbers, $|a|^2 + |b|^2 = |c|^2 + |d|^2$

Actually, for a chosen orthogonal pair, one polarized state is assumed to be |0> and the other is |1>. That is,

$$
\begin{aligned}
|V\rangle &= 1 \text{ and } |H\rangle = 0 \text{ (for a rectilinear state pair) and} \\
|{+45°}\rangle &= 1 \text{ and } |{-45°}\rangle = 0
\end{aligned}
$$

Loosely speaking, a photon can be assumed to be a qubit with one bit of quantum information. Alive and Bob both must first agree on how bits will be encoded in the polarization directions for each filter.

BB84 Protocol Steps

S1: Alice (sender) generates a random sequence of 0s and 1s. Then, she replaces each bit in the binary sequence with a randomly chosen polarization as shown in table-7.1.

Table 7.1: Features of single photons

	Basis	Angle	Polarization	Logic value
Rectilinear	⊕	0°	- (H)	0
Rectilinear	⊕	90°	| (V)	1
Diagonal	⊗	45°	/	0
Diagonal	⊗	-45°	\	1

Any quantum particle can be used to replace the bits. **But photon is preferred because they can be transmitted over longer distances without decoherence.**

S2: Alice sends the photons corresponding to each bit replacement in the binary sequence to Bob using a quantum channel. But it keeps the record of the polarization basis and also the logic value of the transmitted photons.

S3: Bob is unaware of which basis Alice has chosen for a photon. He randomly chooses one of the two bases. If he chooses the same basis as Alice, the polarization is recorded correctly. But if he chooses a different basis, the initial polarization of the received photon is lost and the result is a random polarization. **Note that bit is also possible that sometimes Bob does not register anything because of errors in detection or in transmissions.**

S4: After Bob receives all photons sent by Alice, he acknowledges that he has received and measured all of them. **Note that the bit string of photons as received by Bob is called as a raw key.**

S5: Bob now announces using a public channel, about her choice of basis for each photon. There is no security issue here as Bob reveals only which basis he has used and not the result he/she obtained. **Hence, a hacker can't get any information related to the key formation.**

S6: Alice and Bob compare the bases they selected. They discard all non-matching bases. We can say that both Alice and Bob keep only the bits corresponding to the same bases. **To take the flesh out of it, because both have randomly chosen the bases so there is an equal probability of getting matched and unmatched results.** Therefore, almost 50% of the qubits are available for forming the secret key. **Also note that the key is truly random because neither Alice nor Bob can decide which key will result at the end of the procedure.**

The point to ponder is that BB84 protocol is somewhat inefficient in its use because many key bits (about 50%) are discarded during the key formation process. Later Pasqui-nucci et al. proposed a protocol that uses three orthogonal bases and 6 states to encode the key bits. After that, Scarani proposed another variant of BB84 named as SARG04 (2004).

7.8 EKART 91 (E91)

Ekart 91 is a 3-state protocol. It uses the Einstein-Podolosky-Rosen (EPR) paradox as discussed in previous chapters. Actually, this protocol can be delineated using three polarization states of an EPR photon pair. In BB84, there are 2-stages of communication between Alice and Bob—**one over a quantum channel and the other over a public channel.** An EPR pair of photons is created in randomly selected states and 1 pair is sent to the Alice and the other to Bob using a **quantum channel. The** measurement results are put under 2 categories: -

Group-1: It comprises of bit slots for which some measurement operators are used.

Group-2: It comprises of bit slots for which different measurement operators are used.

Please note that any photons that are not measured in the 1st or the 2nd group are discarded. Also note that the 1st group is used to establish a raw key whereas the 2nd group that includes all the remaining bit slots is called a rejected key.

However, the EPR protocol, (unlike BB84) does not discard the rejected key bits. Instead, they are used to test the presence of a hacker/cracker.

For each measurement where Alice and Bob use the same basis, they should expect the opposite results due to the principle of quantum entanglement. **This means that if Alice and Bob, both interpret their measurements as bits then they each have a bit string which is the binary complement of the other. The point to ponder is that either party can invert their key and share a secret key.** Then they can use this set of common private keys to encrypt and decrypt their messages and communicate secretly. **Practically speaking, each key can be used only once and can't be repeated so as to keep the keys totally random.** The intruder (Eve) can't get any information from the photons during transmission **because the information is formed in a photon only after it is measured. Also because Eve uses a wrong basis, so she doesn't known what the result was.**

In this method of quantum cryptography, EKERT, works on quantum entanglement only. We create a Bell state that gives one member of the EPR pair to Alice and the 2nd member of the EPR pair to Bob. Assume that the state used for the EPR pair is-

$$|\beta_{00}\rangle = (|00\rangle + |10\rangle) / \sqrt{2}$$

We know that Alice and Bob will have measurement results that are completely correlated. On the other hand, if the state used is-

$$|\beta_{01}\rangle = (|01\rangle + |10\rangle) / \sqrt{2}$$

Then Alice and Bob will have measurement results that are perfectly anticorrelated. Alice and Bob measure their respective qubits in randomly chosen bases. Then they communicate over an ordinary channel and find out on which bit positions they used the same basis. They keep these bits to create the key. **Also note that as the measurement results will be perfectly correlated or perfectly anticorrelated, therefore, it is easy for Alice and Bob to find out on which bit positions they used the same basis.** They will keep these bits to create a key.

The point to ponder is that because the measurement results will be perfectly correlated or perfectly anticorrelated so it is easy for Alice and Bob to detect whether or not a hacker is present.

Before we close this chapter, let us solve some problems now.

Example 1: Let p = 3, q = 11. Show how we would encrypt and decrypt a message m = 6 using the RSA algorithm. Is there any other algorithm that can easily crack this RSA encryption scheme?

Solution 1:

Step-1: Create the product, $n = pq = 3 * 11 = 33$

Step-2: We create the quotient, $\Phi = (3 - 1)(11 - 1) = 2 * 10 = 20$

Let $e > 1$ such that e and $\Phi = 20$ have no common factors except 1. Now the smallest number that satisfies this criterion is $e = 3$. To find d, we use the following equation and find the smallest x such that-

$$de = 1 + x\Phi$$

(where d is a natural number).

So, we get-

$$d = (1 + 20x) / 3$$

The smallest value is $x = 1$, that gives-

$$d = (1 + 20) / 3 = 21/3 = 7$$

The encrypted message that is transmitted for $m = 6$ is-

$$c = m^e \bmod n = 6^3 \bmod 33 = 18$$

Alice transmits this signal to Bob who holds the private key d = 7. He decrypts the message using the equation-

$$m = c^d \bmod n = 18^7 \bmod 33 = 6$$

The algorithm given by Peter Shor can easily crack an RSA encryption scheme by a quantum computer as a quantum computer can easily crack an RSA encryption scheme. **Note that this is so because n = pq can be easily factored.**

Example 2: Define what is privacy amplification?

Solution 2: In Quantum Key Distribution (QKD), a refined key is created in a process known as **privacy amplification.** This process involves throwing away of the qubits that Eve (hacker/cracker) could have attempted to measure. **For example,** if the key initially has 20 bits (say) and Eve knew, say about 6 of the bits then the refined key is created by simply throwing away those 6 bits and leaving a 14-bit key.

Example 3: How BB84 QKD works?

Solution 3: Alice (sender) and Bob (receiver) publicly agree to the relationship between spins and bit value as follows: -

Spin	↑	←	↓	→
Bit value	0	0	1	1

This table shows the relationship between the spin and bit values for quantum cryptography.

The Quantum Part

S1: Alice randomly chooses either x or z basis.

S2: Alice sends an **electron in superposition** in the chosen basis, **measures** the spin and **records** the corresponding bit value as 0 or 1. **The electron** is sent to **Bob.**

S3: Bob randomly chooses either the x or z basis.

S4: Bob measures the spin of the electron and **records** whether it was 0 or 1.

S5: Repeat steps S1 to S4 till the desired level of security is obtained.

SUMMARY

The problem in key distribution in secret key cryptography can be removed with the aid of quantum technology. In quantum ecosystem, one can't measure something without causing noise to other related parameter. For detecting qubit, Bob will use a polarization beam splitter. The polarization beam splitter is a device that allows the photons of orthogonal polarization to pass through but shunts the photon of other polarization. **Please understand that it is the quantum nature that dictates 2 things:**

(a) **The same basis beam splitter will pass the received same basis polarized photons.**

(b) **The rectilinear beam splitter will pass the received diagonally polarized photons either as vertical or horizontal polarized photons with equal probability.**

Also note that when both Alice and Bob use the splitter on same basis they will correctly communicate the qubits whereas when they use on different basis, then the chance of matching between sent and received qubits is 50%. If any hacker attempts to hack the photon transmission then only garbage will be acted by both. **This is so because the quantum theory ensures that without changing the phase of the photon, an intercepted photon can't be retransmitted.**

The problem of key distribution can be mitigated by quantum cryptography only. The war between **code-makers and code-breakers** continues to rage on. Hence, quantum cryptography is here for their rescue.

MULTIPLE CHOICE QUESTIONS (MCQS) WITH ANSWERS

1. One-time pad encryption is also known as-
   (a) Vietnam Cipher.
   (b) Vernam Cipher.
   (c) Verna Cipher.
   (d) None of the above.
2. Which of the following are the three principles used in BB84-
   (a) Parallelism, superposition, entanglement.
   (b) Interference, superposition, entanglement.
   (c) No-cloning theorem, measurement collapsing, Irreversible measurements.
   (d) None of the above.
3. When we regularly change the key, it means that we are using-
   (a) One-time pad.
   (b) Padding.
   (c) Cladding.
   (d) None of the above.
4. A technique of quantum cryptography that is based on quantum entanglement is-
   (a) EKERT.
   (b) EPERT.
   (c) ECERT.
   (d) None of the above.
5. In QFD, a refined key is created in a process known as-
   (a) Phase amplification.
   (b) Privacy amplification.
   (c) Amplitude amplification.
   (d) None of the above.
6. Public key cryptography uses a method of encoding and decoding that uses a special case of one-way function called as-
   (a) Trapdoor.
   (b) Corridor.
   (c) Distribution of keys.
   (d) None of the above.
7. Which is the best secure method of transmission of private keys-
   (a) Symmetric key + asymmetric key.
   (b) Symmetric key + QKD.
   (c) Asymmetric key + QKD.
   (d) None of the above.
8. Symmetric algorithms are less impacted by quantum computing than asymmetric algorithms because-
   (a) Their long size makes them quantum safe.
   (b) Their use of diffusion makes them quantum safe.
   (c) They are not predicated on specific mathematical problems that a quantum computer can solve.
   (d) None of the above.
9. The problem of distributing the key of a symmetric cipher is known as-
   (a) Key distribution problem.
   (b) Knapsack problem.

(c) TSP.

(d) None of the above.

10. One of the properties of a photon that can be used to encode a bit is-

(a) Photon's electromagnetic state.

(b) Photon's polarization state.

(c) Photon's excited state.

(d) None of the above.

11. Asymmetric cryptography uses how many keys?

(a) 2

(b) 4

(c) 1

(d) 3

12. In asymmetric-key cryptography, the private key must be-

(a) Shared.

(b) Distributed.

(c) Secret.

(d) None of these.

13. In asymmetric key cryptography, if Alice wants to communicate with Bob, the Bob must know-

(a) Alice's private key.

(b) Alice's public key.

(c) Bob's private key.

(d) All of the above.

14. Sender encrypts the message with his private key, this provides-

(a) Confidentiality.

(b) Authentication.

(c) Both 'a' and 'b'.

(d) Only confidentiality.

15. In RSA, to decrypt a message we need-

(a) Sender's private key.

(b) Sender's public key.

(c) Receiver's private key.

(d) Receiver's public key.

Answers															
1.	(b)	2.	(c)	3.	(a)	4.	(a)	5.	(b)	6.	(a)	7.	(b)	8.	(c)
9.	(a)	10.	(b)	11.	(a)	12.	(c)	13.	(b)	14.	(c)	15.	(c)		

CONCEPTUAL SHORT QUESTIONS WITH ANSWERS

Q1. Give an example of asymmetric encryption from real life.

Ans. 1 Secure Socket Layer (SSL) algorithm which uses public cryptosystem to encrypt your web session when you are making is purchase are also called as asymmetric encryptions.

Q2. What are the rules/protocols for QKD?

Ans. 2 The protocols for quantum key distribution are based on the idea of transmitting non-orthogonal qubit states and then checking for the disturbance in their transmitted states.

Q3. Explain the first QKD protocol, BB84 as proposed by Bennett and Brassard in 1984.

Ans. 3 The following is the protocol-

S1: Alice selects n i.e. the approx. length of the desired encryption key. Then, she generates two random strings of bits 'a' and 'b' of length $(4n + \delta)$.

S2: Alice encodes the bits in string 'a' using the bits in string 'b' to choose the basis (either X or Z) for each qubit in a. she generates $|\psi>$, a block of $(4n + \delta)$ qubits. That is,

$$|\psi\rangle = \bigotimes_{k=1}^{4n+\delta} |\psi\, a_k\, b_k\rangle$$

Where a_k and b_k are the k-th bits of strings 'a' and 'b' respectively.

Please understand that each qubit is in one of the four pure states in two bases, [|0>, |1>]. The four states are as follows: -

$$|\psi\rangle_{00} = |0\rangle$$
$$|\psi\rangle_{10} = |1\rangle$$
$$|\psi\rangle_{01} = (1/\sqrt{2})\,(|0\rangle + |1\rangle)$$
$$|\psi\rangle_{11} = (1/\sqrt{2})\,(|0\rangle - |1\rangle)$$

S3: If ε describes the combined effect of the channel noise and Carol's interference, then the **block of qubits received by Bob is** $\varepsilon\,(|\psi\rangle\langle\psi|)$.

S4: Bob constructs a random string of bits, b', of length (4n + δ). Then, he measures every qubit either in X basis or in Z basis depending on the value of the corresponding bit of b'. So, after his measurement, he constructs the binary string, a'. He informs Alice on a classical channel that he now expects the information about, 'b'.

S5: Alice uses the classical channel to disclose 'b'.

S6: Alice and Bob exchange information over the classical channel

Q4. Distinguish between symmetric and asymmetric cryptography key algorithms.

Ans.4 The following table distinguishes between the two-

Symmetric-Key cryptography	Asymmetric-key cryptography
1. It uses a **single key** for both encryption and decryption of data.	1. It uses **two different keys**—public key for encryption and private key for decryption.
2. Both the communicating parties share the **same algorithm and the key.**	2. Both the communicating parties should have **at least one of the matched pair of keys.**
3. The processes of encryption and decryption are very **fast.**	3. The encryption and decryption processes are **slower** as compared to symmetric-key cryptography.
4. **Key distribution** is a problem.	4. **Key distribution is not** a problem.
5. The size of the encrypted text is **usually same or less** than the original text.	5. The size of the encrypted text is **usually more** than the original text.
6. It can only be used for confidentiality i.e. for **only encryption and decryption of data.**	6. It can be used for **confidentiality of data as well as for integrity and non-repudiation checks** i.e. for digital signatures.
7. **DES and AES are** the commonly used symmetric-key algorithms.	7. **RSA** is the most commonly used asymmetric-key algorithm.

Q5. Encrypt the plaintext 6 using RSA public key encryption algorithm. Use prime numbers 11 and 3 to compute the public key and private key. Also, decrypt the cipher text using the private key.

Ans. 5

Given: $p = 11$ and $q = 3$

Thus, $n = p * q = 11 * 3 = 33$

$\Phi(n) = (p - 1) * (q - 1) = (11 - 1) * (3 - 1) = 10 * 2 = 20$

We choose D = 3 (a number relatively prime to 20 i.e. gcd (20, 3) = 1)

Now, $E * D = 1 \bmod n = E * 3 = 1 \bmod 20$

Or $E = 7$

As already studied, the public key consists of (E, p) and the private key consists of (D, p).

Hence, the public key is (7, 33) and the private key is (3, 33).

The plaintext 6 can be converted into the ciphertext using the public key (7, 33) as follows-

$$C = P^E \bmod n = 6^7 \bmod 33 = 30$$

If we apply the private key to the ciphertext 30, we will get the original plaintext as follows-

$$P = C^D \bmod n = (30)^3 \bmod 33 = 6$$

Q6. List the steps of RSA algorithm for encryption and decryption of messages. Apply these steps to say, p = 11 and q = 3.

Ans. 6 The following are the steps followed: -

S1: Compute n as the product of two primes p and q i.e. n = p * q. These two primes are very large and randomly selected primes.

S2: Compute f (n) = (p – 1) (q – 1).

S3: Select e such that e is relatively prime to f (n).

S4: Select d such that e * d = 1 mod (f (n)), where mod stands for modular operation.

S5: Choose (e, n) as the public key.

S6: Choose (d, n) as the private key.

Please note that in encryption and decryption, receiver's public key (e R, n R) and private key (d R, n R) are used. Also note that encryption is carried out by using m e = m e R mod n R, where m is the plain text and me is the cipher text. And that the decryption is carried out by using m = (m d R) dR mod n R. However, for authentication, sender's public key (e s, n s) and private key (d s, n s) are used. The signature is generated by using m c = m ds mod n s. The signature is authenticated by using m = (m c) e s mod n s.

S1: Select primes, $p = 11, q = 3.$

S2: $n = p * q = 11 * 3 = 33$

$\Phi = (p - 1)(q - 1) = 10 * 2 = 20$

S3: Choose $e = 3.$

Check gcd (e, p-1) = gcd (3, 10) = 1 (as 3 and 10 have no common factors except 1).

And check $\gcd(e, q\text{-}1) = \gcd(3,2) = 1$

So, $\gcd(e, \Phi) = \gcd(e, (p\text{-}1)(q\text{-}1)) = \gcd(3, 20) = 1.$

S4: Compute d such that ed α^{-1} (mod Φ)

i.e. compute $d = e^{-1} \bmod \Phi = 3^{-1} \bmod 20$

i.e. find a value for d such that Φ divides (ed – 1).

i.e. find d such that 20 divides 3d-1.

Simple testing (d = 1, 2, 3,....) gives d = 7.

Checking: ed – 1 = 3.7 -1 = 20, which is divisible by Φ.

S5: **Public key** = (n, e) = (33, 3), used **to encrypt the message.**

Private key = (n d) = (33, 7), used **to decrypt the message.**

Note that this is actually the smallest possible value for the mod n for which the RSA algorithm works.

Say, now we want to encrypt the message, m = 7, then

$$c = m^e \bmod n = 7^3 \bmod 33 = 343 \bmod 33 = 13.$$

So, the ciphertext $c = 13.$

To check decryption, we compute-

$$m` = c^d \bmod n = 13^7 \bmod 33 = 7.$$

Also note that we don't have to calculate the full value of 13 to the power 7. We can make use of the fact that-

$$a = bc \bmod n = (b \bmod n).(c \bmod n) \bmod n$$

Practically speaking, we can break down a potentially large number into its components and combine the results of easier, smaller calculations to calculate the final value.

One way of calculating m` is given below-

$$m` = 13^7 \bmod 33 = 13^{(3+3+1)} \bmod 33 = 13^3.\ 13^3.\ 13 \bmod 33$$
$$= (13^3 \bmod 33).\ (13^3 \bmod 33).\ (13 \bmod 33) \bmod 33$$
$$= (2197 \bmod 33).\ (2197 \bmod 33).\ (13 \bmod 33) \bmod 33$$
$$= 19.19.13 \bmod 33 = 4693 \bmod 33 = 7.$$

Hence, the encrypted cipher can also be decrypted with the help of private key value (33, 7).

Q7. Using public key cryptography system with a = 1, b = 2....etc. Solve the following-

(a) If p = 7 and q = 11, list five legal values for d.

(b) If p = 13 and q = 31 and d =7, find e.

(c) Using p = 5, q = 11 and d = 27, find e and encrypt "abcdefghij".

Ans. 7

(a)

$$p = 7$$
$$q = 11$$
$$d = ?$$

Now, $z = \Phi(n) = (p-1)(q-1)$

$= (7-1)(11-1)$

$= 6 * 10 = 60$

$n = pq = 7 * 11 = 77$

Select integer 'd' which is relatively prime to z.

$\gcd(\Phi(n).d) = 1$

Factors of 60 are 2, 2, 3, 5

So, the value for 'd' is 7, 11, 13, 17, 19

(b) $p = 13 \quad q = 31$ and $d = 7, e = ?$

$z = \Phi(n) = (p-1)(q-1) = (13-1)(31-1) = 12 * 30 = 360$

$n = pq = 13 * 31 = 403$

Compute $ed = 1 \bmod (\Phi(n))$

To compute e, check the condition-

$ed \pmod{(\Phi(n))} = 1$

given: $e = 103$ for $d = 7$

check the value.

$103 * 7 \pmod{360} = 1$

$721 \bmod 360 = 1$

$1 = 1$

Hence, for given d = 7, the value for e = 103.

(c) $p = 5 \quad q = 11$ and $d = 27 \quad e = ?$

$z = \Phi(n) = (p-1)(q-1) = (5-1)(11-1) = 4 * 10 = 40.$

$n = p * q = 5 * 11 = 55$

$ed = 1 \bmod \Phi(n)$

$e_{27} = 1 \bmod (40)$

$e = 3.$

The following table shows this-

Plaintext (P)			Encrypt (C)
Symbolic	**Numeric**	**P^3**	**P^3 mod (55)**
a	1	1	1
b	2	8	8
c	3	27	27
d	4	64	09
e	5	125	15
f	6	216	51

Plaintext (P)			Encrypt (C)
Symbolic	Numeric	P^3	P^3 mod (55)
g	7	343	13
h	8	512	17
i	9	729	14
j	10	1000	10

Please note that the decryption key could not be derived from the encryption key. The encryption algorithm, E and the decryption algorithm, D, has to meet the following three requirements as follows: -

1. D (E (P)) = P.
2. It is difficult to deduce D from E.
3. E can't be broken by a chosen plaintext attack.

Also note that if we apply, D, to an encrypted message, E (P), we get the original plaintext message, P back. For the 2nd condition, we can't deduce D from E. E is the encryption key, so it can't be made public.

Q8. What are the merits and demerits of public key cryptography ad secret key cryptography?

Ans. 8 The main advantage of public-key cryptography is to increase the security. We know that the private keys should never be transmitted or open to anybody.

In a secret-key system, the secret keys must be transmitted since the same key is used for encryption and decryption. It may be possible that a hacker can discover the secret key during transmission. Another merit of public key systems is that they can provide digital signatures that cannot be repudiated. By digital signature, we mean-

Encrypted with private key

Hash function → Message digest ---------------------> Digital signature

Using **hash function/ fast cryptographic algorithm** we can form a **message digest** which is then **encrypted with private key** to form **a digital signature.** They are authentic.

On the other hand, authentication via secret key systems requires the sharing of some secret and the trust of a third party too. As a result a sender can repudiate a previously authenticated message.

Q9. Define what is a digital envelope?

Ans. 9 For encryption, the best solution is to combine public and secret key systems in order to gate both the security benefits of public key systems and the speed advantages of the secret key systems. **Such a protocol is called as a digital envelope.**

Q10. What is a quantum channel?

Ans. 10 In quantum cryptography, we have to send qubits from one location to another. **This process of moving qubits takes place over what is loosely called as a quantum channel. Please understand that this can't be done over classical transmission cables like copper wires.**

Q11. What is the difference between a raw key and a rejected key?

Ans. 11 Any photons that are not measured in the first or the 2nd group are discarded. The 1st group is used to establish a **raw key.** On the other hand, the 2nd group that includes all of the remaining bit slots is called as a **rejected key.**

EXERCISE QUESTIONS

Q1. Consider the following states-

$$|\psi\rangle = a|0\rangle + b|1\rangle \quad |a|^2 + |b|^2 = 1$$

$$|\Phi\rangle = |\psi\rangle \otimes 1/\sqrt{2}\,(|00\rangle + |11\rangle)$$

Show how the measurement of first two qubits of $|\Phi\rangle$ can be used to obtain $|\psi\rangle$ as the last qubit. Alice has the first qubit of $|\Phi\rangle$ and Alice and Bob share the second and the third qubits of $|\Phi\rangle$.

Q2. Say, Alice and Bob exchange 2 billion qubits in order to use the BB84 quantum cryptography protocol. Find out what will be the length of their bit-key? Assume that they do not check for eavesdropping.

Q3. Alice and Bob perform 20 bit key measurements but do not share any information about the bits. What is the probability that Eve will guess the correct 20-bit key?

[**Hint:** $(1/20)^{20} = 10^{-6}$].

Q4. Suppose an eavesdropper, Eve discovers that the no-cloning theorem is wrong and finds a way to clone the state of each photon. How could she use a cloning machine to learn about the entire key?

Q6. Using the RSA algorithm with $p = 3$ and $q = 19$, encrypt and decrypt the message $m = 42$.

Q7. Alice creates an 8 bit string as follows-

$$|0\rangle\,|1\rangle\,|+\rangle\,|0\rangle\,|0\rangle\,|-\rangle\,|+\rangle\,|-\rangle$$

If Bob randomly measures in the following order using the bases $\{|0\rangle, |1\rangle\}\{|0\rangle, |1\rangle\}$, $\{|+\rangle\,|+\rangle\}\,|+\rangle\,|0\rangle, |1\rangle\,|+\rangle\,|+\rangle$. Describe the bit string that Alice and Bob keep.

Q8. For the following, find the private key-

(a) $p = 61, q = 53$.

(b) $p = 17, q = 11$.

Q9. What is the formula for encrypting with RSA?

Q10. How quantum computing solves the key distribution problem?

[**Hints:** symmetric key cryptography

They provide confidential security measure

↓

Key distribution is the major problem

Solutions are-

↙ ↘

Public key cryptography with 2 keys Quantum security.]

Q11. Write RSA algorithm if N = 187 and the encryption key, E = 17, find out the corresponding private key.

Q12. Alice is using a toy version of the DSS signature scheme with a prime modulus P = 47 and generator g = 2 of order q = 23. By chance, Alice generates signatures for two different messages with the same per message random number, k. The hash codes of the two signed messages are 2 and 3 and signatures are (4, 21) and (4, 19) respectively, compute Alice private key.

Q13. Define the following terms-

(a) Plaintext.

(b) Ciphertext.

(c) Cipher.

(d) Cryptanalysis (code breaking).

(e) Cryptology.

Q14. Let p = 3, q = 11 and d = 3. Calculate the public key using RSA technique. Suppose that A wants to send a message M = 107 to B. Sign and verify this message using the RSA digital signature scheme.

Q15. Discuss the main principles of information security?

Q16. Explain One-time pad/ Random Key Encryption method.

Q17. What is Quantum Key Distribution?

Q18. Explain BB84 protocol. What do 84 represent in BB84 protocol? What is a raw key in it?

Q19. Explain Ekert-91, 3-state protocol.

Q20. What are the rules followed for quantum cryptography?

[**Hints:**

1. The value of each bit is encoded on the property of a photon.
2. The propagation of a photon is the oscillation direction of its electric field.
3. When a photon passes through the correct filter, its polarization does not change.
4. When a photon passes through the in-correct filter, its polarization is modified.
5. Light is a stream of photons. But it also behaves as a transverse wave and sometimes as particle.
6. The horizontal photon will pass through a 45° angle.]

Q21. What are the two main problems with secret-key encryption?

Q22. "Quantum cryptography resolves the glitches of secret-key cryptography". Justify this statement.

Q23. What are the three main quantum hardware elements for Quantum Internet?

[**Hints:** quantum channel, quantum repeaters and end nodes are must].

Q24. Construct some use cases based on quantum computing.

[**Hints:** quantum prediction, bank's risk classification, quantum and the automobile industry].

Q25. Write a Python program to simulate BB84 protocol.

Experiments in Quantum Computing Lab. (using Python)

A

APPENDIX A: PRACTICAL PROGRAMS BASED ON QUANTUM COMPUTING (IBM-QISKIT) USING PYTHON.

Experiment No. 1: To study the steps for installation of IBM-QisKit.

Experiment No. 2: To implement basic quantum gates using Qiskit.

Experiment No. 3: To implement NOT, AND, NAND, OR, XOR gates using Qiskit.

Experiment No. 4: To create a single qubit, one classical register to measure the qubit and then apply Pauli-X gate (bit flip) on the qubit and finally measure its value using Qiskit.

Experiment No. 5: To create a basic quantum entanglement circuit using Qiskit.

Experiment No. 6: To create a half-adder quantum circuit using Qiskit.

Experiment No. 7: To implement quantum teleportation using Qiskit.

Experiment No. 8: To implement Grover's algorithm using Qiskit.

Experiment No. 9: To implement a block Sphere showing qubits using Qiskit.

Experiment No. 10:To implement quantum solution to Simon's problem in Qiskit.

Experiment No. 11:To implement quantum solution to Deutsch's problem in Qiskit.

QISKIT-BASED PROGRAMS FOR EXPERIMENTS FROM 1 TO 11.

Experiment No. 1: To study the steps for installation of QISKit.

Solution-1: QISKIT (by IBM) stands for Quantum Information Software kit. It is a powerful tool for the developers and the researchers to explore the potential of quantum computing. It provides a user-friendly interface for programming quantum circuits, simulating quantum algorithms and running experiments on real time hardware. It is built on Python.

The following steps may be followed in order to install Qiskit: -

The supporting Operating Systems:

1. **Windows 7 or later versions.**
2. **MacOS 10.12.6 or later.**
3. **Ubuntu 16.04 or later.**

Prerequsities:

1. **Python 3.5 or later.**
2. **Anaconda, a tool by Python for scientific computing.**

For better and safer programming, use Python virtual environments to cleanly separate Qiskit from other applications. I have installed anaconda3 and qiskit in the following directory-

C:\> Users>HP>anaconda3>lib>site-packages>qiskit

S1: open the terminal: Open the terminal where you want to work and type the following commands-

- Conda creare –n name_of_my_env python=3
- Activate the environment: source activate name_of_my_env

Use conda command to specify the version of Python included with its libraries.

On Windows operating system: -

S1: Install Anaconda.

S2: Search for Anaconda prompt.

S3: Open Anaconda prompt.

Use the following commands-

- conda creatre –n name_of_my_env python = 3
- activate name_of_my_env

Now, install Qiskit package that comes with Terra, Aer, Ignis and Aqua.

- pip install qiskit

Note: If you already have Qiskit installed on your system and want to upgrade, first uninstall it using pip install qiskit and install the latest version using the command-

!pip install qiskit[all]

How to verify the installation?

For listing the packages, use conda list command.

Optional dependencies: If you feel it essential, you can install by using:

1 pip install qiskit-terra[visualization]

2. **Importing Qiskit:**

After the completion of the above given steps, import Qiskit to Python using the command:

import qiskit

Some note on access to IBM Q Systems:

You may also get access to IBM Q Systems. IBM Q gives users an exposure to several real quantum computers and high-performance classical computing simulators through IBM Q Experience with Qiskit.

Steps to follow to set up Qiskit environment:

Step-1: Create a free IBM Q experience account.

Step-2: Go to My Account to view your account settings.

Step-3: Click on Copy token to copy the token. Paste the API token into a text editor for later use to create an account configuration file.

Step-4: Run the commands to store your API token for later use in a file called **qiskitrc.** Replace MY_API_TOKEN with the API token value that you previously stored in your text editor.

We import IBMQ as follows: -

from qiskit import IBMQ

IBMQ.save_account('MY_API_TOKEN')

How to check the version?

In order to check the version of Qiskit that you have installed use the following command-

command qiskit_version_

Input: qiskit._version_

Output: '0.9.1'

To get all of the versions of the Qiskit elements in your environment you may use the following command:

Qiskit._qiskit_version_

Another alternative method given by Google: -

Google has given a free, open working environment named as **Google's colab** (colaboratory). A programmer of Python working on Qiskit programming can directly use colab too. It is an integrated environment with notebooks in Jupyter and with just one click you can run the entire Qiskit code. Also, it is called as **eGoogle colab.** Go to *https://colab.research.google.com/* to use colab.

The Jupyter notebook: Jupyter notebook is an open-source web-based application that acts as a Python programming language interface. To install Jupyter Notebook, we can use a package manager like 'pip'. If Python is not installed, download and install it using the following URL:

https://www.python.org/downloads/

When the Python installation is complete, we can proceed to install Jupyter Notebook as follows:

pip install notebook

After the installation, we can start Jupyter Notebook as follows:

jupyter notebook

Now we can use the Jupyter Notebook to run quantum computing programs. To do this, we must install qiskit using pip command i.e.

!pip install qiskit

Various methods used during qiskit programming

1. **QuantumCircuit:** It is a class in IBM Qiskit that represents a quantum circuit.
2. **transpile:** It is a function provided by IBM Qiskit that transforms a quantum circuit into an optimized version that can be executed on a specific quantum device.
3. **assemble:** It is a function that converts a transpiled quantum circuit into a form that can be executed on a backend, a quantum device or a simulator. It prepares the circuit for execution by converting it into a format that the backend understands. This is required before we submit the circuit for execution.

   So, in nutshell we can say that-

   - **QuantumCircuit** is a class in qiskit package used to construct quantum circuits. For every quantum gate, the related methods are present in this QuantumCircuit class. In fact, a quantum circuit is created in 2 steps:-
   - **Importing QuantumCircuit from qiskit.**
   - **Providing qubits as the first argument and classical bit (optional) as the second argument for a quantum circuit.**
   - **'transpile'** is used to optimize circuits for specific backends.
   - **'assemble'** prepares transpiled circuits for execution on those backends.

   Please note that an integration of all these components is essential for working with IBM's qiskit to design, optimize and run the quantum circuits and related experiments.
4. **draw( ) method:** a method in qiskit that is used to visualize quantum circuits. It provides a graphical representation of the quantum circuit.
5. **barrier( ) method:** a method used to isolate specific parts of a quantum circuit so as to improve the clarity of the circuit. **Also note the following points regarding barrier( ) method-**
   (a) **using a barrier( ) method in a quantum circuit program means that there will be no optimization across that barrier by the compiler or transpiler.**
   (b) **As a rule, quantum gates before the barrier are executed first as compared to quantum gates that exist after the barrier.**
6. **measure( ) method:** As already studied that as we measure a quantum state, then this quantum state collapses to a classical bit only. This measurement of qubit can be done using measure( ) method only. It takes 2 parameters- the qubits to be measured and the classical bits where the measurement outcomes will be stored. It's syntax is-

qc.measure (qubit_list, classical_bit_list)

7. **measure_all( ) method:** A method that is used to add measurement operations to all qubits in a quantum circuit.
8. **append( ) method:** This method allows us to customize and extend quantum circuits with our quantum operations or gates.
9. **copy( ) method:** A method in qiskit that creates a **deep copy of a quantum circuit. A deep copy** actually makes an entirely new and independent copy of the circuit including all its gates and instructions. This copy is separate from the original circuit. **Also note that any modifications made to the copied circuit will not affect the original and vice versa.**
10. **decompose( ) method:** It provides a way to express complex operations in form of elementary gates that can be then executed on the target device.
11. qiskit-chemistry is package, qiskit.chemistry is the module within it and QiskitChemistry is the class within qiskit.chemistry.

    Visualization of quantum data in qiskit:

    There are 2 ways of visualization of quantum data:-

    (a) **Statevector Visualization:** In this laboratory manual, we have used the **plot_bloch_multivector function** to visualize the state of a quantum circuit on the block sphere.

    (b) **Quantum Circuit Visualization:** Qiskit package provides a powerful circuit visualization tool using **qiskit.visualization.** In this lab. Manual, we have used **plot_histogram and plot_state_city functions** to visualize the results of the quantum circuits. Before executing any qiskit code, we should install the qiskit_aer package using the following command:

    !pip install qiskit-aer

12. **plot_state_qsphere( ):** This function is used to define and visualize the state of a quantum system on a **Q-sphere. Q-sphere is a spherical representation that provides a simple way to visualize the quantum state's amplitude and phases.**

Various tools offered by IBM for quantum programming

(a) **IBM Quantum Lab.:** A platform that provides access to quantum hardware.

(b) **IBM Quantum Composer:** It is a web-based GUI that allows users to design and create quantum circuits. It provides a drag-and-drop interface so that the user can use it easily. **Please understand that it is a visual quantum computing interface provided by the IBM Quantum that allows users to design, simulate and execute quantum circuits without requiring deep knowledge of quantum programming languages.** It follows the following steps:-

S1: Access IBM Quantum Composer through the IBM Quantum Experience platform that is a cloud-based platform providing access to real quantum computers, simulators and various quantum resources. You need to create an IBM Quantum account or signing in is needed to get started.

S2: Create a new quantum circuit using the composer interface that provides a grid where we can drag and drop quantum gates onto qubits.

S3: Simulate the quantum circuit by clicking on the "Run" button or the "Simulate" button.

There are four main libraries of qiskit – Terra, Aqua, Aer and Ignis. These four libraries are named after classical elements, earth, water, air and fire. They provide support for everything from hardware emulation and simulation to full-fledged applications.

Terra: Qiskit's low-level codes are located in this Terra library. Open QASM language-based tools for modeling and manipulating quantum circuits and tools for manipulating pulses using Open Pulse are among them. It provides transpilers to improve the performance of quantum circuits on actual hardware like by decreasing the number of CNOT gates. Terra also includes the framework necessary to model physical noise processes. Terra also supplies the interfaces and data structures required to define and pass various quantum computing software constructs between both the different hardware and qiskit libraries.

Aqua: Aqua library supports advanced quantum algorithms. Aqua creates the real quantum circuits utilizing Terra constructions, once the user supplies the application structure and specifications.

Aer: Aer consists of a suite of emulators and imitators for deploying quantum circuits and functions. It facilitates the faster construction of quantum computation by providing an extremely useful and practical means of testing initial versions of such programs.

Ignis: It is a library that consists of all of the concepts and algorithms of methods used to characterize, verify, mitigate and rectify quantum hardware. For carefully classifying and characterizing noise processes in hardware, some methods are like randomized benchmarking and multi-modality tomography simulated evaluations.

Experiment No. 2: To implement basic quantum gates using Qiskit.

Solution-2: The qiskit code along with the output is shown for different basic quantum gates.

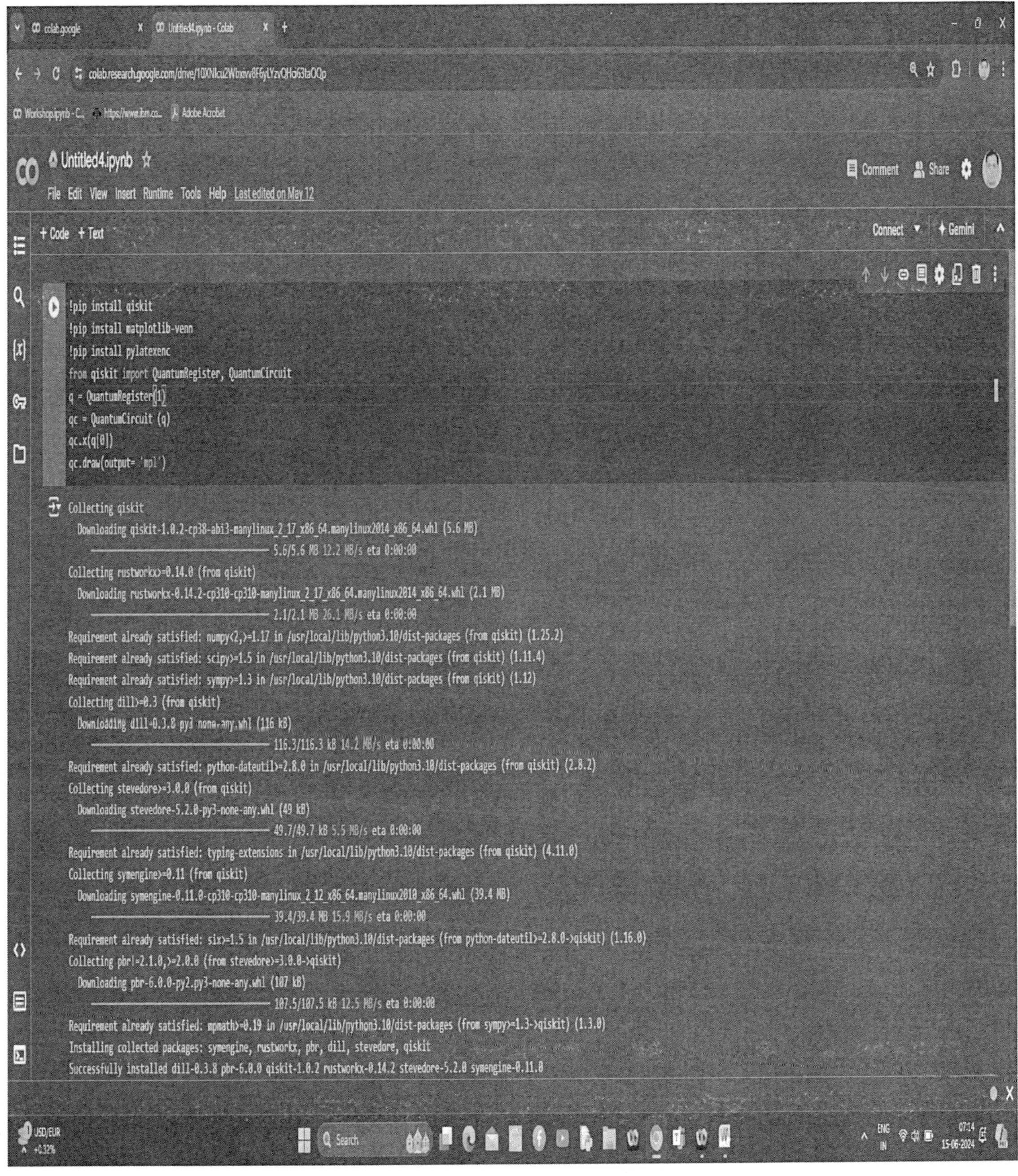

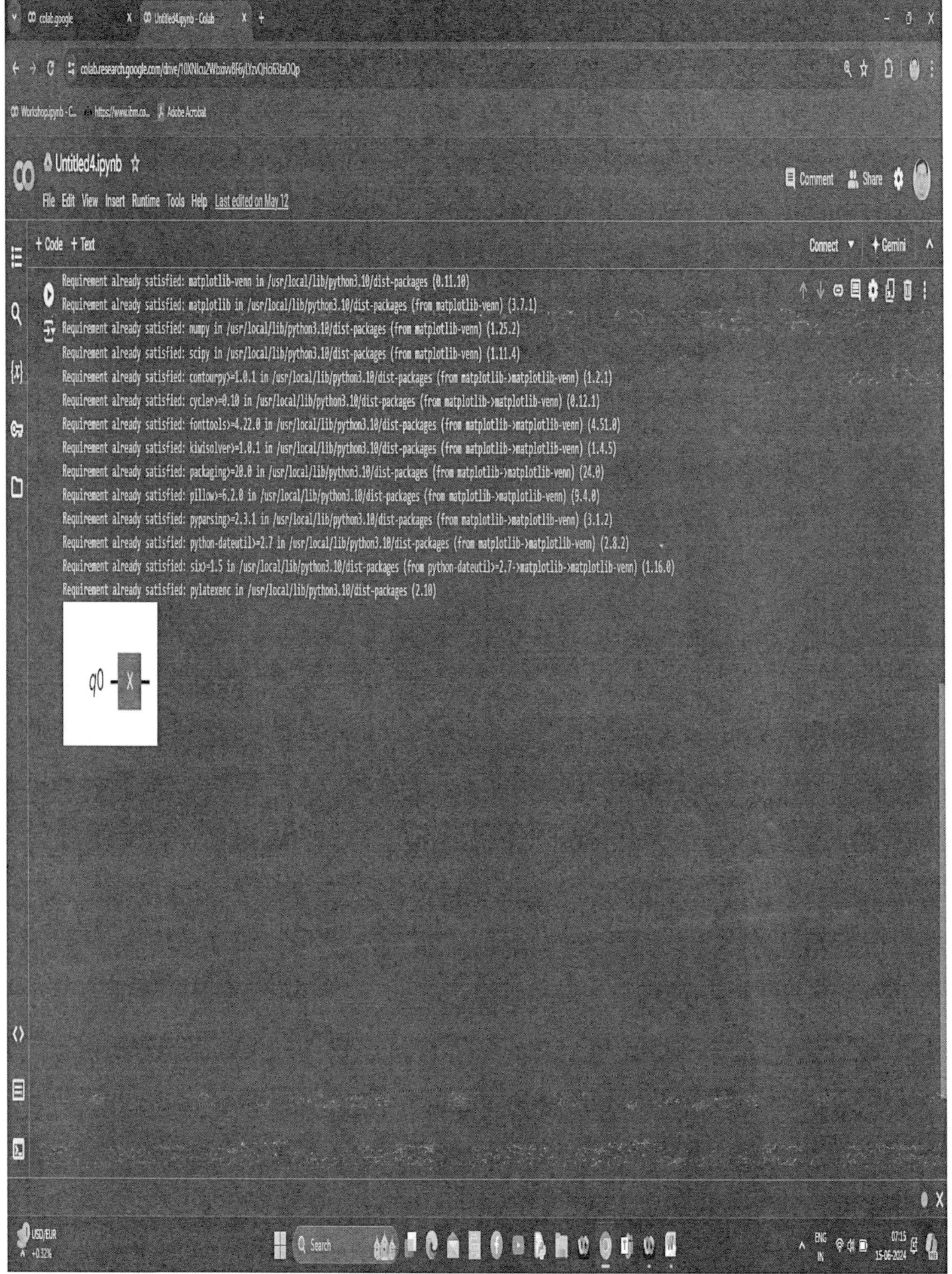
Untitled4.ipynb
File Edit View Insert Runtime Tools Help Last edited on May 12
+ Code + Text
Connect
Gemini
Comment
Share
Requirement already satisfied: matplotlib-venn in /usr/local/lib/python3.10/dist-packages (0.11.10)
Requirement already satisfied: matplotlib in /usr/local/lib/python3.10/dist-packages (from matplotlib-venn) (3.7.1)
Requirement already satisfied: numpy in /usr/local/lib/python3.10/dist-packages (from matplotlib-venn) (1.25.2)
Requirement already satisfied: scipy in /usr/local/lib/python3.10/dist-packages (from matplotlib-venn) (1.11.4)
Requirement already satisfied: contourpy>=1.0.1 in /usr/local/lib/python3.10/dist-packages (from matplotlib->matplotlib-venn) (1.2.1)
Requirement already satisfied: cycler>=0.10 in /usr/local/lib/python3.10/dist-packages (from matplotlib->matplotlib-venn) (0.12.1)
Requirement already satisfied: fonttools>=4.22.0 in /usr/local/lib/python3.10/dist-packages (from matplotlib->matplotlib-venn) (4.51.0)
Requirement already satisfied: kiwisolver>=1.0.1 in /usr/local/lib/python3.10/dist-packages (from matplotlib->matplotlib-venn) (1.4.5)
Requirement already satisfied: packaging>=20.0 in /usr/local/lib/python3.10/dist-packages (from matplotlib->matplotlib-venn) (24.0)
Requirement already satisfied: pillow>=6.2.0 in /usr/local/lib/python3.10/dist-packages (from matplotlib->matplotlib-venn) (9.4.0)
Requirement already satisfied: pyparsing>=2.3.1 in /usr/local/lib/python3.10/dist-packages (from matplotlib->matplotlib-venn) (3.1.2)
Requirement already satisfied: python-dateutil>=2.7 in /usr/local/lib/python3.10/dist-packages (from matplotlib->matplotlib-venn) (2.8.2)
Requirement already satisfied: six>=1.5 in /usr/local/lib/python3.10/dist-packages (from python-dateutil>=2.7->matplotlib->matplotlib-venn) (1.16.0)
Requirement already satisfied: pylatexenc in /usr/local/lib/python3.10/dist-packages (2.10)
q0
X

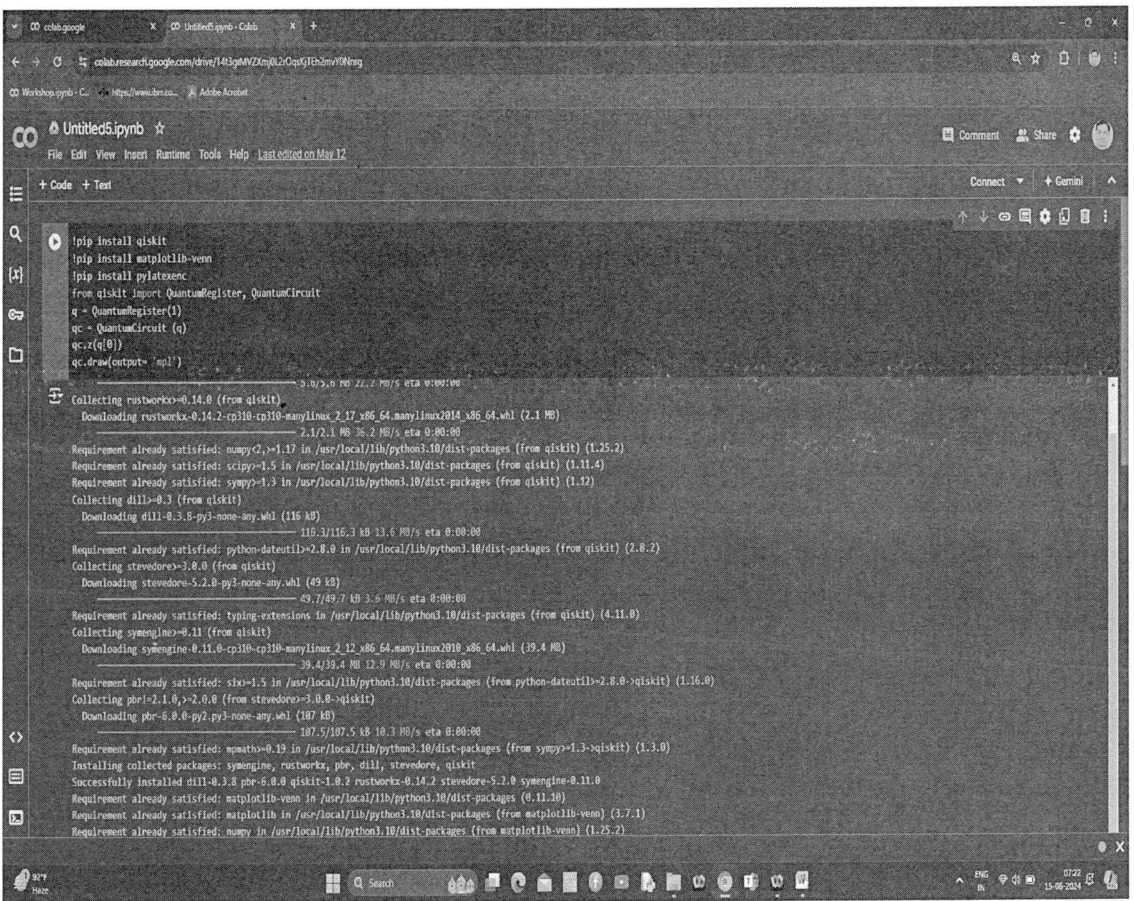
Untitled5.ipynb
File Edit View Insert Runtime Tools Help Last edited on May 12
+ Code + Text
Comment Share
Connect Gemini
!pip install qiskit
!pip install matplotlib-venn
!pip install pylatexenc
from qiskit import QuantumRegister, QuantumCircuit
q = QuantumRegister(1)
qc = QuantumCircuit (q)
qc.z(q[0])
qc.draw(output= 'mpl')
Collecting rustworkx>=0.14.0 (from qiskit)
Downloading rustworkx-0.14.2-cp310-cp310-manylinux_2_17_x86_64.manylinux2014_x86_64.whl (2.1 MB)
2.1/2.1 MB 36.2 MB/s eta 0:00:00
Requirement already satisfied: numpy<2,>=1.17 in /usr/local/lib/python3.10/dist-packages (from qiskit) (1.25.2)
Requirement already satisfied: scipy>=1.5 in /usr/local/lib/python3.10/dist-packages (from qiskit) (1.11.4)
Requirement already satisfied: sympy>=1.3 in /usr/local/lib/python3.10/dist-packages (from qiskit) (1.12)
Collecting dill>=0.3 (from qiskit)
Downloading dill-0.3.8-py3-none-any.whl (116 kB)
116.3/116.3 kB 13.6 MB/s eta 0:00:00
Requirement already satisfied: python-dateutil>=2.8.0 in /usr/local/lib/python3.10/dist-packages (from qiskit) (2.8.2)
Collecting stevedore>=3.0.0 (from qiskit)
Downloading stevedore-5.2.0-py3-none-any.whl (49 kB)
49.7/49.7 kB 3.6 MB/s eta 0:00:00
Requirement already satisfied: typing-extensions in /usr/local/lib/python3.10/dist-packages (from qiskit) (4.11.0)
Collecting symengine>=0.11 (from qiskit)
Downloading symengine-0.11.0-cp310-cp310-manylinux_2_12_x86_64.manylinux2010_x86_64.whl (39.4 MB)
39.4/39.4 MB 12.9 MB/s eta 0:00:00
Requirement already satisfied: six>=1.5 in /usr/local/lib/python3.10/dist-packages (from python-dateutil>=2.8.0->qiskit) (1.16.0)
Collecting pbr!=2.1.0,>=2.0.0 (from stevedore>=3.0.0->qiskit)
Downloading pbr-6.0.0-py2.py3-none-any.whl (107 kB)
107.5/107.5 kB 10.3 MB/s eta 0:00:00
Requirement already satisfied: mpmath>=0.19 in /usr/local/lib/python3.10/dist-packages (from sympy>=1.3->qiskit) (1.3.0)
Installing collected packages: symengine, rustworkx, pbr, dill, stevedore, qiskit
Successfully installed dill-0.3.8 pbr-6.0.0 qiskit-1.0.2 rustworkx-0.14.2 stevedore-5.2.0 symengine-0.11.0
Requirement already satisfied: matplotlib-venn in /usr/local/lib/python3.10/dist-packages (0.11.10)
Requirement already satisfied: matplotlib in /usr/local/lib/python3.10/dist-packages (from matplotlib-venn) (3.7.1)
Requirement already satisfied: numpy in /usr/local/lib/python3.10/dist-packages (from matplotlib-venn) (1.25.2)

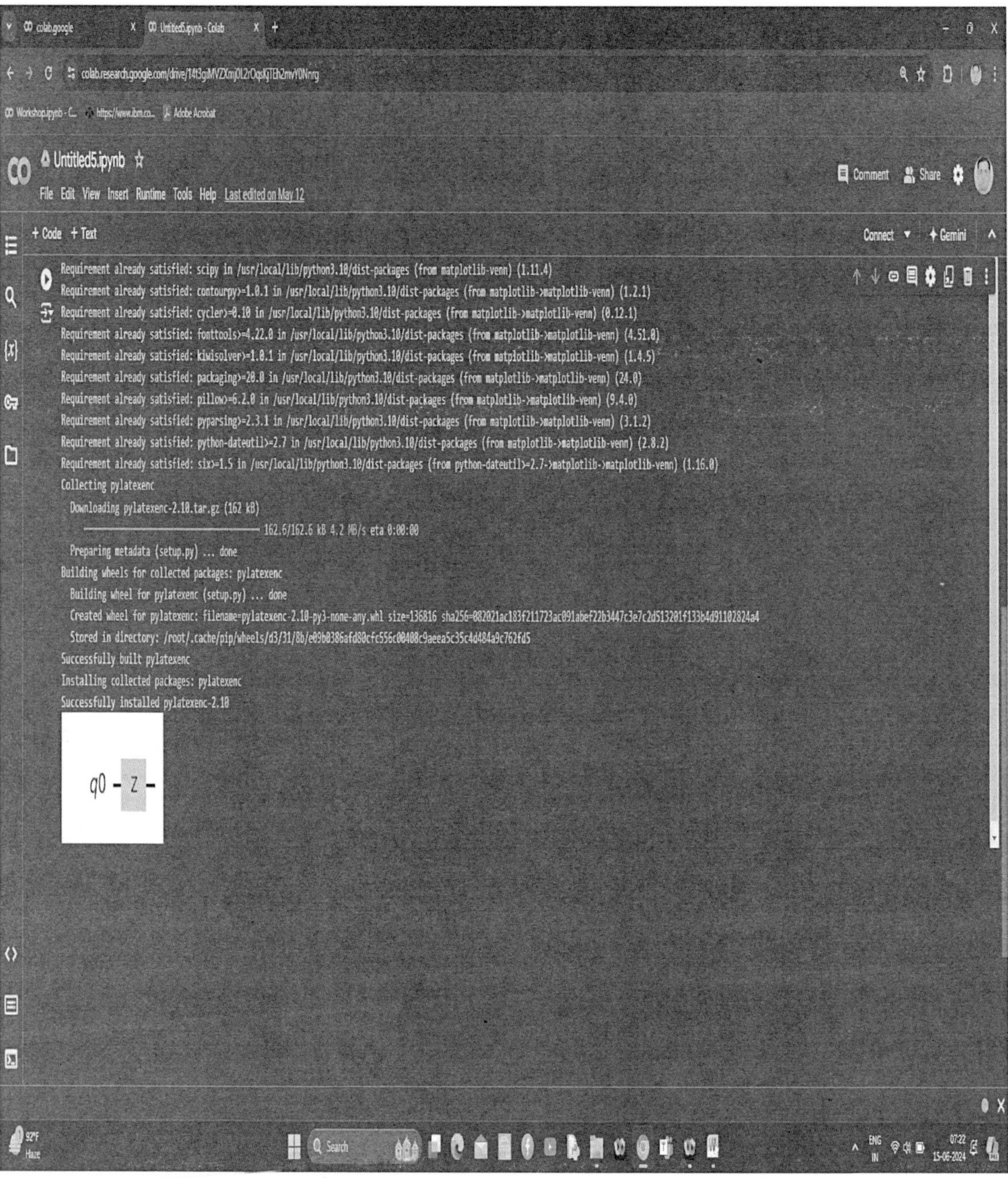
Untitled5.ipynb
File Edit View Insert Runtime Tools Help Last edited on May 12
Requirement already satisfied: scipy in /usr/local/lib/python3.10/dist-packages (from matplotlib-venn) (1.11.4)
Requirement already satisfied: contourpy>=1.0.1 in /usr/local/lib/python3.10/dist-packages (from matplotlib->matplotlib-venn) (1.2.1)
Requirement already satisfied: cycler>=0.10 in /usr/local/lib/python3.10/dist-packages (from matplotlib->matplotlib-venn) (0.12.1)
Requirement already satisfied: fonttools>=4.22.0 in /usr/local/lib/python3.10/dist-packages (from matplotlib->matplotlib-venn) (4.51.0)
Requirement already satisfied: kiwisolver>=1.0.1 in /usr/local/lib/python3.10/dist-packages (from matplotlib->matplotlib-venn) (1.4.5)
Requirement already satisfied: packaging>=20.0 in /usr/local/lib/python3.10/dist-packages (from matplotlib->matplotlib-venn) (24.0)
Requirement already satisfied: pillow>=6.2.0 in /usr/local/lib/python3.10/dist-packages (from matplotlib->matplotlib-venn) (9.4.0)
Requirement already satisfied: pyparsing>=2.3.1 in /usr/local/lib/python3.10/dist-packages (from matplotlib->matplotlib-venn) (3.1.2)
Requirement already satisfied: python-dateutil>=2.7 in /usr/local/lib/python3.10/dist-packages (from matplotlib->matplotlib-venn) (2.8.2)
Requirement already satisfied: six>=1.5 in /usr/local/lib/python3.10/dist-packages (from python-dateutil>=2.7->matplotlib->matplotlib-venn) (1.16.0)
Collecting pylatexenc
Downloading pylatexenc-2.10.tar.gz (162 kB)
162.6/162.6 kB 4.2 MB/s eta 0:00:00
Preparing metadata (setup.py) ... done
Building wheels for collected packages: pylatexenc
Building wheel for pylatexenc (setup.py) ... done
Stored in directory: /root/.cache/pip/wheels/d3/31/8b/e09b0386afd80cfc556c00408c9aeea5c35c4d484a9c762fd5
Successfully built pylatexenc
Installing collected packages: pylatexenc
Successfully installed pylatexenc-2.10
q0 Z

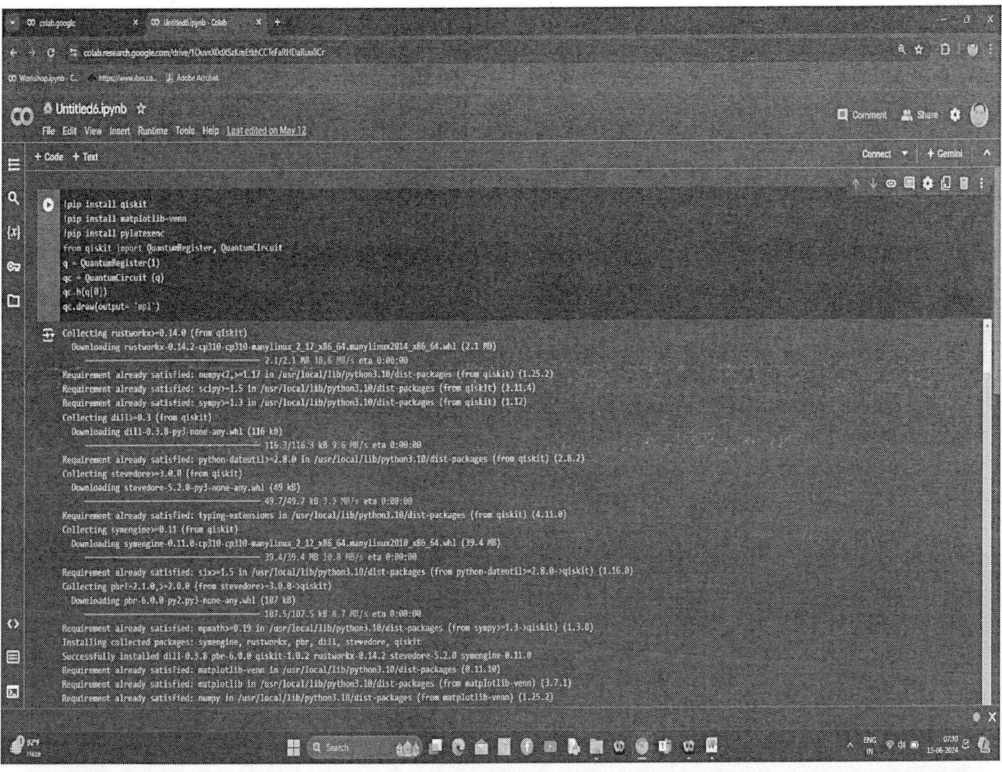
Untitled6.ipynb
File Edit View Insert Runtime Tools Help Last edited on May 12
+ Code + Text
!pip install qiskit
!pip install matplotlib-venn
!pip install pylatexenc
from qiskit import QuantumRegister, QuantumCircuit
q = QuantumRegister(1)
qc = QuantumCircuit (q)
qc.h(q[0])
qc.draw(output= 'mpl')
Collecting rustworkx>=0.14.0 (from qiskit)
Downloading rustworkx-0.14.2-cp310-cp310-manylinux_2_17_x86_64.manylinux2014_x86_64.whl (2.1 MB)
Requirement already satisfied: numpy<2,>=1.17 in /usr/local/lib/python3.10/dist-packages (from qiskit) (1.25.2)
Requirement already satisfied: scipy>=1.5 in /usr/local/lib/python3.10/dist-packages (from qiskit) (1.11.4)
Requirement already satisfied: sympy>=1.3 in /usr/local/lib/python3.10/dist-packages (from qiskit) (1.12)
Collecting dill>=0.3 (from qiskit)
Downloading dill-0.3.8-py3-none-any.whl (116 kB)
Collecting stevedore>=3.0.0 (from qiskit)
Downloading stevedore-5.2.0-py3-none-any.whl (49 kB)
Collecting symengine>=0.11 (from qiskit)
Collecting pbr!=2.1.0,>=2.0.0 (from stevedore>=3.0.0->qiskit)
Downloading pbr-6.0.0-py2.py3-none-any.whl (107 kB)
Installing collected packages: symengine, rustworkx, pbr, dill, stevedore, qiskit
Successfully installed dill-0.3.8 pbr-6.0.0 qiskit-1.0.2 rustworkx-0.14.2 stevedore-5.2.0 symengine-0.11.0

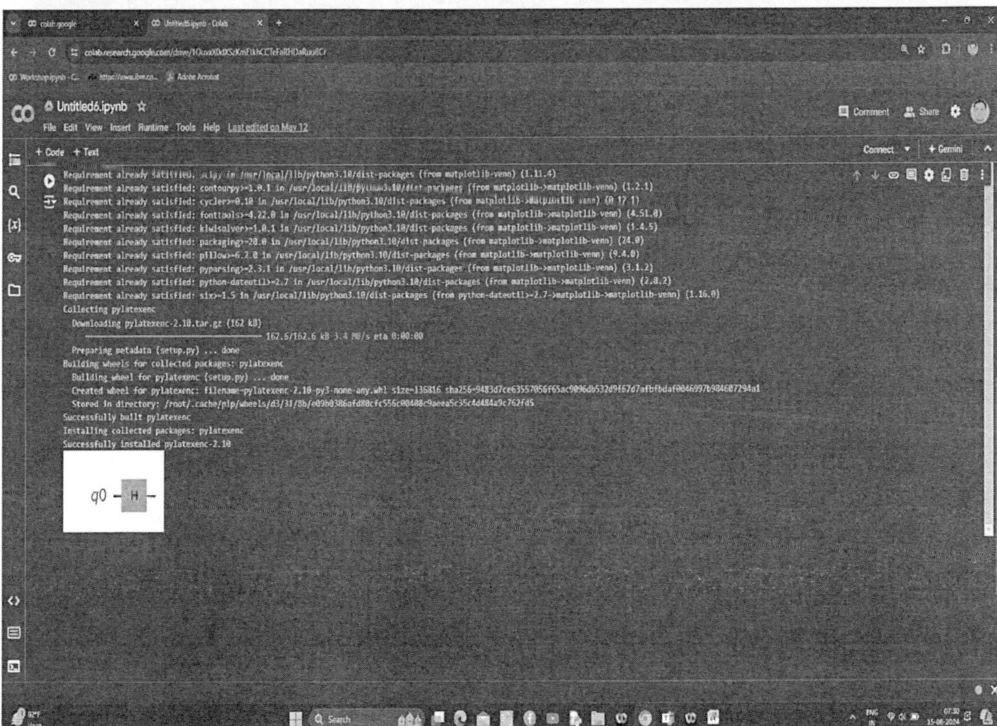
Untitled6.ipynb
File Edit View Insert Runtime Tools Help Last edited on May 12
+ Code + Text
Collecting pylatexenc
Downloading pylatexenc-2.10.tar.gz (162 kB)
Preparing metadata (setup.py) ... done
Building wheels for collected packages: pylatexenc
Building wheel for pylatexenc (setup.py) ... done
Successfully built pylatexenc
Installing collected packages: pylatexenc
Successfully installed pylatexenc-2.10
q0
H

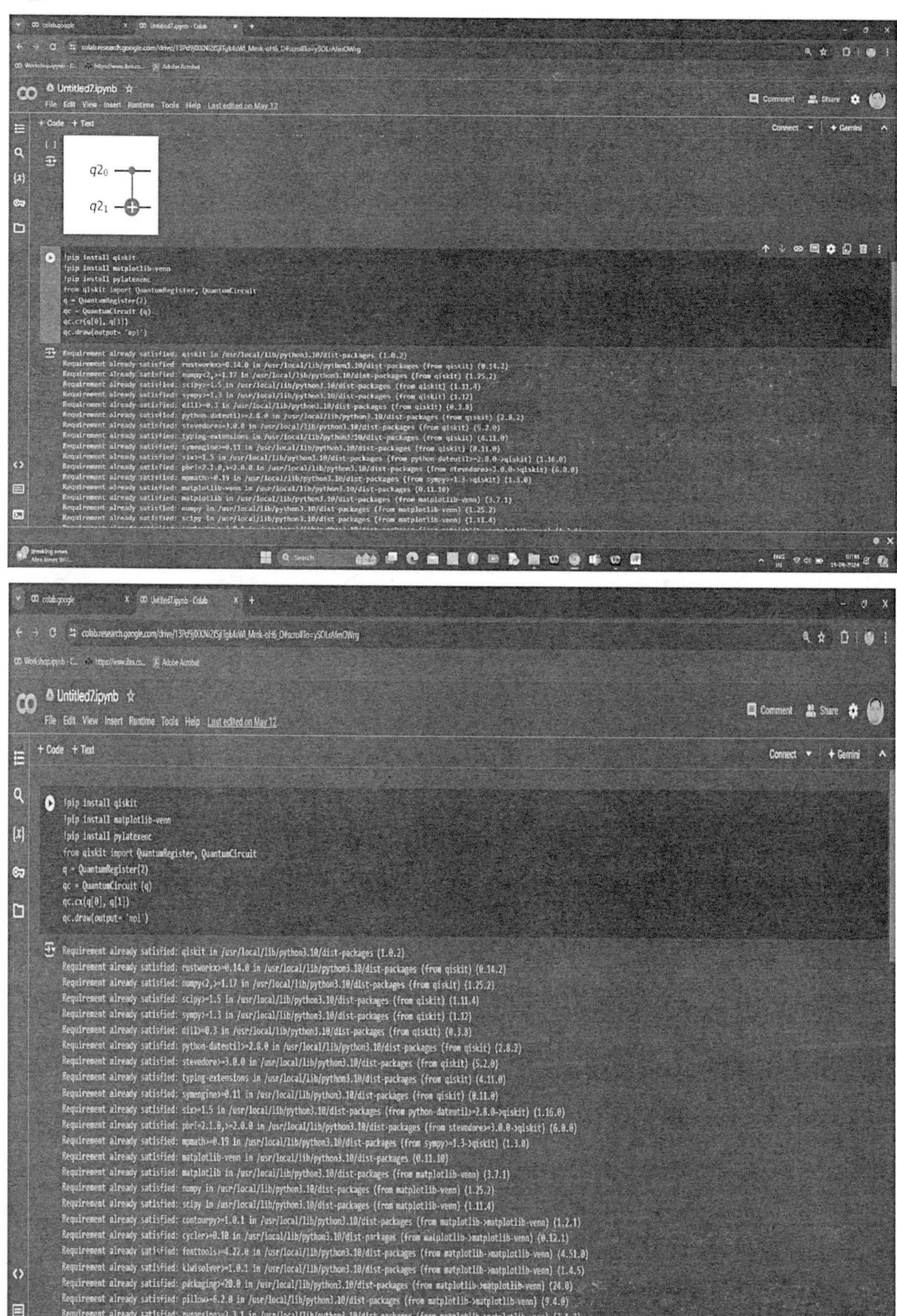

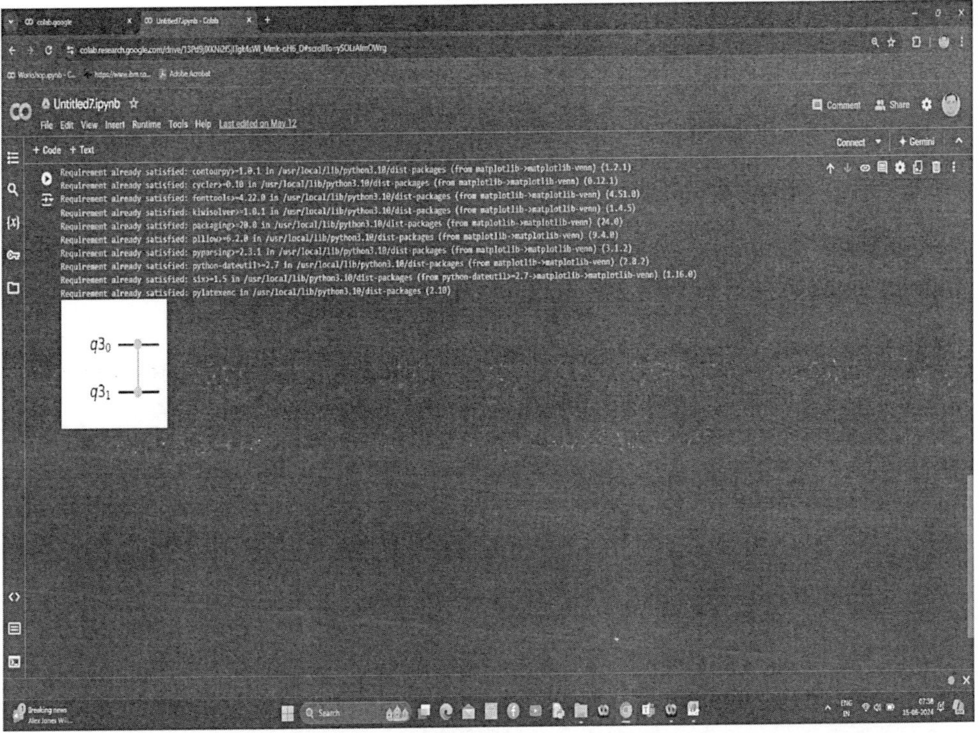
Untitled7.ipynb
$q3_0$
$q3_1$

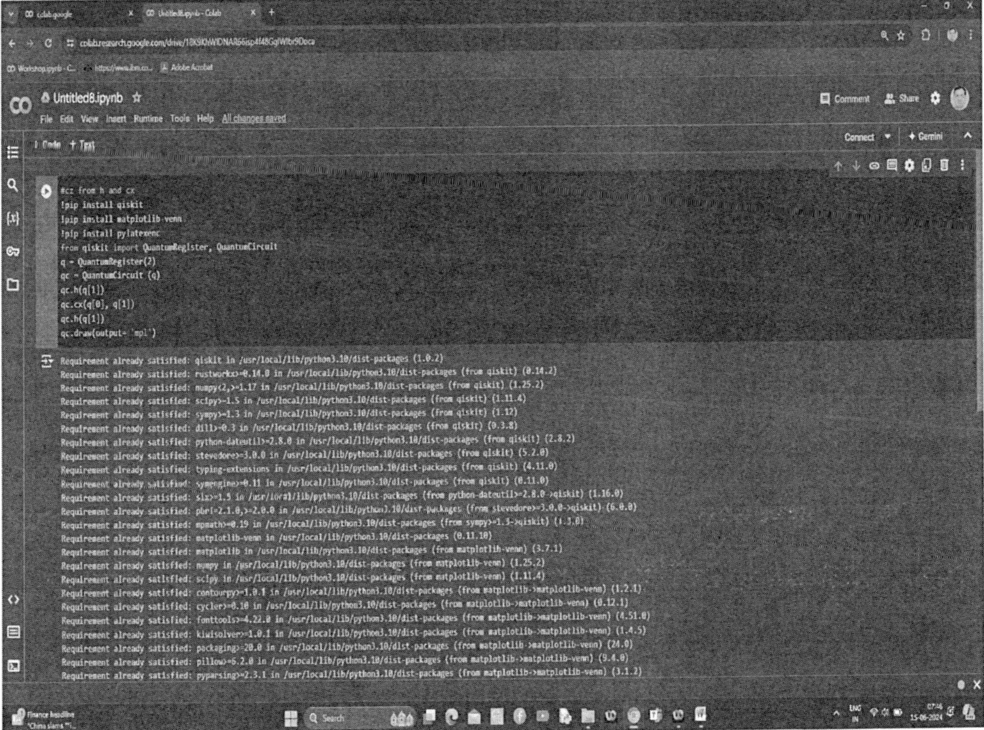
Untitled8.ipynb
#cz from h and cx
!pip install qiskit
!pip install matplotlib-venn
!pip install pylatexenc
from qiskit import QuantumRegister, QuantumCircuit
q = QuantumRegister(2)
qc = QuantumCircuit (q)
qc.h(q[1])
qc.cx(q[0], q[1])
qc.h(q[1])
qc.draw(output='mpl')

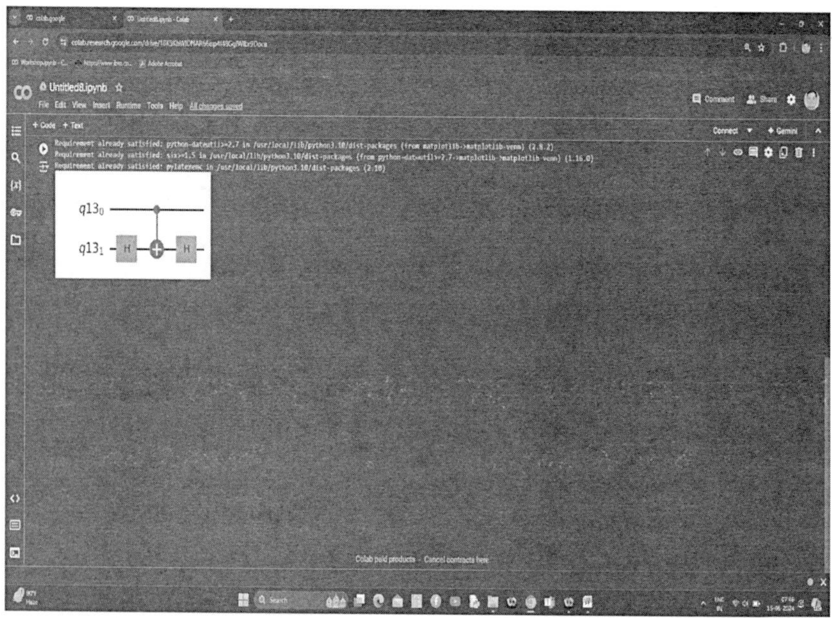
Untitled8.ipynb
File Edit View Insert Runtime Tools Help All changes saved
+ Code + Text
$q13_0$
$q13_1$
H
H

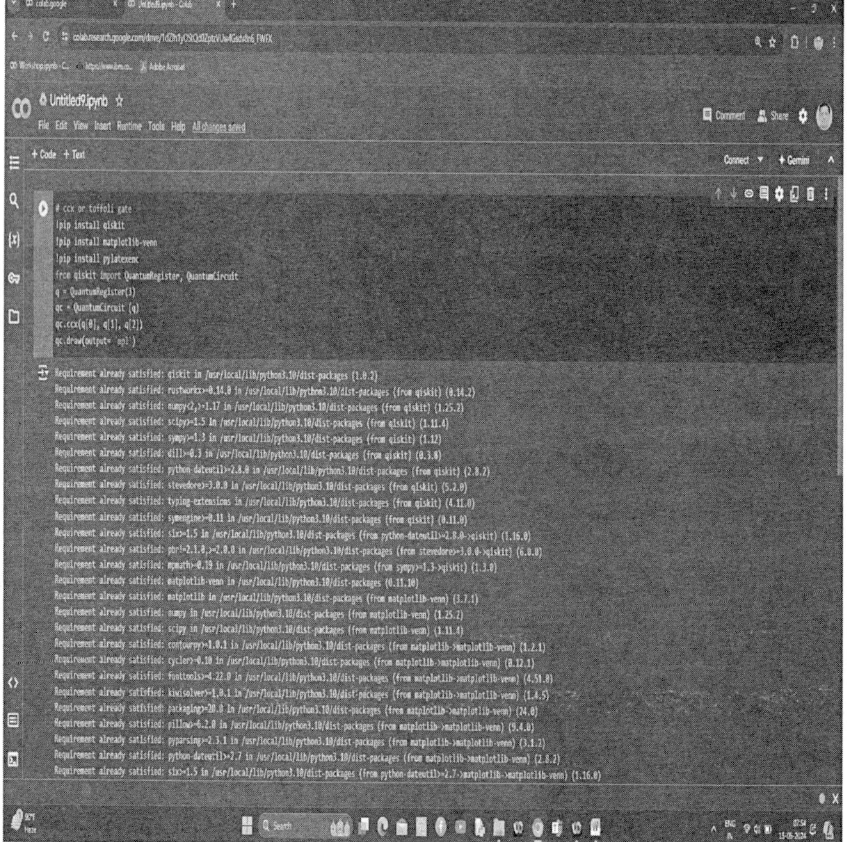
Untitled9.ipynb
File Edit View Insert Runtime Tools Help All changes saved
+ Code + Text
# ccx or toffoli gate
!pip install qiskit
!pip install matplotlib-venn
!pip install pylatexenc
from qiskit import QuantumRegister, QuantumCircuit
q = QuantumRegister(3)
qc = QuantumCircuit (q)
qc.ccx(q[0], q[1], q[2])
qc.draw(output='mpl')
Requirement already satisfied: qiskit in /usr/local/lib/python3.10/dist-packages (1.0.2)

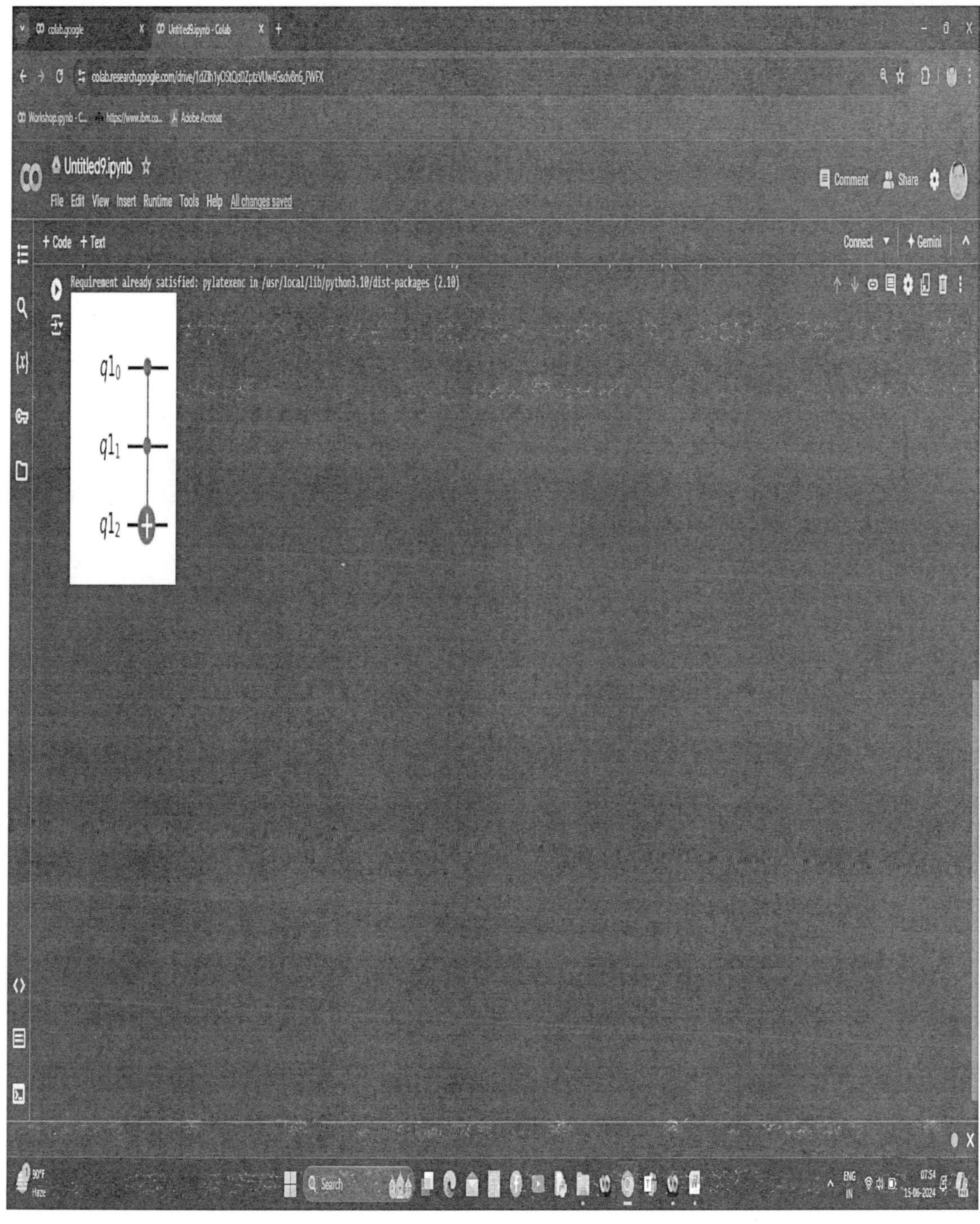
Untitled9.ipynb
File Edit View Insert Runtime Tools Help All changes saved
+ Code + Text
Requirement already satisfied: pylatexenc in /usr/local/lib/python3.10/dist-packages (2.10)
q1_0
q1_1
q1_2

Experiment No. 3: To implement NOT, AND, NAND, OR, XOR gates using Qiskit.

Solution-3: The following is the qiskit code and its outputs for NOT, NAND, OR and XOR gates.

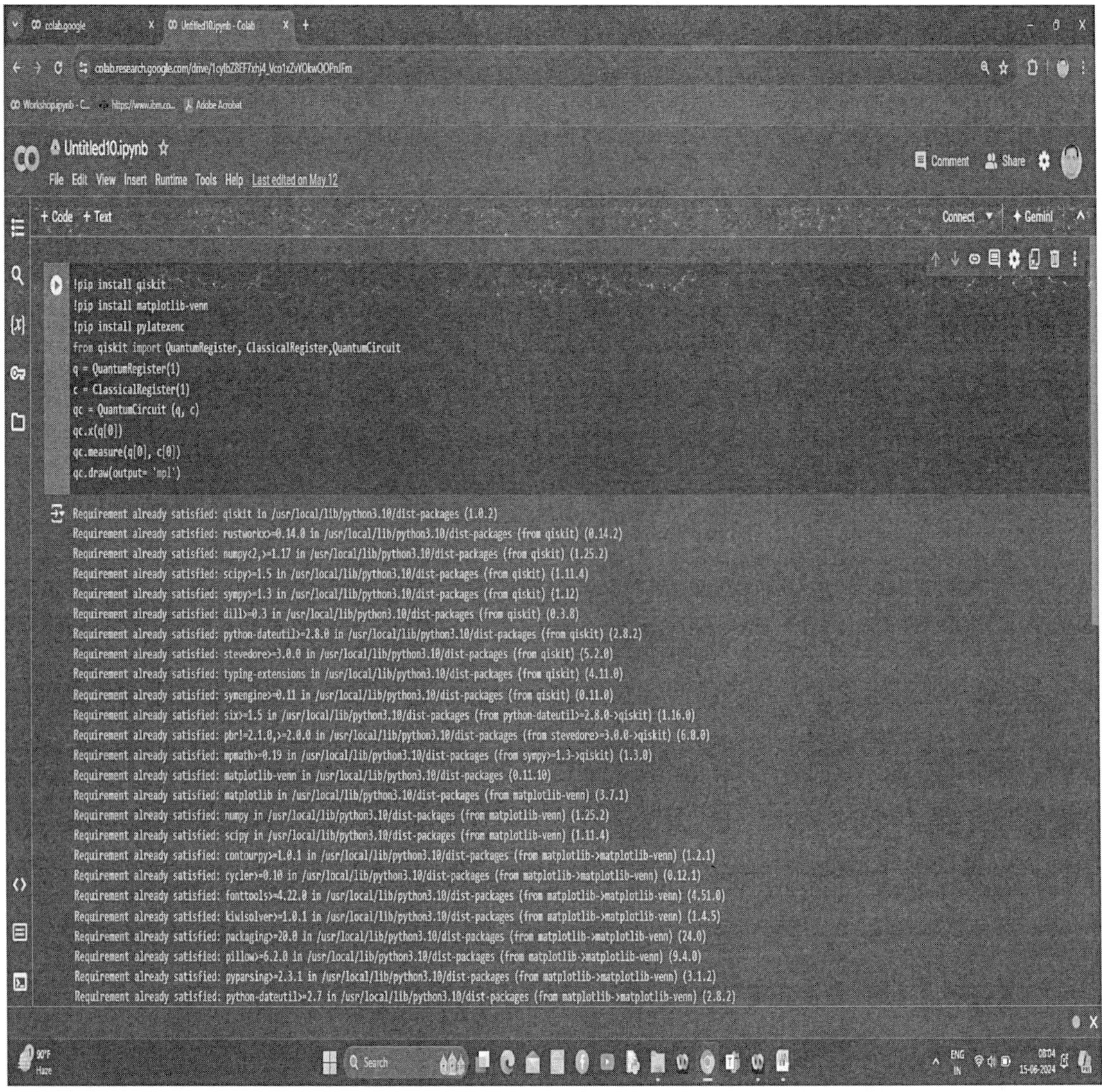

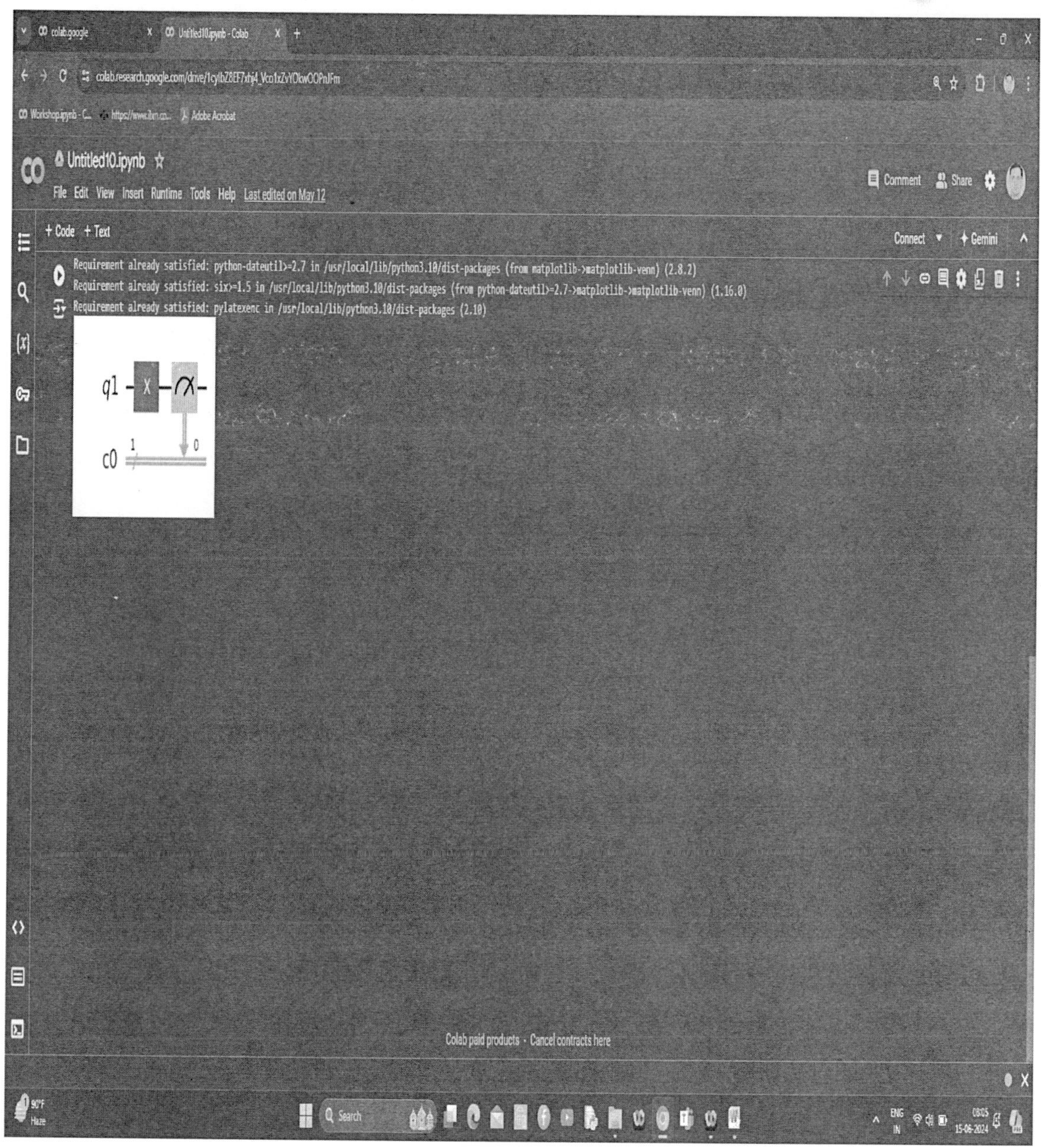
Untitled10.ipynb
File Edit View Insert Runtime Tools Help Last edited on May 12
+ Code + Text
Requirement already satisfied: python-dateutil>=2.7 in /usr/local/lib/python3.10/dist-packages (from matplotlib->matplotlib-venn) (2.8.2)
Requirement already satisfied: six>=1.5 in /usr/local/lib/python3.10/dist-packages (from python-dateutil>=2.7->matplotlib-venn) (1.16.0)
Requirement already satisfied: pylatexenc in /usr/local/lib/python3.10/dist-packages (2.10)
q1
X
c0
1
0
Colab paid products · Cancel contracts here

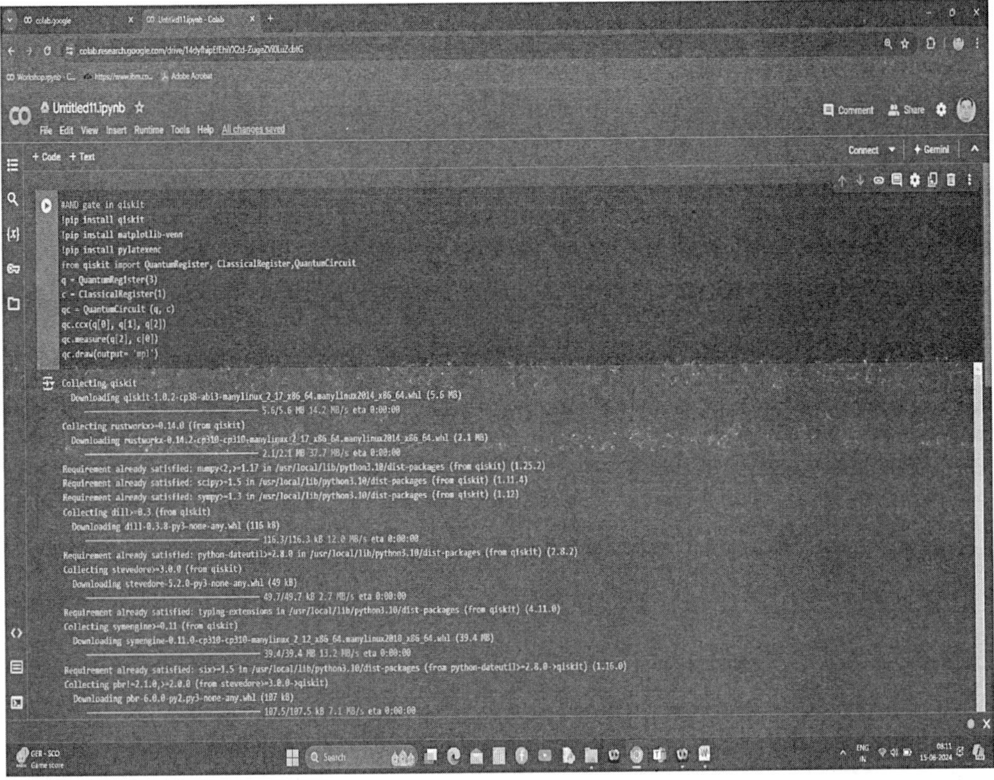
Untitled11.ipynb
File Edit View Insert Runtime Tools Help All changes saved
#AND gate in qiskit
!pip install qiskit
!pip install matplotlib-venn
!pip install pylatexenc
from qiskit import QuantumRegister, ClassicalRegister,QuantumCircuit
q = QuantumRegister(3)
c = ClassicalRegister(1)
qc = QuantumCircuit (q, c)
qc.ccx(q[0], q[1], q[2])
qc.measure(q[2], c[0])
qc.draw(output= 'mpl')
Collecting qiskit
Downloading qiskit-1.0.2-cp38-abi3-manylinux_2_17_x86_64.manylinux2014_x86_64.whl (5.6 MB)
Collecting rustworkx>=0.14.0 (from qiskit)
Downloading rustworkx-0.14.2-cp310-cp310-manylinux_2_17_x86_64.manylinux2014_x86_64.whl (2.1 MB)

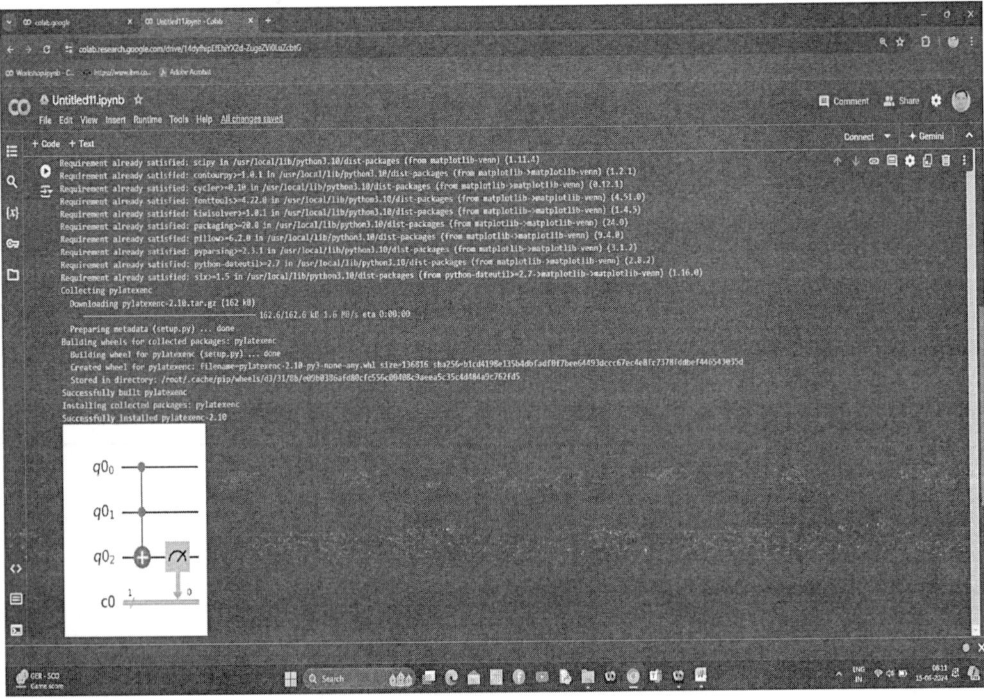
Untitled11.ipynb
Collecting pylatexenc
Downloading pylatexenc-2.10.tar.gz (162 kB)
Successfully built pylatexenc
Installing collected packages: pylatexenc
Successfully installed pylatexenc-2.10
q0₀
q0₁
q0₂
c0
1
0

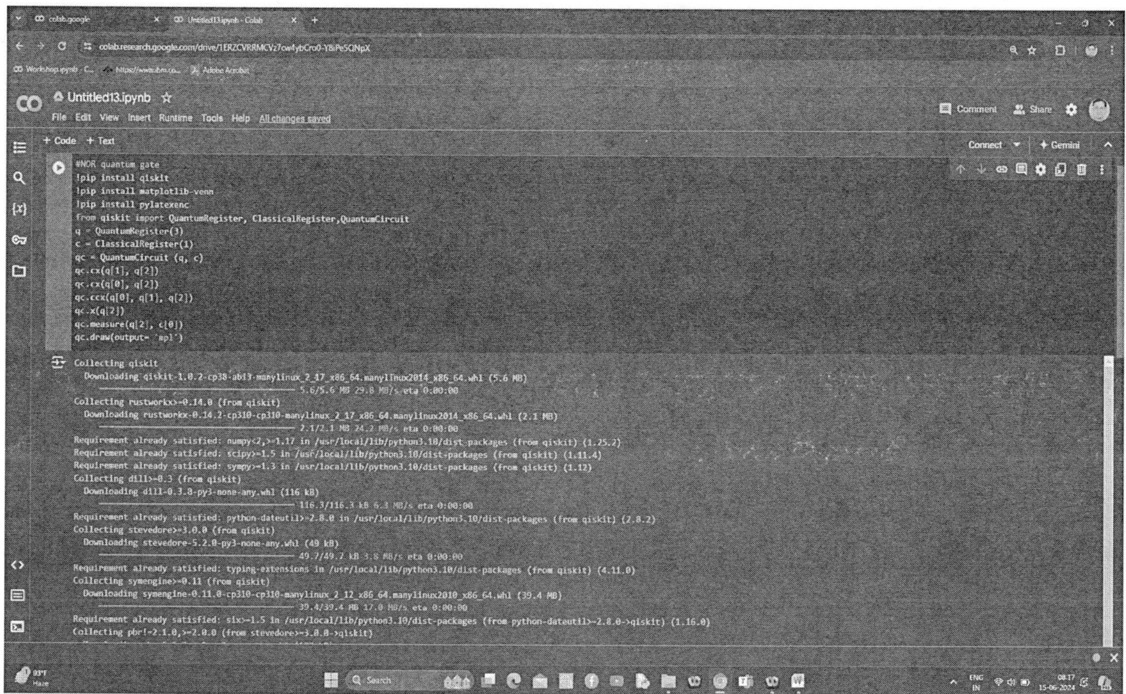
Untitled13.ipynb
File Edit View Insert Runtime Tools Help All changes saved
+ Code + Text
Connect
Gemini
Comment
Share
#NOR quantum gate
!pip install qiskit
!pip install matplotlib-venn
!pip install pylatexenc
from qiskit import QuantumRegister, ClassicalRegister,QuantumCircuit
q = QuantumRegister(3)
c = ClassicalRegister(1)
qc = QuantumCircuit (q, c)
qc.cx(q[1], q[2])
qc.cx(q[0], q[2])
qc.ccx(q[0], q[1], q[2])
qc.x(q[2])
qc.measure(q[2], c[0])
qc.draw(output= 'mpl')
Collecting qiskit
Downloading qiskit-1.0.2-cp38-abi3-manylinux_2_17_x86_64.manylinux2014_x86_64.whl (5.6 MB)
5.6/5.6 MB 29.8 MB/s eta 0:00:00
Collecting rustworkx>=0.14.0 (from qiskit)
Downloading rustworkx-0.14.2-cp310-cp310-manylinux_2_17_x86_64.manylinux2014_x86_64.whl (2.1 MB)
2.1/2.1 MB 24.2 MB/s eta 0:00:00
Requirement already satisfied: numpy<2,>=1.17 in /usr/local/lib/python3.10/dist-packages (from qiskit) (1.25.2)
Requirement already satisfied: scipy>=1.5 in /usr/local/lib/python3.10/dist-packages (from qiskit) (1.11.4)
Requirement already satisfied: sympy>=1.3 in /usr/local/lib/python3.10/dist-packages (from qiskit) (1.12)
Collecting dill>=0.3 (from qiskit)
Downloading dill-0.3.8-py3-none-any.whl (116 kB)
116.3/116.3 kB 6.3 MB/s eta 0:00:00
Requirement already satisfied: python-dateutil>=2.8.0 in /usr/local/lib/python3.10/dist-packages (from qiskit) (2.8.2)
Collecting stevedore>=3.0.0 (from qiskit)
Downloading stevedore-5.2.0-py3-none-any.whl (49 kB)
49.7/49.7 kB 3.8 MB/s eta 0:00:00
Requirement already satisfied: typing-extensions in /usr/local/lib/python3.10/dist-packages (from qiskit) (4.11.0)
Collecting symengine>=0.11 (from qiskit)
Downloading symengine-0.11.0-cp310-cp310-manylinux_2_12_x86_64.manylinux2010_x86_64.whl (39.4 MB)
39.4/39.4 MB 17.0 MB/s eta 0:00:00
Requirement already satisfied: six>=1.5 in /usr/local/lib/python3.10/dist-packages (from python-dateutil>=2.8.0->qiskit) (1.16.0)
Collecting pbr!=2.1.0,>=2.0.0 (from stevedore>=3.0.0->qiskit)
Search

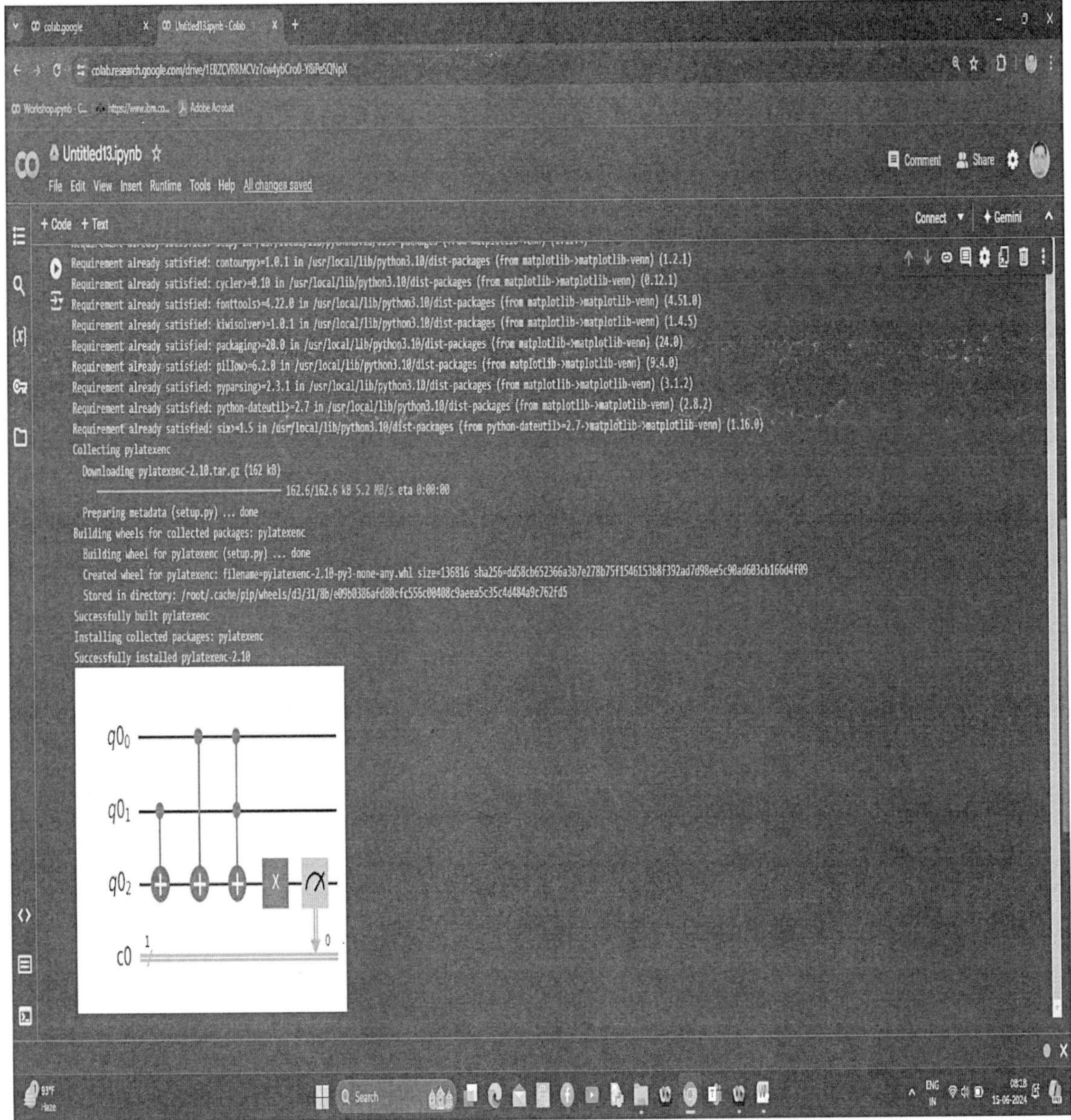

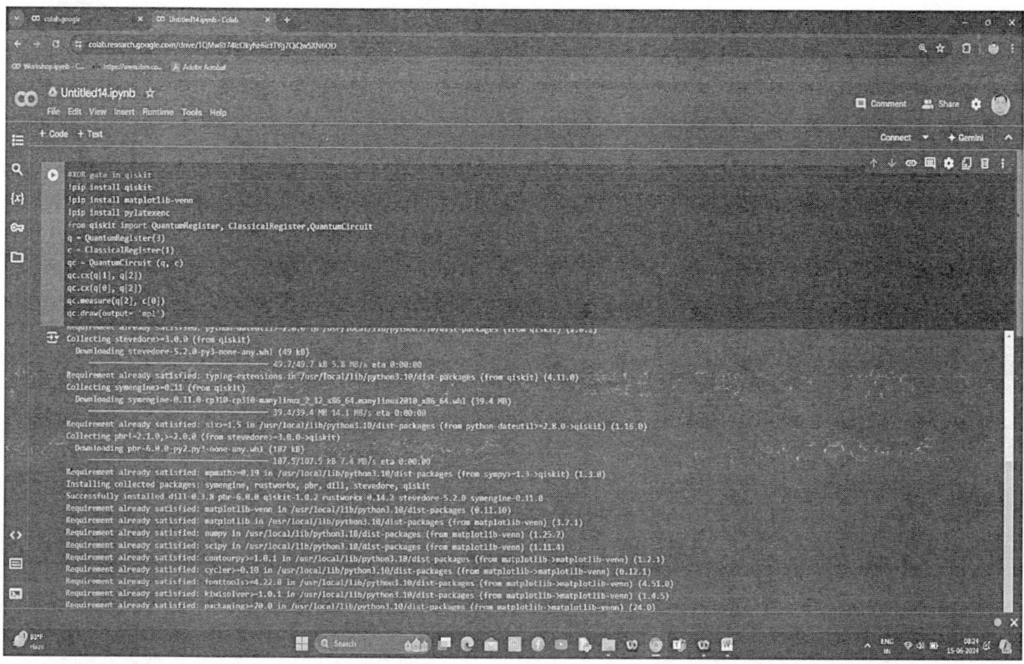


```
Requirement already satisfied: pillow>=6.2.0 in /usr/local/lib/python3.10/dist-packages (from matplotlib->matplotlib-venn) (9.4.0)
Requirement already satisfied: pyparsing>=2.3.1 in /usr/local/lib/python3.10/dist-packages (from matplotlib->matplotlib-venn) (3.1.2)
Requirement already satisfied: python-dateutil>=2.7 in /usr/local/lib/python3.10/dist-packages (from matplotlib->matplotlib-venn) (2.8.2)
Requirement already satisfied: six>=1.5 in /usr/local/lib/python3.10/dist-packages (from python-dateutil>=2.7->matplotlib->matplotlib-venn) (1.16.0)
Collecting pylatexenc
  Downloading pylatexenc-2.10.tar.gz (162 kB)
     ---------------------------------------- 162.6/162.6 kB 3.4 MB/s eta 0:00:00
  Preparing metadata (setup.py) ... done
Building wheels for collected packages: pylatexenc
  Building wheel for pylatexenc (setup.py) ... done
  Created wheel for pylatexenc: filename=pylatexenc-2.10-py3-none-any.whl size=136816 sha256=8225521065201aaa6312d6c4367c9bbaa1d98b092b1a8e66876aa8e8e508fb51
  Stored in directory: /root/.cache/pip/wheels/d3/31/8b/e09b0386afd80cfc556c00408c9aeea5c35c4d484a9c762fd5
Successfully built pylatexenc
Installing collected packages: pylatexenc
Successfully installed pylatexenc-2.10

q0_0
q0_1
q0_2
c0  1  0
```

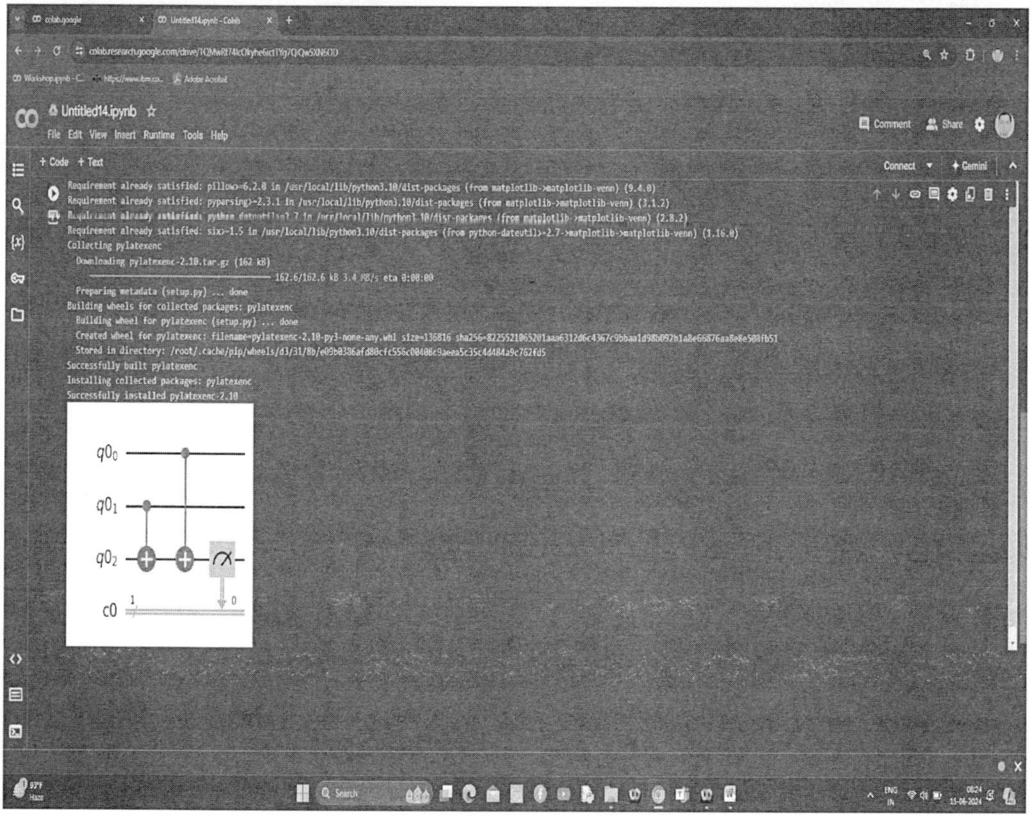

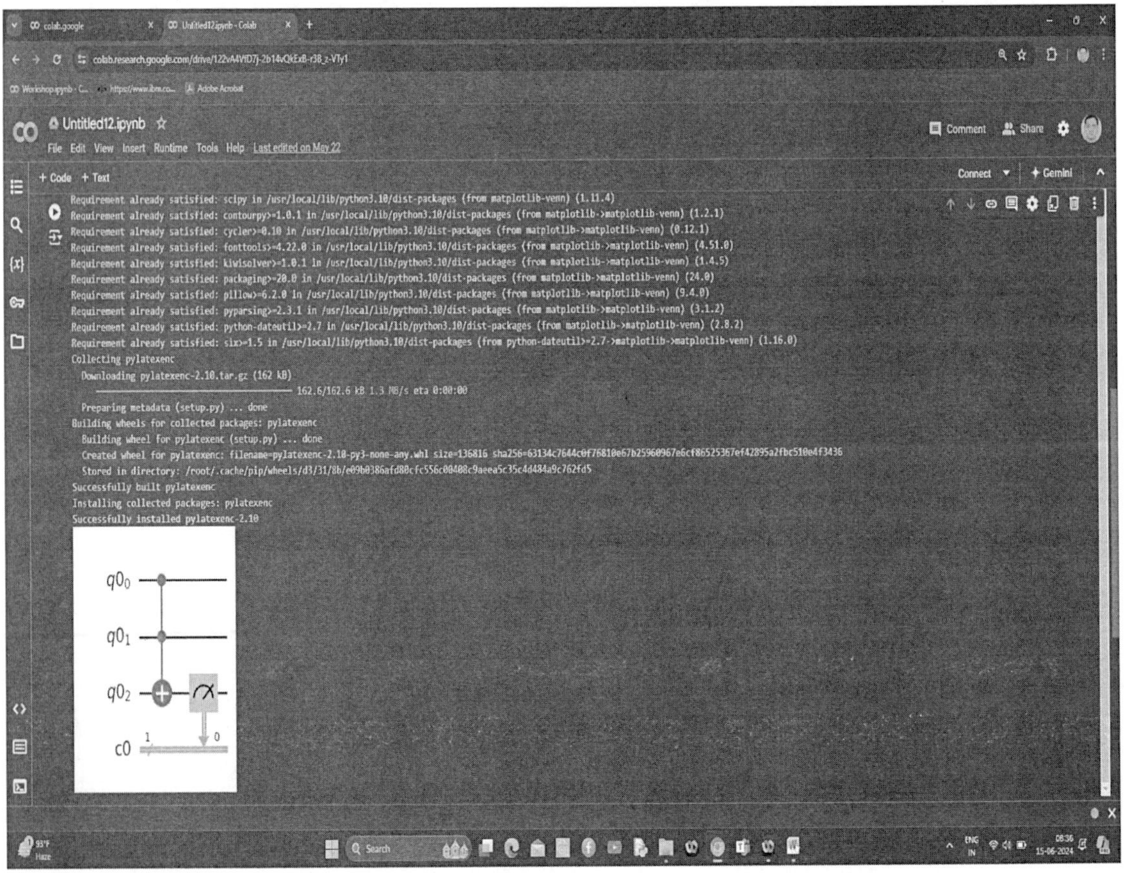

```
Untitled12.ipynb
File Edit View Insert Runtime Tools Help Last edited on May 22
+ Code + Text
Requirement already satisfied: scipy in /usr/local/lib/python3.10/dist-packages (from matplotlib-venn) (1.11.4)
Requirement already satisfied: contourpy>=1.0.1 in /usr/local/lib/python3.10/dist-packages (from matplotlib->matplotlib-venn) (1.2.1)
Requirement already satisfied: cycler>=0.10 in /usr/local/lib/python3.10/dist-packages (from matplotlib->matplotlib-venn) (0.12.1)
Requirement already satisfied: fonttools>=4.22.0 in /usr/local/lib/python3.10/dist-packages (from matplotlib->matplotlib-venn) (4.51.0)
Requirement already satisfied: kiwisolver>=1.0.1 in /usr/local/lib/python3.10/dist-packages (from matplotlib->matplotlib-venn) (1.4.5)
Requirement already satisfied: packaging>=20.0 in /usr/local/lib/python3.10/dist-packages (from matplotlib->matplotlib-venn) (24.0)
Requirement already satisfied: pillow>=6.2.0 in /usr/local/lib/python3.10/dist-packages (from matplotlib->matplotlib-venn) (9.4.0)
Requirement already satisfied: pyparsing>=2.3.1 in /usr/local/lib/python3.10/dist-packages (from matplotlib->matplotlib-venn) (3.1.2)
Requirement already satisfied: python-dateutil>=2.7 in /usr/local/lib/python3.10/dist-packages (from matplotlib->matplotlib-venn) (2.8.2)
Requirement already satisfied: six>=1.5 in /usr/local/lib/python3.10/dist-packages (from python-dateutil>=2.7->matplotlib->matplotlib-venn) (1.16.0)
Collecting pylatexenc
  Downloading pylatexenc-2.10.tar.gz (162 kB)
     ━━━━━━━━━━━━━━━━━━━━━━━━━━━━━━━━ 162.6/162.6 kB 1.3 MB/s eta 0:00:00
  Preparing metadata (setup.py) ... done
Building wheels for collected packages: pylatexenc
  Building wheel for pylatexenc (setup.py) ... done
  Created wheel for pylatexenc: filename=pylatexenc-2.10-py3-none-any.whl size=136816 sha256=63134c7644c0f76810e67b25960967e6cf86525367ef42895a2fbc510e4f3436
  Stored in directory: /root/.cache/pip/wheels/d3/31/8b/e09b0386afd80cfc556c00408c9aeea5c35c4d484a9c762fd5
Successfully built pylatexenc
Installing collected packages: pylatexenc
Successfully installed pylatexenc-2.10
```

q0₀, q0₁, q0₂, c0 (circuit output: Toffoli gate on q0₀, q0₁ → q0₂, then measurement of q0₂ into c0; labels 1, 0)

Experiment No. 4: To create a single qubit, one classical register to measure the qubit and then apply Pauli-X gate (bit flip) on the qubit and finally measure its value using Qiskit.

Solution-4:

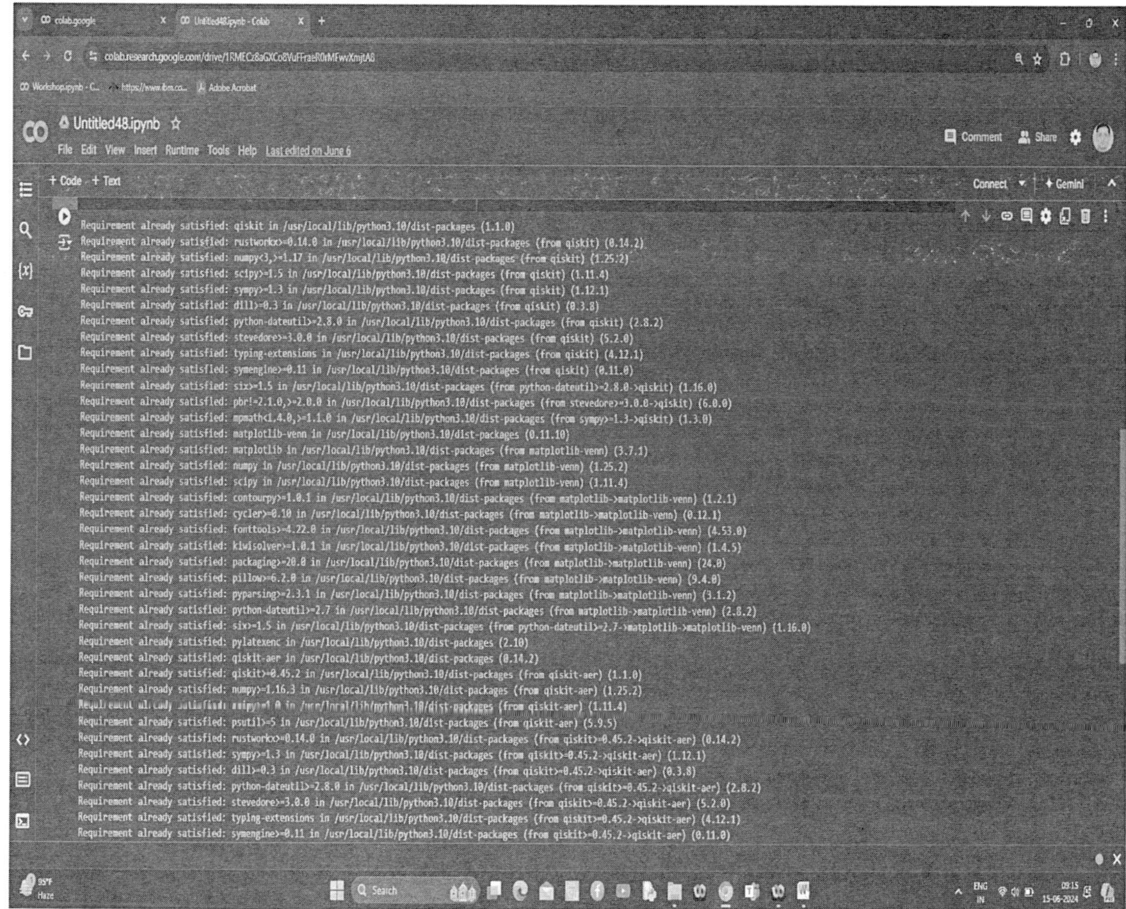

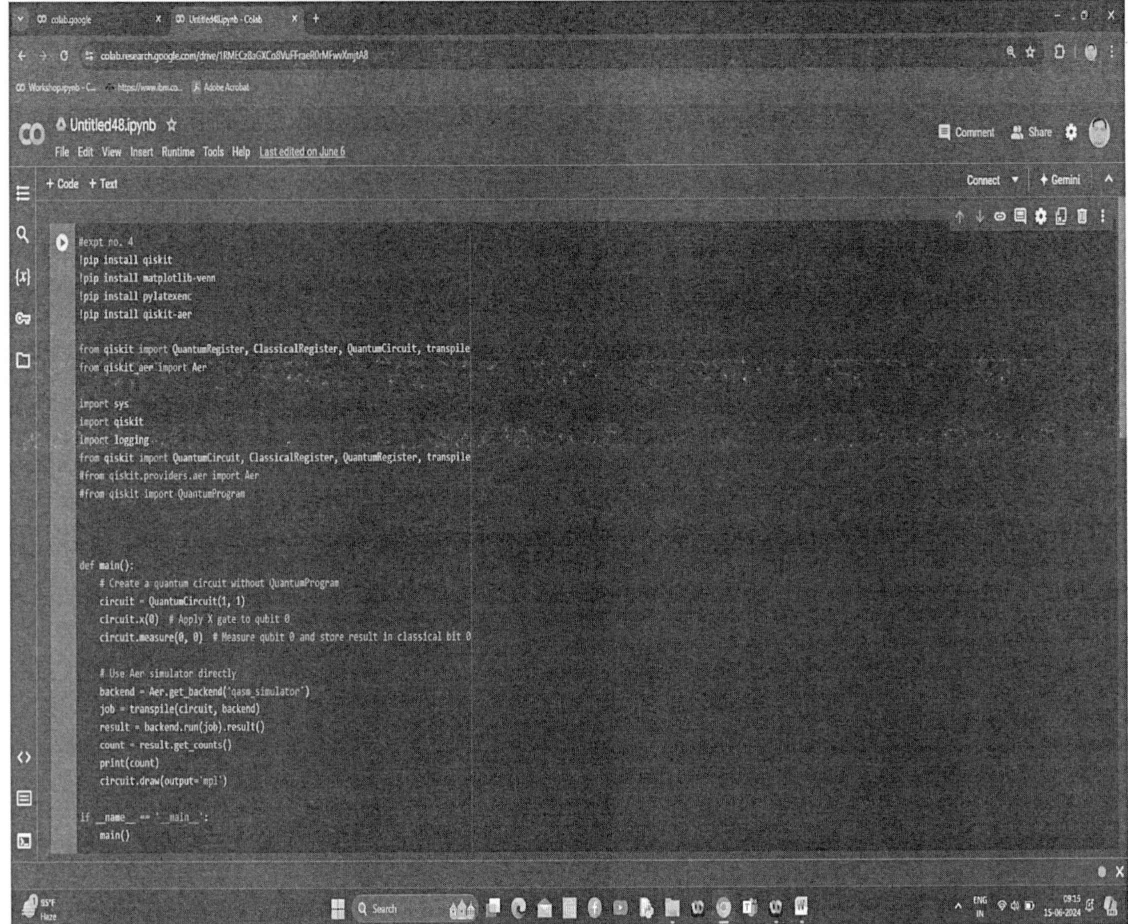
Untitled48.ipynb
File Edit View Insert Runtime Tools Help Last edited on June 6
+ Code + Text
#expt no. 4
!pip install qiskit
!pip install matplotlib-venn
!pip install pylatexenc
!pip install qiskit-aer
from qiskit import QuantumRegister, ClassicalRegister, QuantumCircuit, transpile
from qiskit_aer import Aer
import sys
import qiskit
import logging
from qiskit import QuantumCircuit, ClassicalRegister, QuantumRegister, transpile
#from qiskit.providers.aer import Aer
#from qiskit import QuantumProgram
def main():
# Create a quantum circuit without QuantumProgram
circuit = QuantumCircuit(1, 1)
circuit.x(0) # Apply X gate to qubit 0
circuit.measure(0, 0) # Measure qubit 0 and store result in classical bit 0
# Use Aer simulator directly
backend = Aer.get_backend('qasm_simulator')
job = transpile(circuit, backend)
result = backend.run(job).result()
count = result.get_counts()
print(count)
circuit.draw(output='mpl')
if __name__ == '__main__':
main()

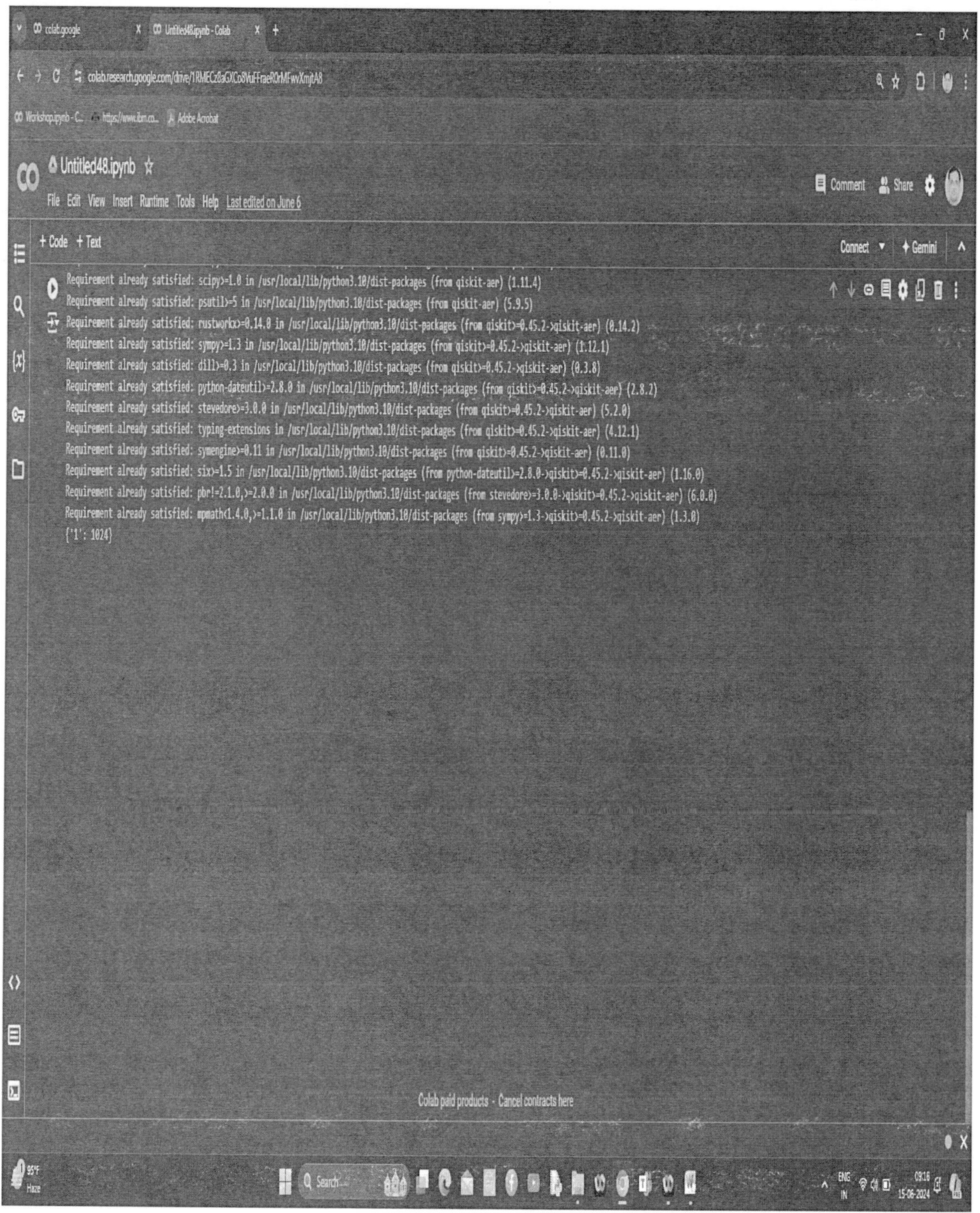
Untitled48.ipynb
File Edit View Insert Runtime Tools Help Last edited on June 6
Requirement already satisfied: scipy>=1.0 in /usr/local/lib/python3.10/dist-packages (from qiskit-aer) (1.11.4)
Requirement already satisfied: psutil>=5 in /usr/local/lib/python3.10/dist-packages (from qiskit-aer) (5.9.5)
Requirement already satisfied: rustworkx>=0.14.0 in /usr/local/lib/python3.10/dist-packages (from qiskit>=0.45.2->qiskit-aer) (0.14.2)
Requirement already satisfied: sympy>=1.3 in /usr/local/lib/python3.10/dist-packages (from qiskit>=0.45.2->qiskit-aer) (1.12.1)
Requirement already satisfied: dill>=0.3 in /usr/local/lib/python3.10/dist-packages (from qiskit>=0.45.2->qiskit-aer) (0.3.8)
Requirement already satisfied: python-dateutil>=2.8.0 in /usr/local/lib/python3.10/dist-packages (from qiskit>=0.45.2->qiskit-aer) (2.8.2)
Requirement already satisfied: stevedore>=3.0.0 in /usr/local/lib/python3.10/dist-packages (from qiskit>=0.45.2->qiskit-aer) (5.2.0)
Requirement already satisfied: typing-extensions in /usr/local/lib/python3.10/dist-packages (from qiskit>=0.45.2->qiskit-aer) (4.12.1)
Requirement already satisfied: symengine>=0.11 in /usr/local/lib/python3.10/dist-packages (from qiskit>=0.45.2->qiskit-aer) (0.11.0)
Requirement already satisfied: six>=1.5 in /usr/local/lib/python3.10/dist-packages (from python-dateutil>=2.8.0->qiskit>=0.45.2->qiskit-aer) (1.16.0)
Requirement already satisfied: pbr!=2.1.0,>=2.0.0 in /usr/local/lib/python3.10/dist-packages (from stevedore>=3.0.0->qiskit>=0.45.2->qiskit-aer) (6.0.0)
Requirement already satisfied: mpmath<1.4.0,>=1.1.0 in /usr/local/lib/python3.10/dist-packages (from sympy>=1.3->qiskit>=0.45.2->qiskit-aer) (1.3.0)
{'1': 1024}
Colab paid products - Cancel contracts here

Experiment No. 5: To create a basic quantum entanglement circuit using Qiskit.

Solution-5:

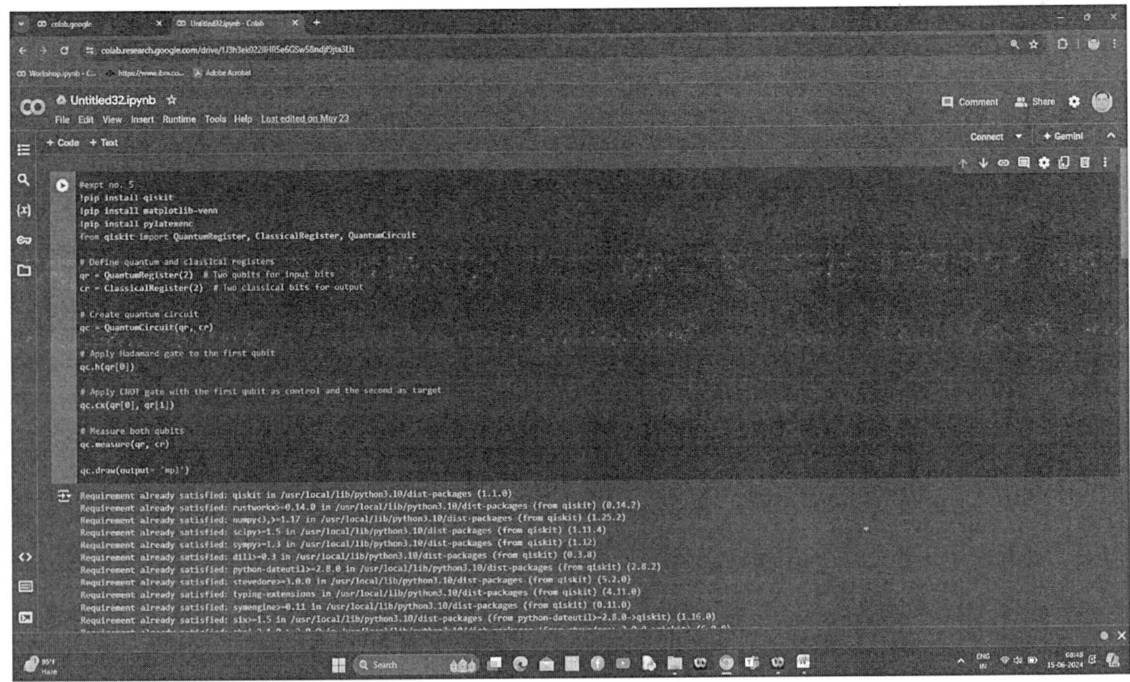

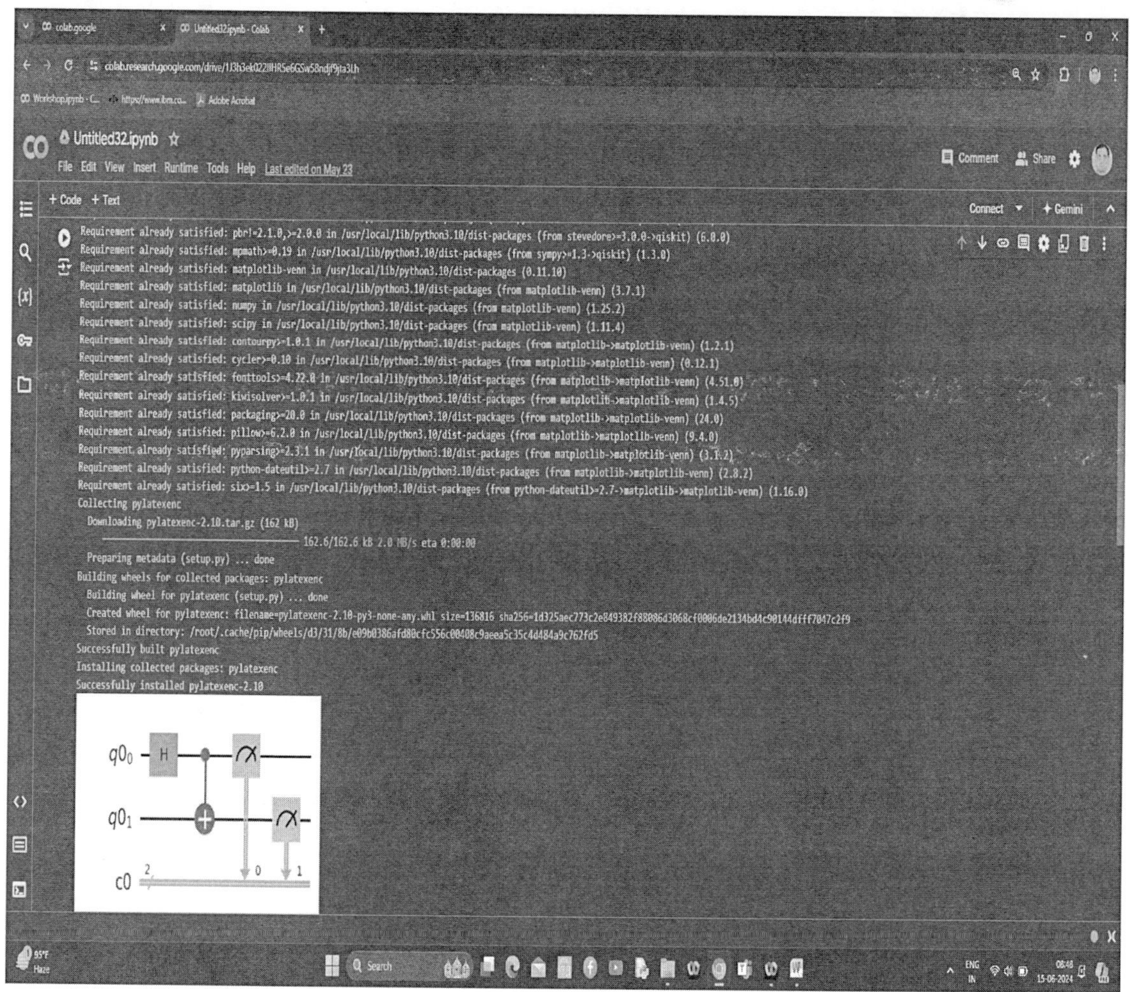
Untitled32.ipynb
File Edit View Insert Runtime Tools Help Last edited on May 23
Comment Share
+ Code + Text
Connect + Gemini
Requirement already satisfied: pbr!=2.1.0,>=2.0.0 in /usr/local/lib/python3.10/dist-packages (from stevedore>=3.0.0->qiskit) (6.0.0)
Requirement already satisfied: mpmath>=0.19 in /usr/local/lib/python3.10/dist-packages (from sympy>=1.3->qiskit) (1.3.0)
Requirement already satisfied: matplotlib-venn in /usr/local/lib/python3.10/dist-packages (0.11.10)
Requirement already satisfied: matplotlib in /usr/local/lib/python3.10/dist-packages (from matplotlib-venn) (3.7.1)
Requirement already satisfied: numpy in /usr/local/lib/python3.10/dist-packages (from matplotlib-venn) (1.25.2)
Requirement already satisfied: scipy in /usr/local/lib/python3.10/dist-packages (from matplotlib-venn) (1.11.4)
Requirement already satisfied: contourpy>=1.0.1 in /usr/local/lib/python3.10/dist-packages (from matplotlib->matplotlib-venn) (1.2.1)
Requirement already satisfied: cycler>=0.10 in /usr/local/lib/python3.10/dist-packages (from matplotlib->matplotlib-venn) (0.12.1)
Requirement already satisfied: fonttools>=4.22.0 in /usr/local/lib/python3.10/dist-packages (from matplotlib->matplotlib-venn) (4.51.0)
Requirement already satisfied: kiwisolver>=1.0.1 in /usr/local/lib/python3.10/dist-packages (from matplotlib->matplotlib-venn) (1.4.5)
Requirement already satisfied: packaging>=20.0 in /usr/local/lib/python3.10/dist-packages (from matplotlib->matplotlib-venn) (24.0)
Requirement already satisfied: pillow>=6.2.0 in /usr/local/lib/python3.10/dist-packages (from matplotlib->matplotlib-venn) (9.4.0)
Requirement already satisfied: pyparsing>=2.3.1 in /usr/local/lib/python3.10/dist-packages (from matplotlib->matplotlib-venn) (3.1.2)
Requirement already satisfied: python-dateutil>=2.7 in /usr/local/lib/python3.10/dist-packages (from matplotlib->matplotlib-venn) (2.8.2)
Requirement already satisfied: six>=1.5 in /usr/local/lib/python3.10/dist-packages (from python-dateutil>=2.7->matplotlib->matplotlib-venn) (1.16.0)
Collecting pylatexenc
Downloading pylatexenc-2.10.tar.gz (162 kB)
162.6/162.6 kB 2.0 MB/s eta 0:00:00
Preparing metadata (setup.py) ... done
Building wheels for collected packages: pylatexenc
Building wheel for pylatexenc (setup.py) ... done
Created wheel for pylatexenc: filename=pylatexenc-2.10-py3-none-any.whl size=136816 sha256=1d325aec773c2e849382f88086d3068cf0006de2134bd4c90144dfff7047c2f9
Stored in directory: /root/.cache/pip/wheels/d3/31/8b/e09b0386afd80cfc556c00408c9aeea5c35c4d484a9c762fd5
Successfully built pylatexenc
Installing collected packages: pylatexenc
Successfully installed pylatexenc-2.10
q0_0
H
q0_1
c0
2
0
1

Experiment No. 6: To create a half-adder quantum circuit using Qiskit.

Solution-6:

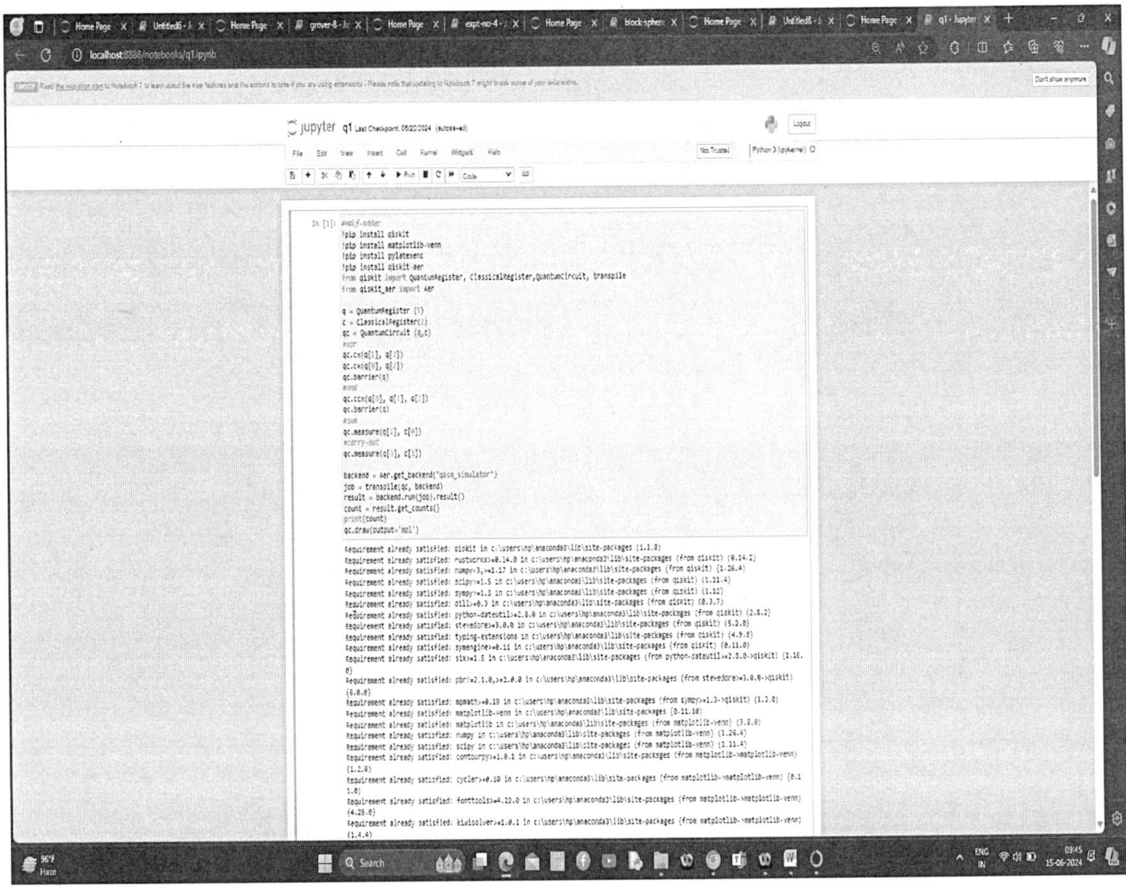

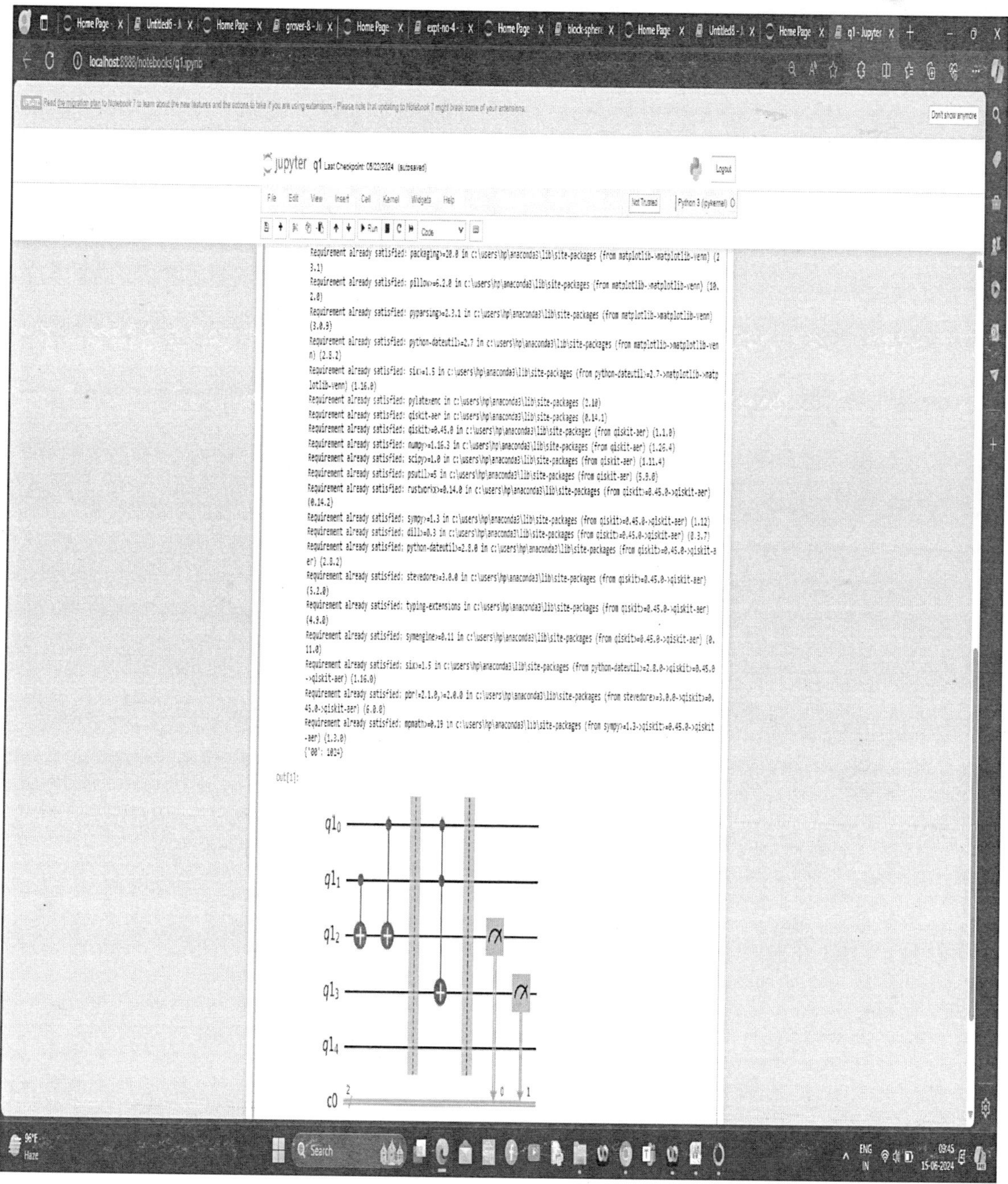
jupyter q1 Last Checkpoint: 05/22/2024 (autosaved)
Logout
File Edit View Insert Cell Kernel Widgets Help
Not Trusted
Python 3 (ipykernel)
Run
Code
Requirement already satisfied: packaging>=20.0 in c:\users\hp\anaconda3\lib\site-packages (from matplotlib->matplotlib-venn) (23.1)
Requirement already satisfied: pillow>=6.2.0 in c:\users\hp\anaconda3\lib\site-packages (from matplotlib->matplotlib-venn) (10.2.0)
Requirement already satisfied: pyparsing>=2.3.1 in c:\users\hp\anaconda3\lib\site-packages (from matplotlib->matplotlib-venn) (3.0.9)
Requirement already satisfied: python-dateutil>=2.7 in c:\users\hp\anaconda3\lib\site-packages (from matplotlib->matplotlib-venn) (2.8.2)
Requirement already satisfied: six>=1.5 in c:\users\hp\anaconda3\lib\site-packages (from python-dateutil>=2.7->matplotlib->matplotlib-venn) (1.16.0)
Requirement already satisfied: pylatexenc in c:\users\hp\anaconda3\lib\site-packages (2.10)
Requirement already satisfied: qiskit-aer in c:\users\hp\anaconda3\lib\site-packages (0.14.1)
Requirement already satisfied: qiskit>=0.45.0 in c:\users\hp\anaconda3\lib\site-packages (from qiskit-aer) (1.1.0)
Requirement already satisfied: numpy>=1.16.3 in c:\users\hp\anaconda3\lib\site-packages (from qiskit-aer) (1.26.4)
Requirement already satisfied: scipy>=1.0 in c:\users\hp\anaconda3\lib\site-packages (from qiskit-aer) (1.11.4)
Requirement already satisfied: psutil>=5 in c:\users\hp\anaconda3\lib\site-packages (from qiskit-aer) (5.9.0)
Requirement already satisfied: rustworkx>=0.14.0 in c:\users\hp\anaconda3\lib\site-packages (from qiskit>=0.45.0->qiskit-aer) (0.14.2)
Requirement already satisfied: sympy>=1.3 in c:\users\hp\anaconda3\lib\site-packages (from qiskit>=0.45.0->qiskit-aer) (1.12)
Requirement already satisfied: dill>=0.3 in c:\users\hp\anaconda3\lib\site-packages (from qiskit>=0.45.0->qiskit-aer) (0.3.7)
Requirement already satisfied: python-dateutil>=2.8.0 in c:\users\hp\anaconda3\lib\site-packages (from qiskit>=0.45.0->qiskit-aer) (2.8.2)
Requirement already satisfied: stevedore>=3.0.0 in c:\users\hp\anaconda3\lib\site-packages (from qiskit>=0.45.0->qiskit-aer) (5.2.0)
Requirement already satisfied: typing-extensions in c:\users\hp\anaconda3\lib\site-packages (from qiskit>=0.45.0->qiskit-aer) (4.9.0)
Requirement already satisfied: symengine>=0.11 in c:\users\hp\anaconda3\lib\site-packages (from qiskit>=0.45.0->qiskit-aer) (0.11.0)
Requirement already satisfied: six>=1.5 in c:\users\hp\anaconda3\lib\site-packages (from python-dateutil>=2.8.0->qiskit>=0.45.0->qiskit-aer) (1.16.0)
Requirement already satisfied: pbr!=2.1.0,>=2.0.0 in c:\users\hp\anaconda3\lib\site-packages (from stevedore>=3.0.0->qiskit>=0.45.0->qiskit-aer) (6.0.0)
Requirement already satisfied: mpmath>=0.19 in c:\users\hp\anaconda3\lib\site-packages (from sympy>=1.3->qiskit>=0.45.0->qiskit-aer) (1.3.0)
{'00': 1024}
Out[1]:
ql0
ql1
ql2
ql3
ql4
c0
2
0
1

Experiment No. 7: To implement quantum teleportation using Qiskit.

Solution-7:

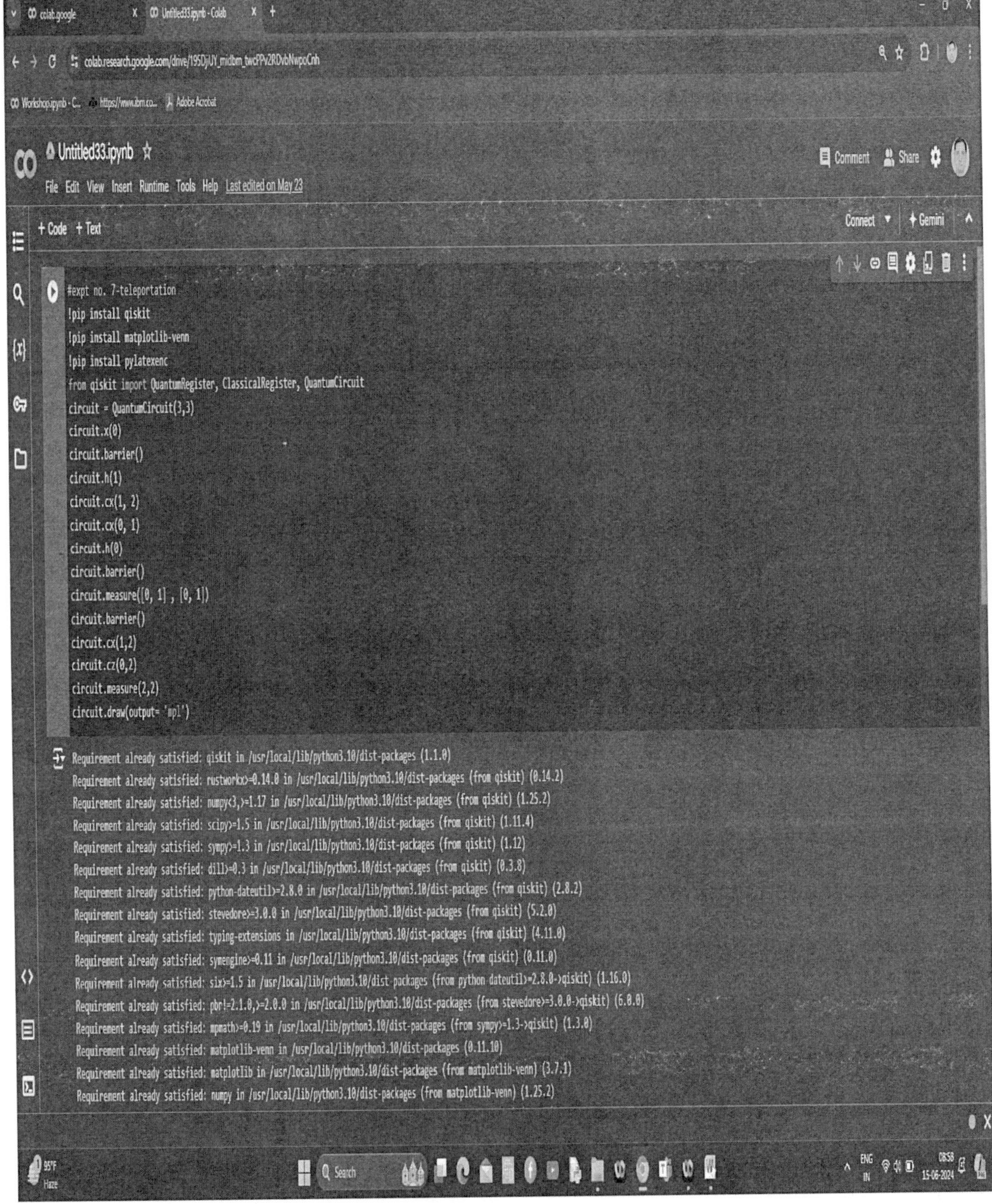

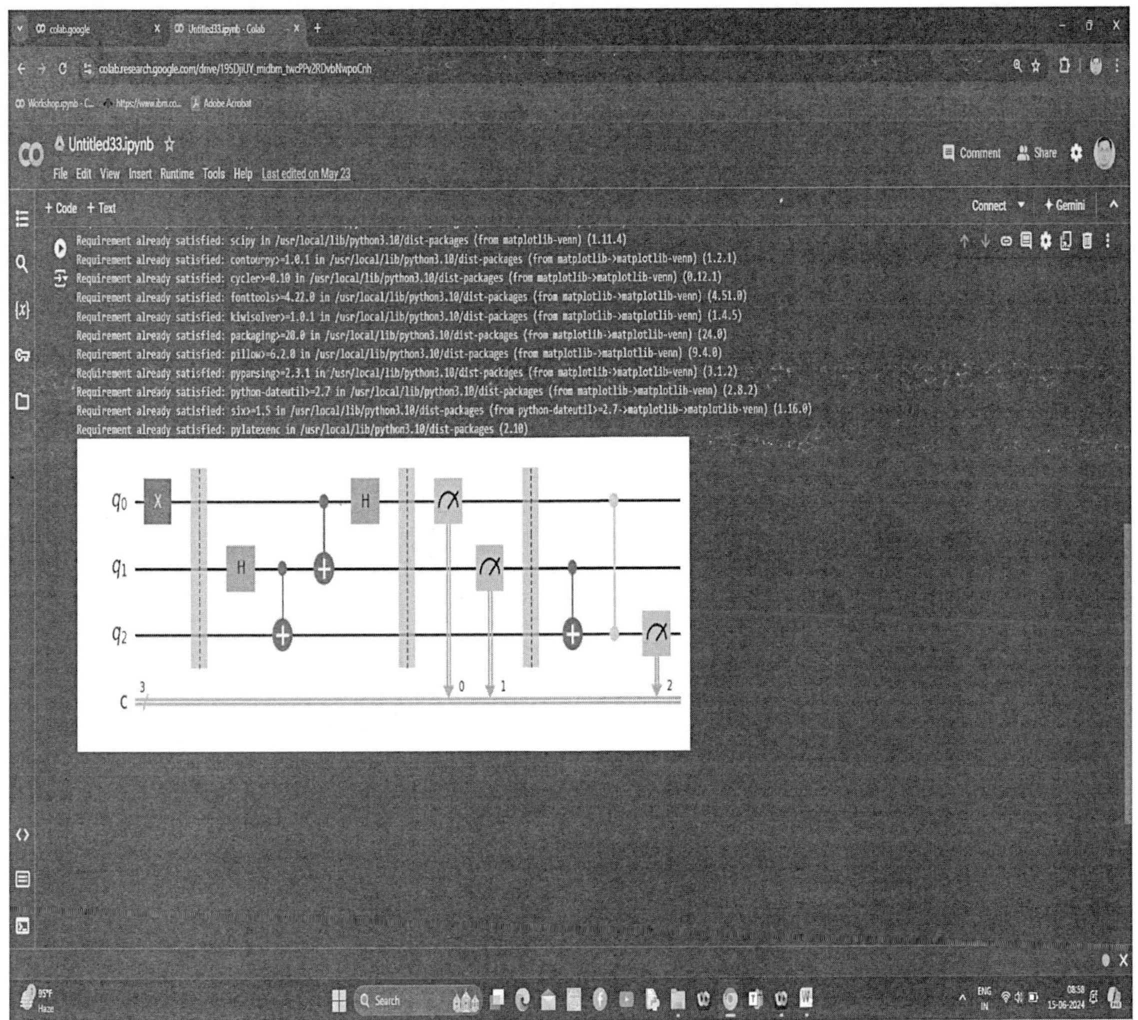
Untitled33.ipynb
File Edit View Insert Runtime Tools Help Last edited on May 23
+ Code + Text
Requirement already satisfied: scipy in /usr/local/lib/python3.10/dist-packages (from matplotlib-venn) (1.11.4)
Requirement already satisfied: contourpy>=1.0.1 in /usr/local/lib/python3.10/dist-packages (from matplotlib->matplotlib-venn) (1.2.1)
Requirement already satisfied: cycler>=0.10 in /usr/local/lib/python3.10/dist-packages (from matplotlib->matplotlib-venn) (0.12.1)
Requirement already satisfied: fonttools>=4.22.0 in /usr/local/lib/python3.10/dist-packages (from matplotlib->matplotlib-venn) (4.51.0)
Requirement already satisfied: kiwisolver>=1.0.1 in /usr/local/lib/python3.10/dist-packages (from matplotlib->matplotlib-venn) (1.4.5)
Requirement already satisfied: packaging>=20.0 in /usr/local/lib/python3.10/dist-packages (from matplotlib->matplotlib-venn) (24.0)
Requirement already satisfied: pillow>=6.2.0 in /usr/local/lib/python3.10/dist-packages (from matplotlib->matplotlib-venn) (9.4.0)
Requirement already satisfied: pyparsing>=2.3.1 in /usr/local/lib/python3.10/dist-packages (from matplotlib->matplotlib-venn) (3.1.2)
Requirement already satisfied: python-dateutil>=2.7 in /usr/local/lib/python3.10/dist-packages (from matplotlib->matplotlib-venn) (2.8.2)
Requirement already satisfied: six>=1.5 in /usr/local/lib/python3.10/dist-packages (from python-dateutil>=2.7->matplotlib->matplotlib-venn) (1.16.0)
Requirement already satisfied: pylatexenc in /usr/local/lib/python3.10/dist-packages (2.10)
q0
q1
q2
C
3
X
H
H
0
1
2

Experiment No. 8: To implement Grover's algorithm using Qiskit.

Solution-8:

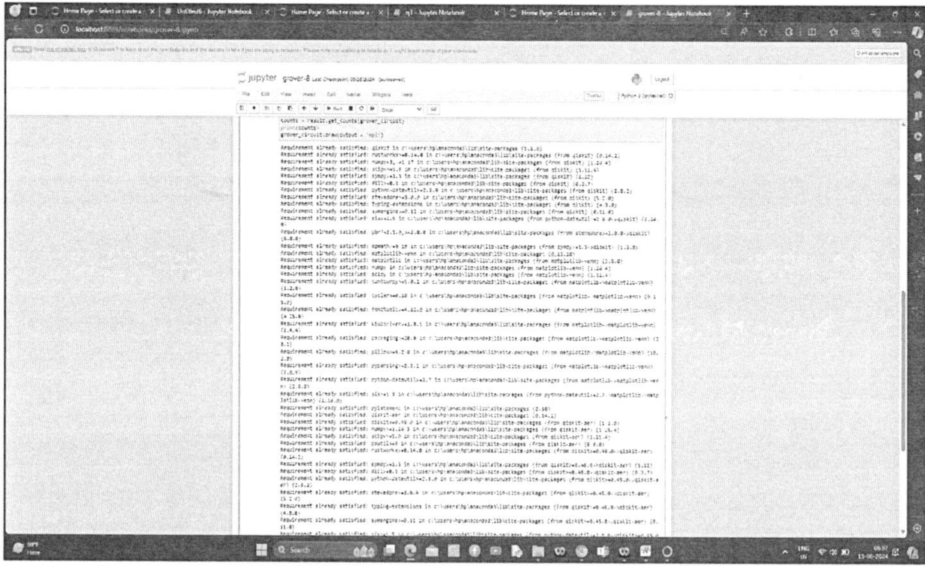

*

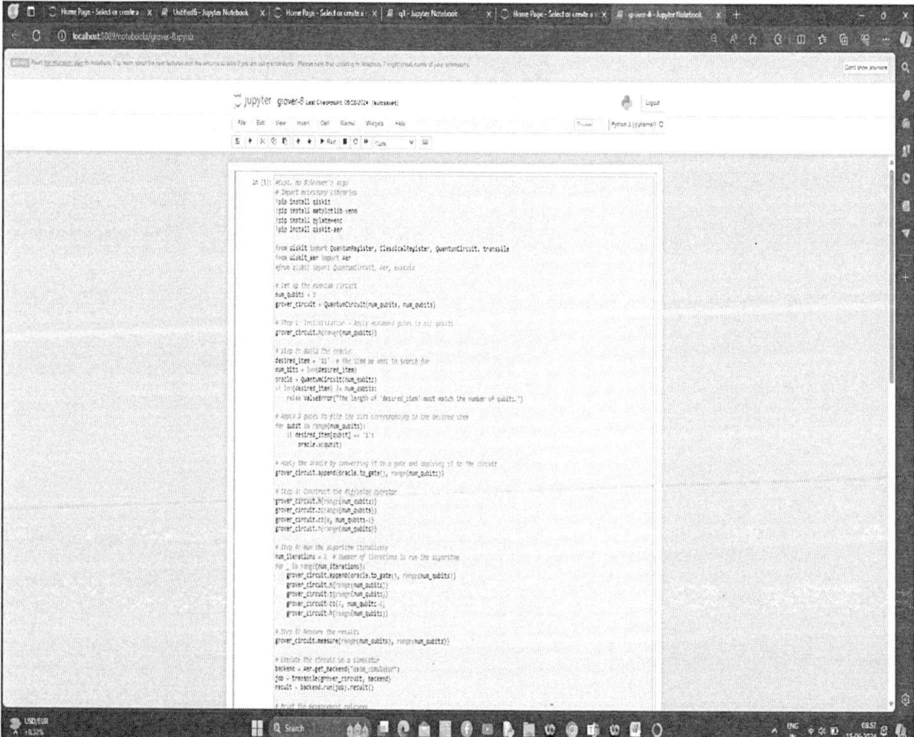

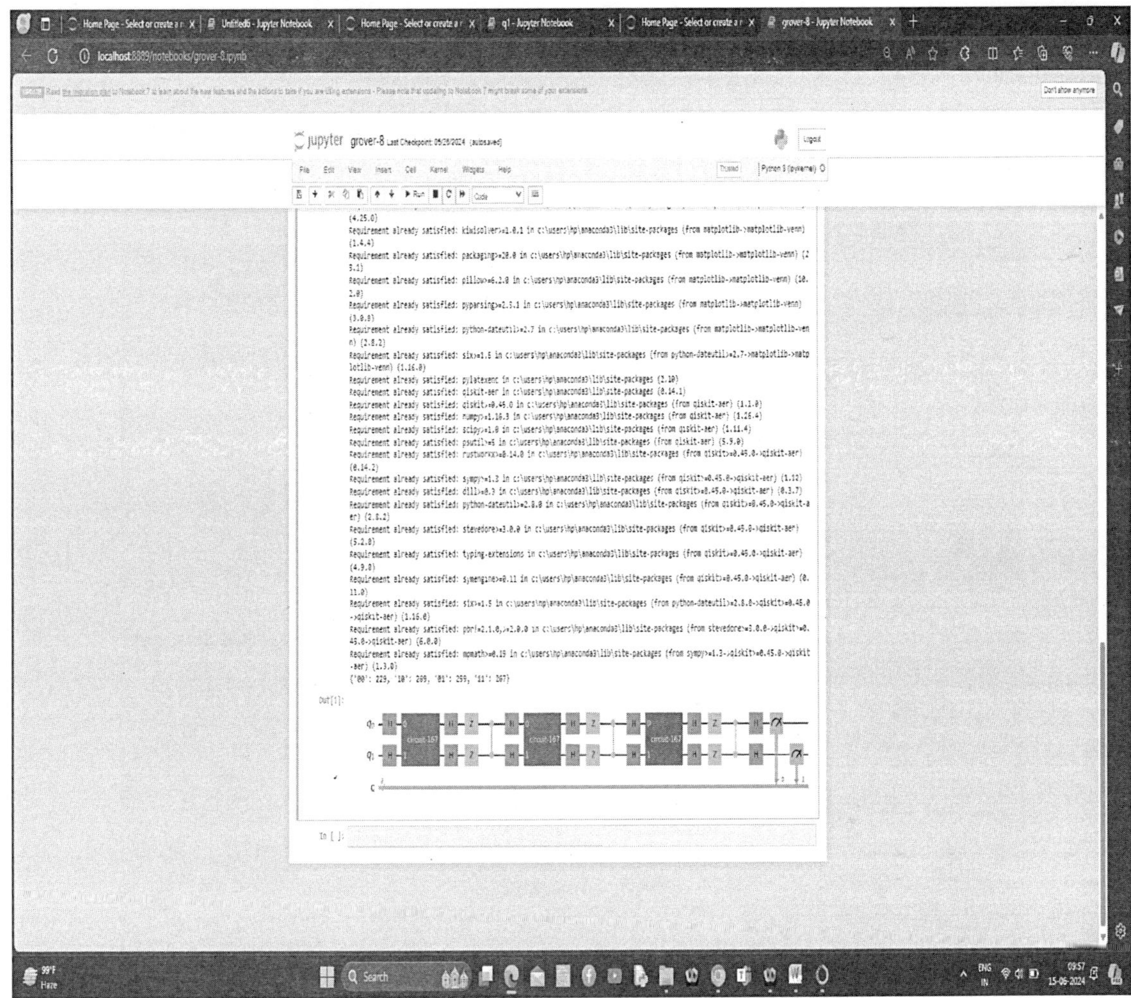

Experiment No. 9: To implement a Block Sphere showing qubits using Qiskit.

Solution-9:

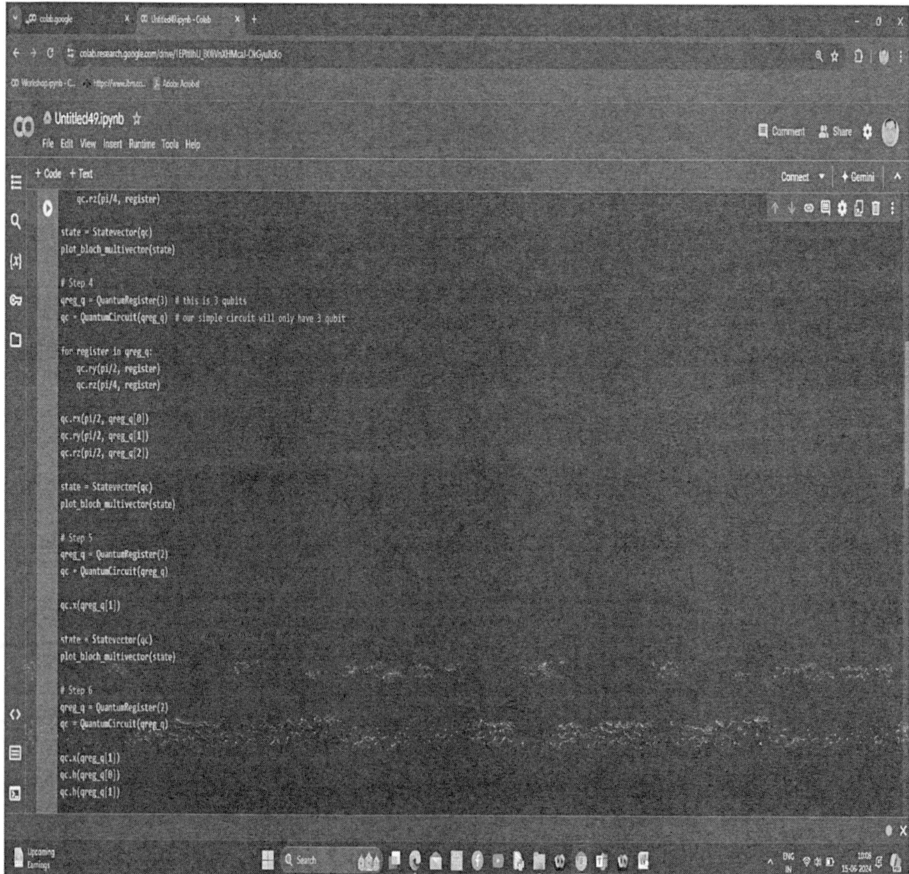

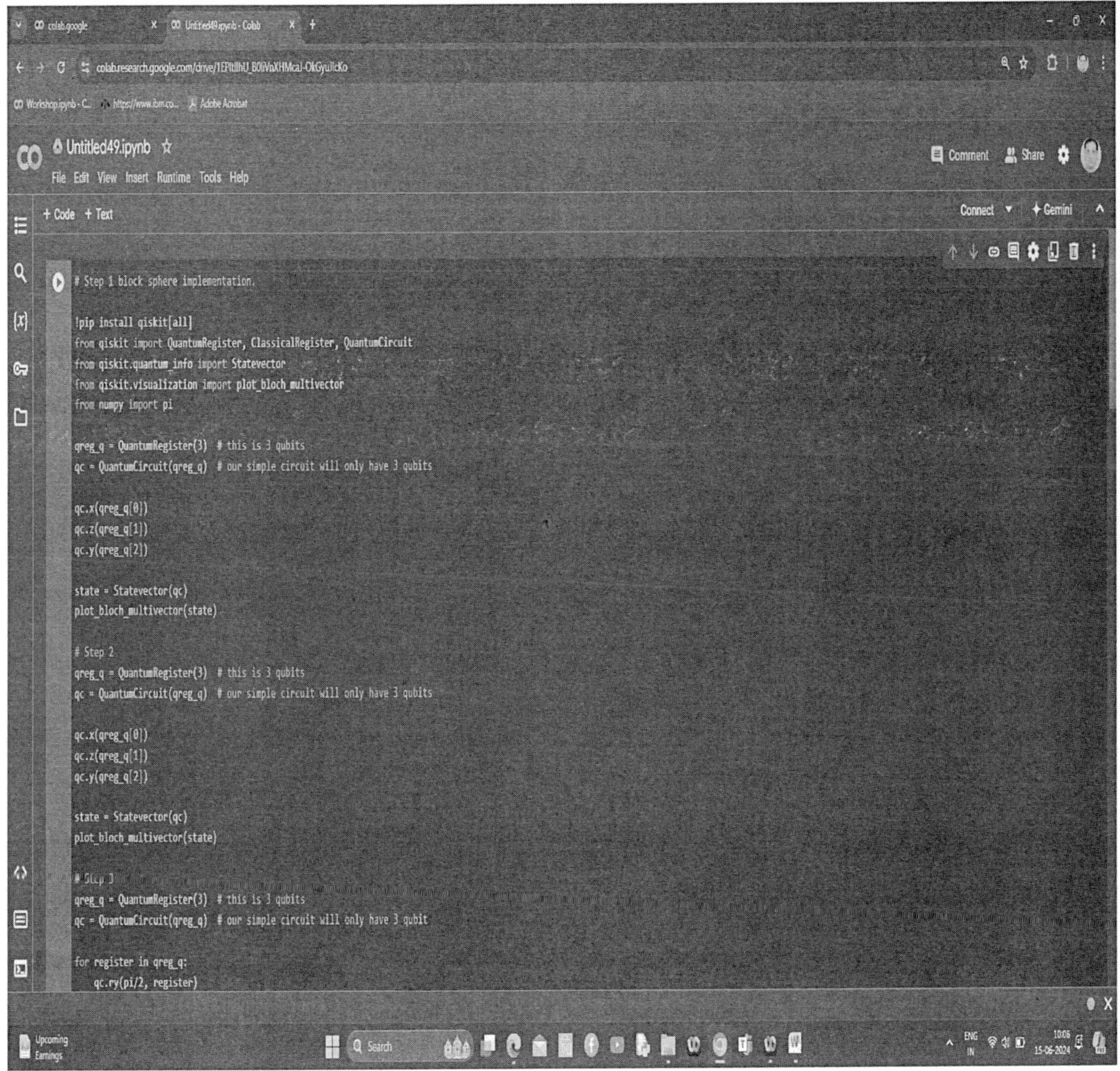
Untitled49.ipynb
File Edit View Insert Runtime Tools Help
+ Code + Text
Connect
Gemini
Step 1 block sphere implementation.
!pip install qiskit[all]
from qiskit import QuantumRegister, ClassicalRegister, QuantumCircuit
from qiskit.quantum_info import Statevector
from qiskit.visualization import plot_bloch_multivector
from numpy import pi
qreg_q = QuantumRegister(3) # this is 3 qubits
qc = QuantumCircuit(qreg_q) # our simple circuit will only have 3 qubits
qc.x(qreg_q[0])
qc.z(qreg_q[1])
qc.y(qreg_q[2])
state = Statevector(qc)
plot_bloch_multivector(state)
# Step 2
qreg_q = QuantumRegister(3) # this is 3 qubits
qc = QuantumCircuit(qreg_q) # our simple circuit will only have 3 qubits
qc.x(qreg_q[0])
qc.z(qreg_q[1])
qc.y(qreg_q[2])
state = Statevector(qc)
plot_bloch_multivector(state)
# Step 3
qreg_q = QuantumRegister(3) # this is 3 qubits
qc = QuantumCircuit(qreg_q) # our simple circuit will only have 3 qubit
for register in qreg_q:
qc.ry(pi/2, register)

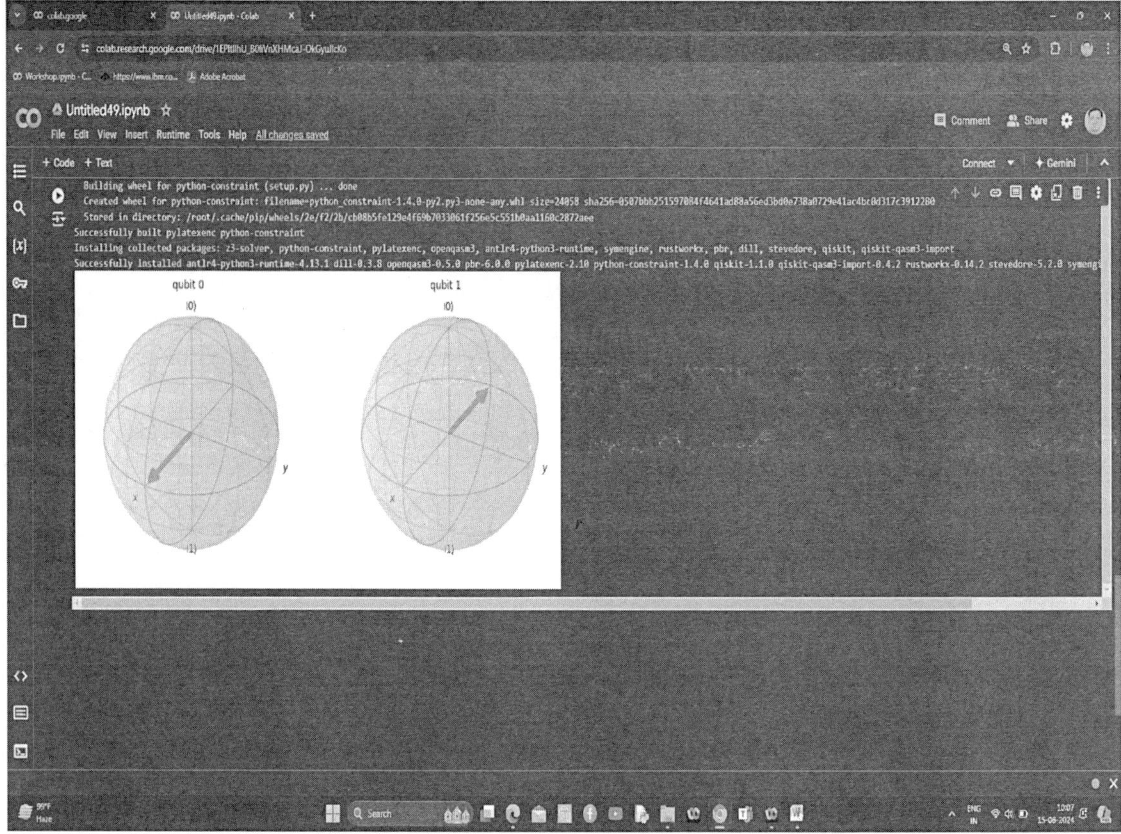
Untitled49.ipynb
File Edit View Insert Runtime Tools Help All changes saved
Building wheel for python-constraint (setup.py) ... done
Successfully built pylatexenc python-constraint
qubit 0
qubit 1

Experiment No. 10: To implement a quantum solution to Simon's problem.

Solution-10:

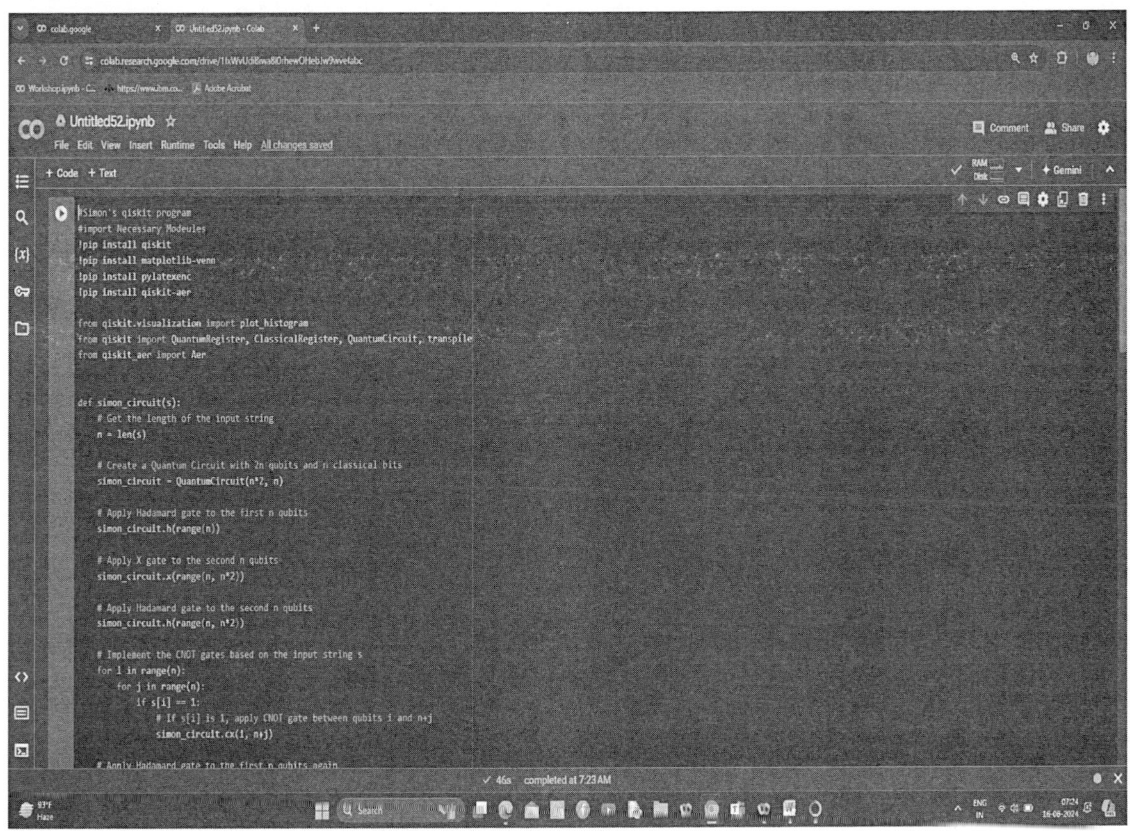

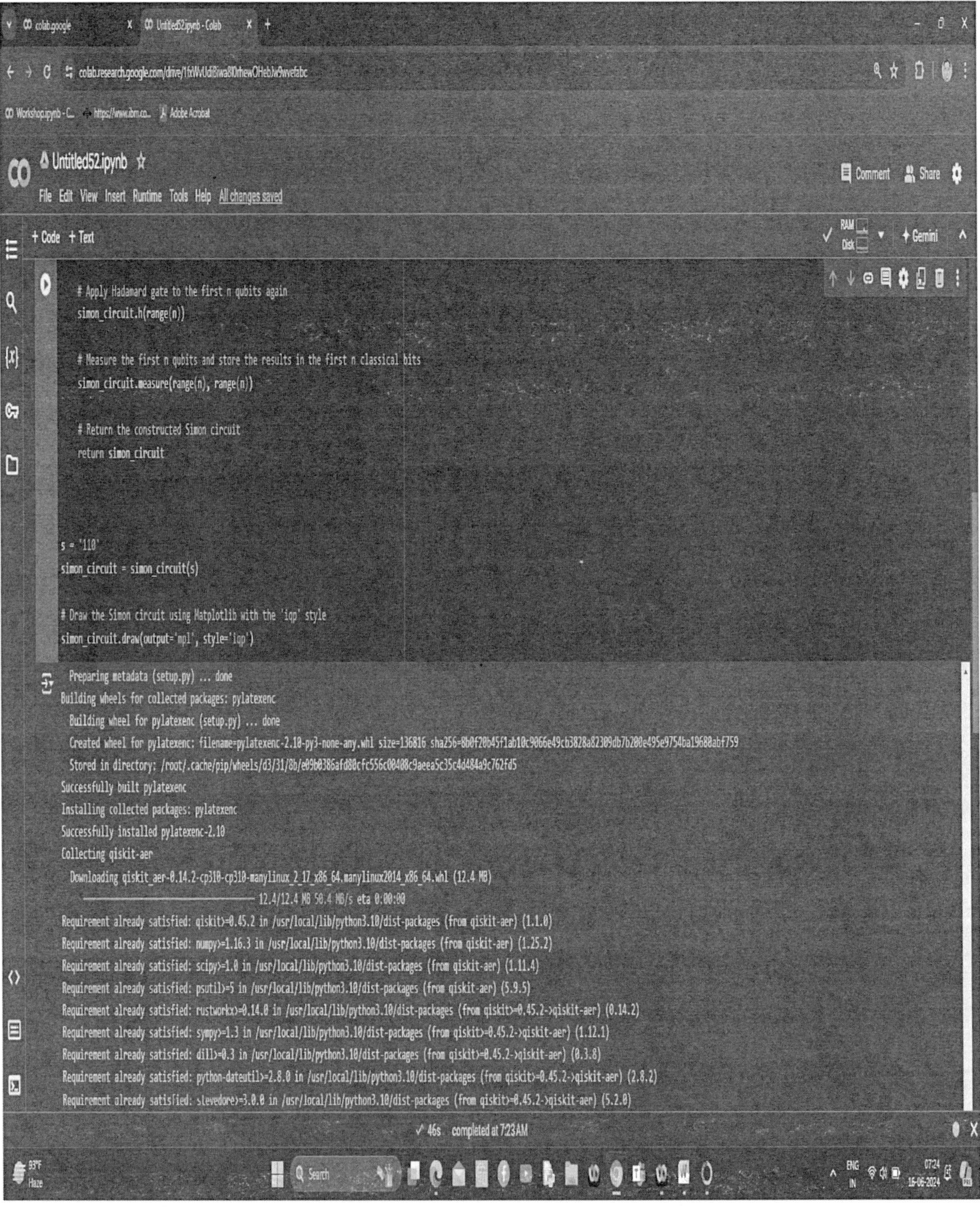

Untitled52.ipynb
File Edit View Insert Runtime Tools Help All changes saved
+ Code + Text
# Apply Hadamard gate to the first n qubits again
simon_circuit.h(range(n))
# Measure the first n qubits and store the results in the first n classical bits
simon_circuit.measure(range(n), range(n))
# Return the constructed Simon circuit
return simon_circuit
s = '110'
simon_circuit = simon_circuit(s)
# Draw the Simon circuit using Matplotlib with the 'iqp' style
simon_circuit.draw(output='mpl', style='iqp')
Preparing metadata (setup.py) ... done
Building wheels for collected packages: pylatexenc
Building wheel for pylatexenc (setup.py) ... done
Created wheel for pylatexenc: filename=pylatexenc-2.10-py3-none-any.whl size=136816 sha256=8b0f20b45f1ab10c9066e49cb3828a82309db7b200e495e9754ba19680abf759
Stored in directory: /root/.cache/pip/wheels/d3/31/8b/e09b0386afd80cfc556c00408c9aeea5c35c4d484a9c762fd5
Successfully built pylatexenc
Installing collected packages: pylatexenc
Successfully installed pylatexenc-2.10
Collecting qiskit-aer
Downloading qiskit_aer-0.14.2-cp310-cp310-manylinux_2_17_x86_64.manylinux2014_x86_64.whl (12.4 MB)
12.4/12.4 MB 50.4 MB/s eta 0:00:00
Requirement already satisfied: qiskit>=0.45.2 in /usr/local/lib/python3.10/dist-packages (from qiskit-aer) (1.1.0)
Requirement already satisfied: numpy>=1.16.3 in /usr/local/lib/python3.10/dist-packages (from qiskit-aer) (1.25.2)
Requirement already satisfied: scipy>=1.0 in /usr/local/lib/python3.10/dist-packages (from qiskit-aer) (1.11.4)
Requirement already satisfied: psutil>=5 in /usr/local/lib/python3.10/dist-packages (from qiskit-aer) (5.9.5)
Requirement already satisfied: rustworkx>=0.14.0 in /usr/local/lib/python3.10/dist-packages (from qiskit>=0.45.2->qiskit-aer) (0.14.2)
Requirement already satisfied: sympy>=1.3 in /usr/local/lib/python3.10/dist-packages (from qiskit>=0.45.2->qiskit-aer) (1.12.1)
Requirement already satisfied: dill>=0.3 in /usr/local/lib/python3.10/dist-packages (from qiskit>=0.45.2->qiskit-aer) (0.3.8)
Requirement already satisfied: python-dateutil>=2.8.0 in /usr/local/lib/python3.10/dist-packages (from qiskit>=0.45.2->qiskit-aer) (2.8.2)
Requirement already satisfied: stevedore>=3.0.0 in /usr/local/lib/python3.10/dist-packages (from qiskit>=0.45.2->qiskit-aer) (5.2.0)
✓ 46s completed at 7:23AM

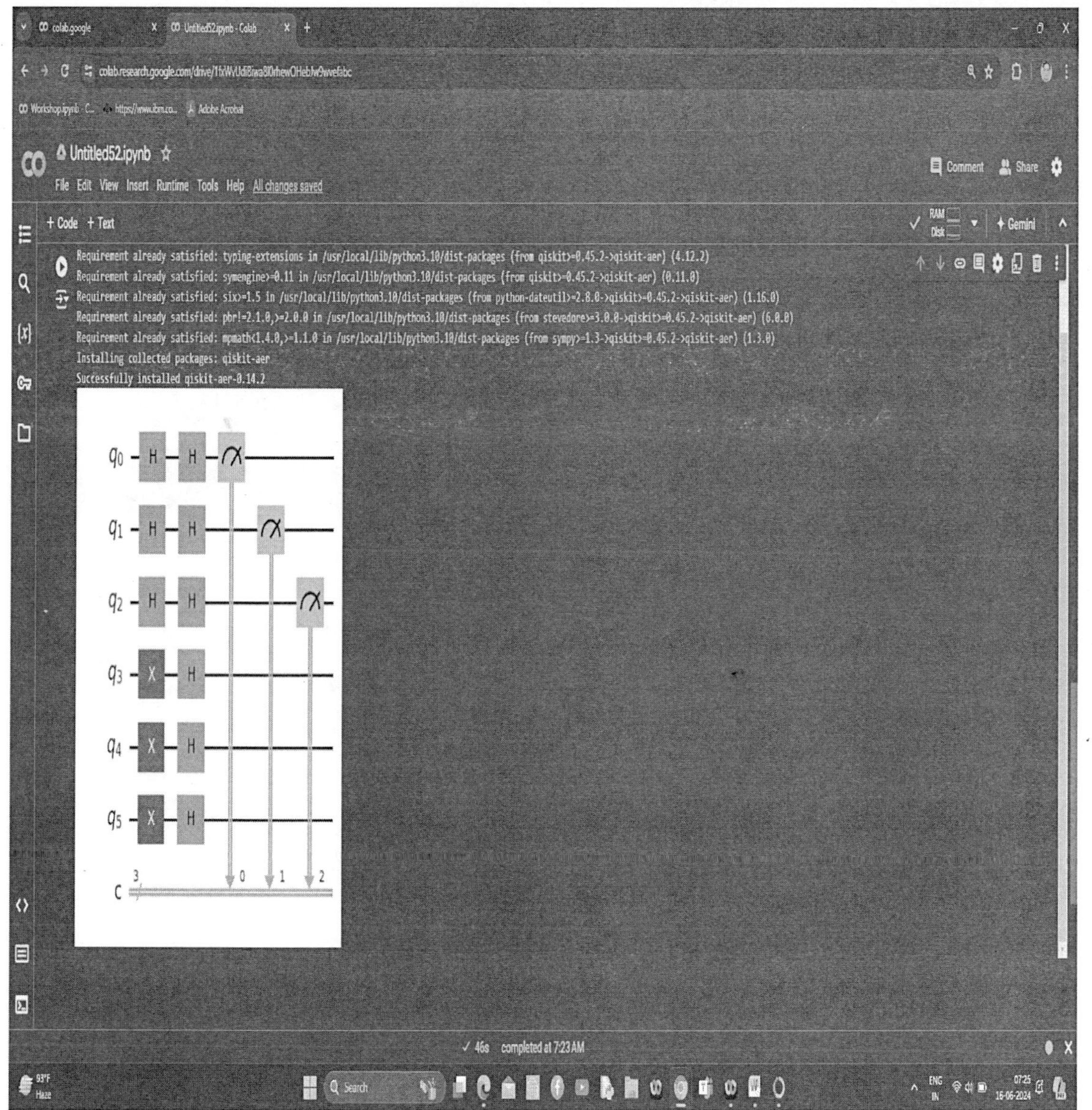
Requirement already satisfied: typing-extensions in /usr/local/lib/python3.10/dist-packages (from qiskit>=0.45.2->qiskit-aer) (4.12.2)
Requirement already satisfied: symengine>=0.11 in /usr/local/lib/python3.10/dist-packages (from qiskit>=0.45.2->qiskit-aer) (0.11.0)
Requirement already satisfied: six>=1.5 in /usr/local/lib/python3.10/dist-packages (from python-dateutil>=2.8.0->qiskit>=0.45.2->qiskit-aer) (1.16.0)
Requirement already satisfied: pbr!=2.1.0,>=2.0.0 in /usr/local/lib/python3.10/dist-packages (from stevedore>=3.0.0->qiskit>=0.45.2->qiskit-aer) (6.0.0)
Requirement already satisfied: mpmath<1.4.0,>=1.1.0 in /usr/local/lib/python3.10/dist-packages (from sympy>=1.3->qiskit>=0.45.2->qiskit-aer) (1.3.0)
Installing collected packages: qiskit-aer
Successfully installed qiskit-aer-0.14.2
q0
q1
q2
q3
q4
q5
c
H
X
3
0
1
2
✓ 46s completed at 7:23 AM

Experiment No. 11: To implement quantum solution to Deutsch's problem in Qiskit.

Solution-11:

```
!pip install qiskit
!pip install matplotlib-venn
!pip install pylatexenc
!pip install qiskit-aer

from qiskit.visualization import plot_histogram
from qiskit import QuantumRegister, ClassicalRegister, QuantumCircuit,
transpile
from qiskit_aer import Aer

def deutsch_algorithm(f):
    # Create a quantum circuit with 2 qubits and 1 classical register
    circuit = QuantumCircuit(2, 1)

    # Apply Hadamard gate on both qubits
    circuit.h([0, 1])

    # Apply X and H gate on the second qubit to create an initial state
|1>
    circuit.x(1)
    circuit.h(1)

    # Apply the quantum oracle (Uf) based on the function f
    if f(0):
        circuit.z(1)
    if f(1):
        circuit.cx(0, 1)

    # Apply Hadamard gate on the first qubit
    circuit.h(0)

    # Measure the first qubit
    circuit.measure(0, 0)

    return circuit

# Define a constant function (always returns 0)
def constant_zero(x):
    return 0

# Define a balanced function (outputs x)
def balanced_identity(x):
    return x

# Choose a function and run the Deutsch algorithm
```

```
f = balanced_identity  # Change this to constant_zero to see the
difference
circuit = deutsch_algorithm(f)

# Simulate the quantum circuit
simulator = Aer.get_backend('qasm_simulator')
result = simulator.run(circuit).result()

# Display the result
counts = result.get_counts(circuit)

# Determine whether the function is constant or balanced
is_constant = len(counts) == 1  # If there is only one measurement
outcome, it's constant
result_type = "constant" if is_constant else "balanced"

print("Measurement result:", counts)
print("Function is", result_type)
```

```
Requirement already satisfied: qiskit in /usr/local/lib/python3.10/dist-packages (1.1.1)
Requirement already satisfied: rustworkx>=0.14.0 in /usr/local/lib/python3.10/dist-packages (from qiskit)
(0.14.2)
Requirement already satisfied: numpy<3,>=1.17 in /usr/local/lib/python3.10/dist-packages (from qiskit) (1.25.2)
Requirement already satisfied: scipy>=1.5 in /usr/local/lib/python3.10/dist-packages (from qiskit) (1.11.4)
Requirement already satisfied: sympy>=1.3 in /usr/local/lib/python3.10/dist-packages (from qiskit) (1.12.1)
Requirement already satisfied: dill>=0.3 in /usr/local/lib/python3.10/dist-packages (from qiskit) (0.3.8)
Requirement already satisfied: python-dateutil>=2.8.0 in /usr/local/lib/python3.10/dist-packages (from qiskit)
(2.8.2)
Requirement already satisfied: stevedore>=3.0.0 in /usr/local/lib/python3.10/dist-packages (from qiskit) (5.2.0)
Requirement already satisfied: typing-extensions in /usr/local/lib/python3.10/dist-packages (from qiskit)
(4.12.2)
Requirement already satisfied: symengine>=0.11 in /usr/local/lib/python3.10/dist-packages (from qiskit)
(0.11.0)
Requirement already satisfied: six>=1.5 in /usr/local/lib/python3.10/dist-packages (from python-
dateutil>=2.8.0->qiskit) (1.16.0)
Requirement already satisfied: pbr!=2.1.0,>=2.0.0 in /usr/local/lib/python3.10/dist-packages (from
stevedore>=3.0.0->qiskit) (6.0.0)
Requirement already satisfied: mpmath<1.4.0,>=1.1.0 in /usr/local/lib/python3.10/dist-packages (from
sympy>=1.3->qiskit) (1.3.0)
Requirement already satisfied: matplotlib-venn in /usr/local/lib/python3.10/dist-packages (0.11.10)
Requirement already satisfied: matplotlib in /usr/local/lib/python3.10/dist-packages (from matplotlib-venn)
(3.7.1)
Requirement already satisfied: numpy in /usr/local/lib/python3.10/dist-packages (from matplotlib-venn) (1.25.2)
Requirement already satisfied: scipy in /usr/local/lib/python3.10/dist-packages (from matplotlib-venn) (1.11.4)
Requirement already satisfied: contourpy>=1.0.1 in /usr/local/lib/python3.10/dist-packages (from matplotlib-
>matplotlib-venn) (1.2.1)
Requirement already satisfied: cycler>=0.10 in /usr/local/lib/python3.10/dist-packages (from matplotlib-
>matplotlib-venn) (0.12.1)
Requirement already satisfied: fonttools>=4.22.0 in /usr/local/lib/python3.10/dist-packages (from matplotlib-
>matplotlib-venn) (4.53.0)
Requirement already satisfied: kiwisolver>=1.0.1 in /usr/local/lib/python3.10/dist-packages (from matplotlib-
>matplotlib-venn) (1.4.5)
Requirement already satisfied: packaging>=20.0 in /usr/local/lib/python3.10/dist-packages (from matplotlib-
>matplotlib-venn) (24.1)
```

```
Requirement already satisfied: pillow>=6.2.0 in /usr/local/lib/python3.10/dist-packages (from matplotlib->matplotlib-venn) (9.4.0)
Requirement already satisfied: pyparsing>=2.3.1 in /usr/local/lib/python3.10/dist-packages (from matplotlib->matplotlib-venn) (3.1.2)
Requirement already satisfied: python-dateutil>=2.7 in /usr/local/lib/python3.10/dist-packages (from matplotlib->matplotlib-venn) (2.8.2)
Requirement already satisfied: six>=1.5 in /usr/local/lib/python3.10/dist-packages (from python-dateutil>=2.7->matplotlib->matplotlib-venn) (1.16.0)
Requirement already satisfied: pylatexenc in /usr/local/lib/python3.10/dist-packages (2.10)
Requirement already satisfied: qiskit-aer in /usr/local/lib/python3.10/dist-packages (0.14.2)
Requirement already satisfied: qiskit>=0.45.2 in /usr/local/lib/python3.10/dist-packages (from qiskit-aer) (1.1.1)
Requirement already satisfied: numpy>=1.16.3 in /usr/local/lib/python3.10/dist-packages (from qiskit-aer) (1.25.2)
Requirement already satisfied: scipy>=1.0 in /usr/local/lib/python3.10/dist-packages (from qiskit-aer) (1.11.4)
Requirement already satisfied: psutil>=5 in /usr/local/lib/python3.10/dist-packages (from qiskit-aer) (5.9.5)
Requirement already satisfied: rustworkx>=0.14.0 in /usr/local/lib/python3.10/dist-packages (from qiskit>=0.45.2->qiskit-aer) (0.14.2)
Requirement already satisfied: sympy>=1.3 in /usr/local/lib/python3.10/dist-packages (from qiskit>=0.45.2->qiskit-aer) (1.12.1)
Requirement already satisfied: dill>=0.3 in /usr/local/lib/python3.10/dist-packages (from qiskit>=0.45.2->qiskit-aer) (0.3.8)
Requirement already satisfied: python-dateutil>=2.8.0 in /usr/local/lib/python3.10/dist-packages (from qiskit>=0.45.2->qiskit-aer) (2.8.2)
Requirement already satisfied: stevedore>=3.0.0 in /usr/local/lib/python3.10/dist-packages (from qiskit>=0.45.2->qiskit-aer) (5.2.0)
Requirement already satisfied: typing-extensions in /usr/local/lib/python3.10/dist-packages (from qiskit>=0.45.2->qiskit-aer) (4.12.2)
Requirement already satisfied: symengine>=0.11 in /usr/local/lib/python3.10/dist-packages (from qiskit>=0.45.2->qiskit-aer) (0.11.0)
Requirement already satisfied: six>=1.5 in /usr/local/lib/python3.10/dist-packages (from python-dateutil>=2.8.0->qiskit>=0.45.2->qiskit-aer) (1.16.0)
Requirement already satisfied: pbr!=2.1.0,>=2.0.0 in /usr/local/lib/python3.10/dist-packages (from stevedore>=3.0.0->qiskit>=0.45.2->qiskit-aer) (6.0.0)
Requirement already satisfied: mpmath<1.4.0,>=1.1.0 in /usr/local/lib/python3.10/dist-packages (from sympy>=1.3->qiskit>=0.45.2->qiskit-aer) (1.3.0)
Measurement result: {'0': 525, '1': 499}
Function is balanced
```

Index

Q